D0321476

# Thailand's Beaches & Islands

written and researched by

## Paul Gray and Lucy Ridout

with additional research by

Claire Saunders, Julia Kelly and Tom Vater

ROUGH GUIDES

www.roughguides.com

N

*Kwai*

2

24

Ayutthaya

*Chao Phraya*

Nakhon Pathom

Kanchanaburi

1

**BANGKOK** ✈

Sa Kaew

Aranyaprathet

Sisophon

4

Samut Songkhram

Chonburi

3

Si Racha

Pattaya ✈

C A M B O D I A

317

Phetchaburi

*Ko Si Chang*

Cha-am

Rayong

Chanthaburi

Hua Hin ✈

3

Trat

♦ *KHAO SAM ROI YOT NATIONAL PARK*

*Ko Samet*

*Ko Chang*

B U R M A

Prachuap Khiri Khan

*G U L F O F T H A I L A N D*

A N D A M A N   S E A

Chumphon ✈

Kaw Thaung

*ANG THONG NATIONAL PARK*

◆ *Ko Tao*

Ranong ✈

41

*Ko Pha Ngan*

4

*KHAO SOK NATIONAL PARK* ♦

Chaiya

*Ko Samui* ✈

*Ko Surin*

Surat Thani ✈

BURMA

LAOS

Takua Pa

401

THAILAND

Khao Lak

*KHAO LUANG NATIONAL PARK* ♦

Bangkok

CAMBODIA

*Ko Similan*

Phang Nga

Nakhon Si Thammarat ✈

A N D A M A N   S E A

Krabi ✈

408

VIETNAM

Phuket ✈

*GULF OF THAILAND*

*Ko Phi Phi*

4

Phatthalung

*Ko Lanta*

Trang ✈

0   200 km

MALAYSIA

Songkhla

Pak Bara

Hat Yai ✈

Pattani

| Meters | |
|---|---|
| | 1000 |
| | 500 |
| | 200 |
| | 100 |
| | 0 |

*KO TARUTAO NATIONAL PARK*

*THALE BAN NATIONAL PARK*

Satun

42

Yala

Narathiwat ✈

*Langkawi*

Kuala Perlis

Kota Bharu

Alor Setar

410

Sungai Kolok

Betong

0      50km

Georgetown

*Penang*

MALAYSIA

## Introduction to
# Thailand's
# Beaches & Islands

**Despite myriad cultural attractions, sand and sea are what most Thailand holidays are about, and with over three thousand kilometres of tropical coastline there are plenty of stunning white-sand beaches to choose from. In addition, the peculiar shape of the country – which is popularly considered to be reminiscent of an elephant's head, with Bangkok as the eye, the East Coast as the chin, and the peninsular Andaman and Gulf coasts forming the trunk – means you can dive, swim and sunbathe all year round, for when the monsoon rains are battering one coast you merely have to cross to the other to escape them.**

Geographical differences have given distinctive character to each of the coasts. The **Andaman Coast** is the most dramatic, edged by sheer limestone cliffs carved by wind and water into strange silhouettes, and interleaved with thick bands of mangrove forest. The **Gulf Coast** begins and ends quietly with relatively flat, featureless stretches to the south of Bangkok and down towards the Malaysian border, but peaks at its midpoint, where the peninsular mountains march into the sea to form the wildly varied landscapes of the Samui archipelago and the Ang Thong National Marine Park. A fair chunk of the **East Coast** is dominated by the rigs of offshore oil and gas exploration, but the islands that lie further out have forested spines and gorgeous

iii

strands. In short, you'll find great beaches on all three coasts: idyllic confections of clear turquoise waters at invitingly balmy temperatures, sand so soft that it squeaks underfoot, and palm trees laden with coconuts.

The Thai royal family started the craze for seaside holidays by making regular trips to Hua Hin in the early 1900s, and the subsequent construction of the Southern Railway Line soon opened up the region to the rest of the population. Inspired by American GIs who'd discovered Thailand's attractions during their R&R breaks from Vietnam, it wasn't long before foreign holidaymakers followed suit, and these days **tourism** is the main industry in nearly all Thailand's coastal areas. Many of the most beautiful spots have been well and truly discovered, and a number have developed into full-blown high-rise resorts which seem to have more in common with the Costa del Sol than the rest of Southeast Asia. But you need only venture a few kilometres from such anomalies to encounter a more traditional scene of fishing communities, rubber plantations and Buddhist temples. Over ninety percent of Thais are **Theravada Buddhists**, and their faith colours all aspects of daily life, from the tiered temple rooftops that dominate the skyline, to the omnipresent saffron-robed monks and the packed calendar of festivals.

## Fact file

● Known as Siam until 1939, Thailand lies wholly within the tropics, covering **511,770 square kilometres** and divided into 76 provinces or *changwat*. The population of **62 million** is made up of ethnic Thais (75 percent) and Chinese (14 percent), with the rest mainly immigrants from neighbouring countries and hill-tribespeople; the national language is *phasaa thai*. **Buddhism** is the national religion, practised by 95 percent of Thais, and Islam the largest minority religion.

● Since 1932 the country has been a constitutional monarchy; **King Bhumibol, aka Rama IX** (being the ninth ruler of the Chakri dynasty), has been on the throne since 1946. The elected National Assembly (*Rathasapha*) has five hundred MPs in the House of Representatives (*Sapha Phuthaen Ratsadon*), led by a prime minister, and two hundred members of the Senate (*Wuthisapha*). With around a dozen major political parties, coalition governments are common.

● **Tourism** is the country's main industry, and its biggest exports are **computers**, **textiles**, **rice**, **tapioca** and **rubber**.

## Sea kayaking

One of the most exciting ways of exploring the sea caves, hidden lagoons and mangrove swamps that characterize southern Thailand's coastlines is by sea kayak. Undisturbed by thrumming engines, you paddle silently between the limestone outcrops, getting a privileged view of the resident birds, reptiles and monkeys. Intriguingly, you may also be guided into a

secret tidal lagoon or *hong*; completely enclosed by impenetrable rock face, these hidden pools inside the outcrops are only accessible via a series of tunnels at a certain point in the tide. Sea kayaking is a popular activity around Krabi (see p.361), Phuket (see p.329), Ko Samui (see p.257) and Trang (see p.402), where reputable tour operators will provide good quality kayaks, instructors and guides – and even someone to paddle for you if necessary.

# Where to go

A irline schedules decree that many beach holidays begin in **Bangkok**, and despite initial impressions, Thailand's crazy, polluted capital is well worth a couple of days of your time. Within the city's historic core you'll find resplendent temples, canalside markets and the opulent indulgence of the eighteenth-century Grand Palace, all of which make a good antidote to the mind-boggling array of markets, boutiques and restaurants in the fashionable downtown area.

Within easy striking distance of Bangkok, the East Coast resort of **Pattaya** is the country's most popular – and least interesting – destination, a concrete warren of hotels and strip joints that makes its money from package tourists

who are unaware of what they're missing. Yet just a few dozen kilometres further east sit the islands of **Ko Samet** and **Ko Chang**, whose superb sands are dotted with beach huts and bungalows designed to appeal to all budgets and tastes.

After an interesting inland diversion at the atmospheric, temple-filled town of **Phetchaburi**, the peninsular Gulf Coast kicks off with the historic resort of **Hua Hin** – now rather disfigured by excessive hotel development, though still a good place for a seafood dinner and a round of golf. The main draw on this side of the peninsula, though, is the Samui archipelago to the south: **Ko Samui** itself is the most developed of the three main islands here, but has kept its good looks and offers an appealing variety of beachside accommodation; **Ko Pha Ngan**, with its small resorts and desolate coves, is still firmly backpacker territory, drawing teenage ravers and solitude seekers in equal parts; while the last outcrop, **Ko Tao**, is the most rustic of the three, but has established itself as one of the world's leading centres for scuba-diving courses.

Across on the other side of the peninsula, the Andaman Coast boasts even more exhilarating scenery and the finest coral reefs in the country, in particular around the spectacular **Ko Similan** island chain, which ranks as one of the best dive sites in the world. The largest Andaman Coast island, **Phuket**, is one of Thailand's top tourist destinations and is graced with a dozen fine beaches; many of these have been overdeveloped with expensive high-rises and throbbing nightlife, but quieter corners can still be found. **Ko Phi Phi** has also suffered under unregulated con-

struction, but its coral-rich sea remains an untainted azure, and the sheer limestone cliffs that characterize the coastline here – and elsewhere around the harbour town and beaches of nearby **Krabi** – are breathtakingly beautiful. The island of **Ko Lanta** has a more understated charm and is a popular destination for families. Inland attractions generally pale in comparison to the coastal splendours, but the rainforests of **Khao Sok National Park** are a notable exception.

Further down the Thai peninsula, in the provinces of the deep south, the edgy relationship between Thai sovereignty and Malaysian Islam – the kind of cultural brew that has characterized Thailand throughout its history – makes this a rewarding region for the more adventurous traveller to explore. The immediate attractions are the teeming sea life and unfrequented sands of **Ko Tarutao National Marine Park** and the islands off **Trang**, while **Songkhla** on the east coast is a good sand-and-see all-rounder, with miles of beach and several diverting museums.

# When to go

T he **climate** of most of Thailand is governed by three seasons: rainy (roughly June through October), caused by the southwest monsoon dumping moisture gathered from the Andaman Sea and the Gulf of Thailand; cool (November to February); and hot (March through May). The **rainy season** is the least predictable of the three, varying in length and intensity from year to year, but usually it gathers force between June and August, coming to a peak in September and October, when unpaved roads are reduced to mud troughs and whole districts of Bangkok are flooded. The **cool season** is the pleasantest time to visit, although temperatures can still reach a

## Rat or raja?

There's no standard system of transliterating Thai script into Roman, so you're sure to find that the Thai words in this book don't always match the versions you'll see elsewhere. Maps and street signs are the biggest sources of confusion, so we've generally gone for the transliteration that's most common on the spot. However, sometimes you'll need to do a bit of lateral thinking, bearing in mind that a classic variant for the town of Satun is Satul, while among street names, Thanon Rajavithi could come out as Thanon Ratwithi – and it's not unheard of to find one spelling posted at one end of a road, with another at the opposite end. See p.457 for an introduction to the Thai language.

broiling 30°C in the middle of the day. In the **hot season**, when temperatures often rise to 35°C in Bangkok, the best thing to do is to hit the beach.

Within this scheme, slight variations are found from region to region. In southern Thailand, temperatures are more consistent throughout the year, with less variation the closer you get to the equator. The rainy season hits the **Andaman Coast** of the southern peninsula harder than anywhere else in the country – heavy rainfall usually starts in May and persists at the same level until October. The **Gulf Coast** of the southern peninsula lies outside this general pattern – with the sea immediately to the east, this coast and its offshore islands feel the effects of the northeast monsoon, which brings rain between October and January. This area suffers less than the Andaman Coast from the southwest monsoon, getting a comparatively small amount of rain between June and September.

Overall, the **cool season** is generally the **best time** to come to Thailand:

as well as having more manageable temperatures and less rain, it offers waterfalls in full spate and the best of the flowers in bloom. Bear in mind, however, that it's also the busiest season, so forward planning is essential.

To find out the current weather situation and seven-day **forecast** in some twenty towns around Thailand, visit the Thai Meteorological Department website at Ⓦ www.tmd.motc.go.th/eng/index.html

## Thailand's Climate

AVERAGE DAILY TEMPERATURES (°C) AND MONTHLY RAINFALL (MM)

| | JAN | FEB | MAR | APR | MAY | JUNE | JULY | AUG | SEPT | OCT | NOV | DEC |
|---|---|---|---|---|---|---|---|---|---|---|---|---|
| **Bangkok** | | | | | | | | | | | | |
| °C | 26 | 28 | 29 | 30 | 30 | 29 | 29 | 28 | 28 | 28 | 27 | 26 |
| mm | 11 | 28 | 31 | 72 | 190 | 152 | 158 | 187 | 320 | 231 | 57 | 9 |
| **Pattaya** | | | | | | | | | | | | |
| °C | 26 | 28 | 29 | 30 | 30 | 29 | 29 | 28 | 28 | 28 | 27 | 26 |
| mm | 12 | 23 | 41 | 79 | 165 | 120 | 166 | 166 | 302 | 229 | 66 | 10 |
| **Ko Samui** | | | | | | | | | | | | |
| °C | 26 | 26 | 28 | 29 | 29 | 28 | 28 | 28 | 28 | 27 | 26 | 25 |
| mm | 38 | 8 | 12 | 63 | 186 | 113 | 143 | 123 | 209 | 260 | 302 | 98 |
| **Phuket** | | | | | | | | | | | | |
| °C | 27 | 28 | 28 | 29 | 28 | 28 | 28 | 28 | 27 | 27 | 27 | 27 |
| mm | 35 | 31 | 39 | 163 | 348 | 213 | 263 | 263 | 419 | 305 | 207 | 52 |

# things not to miss

*It's not possible to explore every inch of Thailand's coastline in one trip – and we don't suggest you try. What follows is a selective taste of the highlights: outstanding beaches, spectacular dives, exuberant festivals and unforgettable temples. They're arranged in five colour-coded categories, so you can browse through to find the very best things to see, do, buy and experience. All highlights have a page reference to take you straight into the guide, where you can find out more.*

**01** **Ko Lanta** Page **379** • Choose from a dozen different beaches on this long, forested island, inhabited by Muslim fishing families and traditional sea gypsy communities.

**02 Full moon party at Hat Rin, Ko Pha Ngan** Page 272 • *Apocalypse Now* without the war . . .

**03 Seafood** Page **44** • Fresh fish, curried with vegetables or steamed whole with ginger and mushrooms, omelettes stuffed with mussels, hot and sour soup with prawns and lemongrass, spicy salads of papaya and crab . . . the only problem is knowing when to stop.

**04 Ko Samet** Page **191** • Petite and pretty, Ko Samet's gorgeous white-sand beaches are justifiably popular.

**05 Ko Pha Ngan** Page 269 • The island is dotted with beautiful beaches, so plump for the seclusion of Bottle Beach or Thong Nai Pan, or gear up for the fun at Hat Rin.

**06 Songkhla** Page **419** • A great all-round base, with miles of sandy beach, some fine restaurants and accommodation, and fascinating sights, including the best museum in the south.

**08 Traditional massage** Page **118** • Combining elements of acupressure and chiropractic, a pleasantly brutal way to help shed jetlag, or simply to end the day.

**09 Loy Krathong** Page **60** • At this nationwide festival held in honour of the water spirits, Thais everywhere float miniature baskets filled with flowers and lighted candles on canals, rivers, ponds and seashores.

**07 Khao Sok National Park** Page **309** • Treehouses, mist-clad outcrops and whooping gibbons make Khao Sok a memorable place to spend the night.

xi

**10** **Phetchaburi** Page **229** • Many of the temples in this charming, historic town date back 300 years and are still in use today.

**11** **Ko Tao** Page **279** • Take a dive course, or just explore this remote island's contours by boat or on foot.

**12** **Diving and snorkelling off Ko Similan** Page **317** • The underwater scenery at this remote chain of national park islands is among the finest in the world.

**13** **Night markets** Page **44** • After-dark gatherings of dramatically lit pushcart kitchens, which are usually the best-value and most entertaining places to eat.

**14** **Songkhran** Page **59** • Thai New Year is the excuse for a national waterfight – don't plan on getting much done if you come in mid-April, just join in the fun.

**15** **Ko Chang, Trat**
Page **211** • Chill out on the long, white sand beaches of Thailand's second-largest, yet still relatively undeveloped, island.

**16** **The Grand Palace, Bangkok**
Page **111** • No visitor should miss this huge complex, which encompasses the country's holiest and most beautiful temple, Wat Phra Kaeo, and its most important image, the Emerald Buddha.

**17** **Rock-climbing** Page **363** • Even novice climbers can enjoy scaling the limestone cliffs on Laem Phra Nang for unbeatable views of the stunning Andaman coastline.

## 18 Krung Ching waterfall, Nakhon Si Thammarat
Page **292** • On the northern flank of Khao Luang, the south's highest mountain, Krung Ching is probably Thailand's most spectacular drop, reachable only by a nature trail through dense, steamy jungle.

## 19 Chatuchak Weekend Market, Bangkok Page **143**
• With over 6000 stalls selling everything from hill-tribe jewellery to cooking pots, Chatuchak Weekend Market is Thailand's top shopping experience.

## 20 Ko Tarutao National Marine Park Page **409** • Spectacular and relatively peaceful islands, with a surprising variety of landscapes and fauna.

## 21 Phuket
Page **319** • It's surprisingly easy to find a tranquil spot on Phuket, especially on the less developed northwest coast.

## 22 Vegetarian festival, Phuket Page **327** •
During Taoist Lent, fasting Chinese devotees test their spiritual resolve with public acts of gruesome self-mortification.

# Underwater Thailand

The Indian Ocean (Andaman Sea) and the South China Sea (Gulf of Thailand) together play host to over 850 species of open-water fish, more than 100 species of reef fish and some 200 species of hard coral. On these pages we highlight just a few of the most interesting examples; for information on the best dive sites and bases, see "Outdoor Activities" in Basics on p.67.

Cabbage patch coral

# Coral

Coral reefs are living organisms composed of a huge variety of marine life forms, but the foundation of every reef is its ostensibly inanimate **stony coral** – hard constructions such as **boulder**, **cabbage patch, mushroom, bushy staghorn** and **brain coral**. Stony coral is composed of whole colonies of polyps – minuscule invertebrates which feed on plankton, depend on algae and direct sunlight for photosynthesis, and extract calcium carbonate (limestone) from sea water in order to reproduce. The polyps use this calcium carbonate to build new skeletons outside their bodies – an asexual reproductive process known as budding – and this is how a reef is formed. It's an extraordinarily slow process, with

Dead man's fingers

Sea fan

colony growth averaging somewhere between 0.5cm and 2.8cm a year.

The fleshy plant-like **soft coral**, such as **dead man's fingers** and **elephant's ear**, generally establishes itself on and around these banks of stony coral, swaying with the currents and using tentacles to trap all sorts of micro-organisms. Soft coral is also composed of polyps, but a variety with flaccid internal skeletons built from protein rather than calcium.

**Horny coral**, like **sea whips** and intricate **sea fans**, looks like a cross between the stony and the soft varieties, while **sea anemones** have much the most obvious, and poisonous, tentacles of any member of the coral family, using them to trap fish and other large prey.

Emperor angelfish

# Reef fish

The algae and plankton that accumulate around coral colonies attract a whole catalogue of fish known collectively as **reef fish**. Most are small in stature, with vibrant colours which serve as camouflage against the coral, flattened bodies and broad tails for easy manoeuvring around the reef, and specially adapted features to help them poke about for food in the tiniest crannies.

Among the most typical and easily encountered reef fish are **angelfish**, distinguishable from butterfly fish (see below) by a short spike extending from the gill cover; the most spectacular family member is the gorgeously coloured **emperor angelfish**.

The **moorish idol** is another fantastic sight, bizarrely shaped with a trailing streamer – or pennant fin – extending from its dorsal fin, a pronounced snout, and dramatic bands of colour.

Moorish idol

Fusilierfish

Similarly eye-catching, the ovoid **surgeonfish** often has a light blue body, a bright yellow dorsal fin and a white "chinstrap". **Butterfly fish** are named for the butterfly-like movements of their thin, flat, colourful bodies, and can swim backwards and sometimes sport eye-like blotches near the tail to confuse predators; some also have elongated snouts for nosing into crevices for food.

Other frequent visitors to the reef that make a memorable sight are the huge shoals of silvery **fusilierfish**, which move as one, changing direction in an eyecatching flash of rippling silver.

Some reef fish, among them the ubiquitous **parrot fish** (for picture see over), eat coral. With the help of a bird-like beak, which is in fact several teeth fused together, the parrot fish scrapes away at the coral, leaving characteristic white scars, and then grinds the fragments down with another set of back teeth – a practice reputedly responsible for the erosion of a great deal of Thailand's reef.

Surgeonfish

# Reef fish
(continued)

Parrotfish

**Anemonefish** are so called because, having covered themselves in the sea anemone's mucus, they are able to move amongst and gain protection from anemone tentacles, which would paralyze other fish on contact. Equally predictable is the presence of cleaner fish, or **cleaner wrasse**, on the edges of every shoal of reef fish. Streamlined, with a long snout and jaws that act like tweezers, a cleaner fish spends its days picking parasites off the skins of other fish such as the normally voracious **grouper fish** – a symbiotic relationship essential to both parties. The commonly sighted **coral hind** is a close but more colourful relative of the grouper.

Anemonefish

Coral hind

Larger, less frequent visitors to Thailand's offshore reefs include the **moray eel**, whose elongated jaws of viciously pointed teeth make it a deadly predator, and the similarly equipped **barracuda**, the world's fastest-swimming fish.

Moray eel

Manta ray

# Sharks and rays

Passive **leopard sharks** and the more excitable **white-tip reef sharks** are quite common off the Andaman coast reefs, but you'd be lucky indeed to encounter a **whale shark,** the largest fish in the world. It's also sometimes possible to swim with a **manta ray**, whose extraordinary flatness, strange wing-like fins, and massive size – up to 6m across and weighing some 1600kg – make it an astonishing presence.

Whale shark

# Turtles

Turtles sometimes paddle around reef waters, too, but all four local species – **leatherback, Olive Ridley, green** and **hawksbill** – are fast becoming endangered in Thailand, so much so that the Royal Forestry Department has placed several of their egg-laying beaches under national park protection, including those at Hat Mai Khao on Phuket, Thai Muang, Ko Surin Tai and Ko Tarutao; see p.331 for more about Thailand's turtles.

**Green turtle**

# Invertebrates

The reef is also home to myriad species of **invertebrates**, including **sea urchins**, which tend to live in shallow areas near shore. They vary not only in colour and size, but also in defence mechanisms: commonest are those with evil-looking black spines which grow up to 35cm in length, but some are covered in short,

**Sea urchin**

Crown-of-thorns starfish

Nudibranch

blunt spines or even excruciatingly painful flower-like pincers. The magnificent **crown-of-thorns starfish** is also protected by highly venomous spines, which cover the twenty or so "arms" that extend from a body that can measure up to 50cm in diameter. Disastrously for many reefs, the crown-of-thorns starfish feeds on coral, laying waste to as much as fifty square centimetres of stony coral in a 24-hour period.

Though ugly, the **sea cucumber**, which looks like a large slug and lies half-buried on the sea bed, is quite harmless. Deceptively slothful in appearance, sea cucumbers are constantly busy ingesting and excreting so much sand and mud that the combined force of those in a three-square-kilometre area can together redistribute one million kilogrammes of sea-bed material a year. Equally intriguing are the many species of hermaphroditic, shell-less mollusc known as **nudibranchs** or sea slugs, which come in an arresting array of patterns and shapes and live in shallow waters.

Crustaceans are more familiar, particularly the ubiquitous **crabs, lobsters** and **shrimps**, though may be more difficult to spot as many are masters of disguise.

Anemone crab

# Hazardous marine life

Thailand is also home to 25 species of **sea snakes**, whose tails are flattened to act as an efficient paddle in water. Most sea snakes are venomous though not aggressive. Of the poisonous ones, the commonest and most easily recognized is the banded sea snake, which is silvery grey with thirty to fifty black bands and a slightly yellow underside at its front end. It grows to 1.5m and inhabits shallow coastal waters, coming onto land to lay its eggs.

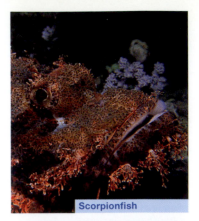
Scorpionfish

Other harmful creatures to be avoided include the highly camouflaged seabed-dwelling **stonefish** and **scorpionfish**, both of whom can be very hard to spot but have extremely poisonous spines which are dangerous when trodden on.

The magnificent **lionfish** should also be admired from afar as its impressive plumes are poisonous if brushed against, as are the tentacles of the **jelly fish.**

The **blue-spotted ray** or **stingray** has two venomous spines on its long tail with which it lashes out when threatened; as it tends to bury itself with almost complete disguise in the mud or sand near reefs, it can be a particular hazard to unwary divers. Also to be wary of is so-called **fire coral** (not actually a true coral but a coral-like brownish encrustation), which is found in shallow waters on the edge of the reef and is covered in a mass of tiny, fuzz-like tentacles that can inflict a painful burn. For advice on how to treat injuries inflicted by these underwater hazards, see Basics p.32.

Lionfish

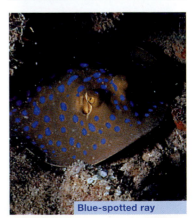
Blue-spotted ray

# contents

# using the Rough Guide

We've tried to make this Rough Guide a good read and easy to use. The book is divided into five main sections, and you should be able to find whatever you want in one of them.

## colour section

The front colour section offers a quick tour of Thailand's Beaches & Islands. The **introduction** aims to give you a feel for the place, with suggestions on where to go and what the weather is like. Next, our authors round up their favourite aspects of Thailand's Beaches & Islands in the **things not to miss** section – whether it's great food, amazing sights or a special hotel. Right after this comes the Rough Guide's full **contents** list.

## basics

You've decided to go and the Basics section covers all the **pre-departure** nitty-gritty to help you plan your trip. This is where to find out which airlines fly to your destination, what paperwork you'll need, what to do about money and insurance, about internet access, food, security, public transport, car rental – in fact just about every piece of **general practical information** you might need.

## guide

This is the heart of the Rough Guide, divided into user-friendly chapters, each of which covers a specific region. Every chapter starts with a list of **highlights** and an **introduction** that helps you to decide where to go, depending on your time and budget.

Likewise, introductions to the various towns and smaller regions within each chapter should help you plan your itinerary. We start most town accounts with information on arrival and accommodation, followed by a tour of the sights, and finally reviews of places to eat and drink, and details of nightlife. Longer accounts also have a directory of practical listings. Each chapter concludes with **public transport** details for that region.

## contexts

Read Contexts to get a deeper understanding of what makes Thailand's Beaches & Islands tick. We include a brief history, articles about **religion** and **the environment**, a detailed further reading section that reviews dozens of **books** relating to the country, and a **language** section which gives useful guidance for speaking Thai, and a glossary of words and terms that are peculiar to the country.

## index & small print

Apart from a **full index**, which includes maps as well as places, this section covers publishing information, credits and acknowledgements, and also has our contact details in case you want to send in updates and corrections to the book – or suggestions as to how we might improve it.

## contents ▶

## basics

## guide ▶

1 Bangkok  2 The East Coast  3 Southern Thailand: The Gulf Coast  4 Southern
Thailand: The Andaman Coast  5 The deep south

## contexts ▶

## index ▶

## chapter map of **Thailand's Beaches & Islands**

# contents

## colour section
**i–xxiv**

Colour map of the country ...................ii
Where to go..............................................v
When to go .............................................vii

Things not to miss ................................ix
underwater thailand............................xv

## basics
**7–76**

Getting there from Britain and Ireland ..9
Getting there from the USA and Canada 12
Getting there from Australia and New
Zealand ...............................................15
Travel via neighbouring countries ......18
Visas and red tape ..............................21
Information, websites and maps ........23
Money, banks and costs ....................26
Insurance ............................................28
Health ..................................................29
Getting around.....................................34
Accommodation ..................................41
Food and drink ....................................44

Telephones, mail and internet access 52
The media ............................................55
Crime and personal safety ..................56
Opening hours and holidays ..............58
Festivals ..............................................59
Entertainment and sport ....................61
Meditation centres and retreats ..........63
Cultural hints ......................................64
Outdoor activities ...............................67
Gay Thailand .......................................70
Disabled travellers .............................72
Travelling with kids .............................73
Directory ..............................................74

## guide
**77–432**

**❶ Bangkok**      **79–168**
Highlights ....................................80
Arrival ..........................................83
Orientation and information ........89
City transport ...............................90
Accommodation ..........................96
Ratanakosin ...............................111
Banglamphu and the Democracy
Monument area ..........................124
Chinatown and Pahurat ............127
Thonburi ....................................131
Dusit ..........................................135
Downtown Bangkok ..................137

Chatuchak and the outskirts ....143
Eating .........................................145
Nightlife and entertainment ......151
Shopping ...................................156
Listings ......................................161
Moving on ..................................164
Travel details .............................168

**❷ The East Coast**    **169–224**
Highlights ...................................170
Si Racha and Ko Si Chang ........173
Pattaya .......................................177
Rayong .......................................190

Ko Samet .......................191
Chanthaburi ....................202
Trat ............................206
Khlong Yai and Ban Hat Lek......209
Laem Ngop.......................209
Overland border crossings into
Cambodia .......................210
Ko Chang .......................211
Ko Mak and Ko Kham .............222
Ko Whai and Ko Lao Ya ..........223
Ko Kud .........................223
Travel details .................223

❸ Southern Thailand: The
Gulf Coast            225–293

Highlights .....................226
Phetchaburi ....................229
Cha-am and around ..............233
Hua Hin ........................235
Khao Sam Roi Yot National Park 241
Prachuap Khiri Khan ............243
Chumphon and around ............243
Chaiya .........................247
Wat Suan Mokkh .................248
Surat Thani ....................249
Ko Samui .......................252
Ang Thong National Marine Park 256
Ko Pha Ngan ....................269
Ko Tao .........................279
Nakhon Si Thammarat ............285
Khao Luang National Park .......291
Sichon .........................292
Travel details .................293

❹ Southern Thailand: The
Andaman Coast         295–390

Highlights .....................296
Ranong .........................300
Kaw Thaung .....................303
Ko Chang .......................304
Ko Pha Yam .....................306
Ko Surin .......................307

Ko Phra Thong ..................309
Khao Sok National Park .........309
Khao Lak and Bang Niang ........312
Ko Similan .....................317
Phuket .........................319
Ao Phang Nga ...................350
Krabi ..........................354
Laem Phra Nang and Ao Nam Mao
................................361
Ao Nang ........................365
Hat Nopparat Thara .............368
Ko Phi Phi .....................369
Ko Lanta Yai ...................379
Ko Bubu and Ko Jum .............388
Travel details .................389

❺ The deep south       391–432

Highlights .....................392
Phatthalung ....................396
Thale Noi Waterbird Park .......398
Trang town .....................398
The coast: Pak Meng to Ban
Chao Mai .......................402
Ko Hai .........................403
Ko Mook ........................404
Ko Kradan ......................405
Ko Libong ......................405
Ko Sukorn ......................406
Satun ..........................407
Thale Ban National Park ........408
Ko Tarutao National Marine Park 409
Ko Phetra National Marine Park ..414
Ko Bulon Lae ...................414
Hat Yai ........................415
Songkhla .......................419
Ko Yo ..........................424
Khu Khut Waterbird Park ........425
Pattani ........................426
Yala ...........................427
Betong .........................427
Narathiwat and around ..........428
Travel details .................432

# contexts                433–462

History ........................435
Religion: Thai Buddhism ........442
The coastal environment ........447

Books ..........................452
Language .......................457
Glossary .......................461

# map symbols

maps are listed in the full index using coloured text

| | | | |
|---|---|---|---|
| ▬▬▬ | International boundary | 🏔 | Mountains |
| ▬ ▬ ▬ | Chapter division boundary | ⬇ | Viewpoint |
| ═══ | Road | ⌂ | Cave |
| ∷∷∷ | Unpaved road | 🌊 | Waterfall |
| - - - - | Path | ⍢ | Lighthouse |
| ▬╫▬ | Railway | ✗ | Airport |
| – – – | Ferry route | ⓘ | Information office |
| ───── | Waterway | © | Telephone |
| ♦ | Point of interest | ⊞ | Hospital |
| ♟ | Border crossing | ⊠ | Post office |
| ▣ | Accommodation | ⚏ | Market |
| ◉ | Restaurants & bars | ▮ | Building |
| ⛺ | Campground | ✚ | Church |
| @ | Internet access | ▦ | Park |
| ⚲ | Temple | ▢ | Beach |
| ▲ | Peak | | |

# basics

# basics

Getting there from Britain and Ireland ..........................................9

Getting there from the USA and Canada ...................................12

Getting there from Australia and New Zealand .........................15

Travel via neighbouring countries ..............................................18

Visas and red tape ......................................................................21

Information, websites and maps .................................................23

Money, banks and costs..............................................................26

Insurance.....................................................................................28

Health..........................................................................................29

Getting around ............................................................................34

Accommodation...........................................................................41

Food and drink.............................................................................44

Telephones, mail and internet access .......................................52

The media ...................................................................................55

Crime and personal safety..........................................................56

Opening hours and holidays........................................................58

Festivals .....................................................................................59

Entertainment and Sport.............................................................61

Meditation centres and retreats..................................................63

Cultural hints...............................................................................64

Outdoor activities........................................................................67

Gay Thailand ..............................................................................70

Disabled travellers.......................................................................72

Travelling with kids......................................................................73

Directory......................................................................................74

# Getting there from **Britain and Ireland**

The fastest and most comfortable way of reaching Thailand is to fly non-stop from London to Bangkok with either Qantas, British Airways, EVA Airways or Thai International – a journey time of about twelve hours. Many scheduled airlines operate indirect flights to Bangkok (ie flights with one or more connections), which usually take up to four hours longer, but work out significantly cheaper; Lauda Air also flies London–Phuket with a change in Vienna. Prices for these vary throughout the year, with airlines such as Lufthansa (who fly via Frankfurt) and Royal Jordanian (who stop off in Amman) offering good deals. A small but growing number of charter flights are now available, especially to Phuket, which can get you into the south of the country quickly and cheaply.

There are no non-stop flights from any regional airports in Britain or from any Irish airports and, rather than routing via London, you may find it convenient to fly to another European hub such as Amsterdam, Frankfurt or Vienna, and take a connecting flight from there. From British regional airports, this can sometimes work out as cheap as an indirect flight via London, but if you're looking to save money from Ireland, you're probably best off getting a cheap flight or ferry to England, then catching your flight to Bangkok from London.

If you're continuing **onward** from Thailand, then consider buying a **one-way London–Bangkok ticket** (from £220 plus airport tax) and shopping around for the next leg of your trip once you arrive (providing you've bought a Thai visa in advance of your trip – see p.21). If you're planning a long trip with several stops in Asia or elsewhere, buying a **round-the-world (RTW) ticket** makes a lot of sense. A typical one-year ticket, costing from £1250 (plus tax), would depart and return to London, taking in Singapore, Bangkok, Bali, Sydney, Auckland, Tahiti, Los Angeles and New York, leaving you to cover the Singapore–Bangkok and LA–NYC legs overland. Alternatively, you might want to consider **open-jaw** tickets, which can be remarkably good value: flying out London–Bangkok, returning Singapore–London starts from as little as £425 in low season with an airline such as Lufthansa.

## Airlines

**British Airways**UK ☎0845/773 3377, Ireland ☎1800/626747, ⊛www.britishairways.com. Daily non-stop flights from Heathrow to Bangkok.
**EVA Airways**UK ☎020/7380 8300, ⊛www.evaair.com.tw. Three non-stop Bangkok flights a week from Heathrow.
**Lauda Air**UK ☎020/7630 5924, ⊛www .laudaair.com. Flies from Gatwick via Vienna twice a week to Bangkok, and once a week to Phuket.
**Lufthansa**UK ☎0845/773 7747, Ireland ☎01/844 5544, ⊛www.lufthansa.co.uk. Five flights a week from Heathrow to Bangkok via Frankfurt
**Qantas**UK ☎0845/774 7767, ⊛www.qantas.com.au. Daily non-stop flights to Bangkok from Heathrow.
**Royal Jordanian Airlines**UK ☎020/7878 6300, ⊛www.rja.com.jo Three flights a week to Bangkok from Heathrow, via Amman.
**Thai International**UK ☎0870/606 0911 or 0161/831 7861, ⊛www.thaiair.com. Daily non-stop Bangkok flights from Heathrow.

## Fares

The most expensive times to fly are July, August and December – you may have to book two to three months in advance for cheaper tickets during these **peak periods**. Check the airline's exact seasonal dates through an agent, as you could make major savings by shifting your departure date by as little as one day.

Discounted **non-stop London–Bangkok** return fares start at around £450 low season, rising to £550 during peak periods. For **indirect flights**, Lufthansa works out among the cheapest in high season, at about £440 inclusive of tax; the best low-season rate at the time of writing is £330 with Royal Jordanian. Some agents offer special discounts (around £400 return) with the more reputable airlines for full-time students and/or under-26s. **Fares to Phuket** with Lauda Air via Vienna range from £575 to £685.

Bear in mind that the £20–30 **departure tax** applicable from British airports is not included in prices quoted by many travel agents; we have not included tax in the example fares detailed above, except where noted. Also, you'll always have to pay an airport departure tax (B500) when leaving Thailand on an international flight.

## Shopping for tickets

There's little point in buying direct from the airlines unless they happen to be running special offers; any reliable **specialist agent** (see below) will normally be able to undercut airline prices by a hefty percentage (the fares mentioned in this section are agents' prices). These discount deals nearly always carry **restrictions** on your length of stay in Thailand (generally limiting you to seven to ninety days) and usually require a fixed departure date from Thailand – check particulars with your agent.

Before making a final decision on who to book with, it's always worth checking out online agents such as www.cheapflights.co.uk and www.ebookers.ie; Teletext (or www.teletext.co.uk), which is especially good for charters; the travel sections in the weekend papers, plus *Time Out* and the *Evening Standard* in London; and free giveaway magazines like *TNT*. Many of the companies advertising in these publications are **bucket shops** who are able to offer extremely cheap deals, but there's a risk attached to companies who don't belong to official travel associations such as ABTA or IATA – if your bucket shop goes bust before you get your ticket, you get no refund. With associated agents, such as those listed below, ABTA and IATA will cover any debts in the case of bankruptcy.

You might also like to consider **courier flights**. The deal involves a package being checked through with your luggage, in return for a cheaper flight. Call up armed with the date you'd like to travel and how long you plan to stay, and they can advise whether flights are available; however, return times and luggage are restricted.

### Discount flight agents in Britain

**Bridge the World**, 47 Chalk Farm Rd, London ☎020/7911 0900, www.bridgetheworld.com. A wide choice of cut-price flights with good deals aimed at the backpacker market – particularly good for RTW tickets.
**Flightbookers**, 177–178 Tottenham Court Rd, London ☎020/7757 3000, www.ebookers.com. Low fares on an extensive range of scheduled flights.
**North South Travel**, Moulsham Mill Centre, Parkway, Chelmsford, Essex ☎01245/608291, www.northsouthtravel.co.uk. Friendly, competitive travel agency, offering discounted fares worldwide; profits are used to support projects in the developing world, especially the promotion of sustainable tourism.
**STA Travel** www.statravel.co.uk. 86 Old Brompton Rd, London ☎020/7361 6144; and over forty other branches in British cities. Worldwide specialists in low-cost flights and tours for students and under-26s, though other customers welcome.
**Trailfinders** www.trailfinders.co.uk. 194 Kensington High St, London ☎020/7938 3939; plus branches in Birmingham, Bristol, Glasgow and Manchester. One of the best-informed and most efficient agents for independent travellers.
**Travelbag**, 52 Regent St, London ☎0870/737 7843, www.travelbag.co.uk. Discount flights to the Far East; official Qantas agent.
**Travel Cuts**, 295a Regent St, London ☎020/7255 2082, www.travelcuts.co.uk. Specializes in budget, student and youth travel and RTW tickets.
**usit CAMPUS**, 52 Grosvenor Gardens, London ☎020/7730 8111, www.usitcampus.co.uk. Student/youth travel specialists, with over fifty branches, including in YHA shops and on university campuses all over Britain.

### Discount flight agents in Ireland

**Joe Walsh Tours** www.joewalshtours.ie. 69 Upper O'Connell St, Dublin ☎01/872 2555; 117 Patrick St, Cork ☎021/277 959. Discount flight agent.
**Silk Road Travel**, 64 South William St, Dublin ☎01/677 1029 or 677 1147. Specialists in Far Eastern destinations.
**Thomas Cook** www.thomascook.co.uk. 118 Grafton St, Dublin ☎01/677 0469; 11 Donegal

Place, Belfast 1 ☎0232/9055 4455. Package holiday and flight agent; also arranges traveller's cheques, insurance and car rental.

**Trailfinders** 4–5 Dawson St, Dublin ☎01/677 7888, ⓦwww.trailfinders.ie. Comprehensive and well-informed flight and travel agent, with excellent RTW ticket offers.

**usit NOW** ⓦwww.usitnow.ie. 19–21 Aston Quay, Dublin ☎01/602 1700; Fountain Centre, College Street, Belfast 1 ☎028/9032 4073, plus branches in Cork, Derry, Galway, Limerick and Waterford. Ireland's main outlet for discounted, youth and student fares.

## Courier flight brokers

**Ben's Travel** 83 Mortimer St, London W1 ☎020/7462 0022, ⓦwww.benstravel.co.uk.
**Bridges Worldwide** Old Mill House, Mill Rd, West Drayton, Middlesex ☎01895/465065 ⓦwww.bridgesworldwide.com.
**International Association of Air Travel Couriers** c/o International Features, 1 Kings Rd, Dorchester, Dorset ☎01305/216920, ⓦwww.courier.org or www.aircourier.co.uk. Agents for lots of courier companies; a small membership fee is required to join.

## Packages

**Package deals** come in two varieties: those offering a return flight and a week or more of accommodation, and specialist tours which organize daytime activities and escorted excursions. Flight and accommodation deals can work out to be good value if you're planning to base yourself in just one or two places, costing around £700 for eight days in Bangkok and Phuket. **Specialist tour** packages, on the other hand, are pretty expensive compared to what you'd pay if you organized everything independently (from about £1400 including flight for a three-week trip), but they do cut out a lot of hassle, and the most adventurous ones often feature activities and itineraries that wouldn't be easy to set up by yourself. Before booking, make sure you know exactly what's included in the price.

## Tour operators

Thailand-wide tour operators based in Bangkok are given on p.167. Prices below exclude international flights except where noted.

**Arc Journeys** ☎020/7681 3175, ⓦwww.travelarc.com. Small group and tailor-made tours. Regular departures include a nine-day overland tour from Bangkok to Singapore, taking in visits to the River Kwai, Hua Hin, Ranong, Krabi and Phuket for £900 per person.

**Bales Worldwide** ☎0870/241 3208, ⓦwww.balesworldwide.co.uk. Traditional high-quality escorted trips, including a fourteen-day "Images of Thailand" tour from £1300 (including flights and some meals) as well as tailor-made itineraries.

**British Airways Holidays** ☎0870/242 4245, ⓦwww.baholidays.co.uk. Beach- and city-based flight and accommodation packages; for example, five nights in Pattaya from £625. Bookings can be made direct or through most travel agents.

**Gecko Travel** ☎023/9237 6799, ⓦwww.geckotravel.co.uk. Southeast Asia specialist operating small-group adventure holidays with off-the-beaten-track itineraries; their 15-day "Reefs and Rainforests" tour of peninsular Thailand starts at £1250 including flights.

**Golden Joy Holidays** ☎0870/241 5187, www.goldenjoy.com. Diving-tour organizers; in Thailand the company specializes in the Andaman Coast, offering tailor-made packages; five days' day-boat diving in Krabi costs from £225.

**Hayes and Jarvis** ☎0870/898 9890, www.hayes-jarvis.com. Tours and hotel-based holidays; five nights in Hua Hin cost £580 including flights. Particularly good on diving destinations; exotic weddings also organized.

**Imaginative Traveller** ☎020/8742 8612, ⓦwww.imaginative-traveller.com. Small-group adventure tours off the beaten track, including a 13-day "Islands and Jungles" package taking in Khao Sok and Ko Pha Ngan for £645.

**Joe Walsh Tours** ☎01/676 0991, ⓦwww.joewalshtours.ie. Well-established Irish tour operator offering twelve-day packages to Bangkok and Pattaya from £1250 including flights.

**Kuoni Travel** ☎020/7499 8636, ⓦwww.kuoni.co.uk. Specializes in two-centre holidays, including flights and accommodation, with good family offers. Eight nights in Bangkok and Phuket from £700. Bookings through most travel agents.

**Magic Of The Orient** ☎01293/537700, www.magic-of-the-orient.com. A wide range of upmarket tailor-made packages, including short tours with your own driver, such as three days in Khao Lak and Khao Sok National Park (£300 per person sharing).

**Peregrine Holidays** ☎01865/559988, ⓦwww.peregrineadventures.co.uk. Soft adventure holidays with upmarket accommodation; their

"Tropical South" tour is an eleven-day trip that covers Khao Sok, Krabi, Ko Phi Phi and Phuket (from £500).
**Skyros** ☏020/7267 4424, ⓦwww.skyros.com. Large selection of holistic courses from a base in the Ao Prao resort on Ko Samet, ranging from yoga to sailing and art. A two-week session including accommodation and half board starts at £700.
**Symbiosis** ☏020/7924 5906, ⓦwww.symbiosis-travel.co.uk. High-quality tailor-made adventure and special-interest packages, including diving, with a commitment to environmentally sensitive and fair-trade tourism; prices start from around £80 a day, including flights and accommodation.
**Thomas Cook Holidays** ☏01733/563200, ⓦwww.tcholidays.com. Mainstream tour operator with seven-night packages to Phuket in five-star accommodation from £700, including flights.

# Getting there from **the USA and Canada**

There are no non-stop flights from North America to Thailand, but plenty of airlines run daily flights to Bangkok from major east- and west-coast cities with only one stop en route. Bear in mind that the layover time between connecting flights can vary not just from carrier to carrier, but between different flights operated by the same airline. The actual flying time is approximately 18 hours from LA via Asia, around an hour longer from New York via Europe. From Canada, you can expect to spend something like sixteen hours in the air flying from Vancouver (via Tokyo) or at least twenty hours from Montreal (via Europe).

Some of the major airlines offer **Circle Pacific** deals, often in partnership with other airlines. Generally valid for one year, these tickets allow you to make a certain number of stopovers en route between the West Coast of the US and Canada and Asia, usually on condition that you travel in an onward direction. Once you factor in the frequent no-backtracking proscription, your possible itinerary may be rather limited, and cost more than a more flexible multi-airline choice. A better bet might be a Circle Pacific ticket booked through a discount travel agent (see p.14): this way, for example, an itinerary starting out and ending in Los Angeles, taking in Tokyo, Hong Kong, Bangkok–Singapore, Jakarta, Denpasar (Bali) and Sydney costs around US$2100.

If Thailand is only one stop on a longer journey, you might also want to consider buying a **round-the-world (RTW) ticket**. Some travel agents can sell you an "off-the-shelf" RTW ticket that will have you touching down in about half a dozen cities (Bangkok is on many itineraries); others will have to assemble one for you, which can be more tailored to your needs but is apt to be more expensive. A typical off-the-shelf itinerary, starting and ending in San Francisco with stops in Hong Kong, Bangkok, Delhi, Mumbai (Bombay), London and Boston costs around US$1500.

## Airlines

**Air Canada** ☏1-888/247-2262, ⓦwww.aircanada.ca. Daily flights to Bangkok from most major Canadian cities via Osaka, Hong Kong or London.
**Air France** US ☏1-800/237-2747, ⓦwww.airfrance.com, Canada ☏1-800/667-2747, ⓦwww.airfrance.ca. Daily flights (though inconveniently scheduled) to Bangkok, via Paris, from over a dozen North American cities.
**Cathay Pacific** ☏1-800/233-2742, ⓦwww.cathaypacific.com. Daily flights via Hong

Kong to Bangkok from New York, Los Angeles, San Francisco and Toronto.

**China Air Lines** ☎1-800/227-5118, 🌐www.china-airlines.com. Flies to Bangkok via Taipei daily from Los Angeles and San Francisco, five times a week from New York, and four times a week (summer only) from Anchorage.

**Delta Airlines** ☎1-800/241-4141, 🌐www.delta.com. Daily flights to Bangkok from most major US cities, via Seoul or Tokyo.

**Finnair**US ☎1-800/950-5000, Canada ☎1-800/461-8651, 🌐www.finnair.fi. Via Helsinki, three Bangkok flights a week from New York, and two summer-only flights a week from Toronto.

**Japan Air Lines** ☎1-800/525-3663, 🌐www.japanair.com. Flies to Bangkok via Tokyo from Chicago, Dallas, Los Angeles, New York, San Francisco, Los Angeles and Vancouver.

**KLM/Northwest**US ☎1-800/374-7747, Canada ☎1-800/361 5073, 🌐www.nwa.com. Daily flights to Bangkok via Japan from San Francisco, Los Angeles, Chicago, Detroit, Seattle and New York, or via Amsterdam from New York.

**Swissair**US ☎1-800/221-4750, Canada ☎1-800/563 5954, 🌐www.swissair.com. Daily flights to Bangkok from Montréal, New York and Toronto via Zürich.

**Thai Airways**US ☎1-800/426-5204, Canada ☎1-800/668-8103, 🌐www.thaiair.com. Daily flights to Bangkok from Los Angeles via Osaka, and from New York via London.

**United Airlines** ☎1-800/241-6522, 🌐www.ual.com. Daily flights to Bangkok from most major US cities, via Tokyo.

## Fares

Regardless of where you buy your ticket, fares will depend on the **season**, with higher fares applying in December, January and from June to August. The prices quoted below assume midweek travel (where there's a difference in price) and exclude taxes.

There doesn't seem to be much logic behind the pricing of published fares **from the US** to Thailand, although it's probably easier to find a reasonable fare on flights via Asia than via Europe, especially if you're departing from the West Coast. Expect to find regular, high-season published fares at around $1200 minimum from the West Coast and at least $1300 from the East Coast or the Midwest, while low-season fares can go for around $750 from the West Coast and $850 from the East Coast or Midwest. A discount travel agent, however,

should be able to dig up, for instance, a high-season fare from LA for around $1050. Be on the lookout also for special limited-offer promotional fares from the major carriers like United Airlines or Thai, which can bring low-season fares down to as little as $600 from the West Coast or $750 from the East Coast.

Air Canada has the most convenient service to Bangkok from the largest number of **Canadian** cities. From Vancouver, expect to pay around CDN$2000 in low season (CDN$300 more in high season), from Toronto, CDN$2300 (CDN$400 more in high season).

## Shopping for tickets

Barring special offers, the cheapest of the airlines' published fares is usually an **APEX** ticket, although this will carry certain restrictions: you will, most likely, have to book and pay up to 21 days before departure, spend at least seven days abroad (maximum stay from one to six months), and you tend to get penalized if you change your schedule.

You can normally cut costs further by going through a specialist flight agent – either a **consolidator**, who buys up blocks of tickets from the airlines and sells them at a discount, or a **discount agent**, who in addition to dealing with discounted flights may also offer special student and youth fares and a range of other travel-related services, such as travel insurance, rail passes, car rentals, tours and the like. Many of these companies sell tickets on the **internet** too, and online-only agents like 🌐www.travelocity.com are worth a try. If you travel a lot, discount **travel clubs** are another option – the annual membership fee may be worth it for benefits such as cut-price air tickets and car rental.

Don't automatically assume that tickets purchased through a travel specialist will be cheapest – once you get a quote, check with the airlines and you may turn up an even better deal. Be advised also that the pool of travel companies is swimming with sharks – exercise caution and *never* deal with a company that demands cash up front or refuses to accept payment by credit card.

Finally, if you're able to fly at short notice, live in or near one of the major North American airport hubs and don't mind fitting into someone else's schedule, then a **courier flight** would probably be your cheapest option. Bangkok isn't as cheap as some courier destinations, but occasionally good bargains and even free flights come up – check regularly at the websites listed below for details.

**Air Brokers International**, 150 Post St, Suite 620, San Francisco ☎1-800/883-3273 or 415/397-1383, ⓦwww.airbrokers.com. Consolidator and specialist in RTW tickets.

**Air Courier Association** ☎1-800/282-1202, ⓦwww.aircourier.org. Courier flight broker; membership costs $50 for one year. A Bangkok flight with them costs $300–550.

**Airtech**, 588 Broadway, Suite 204, New York ☎212/219-7000, ⓦwww.airtech.com. Standby-seat broker; also deals in consolidator fares and courier flights.

**Council Travel** ☎1-800/226-8624 or 617/528-2091, ⓦwww.counciltravel.com. Offices include: 205 E 42nd St, New York ☎212/822 2700; 530 Bush St, Suite 700, San Francisco ☎415/421-3473; 931 Westwood Blvd, Los Angeles ☎310/208-3551; 1153 N Dearborn St, Chicago ☎312/951-0585. Nationwide US organization specializing in student/budget travel.

**Educational Travel Center**, 438 N Frances St, Madison ☎1-800/747-5551 or 608/256-5551, ⓦwww.edtrav.com. Student/youth discount agent.

**High Adventure Travel**, 442 Post St, Suite 400, San Francisco ☎1-800/350-0612 or 415/912-5600, ⓦwww.airtreks.com. RTW and Circle Pacific tickets.

**International Association of Air Travel Couriers** ☎561/582-8320, ⓦwww.courier.org. Courier flight broker with membership fee of around $45 a year.

**Now Voyager**, 74 Varick St, Suite 307, New York ☎212/431-1616, ⓦwww.nowvoyagertravel.com. Consolidator and courier flight broker.

**STA Travel** ☎1800/777-0112, ⓦwww.sta-travel.com. Branches include: 10 Downing St, New York ☎212/627-3111; 7202 Melrose Ave, Los Angeles ☎323/934-8722; 36 Geary St, San Francisco ☎415/391-8407; 297 Newbury St, Boston ☎617/266-6014; 429 S Dearborn St, Chicago ☎312/786-9050; 1905 Walnut St, Philadelphia ☎215/568-7999. Worldwide specialists in independent travel; also student IDs, travel insurance, car rental, etc.

**Travac**, 989 6th Ave, New York ☎1-800/872-8800, ⓦwww.thetravelsite.com. Consolidator and charter broker.

**Travel Avenue**, 10 S Riverside, Suite 1404, Chicago ☎1-800/333-3335, ⓦwww.travelavenue.com. Full-service travel agent that offers discounts in the form of rebates.

**Travel Cuts** ☎1-800/667-2887, ⓦwww.travelcuts.com. Branches include: 187 College St, Toronto ☎416/979-2406; 1613 rue St Denis, Montréal ☎514/843-8511; Student Union Building, University of British Columbia, Vancouver ☎888/FLY CUTS or 604/822-6890). Canadian student travel organization.

## Packages

**Package tours** are often expensive and aimed at those who treasure comfort, but can be excellent value, provided you really want to do all the activities, trips and tours. Those looking for more flexible scheduling would be advised to start with a city package such as those offered by Thai Air (or simply get to Bangkok under their own steam). From the capital, you can then consider a more personal, tailored package to the beaches and islands. All prices quoted below exclude taxes; unless stated otherwise, round-trip flights are from the West Coast.

**Abercrombie & Kent** ☎1-800/323-7308 or 630/954-2944, ⓦwww.abercrombiekent.com. Deluxe ten-day "Highlights of Thailand" tour ($2300 not including flight), plus several other packages which include Thailand as part of a more extensive Asian itinerary.

**Absolute Asia** ☎1-800/736-8187 or 212/627-1950, ⓦwww.absoluteasia.com. Customized tours, covering such specialist interests as archeology and Thai cuisine, as well as a fourteen-day "Discover Thailand" trip taking in Bangkok, the north and Phuket ($1500 excluding international flights).

**Adventures Abroad** ☎1-800/665-3998 or 604/303-1099, ⓦwww.adventures-abroad.com. Small-group specialists with a one-week Thailand tour that starts at about CDN$1100 excluding flights.

**Adventure Center** ☎1-800/228-8747 or 510/654-1879, ⓦwww.adventure-center.com. Over twenty packages, some covering Thailand exclusively, others including Laos, Malaysia or Singapore, from around $500 excluding flight.

**Asia Pacific Adventures** ☎1-800/825-1680 or 818/886-5190, ⊛www.asiapacificadventures.com. Customized tours involving an exciting variety of activities such as sea canoeing, homestays and Thai cooking.

**Asia Trans Pacific Journeys** ☎1-800/642-2742, ⊛www.southeastasia.com. Customized tours and packages; their "Explorer's Thailand" tour lasts sixteen days and costs from $2800 excluding flights.

**EastQuest** ☎1-800/638-3449 or 212/741-1688, ✉earthquest1@aol.com. Customized tours plus adventure or traditional sightseeing packages.

Elderhostel ☎1-877/426-8056, ⊛www.elderhostel.org. Specialists in educational and activity programmes, cruises and homestays for senior travellers; they do an eighteen-day "Discovering Thailand" package costing around $3000 including flights.

**Geographic Expeditions** ☎1-800/777-8183 or 415/922-0448, ⊛www.geoex.com. Among their offerings is a choice of five four-day extensions to a Bangkok stay, including a sea cruise or a trip to Ko Samui (from $1000).

**Goway Travel** ☎1-800/387-8850 or 416/322-1034, ⊛www.goway.com. Wide range of Thailand packages, including three-night tours of Ko Samui and four-nighters in Phuket.

**Himalayan Travel** ☎1-800/225-2380 or 203/743-2349, ⊛www.gorp.com/himtravel.htm. Customized tours plus a range of set packages, including the fifteen-day "Tropical South", which takes in Phuket and costs around $900 excluding flights.

**Journeys International** ☎1-800/255-8735 or 734/665-4407, ⊛www.journeys-intl.com. Established ecotourism operator, offering a five-day "Rainforests & Remote Islands" tour to Thailand from $650 excluding flights.

**Royal Orchid Holidays** ☎1-800/426-5204, ⊛www.thaiair.com. Subsidiary of Thai Airways; does seven-night Bangkok packages from around $900 in low season, including flights, with seaside extensions available. Also regular promotional offers, when prices for a round-trip flight and four nights in a downtown Bangkok hotel can go for between $550 and $900.

**Saga Holidays** ☎1-877/265-6862, ⊛www.sagaholidays.com. Specialists in group travel for senior citizens. Seven nights in Bangkok from $1000 including flights, with seaside extensions available.

# Getting there from **Australia and New Zealand**

There's no shortage of scheduled flights to Bangkok from Australia and New Zealand, with direct services offered by Thai Airways, Qantas and Air New Zealand (flight times from Perth and Sydney are around 9hr, from Auckland around 11hr).

There are a variety of **round-the-world (RTW)** combinations that include Bangkok, with the number of free stopovers ranging from just a few to unlimited. Currently the cheapest is with Qantas/BA, allowing three free stops in each direction for around A$1700/NZ$2100. The most flexible are the mileage-based tickets such as the "Star Alliance 1" offered by the Star Alliance consortium of airlines ( ⊛www.star-alliance.com), and "One World Explorer" by Qantas, Cathay Pacific, British Airways and American Airlines; both tickets allow side trips, back-tracking and open-jaw travel (landing in one city and flying out from another). For example, prices for a RTW ticket from Sydney to Bangkok, London, New York, Los Angeles, Auckland and back to Sydney start at around A$2400/NZ$3000. Ultimately your choice will depend on where you want to travel before or after Bangkok. If your don't want to travel outside Asia, a better option Is a **Circle Asia** ticket. Put together by an alliance of airlines, these tickets allow you to travel via two or more Asian cities en route, but can be a little complicated to arrange as each sector needs to be costed separately, and backtracking isn't allowed.

Indonesia's proximity to Australia and New Zealand makes it the obvious starting point for **overlanding** to Thailand through Asia. There are regular flights to Denpasar in Bali, where you can connect with boat, rail and bus links through Java and/or Sumatra. Northern Sumatra is just a short boat ride from Malaysia and Singapore, and there are regular ferry connections between Medan and Penang, between Dumai and Melaka, and between the Riau islands and Johor Bahru and Singapore. Once in Malaysia or Singapore, you can proceed into Thailand by train, bus or plane (see p.20). Ansett, Qantas and Garuda fares to Denpasar start at A\$800/NZ\$1000. Alternatively, you could fly to Singapore or Kuala Lumpur and then continue overland to Thailand by road or rail. If you'd like to travel in a group, then Intrepid's 29-day "Bali to Bangkok Overland" trip (A\$2100/NZ\$2700 excluding airfare) may be for you.

## Airlines

**Air New Zealand** Australia ☎ 13/2476, New Zealand ☎ 09/357 3000 & 0800/737000, ⓦ www.airnz.com. Several flights a week direct to Bangkok from Auckland, Christchurch, Brisbane and Sydney.

**Ansett** Australia ☎ 13/1414 or 02/9352 6707, New Zealand ☎ 09/336 2364, ⓦ www.ansett.com.au. Several flights a week from major Australian cities and from Auckland to Denpasar and also to Bangkok, Kuala Lumpur and Singapore.

**Egypt Air** Australia ☎ 02/9267 6979, ⓦ www.egyptair.com.eg. Two flights a week direct to Singapore from Sydney.

**Garuda** Australia ☎ 1300/365330, New Zealand ☎ 09/366 1862 & 0800/128510, ⓦ www .garuda-indonesia.com. Several flights a week from major Australian cities and from Auckland to Bangkok, with a stopover in either Denpasar or Jakarta.

**Gulf Air** Australia ☎ 02/9244 2199, New Zealand ☎ 09/308 3366, ⓦ www.gulfairco.com. Three flights a week direct to Singapore from Sydney and Melbourne.

**Malaysia Airlines** Australia ☎ 13/2476, New Zealand ☎ 09/373 2741 & 0800/657472, ⓦ www.mas.com.my. Several flights a week from Brisbane, Sydney, Melbourne, Perth and Auckland, via Kuala Lumpur, to Bangkok, Phuket and Hat Yai.

**Olympic Airways** Australia ☎ 1800/221663 & 02/9251 2044, ⓦ www.olympic-airways.com. Three direct Sydney–Bangkok flights a week.

**Qantas** Australia ☎ 13/1313, New Zealand ☎ 09/357 8900 & 0800/808767, ⓦ www.qantas.com.au. Several flights a week direct to Bangkok from major Australasian cities.

**Royal Brunei Airlines** Australia ☎ 07/3221 7757, ⓦ www.bruneiair.com. Three flights a week to Bangkok via Bandar Seri Begawan from Brisbane, Darwin and Sydney.

**Singapore Airlines** Australia ☎ 02/9350 0262 & 13/1011, New Zealand ☎ 09/303 2129 & 0800/808909, ⓦ www.singaporeair.com. Flights to Bangkok and Phuket, via Singapore: daily from Sydney, Melbourne, Perth and Auckland; four flights a week from Cairns, Brisbane and Christchurch; and three flights a week from Darwin.

**Thai Airways** Australia ☎ 1300/651960, New Zealand ☎ 09/377 3886, ⓦ www.thaiair.com. Flies direct to Bangkok three times a week from Sydney and Auckland, and twice a week from Brisbane, Melbourne, and Perth. Connections available to Hat Yai, Phuket and other Thai destinations.

## Fares

Fares are structured according to **season**; for most airlines high season is from mid-November to mid-January and May to the end of August, when fares rise by about A/NZ\$200–400. Generally airlines have a set fare from major eastern Australian cities (with Ansett and Qantas providing a shuttle service to the main point of departure), while fares from Darwin are around A\$200 cheaper. From Christchurch and Wellington you'll pay NZ\$150–300 more than from Auckland.

**From Australia**, the cheapest direct flights to **Bangkok** are with Olympic Airlines from Sydney (around A\$850/A\$1400 low/high season), while Thai Airways, Air New Zealand, BA and Qantas all weigh in around A\$1000/A\$1500. The best indirect deals are with Royal Brunei, via Bandar Seri Begawan (A\$850/A\$1100), with other airlines up to A\$400 more expensive. To **Singapore**, the best deals are with Gulf Air, Egyptair or Royal Brunei (around A\$700/A\$1200), with Royal Brunei flying to **Kuala Lumpur** for the same prices.

From New Zealand, Qantas offers the best direct low-season fares to Bangkok (around NZ$1100), with Thai Airways only marginally more expensive; Air New Zealand, however, charges a pricey NZ$1500. High-season fares on these airlines are pretty similar, at NZ$1900–2100. In high season, it's slightly cheaper to get an indirect flight to Bangkok with Garuda, though flying via Kuala Lumpur with Malaysia Airlines saves very little. Singapore Airlines flies to **Singapore** for NZ1250/NZ$1900; Malaysia Airlines' fares to **Kuala Lumpur** are about ten percent cheaper.

## Shopping for tickets

Tickets purchased direct from the airlines are usually expensive; the **discount agents** listed below offer much better deals on fares and have the latest information on limited special offers. Flight Centres and STA Travel generally offer the lowest fares. You might also want to have a look on the **internet**; Ⓦwww.travel.com.au and www.travelfor-less.co.nz offer discounted fares, as does Ⓦwww.sydneytravel.com.

### Discount travel agents

**Anywhere Travel** 345 Anzac Parade, Kingsford, Sydney ☏02/9663 0411, Ⓔanywhere@ozemail.com.au. Discounted flights as well as accommodation packages and tours.

**Budget Travel** ☏0800/808040, Ⓦwww.budgettravel.co.nz. 16 Fort St, Auckland ☏09/366 0061, plus branches around the country. Long-established agent dealing with budget air fares and accommodation packages.

**Destinations Unlimited** 220 Queen St, Auckland ☏09/373 4033. Discount fares plus a good selection of tours and holiday packages.

**Flight Centre** Ⓦwww.flightcentre.com.au, Australia: 82 Elizabeth St, Sydney ☏02/9235 3522, plus branches nationwide, nearest branch ☏13/1600; New Zealand: 350 Queen St, Auckland ☏09/358 4310, plus branches nationwide. Competitive discounts on airfares, and a wide range of package holidays and adventure tours.

**Northern Gateway** 22 Cavenagh St, Darwin ☏08/8941 1394, Ⓔoztravel@norgate.com.au. Specialize in low-cost flights to Asia from Darwin.

**STA Travel** Australia: nearest branch ☏13/1776, fastfare telesales ☏1300/360960, Ⓦwww.statravel.com.au; offices at 855 George St, Sydney; 256 Flinders St, Melbourne; other offices in state capitals and major universities. New Zealand: 10 High St, Auckland ☏09/309 0458, fastfare telesales ☏09/366 6673; plus branches in Wellington, Christchurch, Dunedin, Palmerston North, Hamilton and at major universities. Fare discounts for students and under-26s, as well as visas and travel insurance.

**Student Uni Travel** 92 Pitt St, Sydney ☏02/9232 8444; plus branches in Brisbane, Cairns, Darwin, Melbourne and Perth. Student/youth discounts and travel advice.

**Thomas Cook** Australia: 175 Pitt St, Sydney ☏02/9231 2877; 257 Collins St, Melbourne ☏03/9282 0222; plus branches in other state capitals (local branch ☏13 1771, telesales ☏1800/801002). New Zealand: 191 Queen St, Auckland ☏09/379 3920. Low-cost flights, also tours, accommodation and traveller's cheques.

**Trailfinders** Ⓦwww.trailfinders.co.au; offices at 8 Spring St, Sydney ☏02/9247 7666; 91 Elizabeth St, Brisbane ☏07/3229 0887; Hides Corner, Shield St, Cairns ☏07/4041 1199. Independent-travel specialist.

**Travel.com.au** 76–80 Clarence St, Sydney ☏02/9249 5444 & 1800/000447, Ⓦwww.travel.com.au. Flight discounts.

**usit BEYOND** Ⓦwww.usitbeyond.co.nz. Cnr Shortland St and Jean Batten Place, Auckland ☏09/379 4224 or 0800/788336; plus branches in Christchurch, Dunedin, Palmerston North, Hamilton and Wellington. Student/youth travel specialists.

## Package holidays and tours

An **organized tour** is worth considering if you have ambitious sightseeing plans and only a short time to accomplish them, or feel unsure about the language and customs. Most tour companies offer a range of itineraries that take in the major sights and activities. Some of the adventure-oriented tours can help you to get to the more remote areas and include activities such as kayaking and diving.

If you can only manage a short visit and are happy to base yourself in one city or resort, **package holidays** can be an economical and hassle-free way of sampling Thailand. Accommodation/flight packages, Bangkok city stays, fly-drive options and coach tours are offered by a whole host of operators through your travel agent; most can also arrange add-on trips to resort islands, cruises from Bangkok, air passes and rail travel, and can book accommodation in regional Thailand. Sample city-break prices, including international flights, are around A$1200/NZ$1600 for five nights in Bangkok or eight nights in Phuket (the exact price depends on the type of accommodation chosen). Package holidays departing from Darwin, where available, generally cost about A$200 less per person.

## Specialist tour operators and agents

Prices below exclude air fares from Australia and New Zealand except where noted.

**Abercrombie and Kent** Australia ☏03/9699 9766 or 1800/331429, New Zealand ☏ 09/579 3369. Upmarket tours, including four-day luxury train journeys on the Eastern and Oriental Express from Kuala Lumpur to Bangkok (A$2000/NZ$2500).

**Allways Travel** ☏1800/259297, ⓦwww.allwaysdive.com.au. All-inclusive dive packages to prime Thai dive sites.

**Asian Explorer Holidays** ☏07/3832 4266. A selection of accommodation in Bangkok and tours.

**Asian Travel Centre** ☏03/9654 8277. A variety of tours and accommodation in Thailand.

**Birding Worldwide** ☏03/9899 9303, ⓦwww.birdingworldwide.com.au. Three-week bird-watching tours in Thailand's national parks.

**Intrepid Travel** ☏1800/629186, ⓦwww.intrepidtravel.com.au. A host of one- to four-week low-impact, country-wide adventure tours.

Their fifteen-day Southern Thailand trip (A$1200/NZ$1600) explores villages, islands and beaches by day, while spending the nights either camping or staying in a variety of local accommodation.

**New Horizons Holidays** ☏08/9268 3777. Largest Southeast Asian wholesaler in Perth, offering an extensive range of trips to Thailand.

**Padi Travel Network** ☏02/9417 2800 & 1800/678100. Dive packages to the prime sites of the Thai coast.

**Peregrine Adventures** ☏03/9662 2700 & 1300/655433, ⓦwww.peregrine.net.au. Small-group adventure/cultural trips throughout Thailand; act as agents for Gecko's and Exodus' adventure holidays.

**Pro Dive Travel** ☏02/9232 5733 & 1800/820820. Tailored dive packages to some of Thailand's most popular sights.

**San Michele Travel** ☏02/9299 1111 & 1800/222 244, ⓦwww.asiatravel.com.au. Customized rail tours throught Southeast Asia; a favourite is their thirteen-day Singapore–Bangkok journey (A$1700/NZ$2100). They also do city breaks, sightseeing trips, cruises and extended overland tours out of Bangkok.

**Thai Binh Travel** ☏02/9724 2304. Specialists in accommodation and tours throughout Thailand.

**Thailand Travel** ☏08/8272 2166. Specialists in all aspects of travel to Thailand.

**Travel Indochina** ☏02/9321 9133 & 1800/ 640823. Four-day city stays in Bangkok, including day tours, as well as extended tours throughout Thailand.

# ✈ Travel via neighbouring countries

**Sharing land borders with Burma, Laos, Cambodia and Malaysia, Thailand works well as part of many overland itineraries, both across Asia and between Europe and Australia. In addition, Bangkok is one of the major regional flight hubs for Southeast Asia.**

The most popular multiple-stop Circle Asia and round-the-world air tickets often feature a "surface sector" between Bangkok and either Singapore or Bali; in other words it's up to you to find your own way between these places, either by bus, train, boat or locally purchased flight, or some combination of these. Other, more unusual overland routes fly you into China and out of Bangkok, leaving you to make your own way across Vietnam and/or Laos and then into Thailand.

The main restrictions on overland routes in and out of Thailand are determined by **visas**, and by where the permitted land crossings lie. Most passport holders should be able to get an on-the-spot thirty-day entry stamp into Thailand at any of the land borders described below, though you may be asked to show proof of onward travel arrangements, which can be tricky for overlanders. Thirty-day stamps are absolutely non-extendable (though it's easy enough to hop across one of the land borders and return on the same day with another thirty-day stamp), so you might want to apply for a sixty-day tourist visa instead, obtainable in advance from Thai embassies; full details on visa requirements are given on p.21.

You may need to buy visas for your next port of call when in Thailand, and details of visa requirements for travel to Thailand's immediate neighbours are outlined below. All **Asian embassies** are located in Bangkok; see p.162 for contact details.

The right paperwork is also crucial if you're planning to **drive your own car or motorbike into Thailand**. For advice on this, consult The Golden Triangle Rider website @www.geocities.com/goldentriangleride.

Bangkok has become an important centre for **flights** to many parts of Asia, in particular as a transit point for routes between Europe and Vietnam, Laos and Cambodia; indeed on most flights from Europe to Indochina you have no choice but to be routed via Bangkok. In addition it is now also possible to fly into regional Thai airports from nearby countries, for example from Siem Reap in Cambodia to Phuket, from Phnom Penh to Pattaya, and from Singapore to Ko Samui. If you're doing a longer trip around Southeast Asia, you may want to consider buying a Circle ASEAN ticket, sold by the national airlines of Thailand, Brunei, Indonesia, Malaysia, the Philippines, Singapore and Vietnam. The pass entitles you to buy two to six flights between and within these countries for around £75/$110 each sector, depending on the distance; these passes must be bought outside the countries concerned.

## Burma

At the time of writing, there is no overland access from **Burma** into Thailand and access in the opposite direction is restricted: Western tourists are only allowed to make limited-distance day-trips into Burma at a few points, including Kaw Thaung (Victoria Point) near Ranong (see p.303).

There are numerous flights to Bangkok from Burma. Tourists who intend to enter Burma by air can buy four-week tourist **visas** at the Burmese embassy in Bangkok (see p.162) for B800; apply to the embassy and you may be able to collect the same day, or definitely the following day.

## Cambodia

At the time of writing, there are two legal overland **border crossings** from Cambodia into Thailand, but check with other travellers first as border closures are not unheard of.

The most commonly used crossing is at **Poipet**, which lies just across the border from the Thai town of **Aranyaprathet**, at the end of a famously potholed and uncomfortable road. There are reasonable, if time-consuming, public-transport connections to Poipet from Sisophon, Siem Reap and Phnom Penh in Cambodia, and many guest houses in Siem Reap also organize private transport to the border. Bear in mind when arranging transport from your Cambodian departure point that the Thai border closes at 5pm every day, and that the last Aranyaprathet–Bangkok **bus** also leaves at 5pm. Buses from Aranyaprathet take about four and a half hours to reach Bangkok, arriving at the Northern (Mo Chit) Bus Terminal. There are just two **trains** a day from Aranyaprathet to Bangkok, departing at 6.30am and 1.35pm and taking about five and a half hours.

Increasingly popular with travellers is the border crossing in Thailand's Trat province, from Sihanoukville via **Koh Kong** and **Ban Hat Lek** to Trat. The usual route is to get the speedboat from Sihanoukville to Koh Kong, then a taxi-boat from the Koh Kong pier to the Hat Lek border post; however, the Sihanoukville boat doesn't always make it in time before the border closes at 5pm. Minibuses and songthaews run from Ban Hat Lek to Trat, 91km northwest, where you can either pick up a **bus** straight to Bangkok

(4–6hr) or stay the night (see p.206) and then proceed to the popular nearby island of Ko Chang, or continue along Thailand's east coast.

The speedier alternative to the above overland routes is to make use of the daily **flights** operated by Bangkok Airways, including services to Phuket and Bangkok from Phnom Penh and from Siem Reap.

Details on exiting Thailand **into Cambodia** via these crossings are given in the box on p.210. At the time of writing, **visas** for Cambodia are issued to travellers on arrival at Phnom Penh and Siem Reap airports, and at both the Aranyaprathet/Poipet and Hat Lek land borders; if you do need to buy an advance thirty-day visa, you can do so from the Cambodian embassy in Bangkok (see p.162; B1000; two working days) or from travel agents in Bangkok's Banglamphu district (for an extra B200).

## Laos and Vietnam

There are currently five points along the **Lao border** where it's permissible for tourists to cross into north or northeast Thailand: Houayxai (for Chiang Khong); Vientiane (for Nong Khai); Thakhek (for Nakhon Phanom); Savannakhet (for Mukdahan); and Pakxe (for Chong Mek). All these are accessible by various combinations of road and river transport. Lao Aviation operates numerous **flights** to and from Bangkok.

**Visas** are required for all non-Thai visitors to Laos. A fifteen-day visa on arrival can be bought for US$30 (cash only, plus two photos), but is only available to travellers entering Laos at Vientiane Airport, Louang Phabang Airport or at the Friendship Bridge in Nong Khai. If you want to enter Laos via somewhere other than the above border points, or want a longer visa, you must apply in advance from the Lao embassy (see p.162) for around B750–1000, depending

on nationality; you need two passport photos, and processing takes three days (or 24hr for an extra B300). An alternative option is to go through one of the travel agents in Banglamphu, who charge B1200–2000 for a fifteen-day visa, and up to twice as much for a thirty-day visa; allow three working days for processing.

If you have the right Lao visa and Vietnamese exit stamp, you can travel from **Vietnam** to Thailand via Savannakhet in a matter of hours; you'll need to use Vietnam's Lao Bao border crossing, west of Dong Ha, where you can catch a bus to Savannakhet and then a ferry across the Mekhong to Mukdahan. All travellers into Vietnam need to buy a **visa** in advance. Thirty-day visas take four or five working days to process at the embassy in Bangkok (see p.162) and cost B800–2050 depending on your nationality, or B200 extra through a travel agent.

## Malaysia and Singapore

Travelling between Thailand and **Malaysia and Singapore** is straightforward and a very commonly used route. Most Western tourists can spend thirty days in Malaysia and fourteen days in Singapore without having bought a visa beforehand, and transport linking the three countries is excellent.

It's possible to take a **train** all the way from Singapore to Bangkok via Malaysia, a journey of just under 2000km. The journey involves several changes, but the overall trip can be done in around 30 hours at an average cost of about £60/US$90; trains leave at least once a day from both ends. Taking the train from Singapore or Johor Bahru in southern Malaysia, you can opt for the west-coast route, via Kuala Lumpur, or the east-coast route, which goes via Kota Bharu but involves a short taxi ride across the border to Sungai Kolok; the two lines rejoin at the southern Thai town Hat Yai. Travelling from

## The Eastern and Oriental Express

It's possible to travel between Singapore and Bangkok in extreme style by taking the **Eastern and Oriental Express** train – a Southeast Asian version of the Orient Express – which transports its passengers in great comfort and luxury. The journey, via Kuala Lumpur, takes around 41 hours in all, departs approximately once a week from either terminus and costs from £800/$1300 per person all-inclusive. For details, go to ⓦ www.orient-express.com or call ☏020/7805 5100 (UK) or ☏1-800/524-2420 (US); in Australia, Abercrombie and Kent (see p.18) can organize the journey for you.

KL to Hat Yai takes about thirteen hours and costs around £12/US$18 for a second-class sleeper. For the current timetable and ticket prices, visit the Malaysian Railways website @www.ktmb.com.my. Travelling in the reverse direction, you might prefer to change on to a bus or share taxi at Hat Yai (see p.417), and at Sungai Kolok (p.429) you'll have to get a taxi anyway; details of border formalities are given in the relevant accounts.

Plenty of **buses** also cross the Thai–Malaysian border every day. Hat Yai is the major transport hub for international bus connections, and there are regular buses here from Singapore (around £12/US$18; 18hr) and Kuala Lumpur (£9/US$13; 12hr), and buses and share taxis from Penang (£9/US$13; 6hr). You'll also find long-distance buses and minibuses to Bangkok, Krabi, Phuket and Surat Thani from Kuala Lumpur, Penang and Singapore, as well as in the reverse direction. If you're coming from Alor Setar (the nearest big town to the border on Malaysia's west coast) you'll have to get a bus to the border at Bukit Kayu Hitam, then take a share-taxi from the Thai side up to Hat Yai.

It's also possible to travel between Malaysia and Thailand by **ferry**. Frequent boats connect Kuala Perlis and Langkawi with Satun in south Thailand; see p.408 for details.

In addition to the numerous daily **flights** on any number of international airlines from Malaysia and Singapore to Bangkok, Bangkok Airways operates daily flights between Singapore and Ko Samui, while Phuket is served by flights from Kuala Lumpur (Malaysia Airlines) and Singapore (Silk Air). There are also regular flights to Hat Yai from Kuala Lumpur and from Johor Bahru (both Malaysia Airlines), and from Singapore (with Singapore Airlines subsidiary Silk Air).

# Visas and red tape

**There are three main entry categories for Thailand; for all of them your passport must be valid for at least six months from the date of entry. As visa requirements are often subject to change, you should always check with a Thai embassy or consulate, or a reliable travel agent, before departure.**

Most foreign passport holders are allowed to enter the country for **stays of up to thirty days** without having to apply for a visa (New Zealanders are allowed up to ninety days). The period of stay will be stamped into your passport by immigration officials upon entry, but you're supposed to show proof of onward travel arrangements: unless you have a confirmed bus, train or air ticket out of Thailand, you may be put back on the next plane or sent back to get a sixty-day tourist visa from the nearest Thai Embassy. Such thirty-day stays cannot be extended under any but the most exceptional circum-stances, though it's easy enough to get a new one by hopping across the border into a neighbouring country, most conveniently Malaysia, and back again.

If you're fairly certain you may want to stay longer than thirty days, then from the outset you should apply for a **sixty-day tourist visa** from a Thai embassy or consulate, accompanying your application – which always takes several days to process – with your passport and two photos. The sixty-day visa currently costs £8 per entry in the UK, for example – multiple-entry versions are available, which are handy if you're going to be leaving and re-entering Thailand. Entering on a sixty-day visa, you don't need to show proof of onward travel but, as in all countries, it's up to immigration officials at the port of entry as to what expiry date they stamp on your visa, so it's always advisable to dress respectably (see p.65) when crossing borders.

Thai embassies also consider applications for the slightly more expensive **ninety-day non-immigrant visas** (£15 in the UK) as long as you can offer a good reason for your visit, such as study or business (there are different categories of non-immigrant visa for which different levels of proof are needed). As it's quite a hassle to organize a ninety-day visa from outside the country (and generally not feasible for most tourists), you're better off applying for a thirty-day extension to your sixty-day visa once inside Thai borders.

If you **overstay** your visa limits, expect to be fined B100 per extra day when you leave Thailand, though an overstay of a month or more could land you in more serious trouble with immigration officials.

### Thai embassies and consulates abroad

For a full list of Thai diplomatic missions abroad, check out the Thai Ministry of Foreign Affairs' website at ⓦ www.mfa.go.th /embassy/default.htm.
**Australia** Optus Gate, 10 Moore St, Canberra ACT 2600 ☎ 02/6273 1141. Also consulates in Adelaide, Brisbane, Melbourne, Perth and Sydney.
**Canada** 180 Island Park Drive, Ottawa, Ontario K1Y 0A2 ☎ 613/722-4444, ⓦ www.magma.ca/~thaiott; plus consulates in Vancouver, Montréal, Calgary and Toronto.
**Malaysia** 206 Jalan Ampang, 50450 Kuala Lumpur ☎ 03/2148 8222; plus consulates at 4426 Jalan Pengkalan Chepa, 15400 Kota Bharu ☎ 09/748 2545; and 1 Jalan Tunku Abdul Rahman,

10350 Penang ☎ 04/226 9484.
**New Zealand** 2 Cook St, PO Box 17-226, Karori, Wellington ☎ 04/476 8618–19.
**UK** 29 Queens Gate, London SW7 5JB ☎ 0891/600150 or 020/7589 2944; plus consulates in Birmingham, Cardiff, Glasgow, Hull and Liverpool.
**US** 1024 Wisconsin Ave, NW, Suite 401, Washington, DC 20007 ☎ 202/944-3600 or 3608, ⓦ www.thaiembdc.org; plus consulates at 700 North Rush St, Chicago, IL 60611 ☎ 312/644-3129, ⓔ thaichicago@aol.com; 351 East 52nd St, New York, NY 10022 ☎ 212/754-1770, ⓔ thainycg@aol.com; and 611 North Larchmont Blvd, 2nd Floor, Los Angeles, CA 90038 ☎ 323/962-9574, ⓦ www.thai-la.net.

## Visa extensions and re-entry permits

All sixty-day tourist visas can be **extended** in Thailand for a further thirty days, at the discretion of officials; extensions cost B500 and are issued over the counter at immigration offices (*kaan khao muang*) in nearly every provincial capital – most offices ask for one or two photos as well, plus two photocopies of the first four pages and latest Thai visa page of your passport. Immigration offices also issue **re-entry permits** (B500) if you want to leave the country and come back again within the validity of your visa.

## Staying on

Unless you have work or study fixed up before you arrive, **staying on** in Thailand is a precarious affair. Plenty of people do – teaching English, working in resort bars and guest houses, acting as a dive instructor, or even unofficially buying into tourist businesses (farangs are generally barred from owning businesses in Thailand) – but it involves frequent and expensive visa runs to neighbour

### Customs regulations

The duty-free allowance on entry to Thailand is 200 cigarettes (or 250g of tobacco) and a litre of spirits or wine. To export antiques or religious artefacts – especially Buddha images – from Thailand, you need to have a licence granted by the Fine Arts Department, which can be obtained through Bangkok's National Museum on Thanon Na Phra That (☎ 02/226 1661 or 281 0433). Applications take at least a week and need to be accompanied by two postcard-sized photos of the object, taken face-on, and photocopies of the applicant's passport. Some antique shops will organize this for you.

ing countries, and often entails hassle from the local police. All non-residents who acquire income while in Thailand should get a tax clearance certificate from the Revenue Department, which has offices in every provincial capital and on Thanon Chakraphong near Democracy Monument in Bangkok (☎02/282 9899 or 281 5777).

# Information, websites and maps

The efficient Tourism Authority of Thailand (TAT) maintains offices in several cities abroad, where you can pick up a few glossy brochures and get fairly detailed answers to specific pre-trip questions. More comprehensive local information is given at TAT headquarters in Bangkok and its 22 regional branches (all open daily 8.30am–4.30pm), which provide an array of printed information on everything from how to avoid being ripped off to where to learn to dive. In addition, all TAT offices should have up-to-date information on local festival dates and regional transport schedules, but none of them offers accommodation booking and service can be variable. In Bangkok, TAT plays second fiddle to the excellent Bangkok Tourist Bureau, details of which can be found on p.89.

Independent **tour operators** and information desks crop up in tourist spots all over the country and will usually help with questions about the immediate locality, but be on the lookout for self-interested advice, given by staff desperate for commission. As with TAT offices, independent operators won't book accommodation – unless of course they happen to have business links with specific guest houses or hotels.

You'll find plenty of information about Thailand on the **internet** as well, ranging from official government-sponsored sites to travellers' homepages and forums. A selection of the best websites is given on p.25.

## TAT offices abroad

TAT's general website is at ⊕www.tat.or.th.
**Australia**255 George St, Sydney ☎02/9247 7549; 2 Hardy Rd, South Perth ☎08/9474 3646.
**Canada**1393 Royal York Rd, #15, Toronto, Ontario ☎416/614-2625 or 1-800-THAILAND, ℱ416/614-8891.

**New Zealand**Floor 2, 87 Queen St, Auckland ☎09/379 8398.
**UK and Ireland**49 Albemarle St, London ☎020/7499 7679; recorded information on 0839/300800, ⊕www.thaismile.co.uk.
**USA** ☎1-800-THAILAND; 1 World Trade Centre, Suite 3729, New York ☎212/432-0433 or 432-0435, ℱ212/912-0920, ℰttny@aol.com; 611 North Larchmont Blvd, 1st Floor, Los Angeles ☎323/461-9814, ℱ461-9834.

## Maps

One thing neither TAT nor tour operators provide is a decent **map**. For most major destinations, the maps in this book should be all you need, though you may want to supplement them with larger-scale versions of Bangkok and the whole country. Bangkok bookshops are the best source of these maps; where appropriate, detailed local maps and their stockists are recommended in the relevant chapters of the guide. If you want to buy a map before you get there (for outlets at home, see p.24),

23

go for Nelles' 1:1,500,000 map of Thailand, the most consistently accurate of those published abroad, despite leaving many main roads unnumbered. The Bartholomew's 1:1,500,000 is also fairly reliable.

Published by the Roads Association of Thailand in conjunction with Shell, the large-format 1:1,000,000 *Thailand Highway Map* is especially good on **roads**, and is updated annually; it's available at most bookstores in Thailand where English-language material is sold. If you can't get hold of that one, you could go for the set of four 1:1,000,000 regional maps produced by the Highway Department and sold at DK Books all over the country, and in Bangkok at Central department stores. The drawback with this series is that much of the detail is written only in Thai script.

## Travel bookshops and map outlets

### UK

**Blackwell's Map and Travel Shop**, 53 Broad St, Oxford ☎ 01865/792792 ⓦ blackwell.bookshop.co.uk.
**Daunt Books**, 83 Marylebone High St, London ☎ 020/7224 2295; 193 Haverstock Hill, London ☎ 020/7794 4006.
**Heffers Map and Travel**, 20 Trinity Street, Cambridge ☎ 01223/586586, ⓦ www.heffers.co.uk.
**John Smith and Sons**, 26 Colquhoun Ave, Glasgow ☎ 0141/221 7472, ⓦ www.johnsmith.co.uk.
**National Map Centre**, 22–24 Caxton St, London ☎ 020/7222 2466, ⓦ www.mapsnmc.co.uk.
**Stanfords** ⓦ www.stanfords.co.uk. 12–14 Long Acre, London ☎ 020/7836 1321; 29 Corn St, Bristol ☎ 0117/929 9966.
**The Travel Bookshop**, 13–15 Blenheim Crescent, London ☎ 020/7229 5260, ⓦ www.thetravelbookshop.co.uk.

### Ireland

**Easons Bookshop**, 40 O'Connell St, Dublin ☎ 01/873 3811, ⓦ www.eason.ie.
**Fred Hanna's Bookshop**, 27–29 Nassau St, Dublin ☎ 01/677 1255.
**Hodges Figgis Bookshop**, 56–58 Dawson St, Dublin ☎ 01/677 4754, ⓦ www.hodgesfiggis.com.
**Waterstone's** Queens Bldg, 8 Royal Ave, Belfast ☎ 028/9024 7355; 7 Dawson St, Dublin ☎ 01/679

1415; 69 Patrick St, Cork ☎ 021/276 522; ⓦ www.waterstones.com.

### USA

**The Complete Traveller Bookstore**, 199 Madison Ave, New York ☎ 212/685-9007.
**Elliot Bay Book Company**, 101 S Main St, Seattle ☎ 206/624-6600 or 1-800/962-5311, ⓦ www.elliotbaybook.com.
**Map Link**, 30 S La Patera Lane, Unit 5, Santa Barbara ☎ 805/692-6777, ⓦ www.maplink.com.
**Phileas Fogg's Books & Maps**, 87 Stanford Shopping Center, Palo Alto ☎ 1-800/533-3644, ⓦ www.foggs.com.
**Rand McNally**, ⓦ www.randmcnally. com. 444 N Michigan Ave, Chicago ☎ 312/321-1751; 150 E 52nd St, New York ☎ 212/758-7488; 595 Market St, San Francisco ☎ 415/777-3131.
**Travel Books & Language Center**, 4437 Wisconsin Ave, Washington ☎ 1-800/220-2665.

### Canada

**Open Air Books and Maps**, 25 Toronto St, Toronto ☎ 416/363-0719 or 1-800/748-9171.
**Travel Bug Bookstore**, 2667 West Broadway, Vancouver ☎ 604/737-1122, ⓦ www.swifty.com/tbug.
**Ulysses Travel Bookshop**, 4176 St-Denis, Montréal ☎ 514/843-9882, ⓦ www.ulysses.ca.
**World of Maps**, 118 Holland Ave, Ottawa, Ontario ☎ 613/724-6776, ⓦ www.itmb.com.
**World Wide Books and Maps**, 1247 Granville St, Vancouver ☎ 604/687-3320, ⓦ www.worldofmaps.com.

### Australia and New Zealand

**Mapland**, 372 Little Bourke St, Melbourne ☎ 03/9670 4383, ⓦ www.mapland.com.au.
**The Map Shop**, 6 Peel St, Adelaide ☎ 08/8231 2033, ⓦ www.mapshop.net.au.
**Mapworld**, 173 Gloucester Street, Christchurch ☎ 03/374 5399, ⓦ www.mapworld.co.nz.
**Perth Map Centre**, 1/884 Hay St, Perth ☎ 08/9322 5733, ⓦ www.perthmap.com.au.
**Specialty Maps**, 46 Albert St, Auckland ☎ 09/307 2217, ⓦ www.ubd-online.co.nz/maps.
**Travel Bookshop**, Shop 3, 175 Liverpool St, Sydney ☎ 02/9261 8200.
**Walkers Bookshop**, 96 Lake Street, Cairns ☎ 07/4051 2410.
**Worldwide Maps and Guides**, 187 George St, Brisbane ☎ 07/3221 4330.

### Online travel bookstores

**Adventurous Traveler** ⓦ www.adventuroustraveler.com.

Amazon ⓦ www.amazon.co.uk &
www.amazon.com.
Literate Traveler ⓦ www.literatetraveller.com.

## Thailand online

Only general tourist-oriented websites are
listed below. For online accommodation-
booking services see p.43, for diving websites see p.67, and for websites for gay travellers see p.71.

### General Thailand resources

**Accommodating Asia: Thailand**
ⓦ www.accomasia.com/thailand.htm. Has a
particularly good "Travellers Notes" section, with links
to the diaries, travelogues and homepages of recent
travellers to Thailand.
**Bangkok Post** ⓦ www.bangkokpost.net. The
day's main stories from Thailand's leading English-
language daily newspaper, plus archive headlines
and travel stories.
**Geocities** ⓦ www.geocities.com. A vast,
searchable collection of Web pages, including
travellers' reports, virtual tours, and a forum for
travel companions.
**René Hasekamp's Homepage**
ⓦ www.hasekamp.demon.nl/thaiindex.htm.
Constructed by a Dutch man who is married to a
Thai woman, this site lists practical tips and dos and
don'ts for travellers to Thailand, plus info on selected
sights and a handy list of FAQs.
**Thai Focus** ⓦ www.thaifocus.com. Wide-ranging
portal site, offering hotel-booking service, domestic
and international air tickets, car rental, plus a basic
introduction to Thailand's main destinations; the
discounts are nothing special though.
**Tourism Authority of Thailand** (TAT)
ⓦ www.tat.or.th. The official TAT site has general
background on the country, plus links to
accommodation, weather reports and other standard
stuff.
**Tourism Authority of Thailand, London**
ⓦ www.thaismile.co.uk. The official website for the
London TAT office offers special deals on flights to
Thailand, has a page for tourist tips and a travellers'
bulletin board. It also has an innovative section on
Thai culture in the UK, including listings of Thai
restaurants across the country.

### Travellers' resources

**About Ecotourism**
ⓦ www.ecotourism.about.com. Recommended
umbrella site with a wide range of discussions,

articles and links concerning the relationship
between tourism and the environment in Thailand
and elsewhere. Also some links to eco-aware travel
companies.
**Internet Travel Information Service**
ⓦ www.itisnet.com. A really useful resource
specifically aimed at budget travellers. Its
researchers send weekly reports from the road
(Thailand is well covered), so there's heaps of up-to-
the-minute information on things like current
airfares, border crossings, visa requirements as well
as hotel openings and closures.
**Journeywoman** ⓦ www.journeywoman.com.
Highly recommended site aimed at women travellers,
with all sorts of imaginative sections, including "What
Should I Wear?", which features first-hand tips on
acceptable dress in over a hundred different
countries. Also includes travel health information,
travelogues, and advice for solo travellers.
**Open Directory Project**
ⓦ www.dmoz.org/Recreation/Travel/Budget_Travel
/Backpacking. Scores of backpacker-oriented links,
including plenty of Asia-specific ones, plus
travelogues and message boards.
**Rec. travel library** ⓦ www.travel-library.com.
Highly recommended site which has lively pieces on
dozens of travel topics about Thailand and
elsewhere, from the budget travellers' guide to
sleeping in airports, to how to travel light. Excellent
links too.
**Rough Guides** ⓦ www.roughguides.com.
Interactive site for independent travellers, with
forums, bulletin boards, travel tips and features, plus
online travel guides.

### Travellers' forums

**Lonely Planet Thorn Tree**
ⓦ thorntree.lonelyplanet.com. Recommended and
popular travellers' forums, divided into regions (eg
Mainland Southeast Asia) and topics (Travelling with
Kids). A good place to look for travel companions,
exchange information or start a debate.
**Thailand Tips** ⓦ www.thailandtips.com. Thailand-
specific forum for travellers' queries and advice
about everything from elephant round-ups to the
best airport hotel.

### Thailand's regions online

**Bangkok Metro** ⓦ www.bkkmetro.com The online
version of Bangkok's monthly listings magazine
includes archives of features and comprehensive
restaurant and club listings.
**Groovy Map** ⓦ www.groovymap.com. Lively site
from the company who publish wacky, annotated

maps of Bangkok and Phuket, with top-ten lists of things to do by day and night in Bangkok, plus a what's on calendar for the city.

**Phuket Gazette** ⓦwww.phuketgazette.net. Southern Thailand's resort island of Phuket publishes a weekly independent English-language newspaper, and their online version makes interesting reading, with both local and national news stories, editorials and opinion pieces on a good range of subjects.

# Money, banks and costs

Thailand's unit of currency is the baht (abbreviated to "B"), which is divided into 100 satang. Notes come in B10 (brown), B20 (green), B50 (blue), B100 (red), B500 (purple) and B1000 (beige) denominations, inscribed with Arabic as well as Thai numerals, and increasing in size according to value. The coinage is more confusing, because new shapes and sizes circulate alongside older ones. The tiny brass-coloured 25- and 50-satang pieces are rarely used now, as most prices are rounded off to the nearest baht. There are three different silver one-baht coins, all legal tender; the smallest of these is the newest version, and the one accepted by public call-boxes. Silver five-baht pieces are slightly bigger and have a copper rim; ten-baht coins have a small brass centre encircled by a silver ring.

At the time of writing, **exchange rates** were averaging B42 to US$1 and B62 to £1; note that Thailand has no black market in foreign currency. Daily rates are published in the *Bangkok Post* and the *Nation*, and at all foreign exchange counters and kiosks in Thailand. Because of severe currency fluctuations in the late 1990s, some tourist-oriented businesses now quote their prices in dollars, particularly luxury hotels and dive centres.

**Banking hours** are Monday to Friday from 8.30am to 3.30pm, but exchange kiosks in the main tourist centres are always open till at least 5pm, sometimes 10pm, and upmarket hotels change money 24 hours a day. The **Don Muang airport exchange counters** also operate 24 hours (and exchange kiosks at overseas airports with flights to Thailand usually keep Thai currency), so there's little point arranging to buy baht before you leave home, especially as it takes seven working days to order from most banks outside Thailand.

## Costs

In a country where the daily minimum wage is under B165 a day, it's hardly surprising that Western tourists find Thailand an extremely cheap place to travel. At the bottom of the scale, you could manage on a **daily budget** of about B400 (£7/US$10) if you're willing to opt for basic accommodation, stay away from the more expensive resorts like Phuket, Ko Samui and Ko Phi Phi, and eat, drink and travel as the locals do. On this budget, you'll be spending B80–150 for a dorm bed or single room (less if you share the cost of a double room), around B150–200 on three meals (eating mainly at night markets and simple noodle

### Online currency converter

**Bangkok Bank** ⓦbbl.co.th/bankrates/fx _rates_curr.htm. Tells you the day's rate in Thailand for 23 major currencies against the Thai baht; provided by the Bangkok Bank.

shops, and eschewing beer), and the rest on travel (sticking mainly to non-air-con buses and third-class trains) and incidentals. With extras like air-conditioning in rooms (from B300–800 a double in guest houses and simple hotels) and on long-distance buses, taking tuk-tuks (see p.38) rather than buses for cross-town journeys, and a meal and a couple of beers in a more touristy restaurant (B100–150 per person), a day's outlay would look more like B600–800 (£11–14/US$15–20). Staying in comfortable, upmarket hotels and eating in the more exclusive restaurants, you should be able to live in extreme comfort for around B2000 a day (£35/US$50).

Travellers soon get so used to the low cost of living in Thailand that they start **bargaining** at every available opportunity, much as Thai people do. Although it's expected practice for a lot of commercial transactions, particularly at markets and when hiring tuk-tuks and taxis, bargaining is a delicate art that requires humour, tact and patience. If your price is way out of line, the vendor's vehement refusal should be enough to make you increase your offer: never forget that the few pennies or cents you're making such a fuss over will go a lot further in a Thai person's hands than in your own.

On the other hand, making a tidy sum off foreigners is sometimes official practice: at government-run museums and historical parks, for example, foreigners often pay a B40 admission charge while Thais get in for B10. The most controversial **two-tier pricing** system is the recent innovation at most national parks, where foreigners now have to pay B200 entry while Thais pay just B20 (see p.69 for more on this). A number of privately owned tourist attractions follow a similar two-tier system, posting an inflated price in English for foreigners and a lower price in Thai for locals. This is not illegal, but overcharging tourists on fixed-fare public transport is definitely not acceptable – the best way to avoid getting stung by wily conductors on buses and trains is to watch or ask fellow passengers.

### Traveller's cheques, debit and credit cards

The safest way to carry your money is in **traveller's cheques** (a fee of one or two percent is usually levied when you buy them). Sterling and dollar cheques are accepted by banks, exchange booths and upmarket hotels in every sizeable Thai town and resort, and most places also deal in a variety of other currencies; everyone offers better rates for cheques than for straight cash. Generally, a total of B13 in commission and duty is charged per cheque – though kiosks and hotels in isolated places may charge extra. All issuers give you a list of numbers to call in the case of **lost or stolen cheques** and will pay refunds if you can produce the original receipts and a note of your cheque numbers. You'll usually have to notify the police first and then call the issuing company collect to arrange replacements, generally within 24 hours, either by courier or at a local agent.

American Express, Visa, MasterCard and Diners Club **credit cards**, and Visa and MasterCard/Cirrus **debit cards** are accepted at top hotels as well as in some posh restaurants, department stores, tourist shops and travel agents, but surcharging of up to five percent is rife, and theft and forgery are major industries – always demand the carbon copies, and never leave cards in baggage storage. If you have a personal identification number (PIN) for your debit or credit card, you can also withdraw cash from hundreds of 24-hour **ATMs** ("automatic teller machines" or cash dispensers) around the country. Almost every branch of the Bangkok Bank, Bank of Ayudhya, Siam Commercial and Thai Farmers Bank has ATMs that accept **Visa** cards, **MasterCard** and cards on the **Cirrus** network. For an up-to-the-minute list of ATM locations in Thailand, check the relevant websites (ⓦ www.mastercard.com and www.visa.com). There's usually a handling fee of 1.5 percent on every withdrawal, little different from the total amount of fees and commissions payable on traveller's cheques, but it's wise not to rely on plastic alone, which is more tempting to thieves and less easy to replace than the trusty traveller's cheque.

### Wiring money

**Wiring money** through a specialist agent is a fast but expensive way to send and receive money abroad. The funds should be available for collection, usually in local currency, from the company's local agent

27

within twenty minutes of being sent via Western Union or Moneygram; both charge on a sliding scale, so sending larger amounts of cash is better value.

It's also possible to have money wired directly from a bank in your home country to a bank in Thailand, although this is somewhat less reliable because it involves two separate institutions. Your home bank will need the address of the branch bank where you want to pick up the money and the address and telex number of the Bangkok head office, which will act as the clearing house; money wired this way normally takes two working days to arrive, and costs around £25/US$40 per transaction.

# Insurance

If you're unlucky enough to require hospital treatment in Thailand, you'll have to foot the bill – this alone is reason enough to make sure you have adequate travel cover before you leave. Besides covering medical expenses and emergency flights home, a good specialist travel policy should include insurance against loss and theft of money and personal belongings, and possibly cover for damage to rented motorbikes and cars as well. Most standard policies exclude so-called dangerous sports such as scuba-diving, unless an extra premium is paid.

Before shelling out on a new policy, however, it's worth checking whether you are already covered. Many **bank and charge accounts** include some form of travel cover, and insurance is also sometimes included if you pay for your trip with a **credit card** (though usually only medical or accident cover is provided). Some all-risks **home insurance policies** cover your possessions against loss or theft when overseas, and many **private medical schemes** include cover for baggage loss abroad, cancellation or curtailment of your trip and cash replacement as well as sickness or accident. In Canada, provincial health plans usually provide partial cover for medical mishaps overseas, while holders of official student/teacher/youth cards in Canada and the US are entitled to some accident coverage and hospital in-patient benefits. North

## Rough Guides travel insurance

Rough Guides now offers its own **travel insurance**, customized for our readers by a leading UK broker and backed by a Lloyd's underwriter. It's available for anyone, of any nationality or age, travelling anywhere in the world.

There are two main Rough Guide insurance plans: **Essential**, for basic, no-frills cover; and **Premier** – with more generous and extensive benefits. Unlike many policies, the Rough Guides schemes are calculated by the day, so if you're travelling for 27 days rather than a month, that's all you pay for. Alternatively, you can take out annual **multi-trip insurance**, which covers you for any number of trips throughout the year (with a maximum of 60 days for any one trip). If you intend to be away for the whole year, the **Adventurer** policy will cover you for 365 days. Each plan can be supplemented with a "**Hazardous Activities Premium**" if you plan to indulge in sports considered dangerous, such as scuba-diving.

To get a **policy quote** and buy your cover, call the Rough Guide Insurance Line on UK freefone ☎0800/015 0906, US tollfree ☎1-866/220-5588, or if you're calling from elsewhere in the world on ☎(+44)1243/621046. Alternatively, get an online quote and buy your insurance at ⊛www.roughguides.com/insurance.

American students will often find that their student health coverage extends during the vacations and for one term beyond the date of last enrolment.

If **trouble** occurs, make sure you keep all medical bills, and, if possible, contact the insurance company before making any major outlay (for example, on additional con-valescence expenses). If you have anything stolen, get a copy of the police report when you notify them of the incident – otherwise you won't be able to claim. Note also that very few insurers will arrange on-the-spot payments in the event of a major expense or loss; you will usually be reimbursed only after going home.

# Health

Although Thailand's climate, wildlife and cuisine present Western travellers with fewer health worries than in many Asian destinations, it's as well to know in advance what the risks might be, and what preventive or curative measures you should take.

For a start, there's no need to bring huge supplies of non-prescription drugs with you, as Thai **pharmacies** (*raan khai yaa*; typically open daily 8.30am–8pm) are well stocked with local and international branded medicines, and of course they are much less expensive than at home. All pharmacies, whatever size the town, are run by highly trained English-speaking pharmacists, who are usually the best people to talk to if your symptoms aren't acute enough to warrant seeing a doctor.

**Hospital** (*rong phayaabahn*) cleanliness and efficiency vary, but generally hygiene and health-care standards are good and the ratio of medical staff to patients is considerably higher than in most parts of the West. As with head pharmacists, doctors speak

English. All provincial capitals have at least one hospital: if you need to get to one, ask at your accommodation for advice on, and possibly transport to, the nearest or most suitable. In the event of a major health crisis, get someone to contact your embassy (see p.162) or insurance company – it may be best to get yourself flown home.

For a comprehensive, and sobering, account of the health problems which travellers encounter worldwide, consult the *Rough Guide to Travel Health* by Dr Nick Jones. In the UK, pick up the Department of Health's free publication *Health Advice for Travellers*, a comprehensive booklet available at the post office (or by calling the Health Literature Line on ☎0800/555777); the content of the booklet, which contains immunization advice, is constantly updated on Ceefax and at ⊕www.doh.gov.uk/traveladvice/.

## Inoculations

There are no compulsory **inoculation** requirements for people travelling to Thailand from the West, but it makes sense to ensure your polio and tetanus boosters are up to date (they last ten years); most doctors also strongly advise vaccinations against typhoid (shots last three years or oral capsules are available which need boosting annually) and hepatitis A, and in some cases they might also recommend protecting yourself against Japanese encephalitis, rabies, hepatitis B, tuberculosis and diphtheria. If you do decide to have several injections, plan your course at least four weeks in advance.

In the UK and Ireland, the least costly way of getting immunized is to head first to your local health centre (in the UK some immunizations are free under the NHS while other vaccines must be paid for on prescription, but all are administered at no cost by your doctor or health-centre nurse). Though most general practitioners can give advice on inoculation requirements, it's a good idea to come for your appointment armed with a "Health Brief", written information tailored to your journey, provided by return of post by MASTA (see opposite). However, your local health clinic may not administer some of the less common immunizations and you may have to go to a specialist travel clinic: these work out to be expensive but have the advantage of being staffed by tropical-disease specialists; see below.

**North Americans** will have to pay full whack for their inoculations, available at an immunization centre – there's one in every city of any size – or most local clinics. In the US, the doctor's consultation fee is generally $75, and the inoculations cost $75–175 each.

**Australians** and **New Zealanders** can have their jabs administered by their GP for around A$35/NZ$30 per visit plus the cost of the serums. In Australia, sixty percent of the consultation fee is refundable via Medicare, though you still pay for the serums, while Healthcare card-holders are excused the consultation fee and pay only A$2.50 for medicines. In New Zealand, nothing is refundable without medical insurance. In both countries, those who have to pay will find vaccination centres less expensive than doctors' surgeries.

If you forget to have all your inoculations before leaving home, or don't leave yourself sufficient time, you can get them **in Bangkok** at the Australian-run Travmin Bangkok Medical Centre (see p.163 for details), though this is unlikely to work out cheaper than doing it at home. Travmin also advises on and dispenses malaria prophylactics.

### Inoculation centres and information

#### UK and Ireland

**British Airways Travel Clinics** No appointments necessary at 156 Regent St, London (Mon–Fri 9.30am–5.15pm, Sat 10am–4pm; ☎020/7439 9584). BA also operates other appointment-only clinics in the capital and throughout the country (call ☎01276/685040 or check ⊕www.britishairways.com for locations).
**Hospital for Tropical Diseases Travel Clinic** 2nd Floor, Mortimer Market Centre, off Capper Street, London (Mon–Fri 9am–5pm by appointment only; ☎020/7388 9600; £15 consultation fee is waived if you have your injections here). Their recorded Health Line (☎09061/337733, 50p per min) gives hints on hygiene and illness prevention as well as listing appropriate immunizations.
**MASTA** (Medical Advisory Service for Travellers Abroad, ⊕www.masta.org). Call their prerecorded 24hr Travellers' Health Line (in the UK ☎0906/822 4100, 60p per min; in Ireland ☎1560/147000, €1

per min) to request printed health information; in the UK they also provide up-to-date information on malaria on ☎ 0891/600350 (24hr recorded message, 60p per minute).

**Nomad Pharmacy**, 40 Bernard St, London, opposite Russell Square tube station; and 3–4 Turnpike Lane, London (Mon–Fri 9.30am–6pm, ☎ 020/7833 4114 to book appointment; their telephone helpline is ☎ 09068/633414, costing 60p a minute).

**Trailfinders**, 194 Kensington High St, London (Mon–Fri 9am–5pm, Thurs to 6pm, Sat 9.30am–4pm; ☎ 020/7938 3999). This branch of the travel agency has a no-appointments-necessary immunization clinic.

**Travel Health Centre**, Dept of International Health and Tropical Medicine, Royal College of Surgeons in Ireland, Mercers Medical Centre, Stephen's St Lower, Dublin ☎ 01/402 2337. Expert pre-trip advice and inoculations.

## USA and Canada

**International Association for Medical Assistance to Travellers**
ⓦ www.sentex.net/~iamat; 417 Center St, Lewiston ☎ 716/754-4883; and 40 Regal Rd, Guelph, Ontario ☎ 519/836-0102. A non-profit organization supported by donations, which can provide leaflets on various diseases and inoculations.

**Travelers Medical Center**, 31 Washington Square, New York ☎ 212/982-1600. Offers a consultation service on immunizations and treatment of diseases for people travelling to developing countries.

## Australia and New Zealand

**Travellers' Medical and Vaccination Centres**
ⓦ www.tmvc.com.au. Australia: 2/393 Little Bourke St, Melbourne ☎ 03/9602 5788; 7/428 George St, Sydney ☎ 02/9221 7133 and branches in many other cities. New Zealand: 1/170 Queen St, Auckland ☎ 09/373 3531; 147 Armagh St, Christchurch ☎ 03/379 4000; Shop 15, Grand Arcade, 14–16 Willis St, Wellington ☎ 04/473 0991. Travel medicine and vaccination services.

## Mosquito-borne diseases

It isn't only malaria which is spread by **mosquitoes** in Thailand; to a lesser extent, there are risks of contracting both Japanese B encephalitis and dengue fever if you visit during the rainy season. The main message, therefore, is to **avoid being bitten** by mosquitoes. You should smother yourself and your clothes in **mosquito repellent** containing the chemical compound DEET, reapplying regularly (shops, guest houses and department stores all over Thailand stock it but, if you want the highest-strength repellent, or convenient roll-ons or sprays, do your shopping before you leave home). DEET is strong stuff, and if you have sensitive skin a natural alternative is citronella (called Mosi-guard in the UK), made from a blend of Eucalyptus oils, though still use DEET on clothes and nets. At night you should either sleep under a **mosquito net** sprayed with DEET or in a room with screens across the windows. Accommodation in tourist spots nearly always provides screens or a net (check both for holes), but if you're planning to go way off the beaten track or want the security of having your own mosquito net just in case, wait until you get to Bangkok to buy one, where department stores sell them for about an eighth of what you'd pay in the West. **Mosquito coils** – also widely available in Thailand – help keep the insects at bay; electronic "buzzers" are useless. Prophylaxis advice can change from year to year, so it's worth getting the most up-to-date information from your travel health adviser.

### Malaria

Thailand is **malarial**, but the risks involved vary across the country. There is a significant risk of malaria along the **Cambodian border**, including Ko Chang in Trat province; the only anti-malarial drug that is likely to be effective in this area is **Doxycycline**. In most situations you only need to start taking Doxycycline a couple of days before entering a malarial zone; its use should be discussed with your travel health adviser. Elsewhere in Thailand the risk of malaria is considered to be so low that anti-malarial tablets are not advised.

The first **signs of malaria** are remarkably similar to flu, and may take months to appear: if you suspect anything go to a hospital or clinic immediately.

### Dengue fever

Like malaria, **dengue fever**, a debilitating and occasionally fatal viral disease, is on the increase throughout tropical Asia, and is endemic to many areas of Thailand. Unlike

## A traveller's first-aid kit

Among items you might want to carry with you – especially if you're planning to go diving or snorkelling in remote areas – are:

Antiseptic fluid/cream
Antihistamines/antihistamine cream
Bottle of vinegar
Tweezers
Scissors
Plasters/band-aids
Lints and sealed bandages
Imodium, Lomotil or Arret for emergency
  diarrhoea relief
Insect repellent
Sunscreen
Eyedrops
Decongestants
Paracetamol/aspirin
Multivitamin and mineral tablets
Sea-sickness tablets
Rehydration sachets
Hypodermic needles and sterilized skin
  wipes

malaria though, dengue fever is spread by a mosquito (the *Aedes*) which bites during daylight hours – usually in early morning or late afternoon, particularly during and just after the rainy season. Symptoms include fever, a rash, headaches, and fierce joint pain ("breakbone fever" is another name for dengue) and usually develop between five and eight days after being bitten. There is no vaccine against dengue fever; the only treatment is lots of rest, liquids and paracetamol (or any other acetaminophen painkiller, not aspirin), though more serious cases may require hospitalization.

### Japanese encephalitis

If you are travelling for long periods in rural areas between June and September (the rainy season), you may be at risk of contracting **Japanese encephalitis**, a viral inflammation of the brain spread by the *Culex* mosquito which breeds in rice fields. A vaccine is available, and although the risk of travellers catching the disease is low, you should at least consult your health adviser.

## Other health problems

What follows are some of the most common ailments encountered by visitors to Thailand

or the rarely encountered problems that can be easily avoided.

### Poisonous cuts, bites and stings

Wearing protective clothing is a good idea when **swimming**, **snorkelling** or **diving**: a T-shirt will stop you from getting sunburnt in the water, while long trousers can guard against coral grazes. Should you scrape your skin on coral, wash the wound thoroughly with boiled water, apply antiseptic and keep protected until healed. Thailand's seas are home to a few dangerous creatures which you should be wary of, principally jellyfish, poisonous sea snakes, sea urchins and a couple of less conspicuous species – sting rays, which often lie buried in the sand; and stone fish, whose potentially lethal venomous spikes are easily stepped on because the fish look like stones and lie motionless on the sea bed.

If **stung or bitten** you should always seek medical advice as soon as possible, but there are a few ways of alleviating the pain or administering your own first aid in the meantime. If you're stung by a **jellyfish**, the priority treatment is to remove the fragments of tentacles from the skin – without causing further discharge of poison – which is easiest done by applying vinegar to deactivate the stinging capsules. In the case of a poisonous **snake** bite, don't try sucking out the poison or applying a tourniquet: immobilize the limb and stay calm until medical help arrives (all provincial hospitals in Thailand should carry supplies of antivenoms). The best way to minimize the risk of stepping on the toxic **spines** of sea urchins, sting rays and stone fish is to wear thick-soled shoes, though these cannot provide total protection; sea urchin spikes should be removed after softening the skin with ointment, though some people recommend applying urine to help dissolve the spines; for sting ray and stone fish stings, alleviate the pain by immersing the wound in hot water while awaiting help.

### Rabies

**Rabies** is mainly carried by dogs (between four and seven percent of stray dogs in Bangkok are reported to be rabid), but also cats and monkeys, and is transmitted by bites or scratches. Dogs are everywhere in

Thailand and even if kept as pets they're never very well cared for: hopefully their mangy appearance will discourage the urge to pat them as you should steer clear as much as possible. If you are bitten or scratched by an animal, clean and disinfect the wound, preferably with alcohol, and seek medical advice right away.

## Digestive problems

By far the most common travellers' complaint in Thailand, **digestive troubles** are often caused by contaminated food and water, or sometimes just by an overdose of unfamiliar foodstuffs. Break your system in gently by avoiding excessively spicy curries and too much raw fruit in the first few days, and then use your common sense about choosing where and what to eat: if you stick to the most crowded restaurants and noodle stalls you should be perfectly safe. Furthermore, because most Thai dishes can be cooked in under five minutes, you'll rarely have to contend with stuff that's been left to smoulder and stew. You need to be a bit more rigorous about drinking the **water**, though: stick to bottled water, which is sold everywhere, or else opt for boiled water or tea.

Stomach trouble usually manifests itself as simple **diarrhoea**, which should clear up without medical treatment within three to seven days and is best combated by drinking lots of fluids. If this doesn't work, you're in danger of getting **dehydrated** and should take some kind of rehydration solution, either a commercial sachet sold in all Thai pharma-

cies or a do-it-yourself version which can be made by adding a handful of sugar and a pinch of salt to every litre of boiled or bottled water (soft drinks are *not* a viable alternative). Note that anti-diarrhoeal agents such as Imodium are useful for blocking you up on long bus journeys, but only attack the symptoms and may prolong infections. If diarrhoea persists for more than ten days, or if you have blood or mucus in your stools, you may have contracted bacillary or amoebic dysentery, in which case go to a doctor or hospital.

## Heat problems

Aside from the obvious considerations about restricting your exposure to the searing midday sun (using high protection-factor sun creams if you have fair skin, and protecting your eyes with good sunglasses that screen out UV light and your head with a hat), you should avoid **dehydration** by drinking plenty of water and occasionally adding a pinch of salt to fruit shakes. To prevent and alleviate heat rashes, prickly heat and fungal infections, it's a good idea to use a mild antiseptic soap and to dust yourself with prickly heat talcum powder, both of which are sold cheaply in all Thai stores.

## AIDS

**AIDS** is spreading fast in Thailand, primarily because of the widespread sex trade (see p.140). Condoms (*meechai*) are sold in pharmacists, department stores, hairdressers,

## Carrying essential medications

Make sure that you take sufficient supplies of any essential medications and carry the complete supply with you whenever you travel (including on public transport), in case of loss or theft. You should also carry a prescription including the generic name in case of emergency. If travelling for a long time, it may be worth arranging for your doctor or hospital to courier extra supplies to a specific address in Thailand, such as a reputable hotel. It's also a good idea to carry a doctor's letter about your drugs prescriptions with you at all times – particularly when passing through customs at Bangkok airport – as this will ensure you don't get hauled up for narcotics transgressions.

If your medication has to be kept cool, buy a thermal insulation bag and a couple of freezer blocks before you leave home. That way you can refreeze one of the two blocks every day, while the other is in use; staff in most hotels, guest houses, restaurants and even some bars should be happy to let you use their freezer compartment for a few hours. If you use needles and syringes, you should also take a small sharps bin with you, as garbage disposal in Thailand is haphazard and your used syringes might harm someone.

even on street markets. Should you need to have an injection at a hospital, try to check that the needle has been sterilized first; this is not always practicable, however, so you might consider carrying your own syringes.

Don't even consider getting yourself tattooed in Thailand.

Due to rigorous screening methods, the country's **medical blood supply** is now considered safe.

# Getting around

Travel in Thailand is both inexpensive and efficient, if not always speedy. Unless you travel by plane, long-distance journeys in Thailand can be arduous, especially if a shoestring budget restricts you to hard seats and no air-conditioning. Still, the wide range of efficient transport options makes travelling around this country easier than elsewhere in Southeast Asia. Buses are fast and frequent, and can be quite luxurious; trains are slower but safer and offer more chance of sleeping during overnight trips; moreover, if travelling by day you're likely to follow a more scenic route by rail than by road. Inter-town songthaews, share taxis and air-conditioned minibuses are handy, and ferries provide easy access to all major islands. Local transport comes in all sorts of permutations, both public and chartered, with relatively little separating them in terms of cost.

For an idea of the frequency and duration of bus, train, air and ferry services between towns, check the **travel details** at the end of each chapter.

## Inter-town buses

**Buses**, overall the most convenient way of getting around the country, come in two categories: **ordinary** (*rot thammadaa*) and **air-conditioned** (*rot air*), with an additional air-conditioned subcategory known as **tour buses** (*rot tua*). The ordinary and air-conditioned buses are run by Baw Kaw Saw, the government transport company, whereas the misleadingly named tour buses are privately owned and ply the most popular long-distance routes, with no tours involved. Be warned that long-distance overnight buses, particularly the air-conditioned and tour buses, seem to be involved in more than their fair share of accidents; because of this, some travellers prefer to do the overnight journeys by train and then

make a shorter bus connection to their destination.

### Ordinary buses

The orange-coloured **ordinary buses** are incredibly inexpensive and cover most short-range routes between main towns (up to 150km) very frequently during daylight hours. Each bus is staffed by a team of two or three – the driver, the fare collector and the optional "stop" and "go" yeller – who often personalize the vehicle with stereo systems, stickers, jasmine garlands and the requisite Buddha image or amulet. With an entertaining team and eye-catching scenery, journeys can be fun, but there are drawbacks. For a start, the teams work on a commission basis, so they pack as many people in as possible and might hang around for thirty minutes after they're due to leave in the hope of cramming in a few extra. They also stop so often that their average speed of 60kph can only be achieved by hurtling along at breakneck speeds between pick-ups, often propelled by amphetamine-induced craziness. To flag down an ordinary bus from the roadside you should wait at the nearest **bus shelter** or *sala*, usually located at intervals along the main long-distance bus route through town or on the fringes of any decent-sized settlement, for example on the main highway that skirts the edge of town. Where there is only a bus shelter on the "wrong" side of the road, you can be sure that buses travelling in both directions will stop there for any waiting passengers. If you're in the middle of nowhere with no *sala* in sight, any ordinary bus should stop for you if you flag it down.

### Air-conditioned buses

The blue **air-conditioned buses** stop a lot less often (if at all) and cover the distances faster and more comfortably: passengers are allotted specific seats, and on long journeys get blankets, snacks and non-stop videos. On some routes, you also have the option of taking the VIP air-con bus service, which has fewer seats and more leg room. On the down side, air-con buses usually cost one-and-a-half times as much as the ordinary buses (up to twice as much for VIP buses), depart less frequently, and don't cover nearly as many routes – and make sure you have some warm clothes, as temperatures can get chilly, even with the blanket. Not all air-con buses have toilets, so it's always worth using bus station facilities before you board.

### Tour buses

In a lot of cases **tour buses** are indistinguishable from air-conditioned ones, operating the busiest routes at similar prices and with comparable facilities. However, some tour buses – such as those operated by Nakorn Chai and Win Tour – do offer a distinctly better service, with reclining seats and plenty of leg room, for which they charge more than government-run air-con buses. In general these major tour-bus companies operate out of the government bus terminals and provide a consistently good standard of service. The opposite is unfortunately true of a number of the smaller private tour bus companies, several of which have a poor reputation for service and comfort, but

attract their customers with bargain fares and convenient timetables. The long-distance tour buses that run from Thanon Khao San in Banglamphu to Surat Thani are a case in point; travellers on this route frequently complain about shabby furnishings, ineffective air-conditioning, unhelpful (even aggressive) drivers, and a frightening lack of safety awareness – and there are occasional reports of theft from luggage on these routes too. If you're planning to travel this route, you are strongly recommended to go by train instead – the extra comfort and peace of mind are well worth the extra baht.

### Tickets and timetables

**Tickets** for all buses can be bought from the departure terminals, but for ordinary buses it's normal to buy them on board. Air-conditioned buses often operate from a separate station, and tickets for the more popular routes should be booked a day in advance. As a rough indication of **fares**, a trip from Bangkok to Surat Thani should cost about B350 for first class, B175–225 by air-conditioned bus, and B125 by ordinary bus.

Long-distance buses often depart in clusters around the same time (early morning or late at night for example), leaving a gap of five or more hours during the day with no services at all. Local TAT offices often keep up-to-date bus **timetables** in English, or go to the bus terminal the day before you want to leave and check with staff there. That said, if you turn up at a bus terminal in the morning for a medium-length journey (150–300km), you're almost always guaranteed to be on your way within two hours.

## Songthaews, share taxis and air-conditioned minibuses

In rural areas, the bus network is supplemented – or even substantially replaced – by **songthaews** (literally "two rows"), which are open-ended vans (or occasionally cattle-trucks) onto which the drivers squash as many passengers as possible on two facing benches, leaving latecomers to swing off the running board at the back. As well as their essential role within towns (see "Local Transport" on p.37), songthaews ply set routes from larger towns out to their surrounding suburbs and villages, and, where there's no call for a regular bus service, between small towns: some have destinations written on in Thai, but few are numbered. In most towns you'll find the songthaew "terminal" near the market; to pick one up between destinations just flag it down. To indicate to the driver that you want to get out, the normal practice is to rap hard with a coin on the metal railings as you approach the spot (or press the bell if there is one). As a general rule, the cost of inter-town songthaews is comparable to that of air-conditioned buses.

In the deep south they do things with a little more style – **share taxis**, often clapped-out old limos, connect all the major towns, though they are slowly being replaced by more comfortable **air-conditioned minibuses** (for more details, see p.35). These generally depart frequently and cover the distance faster than the ordinary bus service, but can be uncomfortably cramped when filled to capacity and are not ideal for travellers with huge rucksacks.

In many cases, long-distance songthaews and air-con minibuses will drop you at an exact address (for example a particular guest house) if you warn them far enough in advance – it's generally an expected part of the service.

## Trains

Managed by the State Railway of Thailand (SRT), the rail network consists of four main lines radiating out from Bangkok, and a few branch lines. The **Southern Line** extends to Hat Yai, where it branches: one line continues down the west coast of Malaysia, via Butterworth and Kuala Lumpur, to Singapore; the other heads down the eastern side of the peninsula to Sungai Kolok on the Thailand–Malaysia border (20km from Pasir Mas on Malaysia's interior railway). The **Eastern Line** also has two branches, one of which runs from Bangkok to Aranyaprathet on the Cambodian border, the other of which connects Bangkok with Si Racha and Pattaya.

**Fares** depend on the class of seat, whether or not you want air-conditioning, and on the speed of the train; those quoted here exclude the "speed" supplements, which are discussed below. Hard wooden third-class seats cost about the same as an ordinary bus (Bangkok–Surat Thani around B170), and are fine for about three hours, after which numbness sets in. For longer journeys you'd be wise to opt for the padded and often reclining seats in second class (Bangkok–Surat Thani B310, or B450 with air-conditioning). On long-distance trains, you also usually have the option of second-class berths (Bangkok–Surat Thani B410–460, or B560–630 with air-conditioning), with day seats that convert into comfortable curtained-off bunks in the evening. Travelling first class (Bangkok–Surat Thani B1100) means you automatically get a private two-person air-conditioned sleeping compartment, complete with washbasin. Note that you must **buy a ticket before boarding** a train, otherwise you're liable for a fine of B100 on an ordinary train or B200 on a rapid or express train.

There are several different **types of train**: slowest of all is the third-class-only Ordinary service, which is generally (but not always) available only on short and medium-length journeys and has no speed supplement. Next comes the misleadingly named Rapid train (B40 supplement), a trip on which from Bangkok to Surat Thani, for example, takes about twelve hours; the Special Express (B80 supplement) takes half an hour less to cover the same route; and fastest of all is the Special Express Diesel Railcar (also B80 supplement) which does the journey in just nine hours. Note that all long-distance trains have **dining cars**, and rail staff will also bring meals to your seat. Tourist menus are written in English but have inflated prices – ask for the similar but less expensive "ordinary" version, the *menu thammadaa*.

**Booking** at least one day in advance is strongly recommended for second- and first-class seats on all lengthy journeys, and sleepers should be booked as far in advance as possible. It should be possible to make bookings at the station in any major town; for details on how to book trains out of Bangkok, see p.87.

The SRT publishes three clear and fairly accurate free **timetables** in English which detail types of trains and classes available on each route as well as fares and supplementary charges; the best place to get hold of them is over the counter at Bangkok's Hualamphong station or, if you're lucky, the TAT office in Bangkok.

Travel agents overseas sell 7-, 14- and 21-day **rail passes**, covering train journeys

## Train information

If you want to plan ahead, visit the SRT
**website** ⊛www.srt.motc.go.th, which
carries timetables for the main routes as
well as ticket prices. Alternatively, you could
try phoning the 24-hour SRT Hotline on
☎1690, or calling the main Hualamphong
office on ☎02/220 4334.

anywhere in Thailand in non-air-con second-
class seats. However, the passes are generally more trouble than they're worth, as the
country's network is not extensive enough to
make them pay, and many booking offices in
Thailand are at a loss as to how to handle
them, especially if, as is usually the case,
pass-holders want to pay extra for a sleeping berth.

## Ferries

Regular **ferries** connect all major islands
with the mainland, and for the vast majority
of crossings you simply buy your ticket on
board. In tourist areas competition ensures
that prices are kept low, and fares tend to
vary with the speed of the crossing: thus
Phuket–Ko Phi Phi costs between B250 (2hr
30min) and B350 (1hr 30 min). Boats generally operate a reduced service during the
monsoon season (May–Oct along the east
coast and Andaman coast; Nov–Jan on the
Gulf coast); the more remote spots become
inaccessible in these periods. Details on
island connections are given in the relevant
chapters.

## Flights

The domestic arm of **Thai Airways**
(⊛www.thaiairways.com) dominates the
internal flight network, which extends to all
extremities of the country, around two dozen
airports. **Bangkok Airways** (⊛www.bkkair
.co.th) plies some useful additional routes,
including Bangkok–Ko Samui, Bangkok–
Ranong, Ko Samui–Phuket, Ko Samui–Krabi
and Ko Samui–Pattaya, and will be the main
carrier at Trat airport, which is due to open in
2003. There is also a newcomer on the
scene, the Phuket-based **Air Andaman**
(⊛www.airandaman.com), which currently
only flies Phuket–Krabi, Phuket–Surat Thani
and Phuket–Nakhon Si Thammarat, but is

intending to extend its service to include
Phuket–Chumphon, Phuket–Ranong and
Chumphon–Bangkok. If you want to plan
domestic flights before you leave home,
check out the airlines' websites, which list
both schedules and fares for all routes.

All towns served by an airport have at
least one Thai Airways **booking** office;
flights can get booked a long way ahead,
so reserve early if possible – but bear in
mind it costs much less to book in Thailand
than from abroad. The main Bangkok
offices for Thai and Bangkok Airways are
detailed on p.161, and flight durations and
frequencies are listed at the end of each
chapter. If you're planning to use the Thai
Airways' internal network a lot, you can
save money by buying a **Discover
Thailand Airpass** (about £140/US$200),
available only outside Thailand from Thai
Airways' offices and travel agents. The
pass covers four one-way flights in a two-
month period; you fix the routes when you
buy the pass, but dates of travel can be
changed in Thailand.

## Local transport

Most sizeable towns have some kind of **local
transport system**, comprising a network of
buses, songthaews or even longtail boats,
with set fares and routes but not rigid
timetabling; in most cases vehicles leave
when they're full – generally at ten- or twenty-
minute intervals during the busiest time of day
(from about 6am until noon) – and then at
least once an hour until 5 or 6pm.

### Buses and songthaews

Larger cities like Bangkok have a **local bus**
network which usually extends to the suburbs and operates from dawn till dusk
(through the night in Bangkok). Most vehicles display route numbers in Arabic numerals, and you pay the conductor B5–10
depending on your destination (on some
routes you can choose to take air-con
buses, for which you pay a couple of baht
extra).

Within medium-sized and large towns, the
main transport role is often played by
**songthaews**. The size and shape of vehicle
used varies from town to town – and in some
places they're known as "tuk-tuks" from the
noise they make, not to be confused with the

smaller tuk-tuks, described below, that operate as private taxis – but all have the tell-tale two facing benches in the back. In some towns songthaews follow fixed routes; in others they act as communal taxis, picking up a number of people who are going in roughly the same direction and taking each of them right to their destination. Fares within towns range between B5 and B20, depending on distance.

## Longtail boats

Wherever there's a decent public waterway, there'll be a **longtail boat** ready to ferry you along it. Another great Thai trademark, these elegant, streamlined boats are powered by deafening diesel engines – sometimes custom-built, more often adapted from cars or trucks – which drive a propeller mounted on a long shaft that is swivelled for steering. Longtails carry between ten and twenty passengers: in Bangkok and Krabi the majority follow fixed routes, but elsewhere they're for hire at about B100 an hour per boat, more in tourist spots.

## Taxi services

**Taxis** also comes in many guises, and in bigger towns you can often choose between taking a tuk-tuk, a samlor, a motorbike taxi or a car taxi. The one thing common to all modes of chartered transport is that you must establish the **fare** beforehand: although drivers nearly always pitch their first offers too high, they do calculate with traffic and time of day in mind, as well·as according to distance – if successive drivers scoff at your price, you know you've got it wrong. See p.95 for advice on how to avoid being ripped off by Bangkok tuk-tuk drivers.

### Tuk-tuks

Named after the noise of its excruciatingly unsilenced engine, the three-wheeled open-sided **tuk-tuk** is the classic Thai vehicle. Painted in primary colours, tuk-tuks blast their way round towns and cities on two-stroke engines, zipping around faster than any car, and taking corners on two wheels. They aren't as dangerous as they look though, and can be an exhilarating way to get around, as long as you're not too fussy about exhaust fumes. They're also inexpensive: fares start at B10 (B30 in Bangkok)

regardless of the number of passengers – three is the safe maximum, though six is not uncommon.

### Samlors

Tuk-tuks are also sometimes known as samlors (literally "three wheels"), but the real **samlors** are tricycle rickshaws propelled by pedal power alone. Slower and a great deal more stately than tuk-tuks, samlors operate pretty much everywhere except in Bangkok. Forget any qualms you may have about being pedalled around by another human being: samlor drivers' livelihoods depend on having a constant supply of passengers, so your most ethical option is to hop on and not scrimp on the fare. Drivers usually charge a minimum B10 fee and add B10 per kilometre, possibly more for a heavy load. A further permutation are the motorized samlors, where the driver relies on a motorbike rather than a bicycle to propel passengers to their destination. They look much the same as cycle samlors, often sound as noisy as tuk-tuks, and cost something between the two.

### Motorbike taxis

Even faster and more precarious than tuk-tuks, **motorbike taxis** feature both in big towns and out-of-the-way places. In towns – where the drivers are identified by coloured, numbered vests – they have the advantage of being able to dodge traffic jams, but are obviously only really suitable for the single traveller, and motorbike taxis aren't the easiest mode of transport if you're carrying luggage. In remote spots on the other hand, they're often the only alternative to hitching or walking, and are especially useful for getting between bus stops on main roads and to national parks or ancient ruins. Within towns, motorbike-taxi fares are comparable to those for tuk-tuks, but for trips to the outskirts the cost rises steeply – about B100–150 for a twenty-kilometre round trip.

### Car taxis

Generally available only in the biggest towns, air-conditioned **car taxis** charge fares that begin at around B50. Only major towns and resorts such as Bangkok and Phuket have metered taxis, where you must be sure to establish whether or not the meter is actually working before you set off; if it's not, or if you're taxi has no meter, settle on a price at the start.

## Vehicle rental

Despite first impressions, and the obvious mayhem that characterizes Bangkok's roads, **driving yourself around Thailand** is fairly straightforward and unstressful. Many roads, particularly in the south, are remarkably uncongested. Major routes are clearly signed in English, though this only applies to some minor roads – unfortunately there is no perfect English-language map to compensate, though the Nelles map described on p.24 is adequate.

Outside the capital, its immediate environs and the eastern seaboard, local drivers are considerate and noticeably unaggressive; they very rarely use their horns for example, and will often indicate and even swerve away when it's safe for you to overtake. The most inconsiderate and dangerous road-users in Thailand are bus drivers and lorry drivers, many of whom drive ludicrously fast, hog the road, race round bends on the wrong side of the road and use their horns remorselessly; worse still, many of them are tanked up on amphetamines, which makes them quite literally fearless. Bus and lorry drivers are at their worst after dark (many of them only drive then), so you are strongly advised **never to drive at night** – a further hazard being the inevitable stream of unlit bicycles and mopeds in and around built-up areas, as well as poorly signed roadworks which are often not made safe or blocked off from unsuspecting traffic.

As for local **rules of the road**, Thais drive on the left, and the speed limit is 60km/h within built-up areas and 80km/h outside them. More unusually, a major road doesn't necessarily have right of way over a minor, but the bigger vehicle *always* has right of way. An oncoming vehicle flashing its lights means it's coming through no matter what; a right indicator signal from the car in front usually means it's not safe for you to overtake, while a left indicator signal usually means that it is safe to do so.

Theoretically, foreigners need an international driver's **licence** to hire any kind of vehicle, but most companies accept national licences, and the smaller operations (especially bike rentals) may not ask for any kind of proof at all. **Petrol** (*nam man*, which also means oil) costs around B20 a litre. The big fuel stations are the least costly places to fill up (*hai taem*), and many of these also have toilets and simple restaurants, though some of the more decrepit-looking fuel stations on the main highways only sell diesel. Most small villages have easy-to-spot roadside huts where the fuel is pumped out of a large barrel.

### Cars

If you decide to **rent a car**, go to a reputable dealer, preferably an Avis, Budget or SMT branch (see box below) or a rental company recommended by TAT, and make sure you get insurance from them. There are international car-rental places at many regional airports, including Bangkok's Don Muang Airport, which is not a bad place to kick off, as you're on the edge of the city and within fairly easy (signed) reach of the major regional highways. Car rental places in provincial capitals and resorts are listed in the relevant accounts. Prices for a small car start at about B1200 per day, depending on the vehicle's condition, which is generally not bad. In most parts of the country, you can count on covering about 70km per hour if travelling long distances on major highways. If appropriate, consider the option of hiring a driver along with the car, which you can often do for no extra charge on day rentals.

**Jeeps** are a lot more popular with farangs, especially on beach resorts and islands like Pattaya, Phuket and Ko Samui, but they're notoriously dangerous; a huge number of tourists manage to roll their jeeps on steep hillsides and sharp bends. Jeep rental usually works out somewhere between B1000 and B1500.

### Car rental agencies

**Avis** @ www.avisthailand.com, UK
☎ 0870/606 0100, Ireland ☎ 01/605 7555,
US ☎ 1-800/331-1084, Canada 1-800-272
5871, Australia ☎ 13 6333, New Zealand
☎ 09/526 5231 or 0800/655111.

**Budget** @ www.budget.co.th, UK
☎ 0800/181181, Ireland ☎ 1850/575757,
North America ☎ 1-800/527-0700, Australia
☎ 1300/362848, New Zealand
☎ 0800/652227 or 09/375 2270.

**National Car Rental** (**SMT** in Thailand)
@ smtcar@samart.co.th, UK ☎ 0870/536
5365, North America ☎ 1-800/227-7368.

For all cars and jeeps, renters will often ask for a deposit of at least B2000, and will either want to hold onto your passport or take your credit card details as surety.

## Motorbikes

One of the best ways of exploring the countryside is to rent a **motorbike**. Two-seater **80cc** bikes with automatic gears are best if you've never ridden a motorbike before, but aren't really suited for long slogs. If you're going to hit the dirt roads you'll certainly need something more powerful, like a **125cc** trail bike. These have the edge in gear choice and are the best bikes for steep slopes, though an inexperienced rider may find these machines a handful; the less widely available 125cc road bikes are easier to control and much cheaper on petrol.

Rental **prices** for the day usually work out at somewhere between B150 (for a fairly beat-up 80cc) and B350 (for a good trail bike), though you can bargain for a discount on a long rental. As with cars, the renters will often ask for a deposit and your passport or credit-card details, though you're unlikely to have to prove that you've ridden a bike before. Insurance is not often available, so it's a good idea to make sure your travel insurance covers you for possible mishaps.

Before signing anything, **check the bike** thoroughly – test the brakes, look for oil leaks, check the treads and the odometer, and make sure the chain isn't stretched too tight (a tight chain is likelier to break) – and preferably take it for a test run. As you will have to pay an inflated price for any damage when you get back, make a note on the contract of any defects such as broken mirrors, indicators and so on. Make sure you know what kind of petrol the bike takes as well.

As far as **equipment** goes, a helmet is essential – most rental places provide poorly made ones, but they're better than nothing. Helmets are obligatory on all motorbike journeys, and the law is rigidly enforced in major tourist resorts, where on-the-spot fines are the norm. You'll need sunglasses if your helmet doesn't have a visor. As well as being more culturally appropriate, long trousers, a long-sleeved top and decent shoes will provide a second skin if you go over, which most people do at some stage. Pillions should wear long trousers to avoid getting nasty burns from the exhaust. For the sake of stability, leave most of your luggage in baggage storage and pack as small a bag as possible, strapping it tightly to the bike with bungy cords – these are usually provided. Once on the road, oil the chain at least every other day, keep the radiator topped up, and fill up with oil every 300km or so.

For expert **advice** on motorbike travel in Thailand, check out David Unkovich's website ⓦwww.geocities.com/goldentrianglerider.

## Bicycles

The safest and most pleasant way of conveying yourself around certain towns and rural areas is by **bicycle**, except of course in Bangkok. You won't find bike rentals everywhere, but some guest houses keep a few, charging around B20–50 a day.

## Hitching

Public transport being so inexpensive, you should only have to resort to **hitching** in the most remote areas, in which case you'll probably get a lift to the nearest bus or songthaew stop quite quickly. On routes served by buses and trains hitching is not standard practice, but in other places locals do rely on regular passers-by (such as national park officials), and as a farang you can make use of this "service" too. As with hitching anywhere in the world, think twice about hitching solo or at night, especially if you're female. Truck drivers are notorious users of amphetamines (as are a lot of bus drivers), so you may want to wait for a better offer.

# Accommodation

Cheap accommodation can be found all over Thailand: for the simplest double room prices start at around B100 in the outlying regions and B150 in Bangkok, rising to B250 in some resorts. Tourist centres invariably offer a huge range of more upmarket choices, and you'll have little problem finding luxury hotels in these places. In most resort areas rates fluctuate according to demand, plummeting during the off-season and, in some places, rising at weekends throughout the year.

Whatever the establishment, staff expect you to look at the room before taking it; in the budget ones especially, try out the door-lock, check for cockroaches and mosquitoes, and make sure it's equipped with a decent mosquito net or screens. En-suite showers and flush toilets are the norm only in moderately priced and expensive hotels; in the less touristy places you'll be "showering" with a bowl dipped into a large water jar, and using squat toilets.

## Guest houses and hostels

Any place calling itself a **guest house** – which could be anything from a bamboo hut to a three-storey concrete block – is almost certain to provide inexpensive, basic accommodation specifically aimed at Western travellers and priced at around B100–250 for a sparse double room with a fan and (often shared) bathroom. You'll find them in all major tourist centres and even in the most unlikely back-country spots: on the beaches, **bungalows** operate in much the same way.

In the main towns guest houses tend to be concentrated in cheek-by-jowl farang ghettos, but even if you baulk at the travellers' scene that often characterizes these places, guest houses make great places to stay, with attached cafeterias, clued-up English-speaking staff and informative noticeboards. These days, they're providing more and more services and **facilities**, such as internet access, safes for valuables, luggage storage, travel and tour operator desks and their own poste restante. Staying at one out in the sticks, you'll often get involved in local life a lot more than if you were encased in a hotel.

## Accommodation prices

Throughout this guide, guest houses, hotels and bungalows have been categorized according to the price codes given below. These categories represent the minimum you can expect to pay in the high season (roughly July, Aug & Nov–Feb) for a double room. If travelling on your own, expect to pay anything between sixty and one hundred percent of the rates quoted for a double room. Wherever a price range is indicated, this means that the establishment offers rooms with varying facilities – as explained in the write-up. Where an establishment also offers dormitory beds, the prices of these beds are given in the text.

Remember that the top-whack hotels will add seven-percent tax and a ten-percent service charge to your bill – the price codes below are based on net rates after taxes have been added.

| | | | | | |
|---|---|---|---|---|---|
| ❶ under B150 | ❹ B400–600 | ❼ B1200–1800 |
| ❷ B150–250 | ❺ B600–900 | ❽ B1800–3000 |
| ❸ B250–400 | ❻ B900–1200 | ❾ B3000+ |

At the vast majority of guest houses **check-out time** is noon, which means that during high season you should arrive to check in at about 11.30am to ensure you get a room: few places draw up a "waiting list" and they rarely take advance bookings unless they know you already and you've paid a deposit.

The **upmarket guest house** is almost a contradiction in terms, but there are a few such places, charging between B250 and B800 for facilities that may include air-conditioning, bathroom, TV and use of a swimming pool. Beware of pricey guest houses or bungalows in mega-resorts like Pattaya, Phuket and Ko Phi Phi, however, which often turn out to be low-quality fan-cooled establishments making a killing out of unsuspecting holidaymakers.

With just twelve officially registered **youth hostels** in the whole country, it's not worth becoming a YHA member just for your trip to Thailand, especially as card-holders get only a small discount anyway. In general, youth-hostel prices work out the same as guest-house rates and rooms are open to all ages, whether or not you're a member. Online reservations can be made via the Thai Youth Hostels Association website @www.tyha.org.

## Budget hotels

Few Thais use guest houses, opting instead for **budget hotels** offering rooms costing up to B600. Beds in these places are large enough for a couple, and it's quite acceptable for two people to ask and pay for a single room (*hong diaw*). Usually run by Chinese-Thais, these three- or four-storey places are found in every sizeable town, often near the bus station. The rooms are generally clean and usually come with attached bathroom and a fan (or air-conditioning), though they also tend to be staffed by brusque non-English speakers. A number of budget hotels also double as brothels, though as a farang you're unlikely to be offered this sideline, and may not even notice the goings-on anyway.

If the hotel's on a busy main road, as many of them are, try asking for a quiet room (*mii hawng ngiap-kwaa mai*?). Advance bookings are accepted over the phone – if you can make yourself understood – but this is rarely necessary, as such hotels rarely fill up. The only time you may have difficulty finding a budget hotel room is during Chinese New Year (a moveable three-day period in late January or February), when many Chinese-run hotels close and the others get booked up fast.

## Moderate hotels

**Moderate hotels** – priced between B600 and B1200 – can sometimes work out to be good value, offering many of the trimmings of a top-end hotel (TV, fridge, air-conditioning, pool), but none of the prestige. They're often the kind of places that once stood at the top of the range, but were downgraded when the multinational luxury muscled in and hogged the poshest clientele. They still make especially welcome alternatives to the budget hotels in provincial capitals, but, like upmarket guest houses, can turn out to be vastly overpriced in the resorts.

As with the budget hotels, you're unlikely to have trouble finding a room on spec in one of these places, though advance bookings are accepted by phone. Bed size varies a lot more than in the Chinese-run places though, with some making the strict Western distinction between singles and doubles.

## Upmarket hotels

Many of Thailand's **upmarket hotels** belong to international chains like Hilton, Holiday Inn, Le Meridien and Sheraton, maintaining top-quality standards in Bangkok and major resorts at prices of B2400 (£40/US$60) and upward for a double – far less than you'd pay for such luxury accommodation in the West. Some of the best home-grown upmarket hotels are up to B1000 cheaper for equally fine service, rooms equipped with TV, mini-bar and balcony, and full use of the hotel sports facilities and swimming pools. Note that, since the collapse of the baht in 1997, a number of luxury hotels now quote rates in US dollars. All upmarket hotels can be booked in advance, an advisable measure in Phuket or Pattaya during peak season.

## National parks and camping

Unattractive accommodation is one of the big disappointments of Thailand's **national parks**. Generally built to a standard two-roomed format, these dismal concrete

## Booking a hotel online

The following online hotel-booking services offer rates discounted by up to sixty percent on the published prices of selected mid-range and upmarket accommodation. Discounted rates for a double room generally start at US$30, but it is occasionally possible to find rooms for US$20.

### Hotels across Thailand

**Accommodating Asia**
www.accomasia.com/thailand.htm

**Asia Hotels**
www.asia-hotels.com

**Asia Ways**
www.asiaways.com

**Hotel Thailand**
hotelthailand.com

**Island Net**
www.islandnet.com

**Siam Net**
www.siam.net

**Stay In Thailand**
www.stayinthailand.com

**Thai Focus**
www.thaifocus.com

**Thailand Hotels Association**
www.thaihotels.org

**Thailand Hotels and Resorts**
www.hotels.siam.net

### Regional hotels

**Ko Lanta**
www.kohlanta.com

**Ko Samui**
www.sawadee.com

**Krabi**
krabihotels.com
www.krabi.sawadee.com

**Phuket**
www.phuket.com/hotels/index.html

**Trang**
www.trangonline.com

---

bungalows feature in about half the country's parks, and cost an average B500 for four or more beds plus a probably malfunctioning shower. Because most of their custom comes from Thai family groups, park officials are sometimes loathe to discount these huts for lone travellers, though some parks do offer dorm-style accommodation at B100 a bed. In most parks, advance booking is unnecessary except on weekends and national holidays. If you do want to pre-book, then either pay on the spot at the Forestry Department offices (☎02/561 4292–3, ☎579 7099) which are near Kasetsart University on Thanon Phaholyothin, about 4km north of the Mo Chit skytrain terminus – which can be quite a palaver, so don't plan on doing anything else that day – or book on the phone (not much English spoken), then send a baht money order and wait for confirmation. If you turn up without booking, check in at the park headquarters – which is usually adjacent to the visitor centre.

In a few parks, private operators have set up low-cost **guest houses** on the outskirts, and these make much more attractive and economical places to stay.

## Camping

You can usually **camp** in a national park for a minimal fee of B10–30, and some national parks also rent out two-berth tents at anything from B40–200. Unless you're planning an extensive tour of national parks though, there's little point in lugging a tent around Thailand: accommodation everywhere else is too inexpensive to make camping a necessity, and anyway there are no campgrounds inside town perimeters.

Camping is allowed on nearly all **islands and beaches**, many of which are national parks in their own right. Few travellers bother to bring tents for beaches either though, opting for inexpensive bungalow accommodation or simply sleeping out under the stars.

# Food and drink

Thai food is now very popular in most Western countries, with a reputation for using fresh ingredients to quickly create dishes that are fiery but fragrant and subtly flavoured. Lemon grass, basil, coriander, galangal, chilli, garlic, lime juice, coconut milk and fermented fish sauce are some of the vital ingredients that give the cuisine its distinctive taste.

Bangkok is the country's main culinary centre, boasting the cream of gourmet Thai restaurants and the best international cuisines. The rest of the country is by no means a gastronomic wasteland however, and you can eat well and cheaply even in the smallest provincial towns, many of which offer the additional attraction of regional specialities. In fact you could eat more than adequately without ever entering a restaurant, as itinerant food vendors hawking hot and cold snacks materialize in even the most remote spots, as well as on trains and buses, and night markets often serve customers from dusk until dawn.

**Hygiene** is a consideration when eating anywhere in Thailand, but being too cautious means you'll end up spending a lot of money and missing out on some real local treats. Wean your stomach gently by avoiding excessive amounts of chillies and too much fresh fruit in the first few days, and always drink either bottled or boiled water.

You can be pretty sure that any noodle stall or curry shop that's permanently packed with customers is a safe bet, but if you're really concerned about health standards you could stick to restaurants displaying the TAT-approved symbol (also used for shops), which shows a woman seated between two panniers beneath the TAT logo.

Broad **price** categories are appended to restaurant listings throughout this guide: "inexpensive" means you can get a main course for under B60, "moderate" means B60–130, and "expensive" over B130.

## Where to eat

Despite their obvious attractions, a lot of tourists eschew the huge range of Thai places to eat and opt instead for the much "safer" restaurants in **guest houses** and **hotels**. Almost all tourist accommodation has a kitchen and, while some are excellent, the vast majority serve up bland imitations of Western fare alongside equally pale versions of common Thai dishes. However, guest houses do serve comfortingly familiar Western breakfasts – most farangs quickly tire of eating rice three times a day.

Throughout the country most **inexpensive** Thai restaurants and cafés specialize in one general food type or preparation method – a "noodle shop", for example, will do fried noodles and noodle soups, plus a basic fried rice, but they won't have curries or meat or fish dishes. Similarly, a restaurant displaying whole roast chickens and ducks in its window will offer these sliced, usually with chillies and sauces and served over rice, but their menu probably won't extend to noodles or fish, while in "curry shops" your options are limited to the vats of curries stewing away in the hot cabinet.

To get a wider array of low-cost food, it's sometimes best to head for the local **night market** (*talat yen*), a term for the gatherings of open-air night-time kitchens found in every town. Operating usually from about 6pm to 6am, they are typically to be found on permanent patches close to the fruit and vegetable market or the bus station, and as often as not they're the best and most entertaining places to eat, not to mention the least expensive – after a lip-smacking feast of two savoury dishes, a fruit drink and a sweet you'll come away no more than B70–80 the poorer.

A typical night market has some thirty-odd "specialist" pushcart kitchens jumbled together, each fronted by several sets of tables and stools. Noodle and fried-rice vendors always feature prominently, as do sweets stalls, heaped high with sticky rice cakes wrapped in banana leaves or thick with bags of tiny sweetcorn pancakes hot from the griddle – and no night market is complete without its fruit-drink stall, offering banana shakes and freshly squeezed orange, lemon and tomato juices. In the best setups you'll find a lot more besides: curries; barbecued sweetcorn; satay sticks of pork and chicken, fresh pineapple, watermelon and mango; and in coastal towns, heaps of fresh fish. Having decided what you want, you order from the cook or the cook's dogsbody and sit down at the nearest table; there is no territorialism about night markets, so it's normal to eat several dishes from separate stalls and rely on the nearest cook to sort out the bill.

Some large markets, particularly in Bangkok, have separate **food court** areas where you buy coupons first and select food and drink to their value at the stalls of your choice. This is also the modus operandi in the food courts found on the top floor of department stores and shopping centres across the country.

For a more relaxing ambience, Bangkok and the larger towns have a range of **upmarket restaurants**, some specializing in **"royal" Thai cuisine**, which differs from standard fare mainly in the quality of the ingredients and the way the food is presented. As with the nouvelle cuisine of the West, great care is taken over how individual dishes look: they are served in small portions and decorated with carved fruit and vegetables in a way that used to be the prerogative of royal cooks, but has now filtered down to the common folk. The cost of such delights is not prohibitive, either – a meal in one of these places is unlikely to cost more than B500 per person.

## How to eat

Thai food is eaten with a fork (left hand) and a spoon (right hand); there is no need for a knife as food is served in bite-sized chunks, which are forked onto the spoon and fed into the mouth. Steamed **rice** (*khao*) is served with most meals, and indeed the most commonly heard phrase for "to eat" is *kin khao* (literally, "eat rice"); chopsticks are provided

only for noodle dishes, and northeastern sticky-rice dishes are always eaten with the fingers of the right hand, rolled up into small balls and dipped into chilli sauces. Never eat with the fingers of your left hand, which is used for washing after going to the toilet.

So that complementary taste combinations can be enjoyed, the dishes in a Thai meal are served all at once, even the soup, and shared communally. The more people, the more taste and texture sensations; if there are only two of you, it's normal to order three dishes, plus your own individual plates of steamed rice, while three diners would order four dishes and so on. Only put a serving of one dish on your rice plate each time, and then only one or two spoonfuls.

## What to eat

The repertoire of noodles, stir-fries, curries and rice dishes listed below is pretty much standard throughout Thailand. When you get out into the provinces, you'll have the chance to sample a few **specialities** as well, which have evolved either from the cuisines of neighbouring countries or from the crops best suited to that area. Bland food is anathema to Thais and restaurant tables everywhere come decked out with a **condiment set** featuring the four basic flavours: chopped chillies in watery fish sauce; chopped chillies in vinegar; sugar; and ground red pepper – and often extra bowls of ground peanuts and a bottle of chilli ketchup as well.

### Noodle and rice dishes

Thais eat **noodles** (*kway tiaw* or *ba mii*) when Westerners would dig into a sandwich – for lunch, as a late-night snack or just to pass the time – and at B20–30 (around B60 in a posh restaurant) they're the cheapest hot meal you'll find anywhere, whether bought from an itinerant street vendor or ordered in an air-conditioned restaurant. They come in assorted varieties (wide and flat, thin and transparent; made with eggs, soy-bean flour or rice flour) and get boiled up as soups (*kway tiaw nam*), doused in sauces (*kway tiaw rat na*), or stir-fried (*kway tiaw haeng* or *kway tiaw pat*). All three versions include a smattering of vegetables, eggs and meat, but the usual practice is to order the dish with extra chicken, beef, pork or

**B**

**BASICS** | Food and drink

**Southern Thai** cuisine displays a marked Malaysian and Muslim aspect as you near the border and, as you'd expect in a region bounded by sea, the salty flavours associated with seafood are prevalent. Liberal use of **turmeric** is another distinctive feature, which gives many southern dishes a yellow hue, notably *plaa khluk khamin*, grilled fish rubbed with turmeric, garlic and salt. A huge variety of **curries** are dished up in the south, many of them substituting shrimp paste for the fish sauce used elsewhere in Thailand. Three curries that are now found nationally seem to have taken root in Thailand on the peninsula: the rich and usually fairly mild Muslim curry, *kaeng matsaman*; *kaeng phanaeng* (a corruption of Penang, an island off the west coast of Malaysia); a thick, savoury curry also usually made with beef; and the Indian-style chicken curry served over lightly spiced saffron rice, known as *kaeng karii kai*. Other curries are rather more distinctive: *kaeng leuang* ("yellow curry") features fish, turmeric, pineapple, squash, beans and green papaya, while *kaeng tai plaa* is a powerful combination of fish stomach with potatoes, beans, pickled bamboo shoots and turmeric.

Satays feature more down here, as does delicious *hor mok* (sometimes known as *khai plaa mok*), a kind of seafood soufflé made with coconut milk and red curry paste. In Muslim areas, you'll come across *khao mok kai*, the local version of a biryani: chicken and rice cooked with turmeric, cinnamon, cloves and other Indian spices and served with clear chicken soup. Also popular, especially in Phuket, Nakhon Si Thammarat and Trang, is *khanom jiin* (literally, "Chinese pastry"), rice noodles topped with hot, sweet or fishy sauce (the latter Malay-style *naam yaa*, made with ground fish) and served with crispy raw vegetables.

Markets in the south often serve *khao yam* for breakfast, a refreshing salad of dried cooked rice, dried shrimp, grated coconut and lemon grass served with a sweet sauce. You'll find many types of **roti** in the south, too – pancake-like bread sold hot from pushcart griddles and, in its plain form, rolled with sickly sweet condensed milk and sugar. Other versions include *roti kluay* (with banana), *roti khai* (with egg), savoury *mataba* (with minced chicken or beef) and, served with curry sauce for breakfast, *roti kaeng*.

shrimps. Most popular of noodle dishes is *kway tiaw phat thai* (usually abbreviated to *phat thai*), a delicious combination of fried noodles, beansprouts, egg and tofu, sprinkled with ground peanuts and the juice of half a lime, and often spiked with tiny dried shrimps.

**Fried rice** (*khao pat*) is the other faithful standby, much the same price as noodles, and guaranteed to feature on menus right across the country. Curries that come served on a bed of steamed rice are more like stews, prepared long in advance and eaten more as a light meal than a main one; they are usually called *khao na* plus the meat of the chosen dish – thus *khao na pet* is duck curry served over rice.

### Curries, stir-fries, fish, soups and salads

Thai curries (*kaeng*) are based on coconut milk – which gives them a slightly sweet taste and a soup-like consistency – and get their fire from chilli peppers (*phrik*). The best curries are characterized by their **curry pastes**, a subtle blend of freshly ground herbs, spices, garlic, shallots and chilli, the most well known being the red or green curry pastes. It's often possible to request one that's "not too hot" (*mai phet*); if you do bite into a chilli, the way to combat the searing heat is to take a mouthful of plain rice – swigging water just exacerbates the sensation. Alternatively, pick the whole chillies out: contrary to what your eyes might think, the green ones are hotter than the red, and the smaller ones are hotter than the large; thus the tiny green "mouse shit" chillies are small but deadly.

**Stir-fries** tend to be a lot milder, often flavoured with ginger and whole cloves of garlic and featuring a pleasing combination of soft meat and crunchy vegetables or nuts. Chicken with cashew nuts (*kai pat met mamuang*) is a favourite of a lot of farang-orientated places, as is sweet and sour chicken, pork or fish (*kai/muu/plaa priaw waan*). *Pat phak bung* – slightly bitter morning-glory leaves fried with garlic in a black-bean sauce – makes a good vegetable side dish with any of these.

## Fruits of Thailand

One of the most refreshing snacks in Thailand is **fruit** (*phōnlamái*), and you'll find it offered everywhere – neatly sliced in glass boxes on hawker carts, blended into delicious shakes at night market stalls, and served as dessert in restaurants. The fruits described below can be found in all parts of Thailand, though some are seasonal. The country's more familiar fruits are not listed here, but include forty varieties of banana (*klûay*), dozens of different mangoes (*mámûang*), three types of pineapple (*sàppàròt*), coconuts (*mapráo*), oranges (*sôm*), lemons (*mánao*) and watermelons (*taeng moh*). To avoid stomach trouble, peel all fruit before eating it, and use common sense when buying it pre-peeled on the street, avoiding anything that looks fly-blown or seems to have been sitting in the sun for hours.

**Custard apple** (soursop; *nóinà*; July–Sept). Inside the knobbly, muddy green skin you'll find creamy, almond-coloured blancmange-like flesh, having a strong flavour of strawberries and pears with a hint of cinnamon, and many seeds.

**Durian** (*thúrian*; April–June). Thailand's most prized, and expensive, fruit has a greeny-yellow, spiky exterior and grows to the size of a football. Inside, it divides into segments of thick, yellow-white flesh which gives off a disgustingly strong stink that's been compared to a mixture of mature cheese and caramel. Not surprisingly, many airlines and hotels ban the eating of this smelly delicacy on their premises. Most Thais consider it the king of fruits, while most foreigners find it utterly foul in both taste and smell.

**Guava** (*fàràng*; year-round). The apple of the tropics has green textured skin and sweet, crisp flesh that can be pink or white and is studded with tiny edible seeds. Has five times the vitamin C content of an orange and is sometimes eaten cut into strips and sprinkled with sugar and chilli.

**Jackfruit** (*khan'un*; year-round). This large, pear-shaped fruit can weigh up to twenty kilograms and has a thick, bobbly, greeny-yellow shell protecting sweet yellow flesh. Green, unripe jackfruit is sometimes cooked as a vegetable in curries.

**Longan** (*lamyai*; July–Oct). A close relative of the lychee, with succulent white flesh covered in thin, brittle skin.

**Lychee** (*línjìi*; April–May). Under rough, reddish-brown skin, the lychee has sweet, richly flavoured white flesh, rose-scented and with plenty of vitamin C, round a brown, egg-shaped pit.

**Mangosteen** (*mangkùt*; April–Sept). The size of a small apple, with smooth, purple skin and a fleshy inside that divides into succulent white segments which are sweet though slightly acidic.

**Papaya** (paw-paw; *málákaw*; year-round). Looks like an elongated watermelon, with smooth green skin and yellowy-orange flesh that's a rich source of vitamins A and C. It's a favourite in fruit salads and shakes, and sometimes appears in its green, unripe form in salads, notably *sôm tam*.

**Pomelo** (*sôm oh*; Oct–Dec). The largest of all the citrus fruits, it looks rather like a grapefruit, though it is slightly drier and has less flavour.

**Rambutan** (*ngáw*; May–Sept). The bright red rambutan's soft, spiny exterior has given it its name – *rambut* means "hair" in Malay. Usually about the size of a golf ball, it has a white, opaque fruit of delicate flavour, similar to a lychee.

**Rose apple** (*chomphûu*; year-round). Linked in myth with the golden fruit of immortality, the rose apple is small and egg-shaped, with white, rose-scented flesh.

**Sapodilla** (sapota; *lámút*; Sept–Dec). These small, brown, rough-skinned ovals look a bit like kiwi fruit and conceal a grainy, yellowish pulp that tastes almost honey-sweet.

**Tamarind** (*mákhãam*; Dec–Jan). A Thai favourite and a pricey delicacy – carrying the seeds is said to make you safe from wounding by knives or bullets. Comes in rough, brown pods containing up to ten seeds, each surrounded by a sticky, dry pulp which has a sour, lemony taste.

## A food and drink glossary

**Note**: This glossary includes phonetic guidance to assist you with menu selection; a guide to the Thai language appears in Contexts (p.457).

### Basic ingredients

| | |
|---|---|
| Kài | Chicken |
| Mǔu | Pork |
| Néua | Beef, meat |
| Pèt | Duck |
| Ahǎan thaleh | Seafood |
| Plaa | Fish |
| Plaa dùk | Catfish |
| Plaa mèuk | Squid |
| Kûng | Prawn, shrimp |
| Hǒy | Shellfish |
| Hǒy nang rom | Oyster |
| Puu | Crab |
| Khài | Egg |
| Phàk | Vegetables |

### Vegetables

| | |
|---|---|
| Makěua | Aubergine/eggplant |
| Makěua thêt | Tomato |
| Nàw mái | Bamboo shoots |
| Tùa ngâwk | Bean sprouts |
| Phrík | Chilli |
| Man faràng | Potato |
| Man faràng thâwt | Chips |
| Taeng kwaa | Cucumber |
| Phrík yùak | Green pepper |
| Krathiam | Garlic |
| Hèt | Mushroom |
| Tùa | Peas, beans or lentils |
| Tôn hǒrm | Spring onions |

### Noodles

| | |
|---|---|
| Ba mìi | Egg noodles |
| Kwǎy tiǎw (sên yaì/sên lék) | White rice noodles (wide/thin) |
| Ba mìi kràwp | Crisp fried egg noodles |
| Kwǎy tiǎw/ba mìi haêng | Rice noodles/egg noodles fried with egg, small pieces of meat and a few vegetables |
| Kwǎy tiǎw/ba mìi nám (m̄uu) | Rice noodle/egg noodle soup, made with chicken broth (and pork balls) |
| Kwǎy tiǎw/ba mìi | Rice noodles/egg noodles |
| Rât nâ (mǔu) | Fried in gravy-like sauce with vegetables (and pork slices) |
| Phàt thai | Thin noodles fried with egg, beansprouts and tofu, topped with ground peanuts |
| Pàt siyú | Wide or thin noodles fried with soy sauce, egg and meat |

### Rice

| | |
|---|---|
| Khâo | Rice |
| Khâo man kài | Slices of chicken served over marinated rice |
| Khâo mǔu daeng | Red pork with rice |
| Khâo nâ kài/pèt | Chicken/duck served with sauce over rice |
| Khâo niǎw | Sticky rice |
| Khâo pàt | Fried rice |
| Khâo rât kaeng | Curry over rice |
| Khâo tôm | Rice soup (usually for breakfast) |

### Curries and soups

| | |
|---|---|
| Kaeng phèt | Hot, red curry |
| Kaeng phánaeng | Thick, savoury curry |
| Kaeng khǐaw wan | Green curry |
| Kaeng mátsàman | Rich Muslim-style curry, usually with beef and potatoes |
| Kaeng karìi | Mild, Indian-style curry |
| Kaeng sôm | Fish and vegetable curry |
| Tôm khàa kài | Chicken coconut soup |
| Tôm yam kûng | Hot and sour prawn soup |
| Kaeng jèut | Mild soup with vegetables and usually pork |

### Other dishes

| | |
|---|---|
| Hâwy thâwt | Omelette stuffed with mussels |

All seaside restaurants rightly make a big deal out of locally caught **fish** and **seafood**. If you order fish it will be served whole, either steamed or grilled with ginger or chillies. Mussels often get stuffed into a batter and shrimps turn up in everything from soups to fried noodles.

| | | | |
|---|---|---|---|
| *Kài pàt bai kraprao* | Chicken fried with basil leaves | | beans cooked and served in bamboo tubes |
| *Kài pàt nàw mái* | Chicken with bamboo shoots | *Khâo niãw daeng* | Sticky red rice mixed with coconut cream |
| *Kài pàt mét mámûang* | Chicken with cashew nuts | *Khâo niãw thúrian/ mámûang* | Sticky rice mixed with coconut cream, and durian/mango |
| *Kài pàt khîˉng* | Chicken with ginger | *Klûay khàek* | Fried banana |
| *Kài yâang* | Barbecued chicken on a stick | *Lûk taan chêum* | Sweet palm kernels served in syrup |
| *Khài yát sài* | Omelette with pork and vegetables | *Sãngkhayaa* | Coconut custard |
| *Khãnom jiin nám yaa* | Noodles topped with fish curry | *Tàkôh* | Squares of transparent jelly (jello) topped with coconut cream |
| *Kûng chúp paêng thâwt* | Prawns fried in batter | | |

### Drinks (khreûang deùm)

| | |
|---|---|
| *Bia* | Beer |
| *Chaa ráwn* | Hot tea |
| *Chaa yen* | Iced tea |
| *Kaafae ráwn* | Hot coffee |
| *Kâew* | Glass |
| *Khúat* | Bottle |
| *Mâekhõng* (or anglicized "Mekhong") | Thai brand-name rice whisky |
| *Nám klûay* | Banana shake |
| *Nám mánao/sôm* | Fresh, bottled or fizzy lemon/orange juice |
| *Nám plào* | Drinking water (boiled or filtered) |
| *Nám sõdaa* | Soda water |
| *Nám tan* | Sugar |
| *Nám yen* | Cold water |
| *Nom jeùd* | Milk |
| *Ohlíang* | Iced coffee |
| *Sohdaa* | Soda water |
| *Thûay* | Cup |

| | |
|---|---|
| *Laap* | Spicy minced pork flavoured with mint |
| *Mũu prîaw wãan* | Sweet and sour pork |
| *Néua phàt krathiam phrík thai* | Beef fried with garlic and pepper |
| *Néua phàt nám man hõy* | Beef in oyster sauce |
| *Pàt phàk bûng fai daeng* | Morning glory fried in garlic and bean sauce |
| *Pàt phàk lãi yàng* | Stir-fried vegetables |
| *Pàw pía* | Spring rolls |
| *Plaa nêung páe sá* | Whole fish steamed with vegetables and ginger |
| *Plaa rât phrík* | Whole fish cooked with chillies |
| *Plaa thâwt* | Fried whole fish |
| *Sàté* | Satay |
| *Sôm tam* | Spicy papaya salad |
| *Thâwt man plaa* | Fish cake |
| *Yam néua* | Grilled beef salad |
| *Yam plaa mèuk* | Squid salad |
| *Yam thuˋa phuu* | Wing-bean salad |
| *Yam wun sen* | Noodle and pork salad |

### Ordering

| | |
|---|---|
| *Phõm* (male)/ *diichãn* (female) *kin ahãan mangsàwirát/jeh* | I am vegetarian/ vegan |
| *Khãw duù menu?* | Can I see the menu? |
| *Khãw ...* | I would like ... |
| *Sài/mâi sài* | With/without |
| *Khãw check bin?* | Can I have the bill please? |

### Thai sweets (khanõm)

| | |
|---|---|
| *Khanõm beuang* | Small crispy pancake folded over with coconut cream and strands of sweet egg inside |
| *Khâo lãam* | Sticky rice, coconut cream and black |

You can't make a meal out of a Thai **soup**, but it is an essential component in any shared meal, eaten simultaneously with other dishes, not as a starter. Watery and broth-like, soups

are always flavoured with the distinctive tang of lemon grass and kaffir lime leaves, and galangal, and garnished with fresh coriander, and can be extremely hot if the cook adds liberal handfuls of chillies to the pot. Two favourites are *tom kha khai*, a creamy coconut chicken soup; and *tom yam kung*, a prawn soup without coconut milk (the addition of lime juice gives it its distinctive sour flavour).

Another popular part of any proper Thai meal is a spicy, sour **salad** (*yam*), which is often served warm. *Yam* can be made in many permutations – with noodles, meat, seafood, or vegetables for example – but at the heart of every variety is a liberal squirt of fresh lime juice and a fiery sprinkling of chopped chillis, a combination which can take some getting used to. The most prevalent variation on this theme is the national dish of the northeast, *sôm tam*, a spicy green-papaya salad with garlic, raw chillies, green beans, tomatoes, peanuts, and dried shrimps (or fresh crab).

## Sweets

**Sweets** (*khanom*) don't really figure on most restaurant menus, but a few places offer bowls of *luk taan cheum*, a jellied concoction of lotus or palm seeds floating in a syrup scented with jasmine or other aromatic flowers. Coconut milk is a feature of most other desserts, notably delicious coconut ice cream, and a royal Thai cuisine special of coconut custard (*sangkaya*) cooked inside a small pumpkin, whose flesh you can also eat. **Cakes** are sold on the street and tend to be heavy, sticky affairs made from glutinous rice and coconut cream pressed into squares and wrapped in banana leaves.

## Vegetarian food

Although very few Thais are **vegetarian** (*màngsáwirat*), it's rarely impossible to persuade cooks to rustle up a vegetable-only fried rice or noodle dish, though in more out-of-the-way places that's often your only option unless you eat fish – so you'll need to supplement your diet with the nuts, barbecued sweetcorn, fruit and other non-meaty goodies sold by food stalls. In tourist spots, vegetarians can happily splurge on specially concocted Thai and Western veggie dishes, and some restaurants will come up with a completely separate menu if requested. If you're vegan (*jeh*) you'll need to stress when you order that you don't want egg, as eggs get used a lot; cheese and other dairy produce, however, don't feature at all in Thai

cuisine. For an introduction to vegetarianism in Thailand, check out ⓦbangkok.com /healthfood/mangsawirat.shtml.

## Drinks

Thais don't drink water straight from the tap, and nor should you: plastic bottles of drinking **water** (*nam plao*) are sold countrywide, even in the smallest villages, for around B10. Cheap restaurants and hotels generally serve free jugs of boiled water which should be fine to drink, though not as foolproof as the bottles.

Night markets, guest houses and restaurants do a good line in freshly squeezed **fruit juices** such as lemon (*nam manao*) and orange (*nam som*), which often come with salt and sugar already added, particularly upcountry. The same places will usually do **fruit shakes** as well, blending bananas (*nam kluay*), papayas (*nam malakaw*), pineapples (*nam sapparot*) and others with liquid sugar or condensed milk (or yoghurt, to make lassi). Fresh **coconut water** (*nam maprao*) is another great thirst-quencher – you buy the whole fruit dehusked, decapitated and chilled; Thais are also very partial to freshly squeezed **sugar-cane juice** (*nam awy*) which is sickeningly sweet.

Bottled brand-name orange and lemon **soft drinks** are sold all over the place for around B10 (particularly in the ubiquitous 7-11 chain stores). Soft-drink bottles are returnable, so some shops and drink stalls have an amazing system of pouring the contents into a small plastic bag (fastened with an elastic band and with a straw inserted) rather than charging you the extra for taking away the bottle. The larger restaurants keep their soft drinks refrigerated, but smaller cafés and shops add ice (*nam khaeng*) to glasses and bags. Most ice is produced commercially under hygienic conditions, but it might become less pure in transit so be wary – and don't take ice if you have diarrhoea. For those travelling with children, or just partial themselves to **dairy products**, UHT-preserved milk and yoghurt drinks are widely available chilled in shops (especially 7-11 stores), as are a variety of soya drinks.

Weak Chinese **tea** (*nam chaa*) makes a refreshing alternative to water and often gets served in Chinese restaurants and roadside cafés. Posher restaurants keep stronger Chinese and Western teas (*chaa*) and **coffee** (*kaafae*), which is nowadays mostly the ubiquitous instant Nescafé. This is usually the coffee offered to farangs even if freshly ground Thai-grown coffee – notably three kinds of hill-tribe coffee from the mountains of the north – is available. If you would like to try Thai coffee, most commonly found at Chinese-style cafés in the south of the country or at outdoor markets, and prepared through filtering the grounds through a cloth, ask for *kaafae thung* (literally, "bag coffee"), normally served very bitter with sugar as well as sweetened condensed milk alongside a glass of black tea to wash it down with. Fresh Western-style coffee, usually brewed, is mostly limited to farang-orientated places, international-style coffee bars and big hotels, in Bangkok and beach areas. Tea and coffee are normally served black, perhaps with a sachet of coffee whitener on the side.

## Alcoholic drinks

**Beer** (*bia*) is one of the few consumer items in Thailand that's not a bargain due to the heavy taxes levied on the beverage – at B60 for a 330ml bottle it works out roughly the same as what you'd pay in the West (larger, 660ml bottles, when available, are always slightly better value). The most famous beer is the slightly acrid locally brewed Singha, but Kloster, which is also brewed locally and costs about B5–10 more than Singha, is easier on the tongue. Some places also stock a lighter version of Singha called Singha Gold, and another local beer called

Amarit, though it's not widely distributed. Carlsberg and Heineken are now widely found in Thailand, and in the most touristed areas you'll find imported bottles from all over the world. Carlsberg, who part-own a Thai brewery, also produce the ubiquitous Chang (Elephant), usually the cheapest beer available, with a head-banging seven percent alcohol content.

At about B60 for a hip-flask-sized 375ml bottle, the local **whisky** is a lot better value and Thais think nothing of consuming a bottle a night. The most palatable and widely available of these is Mekhong, which is very pleasant once you've stopped expecting it to taste like Scotch; distilled from rice, Mekhong is 35 percent proof, deep gold in colour and tastes slightly sweet. If that's not to your taste, a pricier Thai **rum** is also available, Sang Thip, made from sugar cane, and even stronger than the whisky at forty percent proof. Check the price list carefully when ordering a bottle of Mekhong from a bar in a tourist area, as they often ask up to five times more than you'd pay in a guest house or shop.

You can **buy** beer and whisky in food stores, guest houses and most restaurants at any time of the day; **bars** aren't really an indigenous feature as Thais rarely drink out without eating, but you'll find a fair number of Western-style drinking holes in Bangkok and tourist centres elsewhere in the country, ranging from ultra-hip haunts in the capital to basic, open-to-the-elements **"bar beers"**.

# Telephones, mail and internet access

Thailand boasts a fast and efficient communications network: international mail services are relatively speedy, phoning overseas is possible even from some small islands and internet access is available in every sizeable town and resort.

## Mail

Mail takes around seven days to get between Bangkok and Europe or North America, a little longer from the more isolated areas. Almost all **main post offices** across the country operate a **poste restante** service and will hold letters for two to three months. Mail should be addressed: Name (family name underlined or capitalized), Poste Restante, GPO, Town or City, Thailand. It will be filed by surname, though it's always wise to check under your first initial as well. The smaller post offices pay scant attention to who takes what, but in the busier GPOs you need to show your passport, pay B1 per item received and sign for them. Most GPO poste restantes follow regular post office hours (Mon–Fri 8am–4pm, Sat 8am–noon; some close Mon–Fri noon–1pm and may stay open until 6pm) – exceptions are explained in the guide. **American Express** in Bangkok and Phuket also offer a poste restante facility of up to sixty days to holders of Amex credit cards or traveller's cheques.

Post offices are the best places to buy **stamps**, though hotels and guest houses often sell them too, charging an extra B1 per stamp. An airmail letter of under 10g costs around B17 to send to Europe or Australia and B19 to North America; standard-sized postcards cost B12 (anything smaller or larger costs B15), and aerogrammes B15, regardless of where they're going. All **parcels** must be officially boxed and sealed (for a small fee) at special counters within main post offices or in a private outlet just outside – you can't just turn up with a package and buy stamps for it. The surface rate for a parcel of up to 5kg is B700 to the UK and the US and B540 for Australia, and the package should reach its destination in three months; the airmail parcel service is almost three times as expensive and takes about a week.

## Phones

By and large the Thai phone system works well. Payphones are straightforward enough and generally come in three varieties: red or pale blue for **local calls**, blue or stainless steel for **long-distance calls within Thailand**, and green cardphones for either. Red and pale blue phones take the small one-baht coins and will give you three minutes per B1. Blue and stainless steel ones gobble up B5 coins (inter-provincial rates vary with distance, but on the whole are surprisingly pricey) and are generally unreliable, so you're better off buying a **phonecard**, available in a range of denominations from B25 to B240 from hotels, post offices and a wide variety of shops. In some provincial towns, enterprising mobile-phone owners hang out on the main streets offering cheap long-distance calls.

When **dialling any number in Thailand**, you must always **preface the number with the area code**, even when dialling from the same area. Anything that's prefaced with a ☎01 is a cell phone or satellite phone number (most guest houses on islands like Ko Phi Phi and Ko Chang have satellite phones). Where we've given several line numbers – eg ☎02/431 1802-9 – you can substitute the last digit with any number between 3 and 9. For directory enquiries within Thailand, call ☎1133. One final local idiosyncrasy: Thai phone books list people by their first, not their family names.

An increasing number of tourists are taking their **mobile phones** to Thailand. Visitors

## International dialling codes

If you're dialling from abroad, the international code for Thailand is 66. Calling out of Thailand, dial 001 and then the relevant country code:

Australia 61

Canada 1

Ireland 353

Netherlands 31

New Zealand 64

UK 44

USA 1

Bangkok is seven hours ahead of GMT, twelve hours ahead of Eastern Standard Time and three hours behind Sydney.

For international directory enquiries call ☏100.

from the US need to have a tri-band phone though, and not all foreign networks have links with Thai networks, so check with your phone provider before you travel. Whichever your network, you may well have to ask for the "international bar" to be lifted before you set off. It's also worth checking how much coverage there is for your network within Thailand, and asking in advance for a summary of rates for incoming as well as outgoing calls while you're there; some networks offer flat-rate deals on international usage, which can save you a lot of money.

### International calls

The least costly way of making an international call is to use the **government telephone centre** (open daily, typically 8am–10pm, 24hr in Bangkok), run by the Communications Authority of Thailand, or **CAT**; they're nearly always located within or adjacent to the town's main post office. At government phone centres, you're allotted an individual booth and left to do the dialling.

For international IDD phone calls made on private lines and at government telephone offices, there are three time periods with different **rates**. The most expensive, or **standard**, time to call is from 7am to 9pm (a twenty percent discount applies on Sundays); the **economy** period runs from 9pm to midnight and from 5am to 7am; the **reduced** rate applies between midnight and

5am. The per-minute rate for a call to Europe is around B42 standard, B34 economy, and B30 reduced; for North America and Australia it's B24/20/20. An operator-assisted call always costs slightly more. It's possible to call internationally at government rates on the green public **cardphones**, but for international calls these phones only accept phonecards of B500 and above. (You can use any public long-distance phone to call Laos and Malaysia, and can do so on phonecards of less than B500 if you want.)

If you can't get to one of the official government places, try the slightly more expensive **private international call offices** in tourist areas (such as Bangkok's Thanon Khao San), or the even pricier services offered by the posher hotels. Many guest houses on touristy islands like Ko Samet, Ko Chang and Ko Phi Phi have satellite phones which guests can use to call long distance and overseas.

There's also a private international cardphone system called **Lenso**, which operates in Bangkok and the biggest resorts. The phones are bright orange and have been installed all over the place. To use them, you either need a special Lenso phonecard (available from shops near the phones in B200 and B500 denominations), or you can use a credit card. The main drawback with Lenso phones is that the rates are ten percent higher than government IDD rates.

A BT **chargecard** allows British travellers to charge calls from Thailand to their home phone bill; AT&T, MCI, and other North American long-distance companies enable their customers to make credit-card calls from Thailand (before you leave, call your company's customer service line to find out the toll-free access code in Thailand). Telephone cards such as Australia's Telstra Telecard or Optus Calling Card and New Zealand Telecom's Calling Card can be used to make calls abroad, which are charged back to a domestic account or credit card.

Collect or **reverse-charge calls** can be made free of charge at government phone centres, or from many guest houses and private phone offices, usually for a fee of B100. You can also make Home Country Direct calls from government phone centres, for which you pay a nominal charge to get through to your home country operator, who arranges for you to make a credit-card or reverse-charge call.

## Faxes

Most major post offices offer a domestic and international **fax service** and, as with phone calls, this is where you'll get the cheapest rates – currently around B120 per page to Australia, North America or the UK. Private phone centres will also send faxes for you, as will most guest houses, for which you can expect to pay up to fifty percent more than government rates. Many also offer a "fax restante" service for customers and guests, though as filing systems vary in these places, you might want to check them out before giving fax numbers to your correspondents. Wherever possible, guest house and hotel fax numbers are given in the guide.

## Internet access

Internet access is very widespread and very inexpensive in Thailand. You'll find traveller-oriented **cybercafés** in every touristed town and resort in the country – there are at least twenty in the Banglamphu district of Bangkok, for example – and even islands without land lines, like Ko Samet and Ko Chang, provide (expensive) internet access via satellite phones. In mid-sized towns that don't get much tourist traffic, internet centres are also increasingly popular, making their money from schoolboys who play computer games for hours on end, though travellers are welcome to use these places for emailing as well. Competition keeps prices low: upcountry you could expect to pay as little as B20 per hour, while rates in tourist centres average B1 per minute. Upmarket hotels are the exception, often charging as much as B100 per half-hour or B3–5 per minute. Nearly every mid-sized town in Thailand also offers a public internet service, called **Catnet**, at the government telephone office (usually located inside or adjacent to the main post office).

To use the service, you need to buy a B100 card with a Catnet PIN (available at all phone offices), which gives you three hours of internet time at any of these public terminals.

Before leaving home you should check whether your existing **email account** offers a Web-based service that enables you to pick up your email from any internet terminal in the world. This is becoming increasingly common and is very useful and straightforward, though it can sometimes be a bit slow. If this does not apply to you, it's well worth setting yourself up with a **free email account** for the duration of the trip, either before you leave home or in a cybercafé in Thailand. Several companies offer this free email service, but by far the most popular are those run by Hotmail (Ⓦwww.hotmail.com) and Yahoo (Ⓦwww.yahoo.com). Both Hotmail and Yahoo are completely free to join, and every cybercafé in Thailand will have them bookmarked for speedy access.

If you plan to email from your **laptop** in Thailand, be advised that very few budget guest houses and bungalows have telephone sockets in the room, and that many upmarket hotels charge astronomical rates for international calls. One potentially useful way round the cost issue is to become a temporary subscriber to the **Thai ISP** Loxinfo (Ⓦwww.loxinfo.co.th) who have local dial-up numbers in every province in Thailand. Their Webnet deal is aimed at international businesspeople and tourists and can be bought online; it allows you 25 hours of internet access for B500 or 45 hours for B700. The usual phone plug in Thailand is the American standard RJ11 phone jack. See the Help for World Travellers website (Ⓦwww.kropla.com) for detailed advice on how to set up your modem before you go, and how to hardwire phone plugs where necessary.

# The media

To keep you abreast of world affairs there are several English-language newspapers in Thailand, though a mild form of censorship affects the predominantly state-controlled media, even muting the English-language branches on occasion.

## Newspapers and magazines

Of the hundreds of **Thai-language newspapers and magazines** published every week, the sensationalist tabloid *Thai Rath* attracts the widest readership, the independent *Siam Rath* the most intellectual. Alongside these, two daily **English-language papers** – the *Bangkok Post* and the *Nation* – both adopt a fairly critical attitude to governmental goings-on and cover major domestic and international stories as well as tourist-related issues. Of the two, the *Bangkok Post* tends to focus more on international stories, while the *Nation* has the most in-depth coverage of Thai and Southeast Asian issues. Both detail English-language cinema programmes, TV schedules and expat social events, and are sold at most newsstands in the capital as well as in major provincial towns and tourist resorts; the more isolated places receive their few copies at least one day late. *Bangkok Metro*, the capital's monthly English-language **listings magazine**, is also a good read; as well as reviews and previews of events in the city, it carries lively articles on cultural and contemporary life in Thailand.

You can also pick up **foreign publications** such as *Newsweek*, *Time* and the *International Herald Tribune* in Bangkok, Phuket and Pattaya; expensive hotels sometimes carry air-freighted copies of foreign national newspapers for at least B50 a copy.

## Television

Channel 9 is Thailand's major **TV station**, transmitting news, quiz shows and predominantly imported cartoons and dramas to all parts of the country. Four other networks broadcast to Bangkok – the privately run Channel 3, the military-controlled channels 5 and 7, and the Ministry of Education's Channel 11 – but not all are received in every province. **Cable** networks – available in many mid-range and most upmarket hotel rooms – carry channels from all around the world, including CNN, NBC and MTV from North America, BBC World from the UK, IBC from Australia, the HBO English-language movie channel, and several Star channels from India.

Both the *Bangkok Post* and the *Nation* print the daily TV and cable **schedule**, and they also tell you which English-language programmes are dubbed in Thai. **English soundtracks** for some programmes are transmitted simultaneously on FM radio as follows – Channel 3: 105.5 MHz; Channel 7: 103.5 MHz; Channel 9: 107 MHz; Channel 11: 88 MHz.

## Radio

With a shortwave radio, you can pick up the BBC World Service, Radio Australia, Voice of America and various other international stations on a variety of bands right across the country. Times and wavelengths can change every three months, so get hold of a recent schedule just before you travel. The BBC World Service website (ⓦwww.bbc.co.uk /worldservice) carries current frequency details in a useful format that's designed to be printed out and carried with you. For current listings of all major English-language radio station frequencies while you're in Thailand, consult the *Bangkok Post's* weekly magazine *Real Time*, which comes free with the Friday edition of the paper.

Bangkok is served by a handful of English-language **FM stations**. Radio Thailand broadcasts news, current affairs and sports results in several languages (including English) on 97 MHz from 6am to 11pm. Apart from a few specialist shows, Gold FMX 95.5 pumps out non-stop upbeat chart hits from 5am through to 2am with local and international headlines on the half hour. Proud to dub itself "Bangkok's premier easy-listening station",

Smooth 105 FM rarely veers from the middle of the road; international news breaks in on the hour. Bilingual Soft FM (107FM) follows current and classic music trends, with hourly breaks for CNN news reports. At the opposite end of the taste spectrum, Chulalongkorn University Radio (101.5FM) plays a wide selection of Western jazz every day from 4 to 6.30pm, and classical music from 10.30pm to 1am every night.

# Crime and personal safety

**As long as you keep your wits about you, you shouldn't encounter much trouble in Thailand. Theft and pickpocketing are two of the main problems, but by far the most common cause for concern are the burgeoning number of opportunistic con-artists who manage to dupe ill-informed or over-trusting tourists into unwisely parting with their cash.**

To **prevent theft**, most travellers prefer to carry their valuables with them at all times, either in a money belt, neck pouch or inside pocket, but it's sometimes possible to leave your valuables in a hotel or guest-house locker – the safest lockers are those which require your own padlock, as there are occasional reports of valuables being stolen by hotel staff. Padlock your luggage when leaving it in hotel or guest-house rooms, as well as when consigning it to storage or taking it on public transport. Padlocks also come in handy as extra security on your room, particularly on the doors of beachfront bamboo huts.

Avoiding **scams** means that you must be on your guard against anyone who makes an unnatural effort to befriend you – which, as everywhere else in the world, means treading a fine line between paranoia and healthy suspicion. In one of the more well-known scams in Bangkok, pseudo tourist officials hang around the main train station and take unsuspecting travellers to a disreputable private tour company – falling victim

to this kind of con is rarely dangerous but always frustrating, so it's worth heeding the specific warnings that you'll find throughout the guide. It's also become increasingly common for Bangkok tuk-tuk drivers to pretend that the Grand Palace or other major sight is closed for the day, so that they get to take you on a round-city tour instead; the easiest way to avoid these rip-offs is to take a metered taxi, but for more advice see p.95. Never buy anything from **touts**: gemstone con men prey on greedy and gullible tourists, mostly in Bangkok – for information about buying stones and avoiding stings, see p.160.

On a more dangerous note, beware of **drug** scams: either being shopped by a dealer (there are set-ups at the Ko Pha Ngan full-moon parties) or having substances slipped into your luggage – simple enough to perpetrate unless all fastenings are secured with padlocks. **Drug smuggling** carries a maximum penalty of death and will almost certainly get you five to twenty years in a Thai prison. Despite occasional royal pardons, don't expect special treatment as a farang: because of its reputation as a major source of drugs, Thailand works hard to keep on the right side of the US and in most cases makes a big show of dishing out heavy sentences. Even more alarming, drug enforcement squads are said to receive 25 percent of the market value of seized drugs, so are liable to exaggerate the amounts involved.

**Violent crime** against tourists is not common, but it does occur. There have been several serious attacks on women travellers in the last few years, which are good enough reason to be extra-vigilant wherever you are in Thailand, at whatever time of day. However, bearing in mind that over five million foreign tourists visit Thailand every year, the statistical likelihood of becoming a victim is extremely small. Obvious precautions for travellers of either sex include locking accessible windows and doors at night – preferably with your own padlock (doors in many of the simpler guest houses and beach bungalows are designed for this) – and not travelling alone at night in a taxi or tuk-tuk. Nor should you risk jumping into an unlicensed taxi at Don Muang airport at any time of day: there have been some very violent robberies in these, so take the well-marked authorized vehicles instead or, better still, the airport bus. If you're going hiking on your own for a day, it's a good idea to inform guest-house or hotel staff of where you're planning to go, so they have some idea of where to look for you if necessary.

Be wary of accepting food and drink from strangers, especially on long overnight bus or train journeys, as it may be drugged so as to knock you out while your bags are stolen. This might sound paranoid, but there have been enough drug-muggings for TAT to publish a specific warning about the problem. Unfortunately, it is also necessary for female tourists to think twice about spending time alone with a **monk**, as not all men of the cloth uphold the Buddhist precepts and there have been rapes and murders committed by men wearing the saffron robes of the monkhood (see p.444 for more about the changing Thai attitudes towards the monk-hood).

Among hazards to watch out for in the natural world, **riptides** have claimed too many tourist lives to ignore, particularly off Phuket and Ko Samui during stormy periods of the monsoon season, so always pay attention to warning signs and red flags, and always ask locally if unsure. Crazed **elephants** have gored and occasionally killed tourists at elephant shows and theme parks, usually when baited or scared, for example by a flashgun held too close.

## Reporting a crime or emergency

TAT has a special department for tourist-related crimes and complaints called the Tourist Assistance Center (**TAC**). Set up specifically to mediate between tourists, police and accused persons (particularly shopkeepers and tour agents), TAC has an office in the TAT headquarters on Thanon Rajdamnoen Nok, Bangkok (daily 8.30am–4.30pm; ☎02/281 5051). In **emergencies**, always contact the English-speaking **tourist police** who maintain a toll-free nationwide line (☎1699) and have offices within or adjacent to many regional TAT offices – getting in touch with the tourist police first is invariably more efficient than directly contacting the local police, ambulance or fire service.

## Sexual harassment

Though unpalatable and distressing, Thailand's high-profile sex industry is relatively unthreatening for Western women, with its energy focused exclusively on farang men; it's also quite easily avoided, being contained within certain pockets of the capital and a couple of beach resorts. As for **harassment** from men, it's hard to generalize, but most Western tourists find it less of a problem in Thailand than they do back home. Apart from the main tourist spots, you're more likely to be of interest as a foreigner rather than a woman and, if travelling alone, as an object of concern rather than of sexual aggression.

# Opening hours and holidays

**Most shops open at least Monday to Saturday from about 8am to 8pm, while department stores operate daily from around 10am to 9pm. Private office hours are generally Monday to Friday 8am–5pm and Saturday 8am–noon, though in tourist areas these hours are longer, with weekends worked like any other day. Government offices work Monday to Friday 8.30am–noon and 1–4.30pm, and national museums tend to stick to these hours too, but some close on Mondays and Tuesdays rather than at weekends.**

Most tourists only notice **national holidays** because trains and buses suddenly get extraordinarily crowded: although banks and government offices shut down on these days, most shops and tourist-oriented businesses carry on regardless, and TAT branches continue to dispense information. The only time an inconvenient number of shops, restaurants and hotels do close is during Chinese New Year, which, though not marked as an official national holiday, brings many businesses to a standstill for several days in late January or February. You'll notice it particularly in the south, where most service industries are Chinese-managed.

A brief note on **dates**: Thais use both the Western Gregorian calendar and a Buddhist calendar – the Buddha is said to have died (or entered Nirvana) in the year 543 BC, so Thai dates start from that point: thus 2002 AD becomes 2545 BE (Buddhist Era).

## National holidays

**January 1** Western New Year's Day

**February** (day of full moon) Maha Puja
Commemorates the Buddha preaching to a spontaneously assembled crowd of 1250.

**April 6** Chakri Day
The founding of the Chakri dynasty.

**April** (usually 13–15) Songkhran
Thai New Year

**May 5** Coronation Day

**May** (early in the month) Royal Ploughing Ceremony
Marks start of rice-planting season.

**May** (day of full moon) Visakha Puja
The holiest of all Buddhist holidays, which celebrates the birth, enlightenment and death of the Buddha.

**July** (day of full moon) Asanha Puja
Commemorates the Buddha's first sermon.

**July** (the day after Asanha Puja) Khao Pansa
The start of the annual three-month Buddhist rains retreat, when new monks are ordained.

**August 12** Queen's birthday

**October 23** Chulalongkorn Day
The anniversary of Rama V's death.

**December 5** King's birthday

**December 10** Constitution Day

**December 31** Western New Year's Eve

# Festivals

Hardly a week goes by without some kind of local or national festival being celebrated somewhere in Thailand, and most make great entertainment for participants and spectators alike. All the festivals listed below are spectacular or engaging enough to be worth altering your itinerary for, but bear in mind that for some of the more publicized celebrations you'll need to book transport and accommodation a week or more in advance.

Nearly all Thai festivals have some kind of religious aspect. The most theatrical are generally **Brahmanic** (Hindu) in origin, honouring elemental spirits with ancient rites and ceremonial costumed parades. **Buddhist** celebrations usually revolve round the local temple, and while merit-making is a significant feature, a light-hearted atmosphere prevails, as the wat grounds are swamped with food-

and trinket-vendors and makeshift stages are set up to show *likay* folk theatre, singing competitions and beauty contests.

Few of the **dates** for religious festivals are fixed, so check with TAT for specifics. The names of the most touristy celebrations are given here in English; the more low-key festivals are more usually known by their Thai name (*ngan* means "festival").

## A festival calendar

**Nationwide** (particularly Wat Benjamabophit in Bangkok) Maha Puja: A day of merit-making marks the occasion when 1250 disciples gathered spontaneously to hear the Buddha preach, and culminates with a candlelit procession round the local temple's bot (Feb full-moon day).

**Phetchaburi** Phra Nakhon Khiri fair: A week of *son et lumière* shows at Khao Wang palace (early–mid-Feb).

**Pattani** Ngan Lim Ko Niaw: Local goddess inspires devotees to walk through fire and perform other endurance tests in public (middle of third lunar month – Feb or March).

**Nationwide** (particularly Sanam Luang, Bangkok) Kite fights and flying contests (late Feb to mid-April).

**Nakhon Si Thammarat** Hae Pha Khun That: Southerners gather to pay homage to the Buddha relics at Wat Mahathat, including a procession of long saffron cloth around the chedi (twice a year, coinciding with Maha Puja in Feb and Visakha Puja in May).

**Yala** ASEAN Barred Ground Dove festival: International dove-cooing contests (first weekend of March).

**Nationwide** Songkhran: The most exuberant of the national festivals welcomes the Thai New Year with massive waterfights, sandcastle building in temple compounds and the inevitable parades and "Miss Songkhran" beauty contests (usually April 13–15).

**Pattaya** Pattaya Festival: A week of festivities, including parades, beauty pageants, and fireworks (mid-April).

**Nationwide** (particularly Bangkok's Wat Benjamabophit) Visakha Puja: The holiest day of the Buddhist year, commemorating the birth, enlightenment and death of the Buddha all in one go; the most public and photogenic part is the candlelit evening procession around the wat (May full-moon day).

*continued overleaf*

B

**Sanam Luang, Bangkok** Raek Na: The royal ploughing ceremony to mark the beginning of the rice-planting season; ceremonially clad Brahmin leaders parade sacred oxen and the royal plough, and interpret omens to forecast the year's rice yield (early May).

**Nakhon Si Thammarat** Tamboon Deuan Sip: Merit-making ceremonies to honour dead relatives accompanied by a ten-day fair on the town field (Sept or Oct).

**Phuket and Trang** Vegetarian Festival (Ngan Kin Jeh): Chinese devotees become vegetarian for a nine-day period and then parade through town performing acts of self-mortification such as pushing skewers through their cheeks. Celebrated in Bangkok's Chinatown with most food vendors and restaurants turning vegetarian for about a fortnight (Oct/Nov).

**Nationwide** Tak Bat Devo and Awk Pansa: Offerings to monks and general merrymaking to celebrate the Buddha's descent to earth from Tavatimsa heaven and the end of the Khao Pansa retreat (Oct full-moon day).

**Surat Thani** Chak Phra: The town's chief Buddha images are paraded on floats down the streets and on barges along the river (mid-Oct).

**Nationwide** Thawt Kathin: The annual ceremonial giving of new robes by the laity to the monkhood at the end of the rains retreat (mid-Oct to mid-Nov).

**Nationwide** (especially Krabi) Loy Krathong: Baskets (*krathong*) of flowers and lighted candles are floated on any available body of water (such as ponds, rivers, lakes, canals and seashores) to honour water spirits and celebrate the end of the rainy season. Nearly every town puts on a big show, with bazaars, public entertainments, and fireworks (late Oct or early Nov).

**Krabi** Andaman Festival: To mark the official start of the tourist season, the week leading up to Loy Krathong (see above) sees costumed parades through the town, fishing contests, open-air concerts and nightly bazaars and funfairs (late Oct or early Nov).

**Wat Saket, Bangkok** Ngan Wat Saket: Probably Thailand's biggest temple fair, held around the Golden Mount, with all the usual festival trappings (first week of Nov).

**Hat Nai Harn, Phuket** Phuket King's Cup Regatta: A week of sailing races attracting international competitors (early Dec).

# Entertainment and sport

Most travellers confine their experience of Thai traditional culture to a one-off attendance at a big Bangkok tourist show, but these extravaganzas are far less rewarding than authentic folk theatre, music and sports performances. Traditional sport fits neatly into the same category as the more usual theatrical classifications, not only because it can be graceful, even dance-like, to watch, but because, in the case of Thai boxing, Thai classical music plays an important role in the proceedings. Bangkok has one authentic fixed venue for dance and a couple for Thai boxing; otherwise it's a question of keeping your eyes open in upcountry areas for signs that a travelling troupe may soon turn up.

## Drama and dance

**Drama** pretty much equals **dance** in Thai theatre, and many of the traditional dance-dramas are based on the Hindu epic the *Ramayana* (in Thai, *Ramakien*), a classic adventure tale of good versus evil which is taught in all the schools. Not understanding the plots can be a major disadvantage, so try reading an abridged version beforehand (see "Books", p.452) and check out the wonderfully imaginative murals at Wat Phra Kaeo in Bangkok, after which you'll certainly be able to sort the goodies from the baddies, if little else. There are three broad categories of traditional Thai dance-drama – *khon*, *lakhon* and *likay* – described below in descending order of refinement.

### Khon

The most spectacular form of traditional Thai theatre is **khon**, a stylized drama performed in masks and elaborate costumes by a troupe of highly trained classical dancers. There's little room for individual interpretation in these dances, as all the movements follow a strict choreography that's been passed down through generations: each graceful, angular gesture depicts a precise event, action or emotion which will be familiar to educated *khon* audiences. The dancers don't speak, and the story is chanted and sung by a chorus who stand at the side of the stage, accompanied by a classical *phipat* orchestra.

A typical *khon* performance features several of the best-known **Ramayana** episodes, in which the main characters are recognized by their masks, headdresses and heavily brocaded costumes. Gods and humans don't wear masks, but it's generally easy enough to distinguish the hero Rama and heroine Sita from the action; they always wear tall, gilded headdresses and often appear in a threesome with Rama's brother Lakshaman. Monkey masks are always open-mouthed, almost laughing, and come in several colours: monkey army chief Hanuman always wears white, and his two right-hand men – Nilanol, the god of fire and Nilapat, the god of death – wear red and black respectively. In contrast, the demons have grim mouths, clamped shut or snarling out of usually green faces; Totsagan, king of the demons, wears a green face in battle and a gold one during peace, but always sports a two-tier headdress carved with two rows of faces.

*Khon* is performed regularly at Bangkok's National Theatre and nightly at various cultural shows staged by tourist restaurants in Bangkok, Phuket and Pattaya. Even if you don't see a show you're bound to come across copies of the masks worn by the main *khon* characters, which are sold as souvenirs all over the country and constitute an art form in their own right.

### Lakhon

Serious and refined, **lakhon** is derived from *khon* but is used to dramatize a greater range of stories, including Buddhist *Jataka* tales, local folk dramas and of course the *Ramayana*. The form you're most likely to come across is *lakhon chatri*, which is performed at shrines like Bangkok's Erawan and *lak muang* as entertainment for the spirits and a token of gratitude from worshippers. Usually female, the *lakhon chatri* dancers perform as a group rather than as individual characters, executing sequences which, like *khon* movements, all have minute and particular symbolism. They wear similarly decorative costumes but no masks, and dance to the music of a *phipat* orchestra.

### Likay

**Likay** is a much more popular derivative of *khon* – more light-hearted with lots of comic interludes, bawdy jokes and over-the-top acting and singing. Some *likay* troupes perform *Ramayana* excerpts, but a lot of them adapt pot-boiler romances or write their own. Depending on the show, costumes are either traditional as in *khon* and *lakhon*, modern and Western as in films, or a mixture of both. *Likay* troupes travel around the country doing shows on makeshift outdoor stages wherever they think they'll get an audience; temples sometimes hire them out for fairs and there's usually a *likay* stage of some kind at a festival – if you happen to be in Thailand on the King's Birthday (December 5th), for example, you'll definitely catch a likay show somewhere in town. Performances are often free and generally last for about five hours, with the audience strolling in and out of the show, cheering and joking with the cast throughout. Televised *likay* dramas get huge audiences and always follow romantic plot lines.

### Nang

**Nang** or shadow plays are said to have been the earliest dramas performed in Thailand, but now are rarely seen except in the far south, where the Malaysian influence ensures an appreciative audience for *nang thalung*. Crafted from buffalo hide, the two-dimensional *nang thalung* puppets play out scenes from popular dramas against a backlit screen, while the storyline is told through songs, chants and musical interludes. An even rarer *nang* form is the *nang yai*, which uses enormous cut-outs of whole scenes

rather than just individual characters, so the play becomes something like an animated film. For more on shadow puppets and puppetry, see p.289.

## Film and video

Fast-paced Chinese blockbusters have long dominated the Thai **movie** scene, serving up a low-grade cocktail of sex, spooks, violence and comedy. Not understanding the dialogue is rarely a drawback, as the story lines tend to be simple and the visuals more entertaining than the words. In the cities, Western films are also pretty big, and new releases often get subtitled rather than dubbed. All sizeable towns have a **cinema** or two and tickets generally start at around B50. The king's anthem is always played before every screening, during which the audience is expected to stand up.

Western **videos** come free with your evening meal in beachfront restaurants all over Thailand and dissuade many a traveller from venturing anywhere else of an evening. Even if you steer clear of them, you'll get back-to-back Chinese movies on long-distance air-conditioned buses and in some trains too.

## Thai boxing

**Thai boxing** (*muay Thai*) enjoys a following similar to football or baseball in the West: every province has a stadium and whenever the sport is shown on TV you can be sure that large noisy crowds will gather round the sets in streetside restaurants and noodle shops. The best place to see Thai boxing is at one of Bangkok's two stadiums, which between them hold bouts every night of the week and on some afternoons as well (see p.156).

There's a strong spiritual and **ritualistic** dimension to *muay Thai*, adding grace to an otherwise brutal sport. Each boxer enters the ring to the wailing music of a three-piece *phipat* orchestra, often flamboyantly attired in a lurid silk robe over the statutory red or blue boxer shorts. The fighter then bows, first in the direction of his birthplace and then to the north, south, east and west, honouring both his teachers and the spirit of the ring. Next he performs a slow dance, claiming the audience's attention and demonstrating his prowess as a performer.

Any part of the body except the head may be used as an **offensive weapon** in *muay Thai*, and all parts except the groin are fair targets. Kicks to the head are the blows which cause most knockouts. As the action hots up, so the orchestra speeds up its tempo and the betting in the audience becomes more frenetic. It can be a gruesome business, but it was far bloodier before modern boxing gloves were made compulsory in the 1930s – combatants used to wrap their fists with hemp impregnated with a face-lacerating dosage of ground glass.

For further **information** about Thai boxing, visit ◉www.tat.or.th/do/learn.htm, or contact the Muay Thai Institute at 336/932 Prachathipat, Thanyaburi, Pathum Thani, Bangkok 12130 (☏02/992 0096, 🖷992 0095), which runs forty-hour **training courses** for foreigners at US$160. You can also do one-off training sessions at a gym in central Bangkok, see p.156 for details.

## Takraw

You're very unlikely to stumble unexpectedly on an outdoor bout of *muay Thai*, but you're sure to come across some form of **takraw** game at some point, whether in a public park, a wat compound or just in a backstreet alley. Played with a very light rattan ball (or one made of plastic to look like rattan), the basic aim of the game is to keep the ball off the ground. To do this you can use any part of your body except your hands, so a well-played *takraw* game looks extremely balletic, with players leaping and arching to get a good strike.

There are at least five versions of competitive *takraw*, based on the same principles. The one featured in the Southeast Asian Games and most frequently in school tournaments is played over a volleyball net and involves two teams of three; the other most popular competitive version has a team ranged round a basketball net trying to score as many goals as possible within a limited time period before the next team replaces them and tries to outscore them. Other takraw games introduce more complex rules (like kicking the ball backwards with your heels through a ring made with your arms behind your back) and many assign points according to the skill displayed by individual players rather than per goal or dropped ball. Outside of school playing fields, proper *takraw* tournaments are rare, though they do sometimes feature as entertainment at Buddhist funerals.

# Meditation centres and retreats

Of the hundreds of meditation temples in Thailand, a few cater specifically for foreigners by holding meditation sessions and retreats in English. The meditation taught is mostly vipassana or "insight", which emphasizes the minute observation of internal physical sensation, and novices and practised meditators alike are welcome. To join a one-off class in Bangkok, call to check times and then just turn up; for overnight and longer visits to wats in more remote areas, you usually have to contact the monastery in advance, either directly or through the WFB (see p.64).

Longer retreats are for the serious-minded only. All the temples listed on p.64 welcome both male and female English-speakers, but strict segregation of the sexes is enforced and many places observe a vow of silence. An average day at any one of these monasteries starts with a wake-up call at 4am and includes several hours of group meditation and chanting, as well as time put aside for chores and for personal reflection. However long their stay, all visitors are expected to keep the eight Buddhist precepts, the most restrictive of these being the abstention from food after midday and from alcohol, tobacco, drugs and sex at all times. Most wats ask for a minimal daily donation (around B120) to cover accommodation and food costs. For more information and access details for particular temples, see the relevant sections in the guide.

## Meditation centres and retreat temples

**House of Dhamma Insight Meditation Centre**, 26/9 Soi Chumphon, Soi Lardprao 15, Bangkok ☏02/511 0439, ☎ 512 6083, ✉selena@bkk.loxinfo.co.th. Vipassana meditation classes in English on the second, third and fourth Sunday of the month (2–5pm) – with weekday classes planned in the future – and weekend and week-long retreats organized. Buddhist library and courses in *reiki* and other subjects available.

**Thailand Vipassana Centre** ⊛www.dhamma.org. Dhamma Kamala, 200 Thanon Yoopasuk,

Prachinburi. Frequent ten-day residential courses in a Burmese Vipassana tradition. Foreign students must pre-register by email with Pornphen Leenutaphong on ✉pornphen@bkk.a-net.net.th.

**Wat Khao Tham**, Ban Tai, Ko Pha Ngan, Surat Thani 84280 ⊛ www.watkowtahm.org. Frequent ten-day retreats (Vipassana meditation) led by farang teachers.

**Wat Mahathat**, Thanon Maharat, Ratanakosin, Bangkok. Situated in Section Five of the wat is its International Buddhist Meditation Centre where Vipassana meditation practice is available in English (daily 7–10am, 1–4pm & 6–9pm; ☏02/222 6011 or 01/694 1527 for further information). Participants are welcome to stay in the simple surroundings of the meditation building itself (donation requested) or at a quiet house nearby (B200 per day).

**Wat Suan Mokkh**, Chaiya, Surat Thani ⊛www.suanmokkh.org. Popular Anapanasati (mindfulness with breathing) meditation course held on first ten days of every month.

**World Fellowship of Buddhists (WFB)**, Benjasiri Park, 616 Soi 24, Thanon Sukhumvit, Bangkok ☏02/661 1284, ☎661 0555, ⊛www.wfb-hq.org. The main information centre for advice on English-speaking retreats in Thailand. Holds meditation sessions in English on the first Sunday of every month.

# Cultural hints

Tourist literature has so successfully marketed Thailand as the "Land of Smiles" that a lot of farangs arrive in the country expecting to be forgiven any outrageous behaviour. This is just not the case: there are some things so universally sacred in Thailand that even a hint of disrespect will cause deep offence. TAT publishes a special leaflet on the subject, entitled *Dos and Don'ts in Thailand*, which is also reproduced on their website at ⊛www.tat.or.th – be sure to read it before you travel.

## The monarchy

The worst thing you can possibly do is to bad-mouth the **royal family**. The monarchy might be a constitutional one, but almost

every household displays a picture of King Bhumibol and Queen Sirikit in a prominent position, and respectful crowds mass whenever either of them makes a public appearance. When addressing or speaking about royalty, Thais use a special language full of deference, called *rajasap* (literally "royal language").

Aside from keeping any anti-monarchy sentiments to yourself, you should be prepared to stand when the **King's anthem** is played at the beginning of every cinema programme, and to stop in your tracks if the town you're in plays the **national anthem** over its public address system – many small towns do this twice a day at 8am and again at 6pm, as do some train stations. A less obvious point: as the king's head features on all Thai currency, you should never step on a coin or banknote, which is tantamount to kicking the king in the face.

## Religion

Almost equally insensitive would be to disregard certain religious precepts. Buddhism plays an essential part in the lives of most Thais, and Buddhist monuments should be treated accordingly – which basically means wearing long trousers or knee-length skirts, covering your arms, and removing your shoes whenever you visit one.

All **Buddha images** are sacred, however small, however tacky, however ruined, and should never be used as a backdrop for a portrait photo, clambered over, placed in a position of inferiority, or treated in any manner that could be construed as disrespectful. In an attempt to prevent foreigners from committing any kind of transgression the government requires a special licence for all Buddha statues exported from the country.

**Monks** come only just beneath the monarchy in the social hierarchy, and they too are addressed and discussed in a special language. If there's a monk around, he'll always get a seat on the bus, usually right at the back. Theoretically, monks are forbidden to have any close contact with women, which means, as a female, you mustn't sit or stand next to a monk, or even brush against his robes; if it's essential to pass him something, put the object down so that he can then pick it up – never hand it over directly. Nuns, however, get treated like ordinary women rather than like monks.

## The body

The Western liberalism embraced by the Thai sex industry is very unrepresentative of the majority Thai attitude to the body. **Clothing** – or the lack of it – is what bothers Thais most about tourist behaviour. As mentioned above, you need to dress modestly when entering temples, but the same also applies to other important buildings and all public places. Stuffy and sweaty as it sounds, you should keep shorts and vests for the real tourist resorts, and be especially diligent about covering up and, for women, wearing bras in rural areas. Baring your flesh on beaches is very much a Western practice: when Thais go swimming they often do so fully clothed, and they find topless and nude bathing extremely unpalatable. It's not illegal, but it won't win you many friends.

According to ancient Hindu belief the head is the most sacred part of the **body** and the feet are the most unclean. This belief, imported into Thailand, means that it's very rude to touch another person's head or to point your feet either at a human being or at a sacred image – when sitting on a temple floor, for example, you should tuck your legs beneath you rather than stretch them out towards the Buddha. These hierarchies also forbid people from wearing shoes (which are even more unclean than feet) inside temples and most private homes, and – by extension – Thais take offence when they see someone sitting on the "head", or prow, of a boat. On a more practical note, the **left hand** is used for washing after defecating, so Thais never use it to put food in their mouth, pass things or shake hands – as a farang though, you'll be assumed to have different customs, so left-handers shouldn't worry unduly.

## Social conventions

In fact, Thais very rarely shake hands anyway, using the **wai** to greet and say goodbye and to acknowledge respect, gratitude or apology. A prayer-like gesture made with raised hands, the *wai* changes according to the relative status of the two people involved: Thais can instantaneously assess which *wai* to use when, but as a farang your safest bet is to go for the "stranger's" *wai*, which requires that your hands be raised close to your chest and your fingertips placed just below your chin. If someone makes a *wai* at you, you should definitely *wai* back, but it's generally wise not to initiate.

Public displays of **physical affection** in Thailand are much more acceptable between friends of the same sex than between lovers, whether hetero- or homosexual. Holding hands and hugging is as common among male friends as with females, so if you're given fairly intimate caresses by a Thai acquaintance of the same sex, don't assume you're being propositioned.

Finally, there are three specifically Thai **concepts** you're bound to come across, which may help you comprehend a sometimes *laissez-faire* attitude to delayed buses and other inconveniences. The first, **jai yen**, translates literally as "cool heart" and is something everyone tries to maintain – most Thais hate raised voices, visible irritation and confrontations of any kind. Related to this is the oft-quoted response to a difficulty, **mai pen rai** – "never mind", "no problem" or "it can't be helped" – the verbal equivalent of an open-handed shoulder shrug which has its basis in the Buddhist notion of karma (see "Religion", p.442). And then there's **sanuk**, the wide-reaching philosophy of "fun", which, crass as it sounds, Thais do their best to inject into any situation, even work. Hence the crowds of inebriated Thais who congregate at waterfalls and other beauty spots on public holidays, and the national waterfight which takes place every April on streets right across Thailand.

## Thai names

Although all Thais have a first **name** and a family name, everyone is addressed by their first name – even when meeting strangers – prefixed by the title "Khun" (Mr/Ms); no one is ever addressed as Khun Surname, and even the phone book lists people by their given name. In Thailand you will often be addressed in an Anglicized version of this convention, as Mr Paul or Miss Lucy for example. Bear in mind though, that when a man is introduced to you as Khun Pirom, his wife will definitely not be Khun Pirom as well,

as that would be like calling them Mr and Mrs Paul (or whatever).

Many Thai **first names** come from ancient Sanskrit and have an auspicious meaning; for example, Boon means good deeds, Porn means blessings, Siri means glory and Thawee means to increase. However, Thais of all ages are commonly known by the **nickname** given them soon after birth rather than by their official first name. This tradition arises out of a deep-rooted superstition that once a child has been officially named the spirits will begin to take an unhealthy interest in them, so a nickname is used instead to confuse the spirits. Common nicknames – which often bear no resemblance to the adult's personality or physique – include Yai (Big), Oun (Fat) and Muu (Pig); Lek or Noi (Little), Nok (Bird), Noo (Mouse) and Kung (Shrimp); Neung (Number One/Eldest), Sawng (Number Two), Saam (Number Three); and English nicknames like Apple and Joy.

**Family names** were only introduced in 1913 (by Rama VI, who invented many of the aristocracy's surnames himself), and are used only in very formal situations, always in conjunction with the first name. It's quite usual for good friends never to know each others' surname. Ethnic Thais generally have short surnames like Somboon or Srisai, while the long, convoluted family names – such as Sonthanasumpun – usually indicate Chinese origin, not because they are phonetically Chinese but because many Chinese immigrants have chosen to adopt new Thai surnames and Thai law states that every newly created surname must be unique. Thus anyone who wants to change their surname must submit a shortlist of five unique Thai names – each to a maximum length of ten Thai characters – to be checked against a database of existing names. As more and more names are taken, Chinese family names get increasingly unwieldy, and more easily distinguishable from the pithy old Thai names.

# Outdoor activities

The vast majority of beach itineraries include a stint snorkelling or diving, and the big resorts of Pattaya, Phuket and Ko Samui also offer dozens of other water sports. There is also a developing interest in more unusual outdoor activities, such as rock climbing and kayaking. Golf has also taken off in Thailand, and there are now dozens of courses across the country, the best of them concentrated near the resort towns of Hua Hin (see p.239) and Pattaya (see p.185). Details of water sports at the major resorts are given in the sections on those towns.

## Snorkelling and diving

Thailand has exceptionally rich **marine fauna**, and conditions for coral growth are ideal, with an average sea temperature of about 28°C and very clear waters, so **snorkelling** and **diving** are extremely rewarding. Each coast has at least one resort with a number of equipment-rental shops, diving schools and agencies which organize diving and snorkelling trips to outlying islands, usually at very reasonable prices in worldwide terms. You can dive all year round, too, as the coasts are subject to different monsoon seasons: the diving seasons are from November to April along the Andaman coast, from January to October on the Gulf coast, and all year round on the east coast.

Whether you're snorkelling or diving you should be aware of your effect on the fragile reef structures. Try to minimize your impact by not touching the reefs or asking your boatman to anchor in the middle of one, and don't buy coral souvenirs, as tourist demand only encourages local entrepreneurs to dynamite reefs.

As far as **snorkelling equipment** goes, the most important thing is that you buy or rent a mask that fits. To check the fit, hold the mask against your face, then breathe in and remove your hands – if it falls off, it'll leak water. If you're buying equipment, you should be able to kit yourself out with a mask, snorkel and fins for about B1000; an increasing number of dive centres around the country now sell snorkelling gear as well as dive accessories. Few places rent fins, but a mask and snorkel set usually costs about B50 a day to rent, and if you're going on a snorkelling day-trip they are often included in the price. When renting equipment you'll nearly always be required to pay a deposit of around B200.

### Diving

All diving centres run programmes of one-day **dive trips**, wreck dives and night dives for B1000–1800 plus equipment, and many of the Andaman Coast dive centres (Khao Lak, Phuket, Ko Phi Phi, Ao Nang) also do two- to seven-day liveaboards to the exceptional

## Outdoors Thailand online

**Action Asia** ⊛ www.actionasia.com. Digital lifestyle magazine which carries inspirational features on adventure sports in Thailand and the rest of Southeast Asia.

**Asian Diver** ⊛ www.asian-diver.com. Online version of the divers' magazine, with good coverage of Thailand's diving sites, including recommendations, first-hand dive stories and travellers' reports.

**Dive Thailand Network** ⊛ www.divethailand.net/ontheweb.html. Excellent site with divers' reef reports, masses of links to commercial Thai dive centres, and a bulletin board. Especially good on Andaman Coast diving.

## Thailand's best dives

### The East Coast
Pattaya                              see p.183

### The Andaman Coast
Ao Nang                              see p.365
Burma Banks                          see p.323
Hin Muang and Hin Daeng              see p.323
Ko Lanta                             see p.382
Ko Phi Phi                           see p.372
Ko Racha                             see p.323
Ko Similan                           see p.317
Ko Surin                             see p.307
Laem Phra Nang (Railay)              see p.363
Phuket                               see p.322

### The Gulf Coast
Ko Pha Ngan                          see p.270
Ko Samui                             see p.253
Ko Tao                               see p.282

### The Deep South
Ko Losin                             see p.428
Ko Phetra                            see p.414
Ko Tarutao                           see p.411

reefs off the remote Similan and Surin islands (from around B9000) and even further afield to the impressive Burma Banks. Renting a full set of diving **gear**, including wet suit, from a dive centre costs B600–1000 per day; most dive centres also rent underwater cameras for B1000–1500 per day.

Phuket, Khao Lak, Ao Nang, Ko Phi Phi, Ko Lanta, Ko Tao and Pattaya are the best places to **learn**, and dive centres at all these places offer a range of **courses** from beginner to advanced level, with equipment rental usually included in the cost; Phuket dive centres offer the most competitively priced courses. The most popular courses are the one-day **introductory** or resort dive (a pep talk and escorted shallow dive), which costs anything from B1500 for a very local dive to B4500 for an all-inclusive day-trip to the fabulous Similan Islands; and the four-day **open-water course** which entitles you to dive without an instructor (B7000–12,000 including at least one dive a day). **Insurance** should be included in the price of courses and introductory dives; for qualified divers, it's available from most reputable diving operators in Thailand for around B60 a day, or B250 a month.

Before you sign up for a diving course or expedition, check that the **diving centre** has proof of membership of either **PADI** (Professional Association of Diving Instructors; ⓦ www.padi.com) or **NAUI** (National Association of Underwater Instructors; ⓦ www.naui.org) and ask other people who've done the course or expedition how they rate it. Both PADI and NAUI post up-to-date lists of their affiliated dive centres in Thailand on their websites. In the guide, we've highlighted those dive centres that are accredited PADI **five-star centres**, which are considered by PADI to offer a very high standard of instruction and equipment, but you should always check with other divers first if possible, no matter how many stars your chosen dive centre has garnered.

Most novice and experienced divers prefer to travel to the dive site in a decent-sized **boat** equipped with a radio and emergency medical equipment rather than in a longtail. If this concerns you, be sure to ask the dive company about their boat before you sign up – any company with a good boat will have photos of it to impress potential customers – though you'll find firms that use longtails will probably charge less.

There are currently three **recompression chambers** in Thailand, one in Sattahip on the east coast near Pattaya (see p.184), one on Ko Samui (see p.253), and the other on Ao Patong in Phuket (see p.322). It's a good idea to check whether your dive centre is a member of one of these outfits, as recompression services are extremely expensive for anyone who's not.

## National parks

Over the last forty years almost one hundred areas across Thailand have been singled out for conservation as **national parks**, with the dual aim of protecting the country's natural resources and creating educational and recreational facilities for the public; these parks generally make the best places to observe wildlife. Bird-watchers consider the coastal flats at **Khao Sam Roi Yot National Park** and **Thale Noi Waterbird Park** primary observation spots. Many of southern Thailand's protected reserves are marine parks, incorporating anything from a single beach, such as the turtle-egg-laying grounds on Phuket (see p.330), to an entire archipelago, such as Ko Similan (p.317).

All the national parks are administered by the Royal Forestry Department on Thanon

Phaholyothin, Chatuchak District, Bangkok 10900 (📞02/561 4292–3, 📠579 7099), about forty minutes' bus ride north of Democracy Monument. To book national park bungalows in advance (advisable for weekends and public holidays) you need to pay up front; see "Accommodation" on p.42 for details.

For all their environmental benefits, national parks are a huge source of **controversy** in Thailand, with vested interests such as fishermen, farmers, loggers, poachers and the tourist industry pitted against environmentalists and certain sections of the government. The Royal Forestry Department has itself come in for voluble criticism over the last few years, particularly over the filming of *The Beach* on the national park island of Ko Phi Phi Leh, and in 2000 when – without warning – it raised the **foreigners' entrance fee** levied at most national parks from B20 to B200 (B100 for children). See "The coastal environment" on p.182 for a fuller account of these issues and for a more detailed introduction to Thailand's wildlife.

Because of the drastic hike in entrance fees, you may find yourself having to be selective about which parks to visit. At the more popular parks like Khao Sok you should only have to pay the fee once, however long you stay at the park, even if your accommodation is located outside the entrance gate. And as these parks have plenty of trails and other attractions to keep you occupied, the B200 doesn't seem such bad value. It's the little parks which can only boast of a single waterfall or a lone cave that will probably not seem worth it – at the time of writing not all of these minor attractions were subject to the revised entry fee (those that are have been highlighted in the guide), but the new charges may become more widespread.

Most parks have limited public facilities, very few signposted walking trails, and a paucity of usable maps. Nor are many of the parks well served by public transport – some can take a day to reach from the nearest large town, via a route that entails several bus and songthaew changes and a final lengthy walk. This factor, combined with the expense and poor quality of most national park accommodation, means that if you're planning to do a serious tour of the parks you should consider **bringing a tent** (all parks allow this; see p.43 for details) and be prepared to rent your own transport.

## Rock climbing

The limestone karsts that pepper south Thailand's Andaman coast make ideal playgrounds for **rock climbers**, and the sport has really taken off here in the last decade. Most climbing is centred round East and West Railay beaches on Laem Phra Nang in Krabi province (see p.363), where there are dozens of routes within easy walking distance of tourist bungalows, restaurants and beaches. Several climbing schools have already established centres here, providing instruction, guides and all the necessary equipment. Ko Phi Phi (see p.373) also offers a few interesting routes and a couple of climbing schools. The best place to **learn** rock climbing is Laem Phra Nang: half-day introductory courses cost B800, a full day's guided climbing B1500, and a three-day course B5000. Equipment rental is charged at about B1000 per day for two people. For further details about climbing courses, visit the rock climbing schools' websites listed on p.363.

## Kayaking

**Kayaking, too,** is centred around Thailand's Andaman coast, whose limestone outcrops, sea caves, *hong*s (hidden lagoons), mangrove swamps and picturesque shorelines all make for rewarding paddling (there are also a handful of operators over on Ko Samui – see p.257). And because you've no roaring engine to disturb the wildlife, you often get to see many more creatures than you would in a more conventional boat.

The longest-established **kayaking operator** in Thailand is SeaCanoe (🌐www .seacanoe.com), who always seem to get good reviews; it is due to this trailblazing company that sea kayaking has taken off in Thailand. They run day-trips out of Phuket (see p.329), Phang Nga (p.353) and Ao Nang (p.366), which cost B1700–3000 per person (children aged 4–12 half-price), and also do three- to six-day trips. In typical Thai style, SeaCanoe's success has spawned a lot of copycat operations, most of which are based in Krabi (see p.361), Ao Nang, Laem Phra Nang (see p.363) and Phuket, ranging in price from B1200–2700 for a full day or about B900 for half a day. Some of these operators also rent out kayaks for about B300 per hour, as do a couple of places on Ko Phi Phi as well. Phuket-based Paddle Asia (🌐 www.paddleasia.com) also offers week-long sea kayaking trips around the Trang islands and the Tarutao National Marine Park islands at US$100–150 per person per day.

# Gay Thailand

**Buddhist tolerance and a national abhorrence for confrontation and victimization combine to make Thai society relatively tolerant of homosexuality, if not exactly positive about same-sex relationships. Most Thais are extremely private and discreet about being gay, generally pursuing a "don't ask, don't tell" understanding with their family. However, most Thais are horrified by the idea of gay-bashing and generally regard it as unthinkable to spurn a child or relative for being gay.**

Hardly any public figures are out, yet the predilections of several respected social, political and entertainment figures are widely known and accepted. **Transvestites** (known as *katoey*) and transsexuals are also a lot more visible in Thailand than in the West. You'll find cross-dressers doing ordinary jobs, even in small upcountry towns, and there are a number of transvestites and transsexuals in the public eye too – including national volleyball stars and champion *muay Thai* boxers. The government tourist office vigorously promotes the transvestite cabarets in Pattaya and Phuket, both of which are advertised as family entertainment. *Katoey* also regularly appear as characters in soap operas, TV comedies and films, where they are depicted as harmless figures of fun.

There is no mention of homosexuality at all in Thai **law**, which means that the age of consent for gay sex is sixteen, the same as for heterosexuals. However, this also means that gay rights are not protected under Thai law. This enabled the national Ratchabhat teacher-training institute to implement a bizarre and sudden ban on homosexuals becoming teachers in mid-1997. The ban was greeted with widespread protests and led to a human rights campaign from NGOs at home and abroad, and was eventually dropped.

## The scene

Thailand's **gay scene** is mainly focused on mainstream venues like karaoke bars, restaurants, massage parlours, gyms, saunas and escort agencies. For the sake of discretion, gay venues are usually intermingled with equivalent straight venues. As in the straight scene, venues reflect class and status differences. Expensive international-style places are very popular in Bangkok, attracting upper- and middle-class gays, many of whom have travelled or been educated abroad and developed Western tastes. These places also attract a contingent of Thais seeking foreign sugar daddies.

The biggest concentrations of farang-friendly gay **bars and clubs** are found in Bangkok, Phuket and Pattaya, and are listed in the guide; recently the gay communities of Bangkok and Phuket have both hosted flamboyant **Gay Pride festivals** in November (check upcoming dates on the websites listed opposite). Thailand's gay scene is heavily male, and there are hardly any **lesbian**-only venues, though Bangkok has a few mixed gay bars. Where possible, we've listed lesbian meeting places, but unless otherwise specified, gay means male throughout this guide.

Although excessively physical displays of affection are frowned upon for both heterosexuals and homosexuals, Western gay couples should get no hassle about being seen together in public – it's much more acceptable, and common, in fact, for friends of the same sex (gay or not) to walk hand-in-hand, than for heterosexual couples to do so.

The farang-orientated gay **sex industry** is a tiny but highly visible part of Thailand's gay scene. With its tawdry floor shows and host services, it bears a gruesome resemblance to the straight sex trade, and is similarly most active in Bangkok and Pattaya, and Patong (on Phuket). Like their female counterparts in the heterosexual fleshpots, many of the boys working in the gay sex bars that dominate these districts are under age. A significant number of gay prostitutes are gay by economic necessity rather than by inclination. As with the straight sex scene, we do not list the commercial gay sex bars in the guide.

## Information and contacts for gay travellers

**Anjaree**, PO Box 322, Rajdamnoen PO, Bangkok 10200 ☎ & ⓕ 02/477 1776, ⓔ anjaree@loxinfo.com. General information on the lesbian community in Thailand.

**Dragon Castle's Gay Asia** ⓦ dragoncastle.net. Justifiably bills itself as "Gay Thailand's leading website". Carries informed advice on all aspects of the gay scene, good solid tips on potential dangers and pitfalls, plus plenty of listings and links for further information.

**Dreaded Ned's** ⓦ www.dreadedned.com. Information on almost every gay venue in the country, plus some interesting background on gay Thailand and a book list.

**Gay Media's Gay Guide to Thailand** ⓦ www.gay-media.com. Exhaustive listings of gay-friendly hotels in the major tourist centres; also covers gay bars, clubs and saunas in Bangkok.

**Metro** ⓦ www.bkkmetro.com. Bangkok's monthly listings magazine publishes extensive listings of gay venues and events.

**Pink Ink** ⓦ www.khsnet.com/pinkink. Thailand's first gay and lesbian newsletter in English, featuring listings, gossip columns and news clippings, plus personal ads. Available free from major gay venues in Bangkok.

**Utopia**, 116/1 Soi 23, Thanon Sukhumvit ☎ 02/259 9619, ⓦ www.utopia-asia.com. Bangkok's gay and lesbian centre has a café, noticeboards, gallery and shop, and is a good place to find out what's happening on the gay scene. Their website lists clubs, events and accommodation for gays and lesbians. Utopia also offers a gay tour-guide service, called Thai Friends; it's a strictly non-sexual arrangement and can be organized through the centre or via their website.

# Disabled travellers

Thailand makes few provisions for its disabled citizens and this obviously affects the disabled traveller, but these drawbacks are often balanced out by the affordability of small luxuries such as taxis, comfortable hotels, and personal tour guides, all of which can help smooth the way considerably. Most disabled travellers find Thais only too happy to offer assistance where they can, but hiring a local tour guide to accompany you on a day's sightseeing is particularly recommended – with the help of a Thai speaker you will find it much easier to arrange access to temples, museums and other places that may at first not seem wheelchair-friendly. Government tour guides can be arranged through any TAT office.

Wheelchair users will have a hard time negotiating the uneven pavements, which are high to allow for flooding and invariably lack dropped kerbs, and will find it difficult to board buses and trains. Even crossing the road can be a trial, particularly in Bangkok, where it's usually a question of climbing steps up to a bridge rather than taking a ramped underpass.

One way to cut down the hassle is to go with a **tour**: the extra money is well spent if it guarantees adapted facilities throughout your stay and enables you to explore otherwise inaccessible sights. In the UK, both Kuoni and BA Holidays (see p.11) are used to tailoring package deals to specific needs.

The more expensive international **airlines** tend to be the better equipped: British Airways, Thai International and Qantas all carry aisle wheelchairs and have at least one toilet adapted for disabled passengers. Staff at Bangkok Airport are generally helpful to disabled passengers and, if asked, should be able to whisk you past immigration queues; they will also provide wheelchairs if necessary.

## Contacts for travellers with disabilities

For general **information** on disabled travel abroad, get in touch with the organizations listed below, browse the exhaustive links at ⓦ www.independentliving.org, or post a query on the forum for travellers with disabil-

ities at ⓦ thorntree.lonelyplanet.com. For Thailand-specific information, have a look at ⓦ www.infothai.com/disabled, or try the Council of Disabled People of Thailand (☎ 02/583 3031, ⓕ 583 6518), who can provide limited information on the country's resources for the disabled.

### UK and Ireland

**Access Travel** ☎ 01942/888844, ⓕ 891811, ⓦ www.access.co.uk. Tour operator who can arrange flights, transfer and accommodation for travellers with disabilities.
**Disability Action Group**, 2 Annadale Ave, Belfast BT7 3JH ☎ 028/9049 1011.
**Holiday Care Service** ☎ 01293/774535, minicom 01293/776943ⓕ 784647, ⓦ www.holidaycare.org.uk. Provides free lists of accessible accommodation abroad.
**Irish Wheelchair Association** In the Irish Republic ☎ 01/833 8241, ⓕ 833 3873, ⓔ iwa@iol.ie
**RADAR** (Royal Association for Disability and Rehabilitation) ☎ 020/7250 3222, minicom ☎ 020/7250 4119, ⓦ www.radar.org.uk. A good source of advice on holidays and travel abroad. They produce a guide for long-haul holidays.
**Tripscope** ☎ 08457/585641, ⓕ 020/8580 7022, ⓦ www.justmobility.co.uk/tripscope. This registered charity provides a national telephone information service offering free advice on international transport for those with a mobility problem.

### US and Canada

**Access-Able** ⓦ www.access-able.com. An online resource for travellers with disabilities.

**Directions Unlimited** ☎ 1-800/533-5343 or 914/241-1700. Tour operator specializing in custom tours for people with disabilities.
**Mobility International USA** ☎ 541/343-1284, ⊛ www.miusa.org. Information and referral services, access guides, tours and exchange programmes. Annual membership $35 (includes quarterly newsletter).
**Society for the Advancement of Travelers with Handicaps (SATH)** ☎ 212/447-7284, ⊛ www.sath.org. Non-profit educational organization that has actively represented travelers with disabilities since 1976.
**Travel Information Service** ☎ 215/456-9600. Telephone-only information and referral service.

**Twin Peaks Press** ☎ 360/694-2462 or 1-800/637 2256, ⊛ www.twinpeak.virtualave.net. Publisher of a number of resources for the disabled, including the *Directory of Travel Agencies for the Disabled*, listing more than 370 agencies worldwide.
**Wheels Up!** ☎ 1-888/389-4335, ⊛ www.wheelsup .com. Provides discounted airfares, tour and cruise prices for disabled travelers; also publishes a free monthly newsletter and has a comprehensive website.

## Australia and New Zealand

**ACROD** (Australian Council for Rehabilitation of the Disabled) In Australia ☎ 02/6282 4333, ⊛ www.acrod.org.au.
**Disabled Persons Assembly** In New Zealand ☎ 04/811 9100.

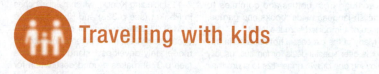

# Travelling with kids

**Travelling through Thailand with kids can be both challenging and rewarding. Thais are very tolerant of children so you can take them almost anywhere without restriction, and they always help break the ice with strangers.**

Even more than their parents, children need protecting from the sun, unsafe drinking water, heat and unfamiliar **food**. All that chilli in particular may be a problem, even with older kids, so if possible try and make a few visits to Thai restaurants in your home country before launching them into the real thing; consider packing a jar of Marmite or equivalent child's favourite, so that you can always rely on toast if the local food doesn't go down so well. As diarrhoea could be dangerous for a child, rehydration solutions (see under "Health", p.33) are vital if your child goes down with it. You should also make sure, if possible, that your child is aware of the dangers of rabies; keep children away from animals, and consider a rabies jab.

For a full briefing about the logistics of travelling with kids in Asia, see *Your Child's Health Abroad* by Dr Jane Wilson-Howarth and Dr Matthew Ellis (Bradt Publications).

You might also want to canvass other travellers' opinions, which you can do by posting your queries on the forum websites (see p.25). For specific advice about kids' health issues, either contact your doctor, or consult one of the travellers' medical services listed on p.30 or, in the UK, call the Nomad Medical Centre (☎ 020/8889 7014), which publishes a special information sheet on keeping kids healthy when abroad.

**Disposable nappies** (diapers) are sold in Thailand at convenience stores, chemists and supermarkets in big resorts and sizeable towns; for longer, more out-of-the-way journeys and stays on lonely islands and beaches, consider bringing some washables as back-up. A changing mat is another necessity. If your baby is on powdered **milk**, it might be an idea to bring some of that too; you can certainly get it in Thailand but it may not taste the same as at home. Dried baby **food**, too, could be worth taking, though you can get

B

BASICS | Travelling with kids

73

international brands in big towns and resorts and some parents find restaurant-cooked rice and bananas go down just as well.

For touring, child-carrier backpacks are ideal, and can weigh less than 2kg. If the child is small enough, a fold-up **buggy** is also well worth packing, though you can buy these cheaply in most moderate-sized Thai towns. Don't expect smooth pavements and plentiful ramps however. Children's **clothes** are also very cheap in Thailand, and have the advantage of being designed for the climate. If you haven't already got beach shoes or sports sandals for your child to swim in (to protect against coral, sea urchins and the like), you can buy these in the big cities and in every resort. Even if you've forgotten a crucial piece of children's equipment, you'll probably find it in Bangkok's well-stocked **children's department store**, Buy Buy Kiddo, (see p.156), which has everything from bottles and dummies to English-language kids' books and games, much of it imported from the West.

Many of the expensive **hotels** listed in this guide offer special deals for families, usually allowing one or two under-12s to share their parents' room for free, so long as no extra bedding is required. It's often possible to cram two adults and two children into the double rooms in inexpensive and mid-range hotels (as opposed to guest houses), as beds in these places are usually big enough for two (see p.42). Few museums or transport companies offer student reductions, but in some cases children get discounts; these vary a lot, one of the more bizarre provisos being the State Railway's regulation that a child aged 3–12 only qualifies for half fare if under 150cm tall – in some stations you'll see a measuring scale painted onto the ticket-hall wall.

A few upmarket hotels arrange special **activities for kids**: *Laguna Resort* hotels complex on Hat Bang Tao, Phuket (see p.333) is particularly recommended for its family-friendly accommodation and special kids' activities camp, as are the *Novotel Phuket Resort*, and the *Holiday Inn*, both on Patong Beach, Phuket (p.339). Several dive centres offer special courses for kids aged 7–11, including Kontiki, which has branches in Phuket (see p.323) and Khao Lak (see p.315). Despite its lack of obvious child-centred activities, many parents find that the moderately developed island of Ko Lanta (see p.379) makes a good destination for kids of all ages, with reasonably priced accommodation, fairly uncrowded sandy beaches and safe seas.

# Directory

**Addresses** Thai addresses can be immensely confusing, mainly because property is often numbered twice, firstly to show which real estate lot it stands in, and then to distinguish where it is on that lot. Thus 154/7–10 Thanon Rajdamnoen means the building is on lot 154 and occupies numbers 7–10. There's an additional idiosyncrasy in the way Thai roads are sometimes named: in large cities a minor road running off a major road is often numbered as a soi ("lane" or "alley", though it may be a sizeable thoroughfare), rather than given its own street name. Thanon Sukhumvit for example – Bangkok's longest – has minor roads numbered Soi 1 to Soi 103, with odd numbers on one side of the road and even on the other; so a Thanon Sukhumvit address could read something like 27/9–11 Soi 15, Thanon Sukhumvit, which would mean the property occupies numbers 9–11 on lot 27 on minor road number 15 running off Thanon Sukhumvit.

**Contact lens solutions** International brands are available from opticians and many department stores.

**Contraceptives** Condoms (*meechai*) are sold in all pharmacies, and birth-control pills can be bought in Bangkok (see p.163); other contraceptives should be brought from home.

**Cookery classes** You can take short courses in authentic Thai cookery at schools in Bangkok, Hua Hin and Phuket; see relevant accounts for details.

**Electricity** Supplied at 220 volts AC and available at all but the most basic beach huts. If you're packing a hair dryer or laptop, bring a set of travel-plug adapters as several plug types are commonly in use, most usually with two round pins, but also with two flat-blade pins, and sometimes with both options. The Help for World Travellers website (ⓦ www.kropla.com) carries pictures of the different sockets used in Thailand.

**Film** The price of film in Thailand is approximately B100 for 36-exposure Fujicolour print film, or B225 for 36-exposure slide film. Slide film is hard to get outside the main tourist centres but video tape is more widely available. Developing film is a lot less expensive than back home and is done in a couple of hours in the main tourist areas, to about the same quality as in the West.

**Laundry services** Guest houses and hotels all over the country run low-cost same-day laundry services. In some places you pay per item, in others you're charged by the kilo; ironing is often included in the price.

**Left luggage** Most major train stations have left-luggage facilities where bags can be stored for up to twenty days; at bus stations you can usually persuade someone official to look after your stuff for a few hours. Many guest houses and hotels also offer an inexpensive and reliable service.

**Tampons** Available from department stores and big supermarkets in every sizeable town and at convenience stores in large resorts.

**Tipping** Some upmarket hotels and restaurants will add an automatic ten-percent service charge to your bill. It is usual to tip hotel bellboys and porters B10–20, and to round up taxi fares to the nearest B10.

# guide

# guide

1. Bangkok ................................................................79–168

2. The east coast .....................................................169–224

3. Southern Thailand: the gulf coast ...........................225–293

4. Southern Thailand: the Andaman coast ................295–390

5. The deep south ....................................................391–432

# Bangkok

CHAPTER 1 # Highlights

* **The Grand Palace** – the country's least missable sight, incorporating its holiest and most dazzling temple, **Wat Phra Kaeo**. p.111

* **Wat Po** – gawp at the Reclining Buddha and the lavish architecture, and leave time for a relaxing massage. p.118

* **The National Museum** – the central repository of the country's artistic riches. p.121

* **The canals of Thonburi** – See the Bangkok of yesteryear on a touristy but memorable longtail boat ride. p.133

* **Jim Thompson's House** – an elegant Thai design classic. p.137

* **Chatuchak Weekend Market** – Six thousand stalls selling everything from triangular cushions to second-hand Levis. p.143.

* **Thai boxing** – Nightly bouts at the national stadia, complete with live musical accompaniment and frenetic betting. p.156

* **Chinatown** – Mile-long alleyway markets, and the world's largest solid-gold Buddha. p.127

* **Thai Craft Museum** – Shop for the best handicrafts, textiles and souvenirs under one roof. p.158

# Bangkok

The headlong pace and flawed modernity of **Bangkok** match few people's visions of the capital of exotic Siam. Spiked with scores of concrete and glass high-rise buildings, it's a vast flatness which holds a population of at least nine million, and feels even bigger. But under the shadow of the skyscrapers you'll find a heady mix of chaos and refinement, of frenetic markets and hushed golden temples, of dispiriting, zombie-like sex shows and early morning almsgiving ceremonies. One way or another, the place will probably get under your skin – and if you don't enjoy the challenge of slogging through jams of buses and tuk-tuks, which fill the air with a chain-saw drone and clouds of pollution, you can spend a couple of days on the most impressive temples and museums, have a quick shopping spree and then strike out for the provinces.

Finding a place to stay in Bangkok is usually no problem: the city has a huge range of **accommodation**, from the murkiest backstreet bunk to the plushest five-star riverside suite, and you don't have to spend a lot to stay in a comfortable place. Getting to your guest house or hotel, however, is a stress-inducing experience, for there can be few cities in the world where **transport** is such a headache. Bumper-to-bumper vehicles create fumes so bad that on some days the city's carbon monoxide emissions come close to the international danger level, and it's not unusual for residents to spend three hours getting to work – and these are people who know where they're going. However, the 1999 opening of the elevated train network called the Bangkok Transit System, or BTS Skytrain, has radically improved public transport in a few parts of the city, notably the Siam Square, Silom and Sukhumvit areas. In areas the Skytrain

---

### Accommodation prices

Throughout this guide, guesthouses, hotels and bungalows have been categorized according to the price codes given below. These categories represent the minimum you can expect to pay in the high season (roughly July, Aug & Nov–Feb) for a double room. If travelling on your own, expect to pay anything between sixty and one hundred percent of the rates quoted for a double room. Wherever a price range is indicated, this means that the establishment offers rooms with varying facilities – as explained in the review. Where an establishment also offers dormitory beds, the prices of these beds are given in the text, instead of being indicated by price code.

Remember that the top-whack hotels will add seven-percent tax and a ten-percent service charge to your bill – the price codes below are based on net rates after taxes have been added.

| | | |
|---|---|---|
| ❶ under B150 | ❹ B400–600 | ❼ B1200–1800 |
| ❷ B150–250 | ❺ B600–900 | ❽ B1800–3000 |
| ❸ B250–400 | ❻ B900–1200 | ❾ B3000+ |

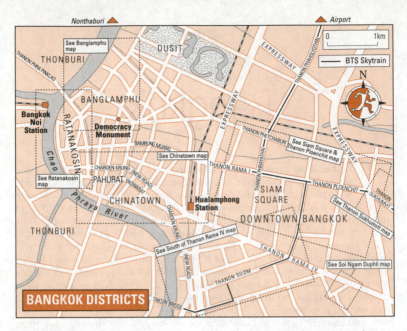

Nonthaburi

Airport

See Banglamphu map

DUSIT

THONBURI

BANGLAMPHU

Bangkok Noi Station

RATANAKOSIN

Democracy Monument

BAMRUNG MUANG

See Chinatown map

CHAROEN KRUNG (NEW ROAD)

See Ratanakosin map

PAHURAT

YAOWARAT

CHINATOWN

Hualamphong Station

THONBURI

See South of Thanon Rama IV map

CHAROEN KRUNG (NEW ROAD)

THANON SILOM

TAKSIN BRIDGE

EXPRESSWAY

EXPRESSWAY

THANON PHRA PINKLAO

Chao

Phraya River

THANON PHETCHABURI

THANON PHAYATHAI

THANON PHAHOLYOTHIN

See Siam Square & Thanon Ploenchit map

THANON RAMA I

THANON PLOENCHIT

SIAM SQUARE

DOWNTOWN BANGKOK

THANON SUKHUMVIT

See Thanon Sukhumvit map

THANON RAMA IV

See Soi Ngam Duphli map

0     1km

BTS Skytrain

N

**BANGKOK DISTRICTS**

doesn't reach, boats provide the fastest means of hopping from one sight to another.

Most budget travellers head for the **Banglamphu** district, where if you're not careful you could end up watching videos all day long and selling your shoes when you run out of money. The district is far from having a monopoly on Bangkok accommodation, but it does have the advantage of being just a short walk from the major sights in the **Ratanakosin** area: the dazzling ostentation of **Wat Phra Kaeo**, the grandiose decay of **Wat Po** and the **National Museum**'s hoard of exquisite works of art. Once those cultural essentials have been seen, you can choose from a whole bevy of lesser sights, including **Wat Benjamabophit** (the "Marble Temple"), especially at festival time, and **Jim**

## City of angels

When Rama I was crowned in 1782, he gave his new capital a grand 43-syllable name to match his ambitious plans for the building of the city. Since then 21 more syllables have been added. Krungthepmahanakhornbowornrattanakosinmahin-tarayutthayamahadilokpopnopparatratchathaniburiromudomratchaniwetma-hasathanamornpimanavatarnsathitsakkathattiyavisnukarprasit is certified by the *Guinness Book of Records* as the longest place name in the world, roughly translating as "Great city of angels, the supreme repository of divine jewels, the great land unconquerable, the grand and prominent realm, the royal and delightful capital city full of nine noble gems, the highest royal dwelling and grand palace, the divine shelter and living place of the reincarnated spirits". Fortunately, all Thais refer to the city simply as Krung Thep, though plenty can recite the full name at the drop of a hat. Bangkok – "Village of the Plum Olive" – was the name of the original village on the Thonburi side; with remarkable persistence, it has remained in use by foreigners since the time of the French garrison.

Thompson's House, a small, personal museum of Thai design.

For livelier scenes, explore the dark alleys of **Chinatown**'s bazaars or head for the water: the great **Chao Phraya River**, which breaks up and adds zest to the city's landscape, is the backbone of a network of **canals and floating markets** that remains fundamentally intact in the west-bank Thonburi district. Inevitably the waterways have earned Bangkok the title of "Venice of the East", a tag that seems all too apt when you're wading through flooded streets in the rainy season; indeed, the city is year by year subsiding into the marshy ground, literally sinking under·the weight of its burgeoning concrete towers.

**Shopping** on dry land varies from touristic outlets selling silks, handicrafts and counterfeit watches, through international fashion emporia and home-grown, street-wise boutiques, to completely and sometimes undesirably authentic marketplaces – notably Chatuchak, where caged animals cringe among the pots and pans. Similarly, the city offers the country's most varied **entertainment**, ranging from traditional dancing and the orchestrated bedlam of Thai boxing, through hip bars and clubs playing the latest imported sounds, to the farang-only sex bars of the notorious Patpong district, a tinseltown Babylon that's the tip of a dangerous iceberg.

# Arrival, orientation, information and city transport

Unless you arrive in Bangkok by train, be prepared for a long slog into the centre. Most travellers' first sight of the city is the International Terminal at Don Muang airport, a slow 25km to the north. Even if you arrive by coach, you'll still have a lot of work to do to get into the centre. Once there, the city is a confusing place to find your way round in, though helpful information centres will help you orientate yourself and get to grips with the public transport system.

## By air

Once you're through immigration at either of the two interconnected **international terminals** at **Don Muang Airport** (queues are often horrendous, owing to the availability of free short-stay visas on the spot), you'll find 24-hour exchange booths, a couple of helpful TAT information desks (daily 8am–midnight; ☏02/523 8972), a round-the-clock Thai Hotels Association accommodation desk, with prices generally cheaper than rack rates, post offices and international telephone facilities, a pricey left-luggage depot (B70 per item

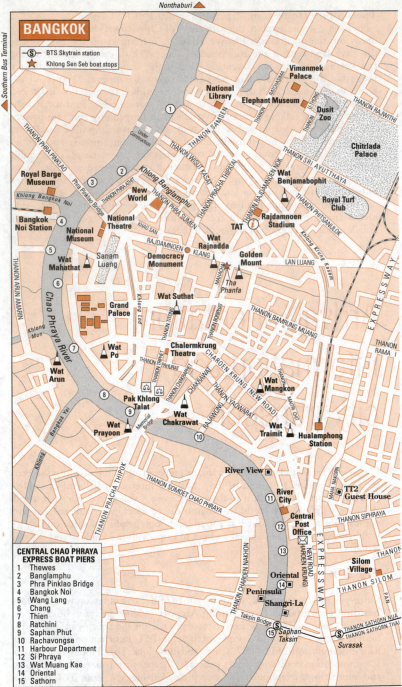

# BANGKOK

Ⓢ BTS Skytrain station
★ Khlong Sen Seb boat stops

**CENTRAL CHAO PHRAYA EXPRESS BOAT PIERS**
1. Thewes
2. Banglamphu
3. Phra Pinklao Bridge
4. Bangkok Noi
5. Wang Lang
6. Chang
7. Thien
8. Ratchini
9. Saphan Phut
10. Rachavongse
11. Harbour Department
12. Si Phraya
13. Wat Muang Kae
14. Oriental
15. Sathorn

Southern Bus Terminal

Nonthaburi

National Library

Vimanmek Palace

Elephant Museum

Dusit Zoo

Chitlada Palace

THANON PHRA PINKLAO

THANON WISUT KASAT

THANON SAMSEN

THANON RATCHASIMA

THANON SRI AYUTTHAYA

THANON RAJWITHI

Under Construction

Khlong Banglamphu

New World

Royal Barge Museum

Khlong Bangkok Noi

Bangkok Noi Station

National Theatre

National Museum

Wat Benjamabophit

Royal Turf Club

Wat Mahathat

Sanam Luang

KHAO SAN

Democracy Monument

RAJDAMNOEN KLANG

Wat Rajnadda

TAT

Rajdamnoen Stadium

Golden Mount

LAN LUANG

THANON ARUN AMARIN

Wat Suthat

Grand Palace

Tha Phanfa

Chao Phraya River

Khlong Mon

Wat Po

Chalermkrung Theatre

THANON BAMRUNG MUANG

THANON RAMA I

Wat Arun

THANON PAHURAT

CHAROEN KRUNG (NEW ROAD)

THANON YAOWARAT

Wat Mangkon

Pak Khlong Talat

Wat Prayoon

Wat Chakrawat

RAJAWONG

Wat Traimit

Hualamphong Station

Memorial Bridge

THANON SOMDET CHAO PHRAYA

River View

River City

TT2 Guest House

THANON SIPHRAYA

Central Post Office

THANON PRACHA THIPOK

THANON CHAROEN NAKHON

Silom Village

Oriental

Peninsula

Shangri-La

THANON SILOM

Taksin Bridge

Saphan Taksin

Surasak

THANON SATHORN NUA

THANON SATHORN

Marriott Royal Garden Hotel

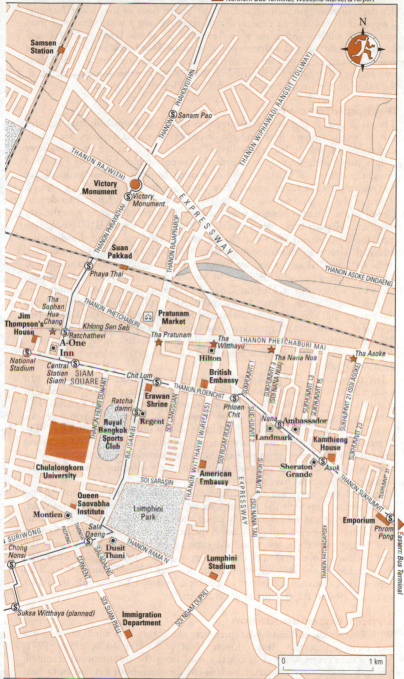

Northern Bus Terminal, Weekend Market & Airport

N

Samsen
Station

THANON RAJWITHI

Sanam Pao

THANON PHAHOLYOTHIN

THANON WIPHAWADI RANGSIT (TOLLWAY)

E X P R E S S W A Y

Victory
Monument

Victory
Monument

THANON PHRAYATHAI

THANON RAJAPRAROP

THANON ASOKE DINDAENG

Suan
Pakkad

Phaya Thai

Tha
Saphan
Hua
Chang

THANON PHETCHABURI

Pratunam
Market

Jim
Thompson's
House

Khlong Sen Seb

Tha Pratunam

Tha
Witthayu

THANON PHETCHABURI MAI

Tha Nana Nua

Tha Asoke

Ratchathevi
A-One
Inn

Hilton

British
Embassy

SUKHUMVIT 1

SUKHUMVIT 3
(SOI NANA NUA)

SUKHUMVIT 13

SUKHUMVIT 15

SUKHUMVIT 21 (SOI ASOKE)

National
Stadium

Central
Station
(Siam)

SIAM
SQUARE

Chit Lom

THANON PLOENCHIT

Phloen
Chit

SUKHUMVIT 2

Nana

Ambassador

SUKHUMVIT 23

Erawan
Shrine

Ratcha-
damri

Regent

THANON RATCHADAMRI

SOI LANGSUAN

THANON WITTHAYU (WIRELESS)

SOI RUAM RUDEE

Landmark

Kamthieng
House

SUKHUMVIT 4

SOI NANA TAI

Sheraton
Grande

Asok

THANON SUKHUMVIT

SUKHUMVIT 31

Royal
Bangkok
Sports
Club

THANON HENRI DUNANT

RAJDAMRI

Chulalongkorn
University

SOI SARASIN

American
Embassy

E X P R E S S W A Y

Queen
Saovabha
Institute

Lumphini
Park

Emporium

Phrom
Pong

Eastern Bus Terminal

Montien

Sala
Daeng

Dusit
Thani

THANON RAMA IV

THANON PATCHADAPISEK

SURIWONG

PATPONG

THANON CONVENT

SALADAENG

Chong
Nonsi

Lumphini
Stadium

Suksa Witthaya (planned)

SOI SUAN PHLU

Immigration
Department

SOI NGAM DUPHLI

0                1 km

per day), an emergency clinic and, on the fourth floor of the newer Terminal 2 opposite *Pizza Hut*, an expensive cybercafé. Among a wide variety of food and drink outlets (particularly in Terminal 2, which boasts Chinese and Japanese restaurants and a British pub that offers 24hr breakfasts), the cheapest and most interesting options are two food centres serving simple Thai dishes, one on the south side of Terminal 2 on the walkway to the domestic terminal, the other on the fourth floor, accessible from Terminals 1 and 2.

### Getting into town

The most economical way of getting into the city is by **public bus**, but this can be excruciatingly slow and the invariably crowded vehicles are totally unsuitable for heavily laden travellers. The bus stop is on the main highway which runs north–south just outside the airport buildings: to find it, head straight out from the northern end of arrivals. Most of the buses run all day and night, with a reduced service after 10pm; see the box on p.92 for a rough sketch of the most useful routes – the TAT office in arrivals has further details. Unless you're already counting your baht, you're better off getting into the city by air-con **airport bus** (daily 4.30am–12.30am; every 30min; B100 payable on bus); the buses depart from outside Terminal 1, Terminal 2 and the domestic terminal (clearly signposted outside each building). Four routes are covered: route AB1 runs along to the west end of Thanon Silom, via Pratunam and Thanon Rajdamri; route AB2 goes to Sanam Luang, via Victory Monument, Democracy Monument, Thanon Tanao (for Thanon Khao San), Thanon Phra Sumen and Thanon Phra Athit; route AB3 runs down the Dindaeng Expressway and along Thanon Sukhumvit to Soi Thonglor via the Eastern Bus Terminal; and route AB4 runs down the Dindaeng Expressway and west along Thanon Ploenchit to Siam Square, then down to Hualamphong train station. A handy colour leaflet available from the TAT desks details which major hotels each route passes.

The **train** to Hualamphong station (see opposite) is the quickest way into town, and ideal if you want to stay in Chinatown, but services are irregular. To reach the station at Don Muang follow the signs from arrivals in Terminal 1 (if in doubt head towards the big *Amari Airport Hotel*, across the main highway, carry on through the hotel foyer and the station is in front of you). Over thirty trains a day make the fifty-minute trip to Hualamphong, with fares starting from B5 in third class (though express trains command surcharges of up to B80), with services most frequent around the early morning – at other times of the day you might have to wait over an hour.

**Taxis** to the centre are comfortable, air-conditioned and not too extravagantly priced, although the driving can be hairy. A wide variety is on offer, from pricey limousines, through licensed metered cabs, down to cheap unlicensed and unmetered vehicles – avoid the latter, as newly arrived travellers are seen as easy prey for robbery, and the cabs are untraceable. Metered taxis, the best option, are operated from clearly signposted counters outside Terminal 1. Even including the B50 airport pick-up fee and B70 tolls for the overhead expressways, a journey to Thanon Ploenchit downtown, for example, should set you back around B250 depending on the traffic.

### Airport accommodation

With time to kill and money to spare between flights, you might want to rest and clean up at the *Amari Airport Hotel* (☎02/566 1020, ℻566 1941, ⓦwww.amari.com; ⑨), just across the road from the international terminal, which rents out very upmarket **bedrooms** for three-hour periods from 8am to 6pm (US$20, no reservations) – far better than the international terminals' day rooms, which are twice the price and designed for transit passengers. To **stay near the airport**, the *Comfort Inn* is a more economical choice (⊤02/552 8929, Ⓕ552 8920, ⒺⓅinap@loxinfo.co.th; ❽) and will pick you up for the five-minute journey from the terminals if you call. Another good option is the huge *Asia Airport Hotel* (⊤02/992 6653, Ⓕ992 6828, Ⓦwww .asiahotel.co.th; ❼), less than ten minutes' drive north of the international terminal, just south of the Rangsit interchange on Thanon Phaholyothin. All rooms are air-conditioned and comfortably furnished, there's a hotel restaurant, a swimming pool and a shopping complex, and free transport to and from the airport; book over the internet for significant discounts. Cheaper still is the *We-Train* guest house, about 3km west of the airport (⊤02/929 2301–10, Ⓕ929 2300, Ⓦwww.wetrain.linethai.co.th; ❹), run by the Association for the Promotion of the Status of Women, where proceeds go to help distressed women and children; in a peaceful lakeside setting, there are dorms (B140), comfortable fan or air-con rooms and a swimming pool.

### Getting to the rest of the country

To catch a connecting **internal flight**, head to the **domestic terminal** at Don Muang, 500m away from Terminal 2, connected by an air-conditioned covered walkway and by a free shuttle bus (daily 5am–midnight; every 15min); the **domestic departure tax** of B30 is always included in the price of your ticket. Facilities here include exchange booths, hotel reservation desks, a post office with international telephones and internet access, and pricey left luggage (B70 per item per day); metered taxi counters can be found outside arrivals on the ground floor, while the airport bus (see opposite) stops outside the northern end of arrivals.

## By train

Travelling to Bangkok by **train** from Malaysia and most parts of Thailand, you arrive at **Hualamphong station**, which is centrally located and served by numerous **city buses**. The most useful of these are bus #53 (non-air-con), which stops on the east side (left-hand exit) of the station and runs to the budget accommodation in Banglamphu; and the #25 and #40 (both non-air-con), which run east to Siam Square (for Skytrain connections) and along Thanon Sukhumvit to the Eastern Bus Terminal; the westbound #25 runs to Tha Thien (for the Grand Palace), while the westbound #40 heads over the river to the Southern Bus Terminal. See p.92 for bus route details. Station **facilities** include a post office, an exchange booth and a Cirrus/MasterCard cashpoint machine (to get to the nearest Visa ATM walk 100m left along Thanon Rama IV to the bank next to *You Sue Vegetarian Restaurant*).

There are two **left-luggage** offices at Hualamphong station. The more secure option is inside the postal service centre at the main entrance, but the opening hours are unhelpfully short (Mon–Fri & Sun 7am–7pm, Sat 8am–4pm) and it's expensive at B30 per day. Alternative storage is available at a cabin halfway down Platform 12, next to the Eastern and Oriental check-in counter; the hours and prices here are more user-friendly (daily 4am–10.30pm; B10 per day for 1–5 days, B15 per day for more than 5 days), but it's not fully enclosed and so doesn't look as secure as the other place. The most economical choice for storing baggage is at the *TT2 Guest House* (see p.102), about fifteen minutes' walk from the station, which provides the same service for only B7 per item per day.

One service the station does not provide is itinerant tourist assistance staff – anyone who comes up to you in or around the station concourse and offers help/information/transport or ticket-booking services is almost certainly a **con-artist**, however many official-looking ID tags are hanging around their necks. This is a well-established scam to fleece new arrivals; the best advice is to avoid them at all costs and turn instead to the friendly and efficient VC Travel and Tour **travel agent** and **accommodation-booking service** (daily 5am–8pm; ☎02/613 6725) on the mezzanine floor above *Coffee Bucks*. The staff here speak excellent English, so this is the place to buy onward rail tickets (no commission) as well as domestic and international flights; they can also arrange discounted accommodation at many hotels (❹ and up) in Bangkok and other major tourist destinations around the country. For more information on buying onward rail tickets see p.165.

A couple of Hua Hin trains pull in at the small and not very busy **Bangkok Noi Station** in Thonburi, which is on the express-boat line (see p.91), just across the Chao Phraya River from Banglamphu and Ratanakosin.

## By bus

**Buses** come to a halt at a number of far-flung spots. All services from the north and northeast terminate at the **Northern Bus Terminal** (**Mo Chit**) on Thanon Kamphaeng Phet 2; some east-coast buses also use Mo Chit (rather than the Eastern Terminal), including several daily services from Pattaya, and a few daily buses from Rayong (for Ko Samet), Chanthaburi and Trat (for Ko Chang and the Cambodian border). The quickest way to get into the city centre from Mo Chit is to hop on to the **Skytrain** at the Mo Chit BTS station, five minutes walk from the bus terminal on Thanon Phaholyothin, and then change on to a city bus if necessary – see p.93 for details of Skytrain routes and fares. Otherwise, it's a long bus, tuk-tuk or taxi ride into town: **city buses** from the Mo Chit area include #2 and #77 to Thanon Silom; regular and air-con #3, and air-con #9, #12 and #32 to Banglamphu; and both regular and air-con #29 to Hualamphong Railway Station; for details of these routes see the box on p.92.

Most buses from the east coast use the **Eastern Bus Terminal** (**Ekamai**) at Soi 40, Thanon Sukhumvit. This bus station is right beside the Ekamai **Skytrain** stop (see p.94), and is also served by lots of **city buses**, including air-con #11 to Banglamphu and regular #59 to the Northern Bus Terminal (see p.92 for details), or you can take a taxi down Soi 63 to Tha Ekamai, a pier on Khlong Sen Seb, to pick up the **canal boat service** to the Golden Mount near Banglamphu (see p.133).

Bus services from Malaysia and the south, as well as from Kanchanaburi, use the **Southern Bus Terminal** (**Sai Tai Mai**) at the junction of Thanon Borom Ratchonni and the Nakhon Chaisri Highway, west of the Chao Phraya River in Thonburi. Drivers on these services nearly always offer to drop passengers on the east side of Thanon Borom Ratchonni before doing a U-turn for the terminus on the west side of the road; if you're heading across the river to Banglamphu or downtown Bangkok you should get off here, along with the majority of the other passengers. Numerous **city buses** run across the river from this bus stop, including air-con #7 to Banglamphu and Hualamphong Station, and air-con #11 to Banglamphu and Thanon Sukhumvit (see p.92 for routes), and they tend to be pretty empty at this point so quite manageable for luggage-bearing tourists. City buses are especially useful here as the Southern Bus Terminal is renowned for its belligerent **taxi** drivers, nearly all of whom refuse to use the meter and quote anything from B250 to B650 for the trip into central Bangkok. If you are keen to take a taxi to your destination, take any west-bound bus for a few stops to get well away from the Bus Terminal zone, then hail a metered taxi.

# Orientation and information

Bangkok can be a tricky place to get your bearings as it's huge and ridiculously congested, with largely featureless modern buildings and no obvious centre. The boldest line on the map is the **Chao Phraya River**, which divides the city into Bangkok proper on the east bank, and **Thonburi**, part of Greater Bangkok, on the west.

The historical core of Bangkok proper, site of the original royal palace, is **Ratanakosin**, which nestles into a bend in the river. Three concentric canals radiate eastwards around Ratanakosin: the southern part of the area between the canals is the old-style trading enclave of **Chinatown** and Indian **Pahurat**, linked to the old palace by Thanon Charoen Krung (aka New Road); the northern part is characterized by old temples and the **Democracy Monument**, west of which is the backpackers' ghetto of **Banglamphu**. Beyond the canals to the north, **Dusit** is the site of many government buildings and the nineteenth-century palace, which is linked to Ratanakosin by the two stately avenues, Thanon Rajdamnoen Nok and Thanon Rajadamnoen Klang.

"New" Bangkok begins to the east of the canals and beyond the main rail line, and stretches as far as the eye can see to the east and north. The main business district and most of the embassies are south of **Thanon Rama IV**, with the port of Khlong Toey at the southern edge. The diverse area north of Thanon Rama IV includes the sprawling campus of Chulalongkorn University, huge shopping centres around **Siam Square** and a variety of other businesses. A couple of blocks northeast of Siam Square stands the tallest building in Bangkok, the 84-storeyed *Baiyoke Sky Hotel*, whose golden spire makes a good point of reference. To the east lies the swish residential quarter off **Thanon Sukhumvit**.

## Information and maps

The **Bangkok Tourist Bureau** (BTB) provides excellent information for tourists on all budgets both from its headquarters, the **Bangkok Information Centre**, located next to Phra Pinklao Bridge at 17/1 Thanon Phra Athit in Banglamphu (daily 9am–7pm; ☎02/225 7612–4), and from its dozen strategically placed information booths around the capital. They all provide reasonable city maps for free, and also run a variety of interesting city tours by boat, bus and bicycle (see p.90). The BTB is the most useful resource for information on the capital, but for destinations further afield you need to visit the **Tourism Authority of Thailand** (**TAT**) which maintains a Tourist Service Centre within walking distance of Banglamphu, at 4 Rajdamnoen Nok (24hr; ☎02/282 9773–4; 24hr freephone tourist assistance ☎1155), a twenty-minute stroll from Thanon Khao San, or a short ride in air-con bus #3. TAT also has a booth in the airport arrivals concourse. If you're staying in Bangkok for more than a couple of days and want to get the most out of the city, it's worth getting hold of *Metro*, a monthly **listings magazine** available for B100 from bookstores, hotel shops and 7–11 shops.

To get around Bangkok without spending much money, you'll need to buy a **bus map**. Of the several available at bookshops, hotels and some guest houses, the most useful is Bangkok Guide's *Bus Routes & Map*, which not only maps all major air-conditioned and non-air-conditioned bus routes but also carries detailed written itineraries of some two hundred bus routes on its flip side. If you can't find a copy, opt for the long-running bright blue and yellow bus map published by Tour 'n' Guide, which maps bus routes as well as the names of dozens of smaller sois; its street locations are not always reliable however, and it can be hard to decipher exact bus routings. The most accurate map for locating small streets and places of interest in the city is *GeoCenter's Bangkok 1:15,000*, best bought before you leave home, though it's also available in some Bangkok bookshops. Serious shoppers might also want to buy a copy of Nancy Chandler's idiosyncratic map of Bangkok, which has lots of annotated recommendations on shops and markets across the city; it's available in most tourist areas.

# City transport

The main form of transport in the city are **buses**, and once you've mastered the labyrinthine complexity of the route map you'll be able to get to any part of the city, albeit slowly. Catching the various kinds of **taxi** can make a serious dent in your budget, and you'll still get held up by the daytime traffic jams. **Boats** are obviously more limited in their range, but they're regular and as cheap as buses, and you'll save a lot of time by using them whenever possible – a journey between Banglamphu and the GPO, for instance, will take around thirty minutes by water, half what it would take on land. The **Skytrain** has a similarly limited range but is also worth using whenever suitable for all or part of your journey; its network coincides with the Chao Phraya River express boats at the vital hub of Sathorn Bridge (Saphan Taksin). **Walking** might often be quicker than travelling by road, but the heat can be unbearable, distances are always further than they look on the map, and the engine fumes are stifling.

If you can't face negotiating the public transport network, any taxi or tuk-tuk driver can be hired for the day to take you around the major or minor sights (B500–800), and every travel agent in the city can arrange this for you as well. Alternatively you can join the open-topped, double-decker **Bangkok Sightseeing Bus** which does a ninety-minute guided tour of Ratanakosin, taking in the Grand Palace and Vimanmek (5 daily, B200); contact the Bangkok Tourist Bureau for details. The BTB also run several quite unusual **tours** of the capital, including a night-time bicycle tour of Ratanakosin (every Sat 7–9.30pm; B290 including bicycle), and a highly recommended 35-kilometre ride along the canal towpaths of Thonburi (see p.133).

## Buses

Bangkok has three types of bus service, and it's not uncommon for one route to be served by the full trio. **Ordinary** (non-air-conditioned) buses come in a variety of colours and sizes, and fares for most journeys range from B3.5 to B5; most routes maintain a 24-hour service. **Air-conditioned** buses subdivide into three varieties: blue (B6–18 according to distance travelled) and orange (B8–20) public buses, and smaller blue private buses (B8–20); most stop at around 10pm, but some of the more popular services run all night. As buses can only go as fast as the car in front, which at the moment is averaging 4km per hour, you'll probably be spending a long time on each journey, so you'd be well advised to pay the extra for cool air – and the air-conditioned buses are usually less crowded, too. It's also possible during the day to travel certain routes on flashy, air-conditioned private **microbuses**, which were designed with the commuter in mind and offer the use of an on-board telephone and newspapers, plus the certainty of a seat (no standing allowed) for a B25 fare (exact money only), which is dropped into a box beside the driver's seat.

Some of the most useful city-bus routes are described in the box on p.92; for a comprehensive roundup of all bus routes in the capital, buy a copy of Bangkok Guide's *Bus Routes & Map* (see opposite), or log on to the Bangkok Mass Transportation website (ⓦwww.bmta.motc.go.th), which also gives details in English of every city-bus route.

## Boats

Bangkok was built as an amphibious city around a network of canals – or **khlongs** – and the first streets were constructed only in the second half of the nineteenth century. Although most of the canals have been turned into roads on the Bangkok side, the Chao Phraya River is still a major transport route for residents and non-residents alike, forming more of a link than a barrier between the two halves of the city, and used by several different kinds of boat.

### Express boats

The Chao Phraya Express Boat Company operates the vital **express-boat** (*reua duan*) service, using large water buses to plough up and down the river, between clearly signed piers (*tha*) which appear on all Bangkok maps – the important central stops are outlined in the box on p.94 and marked on our city map (see pp.84–85). Its usual route, ninety minutes in total, runs between Wat Rajsingkorn, just upriver of Krung Thep Bridge, in the south and Nonthaburi in the north. These **"daily standard"** boats set off every ten to fifteen minutes or so between about 6am and 6.30pm, the last boat in each direction flying a blue flag. Boats do not necessarily stop at every landing – they only pull in if people want to get on or off, and when they do stop, it's not for long – when you want to get off, be ready at the back of the boat in good time for your pier. During rush hours (roughly 6–9am & 4–7pm), certain **"special express"** boats operate limited-stop services on set routes, flying either a **yellow** (Nonthaburi to Rajburana, far downriver beyond Krung Thep Bridge) or a **red and orange flag** (Nonthaburi to Wat Rajsingkorn).

**Tickets** can be bought on board, and cost B6–12 according to distance travelled, or B15–25 on yellow-flag boats. Don't discard your ticket until you're off the boat, as the staff at some piers impose a B1 fine on anyone disembarking without one.

### Cross-river ferries

Smaller than express boats are the slow **cross-river ferries** (*reua kham fak*), which shuttle back and forth between the same two points. Found at every express stop and plenty of other piers in between, they are especially useful for connections to Chao Phraya special express boat stops during rush hours. Fares are B2, which you usually pay at the entrance to the pier.

## Useful bus routes

Except where stated, all buses follow an almost identical route on the return leg of their journey.

**#2** (air-con): *Oriental Hotel*–Thanon Silom–Thanon Rama IV–MBK department store (for Siam Square)–Thanon Phayathai–Chatuchak Weekend Market–Lard Phrao–Suwinthawong.

**#3** (ordinary): Northern Bus Terminal–Chatuchak Weekend market–Thanon Phaholyothin–Thanon Samsen–Thanon Phra Athit (for Banglamphu guest houses)–Thanon Sanam Chai–Thanon Triphet–Memorial Bridge (for Pak Khlong Talat)–Taksin Monument–Wat Suwan.

**#3** (air-con): Southern Bus Terminal–Thanon Borom Ratchonni–Phra Pinklao Bridge (for Banglamphu guest houses)–Democracy Monument–Rajdamnoen Nok (for TAT and boxing stadium)–Wat Benjamabophit–Thanon Sri Ayutthaya (for Thewes guest houses)–Victory Monument–Chatuchak Weekend Market–Rangsit.

**#4** (air-con): Airport–Thanon Rajaprarop–Thanon Silom–Thanon Charoen Krung–Thonburi.

**#7** (air-con): Southern Bus Terminal–Thanon Borom Ratchonni–Phra Pinklao (for Banglamphu guest houses)–Sanam Luang–Thanon Charoen Krung–Thanon Chakrawat–Thanon Yaowarat (for Chinatown and Wat Traimit)–Hualamphong Station–Thanon Rama IV–Bang Na Intersection–Pak Nam.

**#8** (air-con): Wat Po–Grand Palace–Giant Swing (for Wat Suthat)–Thanon Yaowarat–Siam Square–Thanon Ploenchit–Thanon Sukhumvit–Eastern Bus Terminal–Pak Nam (for Ancient City buses).

**#9** (air-con): Nonthaburi–Chatuchak Weekend Market–Victory Monument–Thanon Phitsanulok–Democracy Monument–Rajdamnoen Klang (for Banglamphu guest houses)–Phra Pinklao–Thonburi.

**#10** (air-con): Airport–Chatuchak Weekend Market–Victory Monument–Dusit Zoo–Thanon Rajwithi–Krung Thon Bridge (for Thewes guest houses)–Thonburi.

**#11** (air-con): Southern Bus Terminal–Thanon Borom Ratchonni–Phra Pinklao–Rajdamnoen Klang (for Banglamphu guest houses)–Democracy Monument–Thanon Sukhumvit–Eastern Bus Terminal–Pak Nam (for Ancient City bus).

**#12** (air-con): Northern Bus Terminal–Chatuchak Weekend Market–Thanon Phetchaburi–Thanon Larn Luang–Democracy Monument (for Banglamphu guest houses)–Tha Chang–Pak Khlong Talat.

**#13** (air-con): Airport–Chatuchak Weekend Market–Victory Monument–Thanon Rajaprarop–Thanon Sukhumvit–Eastern Bus Terminal–Sukhumvit Soi 62.

## Longtail boats

**Longtail boats** (*reua hang yao*) ply the khlongs of Thonburi like buses, stopping at designated shelters (fares are in line with those of express boats), and are available for individual rental here and on the river (see p.133). On the Bangkok side, **Khlong Sen Seb** is well served by longtails, which run at least every fifteen minutes during daylight hours from the Phanfa pier at the Golden Mount (handy for Banglamphu, Ratanakosin and Chinatown), and head way out east to Wat Sribunruang, with useful stops at Thanon Phrayathai, aka Saphan Hua Chang (for Jim Thompson's House and Ratchathewi Skytrain stop), Pratunam (for the World Trade Centre and Gaysorn Plaza), Soi Chitlom, Thanon Witthayu (Wireless Rd), and Soi Nana Nua (Soi 3), Soi Asoke (Soi 21), Soi Thonglo (Soi 55) and Soi Ekamai (Soi 63), all off Thanon Sukhumvit. This is your quickest and most interesting way of getting between the west and east parts of town, if you can stand the stench of the canal. You may have trouble actually locating the piers as none are signed in English and they all look

**#15** (ordinary): Bamrung Muang–Thanon Phra Athit (for Banglamphu guest houses)–Grand Palace–Sanam Luang–Democracy Monument–Phanfa (for Khlong Sen Seb and Golden Mount)–Siam Square–Thanon Rajdamri–Thanon Silom–Thanon Charoen Krung (New Road)–Krung Thep Bridge–Thanon Rajadapisek.

**#16** (ordinary): Thanon Srinarong–Thanon Samsen–Thewes (for guest houses)–Thanon Phitsanulok–Siam Square–Thanon Henri Dunant–GPO–Tha Si Phraya.

**#25** (ordinary): Eastern Bus Terminal–Thanon Sukhumvit–Siam Square–Hualamphong Station–Thanon Yaowarat (for Chinatown)–Pahurat–Wat Po and the Grand Palace–Tha Chang.

**#29** (air-con and ordinary): Airport–Chatuchak Weekend Market–Victory Monument–Siam Square–Hualamphong Station.

**#32** (air-con): Thanon Phra Pinklao–Rajdamnoen Klang (for Thanon Khao San guest houses)–Democracy Monument–Victory monument–Northern Bus Terminal.

**#38** (ordinary): Chatuchak Weekend Market–Victory Monument–Thanon Phetchaburi–Soi Asoke–Eastern Bus Terminal.

**#39** (air-con and ordinary): Chatuchak Weekend Market–Victory Monument–Thanon Sri Ayutthaya–Thanon Larn Luang–Democracy Monument–Rajdamnoen Klang (for Thanon Khao San guest houses)–Sanam Luang.

**#40** (ordinary): Eastern Bus Terminal–Thanon Sukhumvit–Thanon Rama 1 (for Siam Square)–Hualamphong Station–Thanon Yaowarat (for Chinatown)–Southern Bus Terminal.

**#53** (ordinary): Hualamphong Station–Thanon Krung Kasem–Thanon Samsen and Thanon Phra Athit (for Banglamphu guest houses)–Sanam Luang (for National Museum and Wat Mahathat)–Thanon Mahathat (for Grand Palace and Wat Po)–Pahurat–Thanon Krung Kasem.

**#56** (ordinary): Circular route: Phra Sumen–Wat Bowoniwes–Thanon Ratchasima (for Vimanmek Palace)–Thanon Rajwithi–Krung Thon Bridge–Thonburi–Memorial Bridge–Thanon Chakraphet (for Chinatown)–Thanon Mahachai–Democracy Monument–Thanon Tanao (for Khao San guest houses)–Thanon Phra Sumen.

**#59** (ordinary): Airport–Chatuchak Weekend Market–Victory Monument–Phanfa (for Khlong Sen Seb and Golden Mount)–Democracy Monument (for Banglamphu guest houses)–Sanam Luang.

**#124** and **#127** (ordinary): Southern Bus Terminal–Tha Pinklao (for ferry to Phra Athit and Banglamphu guest houses).

very unassuming and rickety; see the map on p.84–85 for locations and keep your eyes peeled for a plain wooden jetty – most of which serve boats running in both directions. Once on the boat, state your destination to the conductor when he collects your fare, which will be between B7 and B15. Due to the recent construction of some low bridges, all passengers change on to a different boat at Pratunam and then again at the stop way out east on Sukhumvit Soi 71 – just follow the crowd.

## Skytrain

The long-awaited elevated railway known as the **BTS Skytrain** or *rot fai faa* (ⓦwww.bts.co.th) is now operating in Bangkok, after over thirty years of planning, fudging and building. Although the network is limited, it provides a much faster alternative to the bus, is clean, efficient and vigorously air-conditioned, and – because fares are comparatively high for Bangkokians – is rarely crowded.

## Central stops for the Chao Phraya express boat

1 Thewes (all daily standard and special express boats) – for Thewes guest houses.

2 Banglamphu (daily standard) – for Thanon Khao San and Banglamphu guest houses.

3 Phra Pinklao Bridge (all daily standard and special express boats) – for Thonburi shops and city buses to the Southern Bus Terminal.

4 Bangkok Noi (daily standard) – for trains to Kanchanaburi.

5 Wang Lang (or Prannok; all daily standard and special express boats) – for Siriraj Hospital.

6 Chang (daily standard and red and orange flag) – for the Grand Palace.

7 Thien (daily standard) – for Wat Po, and the cross-river ferry to Wat Arun.

8 Ratchini (aka Rajinee; daily standard).

9 Saphan Phut (Memorial Bridge; daily standard and red and orange flag) – for Pahurat, Pak Khlong Talat (and Wat Prayoon in Thonburi).

10 Rachavongse (aka Rajawong; all daily standard and special express boats) – for Chinatown.

11 Harbour Department (daily standard).

12 Si Phraya (all daily standard and special express boats) – walk north past the *Sheraton Royal Orchid Hotel* for River City shopping complex.

13 Wat Muang Kae (daily standard) – for GPO.

14 Oriental (all daily standard and special express boats) – for Thanon Silom.

15 Sathorn (all daily standard and special express boats) – for Thanon Sathorn.

Numbers correspond to those on the map on pp.84–85.

There are only two Skytrain lines, both running every few minutes from 6am to midnight, with **fares** of around B15–45 per trip depending on distance travelled. Currently, the only **passes** available that are likely to appeal to any visitors cost B250/B300 for ten/fifteen trips (B160/210 for students), but watch out for new deals being introduced.

The **Sukhumvit Line** runs from Mo Chit (stop #N8) in the northern part of the city (near Chatuchak Market and the Northern Bus Terminal), south via Victory Monument (N3) to the interchange, **Central Station** (CS), at Siam Square, and then east along Thanon Ploenchit and Thanon Sukhumvit, via the Eastern Bus Terminal (Ekamai; E7), to On Nut (Soi 77, Thanon Sukhumvit; E9); the whole journey to the eastern end of town from Mo Chit takes around thirty minutes. The **Silom Line** runs from the National Stadium (W1), just west of Siam Square, through Central Station, and then south along Thanon Rajdamri, Thanon Silom and Thanon Sathorn, via Sala Daeng near Patpong (S2), to Saphan Taksin (Sathorn Bridge; S6), to link up with the full gamut of express boats on the Chao Phraya River. Free feeder buses, currently covering seven circular routes mostly along Thanon Sukhumvit, are geared more for commuters than visitors, but pick up a copy of the ubiquitous free BTS **map** if you want more information.

The Skytrain network is just the first phase of a planned integrated city transport programme that will be greatly enhanced by the opening of an underground rail system, currently due in 2002. The subway will run from the central Hualamphong Railway Station, east along Thanon Rama IV, then north up Soi Asoke/Thanon Ratchadapisek before terminating at Mo Chit in the north of the city.

## Taxis

Bangkok **taxis** come in three forms, and are so plentiful that you rarely have to wait more than a couple of minutes before spotting an empty one of any description. Neither tuk-tuks nor motorbike taxis have meters, so you should agree on a price before setting off, and expect to do a fair amount of haggling. Rates for all rise after midnight, and during rush hours when each journey takes far longer.

The most sedate option, Bangkok's metered, air-conditioned **taxi cabs**, is also the most expensive, but well worth the extra in the heat of the day; look out for the "TAXI METER" sign on the roof, which should be illuminated when the cab is available for hire. Fares start at B35, on a clearly visible meter in the front of the vehicle which the driver should reset at the start of each trip, and increase in stages on a combined speed/distance formula. Occasionally, drivers will refuse long, slow, less profitable journeys across town (especially in the middle of the afternoon, when many cabs have to return to the depot for a change of drivers), or, at quieter times of day, will take you on a roundabout, more expensive route to your destination. If a string of metered-cab drivers don't like the sound of your destination, you'll have to try to negotiate a flat fare with one of them, or with one of the now-rare unmetered cabs (denoted by a "TAXI" sign on the roof).

Slightly less stable but typically Thai, **tuk-tuks** can carry three passengers comfortably and are the standard way of making shortish journeys (Banglamphu to Patpong costs at least B80). These noisy, three-wheeled, open-sided buggies fully expose you to the worst of Bangkok's pollution, but are the least frustrating type of city transport – they are a lot nippier than taxi cabs, and the drivers have no qualms about taking semi-legal measures to avoid grid-locks. Be aware, however, that tuk-tuk drivers tend to speak less English than taxi drivers – and there have been cases of robberies and attacks on women passengers late at night. Even during the day it's quite common for tuk-tuk drivers to try and con their passengers into visiting a jewellery or expensive souvenir shop with them, for which they get a hefty commission; the usual tactic involves falsely informing tourists that the Grand Palace is closed (see p.56), and offering instead a ridiculously cheap, even free, city tour – always bear in mind that fuel is around B20/litre and that no honest tuk-tuk driver would make even a short journey for less than B30. Because of the rise in these scams, the Bangkok Tourist Board now advises tourists to take metered taxis instead of tuk-tuks or, failing that, to make sure they take a tuk-tuk with a white "TAXI" sign on the roof, which at least means it's registered to take passengers.

Least costly (a short trip, say from Banglamphu to Wat Po, should cost B20) and quickest of the trio are **motorbike taxis**, though these are rarely used by tourists as they carry only one passenger and are too dangerous to recommend for cross-city journeys. Still, if you've got nerves of steel, pick the riders out by their numbered, coloured vests or find their taxi rank, often at the entrance to a long soi. Crash helmets are compulsory on all main roads in the capital and passengers should insist on wearing one (traffic police fine non-wearers on the spot), though the local press has reported complaints from people who've caught head-lice this way (they suggest wearing a head scarf under the helmet).

# Accommodation

If your time in Bangkok is limited, you should think especially carefully about what you want to do in the city before deciding which part of town to stay in. Traffic jams are so appalling here that you may not want to explore too far from your hotel, and accommodation in some parts of the city is significantly more expensive than others.

For double rooms under B400, your widest choice lies with the **guest houses** of Banglamphu and the smaller, dingier travellers' ghetto that has grown up around Soi Ngam Duphli, off the south side of Thanon Rama IV. Bangkok guest houses are tailored to the independent traveller's needs and often have genuine single rooms with prices to match, a rarity elsewhere; many also have left-luggage rooms. The most inexpensive rooms here are no-frills crash pads: small and often windowless, with thin walls and shared bathrooms. Unless you pay cash in advance, bookings are rarely accepted by guest houses, but it's often worth phoning to establish whether a place is full already. During peak season (Nov–Feb) you may have difficulty getting a room after noon.

**Moderate and expensive** rooms are mainly concentrated downtown around Siam Square and in the area between Thanon Rama IV and Thanon Charoen Krung (New Road), along Thanon Sukhumvit, where the eastern suburbs start, and to a lesser extent in Chinatown. Air-conditioned rooms with hot-water bathrooms can be had for as little as B500 in these areas, but for that you're looking at a rather basic cubicle; you'll probably have to pay more like B1000 for a place with room to breathe, smart furnishings and a swimming pool, or B3000 and over for a room in a five-star, international chain hotel. Details of accommodation **near the airport** are given on p.86.

## Banglamphu

Nearly all backpackers head straight for **Banglamphu**, Bangkok's long-established travellers' ghetto, location of the least expensive accommodation in the city. Within easy reach of the Grand Palace and other major sights in Ratanakosin (a riverfront walkway from Phra Athit to Ratanakosin is in the offing), Banglamphu is served by plenty of **public transport**. All the guest houses listed lie only a few minutes' walk from one of two Chao Phraya Express boat stops (see the box on p.94), and public longtail boats also ply one of the khlongs in the area (see p.92). Useful **bus routes** in and out of Banglamphu include ordinary bus #3, air-con #12 and air-con #32 to and from Mo Chit Northern Bus Terminal; air-con #7 and air-con #11 to and from the Southern Bus Terminal; air-con #11 to and from the Eastern Bus Terminal; and #53 (ordinary) to and from Hualamphong Station. Numerous buses connect Banglamphu with Chatuchak Weekend Market, including air-con #3, #9, #10, #12 and #39; ordinary bus #15 runs to Siam Square; #53 (ordinary) goes to the Grand Palace, and #56 (ordinary) to Chinatown; see p.92 for full details. Airport Bus AB2 also has several stops in Banglamphu (see p86).

At the heart of Banglamphu is the legendary **Thanon Khao San** – almost a caricature of a travellers' centre, crammed with guest houses, dodgy travel agents and restaurants serving yoghurt shakes and muesli, the sidewalks lined with ethnic clothes stalls, racks of bootleg music and software CDs, tattooists and hair-braiders. It's colourful, noisy and a good place to meet other travellers, and is especially enjoyable at night when Khao San is closed to cars and the street throngs with milling shoppers and restaurant tables that spill off the pavements. On the down side, the whole scene can get a bit wearing, and the accommodation on Khao San itself is noisy and poor value, with few places offering windows in their rooms. If you want the benefits of Thanon Khao San without the bustle, try the smaller, quieter roads off and around it: **Soi Chana Songkhram**, which encircles the wat of the same name; **Phra Athit**, running parallel to the Chao Phraya River and packed with trendy Thai café-bars and restaurants (it also has the most useful express-boat stop); or the residential alleyways that parallel Thanon Khao San to the south, **Trok Mayom** and **Damnoen Klang Neua**. About ten minutes' walk north from Thanon Khao San, the **Thanon Samsen sois** offer a more authentically Thai atmosphere, while a further fifteen minutes' walk in the same direction will take you to **Thanon Sri Ayutthaya**, behind the National Library, a seven-minute walk from the **Thewes** express-boat stop, the most attractive area in Banglamphu, where rooms are larger and guest houses smaller. We've listed only the cream of what's on offer in each small area in Banglamphu: if your first choice is full there'll almost certainly be a vacancy somewhere just along the soi, if not right next door.

Banglamphu is well used to serving travellers' needs, so facilities here are second to none. The excellent **Bangkok Information Centre** is on Thanon Phra Athit, and there's a 24-hour tourist information and assistance booth in front of the police station on the west corner of Thanon Khao San. If you plan to stay in Banglamphu, arrange to have **poste restante** sent to one of the area's two post offices rather than to the GPO, which is inconveniently far away on Charoen Krung; the one closest to Khao San is Ratchadamnoen Post Office on the eastern stretch of Soi Damnoen Klang Neua, but Banglamphubon Post Office near Wat Bowoniwes is also very handy (for full details see p.163). Though there are several private companies offering poste restante services in Banglamphu, their service tends to be haphazard at best; the Khao San business that advertises itself as "GPO" is a private operation. Most guest houses will receive faxes for guests, and their numbers are listed below. Almost every alternate building on Thanon Khao San and on the west arm of Soi Ram Bhuttri offers **internet access**, as do many of the guest houses; intense competition keeps the rates very low. There are also Catnet Internet terminals (see Basics, p.54) at the Ratchadamnoen Post Office. Numerous money **exchange** places can be found on Thanon Khao San, including two branches of national banks (with ATMs), dozens of shops and travel agents, and a couple of self-service laundries.

## Thanon Khao San and Soi Damnoen Klang Neua

**Chart Guest House**, 58–60 Thanon Khao San ☎02/282 0171. Clean, comfortable enough hotel in the heart of backpacker land; the cheapest rooms share bathroom and the priciest have air-con. Rooms in all categories are a little cramped, but they all have windows. ❷–❹

**J & Joe House**, 1 Trok Mayom ☎02/281 2949. Simple, inexpensive rooms, all with shared bathrooms, in a traditional wooden house located among real Thai homes (very unusual for Banglamphu) in a narrow alley off Khao San. ❷

**Khao San Palace Hotel**, 139 Thanon Khao San ☎02/282 0578. Clean and well-appointed smallish hotel, where all rooms have attached bathrooms, but only some have windows. The priciest options have air-con and TV. Avoid the rooms overlooking Khao San as they can be noisy at night. ❸–❹

**Lek House**, 125 Thanon Khao San ☎02/281 8441. Classic Khao San guest house, old-style with small, basic rooms and shared facilities, but less shabby than many others in the same price bracket. ❷

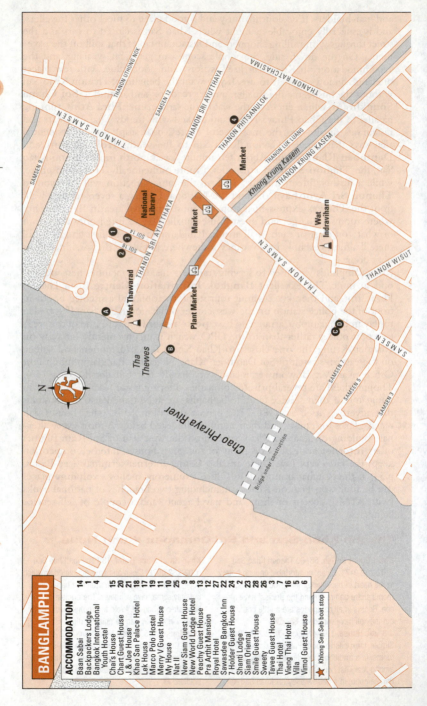

**BANGLAMPHU**

**ACCOMMODATION**

| | |
|---|---|
| Baan Sabai | 14 |
| Backpackers Lodge | 1 |
| Bangkok International Youth Hostel | 4 |
| Chai's House | 15 |
| Chart Guest House | 20 |
| J & Joe House | 21 |
| Khao San Palace Hotel | 18 |
| Lek House | 17 |
| Marco Polo Hostel | 19 |
| Merry V Guest House | 11 |
| My House | 10 |
| Nat II | 25 |
| New Siam Guest House | 9 |
| New World Lodge Hotel | 8 |
| Peachy Guest House | 13 |
| Pra Arthit Mansion | 12 |
| Royal Hotel | 27 |
| Sawasdee Bangkok Inn | 22 |
| 7 Holder Guest House | 24 |
| Shanti Lodge | 2 |
| Siam Oriental | 23 |
| Smile Guest House | 28 |
| Sweety | 26 |
| Tavee Guest House | 3 |
| Thai Hotel | 7 |
| Vieng Thai Hotel | 16 |
| Villa | 5 |
| Vimol Guest House | 6 |

★ Khlong Sen Seb boat stop

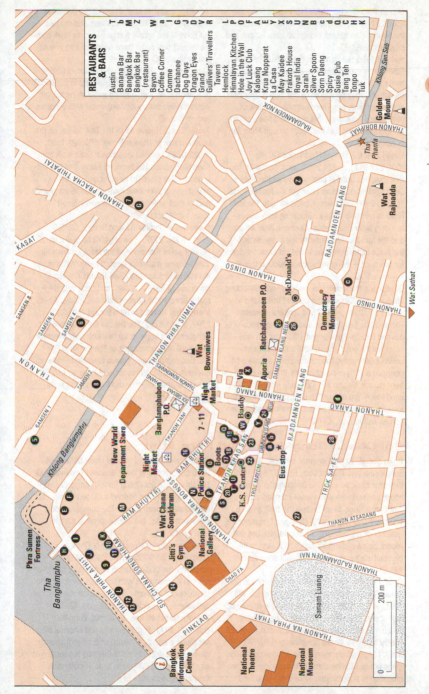

▼ *Wat Suthat*

**RESTAURANTS & BARS**

| | |
|---|---|
| Austin | T |
| Banana Bar | b |
| Bangkok Bar | M |
| Bangkok Bar (restaurant) | Z |
| Bayon | W |
| Coffee Corner | a |
| Comme | I |
| Dachanee | G |
| Dog Days | J |
| Dragon Eyes | D |
| Grand | V |
| Gullivers' Travellers Tavern | R |
| Hemlock | L |
| Himalayan Kitchen | P |
| Hole in the Wall | O |
| Joy Luck Club | F |
| Kaloang | A |
| Krua Nopparat | E |
| La Casa | Y |
| May Kaidee | X |
| Prakorb House | S |
| Royal India | U |
| Sarah | N |
| Silver Spoon | B |
| Sorn Daeng | c |
| Spicy | d |
| Susie Pub | Q |
| Tang Teh | C |
| Tonpo | H |
| Tuk | K |

**Marco Polo Hostel**, 108/7–10 Thanon Khao San ☎02/281 1715. Fairly grim windowless boxes in the heart of the ghetto, though all have air-con and private shower. ❸

**Nat II**, 91–95 Soi Damnoen Klang Neua (aka Soi Post Office) ☎02/282 0211. Large, clean rooms, some with windows, in a fairly quiet location, though you may be woken by the 5am prayer calls at the local mosque. There are only a couple of other guest houses on this road, so it has a friendly, neighbourhood feel to it, even though Khao San is less than 200m away. ❷

**Royal Hotel**, 2 Thanon Rajdamnoen Klang ☎02/222 9111, ℮224 2083. Used mostly for conferences, this hotel is conveniently located just a 5min stroll from Sanam Luang (it's a further 10min or so to the Grand Palace), but getting to Thanon Khao San entails a life-endangering leap across two very busy main roads. All rooms have air-con, and the facilities are perfectly adequate, though the place lacks atmosphere and isn't exactly plush for the price – the grim facade is enough to put anyone off. ❼

**Sawasdee Bangkok Inn**, on a tiny soi connecting Thanon Khao San with the parallel Trok Mayom. ☎02/280 1251, ℮281 7818, ⓦwww.sawasdee -hotels.com. Easy to spot because of its mauve painted facade. Popular and efficiently run mini-hotel, with a good atmosphere and a range of comfortable rooms, though the cheapest are a bit cramped and have no bathroom. Priciest options here include air-con and TV, which makes them good value. You can get Thai massage therapy and lessons on the premises, and there's an attractive garden eating area. ❸–❹

**7 Holder Guest House**, 216/2–3 Soi Damnoen Klang Neua ☎02/281 3682. Clean and modern, but none of the simply furnished rooms have bathrooms and only some have windows. Fan and air-con available. ❷–❸

**Siam Oriental**, 190 Thanon Khao San ☎02/629 0312, ℮629 0310. Guest house right in the middle of Thanon Khao San, offering smallish rooms, all with attached bathrooms and some with windows and air-con. ❸

**Smile Guest House**, 151–161 Trok Sa-ke, off the southern arm of Thanon Tanao ☎02/622 1590, ℮622 0730. Located less than a 5min walk from Khao San, across Rajdamnoen Klang, this is a fairly good-value place that's quiet and out of the tourist ghetto. All rooms have air-conditioning and decent tiled bathrooms, and there's internet access downstairs. ❸

**Sweety**, Soi Damnoen Klang Neua ☎02/280 2191, ℮280 2192, ⓔsweetygh@hotmail.com. Popular place that's one of the least expensive in Banglamphu; it's nicely located away from the fray but convenient for Khao San. Rooms are very small but all have windows, and beds with thick mattresses; some have private bathrooms. ❶–❷

**Vieng Thai Hotel**, Soi Ram Bhuttri ☎02/280 5392, ℮281 8153. The best of the options in Banglamphu's upper price bracket: convenient for the shops and restaurants of Thanon Khao San and Banglamphu, and geared towards tourists not business people. All rooms here have air-con, TV, hot water and mini-bar, and there's a big swimming pool. ❼

## Soi Chana Songkhram and Phra Athit

**Baan Sabai**, 12 Soi Rongmai, between Soi Chana Songkhram and Thanon Chao Fa ☎02/629 1599. Welcome newcomer to the Banglamphu guest-house scene, located in a quiet soi overlooking the Wat Chana Songkhram compound. Built round a courtyard, this large, hotel-style guest house has a range of clean, comfortable, decent-sized en-suite rooms, some of them air-con, and is host to the pleasant *Bangkok Times* restaurant downstairs. ❸–❹

**Chai's House**, 49/4–8 Soi Rongmai, between Soi Chana Songkhram and Thanon Chao Fa ☎02/281 4901, ℮281 8686. Large, clean, simple rooms, all with shared bathrooms. The rate is per person, which makes singles better value than doubles. ❷

**Merry V**, 35 Soi Chana Songkhram ☎02/282 9267. Large, efficiently run and scrupulously clean guest house offering some of the cheapest accommodation in Banglamphu. Rooms are basic and

slightly cramped, and they all share bathrooms. Good noticeboard in the downstairs restaurant. ❷

**My House**, 37 Soi Chana Songkhram ☎02/282 9263. Popular place offering a range of simple but exceptionally clean rooms. The cheapest rooms share bathrooms, the most expensive have air-con. ❷–❹

**New Siam Guest House**, 21 Soi Chana Songkhram ☎02/282 4554, ℮281 7461. Efficiently run place offering comfortably furnished hotel-style rooms; all with fans and windows, and plenty of clothes hooks. The cheapest rooms share bathrooms, the priciest have air-con. ❸–❺

**Peachy Guest House**, 10 Thanon Phra Athit ☎02/281 6471. Popular, cheap and cheerful place set round a small courtyard, with clean if spartan rooms, most with shared bathrooms but some with air-con. Also has B80 dorm beds. Popular with long-stay guests. ❷–❸

**Pra Arthit Mansion**, 22 Thanon Phra Athit ☎02/280 0744, ℹ280 0742, ℹpraarthit@bkk .a-net.net.th. Recommended mid-range place offering very good, comfortable rooms with air-con, TV, hot water and mini-bar. The fifth-floor rooms have the best views of Banglamphu's rooftops. No restaurant, lobby or other hotel facilities, but staff are friendly and the location is quiet and convenient. ❺

## Samsen and Thewes

**Backpackers Lodge**, Soi 14, 85 Thanon Sri Ayutthaya ☎02/282 3231. Quiet, family-run place in the peaceful Thewes quarter of north Banglamphu. Just a handful of simple rooms, all with shared bathroom, and a communal area downstairs. The cheapest accommodation in this area. ❷

**Bangkok International Youth Hostel**, 25/2 Thanon Phitsanulok ☎02/282 0950, ℹ628 7416, ℹwww.tyha.org. Mostly patronized by travelling Thai students: only open to YHA members and nothing special considering the competition. The double rooms have bathrooms, and some have air-con, and there are dorm beds for B70. ❷–❸

**New World Lodge Hotel**, Samsen Soi 2 ☎02/281 5596, ℹ282 5614, ℹwww.new-lodge.com. Good-value, large, unadorned rooms, each with a desk, phone, shower and either fan or air-con. All rooms have balconies, and some have khlong views. The cheapest rooms in the less appealing guest-house wing are simply furnished and have shared bathrooms. ❷–❺

**Shanti Lodge**, Soi 16, 37 Thanon Sri Ayutthaya ☎02/281 2497. Quiet, attractively furnished and comfortable rooms make this deservedly the most popular place in the Thewes area. Facilities range from rooms with shared bathrooms to en-suite ones with air-con. The vegetarian restaurant downstairs is recommended. ❸–❺

**Tavee Guest House**, Soi 14, 83 Thanon Sri Ayutthaya ☎02/282 5983. Good-sized rooms; quiet and friendly and one of the cheaper places in the Thewes quarter. Offers rooms with shared bathroom plus some en-suite ones with air-con, as well as B80 dorm beds. ❷–❹

**Thai Hotel**, 78 Thanon Pracha Thipatai ☎02/282 2831, ℹ280 1299. Comfortable enough, but a little overpriced, considering its slightly inconvenient location. All rooms have air-con and there's a decent-sized pool here too. ❼

**Villa**, 230 Samsen Soi 1 ☎02/281 7009. Banglamphu's most therapeutic guest house, a lovely old Thai house and garden with just ten large rooms, each idiosyncratically furnished in simple, semi-traditional style; bathrooms are shared. Fills up quickly, but it's worth going on the waiting list if you're staying a long time. Rooms priced according to their size. ❸–❹

**Vimol Guest House**, 358 Samsen Soi 4 ☎02/281 4615. Old-style, family-run guest house in a quiet but interesting neighbourhood that has just a couple of other tourist places. The simple, cramped rooms have shared bathrooms and a welcoming atmosphere. ❶

# Chinatown and Hualamphong Station area

Not far from the Ratanakosin sights, **Chinatown (Sampeng)** is one of the most vibrant and quintessentially Asian parts of Bangkok. Staying here, or in one of the sois around the conveniently close **Hualamphong Station**, can be noisy, but there's always plenty to look at, and some people choose to base themselves in this area in order to get away from the travellers' scene in Banglamphu. There are a couple of guest houses and a few moderate and expensive hotels here, in among a cluster of seedier places catering mainly to Thais. All listed accommodation is marked on the map on p.128.

Useful **bus** routes for Chinatown include west-bound air-con #7 and ordinary buses #25, #40 and #53, which all go to Ratanakosin (for Wat Po and the Grand Palace); the east-bound #25 and #40 buses both go to Siam Square, where you change onto the Skytrain system. For more transport details, see p.127.

**Bangkok Center**, 328 Thanon Rama IV ☎02/238 4848, ℹ236 1862, ℹwww.bangkokcentrehotel.com. Handily placed upper-mid-range option with efficient service just across the road from the train station. Rooms are smartly furnished, and all have air-con and TV; there's a pool, restaurant and internet access on the premises. ❻

**Chinatown Hotel**, 526 Thanon Yaowarat ☎02/225 0204, ℹ226 1295,

ⓦ www.chinatown.co.th. Classy Chinese hotel in the heart of the gold-trading district. Comfortably furnished rooms, all with air-con and TV. Kids under 12 can share their parents' rooms for free. ⑤–⑥

**FF Guest House**, 338/10 Trok La-O, off Thanon Rama IV ☏ 02/233 4168. The closest budget accommodation to the station, but very basic indeed and a bit of a last resort. To get there from the station, cross Thanon Rama IV and walk left for 200m, and then right down Trok La-O to the end of the alley. ②

**Krung Kasem Sri Krung Hotel**, 1860 Thanon Krung Kasem ☏ 02/225 0132, ⒡ 225 4705. Mid-range but rather shabby Chinese hotel just 50m across the khlong from the station. All rooms have air-con and TV but could do with an overhaul. ④

**New Empire Hotel**, 572 Thanon Yaowarat ☏ 02/234 6990, ⒡ 234 6997, ⓔ newempirehotel @hotmail.com. Medium-sized hotel right in the thick of the Chinatown bustle, offering fairly run-of-the-mill rooms, with shower and air-con. ④

**River View Guest House**, 768 Soi Panurangsri, Thanon Songvad ☏ 02/235 8501, ⒡ 237 5428. Large but unattractive rooms, with fan and cold water at the lower end of the range, air-con, hot water, TVs and fridges at the top. Great views over the bend in the river, especially from the top-floor restaurant, and handy for Chinatown,

Hualamphong Station and the GPO. Find it through a maze of crumbling Chinese buildings: head north for 400m from River City shopping centre (on the express-boat line) along Soi Wanit 2, before following signs to the guest house to the left. ④–⑤

**TT2 Guest House**, 516 Soi Sawang, off Thanon Maha Nakorn ☏ 02/236 2946, ⒡ 236 3054, ⓔ ttguesthouse@hotmail.com. The best budget place in the station area, though significantly more expensive than *FF*. Clean, friendly and well run with good bulletin boards and traveller-orientated facilities, including left luggage at B7 a day and a small library. All rooms share bathrooms, and there are B100 beds in a three-person dorm. Roughly a 15min walk from either the station or the Si Phraya express-boat stop; to get here from the station, cross Thanon Rama IV, then walk left for 250m and right down Thanon Maha Nakorn as far as the *Full Moon* restaurant (opposite Trok Fraser and Neave), where you turn left and then first right. ③

**White Orchid Hotel**, 409–421 Thanon Yaowarat ☏ 02/226 0026, ⒡ 225 6403. One of the plushest hotels in Chinatown, right at the hub of the gold-trading quarter. All rooms have air-con and TV, and there's a *dim sum* restaurant on the premises. ⑥

# Downtown: Siam Square and Thanon Ploenchit

**Siam Square** – not really a square, but a grid of shops and restaurants between Phrayathai and Henri Dunant roads – and nearby **Thanon Ploenchit** are as central as Bangkok gets, handy for all kinds of shopping, nightlife, the Skytrain and Hualamphong station. There's no budget accommodation here, but a few scaled-up guest houses have sprung up alongside the expensive hotels. Concentrated in their own "ghetto" on **Soi Kasemsan 1**, which runs north off Thanon Rama I just west of Thanon Phrayathai and is the next soi along from Jim Thompson's House (see p.137), these offer an informal guest-house atmosphere, with hotel comforts – air-conditioning and en-suite hot-water bathrooms – at moderate prices. Accommodation here is marked on the map opposite.

**A-One Inn**, 25/13 Soi Kasemsan 1, Thanon Rama I ☏ 02/215 3029, ⒡ 216 4771. The original upscale guest house, owned by a retired police colonel, and still justifiably popular, with helpful staff, satellite TV and a sociable café; no single rooms. ④

**The Bed & Breakfast**, 36/42 Soi Kasemsan 1, Thanon Rama I ☏ 02/215 3004, ⒡ 215 2493. Bright, clean, family-run and friendly, though the rooms – carpeted and with en-suite telephones –

are a bit cramped. As the name suggests, a simple breakfast is included. ④

**Hilton International**, Nai Lert Park, 2 Thanon Witthayu ☏ 02/253 0123, ⒡ 253 6509, ⓦ www.hilton.com. The main distinguishing feature of this member of the international luxury chain is its acres of beautiful gardens, overlooked by many of the spacious, balconied bedrooms; set into the verdant landscaped grounds are a swimming pool, jogging track, tennis courts and popular

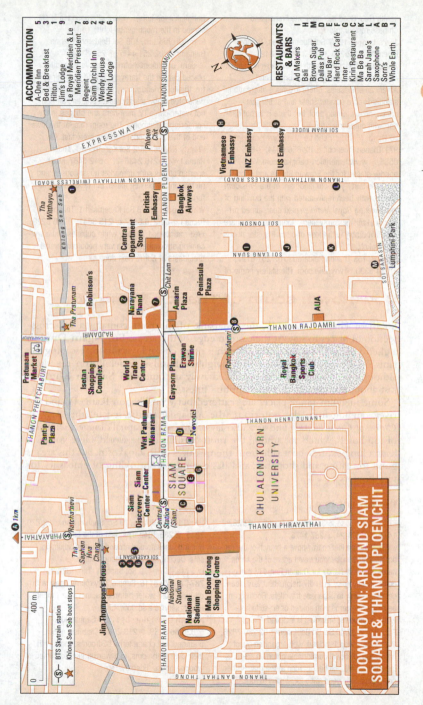

**ACCOMMODATION**

| | |
|---|---|
| A-One Inn | 5 |
| Bed & Breakfast | 3 |
| Hilton | 1 |
| Jim's Lodge | 9 |
| Le Royal Meridien & Le Meridien President | 7 |
| Regent | 8 |
| Siam Orchid Inn | 2 |
| Wendy House | 4 |
| White Lodge | 6 |

**RESTAURANTS & BARS**

| | |
|---|---|
| Ad Makers | I |
| Bali | H |
| Brown Sugar | M |
| Dallas Pub | E |
| Fou Bar | D |
| Hard Rock Café | F |
| Inter | G |
| Kirin Restaurant | C |
| Ma Be Ba | K |
| Sarah Jane's | L |
| Saxophone | A |
| Som's | B |
| Whole Earth | J |

health club. Good deli-café and French and Chinese restaurants. **9**

**Jim's Lodge**, 125/7 Soi Ruam Rudee, Thanon Ploenchit ☎ 02/255 3100–3, ☏ 253 8492, ✉ anant@asiaaccess.net.th. In a relatively peaceful residential area, handy for the British and American embassies; offers luxurious international standards on a smaller scale and at bargain prices; no swimming pool, but there is a roof garden with outdoor jacuzzi. **7**

**Le Royal Meridien** and **Le Meridien President**, 971 Thanon Ploenchit ☎ 02/656 0444, ☏ 656 0555, 🌐 www.lemeridien-bangkok.com. Very handily placed for the Erawan Shrine and shopping, the thirty-year-old landmark of the *President* has recently been rejuvenated with the building of the towering *Royal Meridien* next door, aimed primarily at business travellers. Room rates compare very favourably with those of other five-star hotels in Bangkok. **9**

**Regent**, 155 Thanon Rajdamri ☎ 02/251 6127, ☏ 254 5390, 🌐 www.rih.com. The stately home of Bangkok's top hotels, where afternoon tea is still served in the monumental lobby. **9**

**Siam Orchid Inn**, 109 Soi Rajdamri, Thanon Rajdamri ☎ 02/251 4417, ☏ 255 3144, ✉ siam_orchidinn@hotmail.com. Very handily placed behind the Narayana Phand souvenir centre, this is a friendly, cosy place with an ornately decorated lobby, a tasty restaurant, and air-con, hot water, cable TV, mini-bars and phones in the comfortable bedrooms. The room rate (at the lower end of this price code) includes breakfast. **7**

**Wendy House**, 36/2 Soi Kasemsan 1, Thanon Rama I ☎ 02/216 2436–7, ☏ 612 3487. Most spartan of this soi's upmarket guest houses, and no frills in the service either, but clean and comfortable enough. **4**

**White Lodge**, 36/8 Soi Kasemsan 1, Thanon Rama I ☎ 02/216 8867 or 215 3041, ☏ 216 8228. Well-maintained, shining white cubicles and a welcoming atmosphere, with very good continental breakfasts at *Sorn's* next door. **4**

# Downtown: south of Thanon Rama IV

South of Thanon Rama IV, the left bank of the river contains a full cross-section of places to stay. At the eastern edge of this area is **Soi Ngam Duphli**, a ghetto of budget guest houses which is often choked with traffic escaping the jams on Thanon Rama IV – the neighbourhood is generally on the slide, although the best guest houses, tucked away on quiet **Soi Saphan Khu**, can just about compare with Banglamphu's finest.

Some medium-range places are scattered between Thanon Rama IV and the river, ranging from the notorious (the *Malaysia*) to the sedate (the *Bangkok Christian Guest House*). The area also lays claim to the capital's biggest selection of top hotels, which are among the most opulent in the world. Here you're at least a long express-boat ride from the treasures of Ratanakosin, but this area is good for eating and shopping, and has a generous sprinkling of embassies for visa-hunters.

## Inexpensive

**ETC Guest House**, 5/3 Soi Ngam Duphli ☎ 02/287 1477 or 286 9424, ☏ 287 1478, ✉ ETC@mozart.inet.co.th. Above a branch of the recommended Banglamphu travel agent of the same name, and very handy for Thanon Rama IV, though consequently noisy. Friendly, helpful and very clean, catering mainly to Japanese travellers. Rooms can be dingy, and come with shared or en-suite hot-water bathrooms; breakfast is included. **2**–**3**

**Freddy's 2**, 27/40 Soi Sri Bamphen ☎ 02/286 7826, ☏ 213 2097. Popular, clean, well-organized guest house with plenty of comfortable common areas, including a café and beer garden at the rear. Rather noisy. Especially good rates for singles (B100). **2**

**Lee 3 Guest House**, 13 Soi Saphan Khu ☎ 02/679 7045, ☏ 286 3042. The best of the Lee family of guest houses spread around this and adjoining sois. Decent and quiet, though stuffy. **2**

**Lee Mansion 4**, 9 Soi Saphan Khu ☎ 02/286 7874 or 679 8116. Simple, airy rooms, most with en-suite cold-water bathrooms, in a dour modern tower; service also dour. **2**

**Madam Guest House**, 11 Soi Saphan Khu ☎ 02/286 9289, ☏ 213 2087. Cleanish, often cramped, but characterful bedrooms, some with their own bathrooms, in a warren-like, balconied wooden house. Friendly. **2**

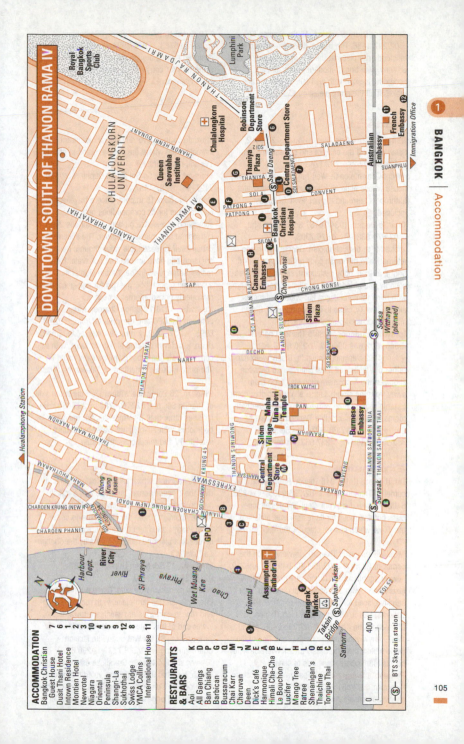

# DOWNTOWN: SOUTH OF THANON RAMA IV

**ACCOMMODATION**

| | |
|---|---|
| Bangkok Christian | 7 |
| Guest House | 6 |
| Dusit Thani Hotel | 1 |
| Intown Residence | 2 |
| Montien Hotel | 3 |
| Newrotel | 10 |
| Niagara | 4 |
| Oriental | 5 |
| Peninsula | 9 |
| Shangri-La | 12 |
| Sukhothai | 8 |
| Swiss Lodge | |
| YMCA Collins | |
| International House | 11 |

**RESTAURANTS & BARS**

| | |
|---|---|
| Aoi | K |
| Ali Gaengs | D |
| Ban Chiang | P |
| Barbican | G |
| Bussaracum | Q |
| Chai Karr | M |
| Charuvan | J |
| Deen | N |
| Dick's Café | E |
| Harmonique | A |
| Himali Cha-Cha | B |
| Le Bouchon | F |
| Lucifer | I |
| Mango Tree | H |
| Ratree | L |
| Shenanigan's | O |
| Thaichine | R |
| Tongue Thai | C |

Royal Bangkok Sports Club

Lumphini Park

THANON RAJDAMRI

THANON RAJDAMRI

CHULALONGKORN UNIVERSITY

Chulalongkorn Hospital

Robinson Department Store

Queen Saovabha Institute

THANON HENRI DUNANT

THANON HENRI DUNANT

THANON PHRAYATHAI

THANON RAMA IV

Thaniya Plaza

Central Department Store

SALADAENG

Sala Daeng (S)

SOI 2

THANIYA

PATPONG 2

PATPONG 1

Bangkok Christian Hospital

SILOM 6

SOI SALADAENG

SOI SALADAENG 2

CONVENT

SUANPHLU

Australian Embassy

French Embassy

Immigration Office

Canadian Embassy

SOLAHUMAN RALDHON

Chong Nonsi

SAP

CHONG NONSI

Chong Nonsi (S)

THANON SILOM

Silom Plaza

Suksa Witthaya (planned)

NARET

DECHO

THANON SI PHRAYA

SOI SUKSA WITTHAYA

TROK VAITHI

PAN

Maha Uma Devi Temple

Silom Village

PRAMUAN

Burmese Embassy

THANON SURIWONG

KRUNG 45

THANON MAHESAK

Central Department Store

SURASAK

SI PHRAYA

Hualamphong Station

THANON MAHA NAKHON

THANON MAHA PHUTHARAM

MAHA PHUTHARAM

Khlong Krung Kasem

CHAROEN KRUNG (NEW ROAD)

THANON CHAROEN KRUNG (NEW ROAD)

CHAROEN PHANIT

Harbour Dept.

River City

Chao Phraya River

Wat Muang Kee

Oriental

Assumption Cathedral

Bangrak Market

GPO

EXPRESSWAY

SI CHAREN

Taksin (S)

Saphan Taksin

SOL 25

Surasak (S)

Surasak

THANON SATHORN NUA

THANON SAT-ORN THAI

SRI VIENG

SURASAK

Sathorn

Sathorn Bridge

(S) — BTS Skytrain station

0        400 m

N

**Sala Thai Daily Mansion**, 15 Soi Saphan Khu ☎02/287 1436. The pick of the area. A clean and efficiently run place at the end of this quiet, shaded alley, with bright, modern rooms (priced according to size) with wall fans; a roof terrace makes it all the more pleasant. ❷–❸

**TTO Guest House**, 2/35 Soi Sri Bamphen ☎02/286 6783, ℻679 7994. Rough, poorly designed rooms, though all with fridge and phone, some with air-con and hot water, in a friendly establishment. ❸

## Moderate

**Bangkok Christian Guest House**, 123 Soi 2, Saladaeng, off the eastern end of Thanon Silom ☎02/234 1852, ℻237 1742, ✉bcgh@loxinfo.co.th. Well-run, orderly missionary house whose plain air-con rooms with hot-water bathrooms surround a quiet lawn. Breakfast included. ❼

**Charlie House**, 1034/36–37 Soi Saphan Khu ☎02/679 8330–1, ℻679 7308, ✉charlie_h_th@yahoo.com. Decent mid-range alternative to the crash pads of Soi Ngam Duphli: bright, air-con lobby restaurant, serving good, reasonably priced food, and small, carpeted bedrooms with minimal floral decor, hot-water bathrooms, air-con and TV, close to Thanon Rama IV. Cheap internet access. No smoking. ❹

**Intown Residence**, 1086/6 Thanon Charoen Krung ☎02/639 0960–2, ℻236 6886, ✉fann4199@asiaaccess.net.th. Clean, welcoming, rather old-fashioned hotel sandwiched between shops on the noisy main road (ask for a room away from the street). Large, slightly chintzy, comfortable rooms come with air-con, hot-water bathrooms, mini-bars, satellite TVs and phones. ❺

**La Residence**, 173/8–9 Thanon Suriwong ☎02/266 5400–1, ℻237 9322, ✉residenc

@loxinfo.co.th. Above *All Gaengs* restaurant, an intimate hotel where the cutesy rooms stretch to TVs and mini-bars. ❼

**Malaysia Hotel**, 54 Soi Ngam Duphli ☎02/679 7127–36, ℻287 1457, ✉malaysia@ksc15.th.com. Once a travellers' legend, famous for its compendious noticeboard, now something of a sleaze pit with a notorious 24hr coffeeshop and massage parlour. The accommodation itself is reasonable value though: the rooms are large and have air-con and hot-water bathrooms; some have fridge, TV and video too. There's a swimming pool (B50 per day for non-guests) and reasonably priced internet access. ❻

**Newrotel**, 1216/1 Thanon Charoen Krung, between the GPO and the *Oriental Hotel* ☎02/630 6995, ℻237 1102, ✉newrotel@idn.co.th. Smart, clean, kitschly decorated and good value, with air-con, hot-water bathrooms, fridges and cable TV. The price includes American or Chinese breakfast. ❼

**Niagara**, 26 Soi Suksa Witthaya, off the south side of Thanon Silom ☎02/233 5783, ℻233 6563. No facilities other than a coffeeshop, but the clean bedrooms, with air-con, hot-water bathrooms, satellite TV and telephones are a snip. ❹

## Expensive

**Dusit Thani Hotel**, 946 Thanon Rama IV, on the corner of Thanon Silom ☎02/236 0450–9, ℻236 6400, ⊕www.dusit.com. Centrally placed top-class hotel, famous for its restaurants, including the *Tiara*, which has spectacular top-floor views. ❾

**Montien Hotel**, 54 Thanon Surawongse, on the corner of Rama IV ☎02/233 7060–9, ℻236 5219, ⊕www.montien.com. Grand, airy and solicitous luxury hotel, with a strongly Thai character, very handily placed for business and nightlife. ❾

**Oriental Hotel**, 48 Oriental Ave, off Thanon Charoen Krung (New Rd) ☎02/236 0400, ℻236 1937, ⊕www.mandarin-oriental.com. One of the world's best, this effortlessly stylish riverside hotel boasts immaculate standards of service. ❾

**Peninsula Bangkok**, 333 Thanon Charoennakorn, Klongsan ☎02/861 2888, ℻861 1112, ⊕www.peninsula.com Superb top-class hotel with

flawless service, which self-consciously aims to rival the *Oriental* across the river, with a stylish modernity that makes its competitor look a little dated. Although it's on the Thonburi side of the Chao Phraya, the hotel operates a shuttle boat across to a pier and reception area by the *Shangri-La Hotel*. ❾

**Pinnacle**, 17 Soi Ngam Duphli ☎02/287 0111–31, ℻287 3420, ⊕www.pinnaclehotels.com. Bland but reliable international-standard place, with rooftop jacuzzi and fitness centre; rates, which are towards the lower end of this category, include breakfast. ❼

**Shangri-La**, 89 Soi Wat Suan Plu, Thanon Charoen Krung ☎02/236 7777, ℻236 8579, ⊕www.shangri-la.com. Grandiose establishment which, for what it's worth, was voted top hotel in the world by *Condé Nast Traveler* readers in 1996. It boasts the longest river frontage of any hotel in

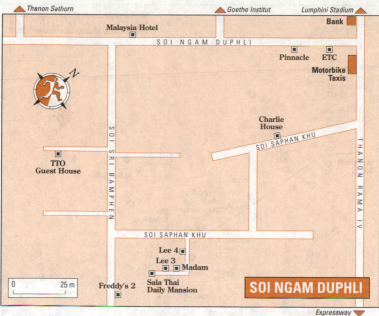

Thanon Sathorn    Goethe Institut    Lumphini Stadium

Bank

Malaysia Hotel

SOI NGAM DUPHLI

Immigration & Ranger

Pinnacle    ETC

Motorbike
Taxis

TTO
Guest House

SOI SRI BAMPHEN

Charlie
House

SOI SAPHAN KHU

THANON RAMA IV

SOI SAPHAN KHU

Lee 4
Lee 3
Madam

Freddy's 2    Sala Thai    **SOI NGAM DUPHLI**
Daily Mansion

0    25 m

Expressway

Bangkok, and makes the most of it with gardens, restaurants – including the award-winning *Salathip* for Thai cuisine – and two pools by the Chao Phraya; the two accommodation wings are linked by free tuk-tuk if you can't be bothered to walk. ❾

**Sukhothai**, 13/3 Thanon Sathorn Thai ☎ 02/287 0222, 🖷 287 4980, 🖝 www.hotelsukhothaibangkok .com. The most elegant of Bangkok's top hotels, its decor inspired by the walled city of Sukhothai: low-rise accommodation coolly furnished in silks, teak and granite, around six acres of gardens and lotus ponds. Good Italian and Thai restaurants. ❾

**Swiss Lodge**, 3 Thanon Convent ☎ 02/233 5345, 🖷 236 9425, 🖝 www.swisslodge.com. Swish, friendly, good-value, solar-powered boutique hotel, just off Thanon Silom and ideally placed for business and nightlife. The imaginatively named theme restaurant *Café Swiss* serves fondue, raclette and all your other Swiss favourites, while the tiny terrace swimming pool confirms the national stereotypes of neatness and clever design. ❽

**YMCA Collins International House**, 27 Thanon Sathorn Thai ☎ 02/287 1900, 287 1996, 🖝 www.ymcabangkok.com. First-class facilities, including swimming pool and cable TV, with no frills. ❼

## Thanon Sukhumvit

**Thanon Sukhumvit** is Bangkok's longest street, continuing east all the way to Cambodia. Packed with high-rise hotels and office blocks, mid-priced foreign-food restaurants, souvenir shops, tailors, bookstores and stall after stall selling fake designer gear, it's a lively place that attracts a high proportion of single male tourists to its enclaves of girlie bars on Soi Nana Tai, Soi Cowboy and the Clinton Entertainment Plaza. But for the most part it's not a seedy area, and is home to many expats and middle-class Thais. Although this is not the place to come if you're on a tight budget, it's a reasonable area for mid-range hotels; the four- and five-star hotels on Sukhumvit tend to be more orientated towards business travellers than tourists, but what they lack in glamour they more than make up for in facilities. The best accommodation here is

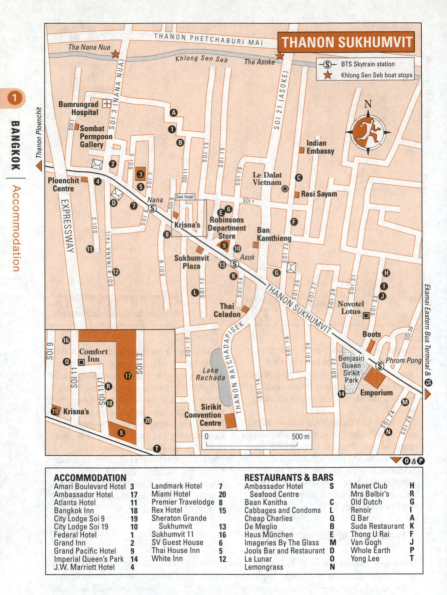

THANON SUKHUMVIT

- Ⓢ BTS Skytrain station
- ★ Khlong Sen Seb boat stops

| ACCOMMODATION | | | RESTAURANTS & BARS | | | |
|---|---|---|---|---|---|---|
| Amari Boulevard Hotel | 3 | Landmark Hotel | 7 | Ambassador Hotel | S | Manet Club | H |
| Ambassador Hotel | 17 | Miami Hotel | 20 | Seafood Centre | | Mrs Balbir's | R |
| Atlanta Hotel | 11 | Premier Travelodge | 8 | Baan Kanitha | C | Old Dutch | G |
| Bangkok Inn | 18 | Rex Hotel | 15 | Cabbages and Condoms | L | Renoir | I |
| City Lodge Soi 9 | 19 | Sheraton Grande | | Cheap Charlies | Q | Q Bar | A |
| City Lodge Soi 19 | 10 | Sukhumvit | 13 | De Meglio | B | Suda Restaurant | K |
| Federal Hotel | 1 | Sukhumvit 11 | 16 | Haus München | E | Thong U Rai | F |
| Grand Inn | 2 | SV Guest House | 6 | Imageries By The Glass | M | Van Gogh | J |
| Grand Pacific Hotel | 9 | Thai House Inn | 5 | Jools Bar and Restaurant | D | Whole Earth | P |
| Imperial Queen's Park | 14 | White Inn | 12 | La Lunar | O | Yong Lee | T |
| J.W. Marriott Hotel | 4 | | | Lemongrass | N | | |

between sois 1 and 21. Advance reservations are accepted at all places listed below and are recommended during high season.

Staying here, you're well served by the **Skytrain**, which has stops all the way along Sukhumvit, making journeys to places such as Siam Square and Chatuchak Weekend Market a fast and hassle-free undertaking. Sukhumvit hotels are also convenient for the Eastern Bus Terminal, with its buses to Pattaya and other east-coast resorts. On the downside, you're a long way from the main Ratanakosin sights, and the sheer volume of traffic on Sukhumvit means that travelling by **bus** across town can take an age – if possible, try to travel to and from Thanon Sukhumvit outside rush hour (7–9am & 3–7pm). Airport Bus AB3 has stops all the way along Thanon Sukhumvit (see opposite); useful buses for getting to Ratanakosin include #8 (air-con) and #25 (ordinary); ordinary buses #25 and #40 go to Hualamphong Station and Chinatown. Full details of bus routes are given on p.92.

A much faster way of getting across town is to hop on one of the longtail **boats** that ply the canals: Khlong Sen Seb, which begins near Democracy Monument in the west of the city, runs parallel with part of Thanon Sukhumvit and has stops at the northern ends of Soi Nana Neua (Soi 3) and Soi Asoke (Soi 21), from where you can either walk down to Thanon Sukhumvit itself, or take a motorbike taxi. This reduces the journey between Thanon Sukhumvit and the Banglamphu/Ratanakosin area to about thirty minutes; for more details on boat routes, see p.92.

## Inexpensive

**The Atlanta**, at the far southern end of Soi 2 ☎02/252 1650, ℉656 8123, ⓦwww.theatlanta hotel.bizland.com. Classic old-style hotel with lots of colonial-era character, welcoming staff, and some of the cheapest accommodation on Sukhumvit. Rooms are simple and a bit scruffy, but all have attached bathrooms; some have air-con and hot water. There are two swimming pools, as well as internet access and a left-luggage facility. The hotel restaurant is recommended, serving an extensive Thai menu which includes lots of vegetarian dishes; classic movies set in Asia are shown in the restaurant every night. ❹–❺
**Miami Hotel**, Soi 13 ☎02/253 5611, ℉253 1266, Ⓔmiamihtl@asiaaccess.net.th. Very popular, long-established budget hotel built around a swimming pool. Large, spartan and slightly shabby rooms; the cheapest have shared bathrooms, the priciest come with air-con. ❸–❺
**Sukhumvit 11**, behind the 7-11 store at 1/3 Soi 11 ☎02/253 5927, ℉253 5929,

ⓦwww.suk11.com. One of the few backpacker-oriented guest houses in this area, with B175 beds in five-person air-con dorms as well as air-con doubles with shared bathroom. Friendly place with informative noticeboards, left luggage and lockers, and a very nice roof terrace/balcony seating area. ❹
**SV Guest House**, Soi 19 ☎02/253 1747, ℉255 7174. Some of the least expensive beds in the area; the rooms, some of which have air-con, are clean and well maintained, and all share bathrooms. ❸
**Thai House Inn**, down a soi beside the *Amari Boulevard* at 1/1 Soi 7 ☎02/255 4698, ℉253 1780, Ⓔthaihouseinn@hotmail.com. Simple, guest-house-style rooms, but reasonably priced for such a central Sukhumvit location. All rooms have air-con, TV and fridge, and there's a Thai-food canteen in the lobby. ❹

## Moderate

**Bangkok Inn**, Soi 11/1 ☎02/254 4834, ℉254 3545, ⓦwww.bangkokinn.cjb.net. A cosy, friendly, German-run place with clean, smart rooms, all of which have air-con, shower, fridge and TV. Central and good value. ❺
**City Lodge**, Soi 19 ☎02/254 4783, ℉255 7340, ⓦwww.amari.com; and Soi 9 ☎02/253 7705, ℉255 4667, same website. Part of the Amari group, these two small, unashamedly mid-range hotels have comfortably equipped rooms with air-con, phone and TV. They are both very centrally located, though the Soi 9 branch suffers from having half its rooms literally overlooking the Nana Skytrain platform. Advance booking advised. ❼
**Federal Hotel**, 27, Soi 11 ☎02/253 0175, ℉253

5332, Ⓔfederalhotel@hotmail.com. Efficiently run, mid-sized hotel at the far end of Soi 11 so there's a feeling of space and a relatively uncluttered skyline; many rooms look out on the appealing poolside seating area. All rooms have air-con, TV and fridge; the upstairs ones are in better condition and worth paying a little extra for. ❺–❻
**Grand Inn**, Soi 3 ☎02/254 9021, ℉254 9020. Small, very central hotel offering sizeable, reasonably priced air-con rooms with TV and fridge. Good value. ❺–❻
**Premier Travelodge**, Soi 8 ☎02/251 3031, ℉253 3195. Well-equipped, centrally located small hotel offering good-value rooms with shower, bathtub, air-con, fridge and TV. ❺

**Rex Hotel**, Soi 34 ⊤ 02/259 0106, ⨍ 258 6635. Adequate rooms with air-con, TV, hot water, and use of the pool. Its location close to the Eastern Bus Terminal and the Ekamai Skytrain stop makes it convenient for east-coast connections, but it's too isolated from the best of Sukhumvit for a longer stay. ❺

**White Inn**, Soi 4 ⊤ 02/251 1662, ⨍ 254 8865. Slightly quaint establishment at the far, quiet end of the soi which cultivates the ambience of an Alpine lodge. There are just eighteen fairly good, comfortable air-con rooms, most with a balcony overlooking the small swimming pool. ❺

## Expensive

**Amari Boulevard Hotel**, Soi 5 ⊤ 02/255 2930, ⨍ 255 2950, ⓦ www.amari.com. Medium-sized, unpretentious and friendly upmarket tourist hotel. Rooms are comfortably furnished and all enjoy fine views of the Bangkok skyline; the deluxe ones have private garden patios as well. There's an attractive rooftop swimming pool and garden terrace which becomes the Thai-food restaurant *Season* in the evenings. ❾

**Ambassador Hotel**, between sois 11 and 13 ⊤ 02/254 0444, ⨍ 254 7503. Sprawling hotel complex on Sukhumvit that's popular with Asian package tourists and has an excellent range of facilities, including over a dozen restaurants. Rooms are a bit faded, though reasonable value. ❽

**Grand Pacific Hotel**, above Robinsons Department Store between sois 17 and 19 ⊤ 02/651 1000, ⨍ 255 2441, ⓦ www.grandpacifichotel.com. Conveniently located four-star hotel with smart, well-maintained rooms and good high-rise views. Facilities include three restaurants, a swimming pool, a gym and a business centre. Good value for its class. ❾

**Imperial Queen's Park**, Soi 22 ⊤ 02/261 9000, ⨍ 261 9530. Enormous and very swish high-rise hotel, whose large, comfortable rooms are nicely decorated with Thai-style furnishings. Facilities include two swimming pools and six restaurants. ❾

**J.W. Marriott Hotel**, between sois 2 and 4 ⊤ 02/656 7700, ⨍ 656 7711, ⓦ www .marriotthotels.com. Deluxe hotel, offering comfortable rooms with sophisticated phone systems and data ports geared towards business travellers. Facilities include three restaurants, a swimming pool, spa and fitness centre. ❾

**Landmark Hotel**, between sois 4 and 6 ⊤ 02/254 0404, ⨍ 253 4259, ⓦ www.landmarkbangkok.com. One of the most luxurious hotels on Sukhumvit, orientated towards the business traveller. Several good restaurants, and shops, in the adjacent Landmark Plaza, plus a fitness club and rooftop pool on the premises. ❾

**Sheraton Grande Sukhumvit**, between sois 12 and 14 ⊤ 02/653 0333, ⨍ 653 0400, ⓦ www .luxurycollection.com. Deluxe accommodation in stylishly understated rooms, all of which offer fine views of the cityscape (the honeymoon suites have their own rooftop plunge pools). Facilities include a gorgeous swimming pool and tropical garden on the ninth floor, a spa with a range of treatment plans, and the trendy *Basil* Thai restaurant. Seventeen and unders stay for free if sharing adults' room. ❾

# The City

Bangkok is sprawling, chaotic and exhausting: to do it justice and to keep your sanity, you need time, boundless patience and a bus map. The place to start is **Ratanakosin**, the royal island on the east bank of the Chao Phraya, where the city's most important and extravagant sights are to be found. On the edges of this enclave, the area around the landmark **Democracy Monument** includes some interesting and quirky religious architecture, a contrast with the attractions of neighbouring **Chinatown**, whose markets pulsate with the much more aggressive business of making money. Quieter and more European in ambience are the stately buildings of the new royal district of **Dusit**, 2km northeast of Democracy Monument. Very little of old Bangkok remains, but the back canals of **Thonburi**, across the river from Ratanakosin and Chinatown, retain a traditional feel quite at odds with the modern high-rise jungle of **downtown Bangkok**, which has evolved across on the eastern perimeter of the city and can take an hour to reach by bus from Ratanakosin. It's here that you'll find the best shops, bars, restaurants and nightlife, as well as a couple of worthwhile sights. Greater Bangkok now covers an area some 30km in diameter; though unsightly urban development predominates, an expedition to **the outskirts** is made worthwhile by several museums and the city's largest market.

# Ratanakosin

When Rama I developed **Ratanakosin** as his new capital in 1782, after the sacking of Ayutthaya and a temporary stay across the river in Thonburi, he paid tribute to its precursor by imitating Ayutthaya's layout and architecture – he even shipped the building materials downstream from the ruins of the old city. Like Ayutthaya, the new capital was sited for protection beside a river and turned into an artificial island by the construction of defensive canals, with a central **Grand Palace** and adjoining royal temple, **Wat Phra Kaeo**, fronted by an open cremation field, **Sanam Luang**; the Wang Na (Palace of the Second King), now doing service as the **National Museum**, was also built at this time. **Wat Po**, which predates the capital's founding, was further embellished by Rama I's successors, who consolidated Ratanakosin's pre-eminence by building several grand European-style palaces (now housing government institutions); Wat Mahathat, the most important centre of Buddhist learning in southeast Asia; the National Theatre and Thammasat University.

Bangkok has expanded eastwards away from the river, leaving the Grand Palace a good 5km from the city's commercial heart, and the royal family have long since moved their residence to Dusit, but Ratanakosin remains the ceremonial centre of the whole kingdom – so much so that it feels as if it might sink into the boggy ground under the weight of its own mighty edifices. The heavy, stately feel is lightened by noisy **markets** along the riverside strip and by **Sanam Luang**, still used for cremations and royal ceremonies, but also functioning as a popular open park and the hub of the modern city's bus system.

Ratanakosin is within easy walking distance of Banglamphu, but is best approached from the river, via the express-boat piers of Tha Chang (for the Grand Palace) or Tha Thien (for Wat Po). A **word of warning**: when you're heading for the Grand Palace or Wat Po, you may well be approached by someone pretending to be a student or an official, who will tell you that the sight is closed when it's not, because they want to lead you on a shopping trip. Although the opening hours of the Grand Palace in particular are sometimes erratic because of state occasions or national holidays, it's far better to put in a bit of extra legwork and check it out for yourself.

## Wat Phra Kaeo and the Grand Palace

Hanging together in a precarious harmony of strangely beautiful colours and shapes, **Wat Phra Kaeo** (Ⓦwww.palaces.thai.net) is the apogee of Thai religious

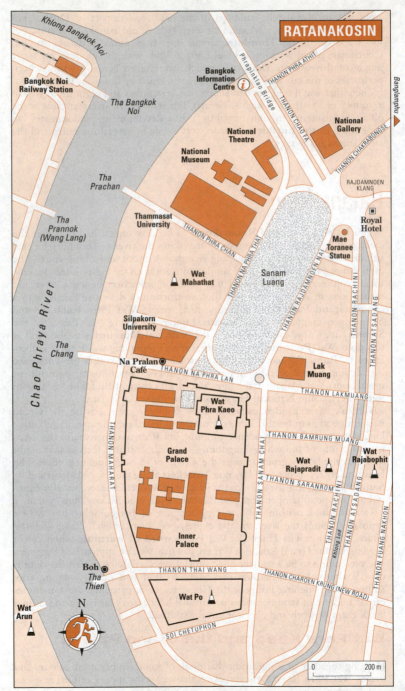

RATANAKOSIN

Khlong Bangkok Noi

Bangkok Noi
Railway Station

Tha Bangkok
Noi

Bangkok
Information
Centre

PhraPinklao Bridge

THANON PHRA ATHIT

THANON CHAO FA

THANON PHRA ATHIT

Banglamphu

National
Gallery

THANON CHAKRABONGSE

RAJDAMNOEN
KLANG

National
Theatre

National
Museum

Tha
Prachan

Thammasat
University

THANON PHRA CHAN

THANON NA PHRA THAI

Sanam
Luang

Royal
Hotel

Mae
Toranee
Statue

THANON RACHINI

THANON ATSADANG

Tha
Prannok
(Wang Lang)

Wat
Mahathat

THANON RAJDAMNOEN NA

Silpakorn
University

Chao Phraya River

Tha
Chang

Na Pralan
Café

THANON NA PHRA LAN

Lak
Muang

THANON LAKMUANG

Wat
Phra Kaeo

THANON MAHARAT

Grand
Palace

THANON BAMRUNG MUANG

THANON SANAM CHAI

Wat
Rajapradit

Wat
Rajabophit

THANON RACHINI

THANON ATSADANG

THANON FUANG NAKHON

THANON SARANROM

Inner
Palace

Khlong Lod

Boh
Tha
Thien

THANON THAI WANG

THANON CHAROEN KRUNG (NEW ROAD)

Wat Po

Wat
Arun

N

SOI CHETUPHON

0          200 m

art and the holiest Buddhist site in the country, housing the most important image, the **Emerald Buddha**. Built as the private royal temple, Wat Phra Kaeo occupies the northeast corner of the huge **Grand Palace**, whose official opening in 1785 marked the founding of the new capital and the rebirth of the Thai nation after the Burmese invasion. Successive kings have all left their mark here, and the palace complex now covers 61 acres, though very little apart from the wat is open to tourists.

The only **entrance** to the complex in 2km of crenellated walls is the Gate of Glorious Victory in the middle of the north side, on Thanon Na Phra Lan. This brings you onto a driveway with a tantalizing view of the temple's glittering spires on the left and the dowdy buildings of the Offices of the Royal Household on the right: this is the powerhouse of the kingdom's ceremonial life, providing everything down to chairs and catering, even lending an urn when someone of rank dies. Turn left at the end of the driveway for the ticket office and entrance turnstiles: **admission** to Wat Phra Kaeo and the palace is B200 (daily 8.30am–3.30pm, palace halls closed Sat & Sun; free tours in English at 10am, 10.30am, 1.30pm & 2pm; personal audioguide B100, with passport or credit card as surety), which includes a free brochure and invaluable map, as well as admission to the Vimanmek Palace in the Dusit area (see p.135). As it's Thailand's most sacred site, you have to show respect by **dressing in smart clothes** – no vests, shorts, see-through clothes, sarongs, miniskirts, fisherman's trousers, slip-on sandals or flip-flops allowed – but, if your rucksack won't stretch that far, head for the office to the right just inside the Gate of Glorious Victory, where suitable garments or shoes can be provided (free, socks B15) as long as you leave some identification (passport or credit card) as surety. If you haven't dressed in the right clothes and haven't brought any ID with you, all is not lost: streetsellers opposite the entrance rent out the required attire (sandals with straps, for example, for B50, with a B50 deposit).

## Wat Phra Kaeo

Entering the temple is like stepping onto a lavishly detailed stage set, from the immaculate flagstones right up to the gaudy roofs. Although it receives hundreds of foreign sightseers and at least as many Thai pilgrims every day, the temple, which has no monks in residence, maintains an unnervingly sanitized look, as if it were built only yesterday. Its jigsaw of structures can seem complicated at first, but the basic layout is straightforward: the turnstiles in the west wall open onto the back of the bot, which contains the Emerald Buddha; to the left, the upper terrace runs parallel to the north side of the bot, while the whole temple compound is surrounded by arcaded walls, decorated with extraordinary murals of scenes from the *Ramayana* (see p.120).

### The approach to the bot

Immediately inside the turnstiles, you're confronted by six-metre tall *yaksha*, gaudy demons from the *Ramayana*, who watch over the Emerald Buddha from every gate of the temple and ward off evil spirits. Less threatening is the toothless old codger, cast in bronze and sitting on a plinth by the back wall of the bot, who represents a Hindu hermit credited with inventing yoga and herbal medicine. Skirting around the bot, you'll reach its **main entrance** on the eastern side, in front of which stands a cluster of grey **statues** which have a strong Chinese feel: next to Kuan Im, the Chinese Goddess of Mercy, is a sturdy pillar topped by a lotus flower, which Bangkok's Chinese community presented to Rama IV during his 27 years as a monk; and two handsome cows which commemorate Rama I's birth in the Year of the Cow. Worshippers make their

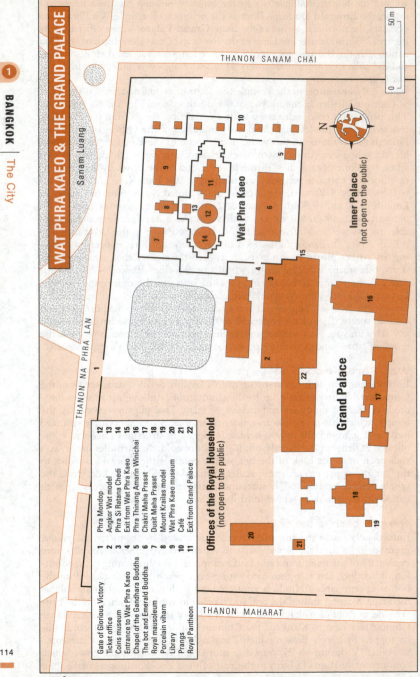

## WAT PHRA KAEO & THE GRAND PALACE

THANON SANAM CHAI

Sanam Luang

0      50 m

N

Wat Phra Kaeo

**Inner Palace**
(not open to the public)

THANON NA PHRA LAN

**Grand Palace**

**Offices of the Royal Household**
(not open to the public)

THANON MAHARAT

Tha Chang

| | | | |
|---|---|---|---|
| Gate of Glorious Victory | 1 | Phra Mondop | 12 |
| Ticket office | 2 | Angkor Wat model | 13 |
| Coins museum | 3 | Phra Si Ratana Chedi | 14 |
| Entrance to Wat Phra Kaeo | 4 | Exit from Wat Phra Kaeo | 15 |
| Chapel of the Gandhara Buddha | 5 | Phra Thinang Amarin Winichai | 16 |
| The bot and Emerald Buddha | 6 | Chakri Maha Prasat | 17 |
| Royal mausoleum | 7 | Dusit Maha Prasat | 18 |
| Porcelain viharn | 8 | Mount Krailas model | 19 |
| Library | 9 | Wat Phra Kaeo museum | 20 |
| Prangs | 10 | Café | 21 |
| Royal Pantheon | 11 | Exit from Grand Palace | 22 |

offerings to the Emerald Buddha in among the statues, where they can look at the image through the open doors of the bot without messing up its pristine interior with candle wax and joss-stick ash.

Nearby in the southeastern corner of the temple precinct, look out for the beautiful country scenes painted in gold and blue on the doors of the **Chapel of the Gandhara Buddha**, a building which was crucial to the old royal rain-making ritual. Adorning the roof are thousands of nagas (serpents), symbolizing water; inside the locked chapel, among the paraphernalia used in the ritual, is kept the Gandhara Buddha, a bronze image in the gesture of calling down the rain with its right hand, while cupping the left to catch it. In times of drought the king would order this week-long ceremony to be conducted, during which he was bathed regularly and kept away from the opposite sex while Buddhist monks and Hindu Brahmins chanted continuously.

### The bot and the emerald Buddha

The **bot**, the largest building of the temple, is one of the few original structures left at Wat Phra Kaeo, though it has been augmented so often it looks like the work of a wildly inspired child. Eight *sema* stones mark the boundary of the consecrated area around the bot, each sheltering in a psychedelic fairy castle, joined by a low wall decorated with Chinese porcelain tiles which depict delicate landscapes. The walls of the bot itself, sparkling with gilt and coloured glass, are supported by 112 golden garudas (birdmen) holding nagas representing the god Indra saving the world by slaying the serpent-cloud which had swallowed up all the water.

Inside the bot, a nine-metre high pedestal supports the tiny **Emerald Buddha**, a figure whose mystique draws pilgrims from all over Thailand and here especially you must act with respect, sitting with your feet pointing away from the Buddha. The spiritual power of the sixty-centimetre jadeite image derives from its legendary past. Reputed to have been created in Sri Lanka, it was discovered when lightning cracked open an ancient chedi in Chiang Rai in the early fifteenth century. The image was then moved around the north, dispensing miracles wherever it went, before being taken to Laos for two hundred years. As it was believed to bring great fortune to its possessor, the future Rama I snatched it back when he captured Vientiane in 1779, installing it at the heart of his new capital as a talisman for king and country.

To this day the king himself ceremonially changes the Buddha's costumes, of which there are three sets, one for each season: the crown and ornaments of an Ayutthayan king for the hot season; a gilt monastic robe dotted with blue enamel for the rainy season, when the monks retreat into the temples; and a full-length gold shawl to wrap up in for the cool season. (The Buddha was granted three new sets of these costumes in 1997, with the old sets put on display in the Wat Phra Kaeo Museum – see p.118.) Among the paraphernalia in front of the pedestal is the tiny, black Victory Buddha, which Rama I always carried with him into war for luck. The two lowest Buddhas were both put there by Rama IX: the one on the left on his sixtieth birthday in 1987, the other when he became the longest-reigning Thai monarch in 1988.

### The upper terrace

The eastern end of the **upper terrace** is taken up with the **Prasat Phra Thep Bidorn**, known as the **Royal Pantheon**, a splendid hash of styles. The pantheon has its roots in the Khmer concept of *devaraja*, or the divinity of kings: inside are bronze and gold statues, precisely life-size, of all the kings since

Bangkok became the Thai capital. The building is open only on special occasions, such as Chakri Day (April 6), when the dynasty is commemorated.

From here you get the best view of the **royal mausoleum**, the **porcelain viharn** and the **library** to the north (all of which are closed to the public) and, running along the east side of the temple, a row of eight bullet-like **prangs**, each of which has a different nasty ceramic colour. Described as "monstrous vegetables" by Somerset Maugham, they represent, from north to south, the Buddha, Buddhist scripture, the monkhood, the nunhood, the Buddhas who attained enlightenment but did not preach, previous emperors, the Bodhisattva and the future Buddha.

In the middle of the terrace, dressed in deep-green glass mosaics, the **Phra Mondop** was built by Rama I to house the *Tripitaka*, or Buddhist scripture. It's famous for the mother-of-pearl cabinet and solid-silver mats inside, but is never open. Four tiny **memorials** at each corner of the mondop show the symbols of each of the nine Chakri kings, from the ancient crown representing Rama I to the present king's sun symbol, while the bronze statues surrounding the memorials portray each king's lucky white elephants, labelled by name and pedigree. A contribution of Rama IV, on the north side of the mondop, is a **scale model of Angkor Wat**, the prodigious Cambodian temple, which during his reign was under Thai rule. At the western end of the terrace, you can't miss the golden dazzle of the **Phra Si Ratana Chedi**, which Rama IV (1851–68) erected to enshrine a piece of the Buddha's breastbone.

### The murals

Extending for over a kilometre in the arcades which run inside the wat walls, the **murals of the Ramayana** depict every blow of this ancient story of the triumph of good over evil, using the vibrant buildings of the temple itself as backdrops, and setting them off against the subdued colours of richly detailed landscapes. Because of the damaging humidity, none of the original work of Rama I's time survives: maintenance is a never-ending process, so you'll always find an artist working on one of the scenes.

The story is told in 178 panels, labelled and numbered in Thai only, starting in the middle of the northern side: in the first episode, a hermit, while out ploughing, finds the baby Sita, the heroine, floating in a gold urn on a lotus leaf and brings her to the city. Panel 109 shows the climax of the story, when Rama, the hero, kills the ten-headed demon Totsagan, and the ladies of the enemy city weep at the demon's death. Panel 110 depicts his elaborate funeral procession, and in 113 you can see the funeral fair, with acrobats, sword jugglers, and tightrope walkers. In between, Sita – Rama's wife – has to walk on fire to prove that she has been faithful during her fourteen years of imprisonment by Totsagan. If you haven't the stamina for the long walk round, you could sneak a look at the end of the story, to the left of the first panel, where Rama holds a victory parade and distributes thank-you gifts.

### The palace buildings

The exit in the southwest corner of Wat Phra Kaeo brings you to the palace proper, a vast area of buildings and gardens, of which only the northern edge is on show to the public. Though the king now lives in the Chitrlada Palace in Dusit, the Grand Palace is still used for state receptions and official ceremonies, during which there is no public access to any part of the palace; in addition the interiors of the Phra Thinang Amarin Winichai and the Dusit Maha Prasat are closed at weekends.

## Phra Maha Monthien

Coming out of the temple compound, you'll first be confronted by a beautiful Chinese gate covered in innumerable tiny porcelain tiles. Extending in a straight line behind the gate is the **Phra Maha Monthien**, which was the grand residential complex of earlier kings.

Only the **Phra Thinang Amarin Winichai**, the main audience hall at the front of the complex, is open to the public. The supreme court in the era of the absolute monarchy, it nowadays serves as the venue for the king's birthday speech; dominating the hall is the *busbok*, an open-sided throne with a spired roof, floating on a boat-shaped base. The rear buildings are still used for the most important part of the elaborate coronation ceremony, and each new king is supposed to spend a night there to show solidarity with his forefathers.

## Chakri Maha Prasat and the Inner Palace

Next door you can admire the facade – nothing else – of the "farang with a Thai hat", as the **Chakri Maha Prasat** is nicknamed. Rama V, whose portrait you can see over its entrance, employed an English architect to design a purely Neoclassical residence, but other members of the royal family prevailed on the king to add the three Thai spires. This used to be the site of the elephant stables: the large red tethering posts are still there and the bronze elephants were installed as a reminder. The building displays the emblem of the Chakri dynasty on its gable, which has a trident (*ri*) coming out of a *chak*, a discus with a sharpened rim.

The **Inner Palace**, which used to be the king's harem (closed to the public), lies behind the gate on the left-hand side of the Chakri Maha Prasat. The harem was a town in itself, with shops, law courts and a police force for the huge all-female population: as well as the current queens, the minor wives and their servants, this was home to the daughters and consorts of former kings, and the daughters of the aristocracy who attended the harem's finishing school. Today, the Inner Palace houses a school of cooking, fruit-carving and other domestic sciences for well-bred young Thais.

## Dusit Maha Prasat

On the western side of the courtyard, the delicately proportioned **Dusit Maha Prasat**, an audience hall built by Rama I, epitomizes traditional Thai architecture. Outside, the soaring tiers of its red, gold and green roof culminate in a gilded *mongkut*, a spire shaped like the king's crown which symbolizes the thirty-three Buddhist levels of perfection. Each tier of the roof bears a typical *chofa*, a slender, stylized bird's head, and several *hang hong* (swan's tails), which represent three-headed nagas. Inside, you can still see the original throne, the **Phra Ratcha Banlang Pradap Muk**, a masterpiece of mother-of-pearl inlaid work. When a senior member of the royal family dies, the hall is used for the lying-in-state: the body, embalmed and seated in a huge sealed urn, is placed in the west transept, waiting up to two years for an auspicious day to be cremated.

To the right and behind the Dusit Maha Prasat rises a strange model mountain, decorated with fabulous animals and topped by a castle and prang. It represents **Mount Krailas**, a version of Mount Meru, the centre of the Hindu universe, and was built as the site of the royal tonsure ceremony. In former times, Thai children had shaved heads except for a tuft on the crown which, between the age of five and eight, was cut in a Hindu initiation rite to welcome adolescence. For the royal children, the rite was an elaborate ceremony that sometimes lasted five days, culminating with the king's cutting of the hair knot. The child was then bathed at the model Krailas, in water representing the original river of the universe flowing down the central mountain.

### The Wat Phra Kaeo Museum

In front of the Dusit Maha Prasat – beside a small, basic **café** – the air-conditioned **Wat Phra Kaeo Museum** (B50) is currently under renovation but you should still be able to get in to see its mildly interesting collection of artefacts associated with the Emerald Buddha and architectural elements rescued from the Grand Palace grounds. Highlights include the Emerald Buddha's original costumes, the bones of various kings' white elephants, and two useful scale models of the Grand Palace, one as it is now, the other as it was when first built.

## Wat Po

Where Wat Phra Kaeo may seem too perfect and shrink-wrapped for some, **Wat Po** (daily 8am–5pm; B20), covering twenty acres to the south of the Grand Palace, is lively and shambolic, a complex arrangement of lavish structures which jostle with classrooms, basketball courts and a turtle pond. Busloads of tourists shuffle in and out of the **north entrance** stopping only to gawp at the colossal Reclining Buddha, but you can avoid the worst of the crowds by using the **main entrance** on Soi Chetuphon to explore the huge compound, where you'll more than likely be approached by friendly young monks wanting to practise their English.

Wat Po is the oldest temple in Bangkok and older than the city itself, having been founded in the seventeenth century under the name Wat Potaram. Foreigners have stuck to the contraction of this old name, even though Rama I, after enlarging the temple, changed the name in 1801 to Wat Phra Chetuphon, which is how it is generally known to Thais. The temple had another major overhaul in 1832, when Rama III built the chapel of the Reclining Buddha, and turned the temple into a public centre of learning by decorating the walls and pillars with inscriptions and diagrams on subjects such as history, literature, animal husbandry and astrology. Dubbed Thailand's first university, the wat is still an important centre for traditional medicine, notably **Thai massage**, which is used against all kinds of illnesses, from backaches to viruses. Thirty-hour training courses conducted here in English, usually over a fifteen-day period, cost B6000 (T 02/221 2974 or E watpottm@netscape.net for more information). Alternatively you can simply turn up and suffer a massage yourself in the ramshackle buildings (open until 6pm) on the east side of the main compound; allow two hours for the full works (B200 per hr; foot reflexology massage B200 for 45min).

### The eastern courtyard

The main entrance on Soi Chetuphon is one of a series of sixteen monumental gates around the main compound, each guarded by stone **giants**, many of them comic Westerners in wide-brimmed hats – ships which exported rice to China would bring these statues back as ballast.

The entrance brings you into the eastern half of the main complex, where a courtyard of structures radiate from the bot – the principal congregation and ordination hall – in a disorientating symmetry. To get to the bot at the centre, turn right and cut through the two surrounding cloisters, which are lined with 394 Buddha images, many of them covered with stucco to hide their bad state of repair – anyone can accrue some merit by taking one away and repairing it.

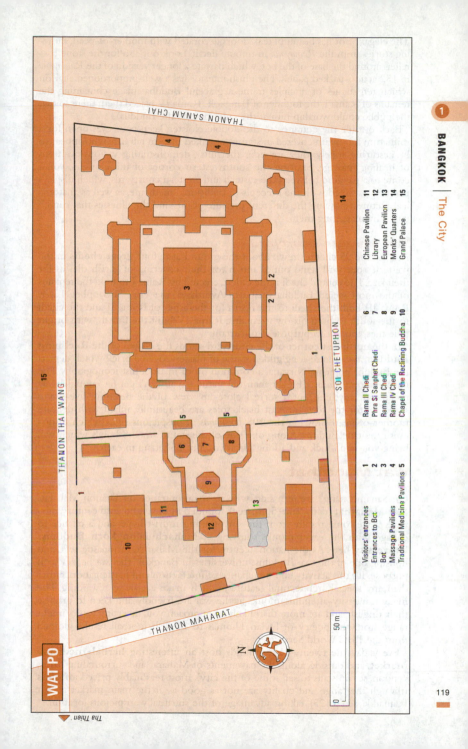

WAT PO

THANON SANAM CHAI

THANON THAI WANG

THANON MAHARAT

SOI CHETUPHON

Tha Thien

N

0    50 m

| Visitors' entrances | 1 | Rama II Chedi | 6 | Chinese Pavilion | 11 |
| Entrances to Bot | 2 | Phra Si Sanphet Chedi | 7 | Library | 12 |
| Bot | 3 | Rama III Chedi | 8 | European Pavilion | 13 |
| Massage Pavilions | 4 | Rama IV Chedi | 9 | Monks' Quarters | 14 |
| Traditional Medicina Pavilions | 5 | Chapel of the Reclining Buddha | 10 | Grand Palace | 15 |

The elegant **bot** has beautiful teak doors decorated with mother-of-pearl, showing stories from the *Ramayana* in minute detail. Look out also for the stone bas-reliefs around the base of the bot, which narrate a longer version of the *Ramayana* in 152 action-packed panels. The plush interior has a well-proportioned altar on which ten statues of disciples frame a graceful Buddha image containing the remains of Rama I, the founder of Bangkok (Rama IV placed them there so that the public could worship him at the same time as the Buddha).

Back outside the entrance to the double cloister, keep your eyes open for a miniature mountain covered in statues of naked men in tall hats who appear to be gesturing rudely: they are *rishis* (hermits), demonstrating various positions of healing massage. Skirting the southwestern corner of the cloisters, you'll come to a pavilion between the eastern and western courtyards, which displays plaques inscribed with the precepts of traditional medicine, as well as anatomical pictures showing the different pressure points and the illnesses that can be cured by massaging them.

### The western courtyard

Among the 95 chedis strewn about the grounds, the four **great chedis** in the western courtyard stand out as much for their covering of garish tiles as for their size. The central chedi is the oldest, erected by Rama I to hold the remains of the most sacred Buddha image of Ayutthaya, the Phra Si Sanphet. Later, Rama III built the chedi to the north for the ashes of Rama II and the chedi to the south to hold his own remains; Rama IV built the fourth, with bright blue tiles, though its purpose is uncertain.

In the northwest corner of the courtyard stands the chapel of the **Reclining Buddha**, a 45-metre-long gilded statue of plaster-covered brick which depicts the Buddha entering Nirvana, a common motif in Buddhist iconography. The chapel is only slightly bigger than the statue – you can't get far enough away to take in anything but a surreal close-up view of the beaming five-metre smile. As for the feet, the vast black soles are beautifully inlaid with delicate mother-of-pearl showing the 108 *lakshanas* or auspicious signs which distinguish the true Buddha. Along one side of the statue are 108 bowls which will bring you good luck and a long life if you put 25 satang in each.

## Wat Mahathat

On Sanam Luang's western side, with its main entrance on Thanon Maharat, **Wat Mahathat** (daily 9am–5pm; free), founded in the eighteenth century, provides a welcome respite from the surrounding tourist hype, and a chance to engage with the eager monks studying at **Mahachulalongkorn Buddhist University** here. As the nation's centre for the Mahanikai monastic sect, and housing one of the two Buddhist universities in Bangkok, the wat buzzes with purpose. It's this activity, and the chance of interaction and participation, rather than any special architectural features, which make a visit so rewarding. The many university-attending monks at the wat are friendly and keen to practise their English, and are more than likely to approach you: diverting topics might range from the poetry of Dylan Thomas to English football results gleaned from the BBC World Service.

Every day the twenty-acre grounds host an interesting **herbal medicine market**, and outside, along the pavements of Maharat and surrounding roads, vendors set up stalls to sell some of the city's most reasonably priced **amulets** (though the range and quality are not as good as at the main market at Wat Rajnadda, see p.125), taking advantage of the spiritually auspicious location.

Situated in Section Five of the wat is its **International Buddhist Meditation Centre** where Vipassana meditation practice is available in English (daily 7–10am, 1–4pm & 6–9pm; ☏02/222 6011 or 01/694 1527 for further information). Participants are welcome to stay in the simple surroundings of the meditation building itself (donation requested) or at a quiet house nearby (B200 per day).

# The National Museum

Near the northwest corner of Sanam Luang, the **National Museum** (Wed–Sun 9am–4pm; B40 including free leaflet with map) houses a colossal hoard of Thailand's chief artistic riches, ranging from sculptural treasures in the north and south wings, through bizarre decorative objects in the older buildings, to outlandish funeral chariots and the exquisite Buddhaisawan Chapel, as well as occasionally staging worthwhile temporary exhibitions (details on ☏02/224 1370). It's worth making time for the free **guided tours in English** (Wed & Thurs 9.30am; details on ☏02/215 8173): they're generally entertaining and their explanation of the choicest exhibits provides a good introduction to Thai religion and culture. The simple **cafeteria** serves good, inexpensive Thai food, especially handy if you linger longer than anticipated – and most people do.

## History and prehistory

The building which houses the information office and bookshop provides a quick whirl through the **history** of Thailand, a display in which a couple of gems are hidden. The first is a black stone inscription, credited to King Ramkhamhaeng of Sukhothai, which became the first capital of the Thai nation (c.1278–99) under his rule. Discovered in 1833 by the future Rama IV, it's the oldest extant inscription using the Thai alphabet. This, combined with the description it records of prosperity and piety in Sukhothai's Golden Age, has made the stone a symbol of Thai nationhood. Further on is a four-foot-tall carved *kinnari*, a graceful half-human, half-bird creature said to live in one of the Himalayan heavens. This delicate masterpiece is from the best period of Thai woodcarving, the seventeenth and early eighteenth centuries, before the fall of Ayutthaya.

The **prehistory** room is entered through a separate door at the back end of the building. Prominent here are bronze artefacts from Ban Chiang in the northeast of Thailand, one of the earliest Bronze Age cultures ever discovered, including the world's oldest socketed tool, an axe head set in a sandstone mould (3600–2300 BC).

## The main collection: southern building

At the back of the compound, two large modern buildings, flanking an old converted palace, house the museum's **main collection**, kicking off on the ground floor of the **southern building**. Look out here for some historic sculptures from the rest of Asia, including one of the earliest representations of the Buddha, from Gandhara in northwest India. Alexander the Great left a garrison at Gandhara, which explains why the image is in the style of Classical Greek sculpture: for example, the *ushnisha*, the supernatural bump on the top of the head, which symbolizes the Buddha's intellectual and spiritual power, is rationalized into a bun of thick, wavy hair.

Upstairs, in the **Dvaravati** rooms (sixth to eleventh centuries), the pick of the stone and terracotta Buddhas is a small head in smooth, pink clay, whose downcast eyes and faintly smiling full lips typify the serene look of this era. You can't miss a voluptuous Javanese statue of elephant-headed Ganesh, Hindu god of wisdom and the arts, which, being the symbol of the Fine Arts Department, is always freshly garlanded. As Ganesh is known as the clearer of obstacles, Hindus always worship him before other gods, so by tradition he has grown fat through getting first choice of the offerings – witness his trunk jammed into a bowl of food in this sculpture.

Room 9 contains the most famous piece of **Srivijaya** art (seventh to thirteenth centuries), a bronze Bodhisattva Avalokitesvara found at Chaiya. With its pouting face and sinuous torso, this image has become the ubiquitous emblem of southern Thailand. The rough chronological order of the collection continues back downstairs with an exhibition of **Khmer** and **Lopburi** sculpture (seventh to fourteenth centuries), most notably some dynamic bronze statuettes and stone lintels. Look out for an elaborate lintel depicting Vishnu reclining on a dragon in the sea of eternity, dreaming up a new universe after the old one has been annihilated in the Hindu cycle of creation and destruction. Out of his navel comes a lotus, and out of this emerges four-headed Brahma, who will put the dream into practice. Nearby, a smooth, muscular stone statue with a sweet smile and downcast eyes shows King Jayavarman VII, last of the great Khmer emperors. Such royal statues are very rare, and the features borrowed from Buddha images suggest that Jayavarman believed that he was close to Buddhahood himself.

## The main collection: northern building

The second half of the survey, in the northern building, begins upstairs with the **Sukhothai** collection (thirteenth to fifteenth centuries), which is short on Buddha images but has some chunky bronzes of Hindu gods and a wide range of ceramics. The **Lanna** rooms (thirteenth to sixteenth centuries) include a miniature set of golden regalia, among them tiny umbrellas and a cute pair of filigree flip-flops, which would have been enshrined in a chedi. An ungainly but serene Buddha head, carved from grainy, pink sandstone, represents the **Ayutthaya** style of sculpture (fourteenth to eighteenth centuries): the faintest incision of a moustache above the lips betrays the Khmer influences which came to Ayutthaya after its conquest of Angkor. A sumptuous scripture cabinet, showing a cityscape of old Ayutthaya, is a more unusual piece, one of a surviving handful of such carved and painted items of furniture.

Downstairs in the **Bangkok** rooms (eighteenth century onwards), a stiffly realistic standing bronze brings you full circle. In his zeal for Western naturalism, Rama V had the statue made in the Gandhara style of the earliest Buddha image displayed in the first room of the museum.

## The funeral chariots

To the east of the northern building, beyond the café on the left, stands a large garage where the fantastically elaborate **funeral chariots** of the royal family are stored. Pre-eminent among these is the Vejayant Rajarot, built by Rama I in 1785 for carrying the urn at his own funeral. The thirteen–metre-high structure symbolizes heaven on Mount Meru, while the dragons and divinities around the sides – piled in five golden tiers to suggest the flames of the cremation – represent the mythological inhabitants of the mountain's forests. Weighing forty tons and pulled by three hundred men, the teak chariot was used as recently as 1985 for the funeral of Queen Rambhai Bharni, wife of Rama VII.

## Wang Na (Palace of the Second King)

The sprawling central building of the compound was originally part of the **Wang Na**, a huge palace stretching across Sanam Luang to Khlong Lod, which housed the "second king", appointed by the reigning monarch as his heir and deputy. When Rama V did away with the office in 1887, he turned the "Palace of the Second King" into a museum, which now contains a fascinating array of Thai *objets d'art*. As you enter (room 5), the display of sumptuous rare gold pieces behind heavy iron bars includes a well-preserved armlet taken from the ruined prang of fifteenth-century Wat Ratburana in Ayutthaya. In adjacent room 6, an intricately carved ivory seat turns out, with gruesome irony, to be a *howdah*, for use on an elephant's back. Among the masks worn by *khon* actors next door (room 7), look out especially for a fierce Hanuman, the white monkey-warrior in the *Ramayana* epic, gleaming with mother-of-pearl.

The huge and varied ceramic collection in room 8 includes some sophisticated pieces from Sukhothai, while the room above (9) holds a riot of mother-of-pearl items, whose flaming rainbow of colours comes from the shell of the turbo snail from the Gulf of Thailand. It's also worth seeking out the display of richly decorated musical instruments in room 15, where you can hear tapes of the unfamiliar sounds they produce.

## The Buddhaisawan Chapel

The second holiest image in Thailand, after the Emerald Buddha, is housed in the **Buddhaisawan Chapel**, the vast hall in front of the eastern entrance to the Wang Na. Inside, the fine proportions of the hall, with its ornate coffered ceiling and lacquered window shutters, are enhanced by painted rows of divinities and converted demons, all turned to face the chubby, glowing **Phra Sihing Buddha**, which according to legend was magically created in Sri Lanka and sent to Sukhothai in the thirteenth century. Like the Emerald Buddha, the image was believed to bring good luck to its owner and was frequently snatched from one northern town to another, until Rama I brought it down from Chiang Mai in 1795 and installed it here in the second king's private chapel. Two other images (in Nakhon Si Thammarat and Chiang Mai) now claim to be the authentic Phra Sihing Buddha, but all three are in fact derived from a lost original – this one is in a fifteenth-century Sukhothai style. It's still much loved by ordinary people and at Thai New Year is carried out onto Sanam Luang, where worshippers sprinkle it with water as a merit-making gesture.

The careful detail and rich, soothing colours of the surrounding 200-year-old **murals** are surprisingly well preserved; the bottom row between the windows narrates the life of the Buddha, beginning in the far right-hand corner with his parents' wedding.

## Tamnak Daeng

On the south side of the Buddhaisawan Chapel, the sumptuous **Tamnak Daeng** (Red House) stands out, a large, airy Ayutthaya-style house made of rare golden teak, surmounted by a multi-tiered roof decorated with carved foliage and swan's-tail finials. Originally part of the private quarters of Princess Sri Sudarak, elder sister of Rama I, it was moved from the Grand Palace to the old palace in Thonburi for Queen Sri Suriyen, wife of Rama II; when her son became second king to Rama IV, he dismantled the edifice again and shipped it here to the Wang Na compound. Inside, it's furnished in the style of the early Bangkok period, with some of the beautiful objects that once belonged to Sri Suriyen, a huge, ornately carved box bed, and the uncommon luxury of an indoor toilet and bathroom.

# Banglamphu and the Democracy Monument area

Best known as the site of the travellers' mecca, Thanon Khao San, the **Banglamphu** district (see map, p.98–99) also holds a couple of noteworthy temples. But the most interesting sights in this part of the city are found to the south and east of **Democracy Monument**, within walking distance of Khao San guest houses and equally accessible from the Grand Palace. The pleasantest way to walk between Banglamphu and the Grand Palace is via the **riverside walkway** that runs alongside the Chao Phraya from the renovated Phra Sumen Fortress at the junction of Phra Athit and Phra Sumen roads; it currently only reaches as far as the Bangkok Information Centre at Phra Pinklao Bridge, but is due to be extended all the way down to Tha Chang, in front of the Grand Palace. If coming from downtown Bangkok the fastest way to get to this area is by longtail canal boat along Khlong Sen Seb (see p.92): the Phanfa terminus for this boat service is right next to the Golden Mount compound, just 30m from Wat Rajnadda. For details on bus and boat services to Banglamphu, see p.96.

## Wat Indraviharn

Located in the northern reaches of the Banglamphu district on Thanon Wisut Kasat, **Wat Indraviharn** (also known as Wat In) is famous for the enormous standing Buddha that dominates its precincts. Commissioned by Rama IV in the mid-nineteenth century to enshrine a Buddha relic from Sri Lanka, the 32-metre-high image certainly doesn't rate as a work of art: its enormous, overly flattened features give it an ungainly aspect, while the gold mirror-mosaic surface emphasizes its faintly kitsch overtones. But the beautifully pedicured foot-long toenails peep out gracefully from beneath devotees' garlands of fragrant jasmine, and you can get reasonable views of the neighbourhood by climbing the stairways of the tower supporting the statue from behind; when unlocked, the doorways in the upper part of the tower give access to the interior of the hollow image, affording vistas from shoulder level. Elsewhere in the wat's compact grounds you'll find the usual amalgam of architectural and spiritual styles, including a Chinese shrine and statues of Ramas IV and V.

For some reason Wat Indraviharn seems to be a favourite hangout for **con-artists**, and the popular scam here is to offer tourists a tuk-tuk tour of Bangkok for a bargain B20 – the driver making his real fee from taking his passengers to a nearby jewellery shop and making it extremely difficult for them to come away empty-handed. Avoid all these hassles by ignoring any tout, persistent tuk-tuk driver or overly helpful "guide" with an ID-card round his neck (there are no official guides), and flag down a passing metered taxi instead.

## Democracy Monument

About 300m southeast of Thanon Khao San, and midway along Rajdamnoen Klang, the avenue that connects the Grand Palace and the new royal district of Dusit, looms the imposing **Democracy Monument**. Begun in 1939 and designed by an Italian sculptor, Corrado Feroci, it was conceived as a testimony to the ideals that fuelled the 1932 revolution and the changeover to a constitutional monarchy, hence its symbolic positioning between the royal residences. Its dimensions are also significant: the four wings tower to a height of 24m, the same as the radius of the monument – allusions to June 24, the date the system was changed; the 75 cannons around the perimeter refer to the year, 2475 BE (Buddhist Era, 1932 AD). The monument contains a copy of the constitution and is a focal point for public events and demonstrations.

## Wat Rajnadda, Loh Prasat and the amulet market

Five minutes' walk southeast of Democracy Monument, at the point where Rajdamnoen Klang meets Thanon Mahachai, stands the assortment of religious buildings known collectively as **Wat Rajnadda**. It's immediately recognizable by the dusky-pink, multi-tiered, castle-like structure called **Loh Prasat** or "Iron Monastery" – a reference to its 37 metal spires, which represent the 37 virtues that lead to enlightenment. Each tier is pierced by passageways running north–south and east–west (fifteen in each direction at ground level), with small meditation cells at each point of intersection. The Sri Lankan monastery on which it is modelled contained a thousand cells; this one probably has half that number.

In the southeast (Thanon Mahachai) corner of the temple compound, Bangkok's biggest amulet market, the **Wat Rajnadda Buddha Center**, comprises at least a hundred stalls selling tiny Buddha images of all designs, materials and prices. Alongside these miniature charms are statues of Hindu deities, dolls and carved wooden phalluses, also bought to placate or ward off disgruntled spirits, as well as love potions and tapes of sacred music. While the amulet

### AMULETS

To gain protection from malevolent spirits and physical misfortune, Thais wear or carry at least one **amulet** at all times. The most popular **images** are copies of sacred statues from famous wats, while others show revered holy men, kings (Rama V is a favourite), healers or a many-armed monk depicted closing his eyes, ears and mouth so as to concentrate better on reaching Nirvana. On the reverse side a *yantra* is often inscribed, a combination of letters and figures also designed to ward off evil, sometimes of a very specific nature: protecting your durian orchards from gales, for example, or your tuk-tuk from oncoming traffic. Individually hand-crafted or mass-produced, amulets can be made from bronze, clay, plaster or gold, and some even have sacred ingredients added, such as the ashes of burnt holy texts. But what really determines an amulet's efficacy is its history: where and by whom it was made, who or what it represents and who consecrated it. Monks are often involved in the making of the images and are always called upon to consecrate them – the more charismatic the monk, the more powerful the amulet. In return, the proceeds from the sale of amulets contributes to wat funds.

Not all amulets are Buddhist-related – there's a whole range of other enchanted objects to wear for protection, including tigers' teeth, rose quartz, tamarind seeds, coloured threads and miniature phalluses. Worn around the waist rather than the neck, the phallus amulets provide protection for the genitals as well as being associated with fertility, and are of Hindu origin.

For some people, amulets are not only a vital form of spiritual protection, but valuable **collectors' items** as well. Amulet-collecting mania is something akin to stamp collecting – there are at least six Thai magazines for collectors, which give histories of certain types, tips on distinguishing between genuine items and fakes, and personal accounts of particularly powerful amulet experiences.

market at Wat Rajnadda is probably the best in Bangkok, you'll find less pricey examples from the streetside vendors who congregate daily along the pavement in front of Wat Mahathat. Prices start as low as B10 and rise into the thousands.

## The Golden Mount

The grubby yellow hill crowned with a gleaming gold chedi just across the road from Wat Rajnadda is the grandiosely named **Golden Mount**, or Phu Khao Tong. It rises within the compound of Wat Saket, and offers a good view of the Grand Palace and distant Wat Arun from its terrace. To reach the walkway up the mount, follow the renovated crenellations of the eighteenth-century Phra Mahakan Fortress, past the small bird and antiques market that operates from one of the recesses, before veering left when signposted.

Wat Saket hosts an enormous annual **temple fair** in the first week of November, when the mount is illuminated with coloured lanterns and the compound seethes with funfair rides, food sellers and travelling performers.

## Wat Suthat and Sao Ching Cha

Located about 1km southwest of the Golden Mount, and a similar distance directly south of Democracy Monument along Thanon Dinso, **Wat Suthat** (daily 9am–9pm; B20) is one of Thailand's six most important temples and contains Bangkok's tallest viharn, built in the early nineteenth century to house the meditating figure of **Phra Sri Sakyamuni Buddha**. This eight-metre-high statue was brought all the way down from Sukhothai by river, and now sits on a glittering mosaic dais surrounded with surreal **murals** that depict the last twenty-four lives of the Buddha rather than the more usual ten. The galleries that encircle the viharn contain 156 serenely posed Buddha images, making a nice contrast to the **Chinese statues** dotted around the viharn's courtyard and that of the bot in the adjacent compound, most of which were brought over from China during Rama I's reign, as ballast in rice boats: check out the depictions of gormless Western sailors and the pompous Chinese scholars.

The area just in front of Wat Suthat is dominated by the towering, red-painted teak posts of **Sao Ching Cha**, otherwise known as the **Giant Swing**, once the focal point of a Brahmin ceremony to honour Shiva's annual visit to earth. Teams of two or four young men would stand on the outsized seat (now missing) and swing up to a height of 25m, to grab between their teeth a bag of gold suspended on the end of a bamboo pole. The act of swinging probably symbolized the rising and setting of the sun, though legend also has it that Shiva and his consort Uma were banned from swinging in their heavenly abode because doing so caused cataclysmic floods on earth – prompting Shiva to demand that the practice be continued on earth as a rite to ensure moderate rains and bountiful harvests. Accidents were so common with the terrestrial version that it was outlawed in the 1930s.

The streets leading up to Wat Suthat and Sao Ching Cha are renowned as the best place in the city to buy **religious paraphernalia**, and are well worth a browse even for tourists. Thanon Bamrung Muang in particular is lined with shops selling everything a good Buddhist could need, from household offertory tables to temple umbrellas and six-foot Buddha images. They also sell special alms packs for devotees to donate to monks; a typical pack is contained within a (holy saffron-coloured) plastic bucket (which can be used by the monk for washing his robes, or himself), and comprises such daily necessities as soap, toothpaste, soap powder, toilet roll, candles and incense.

## Wat Rajabophit

From Wat Suthat, walk south down Thanon Titong for a few hundred metres before turning right (west) on to Thanon Rajabophit, on which stands **Wat Rajabophit** (see map on p.84), one of the city's prettiest temples and another example of Chinese influence. It was built by Rama V and is characteristic of this progressive king in its unusual design, with the rectangular bot and viharn connected by a circular cloister that encloses a chedi. Every external wall in the compound is covered in the pastel shades of Chinese *bencharong* ceramic tiles, creating a stunning overall effect, while the bot interior looks like a tiny banqueting hall, with gilded Gothic vaults and intricate mother-of-pearl doors.

If you now head west towards the Grand Palace from Wat Rajabophit, you'll pass a gold **statue of a pig** as you cross the canal. The cute porcine monument was erected in tribute to one of Rama V's wives, born in the Chinese Year of the Pig. Alternatively, walking in a southerly direction down Thanon Banmo takes you all the way down to the Chao Phraya River and Memorial Bridge, passing some fine old Chinese shop houses and the exuberant flower and vegetable market, Pak Khlong Talat, en route (see p.130).

# Chinatown and Pahurat

When the newly crowned Rama I decided to move his capital across to the east bank of the river in 1782, the Chinese community living on the proposed site of his palace was given no choice but to relocate downriver, to the **Sampeng** area. Two hundred years on, **Chinatown** has grown into the country's largest Chinese district, a sprawl of narrow alleyways, temples and shop houses packed between Charoen Krung (New Road) and the river, separated from Ratanakosin by the Indian area of Pahurat — famous for its cloth and curry houses — and bordered to the east by Hualamphong train station. Real estate in this part of the city is said to be the most valuable in the country, with land prices on the Charoen Krung and Thanon Yaowarat arteries reputed to fetch over a million baht per square metre, and there are over a hundred gold/jewellery shops along Thanon Yaowarat alone. For the tourist, Chinatown is chiefly interesting for its markets and shop houses, its open-fronted warehouses, and remnants of colonial-style architecture, though it also has a few noteworthy temples. The following account covers Chinatown's main attractions and most interesting neighbourhoods, sketching a meandering and quite lengthy route which could easily take a whole day to complete on foot.

Easiest access is to take the Chao Phraya Express **boat** to Tha Rajavongse (Rajawong) at the southern end of Thanon Rajawong, which runs through the centre of Chinatown. This part of the city is also well served by **buses** from downtown Bangkok, as well as from Banglamphu and Ratanakosin; your best bet is to take any Hualamphong-bound bus (see box on p.92) and then walk from the train station; the non-air-con bus #56 is also a useful link from Banglamphu, as it runs along Thanon Tanao at the end of Thanon Khao San and then goes all the way down Mahachai and Chakraphet roads in Chinatown – get off just after the Merry King department store for Sampeng Lane.

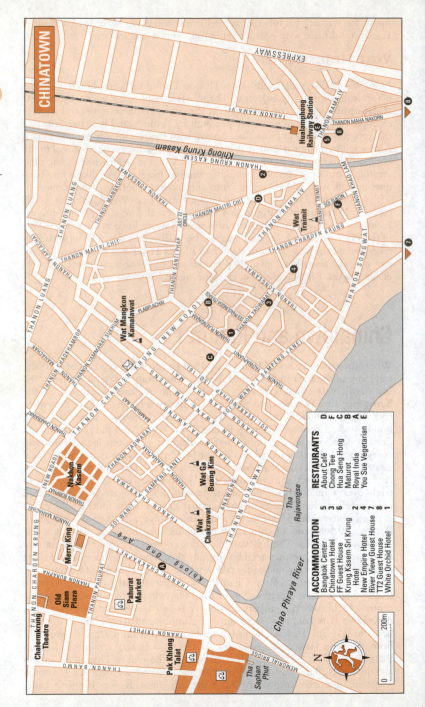

CHINATOWN

EXPRESSWAY

THANON RAMA VI

Hualamphong
Railway Station

THANON RAMA IV

THANON MAHA NAKORN

Khlong Krung Kasem

THANON KRUNG KASEM

THANON SONGSAWAT

THANON MANGKON

THANON MAITRI CHIT

THANON LUANG

THANON MAITRI CHIT

THANON WARACHAK

THANON RAMA IV

THANON TRIMIT

SOI SONI

THANON KHAO LAM

Wat
Traimit

THANON CHAROEN KRUNG

BAY 72
CIRCLE

THANON SANTI PHAP

THANON SONGWAT

Wat Mangkon
Kamalawat

THANON SONGSAWAT

THANON RASSADA

THANON CHAROEN KRUNG

PLABPLACHAI

(NEW ROAD)

THANON RASSAMINIMIT

THANON RASSADA

THANON YAOWARAT

THANON YAOWARAT

SAMPENG LANE)

THANON RATCHAWONG

THANON MAHACHAK

THANON CHAKKRAPHET

THANON CHAKRAPHET

THANON CHAO MAI

(SOI 16)

THANON ISSARANUPHAP

RAMBUNG RAT

WANG THIM TAENG

THANON YAMMABAT SUKHUM

THANON WANIT

THANON WANIT

SOI 1

THANON MAHACHAK

THANON SONGWAT

ANAWONG

THANON ISSARANUPHAP

Nakhon
Kasem

THANON BOPHITAK

Wat Ga
Buang Kim

Merry King

Wat
Chakrawat

THANON CHAROEN KRUNG

THANON MAHACHAI

THANON PAHURAT

Old Siam
Plaza

Pahurat
Market

Chalermkrung
Theatre

THANON TRIPHET

THANON BANMO

Pak Khlong
Talat

Khlong Ong Ang

Khlong Chakphaphet

Tha
Saphan
Phut

MEMORIAL BRIDGE

Chao Phraya River

Tha
Rajavongse

**ACCOMMODATION**
Bangkok Center — 5
Chinatown Hotel — 3
FF Guest House — 6
Krung Kasem Sri Krung
Hotel — 2
New Empire Hotel — 4
River View Guest House — 7
TT2 Guest House — 8
White Orchid Hotel — 1

**RESTAURANTS**
About Café — D
Chong Tee — F
Hua Seng Hong — C
Maturot — B
Royal India — A
You Sue Vegetarian — E

N

0     200m

Coming from downtown Bangkok and/or the Skytrain network, jump on a non-air-con #25 or #40, both of which run from Sukhumvit, via Siam Square to Hualamphong, then Thanon Yaowarat and on to Pahurat.

**Orientation** in Chinatown can be quite tricky: the alleys (known as *trok* rather than the more usual soi) are extremely narrow, their turn-offs and other road signs often obscured by the mounds of merchandise that clutter the sidewalks and the surrounding hoards of buyers and sellers.

## Wat Traimit and the Golden Buddha

Given the confusing layout of the district, it's worth starting your explorations at the eastern edge of Chinatown, just west of Hualamphong station, with the triangle of land occupied by **Wat Traimit** (daily 9am–5pm; B20). Cross the khlong beside the station and walk 200m down (signed) Thanon Tri Mit to enter the temple compound. Outwardly unprepossessing, the temple boasts a quite stunning interior feature: the world's largest solid-gold Buddha is housed here, fitting for a community so closely linked with the gold trade, even if the image has nothing to do with China's spiritual heritage. Over 3m tall and weighing five and a half tons, the **Golden Buddha** gleams as if coated in liquid metal, seated amidst candles and surrounded with offerings of lotus buds and incense. A fine example of the curvaceous grace of Sukhothai art, the beautifully proportioned figure is best appreciated by comparing it with the much cruder Sukhothai Buddha in the next-door bot, to the east.

Cast in the thirteenth century, the image was brought to Bangkok by Rama III, completely encased in stucco – a common ruse to conceal valuable statues from would-be thieves. The disguise was so good that no one guessed what was underneath until 1955 when the image was accidentally knocked in the process of being moved to Wat Traimit, and the stucco cracked to reveal a patch of gold. The discovery launched a country-wide craze for tapping away at plaster Buddhas in search of hidden precious metals, but Wat Traimit's is still the most valuable – it's valued, by weight alone, at $14 million. Sections of the stucco casing are now on display alongside the Golden Buddha.

## Sampeng Lane, Soi Issaranuphap and Wat Mangkon Kamalawat

Leaving Wat Traimit by the Charoen Krung/Yaowarat exit (at the back of the temple compound), walk northwest along Thanon Yaowarat, and make a left turn onto Thanon Songsawat, to reach **Sampeng Lane** (also signposted as Soi Wanit 1), an area that used to thrive on opium dens, gambling houses and brothels, but now sticks to a more reputable (if tacky) commercial trade. Stretching southeast–northwest for about 1km, Sampeng Lane is a fun place to browse and shop, unfurling itself like a ramshackle department store selling everything at bargain-basement rates. Among other things, this is the cheapest place in town to buy Chinese silk pyjama pants, electronic pets and other computer games, sarongs, alarm clocks, underwear and hair accessories. And, to complete this perfect shopping experience, there are food stalls every few steps to help keep up your energy.

For a rather more sensual experience, take a right about halfway down Sampeng Lane, into **Soi Issaranuphap** (also signed in places as Soi 16). Packed with people from dawn till dusk, this long, dark alleyway, which also traverses Charoen Krung (New Road), is where you come in search of ginseng roots (essential for good health), quivering fish heads, cubes of cockroach-killer chalk, and pungent piles of cinnamon sticks. You'll see Chinese grandfathers discussing business in darkened shops, ancient pharmacists concocting bizarre potions to order, alleys branching off in all directions to gaudy Chinese temples and market squares. Soi Issaranuphap finally ends at the Thanon Plaplachai intersection amid a flurry of shops specializing in paper **funeral art**. Believing that the deceased should be well provided for in their afterlife, Chinese buy miniature paper replicas of necessities to be burned with the body: especially popular are houses, cars, suits of clothing and, of course, money.

If Soi Issaranuphap epitomizes traditional Chinatown commerce, then **Wat Mangkon Kamalawat** (also known as Wat Leng Nee Yee or, in English, "Dragon Flower Temple") stands as a superb example of the community's spiritual practices. Best approached via its dramatic multi-tiered gateway 10m up Charoen Krung (New Road) from the Soi Issaranuphap junction, Wat Mangkon receives a constant stream of devotees, who come to leave offerings at one or more of the small altars inside this important Mahayana Buddhist temple. As with the Theravada Buddhism espoused by the Thais, Mahayana Buddhism (see "Religion: Thai Buddhism" in Contexts) fuses with other ancient religious beliefs, notably Confucianism and Taoism, and the statues and shrines within Wat Mangkon cover the whole spectrum. Passing through the secondary gateway, under the glazed ceramic gables topped with undulating Chinese dragons, you're greeted by a set of four outsize statues of bearded and rather forbidding sages, each clasping a symbolic object: a parasol, a pagoda, a snake's head and a mandolin. Beyond them, a series of Buddha images swathed in saffron netting occupies the next chamber, a lovely open-sided room of gold paintwork, red-lacquered wood, lattice lanterns and pictorial wall panels inlaid with mother-of-pearl. Elsewhere in the compound are little booths selling devotional paraphernalia, a Chinese medicine stall and a fortune-teller.

## Wat Ga Buang Kim

Less than 100m up Charoen Krung (New Road) from Wat Mangkon, a left turn into Thanon Rajawong, followed by a right turn into Thanon Anawong and a further right turn into the narrow, two-pronged Soi Krai brings you to the typical neighbourhood temple of **Wat Ga Buang Kim**. Here, as at Thai temples upcountry, local residents socialize in the shade of the tiny, enclosed courtyard and the occasional worshipper drops by to pay homage at the altar. This particular wat is remarkable for its exquisitely ornamented "vegetarian hall", a one-room shrine with altar centrepiece framed by intricately carved wooden tableaux – gold-painted miniatures arranged as if in sequence, with recognizable characters reappearing in new positions and in different moods. The hall's outer wall is adorned with small tableaux, too, the area around the doorway at the top of the stairs peopled with finely crafted ceramic figurines drawn from Chinese opera stories. The other building in the wat compound is a stage used for Chinese opera performances.

## Pak Khlong Talat

A browse through the 24-hour **flower and vegetable market**, **Pak Khlong Talat**, is a fine and fitting way to round off a day in Chinatown, though if you're an early riser it's also a great place to come before dawn, when market gardeners from Thonburi boat and truck their freshly picked produce across the Chao Phraya ready for sale to the shopkeepers, restaurateurs and hoteliers.

Occupying an ideal position close to the river, the market has been operating from covered halls between the southern ends of Thanon Banmo, Thanon Chakraphet and the riverbank since the nineteenth century and is the biggest wholesale market in the capital. The flower stalls, selling twenty different varieties of cut orchids and myriad other tropical blooms, spill on to the streets along the riverfront as well and, though prices are lowest in the early morning, you can still get some good bargains here in the afternoon.

The Chao Phraya Express Boat service stops just a few metres from the market at Tha Saphan Phut, and numerous city **buses** stop in front of the pier, including the northbound ordinary #3 and air-con #12, which both run to Banglamphu (see p.92).

# Thonburi

Bangkok really began across the river from Ratanakosin in the town of **Thonburi**. Devoid of grand ruins and isolated from central Bangkok, it's hard to imagine Thonburi as a former capital of Thailand, but so it was for fifteen years, between the fall of Ayutthaya in 1767 and the establishment of Bangkok in 1782. General Phrya Taksin chose to set up his capital here, strategically near the sea and far from the marauding Burmese, but the story of his brief reign is a chronicle of battles that left little time and few resources to devote to the building of a city worthy of its predecessor. When General Chao Phraya displaced the demented Taksin to become Rama I, his first decision as founder of the Chakri dynasty was to move the capital to the more defensible site across the river. It wasn't until 1932 that Thonburi was linked to its replacement by the **Memorial Bridge** (aka Phra Buddha Yodfa Bridge), built to commemorate the one-hundred-and-fiftieth anniversary of the foundation of the Chakri dynasty and of Bangkok, and dedicated to Rama I, whose bronze statue sits at the Bangkok approach. Thonburi retained its separate identity for another forty years until, in 1971, it officially became part of Bangkok.

As well as the imposing riverside structure of Wat Arun, Thonburi also offers a fleet of royal barges. In addition, life on this side of the river still revolves around the khlongs, on which vendors of food and household goods paddle their boats through the residential areas, and canalside factories transport their wares to the Chao Phraya River artery. The **architecture** along the canals ranges from ramshackle, makeshift homes balanced just above the water – and prone to flooding during the monsoon season – to villa-style residences where the river is kept at bay by lawns, verandas and concrete. Venture on to the Thonburi backroads just three or four kilometres west of the river and you find yourself surrounded by market gardens, nurseries and rural homes, with no hint of the throbbing metropolis across on the other bank. Modern Thonburi, on the other hand, sprawling to each side of Thanon Phra Pinklao, consists of the prosaic line-up of department stores, cinemas, restaurants and markets found all over urbanized Thailand.

**Getting to Thonburi** is simply a matter of crossing the river – use one of the numerous bridges (Memorial and Phra Pinklao are the most central), take a cross-river ferry, or hop on the express ferry, which makes three stops around the riverside Bangkok Noi station, just south of Phra Pinklao Bridge. The Southern Bus Terminal is also in Thonburi, at the junction of Thanon Borom

## Exploring Thonburi by boat and bike

One of the most popular ways of seeing the sights of Thonburi is by **longtail boat**, taking in Wat Arun and the Royal Barge Museum, then continuing along Thonburi's network of small canals. The easiest place to organize boat tours is at the Bangkok Information Centre, where staff can help hire a boat for you at Tha Wang Nah pier, next to their office on Thanon Phra Athit in Banglamphu (B400 per hour for a boat carrying up to six passengers). Most people however hire boats from Tha Chang, which is conveniently located in front of the Grand Palace, but is renowned for its aggressive and unscrupulous touts and boatmen and is best avoided; if you do go for this option, bear the B400 per hour price in mind, but expect to be charged up to B1500 per boat for a two-hour tour.

A less expensive option is to use the **public longtails** that run bus-like services along back canals from central Bangkok-side piers, departing every ten to thirty minutes and charging from B15–30 a round trip. Potentially interesting routes include the Khlong Bangkok Noi service from Tha Chang; the Khlong Mon service from Tha Thien, in front of Wat Po; the Khlong Bang Waek service from Tha Saphan Phut, at Memorial Bridge; and the Khlong Om service from Tha Nonthaburi. There have however been recent reports that taxi-boat drivers are making it impossible for tourists to board the public services from Tha Chang and Tha Thien, so the tourist office suggests starting in Nonthaburi instead.

A fixture of the upper-bracket tourist round is the organized **canal tour** to see Thonburi's Wat Sai **floating market**. This has become so commercialized and land-based that it can't be recommended wholeheartedly, but if you're short for time and set on seeing fruit- and flower-laden paddle boats, then join the longtail Wat Sai market tours from Tha Chang or from Tha Orienten (at the *Oriental Hotel*); these tours leave at around 7am and cost from B400 per person. **Taling Chan floating market**, fairly contrived but picturesque nonetheless, operates every Saturday and Sunday from 9am to 4pm on Khlong Chakphra in front of Taling Chan District Office, a couple of kilometres west of Bangkok Noi station. It can be visited as part of a chartered longtail tour, or you can make your own way there on bus #79 from Democracy Monument/Ratchadamnoen Klang, getting out at Khet Taling Chan, and either watching from the banks or hiring a longtail from the market. Alternatively, every weekend, the Mitchaophya Boat Company (☎02/225 6179) runs a boat **tour** that departs from Tha Chang at 9am and takes in the Royal Barges Museum, floating markets, and the island of Ko Kred, returning at 4pm (Sat & Sun; B200, children B150).

The most peaceful way to enjoy the canals of Thonburi is to join the monthly 35-kilometre **bicycle tour** organized by the Bangkok Tourist Bureau on Thanon Phra Athit in Banglamphu (☎02/225 7612–4; B650 including bike rental). The tour currently takes place from 7am to 4.30pm on the first Sunday of every month, but there are plans to make it a weekly event, so call ahead to check.

Ratchonni and the Nakhon Chaisri Highway, and all public and air-conditioned buses to southern destinations leave from here.

## Wat Arun

Almost directly across the river from Wat Po rises the enormous five-pranged **Wat Arun** (daily 7am–5pm; B20), the Temple of Dawn, probably Bangkok's most memorable landmark and familiar as the silhouette used in the TAT logo. It looks particularly impressive from the river, as you head downstream from the Grand Palace towards the *Oriental Hotel*, but is ornate enough to be well worth stopping off for a closer look. All boat tours include half an hour here, but Wat Arun is also easily visited by yourself, although tour operators will try to persuade you otherwise: just take a B2 cross-river ferry from the pier adjacent to the Chao Phraya Express Boat pier at Tha Thien.

A wat has occupied this site since the Ayutthaya period, but only in 1768 did it become known as the Temple of Dawn – when General Phrya Taksin reputedly reached his new capital at the break of day. The temple served as his royal chapel and housed the recaptured Emerald Buddha for several years until the image was moved to Wat Phra Kaeo in 1785. Despite losing its special status after the relocation, Wat Arun continued to be revered and was reconstructed and enlarged to its present height of 104m by Rama II and Rama III.

The Wat Arun that you see today is a classic prang structure of Ayutthayan style, built as a representation of Mount Meru, the home of the gods in Khmer mythology. Climbing the two tiers of the square base that supports the **central prang**, you not only enjoy a good view of the river and beyond, but also get a chance to examine the tower's curious decorations. Both this main prang and the four minor ones that encircle it are covered in bits of broken porcelain, arranged to create an amazing array of polychromatic flowers (local people gained much merit by donating their crockery for the purpose). Statues of mythical figures such as *yaksha* demons and half-bird, half-human *kinnari* support the different levels and, on the first terrace, the mondops at each cardinal point contain statues of the Buddha at the most important stages of his life: at birth (north), in meditation (east), preaching his first sermon (south) and entering Nirvana (west). The second platform surrounds the base of the prang proper, whose closed entranceways are guarded by four statues of the Hindu god Indra on his three-headed elephant Erawan. In the niches of the smaller prangs stand statues of Phra Pai, the god of the wind, on horseback.

## Royal Barge Museum

Until about twenty years ago, the king would process down the Chao Phraya River to Wat Arun in a flotilla of royal barges at least once a year, on the occasion of Kathin, the annual donation of robes by the laity to the temple at the end of the rainy season. Fifty-one barges, filling the width of the river and stretching for almost 1km, drifted slowly to the measured beat of a drum and the hypnotic strains of ancient boating hymns, chanted by over two thousand oarsmen whose red, gold and blue uniforms complemented the black and gold craft.

The 100-year-old boats are becoming quite frail, so such a procession is now a rare event – the last was in 1999, to mark the king's 72nd birthday. The three elegantly narrow vessels at the heart of the ceremony now spend their time moored in the **Royal Barge Museum** on the north bank of Khlong Bangkok Noi (daily 8.30am–4.30pm; B30). Up to 50m long and intricately lacquered and gilded all over, they taper at the prow into magnificent mythical figures after a design first used by the kings of Ayutthaya. Rama I had the boats copied and, when those fell into disrepair, Rama V commissioned the exact reconstructions still in use today. The most important of the trio is *Sri Suphanahongse*, which bears the king and queen and is instantly recognizable by the fifteen-foot-high prow representing a golden swan. In front of it floats *Anantanagaraj*, fronted by a magnificent seven-headed naga and bearing a Buddha image, while the royal children bring up the rear in *Anekchartphuchong*, which has a monkey god from the *Ramayana* at the bow.

The museum is a feature of most canal tours. To get there on your own, cross the Phra Pinklao Bridge (served by air-con buses #3, #7, #9, #11 or #32), and take the first left (Soi Wat Dusitaram), which leads to the museum through a jumble of walkways and houses on stilts. Alternatively, take a ferry to Bangkok Noi station (Tha Rot Fai); from there follow the tracks until you reach the bridge over Khlong Bangkok Noi, cross it and follow the signs. Either way it's about a ten-minute walk.

# Dusit

Connected to Ratanakosin via the boulevards of Rajdamnoen Klang and Rajdamnoen Nok, the spacious, leafy area known as **Dusit** has been a royal district since the reign of Rama V (1860–1910). The first Thai monarch to visit Europe, Rama V returned with radical plans for the modernization of his capital, the fruits of which are most visible in Dusit: notably **Vimanmek Palace** and **Wat Benjamabophit**, the so-called Marble Temple. Today the peaceful Dusit area retains its European feel, and much of the country's decision-making goes on behind the high fences and impressive facades along its tree-lined avenues: Government House is here, and the king lives on the eastern edge of the area, in the Chitrlada Palace.

From Banglamphu, you can get to Dusit by taking the west-bound #56 **bus** from Thanon Tanao or Thanon Phra Sumen and getting off on Thanon Ratchasima. From downtown Bangkok, easiest access is by bus from the Skytrain stop at Victory Monument; there are many services from here, including air-con #10 and #16, both of which run all the way along Thanon Rajwithi. Vimanmek is also served by the open-topped Bangkok Sightseeing Bus (see p.90).

## Vimanmek Palace and the Royal Elephant National Museum

**Vimanmek Palace** (daily 9.30am–4pm; compulsory free guided tours every 30min, last tour 3.15pm; B50, or free with a Grand Palace ticket, which remains valid for one month) was built by Rama V as a summer retreat on Ko Si Chang (see p.176), from where it was transported bit by bit in 1901. Built almost entirely of golden teak without a single nail, the L-shaped "Celestial Residence" is encircled by verandas that look out onto well-kept lawns, flower gardens and lotus ponds. The ticket price also covers entry to half a dozen other small museums in the palace grounds, including the Support Museum and Elephant Museum described below, and all visitors are treated to free performances of traditional Thai dance daily at 10.30am & 2pm. Note that the same **dress rules** apply here as to the Grand Palace (see p.113). The main **entrance** to the extensive Vimanmek Palace compound is on Thanon Rajwithi, but there are also ticket gates on Thanon Ratchasima, and opposite Dusit Zoo on Thanon U-Thong.

### Vimanmek Palace

Vimanmek soon became Rama V's favourite palace, and he and his enormous retinue of officials, concubines and children stayed here for lengthy periods between 1902 and 1906. All of Vimanmek's 81 rooms were out of bounds to male visitors, except for the king's own apartments, in the octagonal tower, which were entered by a separate staircase.

On display inside is Rama V's collection of artefacts from all over the world, including *bencharong* ceramics, European furniture and bejewelled Thai betel-nut sets. Considered progressive in his day, Rama V introduced many newfangled ideas to Thailand: the country's first indoor bathroom is here, as is the earliest typewriter with Thai characters, and some of the first portrait paintings – portraiture had until then been seen as a way of stealing part of the sitter's soul.

## The Support Museum

Elsewhere in the Vimanmek grounds several small throne halls have been converted into tiny museums displaying royal portraits, antique clocks and other collectors' items. The most interesting of these is the **Support Museum Abhisek Dusit Throne Hall**, showcasing the exquisite handicrafts produced under Queen Sirikit's charity project, Support, which works to revitalise traditional Thai arts and crafts. Outstanding exhibits include a collection of handbags, baskets and pots woven from the *lipao* fern that grows wild in southern Thailand; jewellery and figurines inlaid with the iridescent wings of beetles; gold and silver nielloware; and lengths of intricately woven silk from the northeast.

## Royal Elephant National Museum

Just inside the eastern, Thanon U-Thong, entrance to the Vimanmek compound stand two whitewashed buildings that once served as the stables for the king's white elephants. Now that the sacred pachyderms have been relocated, the stables have been turned into the **Royal Elephant National Museum**. Inside you'll find some interesting pieces of elephant paraphernalia, including sacred ropes, mahouts' amulets and magic formulae, as well as photos of the all-important ceremony in which a white elephant is granted royal status.

In Thailand the most revered of all elephants are the so-called **white elephants** – actually tawny brown albinos – which are considered so sacred that they all, whether wild or captive, belong to the king by law. The present king, Rama IX, has twelve, the largest royal collection to date. Before an elephant can be granted official "white elephant" status, it has to pass a stringent assessment of its physical and behavioural characteristics. Key qualities include a paleness of seven crucial areas – eyes, nails, palate, hair, outer edges of the ears, tail and testicles – and an all-round genteel demeanour, manifested, for instance, in the way in which it cleans its food before eating, or in a tendency to sleep in a kneeling position. The expression "white elephant" probably derives from the legend that the kings used to present certain enemies with one of these exotic creatures. The animal required expensive attention but, being royal, could not be put to work in order to pay for its upkeep. The recipient thus went bust trying to keep it.

# Dusit Zoo (Khao Din)

Just across Thanon U-Thong is **Dusit Zoo**, also known as **Khao Din** (daily 8am–6pm; B30, children B5); once part of the Chitrlada Palace gardens, it is now a public park. All the usual suspects are here, including big cats, elephants, orang-utans, chimpanzees and a reptile house, but the enclosures are pretty basic and not especially heart-warming. However, it's a reasonable place for kids to let off steam, with plenty of shade, a full complement of English-language signs, a lake with pedalos and lots of foodstalls. The main entrance to the zoo is on Thanon Rajvithi and there's another one across from the Vimanmek elephant museum on Thanon U-Thong.

## Wat Benjamabophit

Ten minutes' walk southeast from Vimanmek and the zoo along Thanon Sri Ayutthaya, **Wat Benjamabophit** (daily 7am–5pm; B20) is the last major temple to have been built in Bangkok. It's an interesting fusion of classical Thai and nineteenth-century European design, with its Carrara marble walls – hence the touristic tag "The Marble Temple" – complemented by the bot's unusual stained-glass windows, Victorian in style but depicting figures from Thai mythology. Inside, a fine replica of the highly revered Phra Buddha Chinnarat image of Phitsanulok presides over the small room containing Rama V's ashes. The courtyard behind the bot houses a gallery of Buddha images from all over Asia, set up by Rama V as an overview of different representations of the Buddha.

Wat Benjamabophit is one of the best temples in Bangkok to see religious **festivals** and rituals. Whereas monks elsewhere tend to go out on the streets every morning in search of alms, at the Marble Temple the ritual is reversed, and merit-makers come to them. Between about 6 and 7.30am, the monks line up on Thanon Nakhon Pathom, their bowls ready to receive donations of curry and rice, lotus buds, incense, even toilet paper and Coca-Cola; the demure row of saffron-robed monks is a sight that's well worth getting up early for. The evening candlelight processions around the bot during the Buddhist festivals of Maha Puja (in Feb) and Visakha Puja (in May) are among the most entrancing in the country.

# Downtown Bangkok

Extending east from the rail line and south to Thanon Sathorn, **downtown Bangkok** is central to the colossal expanse of Bangkok as a whole, but rather peripheral in a sightseer's perception of the city. This is where you'll find the main financial district, around Thanon Silom, and the chief shopping centres, around Siam Square, in addition to the smart hotels and restaurants, the embassies and airline offices. Scattered widely across the downtown area are just a few attractions for visitors, including the noisy and glittering **Erawan Shrine**, and three attractive museums housed in traditional teak buildings: **Jim Thompson's House**, the **Kamthieng House** and the **Suan Pakkad Palace Museum**. The infamous **Patpong** district hardly shines as a tourist sight, yet, lamentably, its sex bars provide Thailand's single biggest draw for farang men.

If you're heading downtown from Banglamphu, allow at least an hour to get to any of the places mentioned here by **bus**. To get to the southern part of the area, take an **express boat** downriver and then change onto the **Skytrain** or a bus if necessary. For other parts of the downtown area, it might be worth considering the regular **longtails** on Khlong Sen Seb, which runs parallel to Thanon Phetchaburi. They start at the Golden Mount, near Democracy Monument, and have useful stops at Saphan Hua Chang on Thanon Phrayathai (for Jim Thompson's House) and Pratunam (for the Erawan Shrine).

## Jim Thompson's House

Just off Siam Square at 6 Soi Kasemsan 2, Thanon Rama I, **Jim Thompson's House** (daily from 9am, viewing on frequent 45-minute guided tours in several languages, last tour 4.30pm, café and shop open until 5.30pm; B100, under-25s B50; ⓦwww.jimthompson.com) is a kind of Ideal Home in elegant Thai style, and a peaceful refuge from downtown chaos. The house was the residence of the legendary American adventurer, entrepreneur, art collector and all-round character whose mysterious disappearance in the jungles of Malaysia in 1967 has made him even more of a legend among Thailand's farang community. Apart from putting together this beautiful home, Thompson's most concrete contribution was to turn traditional silk-weaving from a dying art into the highly successful international industry it is today.

The grand, rambling **house** is in fact a combination of six teak houses, some from as far afield as Ayutthaya and most over 200 years old. Like all traditional houses, they were built in wall sections hung together without nails on a frame of wooden pillars, which made it easy to dismantle them, pile them onto a barge and float them to their new home. Although he had trained as an architect, Thompson had more difficulty in putting them back together again; in the end, he had to go back to Ayutthaya to hunt down a group of carpenters who still practised the old house-building methods. Thompson added a few unconventional touches of his own, incorporating the elaborately carved front wall of a Chinese pawnshop between the drawing room and the bedroom, and reversing the other walls in the drawing room so that their carvings faced into the room.

The impeccably tasteful **interior** has been left as it was during Thompson's life, even down to the cutlery on the dining table. Complementing the fine artefacts from throughout Southeast Asia is a stunning array of Thai arts and crafts, including one of the best collections of traditional Thai paintings in the world. Thompson picked up plenty of bargains from the Thieves' Quarter (Nakhon Kasem) in Chinatown, before collecting Thai art became fashionable and expensive. Other pieces were liberated from decay and destruction in upcountry temples, while many of the Buddha images were turned over by ploughs, especially around Ayutthaya. Some of the exhibits are very rare, such as a seventeenth-century Ayutthayan teak Buddha, but Thompson also bought pieces of little value and fakes simply for their looks – a shopping strategy that's all the more sensible in the jungle of today's Thai antiques trade.

## Suan Pakkad Palace Museum

The **Suan Pakkad Palace Museum** (daily 9am–4pm; B100), 352–4 Thanon Sri Ayutthaya, stands on what was once a cabbage patch but is now one of the finest gardens in Bangkok. Most of this private collection of beautiful Thai objects from all periods is displayed in six traditional wooden houses, which were transported to Bangkok from various parts of the country. You can either take a mediocre guided tour in English (free) or explore the loosely arranged collection yourself (a free handout is usually available and some of the exhibits are labelled). The attached **Marsi Gallery** has recently opened to display some interesting temporary exhibitions of contemporary art (daily 9am–6pm; ☎02/246 1775–6 for details).

The highlight here is the renovated **Lacquer Pavilion**, across the reedy pond at the back of the grounds. Set on stilts, the pavilion is actually an amalgam of two eighteenth- or late seventeenth-century temple buildings, a *ho trai* (library) and a *ho khien* (writing room), one inside the other, which were found between Ayutthaya and Bang Pa-In. The interior walls are beautifully decorated with gilt on black lacquer: the upper panels depict the life of the Buddha while the lower ones show scenes from the *Ramayana*. Look out especially for the grisly details in the tableau on the back wall, showing the earth goddess drowning the evil forces of Mara. Underneath are depicted some European dandies on horseback, probably merchants, whose presence suggests that the work was executed before the fall of Ayutthaya in 1767.

The carefully observed details of daily life and nature are skilful and lively, especially considering the restraints which the **lacquering technique** places on the artist, who has no opportunity for corrections or touching up: the design has to be punched into a piece of paper, which is then laid on the panel of black lacquer (a kind of plant resin); a small bag of chalk dust is pressed on top so that the dust penetrates the minute holes in the paper, leaving a line of dots on the lacquer to mark the pattern; a gummy substance is then applied to the background areas which are to remain black, before the whole surface is covered in microscopically thin squares of gold leaf; thin sheets of blotting paper, sprinkled with water, are then laid over the panel, which when pulled off bring away the gummy substance and the unwanted pieces of gold leaf that are stuck to it, leaving the rest of the gold decoration in high relief against the black background.

The **Ban Chiang House** has a very good collection of elegant, whorled pottery and bronze jewellery, which the former owner of Suan Pakkad Palace, Princess Chumbot, excavated from tombs at Ban Chiang, the major Bronze Age settlement in northeast Thailand. Scattered around the rest of the museum are some attractive Thai and Khmer religious sculptures among an eclectic jumble of artefacts: fine ceramics as well as some intriguing kiln-wasters, failed pots which have melted together in the kiln to form weird, almost rubbery pieces of sculpture; an extensive collection of colourful papier-mache *khon* masks; beautiful betel-nut sets; elegant monks' ceremonial fans; and some rich teak carvings, including a 200-year-old temple door showing episodes from *Sang Thong*, a folk tale about a childless king and queen who discover a handsome son in a conch shell.

## The Erawan Shrine

For a break from high culture drop in on the **Erawan Shrine** (*Saan Phra Pom* in Thai), at the corner of Ploenchit and Rajdamri roads. Remarkable as much for its setting as anything else, this shrine to Brahma, the ancient Hindu creation god, and Erawan, his elephant, squeezes in on one of the busiest and noisiest corners of modern Bangkok, in the shadow of the *Grand Hyatt Erawan Hotel* – whose existence is the reason for the shrine. When a string of calamities held up the building of the original hotel in the 1950s, spirit doctors were called in, who instructed the owners to build a new home for the offended local spirits: the hotel was then finished without further mishap.

The main structure shines with lurid glass of all colours and the overcrowded precinct around it is almost buried under scented garlands and incense candles. You might also catch a lacklustre group of traditional dancers performing here to the strains of a small classical orchestra – worshippers hire them to give thanks for a stroke of good fortune. To increase their future chances of such good fortune, visitors buy a bird or two from the flocks incarcerated in cages here; the bird-seller transfers the requested number of captives to a tiny handheld cage, from which the customer duly liberates the animals, thereby accruing merit. People set on less abstract rewards will invest in a lottery ticket from one of the physically disabled sellers: they're thought to be the luckiest you can buy.

# Patpong

Concentrated into a small area between the eastern ends of Silom and Suriwong roads, the neon-lit go-go bars of the **Patpong** district loom like rides in a tawdry sexual Disneyland. In front of each bar, girls cajole passers-by with a lifeless sensuality while insistent touts proffer printed menus detailing the degradations on show. Inside, bikini-clad or topless women gyrate to Western music and play hostess to the (almost exclusively male) spectators; upstairs, live shows feature women who, to use Spalding Gray's phrase in *Swimming to Cambodia*, "do everything with their vaginas except have babies".

## Thailand's sex industry

Bangkok owes its reputation as the carnal capital of the world to a highly efficient sex industry adept at peddling fantasies of cheap sex on tap. More than a thousand sex-related businesses operate in the city, but the gaudy neon fleshpots of Patpong give a misleading impression of an activity that is deeply rooted in Thai culture – the overwhelming majority of Thailand's prostitutes of both sexes (estimated at anywhere between 200,000 and 700,000) work with Thai men, not farangs. It is a phenomenally lucrative industry – according to a Chulalongkorn University study, the 1993 income from the trafficking of women in Thailand amounted to US$20–23 billion, or two-thirds of the national budget.

Prostitution and polygamy have long been intrinsic to the Thai way of life. Until Rama VI broke with the custom in 1910, Thai kings had always kept a retinue of concubines around them, a select few of whom would be elevated to the status of wife and royal mother, the rest forming a harem of ladies-in-waiting and sexual playthings. The practice was aped by the status-hungry nobility and, from the early nineteenth century, by newly rich merchants keen to have lots of sons and heirs. Though the monarch is now monogamous, many men of all classes still keep mistresses, known as *mia noi* (minor wives), a tradition bolstered by the popular philosophy which maintains that an official wife (*mia luang*) should be treated like the temple's main Buddha image – respected and elevated upon the altar – whereas the minor wife is an amulet, to be taken along wherever you go. For those not wealthy enough to take on *mia noi*, prostitution is a far less costly and equally accepted option. Statistics indicate that at least forty percent of sexually active Thai men are thought to use the services of prostitutes twice a month on average, and it's common practice for a night out with the boys to wind up in a brothel or massage parlour.

The **farang sex industry** is a relatively new development, having had its start during the Vietnam War, when the American military set up seven bases around Thailand. The GIs' appetite for "entertainment" fuelled the creation of instant redlight districts near the bases, attracting women from surrounding rural areas to cash in on the boom; Bangkok joined the fray in 1967, when the US secured the right to ferry soldiers in from Vietnam for R&R breaks. By the mid-1970s, the bases had been evacuated but the sex infrastructure remained and tourists moved in to fill the vacuum, lured by advertising that diverted most of the traffic to Bangkok and Pattaya. Sex tourism has since grown to become an established part of the Thai economy, the two-million-plus foreign males who arrive each year representing foreign-exchange earnings of B50 billion. Even the highly respectable *Bangkok Post* publishes a weekly column on sex-industry news and gossip.

The majority of the women who work in the Patpong bars come from the poorest rural areas of north and northeast Thailand. **Economic refugees** in search of a better life, they're easily drawn into an industry in which they can make in a single night what it takes a month to earn in the rice fields. Reinforcing the social

Patpong was no more than a sea of mud when the capital was founded on the marshy riverbank to the west, but by the 1960s it had grown into a flash district of nightclubs and dance halls for rich Thais, owned by a Chinese millionaire godfather who gave his name to the area. In 1969, an American entrepreneur turned an existing teahouse into a luxurious nightclub to satisfy the tastes of soldiers on R&R trips from Vietnam, and so Patpong's transformation into a Western sex reservation began. At first, the area was rough and violent, but over the years it has wised up to the desires of the affluent farang, and now markets itself as a packaged concept of Oriental decadence. The centre of the skin trade lies along the interconnected sois of **Patpong 1 and 2**, where lines

obligation to contribute an equal share to the family income is the pervasive Buddhist notion of **karma**, which holds that your lot, however unhappy, is the product of past-life misdeeds and can only be improved by making sufficient merit to ensure a better life next time round.

While most women enter the racket presumably knowing at least something of what lies ahead, younger girls definitely do not. **Child prostitution** is rife: an estimated ten percent of prostitutes are under 14, some are as young as 9. They are valuable property: in the teahouses of Chinatown, a prepubescent virgin can be rented to her first customer for B5000, as sex with someone so young is believed to have rejuvenating properties. Most child prostitutes have been sold by desperate parents as **bonded slaves** to pimps or agents, and are kept locked up until they have fully repaid the money given to their parents, which may take two or more years.

Despite its ubiquity, prostitution has been **illegal** in Thailand since 1960, but sex-industry bosses easily circumvent the law by registering their establishments as bars, restaurants, barbers, nightclubs or massage parlours, and making payoffs to the police. Sex workers, on the other hand, often endure exploitation and violence from employers, pimps and customers rather than face fines and long rehabilitation sentences in prison-like reform centres. Life is made even more difficult by the fact that abortion is illegal in Thailand. In an attempt to redress some of the iniquities, and protect the youngest prostitutes at least, an amendment to the **anti-prostitution law**, passed in April 1996, attempts to treat sex workers as victims rather than criminals. Besides penalizing parents who sell their children to the flesh trade, the amended law is supposed to punish owners, managers and customers of any place of prostitution with a jail sentence or a heavy fine, but this has been met with some cynicism, owing to the number of influential police and politicians allegedly involved in the sex industry. Under this amendment anyone caught having sex with an under-15 is charged with rape, though this has apparently resulted in an increase in trafficking of young children from neighbouring countries as they are less likely to seek help.

In recent years, the spectre of **AIDS** has put the problems of the sex industry into sharp focus: according to a joint study by Chulalongkorn University and the European Union, there are currently around one million HIV carriers in Thailand, and there have been over 270,000 AIDS-related deaths in the country since 1985, a disproportionate number of them in the northern provinces. Since 1988, the government has conducted an aggressive, World Health Organization-approved AIDS awareness campaign, a vital component of which has been to send health officials into brothels to administer blood tests and give out condoms. The programme seems to have had some effect, and the number of new HIV infections declined sharply between 1993 and 1996, though there was a rise during the period following the economic crisis of 1997.

of go-go bars share their patch with respectable restaurants, a 24-hour super-market and an overabundance of chemists. By night, it's a thumping theme park, whose blazing neon promises tend towards self-parody, with names like *French Kiss* and *Love Nest*. Budget travellers, purposeful safari-suited business-men and noisy lager louts throng the streets, and even the most demure tourists – of both sexes – turn out to do some shopping at the night market down the middle of Patpong 1, where hawkers sell fake watches, bags and designer T-shirts. By day, a relaxed hangover descends on the place. Bar-girls hang out at food stalls and cafés in respectable dress, often recognizable only by their faces, pinched and strained from the continuous use of antibiotics and heroin in an attempt to ward off venereal disease and boredom. Farang men slump at the bars on Patpong 2, drinking and watching videos, unable to find anything else to do in the whole of Bangkok.

The small dead-end alley to the east of Patpong 2, **Silom 4** (ie Soi 4, Thanon Silom), hosts Bangkok's hippest nightlife, its bars, clubs and pavements heaving at weekends with the capital's brightest and most over-privileged young things. A few gay venues still cling to Silom 4, but the focus of the scene has recent-ly shifted to **Silom 2**. In between, **Thaniya Road**'s hostess bars and one of the city's swishest shopping centres, Thaniya Plaza, cater mostly to Japanese tourists, while **Soi 6** (Soi Tanatawan) to the west of Patpong attracts a curious mix of Korean and hardcore gay visitors.

## Ban Kamthieng

Another reconstructed traditional Thai residence, **Ban Kamthieng** (Tues–Sat 9am–5pm; entry by donation until renovations are completed in 2002) was moved in the 1960s from Chiang Mai to 131 Soi Asoke (Soi 21), off Thanon Sukhumvit, and set up as an ethnological museum by the Siam Society. It dif-fers from both Suan Pakkad and Jim Thompson's House in being the home of a rural family, and the objects on display give a fair representation of country life in northern Thailand.

The house was built on the banks of the River Ping in the mid-nineteenth century, and the ground-level display of farming tools and fish traps evokes the upcountry practice of fishing in flooded rice paddies to supplement the supply from the rivers. Upstairs, the main rooms of the house are much as they would have been 150 years ago – the raised floor is polished and smooth, sparsely fur-nished with only a couple of low tables and seating mats, and a betel-nut set to hand; notice how surplus furniture and utensils are stored in the rafters. The rectangular lintel above the door to the inner room is a *hum yon*, carved in flo-ral patterns that represent testicles and designed to ward off evil spirits. The gar-den, too, is as authentic as possible: walking along the open verandah between the kitchen and the granary, you'll see areca palm trees to your left, the red fruit of which – the betel nut – is mildly narcotic and a favourite chew of upcoun-try villagers.

Next door to Kamthieng House, in the same compound, is the more recent-ly acquired **Sangaroon House**, built here to house the folk-craft collection of Thai architect and lecturer Sangaroon Ratagasikorn. Upon his return to Thailand after studying in America under Frank Lloyd Wright, Sangaroon became fascinated by the efficient designs of rural utensils and began to col-lect them as teaching aids. Those on display include baskets, fishing pots and *takraw* balls, all of which fulfil his criteria of being functional, simple and beau-tiful.

# Chatuchak and the outskirts

The amorphous clutter of Greater Bangkok doesn't harbour many attractions, but **Chatuchak Weekend Market**, and the cultural theme park of **Muang Boran** are both well worth making the effort for.

## Chatuchak Weekend Market

With six thousand open-air stalls to peruse, and wares as diverse as Laotian silk, Siamese kittens and designer lamps to choose from, the enormous **Chatuchak Weekend Market** (Sat & Sun 7am–6pm) is Bangkok's most enjoyable shopping experience. It occupies a huge patch of ground between the Northern Bus Terminal and Mo Chit Skytrain station (N8), and is best reached by Skytrain if you're coming from downtown areas. The Mo Chit stop is the most convenient, but some people prefer to get off at Saphan Kwai (N7) and then walk through the amulet stalls that line the road up to the southern (handicraft) part of the market. Coming from Banglamphu, you can either get a bus to the nearest Skytrain stop (probably Ratchathewi or Phya Thai) and then take the train, or take the #3 or #9 bus all the way from Rajdamnoen Klang (1hr).

Though its primary customers are Bangkok residents in search of inexpensive clothes and home accessories, Chatuchak also has plenty of collector- and tourist-orientated **stalls**. Best buys include antique lacquerware, unusual sarongs, cotton clothing and crafts from the north, jeans, traditional musical instruments, silver jewellery and ceramics, particularly the five-coloured *bencharong*. The market is divided into 26 numbered **sections**, plus a dozen unnumbered ones, each of which is more or less dedicated to a certain range of goods, for example household items, plants, used books or handicrafts. If you have several hours to spare, it's fun just to browse at whim, but if you're looking for souvenirs, handicrafts or traditional textiles you should start with sections 22, 24, 25 and 26, which are all in a cluster at the southwest (Saphan Kwai) end of the market; the "Dream" section behind the TAT office is also full of interesting artefacts. *Nancy Chandler's Map of Bangkok* has a fabulously detailed and informatively annotated map of all the sections in the market, but should be bought before you arrive. Alternatively, drop in at the TAT office, located in the Chatuchak market building on the southwest edge of the market, across the car park, as they dish out smaller but useful plans of the market for free.

The market also contains a large, and controversial, **wildlife** section and has long been a popular clearing-house for protected and endangered species such as gibbons, palm cockatoos and Indian pied hornbills, many of them smuggled in from Laos and Cambodia and sold to private animal collectors and foreign zoos, particularly in eastern Europe. The illegal trade goes on beneath the counter, but you're bound to come across fighting cocks around the back (demonstrations are almost continuous), miniature flying squirrels being fed milk through pipettes, and iridescent red and blue Siamese fighting fish, kept in individual jars and shielded from each other's aggressive stares by sheets of cardboard.

There's no shortage of **food** stalls inside the market compound, particularly at the southern end, where you'll find plenty of places serving inexpensive *pat thai* and Isaan snacks. Close by these stalls is a classy little juice bar called *Viva* where you can rest your feet while listening to the manager's jazz tapes. The biggest restaurant here is *Toh Plue*, behind TAT on the edge of the Dream section, which makes a good rendezvous point. For vegetarian sustenance, head for *Chamlong's* (also known as *Asoke*), an open-air, cafeteria-style restaurant just outside the market on Thanon Kamphaeng Phet (across Thanon Kamphaeng Phet 2), set up by Bangkok's former governor as a service to the citizenry (Sat & Sun 8am–noon). You can **change money** (Sat & Sun 7am–7pm) in the market building at the south end of the market, across the car park from the stalls area, and there's an ATM here too.

### Muang Boran Ancient City

The brochure for **Muang Boran Ancient City** (daily 8am–5pm; B50, children B25), 33km southeast of the city, sells the place as a sort of cultural fast-food outlet – "a realistic journey into Thailand's past in only a few hours, saving you the many weeks of travel and considerable expense of touring Thailand yourself". The open-air museum is a considerably more authentic experience than its own publicity makes out, showcasing past and present Thai artistry and offering an enjoyable introduction to the country's architecture. To get there from Bangkok, take a bus to **Samut Prakan** on the edge of built-up Greater Bangkok, then a songthaew; air-conditioned **buses** #8 and #11 from Banglamphu/Thanon Rama I/Thanon Sukhumvit, and regular bus #25 from Sanam Luang/Charoen Krung/Thanon Rama I/Thanon Sukhumvit all go to Samut Prakan, where you need to change on to songthaew #36 which passes the entrance to Muang Boran.

Some of Muang Boran's ninety-odd buildings are originals, including a rare scripture library rescued from Samut Songkhram. Others are painstaking reconstructions from contemporary documents (the Ayutthaya-period Sanphet Prasat palace is a particularly fine example) or scaled-down copies of famous monuments such as the Grand Palace. A sizeable team of restorers and skilled craftspeople maintains the buildings and helps keep some of the traditional techniques alive; if you come here during the week you can watch them at work.

# Eating, drinking, entertainment and shopping

As you'd expect, nowhere in Thailand can compete with Bangkok's diversity when it comes to eating and entertainment and, although prices are generally higher here than in the provinces, it's still easy to have a good time while on a budget. Bangkok boasts an astonishing fifty thousand **places to eat** – that's almost one for every hundred citizens – ranging from grubby streetside noodle shops to the most elegant of restaurants. Below we run through the best of the city's indigenous eateries, with a few representatives of the capital's numerous ethnic minorities.

Bangkok's **bars** and **clubs** have not always been the city's strongest suit, but a vibrant house and techno scene has now emerged around the fringes of Patpong, and the number of trendy restaurant–bars in the Banglamphu area has recently mushroomed. Getting back to your lodgings is no problem in the small hours: many bus routes run a reduced service throughout the night, and tuk-tuks and taxis are always at hand – though it's probably best for unaccompanied women to avoid using tuk-tuks late at night.

Introductions to more traditional elements of Thai culture are offered by the raucous ambience of the city's **boxing arenas**, its **music and dancing** troupes and its profusion of **shops**, stalls and markets – all of them covered here.

# Eating

Thai restaurants of all types are found all over the city. The best **gourmet Thai** restaurants operate from the downtown districts around Sukhumvit and Silom roads, proffering wonderful royal, traditional and regional cuisines that definitely merit an occasional splurge. Over in Banglamphu, Thanon Phra Athit has become famous for its dozen or so trendy little restaurant–bars, each with distinctive decor and a contemporary Thai menu that's angled at young Thai diners. At the other end of the scale there are the **night markets** and **street stalls**, so numerous in Bangkok that we can only flag the most promising areas – but wherever you're staying, you'll hardly have to walk a block in any direction before encountering something appealing.

For the non–Thai cuisines, Chinatown naturally rates as the most authentic district for pure **Chinese** food; likewise neighbouring Pahurat, the capital's Indian enclave, is best for unadulterated **Indian** dishes. The place to head for Western, **travellers' food** – from herbal teas and hamburgers to muesli – as well as a hearty range of veggie options is Thanon Khao San, packed with small, inexpensive tourist restaurants; standards vary, but there are some definite gems among the blander establishments.

**Fast food** comes in two forms: the mainly Thai version, found on the upper floor **food courts** of department stores all over the city, and the old Western fallbacks like *McDonald's* and *KFC* that mainly congregate around Thanon Sukhumvit, Siam Square and Thanon Ploenchit – an area that also has its share of decent Thai and foreign restaurants. In addition, downtown Bangkok has a good quota of **coffee shops**, including several branches of Black Canyon and Starbucks, the latter expensive but usually graced with armchairs and free newspapers.

The restaurants listed below are graded by three general price categories based on the cost of a main dish: inexpensive (under B60), moderate (B60–130) and expensive (over B130). In the more expensive places you may have to pay a service charge and seven percent government tax. Most restaurants in Bangkok are open daily for lunch and dinner; we've noted exceptions in the listings below. All the restaurants have English menus unless stated; telephone numbers are given for the more popular or out-of-the-way places, where bookings may be advisable.

# Banglamphu and Democracy area

Banglamphu is a great area for eating. **Khao San** is stacked full of guest-house restaurants serving the whole range of cheap and cheerful travellers' fare; there are also some good veggie places here, as well as Indian, Israeli and Italian joints. For a complete contrast you need only walk a few hundred metres down to riverside **Thanon Phra Athit**, where the pavement positively heaves with arty little café–restaurants; these are patronized mainly by students from Thammasat University up the road, but most offer English-language menus to any interested farangs. The food in these places is generally modern Thai, nearly always very good and reasonably priced. There are also some recommended trendy Thai places on the Banglamphu **fringes**, plus a few traditional options too. For restaurant locations see the map on pp.98–99.

## Around Khao San

**Coffee Corner**, west end of Trok Mayom/Damnoen Klang Neua. Makeshift alleyway café serving ten different blends of freshly brewed coffee, plus espressos and cappuccinos. Inexpensive.

**Himalayan Kitchen**, 1 Thanon Khao San. First-floor restaurant with good bird's-eye views of Khao San action. Both the food and the decor draw their inspiration from Nepal, with religious *thanka* paintings on the wall and thalis (veg and non-veg) on the menu. Moderate.

**La Casa**, Thanon Khao San. Stylish Italian place that's the sister operation of the Chiang Mai restaurant. All the standard pizza and pasta formulae are here, plus there are some innovative pasta salads, including a recommended Greek-style one with basil, olives, capers and anchovies. And if you're feeling particularly adventurous you can round off with fettucine doused in chocolate sauce and ice cream. Moderate to expensive.

**May Kaidee**, 123–125 Thanon Tanao, though actually on the parallel soi to the east; easiest access is to take first left on Soi Damnoen Klang Neua (Soi Post Office). Simple, soi-side foodstall plus tables serving the best vegetarian food in Banglamphu. Try the tasty green curry with coconut, the curry-fried tofu with vegetables or the sticky black-rice pudding. Shuts about 9pm. Inexpensive.

**Night markets**, in front of 7/11 at the Thanon Tani/Soi Ram Bhuttri intersection, and at the Soi Ram Bhuttri/Thanon Chakrabongse intersection. Small knots of hot-food stalls serving very cheap night-market fare including *pat thai*, *kway tiaw nam*, satay, fresh fruit juices and cold beer. Sets up around 5.30pm and keeps going until the early hours.

**Prakorb House**, Thanon Khao San. Archetypal travellers' haven, with only a few tables, and an emphasis on wholesome ingredients. Herbal teas, mango shakes, delicious pumpkin curry, and lots more besides. Inexpensive.

**Royal India**, opposite Boots on Thanon Khao San. Excellent Indian food in copious quantities at this very popular branch of the Pahurat original. Inexpensive to moderate.

**Sarah**, off Thanon Chakrabongse, between the Shell petrol station and the police station. Inexpensive Israeli restaurant, serving hearty plate-fuls of workaday falafels, hummus, salads and dips.

**Sorn Daeng**, southeast corner of Democracy Monument. Standard Thai dishes including southern curries like the rich sweet beef *kaeng mat-saman*. Inexpensive.

## Phra Athit area

**Hemlock**, 56 Thanon Phra Athit, next door but one from *Pra Arthit Mansion*; the sign is visible from the road but not from the pavement (☎02/282 7507). Small, stylish, highly recommended air-con restaurant that's very popular with students and young Thai couples. Offers a long and interesting menu of unusual Thai dishes, including banana flower salad (*yam hua plii*), coconut and mushroom curry, grand lotus rice and various *larb* and

fish dishes. The traditional *miang* starters (shiny green wild tea leaves filled with chopped vegetables, fish and meat) are also very tasty, and there's a good vegetarian selection. Mon–Sat 5pm–midnight; worth reserving a table on Friday and Saturday nights. Moderate.

**Joy Luck Club**, opposite the fort at the point where Thanon Phra Athit turns into Thanon Phra Sumen. Despite its name, the only thing that's noticeably Chinese about this cute little art-house café–restaurant is the red lanterns hanging outside. Inside are just half a dozen tables, modern art on the walls and occasional live music. The Thai food is delicious, and there's a big veggie menu too, including various green and matsaman curries, plus lots of cocktails. Inexpensive to moderate.

**Krua Nopparat**, 130–132 Thanon Phra Athit. The decor in this unassuming air-con restaurant is noticeably plain compared with all the arty joints on this road, but the Thai food is good – try the eggplant wingbean salad and the battered crab – and the prices very inexpensive.

**Tonpo**, Thanon Phra Athit, next to Tha Banglamphu express boat pier. Sizeable seafood menu and a relatively scenic riverside location; good place for a beer and a snack at the end of a long day's sightseeing. Moderate.

**Tuk**, corner of Soi Ram Bhuttri and Soi Chana Songkhram. The perfect breakfast place, with lots of options, ranging from American and European to Israeli and Chinese, plus wholemeal bread and good yoghurt. Inexpensive.

## Samsen, Thewes and the fringes

**Bangkok Bar**, 591 Thanon Phra Sumen. Housed in an elegant 150-year-old canalside house, complete with high ceilings, wooden floors and fine fretwork, this place is well worth trying both for its setting and for its good-value upmarket Thai cuisine. There's a gallery upstairs to entertain you while you're waiting for food. Recommendations include seafood with young coconut, fish-head curry and deep-fried pillows of tofu. Moderate.

**Dachanee**, 18/2 Thanon Pracha Thipatai, near *Thai Hotel*. Standard Thai fare such as fiery *tom yam*, plus tasty extras like tofu- and beansprout-stuffed *khanom buang* (crispy Vietnamese-style pancakes), in an air-con restaurant. Inexpensive to moderate.

**Dragon Eyes**, Thanon Samsen, on the corner of Thanon Wisut Kasat. Small restaurant popular with young Thai couples. Stylish renditions of standard Thai dishes – try the *khao pat* with added fruit and nuts, or the chilli-fried chicken with cashews (*kai pat met mamuang himapaan*). Huge selection of bar drinks as well and, as you'd expect from a place managed by a *Bangkok Post* music critic, a fine range of music. Daily except Sun 6.30pm–midnight. Moderate.

**Isaan restaurants**, behind the Rajdamnoen Boxing Stadium on Thanon Rajdamnoen Nok. At least five restaurants in a row serving northeastern fare to hungry boxing fans: take your pick for hearty plates of *kai yang* and *khao niaw*. Inexpensive.

**Kainit**, 68 Thanon Titong, next to Wat Suthat. Rather formal Italian restaurant that's mainly patronized by expats, but also works fine as a lunch–time treat after visiting Wat Suthat next door. The pizza and pastas are tasty but expensive.

**Kaloang**, beside the river at the far western end of Thanon Sri Ayutthaya. Flamboyant service and excellent seafood attracts an almost exclusively Thai clientele to this open-air riverside restaurant. Try the fried rolled shrimps served with a sweet dip, the roast squid cooked in a piquant sauce, or the steamed butter fish. Expensive.

**Na Pralan**, almost opposite the Gate of Glorious Victory, Thanon Na Phra Lan. Technically in Ratanakosin (it's marked on the map on p.112) but very close to Banglamphu, this small café, only a couple of doors up the street from the Silpakorn University Art College, is ideally placed for refreshment after your tour of the Grand Palace. Popular with students, it occupies a quaint old air-con shophouse with battered, arty decor. The menu, well thought out with some unusual twists, offers tasty daily specials – mostly one-dish meals with rice – and a range of Thai desserts, coffees, teas and beers. Mon–Sat 10am–10pm. Inexpensive.

**Silver Spoon**, beside the Tha Thewes express-boat pier at 2/1 Thanon Krung Kasem. Popular place for seafood – and riverine breezes, with decent Chao Phraya views and a huge menu including baked cottonfish in mango sauce, steamed snakehead fish with chillies, and *tom yam kung*. Moderate.

**Tang Teh**, 269–271 Thanon Wisut Kasat, corner of Thanon Samsen. Quality Thai restaurant, with contemporary art on the walls and high-class food on the menu. Fried catfish with cashews and chilli sauce recommended, as are the superb fishcakes and the steamed sea bass with Chinese plum sauce; also a fairly interesting veggie menu, and home-made ice cream. Moderate.

# Chinatown and Pahurat

The places listed below are marked on the map on p.128.

## Yellow-flag heaven for veggies

Every autumn, for nine days during the ninth lunar month (October or November), Thailand's Chinese community goes on a **meat-free** diet in order to mark the onset of the Vegetarian Festival (Ngan Kin Jeh), a sort of Taoist version of Lent. Though the Chinese citizens of Bangkok don't go in for skewering themselves like their compatriots in Trang and Phuket (see p.327), they do celebrate the Vegetarian Festival with gusto: nearly every restaurant and foodstall in Chinatown turns vegetarian for the period, flying small yellow flags to show that they are upholding the tradition. For vegetarian tourists this is a great time to be in town – just look for the yellow flag and you can be sure all dishes will be one hundred percent vegan. Many hotel restaurants also get in on the act during the Vegetarian Festival, running special veggie promotions for a week or two.

**Chong Tee**, 84 Soi Sukon 1, Thanon Trimit, between Hualamphong station and Wat Traimit. Delicious pork satay and sweet toast. Inexpensive.

**Hua Seng Hong**, 371 Thanon Yaowarat. Not too hygienic, but the food is good. Sit outside on the jostling pavement for delicious egg noodle soup with pork, duck or *wonton*, or good-value shark's fin soup; or venture inside to the air-con restaurant, where the main thrust is fish and seafood (try the asparagus with scallop), though pricey Chinese specialities like goose feet, smoked whole baby pig and bird's nest are also on offer. If you've still got room for more, head for the stall outside selling delicious *bua loy nga dam nam khing*, soft rice dumplings stuffed with bitter-sweet black sesame in ginger soup (evenings only; inexpensive). Moderate.

**Maturot**, Soi Phadungdao (aka Soi Texas), Thanon Yaowarat. In a soi famous for its seafood stalls, the fresh, meaty prawns served up here, accompanied by *pak bung fai daeng* (fried morning glory) and

*tom yam kung*, stand out. Evenings only, until late. Inexpensive to moderate.

**Royal India**, just off Thanon Chakraphet. Serves the same excellent curries as its Banglamphu branch, but attracts an almost exclusively Indian clientele. Inexpensive to moderate.

**White Orchid Hotel**, 409–421 Thanon Yaowarat. Recommended for its *dim sum*, with bamboo baskets of prawn dumplings, spicy spare ribs, stuffed beancurd and the like, served in three different portion sizes. *Dim sum* 11am–2pm & 5–10pm. All-you-can-eat lunch-time buffets also worth considering. Moderate to expensive.

**You Sue Vegetarian**, 75m east of Hualamphong station at 241 Thanon Rama IV; directly across the road from the sign for the *Bangkok Centre Hotel*. Cheap and cheerful Chinese vegetarian café, where standard Thai curries and Chinese one-pot dishes are made with high-protein meat substitutes. Daily 6am–10pm.

# Downtown: Siam Square and Thanon Ploenchit

The map on p.103 shows the places listed below.

**Bali**, 15/3 Soi Ruam Rudee ✆02/250 0711. Top-notch Indonesian food in a cosy nook; closed Mon lunch. Moderate to expensive – blow out on seven-course *rijstaffel* for B250.

**Café Botanica**, 1st Floor, Gaysorn Plaza, Thanon Ploenchit ✆02/656 1305–6. A haven for footsore shoppers but worth a detour in its own right: excellent Thai and Western food, with an especially good choice of Thai salads and noodles, in a sophisticated, open-plan setting. Daily 10am–9.30pm. Moderate.

**Inter**, 432/1–2 Soi 9, Siam Square ✆02/251 4689. Efficient Thai restaurant that's popular with

students and shoppers, serving good one-dish meals and more expensive curries in a no-frills, fluorescent-lit canteen atmosphere. Daily 10am–10pm. Inexpensive.

**Kirin Restaurant**, 226/1 Soi 2, Siam Square. Swankiest and best of many Chinese restaurants in the area; for a blow-out, order the delicious *ped pak king*, duck cooked with vegetables and ginger. Expensive.

**Kroissant House**, ground floor of World Trade Centre, corner of Thanon Rama I and Thanon Rajdamri. Fine Italian ice creams, cakes and pastries – a good choice for breakfast.

**Ma Be Ba**, 93 Soi Lang Suan ☎02/254 9595. Lively, spacious and extravagantly decorated Italian restaurant dishing up excellent pizzas and daily pasta specials, usually seafood, from a huge open kitchen. Daily 11am–2.30pm & 5.30pm–1am (last food orders 11.30pm). Expensive.

**Mah Boon Krong Food Centre**, 6th Floor, MBK shopping centre, corner of Rama I and Phrayathai roads. Increase your knowledge of Thai food here: ingredients, names and pictures of dishes (including plenty of vegetarian ones, and a wide range of desserts) from all over the country are displayed at the various stalls. Inexpensive.

**Sarah Jane's**, Ground Floor, Sindhorn Tower 1, 130–132 Thanon Witthayu ☎02/650 9992–3. Long-standing restaurant, popular with Bangkok's Isaan population, serving excellent, simple north-eastern food. It's in slick but unfussy modern premises that can be slightly tricky to find at night, towards the rear of a modern office block. Moderate.

**Sorn's**, 36/8 Soi Kasemsan 1, Thanon Rama I. In this quiet lane of superior guest houses, a laid-back hangout with an atmosphere like a beachside guest-house restaurant. Delicious versions of standard Thai dishes – the *tom kha kai* is especially good – as well as Western meals, varied breakfasts, good coffee and a full-service bar with reasonably priced wine. Moderate.

**Talat Samyarn** (Samyarn Market), set back on the west side of Thanon Phrayathai, near the corner of Rama IV. Great area for stall-grazing, always busy with Chulalongkorn University students. Inexpensive.

**Whole Earth**, 93/3 Soi Langsuan ☎02/252 5574. The best veggie restaurant in Bangkok, serving interesting and varied Thai and Indian-style food (plus some dishes for carnivores) in a relaxing atmosphere. Moderate.

**Zen**, 6th Floor, World Trade Center, corner of Thanon Rama I and Thanon Rajdamri ☎02/255 6462; and 4th Floor, Siam Center, Thanon Rama I ☎02/658 1183–4. Good-value Japanese restaurant with wacky modern wooden design and seductive booths. Among a huge range of dishes, the complete meal sets (with pictures to help you choose) are filling and particularly good. Moderate to expensive.

# Downtown: south of Thanon Rama IV

The places listed below are marked on the maps on p.105 and p.107.

**Akane Japanese Noodle**, Central department store, Thanon Silom (plus branches around town, including in the World Trade Center, corner of Rajdamri and Rama I). Deliciously authentic *soba*, *udon*, *ramen* and *sushi* dishes in unpretentious café-style surrounds. Daily 11am–10pm. Moderate.

**All Gaengs**, 173/8–9 Thanon Suriwong. Large menu of tasty curries (*kaeng*, sometimes spelt *gaeng*) served in cool, modern surrounds. Closed Sat & Sun lunch times. Moderate.

**Angelini's**, *Shangri-La Hotel*, 89 Soi Wat Suan Plu, Thanon Charoen Krung (New Rd) ☎02/236 7777. One of the capital's best Italians, pricey but not too extravagant. The setting is lively and relaxed, with open-plan kitchen and big picture windows onto the pool and river, though the music can be obtrusive. Whether you're vegetarian or not, it's worth plumping for the pumpkin ravioli with truffle butter sauce; otherwise, there are some unusual main courses as well as old favourites like *ossobucco*, or you can invent your own wood-oven-baked pizza. Daily 11am–late.

**Aoi**, 132/10–11 Soi 6, Thanon Silom ☎02/235 2321–2; branch in Emporium on Thanon Sukhunvit ☎02/664 8590. The best place in town for a Japanese blowout, justifiably popular with the expat community. Excellent authentic food and elegant decor. Lunch sets available and a sushi bar. Expensive.

**Ban Chiang**, 14 Thanon Srivieng, between Silom and Sathorn roads ☎02/236 7045. Fine Thai cuisine in an elegant wooden house. Moderate to expensive.

**Bussaracum**, 139 Sethiwan Building, Thanon Pan ☎02/266 6312–8. Superb royal Thai cuisine. Expensive, but well worth it.

**Chai Karr**, 312/3 Thanon Silom ☎02/233 2549. Opposite *Holiday Inn*. Folksy, traditional-style wooden decor is the setting for a wide variety of standard Thai and Chinese dishes, followed by liqueur coffees and coconut ice cream. Daily 11.30am–9pm. Moderate.

**Charuvan**, 70–2 Thanon Silom, near the entrance to Soi 4. Clean but lackadaisical place, with an air-con room, specializing in inexpensive and tasty duck on rice; the beer's a bargain too.

**Deen**, 786 Thanon Silom, almost opposite Silom Village (no English sign). Small, basic Muslim café with air-con (no smoking), which offers Thai and Chinese standard dishes with a southern Thai twist, as well as spicy Indian-style curries and specialities such as *grupuk* (crispy fish) and *roti*. Mon–Sat 11am–9.30pm. Inexpensive to moderate.

**Harmonique**, 22 Soi 34, Thanon Charoen Krung, on the lane between Wat Muang Kae express-boat pier and the GPO ☏02/237 8175. A relaxing, welcoming restaurant that's well worth a trip: tables are scattered throughout several converted houses, decorated with antiques, and a quiet, leafy courtyard, and the Thai food is varied and excellent – among the seafood specialities, try the crab curry. Daily 10am–10pm. Moderate.

**Himali Cha-Cha**, 1229/11 Thanon Charoen Krung, south of GPO ☏02/235 1569. Fine north Indian restaurant founded by a character who was chef to numerous Indian ambassadors, and now run by his son; good vegetarian selection. Moderate.

**Laicram**, 2nd Floor, Thaniya Plaza, east end of Thanon Silom. Small, proficient restaurant offering some unusual specialities from around Thailand on a huge menu, plus loads of veggie dishes and traditional desserts. Moderate.

**Le Bouchon**, 37/17 Patpong 2, near Thanon Suriwong ☏02/234 9109. Cosy, welcoming French bistro serving unpretentious food; much frequented by the city's French expats. Daily 11am–11.30pm. Expensive.

**Mango Tree**, 37 Soi Tantawan, Thanon Suriwong ☏02/236 2820. Excellent authentic Thai food in a surprisingly peaceful haven between Suriwong and Silom, where you can eat indoors or out in the garden to the live strains of a traditional Thai ensemble. Highly rated by Bangkokians, so definitely worth booking. Moderate to expensive.

**Mei Jiang**, *Peninsula Hotel*, 333 Thanon Charoennakorn, Klongsan. Probably Bangkok's best Chinese restaurant, with beautiful views of the hotel gardens and the river. It's designed like an elegant teak box, without the gaudiness of many Chinese restaurants, and staff are very attentive. Specialities include duck smoked with tea and excellent lunch-time *dim sum* – a bargain at around B65 a dish. Expensive.

**Ranger**, Mahamek Driving Range, south end of Soi

Ngam Duphli, by the Ministry of Aviation compound ☏02/679 8964. Unusual location in a golf driving range, but the setting for the restaurant itself is cute and pastoral, on tree-shaded platforms above a quiet, lotus-filled pond. Specialities include *yam hua pree*, delicious banana flower salad with dried shrimp and peanuts; some veggie dishes are available, and the service is friendly and attentive. Daily 6am–10pm. Moderate.

**Ratree Seafood**, opposite Thaniya Plaza, Soi 1, Thanon Silom. Famous street stall, surrounded by many similar competitors, with twenty or so tables in the adjoining alley. Temptingly displayed is all manner of fresh seafood (the specialities are *poo chak ka chan* – oily, orange, medium-sized sea crab – and barbecued fish) and there's noodle soup too. Evenings only. Inexpensive to moderate.

**Sui Heng**, mouth of Soi 65, Thanon Charoen Krung, south of Sathorn Bridge. In a good area for stall-grazing, a legendary Chinese street vendor who has been selling one dish for over seventy years: *khao man kai*, tender boiled chicken breast served with delicious broth and garlic rice. Evenings only, until late. Inexpensive.

**Thaichine**, 233 Thanon Sathorn ☏02/212 6401. In a grand, century-old building that was formerly the Thai-Chinese Chamber of Commerce, this is an elegant, comfortable restaurant, where the eclectic Asian decor matches the menu's delicious combination of Thai, Vietnamese and Chinese dishes. Daily 10am–11pm. Moderate.

**Tongue Thai**, 18–20 Soi 38, Thanon Charoen Krung ☏02/630 9918–9. In front of the Oriental Place shopping mall. Very high standards of food and cleanliness, with charming, unpretentious service, in an elegantly decorated 100-year-old shophouse. Veggies are amply catered for with delicious dishes such as tofu in black bean sauce and deep-fried banana flower and corn cakes, while carnivores should try the fantastic beef curry (*panaeng neua*). Expensive.

## Thanon Sukhumvit

See the map on p.108 for locations of the places listed below.

**Ambassador Hotel Seafood Centre**, inside the *Ambassador Hotel* complex, between sois 11 and 13. Cavernous hall of a restaurant that spills over into a covered courtyard with over a dozen stalls serving all manner of fish and seafood dishes, including soups and barbecued fish. Moderate.

**Baan Kanitha**, Soi 23. The big attraction at this long-running favourite haunt of Sukhumvit expats is the setting in a traditional Thai house. The food is upmarket Thai and includes lots of fiery salads

(*yam*), and a good range of *tom yam* soups, green curries and seafood curries. Expensive.

**Basil**, *Sheraton Grande Hotel*, between sois 12 and 14. Mouthwateringly fine traditional Thai food with a modern twist is the order of the day at this trendy, relatively informal restaurant. Recommendations include the grilled river prawns with chilli, the *matsaman* curry (both served with red and green rice) and the surprisingly delicious durian cheesecake. Vegetarian menu on request. Expensive.

**Cabbages and Condoms**, Soi 12. Run by the Population and Community Development Association of Thailand (PDA): diners are treated to authentic Thai food in the Condom Room, and relaxed scoffing of barbecued seafood in the beer garden. Try the *plaa samlii* (fried cottonfish with mango and chilli) or the *kai haw bai toey* (marinated chicken baked in pandanus leaves). All proceeds go to the PDA, and there's an adjacent shop selling all kinds of double-entendre T-shirts, keyrings and of course condoms. Moderate.

**De Meglio**, Soi 11. Upmarket Italian presided over by a chef who was trained by Anton Mosiman. Antipastos here are unusual Thai–Italian hybrids, and the linguini with clams and the crab cannelloni with fennel salad are recommended. Authentic wood-fired pizzas a speciality. Expensive.

**Emporium Food Court**, 5th Floor, Emporium Shopping Centre, between sois 22 and 24. Typical food court of twenty stalls selling very cheap but reasonable quality Thai standards including fishball soup, fried chicken and satay. Buy coupons at the entrance booth and find a window table for pleasant views over Queen Sirikit park. For something more upmarket, there are a dozen small restaurant concessions on the same floor as the food court, ranging from Italian to Japanese.

**Haus München**, Soi 15. Hearty helpings of authentic German classics, from pigs' knuckles to *bratwurst*, served in a restaurant that's modelled on a Bavarian lodge. Moderate.

**Jools Bar and Restaurant**, Soi 4, a short walk from the Soi Nana go-go strip. Hearty British fare of the meat-and-two-veg variety dished out in the upstairs room of a popular British-run pub. Moderate.

**Lemongrass**, Soi 24 ☎02/258 8637. Scrumptious Thai nouvelle cuisine in a converted traditional house; vegetarian menu on request. The minced chicken with ginger is a particular winner. Advance reservations recommended. Moderate to expensive.

**Mrs Balbir's**, Soi 11/1. Deservedly popular veg and non-veg Indian restaurant run by TV cook Mrs Balbir. Specialities include the spicy dry chicken and lamb curries (*masala kerai*) and the daily all-you-can-eat veggie buffet, which is highly recommended at B150 per person. Indian cookery courses held here every week – see Listings on p.162 for details.

**Nipa**, 3rd Floor of Landmark Plaza, between sois 4 and 6. Tasteful traditional Thai-style place with a classy menu that features an adventurous range of dishes, including spicy fish curry, several *matsaman* and green curries, excellent *som tam* and mouthwatering braised spare ribs. Also offers a sizeable vegetarian selection. Regular cookery classes are held here – see Listings on p.162 for details. Last orders at 10.15pm. Moderate to expensive.

**Suda Restaurant**, Soi 14. Unpretentious locals' hangout, patronized by office workers at lunch time, but open till midnight. Standard *kap khao* (dishes served with rice) and noodle dishes, plus some fish: fried tuna with cashews and chilli recommended. Inexpensive to moderate.

**Thong U Rai**, 22/4–5 Soi 23. Highly recommended bohemian place decked out with paintings and antique curios; serves mid-priced Thai food including especially good minced chicken marinaded in limes.

**Whole Earth**, a 10min walk down Soi 26 at #71. Vegetarian restaurant serving meat-free Thai and Indian food plus a few dishes for carnivores (there's another branch off Thanon Ploenchit; see p.149). The mushroom and tofu *larb* served over baked rice is worth the walk, especially if you can get one of the low tables on the first floor where there's more atmosphere than in the ground floor restaurant. Moderate.

**Yong Lee**, corner of Soi 15. One of the few unpretentious and refreshingly basic rice-and-noodle shops on Sukhumvit. Inexpensive.

# Nightlife and entertainment

For many of Bangkok's visitors, nightfall in the city is the signal to hit the **sex bars**, the neon sumps that disfigure three distinct parts of town: along Sukhumvit Road's Soi Cowboy (between sois 21 and 23) and Nana Plaza (Soi 4) and, most notoriously, in the two small sois off the east end of Thanon Silom known as Patpong 1 and 2. But within spitting distance of the beer bellies flopped onto Patpong's bars lies **Silom 4**, Bangkok's most happening after-dark haunt, pulling in the cream of Thai youth and tempting an increasing number of travellers to stuff their party gear into their rucksacks: Soi 4, the next alley off Thanon Silom to the east of Patpong 2, started out as a purely **gay** area but now offers a range of styles in gay, mixed and straight pubs, dance bars and clubs. The city's other main gay areas are the more exclusive Silom 2 (towards Thanon Rama IV), and the rougher, mostly Thai bars of Thanon Sutthisarn near the Chatuchak Weekend Market. As with the straight scene, the majority of gay bars feature go-go dancers and live sex shows. Those listed here do not.

On the cultural front, **Thai dancing** is the most accessible of the capital's performing arts, particularly when served up in bite-size portions on tourist restaurant stages. **Thai boxing** is also well worth watching: the live experience at either of Bangkok's two main national stadiums far outshines the TV coverage.

## Bars and clubs

For convenient drinking and dancing, we've split the most recommended of the city's bars and clubs into three central areas. In **Banglamphu**, there are two main centres for night-time entertainment. The bars and clubs on and around Thanon Khao San are aimed at young Western travellers, with pool tables, cheap beer and either a programme of back-to-back video showings or a DJ with a good loud set of turntables; some of these places also attract crowds of young Thai drinkers. Khao San itself becomes a traffic-free zone after about 7pm and the kerbside tables make great places to nurse a few beers and watch the parade of other travellers; most of the stalls and shops stay open till 11pm or later, so this is also a good time to browse. A couple of blocks further west, Thanon Phra Athit is more of a Thai scene, though again there are always some farang drinkers in the mix. Here, the style-conscious little restaurant–bars have their tables spill over on to the pavement, and the live music is likely to be a lone piano player or guitarist.

**Downtown** bars, which tend to attract both farang and Thai drinkers, are concentrated on adjoining Soi Langsuan and Soi Sarasin (between Thanon Ploenchit and Lumphini Park), and in studenty Siam Square, as well as around the east end of Thanon Silom. Langsuan and Sarasin have their fair share of live-music bars, but the Western covers and bland jazz on offer are often less than inspiring; the better live-music venues are listed below. If, among all the choice of nightlife around Silom, you do end up in one of Patpong's sex bars, be prepared to shell out up to B600 for a small beer. Though many Patpong bars trumpet the fact that they have no cover charge, almost every customer gets ripped off in some way, and stories of menacing bouncers are legion. **Thanon Sukhumvit** watering holes tend to be either British-style pubs, barbeers (open-sided drinking halls with huge circular bars) packed full of hostesses, or full-on girlie bars.

During the cool season (Nov–Feb), an evening out at one of the seasonal **beer gardens** is a pleasant way of soaking up the urban atmosphere (and the traffic fumes). You'll find them in hotel forecourts or sprawled in front of shopping centres – the huge beer garden that sets up in front of the World Trade Centre on Thanon Rajdamri is extremely popular, and recommended; beer is served in pitchers here and bar snacks are available too.

### Banglamphu, Ratanakosin and Hualamphong

All the bars listed below are marked on the map on pp.98–99.

**About Café**, a 5min walk from Hualamphong Station at 418 Thanon Maitri Chit (see map on p.128). Arty café–bar that's popular with trendy young Thais. There's a gallery space upstairs and exhibits usually spill over into the ground floor eating and drinking area, where tables and sofas are scattered about in an informal and welcoming fashion. Mon–Sat 10am–midnight.

**Austin**, just off Thanon Khao San, in the scrum behind *D&D Guest House*. Named in honour of the car (hence the neon silhouette), this homely three-floored bar plays loud music and is hugely popular with students from nearby Thammasat University, though it has yet to attract much of a farang crowd. The favoured drink is a jug of Sang Som rum over ice, mixed with soda and lemon and served with straws to share with your mates. Also on offer are lots of cocktails and fairly pricey beer.

**Banana Bar**, Trok Mayom/Damnoen Klang Neua. Half a dozen tiny cubbyhole bars open up on this alley every night, each with just a handful of alley-side chairs and tables, loud music on the tape player, and a trendy bartender.

**Bangkok Bar**, west end of Soi Ram Bhuttri. Not to be confused with the restaurant of the same name on Thanon Phra Sumen, this small, narrow dance bar is fronted by a different DJ every night and draws capacity crowds of drinkers and clubbers.

**Bayon**, Thanon Khao San. Sizeable but not terribly exciting upstairs dance floor playing disco and rave classics and serving mid-priced drinks to a mixed crowd of Thais and farangs till around 2am.

**Boh**, Tha Thien, Thanon Maharat. When the Chao Phraya express boats stop running around 7pm, this bar takes over the pier with its great sunset views across the river. Beer and Thai whisky with accompanying spicy snacks and loud Thai pop music – very popular with university students.

**Comme**, opposite *Tonpo* riverside restaurant at the northern end of Thanon Phra Athit. One of the most sophisticated bar–restaurants on this trendy road, where you can choose between the air-con section and the open-fronted streetside. Serves decent Thai food and well-priced drinks. Daily 6pm–2am.

**Dog Days**, 100/2–6 Thanon Phra Athit. Quirky little bar–restaurant with a canine theme, a cosy atmosphere, and mid-priced food and drink. Tues–Sun 5pm–midnight.

**Grand Guest House**, middle of Thanon Khao San. Cavernous place lacking in character but popular because it stays open 24hr. Videos are shown non-stop, usually movies in the day and MTV in the early hours.

**Gullivers' Travellers Tavern**, Thanon Khao San. Backpacker-oriented air-con sports pub with two pool tables, sixteen TV screens, masses of sports memorabilia and reasonably priced beer. Stays open until at least 2am.

**Hole in the Wall Bar**, Thanon Khao San. Small, low-key drinking-spot at the heart of the back-packers' ghetto. Dim lighting, a more varied than average CD selection and competitively priced beer.

**Spicy**, Thanon Tanao. Fashionably modern, neon-lit youthful hangout, best for beer, whisky and snacks, but serves main dishes too. Daily 6pm–2am.

**Susie Pub**, next to *Marco Polo Guest House* off Thanon Khao San. Big, dark, phenomenally popular pub that's usually standing-room-only after 9pm. Has a pool table, decent music, resident DJs and cheapish beer. Packed with farangs and young Thais. Daily 11am–2am.

## Siam Square, Thanon Ploenchit and northern downtown

The venues listed below are marked on the map on p.103.

**Ad Makers**, 51/51 Soi Langsuan ⏀02/652 0168. Friendly, spacious bar with Wild West-style wooden decor, featuring nightly "songs for life" (Thai folk music blended with Western prog and folk rock) bands; cheap drinks.

**Brown Sugar**, 231/19–20 Soi Sarasin ⏀02/250 0103. Chic, pricey, lively bar, acknowledged as the capital's top jazz venue.

**Concept CM$^2$**, *Novotel*, Soi 6, Siam Square ⏀02/255 6888. More theme park than nightclub, with live bands and various, barely distinct entertainment zones, including karaoke and an Italian restaurant. Admission price depends on what's on; drinks are pricey.

**Dallas Pub**, Soi 6, Siam Square ⏀02/255 3276. Typical dark, noisy "songs for life" hangout – buffalo skulls, Indian heads, American flags – but a lot of fun: singalongs to decent live bands, dancing round the tables, cheap beer and friendly, casual staff.

**Fou Bar**, 264/4–6 Soi 3, Siam Square. Smart, modernist but easy-going hangout for students and 20-somethings, with reasonably priced drinks, a good choice of accompanying snacks and some interesting Thai/Italian crossovers for main dishes. Hard to find above a juice bar/internet café by Siam Square's Centerpoint.

**Hard Rock Café**, Soi 11, Siam Square. Genuine outlet of the famous chain, better for drink than food. Big sounds, brash enthusiasm, bank-breaking prices.

**Saxophone**, 3/8 Victory Monument (southeast corner), Thanon Phrayathai ⏀02/246 5472. Lively, spacious venue that hosts nightly jazz, blues, folk and rock bands and attracts a good mix of Thais and farangs; decent food, relaxed drinking atmosphere and, all things considered, reasonable prices.

## Southern downtown: south of Thanon Rama IV

See the map on p.105 for locations of the venues listed below.

**The Barbican**, 9/4–5 Soi Thaniya, east end of Thanon Silom ☎02/234 3590. Stylishly modern fortress-like decor to match the name: dark woods, metal and undressed stone. With Guinness on tap and the financial pages posted above the urinals, it could almost be a smart City of London pub – until you look out of the windows onto the soi's incongruous Japanese hostess bars. Good food, DJ sessions and happy hours Mon–Fri 5–7pm.

**Deeper**, Soi 4, Thanon Silom. Long-running hardcore dance club, done out to give an underground feel, all metal and black. Closed after a police raid at the time of writing, but unlikely to remain so.

**Hyper**, Soi 4, Thanon Silom. Long-standing Soi 4 people-watching haunt, with laid-back music and a fun crowd.

**Lucifer**, 76/1–3 Patpong 1. Popular rave club in the dark heart of Patpong, largely untouched by the sleaze around it. Done out with mosaics and stalactites like a satanic grotto, with balconies to look down on the dance-floor action. *Radio City*, the interconnected bar downstairs, is only slightly less raucous, with live bands and tables out on the sweaty pavement.

**Shenanigans**, 1/5 Thanon Convent, off the east end of Thanon Silom ☎02/266 7160. Blarney Bangkok-style: a warm, relaxing Irish pub, tastefully done out in wood, iron and familiar knick-knacks and packed with expats, especially on Fri night. Guinness and Kilkenny Bitter on tap (happy hour 4–7.30pm), very expensive Irish food such as Belfast chaps (fried potatoes) and good veggie options (Mon–Thurs set lunches are better value), as well as a fast-moving rota of house bands.

**Tapas Bar**, Soi 4, Thanon Silom. Cramped, vaguely Spanish-orientated bar (but no tapas), whose outside tables are probably the best spot for checking out the comings and goings on the soi; inside, there's house and garage downstairs, chilled-out ambient and funk upstairs.

## Thanon Sukhumvit

The places listed below are marked on the map on p.108.

**Cheap Charlies**, Soi 11, Thanon Sukhumvit. Hugely popular, long-running pavement bar where it's standing room only, but at a bargain B50 for a bottle of beer it's worth standing.

**Imageries By The Glass**, 2, Soi 24, Thanon Sukhumvit. Usually packed out with Thai couples who come to hear the nightly live music from the roster of different vocalists including rock-, pop- and folk-singers. Pricey drinks. Mon–Sat 6pm–1.30am.

**Jools Bar and Restaurant**, Soi 4, Thanon Sukhumvit, a short walk from the Soi Nana go-go strip. Easy-going British-run pub, popular with expat drinkers (photos of regular customers plaster the walls). The cosy downstairs bar is mainly standing room only, and traditional British food is served at tables upstairs.

**La Lunar**, near *Four Wings Hotel* on Soi 26, Thanon Sukhumvit. Swanky, well-designed place, whose various levels encompass a balconied disco with plenty of room to dance, a sushi bar and a pub with live bands. You need to dress up a bit to get in. B500 including two drinks.

**Manet Club**, **Renoir Club**, **Van Gogh Club**, Soi 33, Thanon Sukhumvit. Three very similar, unexciting, not at all Parisian bars, all almost next door to one another, that are best visited during happy hour (4–9pm).

**Old Dutch**, Soi 23, Thanon Sukhumvit, at the mouth of the Soi Cowboy strip. Cool, dark, peaceful oasis at the edge of Sukhumvit's frenetic sleaze; a reasonable basic menu and a big stock of current US and European newspapers make this an ideal daytime or early evening watering hole.

**Q Bar**, far end of Soi 11. Very dark, very trendy, New York-style bar occupying two floors and a terrace. Appeals to a mixed crowd of fashionable people, particularly on Fri and Sat nights when the DJs fill the dance floor and there's a B300 cover charge that includes two free drinks. Arrive before 11pm if you want a seat; shuts about 2am.

## Gay scene

**The Balcony**, Soi 4, Thanon Silom. Unpretentious, fun place with a large, popular terrace, cheap drinks and decent Thai, Indian and Western food; karaoke and regular talent nights.

**Dick's Café**, 894/7–8 Soi Pratuchai, Thanon Suriwong. Stylish day-and-night café (daily noon–4am) on a quiet soi opposite the prominent Wall St Tower, ideal for cheap drinking, pastries or just chilling out.

**Disco Disco**, Soi 2, Thanon Silom. Small, well-designed bar/disco, with reasonably priced drinks and good dance music for a fun young crowd.

**DJ Station**, Soi 2, Thanon Silom. Highly fashionable but unpretentious disco, packed at weekends, attracting a mix of Thais and farangs; midnight cabaret show. B100 including one drink (B200 including two drinks Fri & Sat).

**Freeman Dance Arena**, 60/18–21 Thanon Silom (in the soi beside 7-11 store, between Soi Thaniya and Thanon Rama IV). Busy, compact disco playing poppy dance music; regular cabaret shows and chill-out tables out on the soi.

**The Icon**, 90–96 Soi 4, Thanon Silom. Nightclub with good sounds and a large dance floor; singing impersonators at 10.30pm, male dance cabaret at 11.45pm. B200 including two drinks.

**JJ Park**, 8/3 Soi 2, Thanon Silom. Classy, Thai-orientated bar/restaurant, for relaxed socializing rather than raving, with live Thai music, comedy shows and good food.

**Sphinx**, 98–104 Soi 4, Thanon Silom. Chic decor, terrace seating and good food attract a sophisticated crowd to this ground-floor bar and restaurant; karaoke and live music upstairs.

**Telephone Bar**, 114/11–13 Soi 4, Thanon Silom. Cruisey, long-standing eating and drinking venue with good Thai cuisine and a terrace on the alley.

**Utopia**, 116/1 Soi 23 (Soi Sawadee), Thanon Sukhumvit ☎02/259 9619, ⊛ www.utopia-asia .com. Bangkok's first gay and lesbian community venue, comprising a shop for books, magazines, fashion and gifts, gallery, cosy café and bar with weekly women-only nights (currently Fri). "Thai Friends" scheme for visitors to be shown around the city by English-speaking gay Thais. Daily noon–midnight.

**Vega**, Soi 39, Thanon Sukhumvit. Trendy bar-restaurant run by a group of lesbians. The live music, karaoke and dance floor attract a mixed, fashionable crowd.

## Culture shows

Only in Bangkok can you be sure to catch a live display of non–tourist-oriented traditional dance or theatre; few of the outlying regions have resident troupes, so authentic performances elsewhere tend to be sporadic and may not coincide with your visit. The main venue is the National Theatre (☎02/224 1342, Mon–Fri 8.30am–4.30pm), next to the National Museum on the northwest corner of Sanam Luang, which puts on special medley shows of **drama and music** from all over the country, performed by students from the attached College of the Performing Arts. From November through May, these take place almost every Saturday, and there are also similar shows throughout the year on the last Friday of every month. Spectacular and authentic, the performances serve as a tantalizing introduction to the theatre's full-length shows, which include *lakhon* (classical) and *likay* (folk) theatre and the occasional *nang thalung* (shadow-puppet play). Tickets for these start at around B100; programme details can be checked by calling the theatre or TAT.

Many tourist restaurants feature nightly **culture shows** – usually a hotch-potch of Thai dancing and classical music, with a martial–arts demonstration thrown in. Worth checking out are *Baan Thai* (☎02/258 5403), a traditional teak house on Soi 32, Thanon Sukhumvit, where diners are served a set meal during the show (performances at 8.45pm; B550), and the outdoor restaurant in *Silom Village* (☎02/234 4581) on Thanon Silom which also stages a nightly fifty-minute show (7.30pm; B450) to accompany the set menu. In Banglamphu, all tour agents offer a dinner show package including transport for around B600 per person.

**Thai dancing** is performed for its original ritual purpose – to thank benevolent spirits for answered prayers – usually several times a day, at the Lak Muang Shrine behind the Grand Palace and the Erawan Shrine on the corner of Thanon Ploenchit (see p.139).

## Thai boxing

The violence of the average **Thai boxing** match may be off-putting to some, but spending a couple of hours at one of Bangkok's two main stadiums can be immensely entertaining, not least for the enthusiasm of the spectators and the ritualistic aspects of the fights. Bouts, advertised in the English-language newspapers, are held in the capital every night of the week at the **Rajdamnoen Stadium**, next to the TAT office on Rajdamnoen Nok Avenue (Mon, Wed & Thurs 6pm & 9pm, Sun 5pm), and at **Lumphini Stadium** on Thanon Rama IV (Tues & Fri 6.30pm, Sat 5pm & 8.30pm). Tickets go on sale one hour before and, unless the boxers are big stars, start at B220, rising to B1000 for a ringside seat; tickets for the Sunday bouts at Rajdamnoen cost from B50. You might have to queue for a few minutes, but there's no need to get there early unless there's a really important fight on.

Sessions usually feature ten bouts, each consisting of five three-minute rounds (with two-minute rests in between each round), so if you're not a big fan it may be worth turning up an hour late, as the better fights tend to happen later in the billing. It's more fun if you buy one of the less expensive standing tickets, enabling you to witness the wild gesticulations of the betting aficionados at close range.

To engage in a little Muay Thai yourself, try Jitti's Gym off Thanon Chakrabongse in Banglamphu, which holds open *muay Thai* **classes** every afternoon (3–6pm; B300; ☏02/282 7854).

# Shopping

Bangkok has a good reputation for **shopping**, particularly for silk, gems, and fashions, where the range and quality is streets ahead of other Thai cities, and of many other Asian capitals as well. Antiques and handicrafts are good buys too, and some shops stock curiosities from the most remote regions of the country alongside the more typical items. As always, watch out for old, damaged goods being passed off as antiques: if you're concerned about the quality or authenticity of your purchases, stick to TAT-approved shops. Bangkok also has the best English-language bookshops in the country. Department stores and tourist-orientated shops in the city keep late hours, opening at 10 or 11am and closing at about 9pm.

Downtown Bangkok is full of smart, multistoreyed **shopping plazas** where you'll find the majority of the city's fashion stores, as well as designer lifestyle goods and bookshops. You're more likely to find useful items in one of the city's numerous **department stores**, most of which are also scattered about the downtown areas. The Central department stores (on Silom and Ploenchit roads) are probably the city's best, but Robinson's (on Sukhumvit Soi 19, Thanon Rajdamri and at the Silom/Rama IV junction) are also good. Should you need to buy **children's gear**, you'll find everything you can think of, and more, in the children's department store Buy Buy Kiddo on Sukhumvit Soi 12.

For travellers, spectating, not shopping, is apt to be the main draw of Bangkok's neighbourhood **markets** – notably the bazaars of Chinatown (see p.129) and the blooms and scents of Pak Khlong Talat, the flower and vegetable market just west of Memorial Bridge (see p.130). The massive Chatuchak Weekend Market is an exception, being both a tourist attraction and a

## Counterfeit culture

Faking it is big business in Bangkok, a city whose copyright regulations carry about as much weight as its anti-prostitution laws. Forged **designer clothes** and accessories are the biggest sellers; street vendors along Patpong, Silom, Sukhumvit and Khao San roads will flog you a whole range of inexpensive lookalikes, including Tommy Hilfiger shirts, D&G jeans, Calvin Klein wallets, Prada bags and Hermes scarves.

Along Patpong, after dark, plausible would-be **Rolex**, **Cartier and Tag watches** from Hong Kong and Taiwan go for about B500 – and are fairly reliable considering the price. If your budget won't stretch to a phoney Rolex Oyster, there are plenty of opportunities for lesser expenditure at the stalls concentrated on Thanon Khao San, where pirated **music CDs** and **software and games CD-ROMs** are sold at a fraction of their normal price. Quality is usually fairly high but the choice is often less than brilliant, with a concentration on mainstream pop and rock albums. Finally, several stallholders along Thanon Khao San even make up passable international **student and press cards** – though travel agencies and other organizations in Bangkok aren't easily fooled.

marvellous shopping experience; see p.143 for details. If you're planning on some serious market exploration, get hold of *Nancy Chandler's Map of Bangkok*, an enthusiastically annotated creation which includes special sections on the main areas of interest. With the chief exception of Chatuchak, most markets operate daily from dawn till early afternoon; early morning is often the best time to go to beat the heat and crowds. The Patpong **night market**, which also spills out on to Thanon Silom, is *the* place to stock up on fake designer goods, from pseudo-Rolex watches to Tommy Hilfiger shirts; the stalls open at about 5pm until late into the evening.

Among the more **esoteric** items you can buy in Bangkok are fossils and Thai wine. The tiny House of Gems (Khun Boonman) at 1218 Thanon Charoen Krung (New Rd), near the GPO, deals almost exclusively in **fossils**, minerals and – no kidding – dinosaur droppings. Ranging from sixty million to two hundred million years old, these petrified droppings (properly known as coprolite) were unearthed in the mid-1980s in Thailand's Isaan region; weighing from 150 grams to 8 kilograms, they are sold at B7 per gram. Also on sale here, from B5 to B500 each, are tektites, pieces of glassy rock found in Thai fields and thought to be the 750,000-year-old products of volcanic activity on the moon. As for **wine**, Maison du Vin, 2nd Floor, Thaniya Plaza, Thanon Silom (☎02/231 2185), sells a better-than-passable Chateau de Loei red and white, made by an eccentric Frenchman from grapes grown on the slopes of Phu Reua in Thailand's Isaan region.

## Handicrafts and traditional textiles

Samples of nearly all regionally produced **handicrafts** end up in Bangkok, so the selection is phenomenal. Many of the shopping plazas have at least one classy handicraft outlet, and competition keeps prices in the city at upcountry levels, with the main exception of household objects – particularly wickerware and tin bowls and basins – which get palmed off relatively expensively in Bangkok. Handicraft sellers in Banglamphu tend to tout a limited range compared with the shops downtown, but several places on Thanon Khao San sell reasonably priced triangular pillows (*mawn khwaan*) in traditional fabrics, which make fantastic souvenirs but are heavy to post home; some places sell unstuffed versions which are simple to mail home, but a pain to fill when you return.

This is also a good place to pick up Thai shoulder bags woven to all specifications and designed with travellers' needs in mind. The cheapest place to buy traditional northern and northeastern textiles – including sarongs, triangular pillows and farmers' shirts – is **Chatuchak Weekend Market** (see p.143), and you might be able to nose out some interesting handicrafts here too.

**Come Thai**, 2nd Floor, Amarin Plaza (the Sogo building), Thanon Ploenchit. Currently has no English sign, but easily spotted by its carved wooden doorframe. Impressive range of unusual handwoven silk and cotton fabrics, much of it made up into traditional-style clothes such as Chinese mandarin shirts and short fitted jackets.

**Kealang**, 2nd Floor, Amarin Plaza, Thanon Ploenchit. Huge variety of *bencharong* pots and vases, as well as other multicoloured Thai-Chinese ceramics.

**Khomapastr**, 1st Floor, River City shopping complex, off Thanon Charoen Krung (New Rd). Unusual choice of attractive patterned cotton, in lengths or made up into items such as quirky cushion covers, attractive shirts and *mawn khwaan*.

**Krishna's**, between sois 9 and 11, Thanon Sukhumvit. The four-storey building is crammed full of artefacts from all over Asia and, though mass-produced metallic statuettes and Balinese masks seem to dominate, there are enough interesting curios (such as Nepalese jewellery and Japanese *netsuke* ornaments) to reward a thorough browse.

**The Legend**, 2nd Floor, Amarin Plaza, Thanon Ploenchit, and 3rd Floor, Thaniya Plaza, Thanon Silom. Stocks a small selection of well-made Thai handicrafts, from wood and wickerware to fabrics and ceramics, at reasonable prices.

**Narayana Phand**, 127 Thanon Rajdamri. This government souvenir centre was set up to ensure the preservation of traditional crafts and to maintain standards of quality, and makes a reasonable one-stop shop for last-minute presents. It offers a huge assortment of very reasonably priced goods from all over the country, including *khon* masks and shadow puppets, musical instruments and kites, nielloware and celadon, and hill-tribe crafts. Unfortunately the layout is not very appealing and the place feels like a warehouse.

**Prayer Textile Gallery**, 197 Thanon Phrayathai, on the corner of Thanon Rama I. Traditional fabrics from the north and the northeast, as well as from Laos and Cambodia. The selection is good, but prices for these textiles are getting surprisingly high, particularly for those now classified as antiques.

**Rasi Sayam**, a 10min hike down Sukhumvit Soi 23, opposite *Le Dalat Vietnamese* restaurant. Very classy handicraft shop, specializing in eclectic and fairly pricey decorative and folk arts such as tiny betel-nut sets woven from *lipao* fern, sticky rice lunch baskets, coconut wood bowls, and *mut mee* textiles. Mon–Sat 9am–5.30pm.

**Silom Village**, 286/1 Thanon Silom, just west of Soi Decho. A complex of wooden houses that attempts to create a relaxing, upcountry atmosphere as a backdrop for its pricey fabrics and occasionally unusual souvenirs, such as grainy *sa* paper made from mulberry bark.

**Sukhumvit Square**, between sois 8 and 10, Thanon Sukhumvit. This open-air night-bazaar-style plaza doesn't really get going till nightfall, when it's well worth dropping by to check out the range of quality handicrafts, artefacts, antiques, textiles and clothing sold in the 50 little shops here.

**Tamnan Mingmuang**, 3rd Floor, Thaniya Plaza, Soi Thaniya, east end of Thanon Silom. Subsidiary of The Legend which aims to foster and popularize crafts from all over the country. Among the unusual items on offer are trays and boxes for tobacco and betel nut made from *yan lipao* (intricately woven fern vines), and bambooware sticky rice containers, baskets and lamp shades.

**Thai Celadon**, Sukhumvit Soi 16 (Thanon Ratchadapisek). Classic celadon stoneware made without commercial dyes or clays and glazed with the archetypal blues and greens that were invented by the Chinese to emulate the colour of precious jade. Mainly dinner sets, vases and lamps, plus some figurines.

**Thai Craft Museum**, 2nd & 3rd Floor of Gaysorn Plaza, entrances on Thanon Ploenchit and on Thanon Rajdamri. Most of the top two floors of Gaysorn Plaza shopping centre are taken over by this collection of three hundred different outlets selling classy, high-quality crafts, textiles, jewellery, art, clothes and souvenirs, much of which is commissioned from villages around the country. You won't find absolute bargains here, but you get what you pay for. The best one-stop souvenir shop in the capital.

**Via**, 55 Thanon Tanao, Banglamphu. A specialist outlet for miniature reproduction traditional Thai boats. The scale models are all made from teak with fine attention to detail, and cover a dozen different styles of boat including rice barges, royal boats and longtails. Prices from B2000.

# Clothes and Thai silk

Noted for its thickness and sheen, **Thai silk** became internationally recognized only about forty years ago after the efforts of American Jim Thompson (see pp.137–138). Much of it comes from the northeast, but you'll find the lion's share of outlets and tailoring facilities in the capital. Prices start at about B350 per metre for two-ply silk (suitable for thin shirts and skirts), or B500 for four-ply (for suits).

Bangkok can be a great place to have **tailored clothes** made: materials don't cost much, and work is often completed in only 24 hours. On the other hand, you may find yourself palmed off with artificial silk and a suit that falls apart in a week. Inexpensive silk and tailoring shops crowd Silom, Sukhumvit and Khao San roads, but many people opt for hotel tailors, preferring to pay more for the security of an established business. Be wary of places offering ridiculous deals – when you see a dozen garments advertised for a total price of less than $200, you know something's fishy – and look carefully at the quality of samples before making any decision. If you're staying in Banglamphu, keep an eye on guest-house noticeboards for cautionary tales from other travellers.

Thanon Khao San is lined with stalls selling low-priced **ready-mades**: the tie-dyed shirts, baggy cotton trousers, embroidered blouses and ethnic-style outfits are all aimed at backpackers and New Age hippies; the stalls of Banglamphu Market, around the edges of the abandoned New World department store, have the best range of inexpensive Thai fashions in this area. For the best and latest fashions, however, check out the shops in the Siam Centre and the Siam Discovery Centre, both across from Siam Square, and the high-fashion outlets at the upmarket Emporium on Sukhumvit. **Shoes** and **leather goods** are good buys in Bangkok, being generally handmade from high-quality leather and quite a bargain: check out the "booteries" along Thanon Sukhumvit.

**Ambassador Fashions**, 1/10–11 Soi Chaiyot, off Sukhumvit Soi 11 (☎02/253 2993). Long-established and reputable tailor, well versed in making both men's and women's wear. Clothes can be made within 24hr if necessary. Call for free pick-up in Bangkok.

**Emporium**, between sois 22 and 24 on Thanon Sukhumvit. Enormous and rather glamorous shopping plaza, with a good range of fashion outlets, from exclusive designer wear to trendy high-street gear. Brand name outlets include Versace, Chanel and Louis Vuitton.

**Jim Thompson's Thai Silk Company**, main shop at 9 Thanon Suriwong, plus branches in the World Trade Center, Central department store on Thanon Ploenchit, at Emporium on Thanon Sukhumvit, and at many hotels around the city. A good place to start looking for traditional Thai fabric, or at least to get an idea of what's out there. Stocks silk and cotton by the yard and ready-made items from dresses to cushion covers, which are well designed and of good quality, but pricey. They also have a home furnishings section and a good tailoring service.

**Khanitha**, branches at 111/3–5 Thanon Suriwong and the *Oriental* hotel. Specialize in women's suits, evening wear and dressing gowns, tailored from the finest Thai silk.

**Mah Boon Krong (MBK)**, at the Rama I/Phrayathai intersection. Labyrinthine shopping centre which houses hundreds of small, mostly fairly inexpensive outlets, including plenty of high-street fashion shops.

**Narry's**, 155/22 Sukhumvit Soi 11/1 ☎02/254 9184, ◉www.narry.com. Good-value, award-winning tailor of men's and women's clothes. Finished items ready within 24hr if necessary. Call for free pick-up in Bangkok.

**Peninsula Plaza**, Thanon Rajdamri. Considered the most upmarket shopping plaza in the city, so come here for Louis Vuitton and the like.

**Siam Centre**, across the road from Siam Square. Particularly good for local labels as well as international high-street chains; Kookaï, Greyhound and Soda Pop are typical outlets.

**Siam Discovery Centre**, across the road from Siam Square. Flash designer gear, including plenty of name brands like D&G, Morgan, Max Mara and YSL.

**Siam Square**. Worth poking around the alleys here, especially near what's styled as the area's

"Centerpoint" between sois 3 and 4. All manner of inexpensive boutiques, some little more than booths, sell colourful street gear to the capital's fashionable students and teenagers.

## Books

English-language **bookstores** in Bangkok are always well stocked with everything to do with Thailand, and most carry fiction classics and popular paperbacks as well. The capital's few **secondhand** bookstores are surprisingly poor value, but you might turn up something worthwhile – or earn a few baht by selling your own cast-offs – in the shops and stalls along Thanon Khao San.

**Aporia**, Thanon Tanao, Banglamphu. Run by knowledgeable book-loving staff, Banglamphu's main outlet for new books keeps a good stock of titles on Thai and Southeast Asian culture and has a decent selection of travelogues, plus some English-language fiction. Also sells secondhand books.

**Asia Books**, branches on Thanon Sukhumvit between sois 15 and 19, in Landmark Plaza between sois 4 and 6, in Times Square between sois 12 and 14, and in Emporium between sois 22 and 24; in Peninsula Plaza on Thanon Rajdamri; in Siam Discovery Centre on Thanon Rama I; and in Thaniya Plaza near Patpong off Thanon Silom. English-language bookstore that's especially recommended for its books on Asia – everything from guidebooks to cookery books, novels to art (the Sukhumvit 15–19 branch has the very best Asian selection). Also stocks bestselling novels and coffee-table books.

**Books Kinokuniya**, 3rd Floor, Emporium Shopping Centre, between sois 22 and 24 on Thanon Sukhumvit. Huge English-language bookstore with a broad range of books ranging from bestsellers to travel literature and from classics to sci-fi; not so hot on books about Asia though.

**Central Department Store**, most convenient branches on Thanon Silom; Paperback fiction, maps and reference books in English.

**DK (Duang Kamol) Books**, branches on the 3rd Floor of the MBK shopping centre, corner of Rama I and Phrayathai roads; at 244–6 Soi 2, Siam Square; and at 180/1 Thanon Sukhumvit between sois 8 and 10. One of Thailand's biggest bookseller chains, DK is especially good for maps and books on Thailand.

**Shaman Books**, two branches on Thanon Khao San, Banglamphu. The best-stocked and most efficient secondhand bookshop in the city, where all books are displayed alphabetically as well as being logged on the computer – which means you can locate your choice in seconds. Lots of books on Asia (travel, fiction, politics and history) as well as a decent range of novels and general interest books. Don't expect bargains though.

## Gems and jewellery

Bangkok boasts the country's best **gem and jewellery** shops, and some of the finest lapidaries in the world, making this *the* place to buy cut and uncut stones such as rubies, blue sapphires and diamonds. The most exclusive gem outlets are scattered along Thanon Silom – try Mr Ho's at number 987 – but many tourists prefer to buy from hotel shops, like Kim's inside the *Oriental*, where reliability is assured. Other recommended outlets include Johnny's Gems at 199 Thanon Fuang Nakhon, near Wat Rajabophit in Ratanakosin; Merlin et Delauney at 1 Soi Pradit, off Thanon Suriwong; and Uthai's Gems, at 28/7 Soi Ruam Rudee, off Thanon Ploenchit. For cheap and cheerful silver earrings, bracelets and necklaces, you can't beat the traveller-oriented jewellery shops along Thanon Khao San in Banglamphu.

While it's unusual for established jewellers to fob off tourists with glass and paste, a common **scam** is to charge a lot more than what the gem is worth based on its carat weight. Get the stone tested on the spot, and ask for a written guarantee and receipt. Be extremely wary of touts and the shops they recommend, and note that there are no TAT-endorsed jewellery shops despite any information you may be given to the contrary. Unless you're an experienced gem trader, don't even consider buying gems in bulk to sell at a supposedly vast profit elsewhere: many a gullible traveller has invested thousands of baht on a handful of worthless multicoloured stones. If you want independent professional advice or precious stones certification, contact the Asian Institute of Gemological Sciences, located inside the Jewelry Trade Center Building, 919/298 Thanon Silom (☎02/267 4315–9). For more on Thailand's ruby and sapphire industry, see p.204.

## Antiques and paintings

Bangkok is the entrepôt for the finest Thai, Burmese and Cambodian **antiques**, but the market has long been sewn up, so don't expect to happen upon any undiscovered treasure. Even experts admit that they sometimes find it hard to tell real antiques from fakes, so the best policy is just to buy on the grounds of attractiveness. The River City shopping complex, off Thanon Charoen Krung (New Rd), devotes its third and fourth floors to a bewildering array of pricey treasures and holds an auction on the first Saturday of every month (viewing during the preceding week). The other main area for antiques is the stretch of Charoen Krung that runs between the GPO and the bottom of Thanon Silom. Here you'll find a good selection of reputable individual businesses specializing in wood carvings, bronze statues and stone sculptures culled from all parts of Thailand and neighbouring countries as well. Remember that most antiques require an export permit (see p.22).

Street-corner stalls all over the city sell poor quality mass-produced traditional Thai **paintings**, but for a huge selection of better quality Thai art, visit Sombat Permpoon Gallery on Soi 1, Thanon Sukhumvit, which carries thousands of canvases, framed and unframed, spanning the range from classical Ayutthayan-era-style village scenes to twenty-first-century abstracts. The gallery does have works by famous Thai artists like Thawan Duchanee, but prices for the more affordable works by less well-known painters start at B1500.

# Listings

**Airport enquiries** General enquiries ☎02/535 1111; international departures ☎02/535 1254 or 535 1386; international arrivals ☎02/535 1310, 535 1301 or 535 1149; domestic departures ☎02/535 1192; domestic arrivals ☎02/535 1253. **Airlines** Thai Airlines' main offices are at 485 Thanon Silom (☎02/234 3100–19) and at 6 Thanon Lan Luang near Democracy Monument (☎02/280 0060); the central Bangkok Airways office is at 1111 Thanon Ploenchit (☎02/254 2903); and Air Andaman is at 87 Nailert Bldg., 4th Floor, Unit 402a, Thanon Sukhumvit, (☎02/251 4905). International airlines with offices in Bangkok include Aeroflot, 7 Thanon Silom (☎02/233 6965); Air France, Unit 2002, 34 Vorwat Bldg, 849 Thanon Silom (☎02/635 1186–7); Air India, 1 Pacific Place, between sois 4 and 6, Thanon Sukhumvit (☎02/254 3280); Air Lanka,

Charn Issara Tower, 942/34–35 Thanon Rama IV (☎02/236 4981); Air New Zealand/Ansett, Sirindhorn Bldg, Thanon Witthayu (Wireless Rd; ☎02/254 5440); Biman Bangladesh Airlines, Chongkolnee Building, 56 Thanon Suriwong (☎02/235 7643); British Airways, 14th Floor, Abdullrahim Place, opposite Lumphini Park, 990 Thanon Rama IV (☎02/636 1747); Canadian Airlines, 6th Floor, Maneeya Centre, 518/5 Thanon Ploenchit (☎02/254 0960); Cathay Pacific, Ploenchit Tower, 898 Thanon Ploenchit (☎02/263 0616); China Airlines, Peninsula Plaza, 153 Thanon Rajdamri (☎02/253 4242–3); Egyptair, CP Tower, 313 Thanon Silom (☎02/231 0505–8); Emirates, 356/1 Thanon Vibhavadi Rangsit (☎02/531 6585); Eva Air, 2nd Floor, Green Tower, Thanon Rama IV (☎02/367 3388); Finnair, Don Muang Airport (☎02/535 2104); Garuda, Lumphini Tower,

1168/77 Thanon Rama IV (☎02/285 6470–3); Gulf Air, Maneeya Building, 518/5 Thanon Ploenchit (☎02/254 7931–4); Japan Airlines, 254/1 Thanon Rajadapisek (☎02/274 1401–9); KLM, 19th Floor, Thai Wah Tower 2, 21/133 Thanon Sathorn Thai (☎02/679 1100 ext. 11); Korean Air, Kongboonma Building, 699 Thanon Silom (☎02/635 0465); Lao Aviation, Silom Plaza, Thanon Silom (☎02/237 6982); Lauda Air, Wall Street Tower, 33/37 Thanon Suriwong (☎02/233 2544); Lufthansa, Q-House, Soi 21, Thanon Sukhumvit (☎02/264 2400); Malaysia Airlines, 98–102 Thanon Suriwong (☎02/236 4705); Myanmar Airlines, 23rd Floor, Jewelry Trade Center Building, Unit H1, 919/298 Thanon Silom (☎02/630 0338); Northwest, 4th Floor, Peninsula Plaza, 153 Thanon Rajdamri (☎02/254 0790); Olympic Airways, 4th Floor, Charn Issara Tower, 942/133 Thanon Rama IV (☎02/237 6141); Pakistan International (PIA), 52 Thanon Suriwong (☎02/234 2961–5); Philippine Airlines, Chongkolnee Building, 56 Thanon Suriwong (☎02/233 2350–2); Qantas Airways, 14th Floor, Abdullrahim Place, opposite Lumphini Park, 990 Thanon Rama IV (☎02/636 1747); Royal Air Cambodge, 17th Floor, Two Pacific Place Building, Room 1706, 142 Thanon Sukhumvit (☎02/653 2261–6); Royal Nepal, 1/4 Thanon Convent (☎02/233 5957); Singapore Airlines, Silom Centre, 2 Thanon Silom (☎02/236 0440); Swissair, 21st Floor, Abdullrahim Place, opposite Lumphini Park, 990 Thanon Rama IV (☎02/636 2150); United Airlines, 14th Floor, Sirindhorn Bldg, 130 Thanon Witthayu (☎02/253 0558); Vietnam Airlines, 7th Floor, Ploenchit Center Building, Sukhumvit Soi 2 (☎02/656 9056–8).

**American Express** c/o Sea Tours, 128/88–92, 8th Floor, Phrayathai Plaza, 128 Thanon Phrayathai, Bangkok 10400 (☎02/216 5934–6). Amex credit-card and traveller's-cheque holders can use the office (Mon–Fri 8.30am–5.30pm, Sat 8.30am–noon) as a poste restante, but mail is only held for sixty days. To report lost cards or cheques call ☎02/273 0044 (cards, office hours), ☎02/273 5296 (travellers' cheques, office hours), or ☎02/273 0022 (after hours for both cards and cheques).

**Car rental** Avis ⊚www.avis.com; Head Office, 2/12 Thanon Witthayu (Wireless Rd) ☎02/255 5300–4; also at Don Muang International Airport (☎02/535 4052); the *Grand Hyatt Erawan Hotel*, 494 Thanon Rajdamri (☎02/254 1234); *Le Meridien Hotel*, 971 Thanon Ploenchit (☎02/253 0444); and the *Amari Airport Hotel*, Don Muang International Airport (☎02/566 1020–1). Budget ⊚www.budget.co.th; Head Office, 19/23 Building A, Royal City Avenue, Thanon New Phetchaburi

(☎02/203 0250); and at *Comfort Suites Airport Hotel*, 88/107 Thanon Vibhavadi (☎02/973 3752). SMT Rent-A-Car (part of National) ⊜smtcar@samart.co.th; Head Office (☎02/722 8487); and at *Amari Airport Hotel*, Don Muang International Airport (☎02/928 1525); plus numerous others on Sukhumvit and Ploenchit roads.

**Cookery classes** Nearly all the five-star hotels will arrange a Thai cookery class for guests if requested; the most famous is held at the *Oriental* hotel (☎02/437 6211), which mainly focuses on demonstrating culinary techniques and runs for four mornings a week; the Saturday-morning Benjarong Cooking Class at the *Dusit Thani* hotel (☎02/236 6400) takes a more hands-on approach, as does the *Nipa Thai* restaurant (☎02/254 0404 ext 4823), which runs one- to five-day cookery courses on demand, and regular fruit-carving lessons (daily 2–4pm) at the restaurant on the third floor of the Landmark Plaza, between sois 4 and 6 on Thanon Sukhumvit. *Mrs Balbir's* restaurant on Soi 11 Thanon Sukhumvit (☎02/651 0498) holds regular, inexpensive, classes in Thai cookery (Fri 10.30–11.30am) and Indian cookery (Tues 10.30am–noon).

**Couriers** DHL Worldwide, Grand Amarin Tower, Thanon New Phetchaburi (☎02/658 8000).

**Directory enquiries** Bangkok ☎13, for numbers in the rest of the country ☎183.

**Embassies and consulates** Australia, 37 Thanon Sathorn Thai (☎02/287 2680); Burma (Myanmar), 132 Thanon Sathorn Nua (☎02/233 2237); Cambodia, 185 Thanon Rajdamri (enter via Thanon Sarasin; ☎02/254 6630); Canada, Boonmitr Building, 138 Thanon Silom (☎02/237 4125); China, 57/2 Thanon Rajadapisek (☎02/245 7033); India, 46 Soi 23, Thanon Sukhumvit (☎02/258 0300); Indonesia, 600–602 Thanon Phetchaburi (☎02/252 3135–40); Ireland, either contact the UK embassy, or call the Irish embassy in Malaysia (☎001 60 3/2161 2963); Korea, 51 Soi 26, Thanon Sukhumvit (☎02/278 5118); Laos, 520 Ramkhamhaeng Soi 39 (☎02/539 6667–8, extension 103); Malaysia, 35 Thanon Sathorn Tai (☎02/287 3979); Nepal, 189 Soi 71, Thanon Sukhumvit (☎02/391 7240); Netherlands, 106 Thanon Witthayu (Wireless Rd; ☎02/254 7701–5); New Zealand, 93 Thanon Witthayu (☎02/254 2530); Pakistan, 31 Soi 3, Thanon Sukhumvit (☎02/253 0288–90); Philippines, 760 Thanon Sukhumvit, opposite Soi 47 (☎02/259 0139–40); Singapore, 129 Thanon Sathorn Thai (☎02/286 2111); Sri Lanka, 75/84 Soi 21, Thanon Sukhumvit (☎02/261 1934–8); Vietnam, 83/1 Thanon Witthayu (☎02/251 5835–8); UK, 1031 Thanon Witthayu (☎02/253 0191–9); US, 20 Thanon

Witthayu (☎ 02/205 4000).

**Emergencies** For all emergencies, either call the tourist police (free 24hr phoneline ☎ 1699), visit the Banglamphu Police Station at the west end of Thanon Khao San, or contact the Tourist Police Headquarters, 23rd Floor, 26/56 TPI Tower Bldg, Thanon Chantadmai, Tungmahamek, Sathorn (☎ 02/678 6800–9).

**Exchange** The airport exchange desk and those in the upmarket hotels are open 24hr; many other exchange desks stay open till 8pm, especially along Khao San, Sukhumvit and Silom roads. If you have a MasterCard/Cirrus or Visa debit or credit card, you can also withdraw cash from hundreds of ATMs around the city, at branches of the Bangkok Bank, the Bank of Ayudhaya, Thai Farmers Bank and Siam Commercial Bank.

**Hospitals and clinics** If you haven't picked up vaccinations and malaria advice in your home country, or if you need contraceptives or family planning advice, contact the Australian-run Travmin Bangkok Medical Centre, 8th Floor, Alma Link Building, next to Central Department Store at 25 Soi Chitlom, Thanon Ploenchit (☎ 02/655 1024–5; outside clinic hours, call the same number for emergency contacts; B650 per consultation); there's a general clinic here, too. Most expats rate the private Bumrungrad Hospital at 33 Soi 3, Thanon Sukhumvit (☎ 02/253 0250) as the best and most comfortable in the city. Other recommended hospitals and clinics include Bangkok Adventist Hospital (aka Mission Hospital), 430 Thanon Phitsanulok (☎ 02/281 1422); Samitivej Sukhumvit Hospital, 133, Soi 49, Thanon Sukhumvit (☎ 02/392 0011–19); Bangkok Nursing Home Hospital (BNH), 9 Thanon Convent (☎ 02/632 0550); Bangkok Christian Hospital, 124 Thanon Silom (☎ 02/233 6981–9); Dental Polyclinic, 211–13 Thanon New Phetchaburi (☎ 02/314 5070); and Pirom Pesuj Eye Hospital, 117/1 Thanon Phrayathai (☎ 02/252 4141). For rabies advice and treatment, you can also go to the Queen Saovabha Memorial Institute (QSMI) attached to the Snake Farm on Thanon Henri Dunant (☎ 02/252 0161; Mon–Fri 8.30–10.30am & noon–1pm).

**Immigration office** About 1km down Soi Suan Plu, off Thanon Sathorn Thai (Mon–Fri 8am–noon & 1–4pm; ☎ 02/287 3101–10). Visa extensions take about an hour.

**Internet access** Banglamphu is packed with internet cafés, in particular along Thanon Khao San and Soi Ram Bhuttri where almost every other business offers internet access; many guest houses offer have internet access too. Competition keeps prices very low, so this is the best area of the city for all cyber activities. The Ratchadamnoen Post Office on Banglamphu's Soi Damnoen Klang Neua (daily 8am–10pm) also has public Catnet internet booths (see p.54 for details). Outside Banglamphu, mid-range and upmarket hotels also offer internet access, but at vastly inflated prices. Thanon Sukhumvit has a number of makeshift phone/internet offices, as well as several more formal and more clued-up internet cafés, including *Cybercafé*, 2nd Floor, Ploenchit Center, Soi 2 Thanon Sukhumvit (daily 10am–9.30pm); and Time Internet Centre on the second floor of Times Square, between sois 12 and 14 (daily 9am–midnight); the Soi Nana Post Office between sois 4 and 6 also has some Catnet internet terminals. Around Siam Square, try Bite Time, 7th Floor, Mah Boon Krong Shopping Centre (daily 11am–10pm); in the Silom area, head for Explorer on Patpong 1 (Mon–Fri & Sun 2pm–1am; Sat 2–10pm). There are also Catnet terminals at the post office counters inside Don Muang Airport.

**Language Courses** AUA (American University Alumni), 179 Thanon Rajdamri (☎ 02/252 8398) and Union Language School, CCT Building, 109 Thanon Suriwong (☎ 02/233 4482) run regular, recommended Thai language courses.

**Laundries** Nearly all guest houses and hotels offer same-day laundry services; if yours doesn't, either look for one that does, or use one of the two self-service laundries on Thanon Khao San.

**Left luggage** At Don Muang airport (international and domestic; B70 per day), Hualamphong train station (B10–30 per day; see p.87), and at most hotels and guest houses (B7–10 per day).

**Mail** The GPO is at 1160 Thanon Charoen Krung (New Rd), a few hundred metres left of the exit for Wat Muang Kae express-boat stop. Poste restante can be collected here Mon–Fri 8am–8pm, Sat, Sun & holidays 8am–1pm; letters are kept for three months. The parcel packing service at the GPO operates Mon–Fri 8am–4.30pm, Sat 9am–noon. If you're staying in Banglamphu, it's more convenient to use the poste restante service at one of the two local post offices. The one closest to Khao San is Ratchadamnoen Post Office on the eastern stretch of Soi Damnoen Klang Neua (Mon–Fri 8.30am–5pm, Sat 9am–noon; letters are kept for two months and should be addressed c/o Poste Restante, Ratchadamnoen PO, Bangkok 10002. Banglamphu's other post office is on Soi Sibsam Hang, just west of Wat Bowoniwes (Mon–Fri 8.30am–5pm, Sat 9am–noon); its poste restante address is Banglamphubon PO, Bangkok 10203. You can also send and receive faxes there on Ⓕ 02/281 1579; or use your guest house or hotel fax number. In the Sukhumvit area, poste restante can be sent to the Thanon Sukhumvit post office between sois 4 and 6, c/o Nana PO, Thanon Sukhumvit, Bangkok 10112.

**Massage** Traditional Thai massage sessions and courses are held at Wat Po (see p.118), and at dozens of guest houses in Banglamphu.

**Meditation centres and retreats** The main centres are the House of Dhamma Insight Meditation Centre, Wat Mahathat; and World Fellowship of Buddhists; see p.64 for details.

**Pharmacies** There are English-speaking staff at most of the capital's pharmacies, including the numerous branches of the British chain, Boots the Chemist (they have outlets on Thanon Khao San as well as in the Times Square plaza and Emporium shopping centre, both on Thanon Sukhumvit).

**Telephones** The least expensive places to make international calls are the public telephone offices in or adjacent to post offices. The largest and most convenient of these is in the compound of the GPO on Thanon Charoen Krung (New Rd), which is open 24hr and also offers a fax service and a free collect-call service (see p.163 for location details). The post offices at Hualamphong station, on Thanon Sukhumvit (see p.163) and on Soi Sibsam Hang in Banglamphu (see p.163) also have international telephone offices attached, but these close at 8pm; the Ratchadamnoen phone office on Soi Damnoen Klang Neua opens daily 8am–10pm.

Many private telephone offices claim that they offer the same rates as the public phone offices, but they are almost always at least ten percent more expensive.

**Travel agents** Diethelm Travel is a huge, recommended agent with branches all over Thailand and Indochina, in Bangkok they're at 12th Floor, Kian Gwan Building II, 140/1 Thanon Witthayu (Wireless Rd) (☎02/255 9200, ⓕ255 9192, ⓦwww.diethelm-travel.com). They sell tickets for domestic and international flights and tours, and are particularly good on travel to Burma, Cambodia, Laos and Vietnam. VC Travel and Tour, Mezzanine Floor, Hualamphong Railway (☎02/613 6725, ⓕ613 6727), is a friendly and efficient travel agent who also provides an accommodation-booking service and sell train tickets at no commission. Also recommended are Educational Travel Centre (ETC), *Royal Hotel*, Room 318, 2 Rajdamnoen Klang (☎02/224 0043, ⓕ622 1420, ⓔETC@mozart.inet.co.th); 180 Thanon Khao San (☎282 2958); 5/3 Soi Ngam Duphli (☎287 1477 or 286 9424); Exotissimo, 755 Thanon Silom (☎02/223 1510) and 21/17 Soi 4, Thanon Sukhumvit (☎02/253 5240) ⓔexotvlth@linethai.co.th; NS Tours, c/o *Vieng Thai Hotel*, Soi Ram Bhuttri, Banglamphu (☎02/629 0509); and STA Travel, 14th Floor, Wall Street Tower, 33 Thanon Suriwong (☎02/236 0262).

# Moving on

**Public transport** between Bangkok and the beaches is inexpensive and plentiful, if not particularly speedy. Bangkok is also an unrivalled place to make arrangements for onward travel from Thailand – all the major Asian embassies are here, so getting the appropriate **visas** should be no problem and the city's travel agents can offer some amazing flight deals.

The cheapest of these deals come from agents who don't belong to the **Association of Thai Travel Agents** (ATTA), though many of these are transient and not altogether trustworthy. Thanon Khao San is a notorious centre of such fly-by-night operations. If you do buy from a non-ATTA outlet it's a good idea to ring the airline and check your reservation yourself – don't hand over any money until you've done that and have been given the ticket. The slightly more expensive ATTA agencies still work out good value by international standards: to check if an agency is affiliated either get hold of the TAT list, ask for proof of membership or call the ATTA office (☎02/237 6046–8). Some tried and tested travel agents are given in "Listings", above.

The **international departure tax** on all foreigners leaving Thailand by air is B500; buy your voucher near the check-in desks at the airport.

# Travel within Thailand

Having to change trains or buses in Bangkok might sound a tiresome way to travel the country, but it has its advantages – breaking up what would otherwise be an unbearably long trip, and giving the chance to confirm plane tickets and stock up on supplies not so widely available elsewhere.

## By train

All trains depart from **Hualamphong Station** except the twice-daily service to Nakhon Pathom and Kanchanaburi, and a couple of the Hua Hin trains, which leave from **Bangkok Noi Station** (also referred to as **Thonburi Station**). The "Information" booth at Hualamphong station keeps English-language timetables, or you can try phoning the Train Information Hotline on ☏1690; the State Railway of Thailand website (Ⓦwww.srt.motc.go.th) carries an English-language timetable and fare chart for major destinations. For a guide to destinations and journey times from Bangkok, see Travel Details on p.168. For details on city transport to and from Hualamphong, left-luggage facilities at the station, and a warning about con-artists operating at the station, see the section on Arriving in Bangkok on p.87.

   **Tickets** for overnight trains and other busy routes should be booked at least a day in advance (or at least a week in advance for travel on national holidays), and are best bought from Hualamphong. The clued-up English-speaking staff at VC Travel and Tour on the mezzanine floor of the station concourse (daily 5am–8pm; ☏02/613 6725), above *Coffee Bucks*, sell all types of rail tickets at no commission, and can also book discounted mid-range accommodation at your destination. Alternatively, during normal office hours you can buy rail tickets from the clearly signed State Railway **advance booking office** at the back of the station concourse (daily 8.30am–4pm); at other times you can buy them from ticket counter #2 (daily 5–8.30am & 4–10pm), which is also the place to apply for ticket refunds. Train tickets can also be bought through almost any travel agent and through some hotels and guest houses for a booking fee of about B50. In addition to all types of normal rail ticket, both VC Travel and the Advance Booking Office, sell joint rail and boat or rail and bus tickets, to Ko Samui, Ko Pha Ngan, Ko Tao, Ko Phi Phi and Phuket. Sample prices include B750 to Ko Samui (second-class sleeper and boat ticket) and B800 to Phuket (second-class sleeper and bus transfer).

## By bus

Bangkok's three main bus terminals are distributed around the outskirts of town. Leave plenty of time to get to the bus terminals, especially if setting off from Banglamphu, from where you need at least an hour and a half (outside rush hour) to get to the Eastern Bus Terminal, and a good hour to get to the Northern or Southern terminals. Seats on regular long-distance buses don't need to be **booked** in advance, but air-conditioned ones should be reserved ahead of time either at the relevant bus station or through hotels and guest houses. Agencies sometimes provide transport to the bus station for an additional charge.

   The **Northern Bus Terminal** or **Sathaanii Mo Chit** (departure info for both air-con and regular services on ☏02/936 2860) is the departure point for a few buses to the east-coast destinations of Pattaya, Chanthaburi and Trat, though there are more regular services to the east coast from the Eastern Bus Terminal. The Northern Bus Terminal is on Thanon Kamphaeng Phet 2, near Chatuchak Weekend Market in the far north of the city; the fastest way to get there is to take the BTS Skytrain to its northernmost terminus, Mo Chit (N8) on Thanon Phaholyothin, which is just a few minutes' walk from the bus terminal. Alternatively, you can take several city buses to Mo Chit, including #2 and #77 from Thanon Silom; both regular and air-con #3, and air-con #9, #12 and #32 from Banglamphu; and both regular and air-con #29 from Hualamphong Railway Station; see p.92 for bus route details.

The **Eastern Bus Terminal**, or **Sathaanii Ekamai** (air-con services ⊤02/391 2504; regular services ⊤02/391 8097), at Thanon Sukhumvit Soi 40, serves east-coast destinations such as Pattaya, Ban Phe (for Ko Samet) and Trat (for Ko Chang). The Skytrain stops right by the bus terminal at Ekamai station, as do city buses #11 (from Banglamphu) and #59 (from the Northern Bus Terminal); see p.92 for bus route details. Or you can take the Sen Seb canal boat service from the Golden Mount (see p.92) to Tha Ekamai (Thanon Sukhumvit Soi 63) and then hop into a taxi down Soi 63 to the bus terminal.

The **Southern Bus Terminal**, or **Sathaanii Sai Tai Mai** (air-con services ⊤02/435 1199; regular services ⊤02/434 5557) is at the junction of Thanon Borom Ratchonni and the Nakhon Chaisri Highway, west of the Chao Phraya River in Thonburi. It handles departures to all points south of the capital, including Hua Hin, Chumphon (for Ko Tao), Surat Thani (for Ko Samui), Phuket and Krabi (for Ko Phi Phi and Ko Lanta), as well as departures for destinations west of Bangkok, such as Kanchanaburi. Regular and air-conditioned buses leave from different sections of the Southern Bus Terminal, and anyone there will be able to point you in the right direction for your bus. To get here, take city bus #7 (air-con) from Banglamphu or Hualamphong Station, or air-con #11 from Banglamphu or Thanon Sukhumvit and (see p.92 for bus route details).

## Budget transport

Many Bangkok tour operators offer **budget transport** to major tourist destinations such as Surat Thani, Krabi, Ko Samet and Ko Chang. In many cases this works out as cheap if not cheaper than the equivalent fare on a public air-con bus and, as most of the budget transport deals leave from the Thanon Khao San area in Banglamphu, they're often more convenient. The main drawbacks, however, are the **lack of comfort** and **poor safety**.

For the shorter trips, for example to **Ko Samet** (around B300 including boat) and **Ko Chang** (B480), transport operators always take passengers in minibuses which, if crowded, can be unbearably cramped, and often have insufficient air-conditioning. Drivers usually go as fast as possible, which some travellers find scary. For destinations further afield, such as **Surat Thani** (11hr), travellers are usually taken by larger tour bus; again these tend to be clapped-out old things and drivers on these journeys have an even worse safety record. **Security** on these buses is also a problem, so keep your luggage locked or within view, and passengers often find themselves dumped on the outskirts of their destination city, at the mercy of unscrupulous touts. If you are planning a journey to Surat Thani, consider taking the train instead – the extra comfort and peace of mind are well worth the extra baht.

If you're heading for an **island** (such as **Ko Samui**, **Ko Tao** or **Ko Chang**), your bus should get you to the ferry port in time to catch the boat, though there have been complaints from travellers that this does not always happen;

always check whether your bus ticket covers the ferry ride. Sample prices for joint bus and boat tickets include B420 for Ko Samui, B520 for Ko Pha Ngan, B570 for Ko Tao, and B570 for Ko Phi Phi.

The best overall advice is to consult other travellers before booking with budget transport operators, and to be prepared for the ride not to be especially comfortable. **Tour operators** open up and go bust all the time, particularly in the Thanon Khao San area, so ask around for recommendations or make your arrangements through a reputable hotel or guest house; never hand over any money until you see the ticket.

## By air

Domestic **flights** should be booked as far in advance as possible, though tickets can be bought at the airport if available; the domestic departure tax is included in the price of the ticket. Thai Airways is the main domestic carrier and flies to over twenty major towns and cities; Bangkok Airways currently covers just a few routes from the capital, including Ko Samui, Ranong and Hua Hin. All domestic flights leave from Don Muang airport (see p.83); for details on hotels within ten minutes' drive of the airport see p.86; and for airline phone numbers see Listings, p.161.

The fastest, most expensive way of **getting to the airport** is by **metered taxi**, which can cost anything from B120 to B350 (plus B40 expressway toll), depending on where you are and how bad the traffic is. If you leave the downtown areas before 7am you can get to the airport in half an hour, but at other times you should set off at least an hour before you have to check in.

### Package tours and tour operators

If your time is short and you want to pack as much as you can into your stay, you might consider booking a **package tour** once you're in Thailand; some recommended tour operators are listed below. A number of tour operators offer inexpensive packages, with deals that range from overnight trips to tailor-made tours of a week or more. All of them include transport and budget accommodation, and most include food as well; prices start at around B1000 for two-day packages. One of the most popular packages includes two to four nights in **Khao Sok** national park (trekking, river-rafting and elephant riding). There are also a number of **specialist activity tours**, which are well worth investigating, including rock climbing, kayaking, diving and cycling.

**Bike and Travel**, 802/756 River Park, Mu 12, Thanon Phaholyothin (℡02/990 0274, ⊛www.cyclingthailand.com). Weekend cycling and canoeing trips all over Thailand, tailored for different levels of fitness.

**Lost Horizons**, Ban Chaophraya Rm 1907, Somded Chaophraya Soi 17 (℡02/863 3180, ℻863 1301, ⊛www.losthorizonsasia.com). Manage and own several mid-priced eco-resorts in secluded spots in southern Thailand, and arrange all-inclusive soft-adventure tours to destinations including Khao Sok, the River Kwai, and Bangkok canals.

**Nature Trails**, 549 Thantip Soi 2, Thanon Sukhapibaan 3 (℡02/374 6610, ℻735 0638, ⊛www.ntrails.co.th). Regular bird- and butterfly-watching weekends in Thailand's national parks.

**Planet Scuba and Wild Planet**, across from Thanon Khao San on Thanon Chakrabongse, Banglamphu (℡02/629 0977, ℻629 0976, ⊛www.wildplanet.co.th). Five-star PADI dive centre and adventure tour operator which runs a regular programme of activity packages, including dive packages to Ko Tao and Pattaya.

Every guesthouse and travel agent in Banglamphu, and many hotels else-where in the city, can book you on to one of the **private minibuses** to the airport. Those running from Banglamphu depart approximately every hour, day and night, and cost B60–80; though you'll get picked up from your accom-modation, you should book yourself on to a minibus that leaves at least an hour and a half before check-in commences as it can take up to 45 minutes to pick up all passengers, after which there's the traffic to contend with.

The **airport bus services** that are so useful when arriving at Don Muang are less reliable on the outward journey, mainly because the traffic often makes it impossible for them to stick to their half-hourly schedules; at B100 it's not a risk worth taking.

As with in-bound **trains**, schedules for trains from Hualamphong to Don Muang are not helpfully spread throughout the day, but the service is cheap and fast if the timetable fits yours. A number of **city buses** run from the city to the airport and are detailed on p.92; they are slow and crowded however.

## Travel details

### Trains

**Bangkok Hualamphong Station** to: Aranyaprathet (2 daily; 5–6hr); Butterworth (daily; 23hr); Chumphon (9 daily; 6hr 45min–8hr 20min); Don Muang Airport (30 daily; 50min); Hat Yai (5 daily; 14–16hr); Hua Hin (9 daily; 3–4hr); Nakhon Si Thammarat (2 daily; 15hr); Pattaya (1 daily; 3hr 45min); Phatthalung (5 daily; 12–15hr); Si Racha (1 daily; 3hr 15min); Surat Thani (10 daily; 9–12hr); Trang (2 daily; 16hr); Yala (4 daily; 15–20hr).

**Bangkok Noi Station** to: Hua Hin (2 daily; 4hr–4hr 30min).

### Buses

**Eastern Bus Terminal** to: Ban Phe, for Ko Samet (12 daily; 3hr); Chanthaburi (18 daily; 5–7hr); Pattaya (every 40min; 2hr 30min); Rayong (every 15min; 2hr 30min); Si Racha, for Ko Si Chang (every 30min; 2–3hr); Trat, for Ko Chang (21 daily; 6–8hr).

**Northern Bus Terminal** to: Chanthaburi (3 daily; 3hr); Pattaya (every 30min until 5pm; 2–3hr); Rayong (2 daily; 2hr 30min); Trat (3 daily; 4hr).

**Southern Bus Terminal** to: Chumphon (9 daily; 7hr); Hat Yai (every 30min; 13hr); Hua Hin (every 25min; 3–3hr 30min); Ko Samui (3 daily; 15hr); Krabi (9 daily; 12–14hr); Nakhon Si Thammarat (10 daily; 12hr); Narathiwat (3 daily; 17hr); Pattani (3 daily; 16hr); Phang Nga (4 daily; 11hr–12hr 30min); Phatthalung (4 daily; 13hr); Phuket (at least 10 daily; 14–16hr); Ranong (7 daily; 9–10hr); Satun (2 daily; 16hr); Sungai Kolok (3 daily; 18–20hr); Surat Thani (7 daily; 11hr); Takua Pa (10 daily; 12–13hr); Trang (8 daily; 14hr); Yala (4 daily; 19hr).

### Flights

**Bangkok** to: Hat Yai (6 daily; 1hr 25min); Hua Hin (1 daily; 30min); Ko Samui (12–14 daily; 1hr 20min); Nakhon Si Thammarat (1–2 daily; 1hr 15min); Narathiwat (1 daily; 3hr); Phuket (14 daily; 1hr 20min); Ranong (4 weekly; 1hr 20min); Surat Thani (2 daily; 1hr 10min); Trang (1–2 daily; 1hr 30min); U-Tapao, for Pattaya (1–2 daily; 20min).

# The east coast

# CHAPTER 2

# Highlights

✳ **Ko Si Chang** – Tiny, barely touristed island with craggy coastlines and an appealingly laid-back ambience. p.174

✳ **Diving from Pattaya** – Away from the girlie bars and high-rise hotels, there's rewarding year-round wreck and reef diving nearby. p.183

✳ **Ko Samet** – Pretty (and popular) little island fringed with dazzlingly white beaches. p.191

✳ **Chanthaburi** – Watch gem dealers polishing piles of uncut sapphires, and explore the Vietnamese quarter. p.202

✳ **Ko Chang** – Large, sparsely populated island, with several good beaches and lots of accommodation. p.211

✳ **Ko Mak** – Stay in a teepee-hut on this diminutive island with fine white-sand beaches. p.222

# The east coast

Located within easy reach of the capital, the **east coast** resorts and islands attract a mixed crowd of weekending Bangkokians, pleasure-seeking expats and budget-conscious backpackers. Transport connections are good, prices are generally more reasonable than at the biggest southern resorts and, if you're heading overland to Cambodia, the east coast beaches make the perfect chance to indulge yourself en route before adventuring into more challenging territory across the border. You'll find the whitest beaches on the offshore islands – the five-hundred-kilometre string of mainland strands are disappointingly grey and the resorts here cater more for Thai groups than solitary horizon-gazing farangs. In addition, the discovery of oil and natural gas fields in these coastal waters has turned pockets of the first hundred-kilometre stretch into an unsightly industrial landscape of refineries and depots, sometimes referred to as the Eastern Seaboard. Offshore, however, it's an entirely different story, with island beaches as peaceful and unsullied as many of the more celebrated southern retreats.

The first worthwhile stop comes 100km east of Bangkok at the less than scintillating town of **Si Racha**, which is the point of access for tiny **Ko Si Chang**, whose dramatically rugged coastlines and low-key atmosphere make it a restful haven. In complete contrast, **Pattaya**, just half an hour south, is Thailand's number-one package-tour destination, its customers predominant-

## Accommodation prices

Throughout this guide, guest houses, hotels and bungalows have been categorized according to the price codes given below. These categories represent the minimum you can expect to pay in the high season (roughly July, Aug & Nov–Feb) for a double room. If travelling on your own, expect to pay anything between sixty and one hundred percent of the rates quoted for a double room. Wherever a price range is indicated, this means that the establishment offers rooms with varying facilities – as explained in the write-up. Wherever an establishment also offers dormitory beds, the prices of these beds are given in the text, instead of being indicated by price code.

Remember that the top-whack hotels will add seven percent tax and a ten percent service charge to your bill – the price codes below are based on net rates after taxes have been added.

| | | |
|---|---|---|
| ❶ under B150 | ❹ B400–600 | ❼ B1200–1800 |
| ❷ B150–250 | ❺ B600–900 | ❽ B1800–3000 |
| ❸ B250–400 | ❻ B900–1200 | ❾ B3000+ |

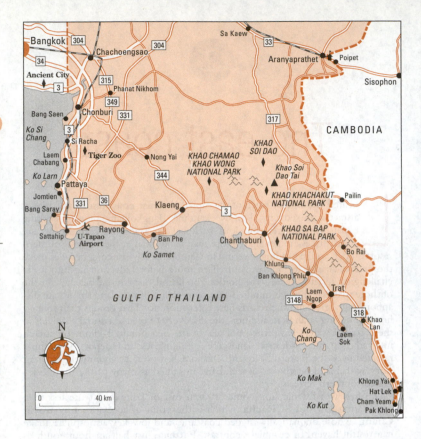

ly middle-aged Western and Chinese males enticed by the resort's sex-market reputation and undeterred by its notoriety as the country's most polluted beach. Things soon look up, though, as the coast veers sharply eastwards towards Ban Phe, revealing the island of **Ko Samet**, the prettiest of all the beach resorts within comfortable bus-ride range of Bangkok.

East of Ban Phe, the landscape starts to get more lush and hilly as the coastal highway nears **Chanthaburi**, the dynamo of Thailand's gem trade and one of only two provincial capitals in the region worth visiting. The other appealing inland city is **Trat**, 68km further along the highway and an important departure point for **Ko Chang**, a huge forested island with long, fine beaches, plentiful accommodation and a host of smaller, less developed islets off its coasts. East of Ko Chang lies the Cambodian border post of Ban Hat Lek, one of two points – the other being Aranyaprathet, a little way north – where it is currently legal to **cross overland into Cambodia**; details of these border crossings are given on p.120.

Highway 3 extends almost the entire length of the east coast – beginning in Bangkok as Thanon Sukhumvit, and known as such when it cuts through towns – and hundreds of **buses** ply the route, connecting all major mainland destinations. Buses from Bangkok's Eastern (Ekamai) Bus Terminal serve all the provincial capitals and tourist spots; there are a few services here from Bangkok's Northern (Mo Chit) Bus Terminal as well, and tourist minibuses run direct from Banglamphu in Bangkok to the ferry piers for Ko Samet and Ko Chang. One Eastern Line **train** a day runs in each direction between Bangkok, Si Racha and Pattaya, and there are two trains a day from Bangkok to Aranyaprathet and back. There's an **airport** at U-Tapao naval base, midway between Pattaya and Rayong, served by Bangkok Airways **flights** to and from Ko Samui and Phnom Penh in Cambodia; an airport is also scheduled to open in Trat in 2003.

# Si Racha and Ko Si Chang

Almost 30km southeast of Bangkok, Highway 3 finally emerges from the urban sprawl at the fishing town of Samut Prakan. It then follows the edge of the plain for a further 50km before reaching the provincial capital of **Chonburi**, whose only real attraction is its annual October bout of buffalo racing. Thai holidaymakers are very keen on the expensive beach resort of Bang Saen, 10km south of Chonburi, particularly as a day-trip break from Bangkok. As an off-the-beaten-track experience, however, the nearby island of **Ko Si Chang** is more rewarding, with the possibility of a night in an atmospheric waterside hotel on the mainland at **Si Racha** on the way there or back.

## Si Racha and around

Access to Ko Si Chang is from the fishing port and refinery town of **SI RACHA**, famous throughout Thailand as the home of *nam phrik Si Racha*, the orange-coloured, chilli-laced ketchup found on every restaurant and kitchen table in the country. You'll probably only find yourself staying here if you miss the last boat to the island, though the idiosyncratic seafront hotels make this an unexpectedly enjoyable experience, and the town is not without charm, especially at twilight, when the rickety, brightly painted fishing boats load up with ice and nets before setting off into the night. Si Racha's other claim to fame is its Tiger Zoo, an increasingly popular tourist attraction.

### Practicalities

**Buses** to Si Racha leave Bangkok's Eastern (Ekamai) Bus Terminal every thirty minutes and take about two hours. Air-conditioned buses stop near Laemtong department store on Thanon Sukhumvit (Highway 3), from where you can take a samlor or tuk-tuk to the pier for **ferries to Ko Si Chang** (for details of these see p.174); most regular buses stop nearer the waterfront, on Thanon Chermchompon (also spelt Thanon Jermjompol), within walking distance of the pier. There are also direct buses between Si Racha and Rayong (for Ban Phe and Ko Samet), Pattaya, and Trat (for Ko Chang). White songthaews from Naklua (the northern suburb of Pattaya, see p.180) run around twice an hour to Si Racha, dropping passengers near the clocktower on the southern edge of town. One **train** a day in each direction connects Si Racha with Bangkok; the **train station** is on the eastern edge of the town and is most easily reached by tuk-tuk.

Strung out along the wooden jetties are the simple, cabin-like rooms of three pleasant waterfront **hotels**, all of which are on Thanon Chermchompon, within five minutes' walk of the Ko Si Chang pier. The English-speaking managers give a slight advantage to *Sri Wattana* on the (unmarked) Soi 8 at 35 Thanon Chermchompon (T038/311037; **2**), but the adjacent *Siwichai* at 38 Thanon Chermchompon (T038/311212; **2–4**) is just as pleasant, as is the *Samchai* – which also has some air-con rooms – at the end of the signposted Soi 10, officially 3 Thanon Chermchompon (T038/311234; **2–3**). For **eating**, try any of the seafood restaurants along Thanon Chermchompon, especially the Chinese-style *Chua Lee* between sois 8 and 10, or the night-market stalls by the clock tower further south down the road.

### Sriracha Tiger Zoo

Nine kilometres southeast of Si Racha, the **Sriracha Tiger Zoo** (daily 9am–6pm; B250, children B150) is usually visited by day-trippers from Pattaya, but is also easily accessible from Si Racha. Said to be the most successful tiger breeding centre in the world, the zoo currently has some two hundred Bengal tigers in its care, as well as thousands of crocodiles and a host of other typical zoo creatures, including elephants, camels, wallabies and Peruvian guinea pigs. One of the zoo's philosophies is that different animals should interact with each other as if they were members of the same family, so you're quite likely to see tiger cubs being suckled by pigs, and ducks hanging out with the crocodiles. Visitors are usually allowed to cuddle the zoo-bred baby tigers, and elephant shows, pig racing and an animal circus are staged several times a day.

All tour companies in Pattaya (see p.177) offer day-trips to the Tiger Zoo. Alternatively, there is **public transport** there from the southern edge of Si Racha town centre: walk south a few hundred metres down Thanon Sukhumvit from the town centre as far as Robinson's department store (get off here if coming by bus **from Pattaya**), then cross the road onto minor road 3241 and wait outside the Assumption College for a songthaew (at least hourly; 20min) to the zoo.

## Ko Si Chang

The unhurried pace and the absence of consumer pressures make tiny, rocky **Ko Si Chang** a satisfying place to hang out for a few days. Unlike most other east-coast destinations, it offers no real beach life – fishing is the major source of income, and there's little to do here but explore the craggy coastline and gaze at the horizon, though there are several appealing hotels and guest houses.

### Practicalities

**Ferries** to Ko Si Chang leave from Si Racha and run approximately hourly from 6am to 8pm. Nearly all the ferries depart from the pier at the end of Si Racha's Soi 14, off Thanon Chermchompon, though occasionally they set off instead from Wat Ko Loi, the "island temple" at the end of the very long causeway 400m further along. The hop across to Ko Si Chang should take about forty minutes, but this varies according to how many passengers need to be transferred to and from the cargo ships between which the ferries weave.

On **arrival**, you'll probably dock at Ko Si Chang's Tha Bon, the more northern of the two piers on the east coast, though some boats pull in at Tha Lang. The first boat back to the mainland leaves at 6am and the last at 6pm; all but the 6.40am departing boats stop off at Tha Lang on their way back.

Both piers connect with Thanon Asadang, a small ring road on which you'll find the market, shops and most of the island's houses. The rest of the island is accessible only by paths and tracks. It's easy enough to walk from place to place, the simplest point of reference for **orientation** being *Tiew Pai Guest House*, which stands at the southwest "corner" of Thanon Asadang, about 750m from Tha Lang. Alternatively, you can jump in one of the bizarrely elongated 1200cc motorbike **samlors** which, as there are probably fewer than a dozen private cars on Ko Si Chang, virtually monopolize the roads. A ride from the pier to any of the guest houses in one of these contraptions costs about B30, and a tour of the island will set you back around B250; some of the drivers speak good English. You can rent **motorbikes** (B250 per day) and **mountain bikes** (B50) from *Sripitsanu Bungalows*, whose managers can also arrange

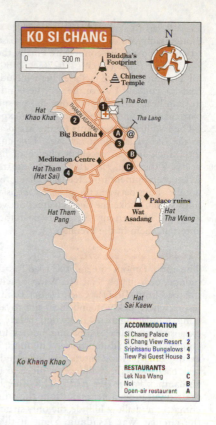

boat trips to nearby islands for B1000–1600 per boat with up to twenty passengers.

There are **exchange facilities** (but no ATM) at the Thai Farmers Bank near the market between the two piers. The post office and hospital are near Tha Bon, and **internet access** is available inside the video rental store near Tha Lang. For a fee of B50, non-guests can use the **swimming pool** at *Sichang Palace Hotel*.

## Accommodation and eating

There's a surprising range of **accommodation** on Ko Si Chang, including some places with superb sea views. Most backpackers stay in the centrally located *Tiew Pai Guest House* (☎038/216084; ❸–❺), where rooms range from simple doubles with shared bathrooms to air-conditioned ones with private facilities. The restaurant serves a good range of food and the friendly managers speak English. If you prefer a coastal spot, and are willing to pay a bit more, your first choice should be *Sripitsanu Bungalows* (☎038/216336, ✉sripitsanu@hotmail.com; ❹), which has just half a dozen comfortably furnished bungalows almost right at the edge of the Hat Tham cliff – some of the lower rooms are actually built into the rockface. It's a really relaxing place, run by a well-informed couple. Further along the coast, at Hat Khao Khat, *Si Chang*

*View Resort* (☎038/216210, ℻216211; ❹–❺) occupies another prime spot, though sadly you can't see the rugged coastline clearly from the otherwise very attractive fan and air-con rooms. Finally, the most upmarket place on the island is *Si Chang Palace* (☎038/216276, ℻216030; ❼–❽), set across from Tha Bon on Thanon Asadang; facilities here include a swimming pool, and all rooms have air-con and TV. For the very best and personally selected sea views, nothing can beat **camping** on your chosen spot: the cliffs at Hat Khao Khat are a particularly popular site, though quite exposed.

The two best **restaurants** on the island are southeast of *Tiew Pai*, on the road to the old palace. Both *Lek Naa Wang* and *Noi* serve up recommended Thai food, including an excellent choice of fish and seafood dishes, at moderate prices. Otherwise, *Tiew Pai* does decent travellers' food (with nightly karaoke-style entertainment from teenage Thai girls at night) and there are several small noodle shops between the piers. As the island caters for the crews of the cargo ships which choke the deep channel between Ko Si Chang and the mainland, a couple of open-air restaurants near the piers employ singing hostesses to entertain them in the evenings.

## Around the island

The most famous site on the island is the overgrown ruins of **Rama V's palace**, near pebbly Hat Tha Wang beach on the southeast coast (just follow the road from *Tiew Pai Guest House*). Built here in the 1890s as a sort of health resort where sickly members of the royal family could recuperate in peace, King Chulalongkorn's teakwood palace formed the heart of a grand and extensive complex comprising homes for royal advisers, quarters for royal concubines and administrative buildings. By the turn of the century, however, the king had lost interest in his island project and so in 1901 his golden teak palace was moved piece by piece to Bangkok, and reconstructed there as Vimanmek Palace (see p.135). The other buildings were left to disintegrate in their own good time: aside from the stone steps and balustrades which still cling to the shallow hillside, the only structure on the site to survive intact was the circular **Wat Asadang**, right at the top and surmounted by a chedi. Nonetheless it's an evocative site and a pleasant focus for a not particularly strenuous outing; you can walk to the ruins in less than half an hour from *Tiew Pai*.

The main beach on the west coast, and the most popular one on the island, is **Hat Tham Pang**, a kilometre-long stretch of sand complete with deckchairs and beach umbrellas for rent. A samlor to this beach costs around B70 from *Tiew Pai*. North of Hat Tham Pang, and also accessible via a fork off Thanon Asadang opposite *Tiew Pai*, you'll find the Tham Yai Prik meditation centre and the dramatically situated *Sripitsanu Bungalows*, both located above a tiny, rocky cove known as **Hat Tham** or Hat Sai.

Back down on the ring road, continuing in a northwesterly direction, you'll pass beneath the gaze of a large yellow Buddha before reaching the rocky northwest headland of **Khao Khat**, a few hundred metres further along Thanon Asadang. The uninterrupted panorama of open sea makes this a classic sunset spot, and it's safe enough for cliffside scrambling.

From here the road heads east to reach the gaudy, multi-tiered Chinese temple, **Saan Chao Paw Khao Yai** (Shrine of the Father Spirit of the Great Hill), stationed at the top of a steep flight of steps and commanding a good view of the harbour and the mainland coast. Established here long before Rama V arrived on the island, the shrine was dedicated by Chinese seamen who saw a strange light coming out of one of the **caves** behind the modern-day temple. The caves, now full of religious statues and offertory paraphernalia, are visited by boatloads of Chinese pilgrims, particularly over Chinese New Year.

Continue on up the cliffside to reach the small pagoda built for Rama V and enshrining a **Buddha's Footprint**. Two very long, very steep flights of stairs give access to the footprint: the easternmost one starts at the main waterfront entrance to the Chinese temple and takes you past a cluster of monks' meditation cells, while the westerly one rises further west along the ring road and offers the finest lookouts. It's well worth the vertiginous ascent, not least for the views out over Thailand's east coast; looking down over a gulf congested with cargo boats from Bangkok, you'll see the tiny island of Ko Khram and, clearly visible on the horizon, the Si Racha coast.

# Pattaya

With its murky sea, streets packed with high-rise hotels and touts on every corner, **PATTAYA** is the epitome of exploitative tourism gone mad. But most of Pattaya's visitors don't mind that the place looks like Torremolinos or that the new water treatment plant has only recently stopped businesses from dumping their sewage straight into the bay – what they are here for is sex. The town swarms with male and female **prostitutes**, spiced up by a sizeable population of transvestites (*katoey*), and plane-loads of Western men flock here to enjoy their services in the rash of go-go bars and massage parlours for which "Patpong-on-Sea" is notorious. The ubiquitous signs trumpeting "Viagra for Sale" say it all. Pattaya also has the largest **gay scene** in Thailand, with several exclusively gay hotels and a whole area given over to gay sex bars.

Pattaya's evolution into sin city began with the Vietnam War, when it got fat on selling sex to American servicemen. Tempted by the dollars, outside investors moved in, local landowners got squeezed out, and soon the place was unrecognizable as the fishing village it once was. When the soldiers and sailors left in the mid-1970s, Western tourists were enticed to fill their places, and as the seaside Sodom and Gomorrah boomed, ex-servicemen returned to run the sort of joints they had once blown their dollars in. Almost half the bars, cafés and restaurants in Pattaya are Western-run, specializing in home-from-home menus of English breakfasts, sauerkraut and bratwurst, hamburgers and chips. More recently, there is said to have been an influx of criminal gangs from Germany, Russia and Japan, who reportedly find Pattaya a convenient centre for running their rackets in passport and credit-card fraud as well as child pornography and prostitution.

Yet Pattaya does have its good points even if you don't fit the lecherous profile of the average punter, as attested by the number of **families** and older couples who choose to spend their package fortnights here. Although very few people swim off Pattaya's shore, the beach itself is kept clean so lots of tourists make use of the deckchairs and parasols that line its length, stirring only to beckon one of the iced-drink vendors. Pattaya's watersports facilities are among the best in the country, and there are masses of tourist-oriented theme parks, cultural attractions and golf courses within day-tripping distance. Holidaying here is not cheap (with no makeshift, low-budget bamboo huts for backpackers, and few bargain foodstalls), but travellers on a modest budget can find good accommodation at relatively low cost.

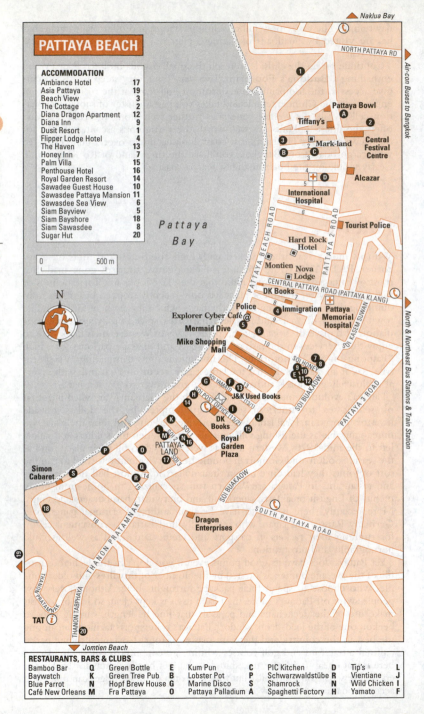

# PATTAYA BEACH

**ACCOMMODATION**

| | |
|---|---|
| Ambiance Hotel | 17 |
| Asia Pattaya | 19 |
| Beach View | 3 |
| The Cottage | 2 |
| Diana Dragon Apartment | 12 |
| Diana Inn | 9 |
| Dusit Resort | 1 |
| Flipper Lodge Hotel | 4 |
| The Haven | 13 |
| Honey Inn | 7 |
| Palm Villa | 15 |
| Penthouse Hotel | 16 |
| Royal Garden Resort | 14 |
| Sawadee Guest House | 10 |
| Sawasdee Pattaya Mansion | 11 |
| Sawasdee Sea View | 6 |
| Siam Bayview | 5 |
| Siam Bayshore | 18 |
| Siam Sawasdee | 8 |
| Sugar Hut | 20 |

0        500 m

Naklua Bay

NORTH PATTAYA RD

Air-con Buses to Bangkok

Pattaya Bowl

Tiffany's

Mark-land

Central Festival Centre

Alcazar

International Hospital

Tourist Police

Hard Rock Hotel

Montien

Nova Lodge

CENTRAL PATTAYA ROAD (PATTAYA KLANG)

DK Books

Police

Explorer Cyber Café

Mermaid Dive

Mike Shopping Mall

Immigration

Pattaya Memorial Hospital

North & Northeast Bus Stations & Train Station

SOI HONEY

SOI YAMATO

J&K Used Books

DK Books

SOI POST OFFICE (13/2)

SOI BUAKAOW

SOI 1

PATTAYA-LAND

Royal Garden Plaza

SOI 2/003

Simon Cabaret

SOUTH PATTAYA ROAD

SOI BUAKAOW

PATTAYA 3 ROAD

SOI KASEM SUWAN

PATTAYA 2 ROAD

PATTAYA BEACH ROAD

Dragon Enterprises

THANON PRATAMNAK

THANON PRATAMNAK

THANON TABPHAYA

TAT

Jomtien Beach

P a t t a y a   B a y

N

**RESTAURANTS, BARS & CLUBS**

| | | | | | | | | | |
|---|---|---|---|---|---|---|---|---|---|
| Bamboo Bar | Q | Green Bottle | E | Kum Pun | C | PIC Kitchen | D | Tip's | L |
| Baywatch | K | Green Tree Pub | B | Lobster Pot | P | Schwarzwaldstübe | R | Vientiane | J |
| Blue Parrot | N | Hopf Brew House | G | Marine Disco | S | Shamrock | N | Wild Chicken | I |
| Café New Orleans | M | Fra Pattaya | O | Pattaya Palladium | A | Spaghetti Factory | H | Yamato | F |

## Orientation

Pattaya comprises three separate bays. At the centre is the four-kilometre **Pattaya Beach**, the noisiest, most unsightly zone of the resort, crowded with yachts and tour boats and fringed by a sliver of sand and a paved beachfront walkway. Known by its English name, and signed as such, **Pattaya Beach Road** (Thanon Hat Pattaya) runs the length of the beach and is connected to the parallel Pattaya 2 Road (Thanon Pattaya Sawng) by a string of sois numbered from 1 in the north to 17 in the south. The core of this block, between sois 6 and 13, is referred to as **Central Pattaya** and is packed with hotels, restaurants, bars, fast-food joints, souvenir shops and tour operators. During the day this is the busiest part of the resort, but after dark the neon zone south of Soi 13/2 – **South Pattaya** – takes over. Known locally as "the strip", this is what Pattaya's really about, with sex for sale in go-go bars, discos, massage parlours and open-sided "bar-beers". The town's enclave of gay sex bars is here too, focused mainly on the interlinked network of small lanes known as **Pattayaland** sois 1, 2 and 3, but actually signed as Sois 13/3, 13/4 and 13/5, between the Royal Garden Plaza and Soi 14. Pattaya Beach Road continues south from its junction with South Pattaya Road (Thanon Pattaya Tai) all the way down to the *Siam Bayshore Hotel*; this stretch of road is also known as **Walking Street** because it's pedestrianized every evening from 7pm, though proposed development may put a stop to that. **North Pattaya**, between Central Pattaya Road (Thanon Pattaya Klang) and North Pattaya Road (Thanon Hat Pattaya Neua), also has its "bar-beers", but is a more sedate, upmarket district.

The southerly bay, **Jomtien Beach**, is also fronted by enormous high-rises, many of which are condominiums, though there are some low-rise mid-priced hotels along the beachfront road, Jomtien Beach Road (Thanon Hat Jomtien), as well. Fourteen kilometres long, it is safer and a little cleaner than Pattaya Beach, and is considered Thailand's number-one windsurfing spot. Trees provide shade in some stretches and in other parts there are sun loungers with parasols for rent. The far northern tip of Jomtien, beyond the end of the road, is mainly a gay cruising beach. The atmosphere in Jomtien is almost sleepy in comparison to Pattaya, with just a handful of restaurant-shacks, the occasional minimarket, and half-a-dozen bar-beers between the hotels and condos.

**Naklua Bay**, around the northerly headland from Pattaya Beach, is the quietest of the three enclaves, and has managed to retain its fishing harbour and indigenous population despite the onslaught of condominiums, holiday apartments and expat homes. Most of the accommodation here is in time-shared condos, and there's no decent beach.

## Arrival and information

Most people **arrive** in Pattaya direct **from Bangkok**, either by public **bus** from the Eastern (Ekamai) Bus Terminal (every 30min until 10.30pm; 2–3hr), the Northern (Mo Chit) Bus Terminal (every 30min until 5pm; 2–3hr), or by air-conditioned tour bus from a Bangkok hotel or Don Muang airport (3 daily; 2hr 30min). Air-con buses to and from Bangkok and the airport use the bus station on North Pattaya Road, from where share-taxis deliver travellers to the hotel of their choice for B40 per person. Non-air-con buses use the Baw Kaw Saw government bus station on Thanon Chaiyapruk in Jomtien. **From Si Racha** it's a thirty-minute ride to Pattaya in one of the frequent buses or songthaews, and you'll probably get dropped just east of the resort on Thanon Sukhumvit, from where songthaews will ferry you into town; a few Si Racha songthaews will take you all the way. Buses **from Rayong** and **Trat** generally drop passengers on Thanon Sukhumvit as well. To travel to Rayong (for Ban Phe and Ko Samet) or Trat (for Ko Chang), you need to wait at one of the bus *sala* on Thanon Sukhumvit and flag down any of the frequent government buses that pass. Malibu Travel offers a faster and more direct B150 minibus service between Pattaya and the Ban Phe pier; the ticket includes pick-up from your hotel and can be booked through most hotels and tour agents in Pattaya.

Pattaya is on a branch line of the eastern rail line, and there is one **train** a day in each direction between the resort and Bangkok, which takes almost four hours. Though this seems a lot longer than the bus, it can work out faster if you factor in the time it takes to cross Bangkok to the Eastern Bus Terminal. Pattaya's **train station** is on Thanon Sukhumvit, about 500m north of the Central Pattaya Road interesction.

Pattaya's U-Tapao **airport** (☏038/245595) is located at the naval base near Sattahip, about 25km south of the resort; it's served by Bangkok Airways flights to and from Ko Samui and Phnom Penh in Cambodia (through flights to Siem Reap are planned). If you're travelling to Cambodia from U-Tapao you'll have to pay a B400 departure tax at the airport; the domestic departure tax of B30 is included in the price of the ticket.

### Information

The **TAT** office is inconveniently located at 609 Thanon Pratamnak (sometimes referred to as Cliff Road) between South Pattaya and Jomtien (daily 8.30am–4.30pm; ☏038/428750, ☏429113, ☏tatpty@chonburi.ksc.co.th). The *Pattaya Mail* prints local news stories, entertainment listings and details of community events; it comes out every Friday and is available at most newsstands and bookstores. There are several free what's-on magazines published in Pattaya, which are dished out at tour agencies and pricier hotels.

### Transport

The easiest way to get around Pattaya is by **songthaew** – though on all routes beware of being overcharged. Most follow a standard anticlockwise route up Pattaya 2 Road as far as North Pattaya Road and back down Pattaya Beach Road, for a fixed fee of B10 per person. Never jump in a parked songthaew, as you'll be charged for chartering the whole vehicle; instead just flag down a passing one and press the bell when you want to get off. Songthaews **to Jomtien** leave from the junction of Pattaya 2 Road and South Pattaya Road (but can be flagged down anywhere along their route) and cost B10 to Thanon Boonkanjana. Songthaews **to Naklua** start from the junction of Pattaya 2 Road and Central Pattaya Road and cost B10 to Naklua Soi 12.

The alternative is to rent your own transport: Pattaya Beach Road is full of touts offering motorbikes and jeeps for rent. **Motorbike rental** costs from B150 to B700 per day depending on the bike's size; beware of faulty vehicles, and of scams – some people have reported that rented bikes get stolen from tourists by touts so they can keep the customer's deposit. Avis **car rental** (☏038/361627, ⊛www.avisthailand.com) have an office inside the *Dusit Resort Hotel* in North Pattaya, Budget (☏038/720613, ⊛www.budget.co.th)

has an office off Soi Diana Inn, and many of the motorbike touts also rent out jeeps for about B1000 per day.

## Accommodation

Really cheap **hotels** are almost impossible to find in Pattaya, and a depressing number of the lowest-priced options suffer from poor maintenance, musty rooms and unfriendly staff. Only one of the "inexpensive" hotels listed below has rooms for B150, but there are a number of places offering fan rooms for B250 and air-con rooms for B300. Rooms that cost B400 and up usually offer reasonable facilities, including air-conditioning, TV and use of a swimming pool as well. Advance reservations are advisable to stay in the best-value hotels. Prices in all categories plummet by up to fifty percent when demand is slack, so it's often worth asking around two or three places before checking in. If your budget can't stretch to B250, you may have to resort to one of the less pricey "rooms for rent" advertised in the shops along Pattaya 2 Road between Soi 11 and Soi 13/2 (Soi Post Office), along Soi 13/2 itself, on Soi 13/1 (Yamato) and on Soi Buakaow. These tend to be dingy back rooms, and usually operate only until the owner finds something more lucrative to do with the premises.

Bear in mind that the sex industry ensures that all rooms have beds large enough for at least two people; rates quoted here are for "single" rooms with one big double bed (a "double" room will have two big double beds and cost more). Another effect of the sex industry is that hotel guests are often assumed to be untrustworthy, so when checking in you're likely to be asked for a deposit against the loss of your room key and against the use of your mini-bar and phone. Though all hotels are easy-going about gay couples, we've listed a couple of exclusively gay hotels as well.

Some people prefer to stay on **Jomtien Beach**, which is quieter and has a bit more of a beach scene, but lacks the shops and restaurants of Pattaya — as well as the go-go bars. Prices here are about the same as on Pattaya Beach.

### Pattaya

**Inexpensive and moderate**

**Ambiance Hotel**, 325/91 Pattayaland Soi 3 (Soi 13/5), South Pattaya ☎038/424099, ☎424626. Well-appointed hotel aimed at gay customers and located right in the heart of the gay district. Has just thirty rooms, all of them furnished with air-con, TV and mini-bar. ⑤–⑦

**Beach View**, Soi 2, Pattaya Beach Rd, North Pattaya ☎038/422660, ☎422664. Medium-sized mid-range high-rise with swimming pool just across the road from the beach. Many rooms have sea view and some have air-con. Extremely reasonable for its class. ④–⑤

**The Cottage**, off Pattaya 2 Rd, North Pattaya ☎038/425660, ☎425650. Excellent-value, well-appointed fan and air-con bungalows, attractively designed and pleasantly located in a quiet garden compound a good distance off the main road. Convenient for the shops and restaurants in the

Central Festival Centre complex. Facilities include two small swimming pools, a bar and a restaurant. ④–⑤

**Diana Dragon Apartment**, 198/16 Soi Diana Inn, opposite Soi 11, Central Pattaya ☎038/423928, ☎411658. Enormous fan and air-con rooms with fridge, and use of the pool at *Diana Inn*, 100m away; favoured by long-stay tourists. Very good value. ③

**Diana Inn**, 216/3–9 Pattaya 2 Rd, opposite Soi 11, Central Pattaya ☎038/429675, ☎424566, ﹫www.golfasia.com. Popular, centrally located mid-range hotel with rather dark, faded rooms, most with air-con and TV. Swimming pool and buffet breakfast included in the price. ③–⑤

**Flipper Lodge Hotel**, 520/1 Soi 8, Pattaya Beach Rd, Central Pattaya ☎038/426401, ☎426403, ﹫flippers@ptty.loxinfo.co.th. Very good-value mid-range hotel at the lower end of this price category. Smart air-con rooms, all with TV, some with sea view, and two swimming pools, one of them on the rooftop. Advance reservations advisable. **5 – 6**

**The Haven**, 185 Soi 13, Pattaya Beach Rd, Central Pattaya ☏ 038/710988, ℻ 426200, ✉ fobe@loxinfo.co.th. Small, friendly establishment offering fifteen clean, comfortable and remarkably good value air-con rooms set around a small courtyard with a swimming pool and seafood restaurant. All rooms have TV, video player and phone. Fairly peaceful despite being in a soi that's lined with bar-beers. **5**

**Honey Inn**, 529/2 Soi Honey Inn, opposite Soi 10, Pattaya 2 Rd, Central Pattaya ☏ 038/428117. Mid-sized hotel with swimming pool offering large, air-con rooms in fairly good condition, all with a decent balcony and TV. **4**

**Palm Villa**, 485 Pattaya 2 Rd, opposite Soi 13/2, Central Pattaya ☏ & ℻ 038/429099. Peaceful haven close to the nightlife, with small garden, a swimming pool, and sizeable fan and air-con rooms. **3 – 4**

**Penthouse Hotel**, Pattayaland Soi 2 (Soi 13/4), South Pattaya ☏ 038/429639, ℻ 421747. Small hotel for gay tourists offering inexpensive, good-value air-con rooms, all with TV. Located in the gay district. **4**

**Sawasdee Guest House**, 502/1 Soi Honey Inn, opposite Soi 10, Pattaya 2 Rd, Central Pattaya ☏ 038/425360, ℻ 720261, ⓦ www.sawasdee-hotels.com. The cheapest branch of the excellent Sawasdee chain of budget hotels has the most inexpensive rooms in Pattaya, decently if spartanly outfitted and available with fan or air-con. **2 – 3**

**Sawasdee Pattaya Mansion**, 367 Soi Diana Inn, Central Pattaya ☏ 038/720563, ℻ 720261, ⓦ www.sawasdee-hotels.com. Perhaps the nicest of all the Sawasdee hotels, this one has appealingly cosy rooms with TV and air-con, a small pool and a friendly atmosphere. **3 – 4**

**Sawasdee Sea View**, 302/1 Soi 10, Central Pattaya ☏ 038/710566, ℻ 720261, ⓦ www.sawasdee-hotels.com. Recommended place occupying a great location in a still quiet soi just a few dozen metres off the beachfront road. Rooms are smallish but clean, air-conditioned and fairly well kept; the pricier ones have TV, and some rooms on the upper floors do indeed have a faint sea view. **3 – 4**

**Siam Sawsadee**, corner of Soi Honey Inn and Soi Buakaow, Central Pattaya ☏ 038/720330, ℻ 720261, ⓦ www.sawasdee-hotels.com. Breezy, good-value hotel with a swimming pool and 206 big, comfortable rooms, all with air-con, TV and fridge. **4**

### Expensive

**Asia Pattaya**, 325 Thanon Pratamnak (Cliff Rd), South Pattaya ☏ 038/250602–6, ℻ 250496, ⓦ www.asiahotel.co.th. Attractively placed on a private bay between the *Royal Cliff* and Jomtien Beach. Extensive facilities including nine-hole golf course, tennis courts, swimming pool and snooker tables. **8 – 9**

**Dusit Resort**, 240/2 Pattaya Beach Rd, North Pattaya ☏ 038/425611–4, ℻ 428239, ⓦ www.dusit.com. In the thick of the high-rises, it has an excellent reputation for high-quality service and facilities, which include two pools, a gym, tennis and squash courts. **9**

**Royal Garden Resort**, 218 Pattaya Beach Rd, Central Pattaya ☏ 038/412120, ℻ 429926, ⓦ www.royal-garden.com. Set right in the heart of the resort, across the road from the beach, and enclosed by a tropical garden, this well-equipped hotel has standard-issue top-notch rooms, floodlit tennis courts, a huge pool and a spa. **8 – 9**

**Siam Bayshore**, 559 Pattaya Beach Rd ☏ 038/428678, ℻ 428730, ⓦ www.siamhotels.com. At the far southern end of the South Pattaya strip, set in a secluded wooded spot overlooking the beach, this popular hotel comprises 270 rooms spread over twelve wings and is set in exceptionally lush tropical gardens. Many rooms have balconies offering uninterrupted sea views, and there are two pools as well as tennis courts and snooker, table-tennis and badminton facilities. **8 – 9**

**Siam Bayview**, Pattaya Beach Rd, on the corner of Soi 11, Central Pattaya ☏ 038/423871, ℻ 423879, ⓦ www.siamhotels.com. Very centrally located upscale hotel that has smart, good-sized rooms, many of them with ocean views. Good value considering its location and facilities, which include two swimming pools, tennis courts, snooker and several restaurants. **8 – 9**

**Sugar Hut**, 391/18 Thanon Tabphaya, midway between South Pattaya and Jomtien ☏ 038/251686, ℻ 251689, ⓦ www.sugarhut.co.th. The most unusual, least corporate accommodation in Pattaya comprises a charming collection of just 33 Ayutthaya-style traditional wooden bungalows set in a fabulously lush garden with three swimming pools. The bungalows are in tropical-chic style, with low beds, open-roofed shower rooms, mosquito nets and private verandas; the more expensive ones have a sitting room as well. It's an appealingly laid-back place but best with your own transport as it's nowhere near the restaurants, shops or sea. **9**

## Jomtien Beach

**DD Inn**, just back from the beach, on a tiny soi opposite *KFC* at the far north end of Beach Rd ☎038/232995, ✉ddinnguesthouse@hotmail.com. Friendly, good-value guest-house-style little hotel in an ideal spot just a few metres from the beach. Rooms with balconies are slightly pricier, but all rooms come with air-con, TV, hot water – and duvets! Recommended. ❹

**Grand Jomtien Palace**, 365 Beach Rd, at the corner of Thanon Wat Boonkanjana (aka Wat Bun) ☎038/231405, ☎231404, ✉grandjt@ptty2.loxin-fo.co.th. Upmarket high-rise hotel where many of the comfortable, air-con rooms have a decent sea view. Facilities include a swimming pool, a beer garden and restaurant, and a small shopping arcade. ❽

**JB Guest House**, 75/14 Soi 5 (Soi Post Office), off Beach Rd ☎038/231581. Exceptionally good-value rooms in this small, friendly, Bangkok-style guest-house. All rooms have TV and hot water; you pay slightly more for air-con. ❸

**Mermaid's Beach Resort**, 75/102 Soi 7, off Beach Rd ☎038/232210, ☎231908. Nicely appointed, mid-range, low-rise hotel that's smartly furnished and well maintained. There's a swimming pool, dive centre, restaurant and baby-sitting service, and all 120 rooms have air-con and TV. Price depends on whether you want a view of the pool or the street. ❺–❼.

**Sea Breeze Hotel**, next to Soi 10 on Beach Rd ☎038/231056, ☎231059. Decent sized air-con rooms, all with TV and most overlooking a garden. Swimming pool and pool table on the premises. ❺

**Silver Sand Villa**, next to Soi White House at the northern end of Beach Rd ☎038/231288, ☎232491, ✉sweetsea@cbi.cscom.com The huge, nicely furnished air-con rooms in the old wing are good value, but you need to book ahead for a view of the pool (rather than a wall); most of the rooms are wheelchair-accessible. Rooms in the new wing are more expensive; though plainly furnished, they all have balconies and pool views. Two swimming pools and restaurant. ❺–❼

**Surf House**, between Sois 5 and 7 at the north end of Beach Rd ☎038/231025, ☎231029. Popular mid-range place across from the beach. Rooms are a bit faded, but all have air-con and TV, and some have a sea view. ❺

# Daytime activities

Most tourists in Pattaya spend the days recovering from the night before: not much happens before midday, breakfasts are served until early afternoon, and the hotel pool generally seems more inviting than a tussle with water-skis. But the energetic are well catered for, with a decent range of dive centres, water-sports facilities, golf courses and theme parks to enjoy.

## Snorkelling and scuba diving

Snorkelling and scuba diving are popular in Pattaya, though if you've got the choice between diving here or off the Andaman coast (see pp.322–323), go for the latter – the reefs there are a lot more spectacular. The big advantage of Pattaya is that it can be dived year-round. The main destinations for local **dive trips** are the group of "outer islands" about 25km from shore, which include Ko Rin, Ko Man Wichai and Ko Klung Badaan, where you have a good chance of seeing big schools of barracuda, jacks and tuna, as well as moray eels and blue-spotted stingrays. There are also two rewarding wreck dives in the Samae San/Sattahip area: the 21-metre-deep freighter *Phetchaburi Bremen*, which went down in the 1930s; and the 64-metre-long cargo ship *Hardeep*, which was sunk during World War ll and can be navigated along the entire length of its interior. A one-day dive trip including two dives, equipment and lunch generally costs around B3000, with accompanying snorkellers paying B800. Several companies along Pattaya Beach Road run **snorkelling** trips to nearby Ko Larn and Bamboo Island, though mass tourism has taken its toll on these two islands and their coral.

Pattaya is also an easy place to learn to dive: one-day introductory dives start at about B3000, and four-day open-water **courses** average out at B12,000. Be

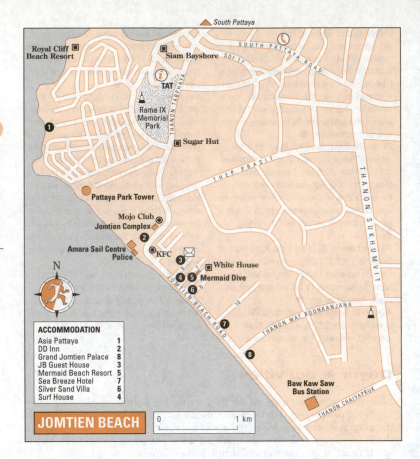

**JOMTIEN BEACH**

ACCOMMODATION

| | |
|---|---|
| Asia Pattaya | 1 |
| DD Inn | 2 |
| Grand Jomtien Palace | 8 |
| JB Guest House | 3 |
| Mermaid Beach Resort | 5 |
| Sea Breeze Hotel | 7 |
| Silver Sand Villa | 6 |
| Surf House | 4 |

0       1 km

careful when signing up for a dive course or expedition: unqualified instructors and dodgy equipment are a fact of life in Pattaya, and it's as well to question other divers about all operators, TAT-approved or not (see p.67 of Basics for more guidelines). The local **recompression chamber** is at the Apakorn Kiatiwong Naval Hospital (☎038/601185) in Sattahip, 26km south of Pattaya; it's open 24 hours. TAT-approved dive shops that run diving expeditions and internationally certificated courses include:

**Aquarelax Diving Center**, 183/31 Soi 13/2 (Soi Post Office), Central Pattaya ☎038/710900, ☏7109-01, ✉www.dive-pattaya.com. PADI Five-Star Instructor Development Centre; German management.

**Dave's Divers Den**, 190/11 Central Pattaya Rd, Central Pattaya ☎038/420411, ☏360095, ✉drd @loxinfo.co.th. Pattaya's longest-running dive centre.

**Mermaid's Dive Centre**, Soi White House, Jomtien ☎038/232219, ☏232221, ✉www .mermaiddive.com; and between sois 10 and 11

on Beach Rd, Central Pattaya. PADI Five-Star Instructor Development Centre.

**Paradise Scuba Divers**, *Siam Bay View Hotel*, corner Soi 10, Pattaya Beach Rd, Pattaya ☎038/710567, ✉lscuba@loxinfo.co.th. PADI Five-Star dive centre.

**Seafari Sports Center**, 359/2 Soi 5, Pattaya Beach Rd, North Pattaya ☎038/429060, ☏361356, ✉www.seafari.net. PADI Five-Star Instructor Development Centre; American management.

## Water sports

Jomtien Beach is the place for **windsurfing**, **water-skiing**, **jet-skiing** and **parasailing** (the latter is also popular in North Pattaya): you can either book up in the outlets along Pattaya's Beach Road or head down to Jomtien itself and sign up there. One of Jomtien's biggest watersports outlets is the Amara Sail Centre, located on the beach just north of the police station and the Thanon Tabphaya/Beach Road junction. *Surf House Kitchen* restaurant between sois 5 and 7 at the north end of Jomtien's Beach Road also rents out water-sports equipment, as do several nearby shops, and there are heaps of jetskis for rent on the beach north of Soi 5. Average prices start at about B1000 per hour for water-skiing, B500 for windsurfing, and B500 for one round of parasailing. Or you might want to try **cable skiing** at the Lakeland lagoon (daily 10am–9pm; B300 for 2hr) on Thanon Sukhumvit, about 5km north of Pattaya. *Deutsches House* restaurant on Soi 4, North Pattaya (⊤038/428725) runs day-long **deep-sea fishing** expeditions for about B2000 per person; you could also try asking about fishing trips at the *Shamrock* bar on Pattayaland Soi 2 (Soi 13/4) in Central Pattaya.

## Land sports

All top-end hotels have **tennis courts** and some offer badminton and gym facilities too, though these are generally open only to guests. The Pattaya Bowl, just north of Soi 1, Pattaya 2 Road in North Pattaya (daily 10am–midnight), has twenty **bowling** lanes (B60–80 per game); there's a **shooting range** at *Tiffany's* on Pattaya 2 Road, North Pattaya (daily 9am–10pm; B120), and a **go-kart circuit** in Jomtien that's suitable for 7-year-olds as well as adults (daily 9.30am–6.30pm; B100–200 for 10min). And at weekends there's always the prospect of watching a **speedway race** at the Bira International Circuit, 14km northeast of Pattaya on Highway 36 (B80–150). Six bouts of **Thai boxing** are staged at 8pm every Thursday night at the Sityodtong stadium, near the Siam Country Club on the far eastern fringes of Pattaya; tickets cost B400, plus B100 for return transport and can be bought through Dragon Enterprises (⊤038/427585), on Soi Day-Night Hotel in South Pattaya.

There are currently seventeen international-standard **golf courses** within easy reach of Pattaya, some of them designed by famous golfers. Visitors' green fees average B750 on a weekday, B1500 on a weekend, plus B200 for a caddy, and a set of clubs can usually be rented for B200–300. One popular option is to join the golf **package** run by Golf Bus (⊤038/720370), which includes transport to and from the Phoenix Golf and Country Club and all fees except club rental (B1500 on weekdays, or B2100 weekends). The *Diana Inn* at 216/3–9 Pattaya 2, opposite Soi 11, Central Pattaya (⊤038/429675, ⓦwww.golfasia.com), also organizes all-inclusive golfing packages to local courses. The following courses are all less than an hour's drive from Pattaya, with the closest listed first and the furthest last; for directions, either call the course or ask at your hotel. Phoenix Golf and Country Club (27 holes; ⊤038/239391), Siam Country Club (18 holes; ⊤038/249381); Laem Chabang International Country Club (27 holes; ⊤038/338351); and Eastern Star Golf Course (18 holes; ⊤038/630410).

## Theme parks and other attractions

One of the most enjoyable attractions in the resort is **Ripley's Believe It Or Not** (daily 11am–11pm; B280), located on the third floor of the Royal Garden Plaza shopping and entertainments centre on Pattaya Beach Road. It's part of a worldwide chain of similar curiosity museums inspired by the bizarre collections of the early twentieth-century American cartoonist and adventurer Robert Leroy Ripley, and displays lots of outlandish objects (including fetishes, torture contraptions and tribal masks), and real-life novelties from Thailand and further afield (such as models of the world's tallest, smallest and fattest men), as well as an exhibition on sharks. Amazing facts are presented in a lively way which makes it fun for all the family, so long as the kids have a penchant for the gruesome. When the kids tire of Ripley's they can always play on the arcade games, dodgems and ride-simulators found nearby on the same floor of the plaza.

Advertised as the only one of its kind in the world, the **Museum of Bottle Art** (daily 11am–8pm; B100), 100m south of the bus station on Thanon Sukhumvit, contains three hundred pieces of art in bottles, all of them painstakingly assembled by Dutch expat Pieter Bij de Leij. The artist has spent the best part of his 60-plus years pursuing this hobby and the result is a huge collection of miniature replicas – including Dutch windmills, Thai temples, a Saudi mosque and a British coach and horses – encased in glass bottles. He is usually on hand to demonstrate his technique, and there's also a video showing him at work. To get to the museum, take an eastbound songthaew along Central Pattaya Road, get off as soon as you reach Thanon Sukhumvit, and walk 200m south.

The hugely ambitious **Sanctuary of Truth**, also known as **Wang Boran** and **Prasat Mai** (daily 8am–6pm; B500; ☎038/225407), is also a kind of replica, but on a 1:1 scale. It's a huge temple-palace designed to evoke the great ancient Khmer sanctuaries of Angkor and built entirely of wood. Begun in 1981, the sanctuary is still a work-in-progress (and still a hard-hat zone), with construction workers and woodcarvers swarming over the site and as yet no English-language tourist information available, but if you have an interest in ancient Khmer architecture or modern Thai woodcraft then it's probably worth the steep entry fee. The sanctuary is located behind imposing crenellated walls off the west end of Naklua Soi 12, close to the *Garden Sea View* hotel; to get there from Central Pattaya, take a Naklua-bound songthaew as far as Soi 12, then a B10 motorbike taxi. Built in a fabulously dramatic spot beside the sea, the temple rises to 105m at its highest point (each of the central pillars is made from a single tree) and fans out into four gopura, or entrance pavilions, each of which is covered in symbolic religious and mythological woodcarvings. The **carvings** on the north (seaside) gopura are inspired by Cambodian mythology, and include a tower above the gopura that's crowned with an image of the four-headed Hindu god Brahma, plus a lotus flower and two three-headed elephants; those on the east gopura refer to China, so the Mahayana Buddhist *bodhisattva*s have Chinese faces; the carvings on the west gopura evoke India and include scenes from the Hindu epic the *Mahabarata*; and the southern entrance has images from Thailand, such as scenes from the Hindu tale the *Ramayana*.

There are several theme parks, "culture villages" and wildlife parks on the outskirts of Pattaya, all well signed off the main roads. **Mini Siam**, just north of the North Pattaya Road/Thanon Sukhumvit intersection, is just what it sounds like: two hundred of Thailand's most precious monuments reconstructed to 1:25 scale; Mini Europe is supposedly coming soon. **Nong Nooch Village**, 18km south of Pattaya off Thanon Sukhumvit, serves life-sized Thai culture in the form of traditional dancing and elephant rides against the backdrop of an attractively landscaped park. It's a popular feature of many tour-operators' programmes (B350 half-day), but it's worth coming here if you're into flowers: the **orchid garden** is said to be the world's largest. The **Elephant Village**, 6km northeast of Pattaya, offers ninety-minute elephant "treks" round its park for B700, plus the option of doing some rafting as well; there's also an elephant training show every afternoon (B400). For details and transport, call ☏038/361868, or contact *Novotel Tropicana Hotel*, off Soi 6, Pattaya Beach Road. **Sriracha Tiger Zoo**, about 30km north of Pattaya, also offers the chance to interact with creatures of the wild, and is described on p.174.

Plenty of agents fix up **day-trips** to tourist spots further afield, like Ko Samet (B800), the River Kwai (B1500) and Bangkok (B1500), though the journey times for all these are so long as to make them hardly worth the effort.

## Shopping

Pattaya is not a bad place for **shopping**, though unless you're keen to snap up dozens of fake designer boxer shorts and mass-produced woodcarvings you're probably best keeping away from the ubiquitous street stalls that clog the pavements of Pattaya Beach Road day and night. Better to retreat inside one of the resort's glossy shopping plazas – like the Central Festival Centre on Pattaya 2 Road in North Pattaya, which has a tempting array of fairly classy shops, ranging from designer clothes outlets such as D&G to smart gift and handicraft shops; there's also a cineplex (see p.190), several restaurants and a food court. Pattaya's other main shopping centre is Royal Garden Plaza in South Pattaya, where you'll find international fashion outlets like Timberland, as well some handicraft stalls, Boots the Chemist, *Pizza Hut* and *McDonald's*, lots of coffee shops, Ripley's Believe it or Not (see p.185) and a cinema screen.

Pattaya boasts Thailand's best English-language **bookshops** outside Bangkok. DK Books (daily 8am–11pm) on Soi 13/2 (Soi Post Office) stocks a phenomenal range of books on Asia, from guidebooks to novels to coffee-table glossies, and has a pile of anecdotal "farang in Thailand" and "confessions of a bar girl" literature too; there's a much smaller branch of DK north up Beach Road, on the corner of Central Pattaya Road. Bookazine on the corner of Pattayaland 1 (Soi 13/3) and Beach Road in South Pattaya also has an impressive range of books on Asia, as well as several shelves of novels and general-interest titles; their magazine section is unrivalled, and you should be able to find almost any major international newspaper or magazine here. J&K Used Books, which occupies an upstairs room above a grocery shop on Soi 13/1 (Soi Yamato), keeps a small stock of inexpensive secondhand novels and non-fiction titles, arranged alphabetically and catalogued on computer.

## Eating

Overall, **food** in Pattaya is expensive compared to the rest of the country and not nearly as interesting. The scores of expat restaurateurs in Pattaya have made Western food the resort's primary dining option, a generally dismal situation worsened by the host of fast-food joints along Pattaya Beach Road – *McDonald's*, *KFC*, *Mr Donut* and so on. For inexpensive Thai food, hunt out the curry and noodle vendors on Soi Kasem Suwan – they are concentrated between Central Pattaya Road and Soi Honey, but might pitch up anywhere. Top-quality Thai restaurants are a bit thin on the ground – not surprisingly, given the setting, there's more of an emphasis on seafood than on classical cuisine. Most hotels offer fairly good value all-you-can eat breakfast buffets for around B75 per head, the majority of which are open to non-guests as well.

**Baywatch**, Pattaya Beach Rd, between Pattayaland sois 1 and 2 (sois 13/3 and 13/4), Central Pattaya. Open 24hr, this is a good, if pricey, place to get your all-day breakfast, complete with sea view and sidewalk vantage point. Cappuccinos, filter coffees, burgers, sandwiches and pancakes.

**Blue Parrot**, Pattayaland Soi 2 (Soi 13/4), Central Pattaya. Mexican café and bar, good for moderately priced lunchtime tacos, enchiladas and chilli.

**Café New Orleans**, Pattayaland Soi 2 (Soi 13/4), Central Pattaya. Specializing in mid-priced Cajun and Creole dishes, this place is especially recommended for its tasty baby back ribs and its all-you-can-eat lunchtime deals on weekends.

**Fra Pattaya**, South Pattaya Rd, South Pattaya. Big menu of moderately priced staple Thai and Chinese dishes; authentic taste and workaday atmosphere.

**Lobster Pot**, opposite Soi 14, Pattaya Beach Rd, South Pattaya. Enormous, moderately priced seafront restaurant specializing in fresh seafood, in particular tiger prawns and giant lobsters.

**PIC Kitchen**, Soi 5, North Pattaya. One of Pattaya's finest traditional Thai restaurants, set in a stylish series of teak buildings. Mouth-watering, mid-priced menu of elegantly presented curry, seafood, rice, noodle and vegetarian dishes. Nightly live jazz from 7pm.

**Royal Garden Plaza Food Court**, top floor of the Royal Garden Plaza, Pattaya Beach Rd, Central Pattaya. Lots of hot-food stalls serving specialities from different parts of Thailand, plus Japanese and Italian options too. Not exactly haute cuisine, but fast, hassle-free and fairly inexpensive for Pattaya.

Decide what you want and then buy coupons to the right value.

**Schwarzwaldstube**, Soi 15, Central Pattaya. Hearty Swiss and German dishes with lots of reasonably priced steak and an unusually good cheese selection.

**Spaghetti Factory**, corner of Soi 13/2 (Soi Post Office) and Pattaya Beach Rd, Central Pattaya. Pleasant and popular streetside branch of this chain restaurant. Hearty portions of pasta and pizza at moderate prices.

**Sugar Hut**, 391/18 Thanon Tabphaya, mid-way between South Pattaya and Jomtien. Attached to the delightful tropical hotel described on p.182, this restaurant gives you the chance to soak up the ambience and enjoy the tropical gardens without shelling out for a bungalow. Food is served in an open-sided *sala* and is mainly classy (and expensive) traditional Thai; recommendations include fried catfish in coconut milk and chilli, and chicken baked with pineapple. Worth the splurge.

**Tip's**, 22/10 Pattaya Beach Rd, between Pattayaland sois 2 and 3 (sois 13/4 and 13/5), South Pattaya. Long-running Pattaya institution offering over a dozen different set breakfasts at cheap prices.

**Vientiane**, between sois 13/1 and 13/2 on Pattaya 2 Rd. Specializes in moderately priced Southeast Asian food, including Lao-inspired curries and some Indonesian dishes.

**Yamato**, Soi 13/1 (Soi Yamato), Central Pattaya. Good-value, relatively inexpensive Japanese fare including sushi, *soba* and *udon* dishes, *tempura* and *sashimi*. Open evenings only during the week, and for lunch and dinner at weekends.

## Drinking and nightlife

Entertainment is Pattaya's *raison d'être* and the **nightlife** is what most tourists come for, as do oilfield workers from the Arabian Gulf and US marines on R&R. Of the four hundred-odd **bars** in Pattaya, the majority are the so-called "bar-beers", relatively innocent open-air drinking spots staffed by hostesses whose primary job is to make you buy beer not bodies. However, sex makes more money than booze in Pattaya – depending on who you believe, there are between six thousand and twenty thousand Thais working in Pattaya's sex industry, a workforce that includes children as young as 10. It's an all-pervasive trade: the handful of uninspiring discos depend more on prostitutes than on ravers, while the transvestite cabarets attract audiences of thousands.

### Bars

Pattaya's often nameless outdoor **"bar-beers"** group themselves in clusters all over North, Central and South Pattaya. The set-up is the same in all of them:

the punters – usually lone males – sit on stools around a brashly lit circular bar, behind which the hostesses keep the drinks, bawdy chat and well-worn jokes flowing. Beer is generally quite inexpensive at these places, the atmosphere low-key and good-humoured, and couples as well as single women drinkers are almost always made welcome.

Drinks are a lot more expensive in the bouncer-guarded **go-go bars** on the South Pattaya "strip" where near-naked hostesses serve the beer and live sex shows keep the boozers hooked through the night. The scene follows much the same pattern as in Patpong, with the women dancing on a small stage in the hope they might be bought for the night – or the week. Go-go dancers, shower shows and striptease are also the mainstays of the **gay scene**, centred on Pattayaland Soi 3 (Soi 13/5), South Pattaya.

There's not a great deal of demand for bars where the emphasis is on simple companionable drinking, but those listed below are comparatively low-key and welcoming. Most are open-sided streetside joints, with a few bar stools and a number of chairs set out around low tables in the front. Even here, bartenders are nearly always young and female, and many of them earn extra money by occasionally sleeping with customers.

**Bamboo Bar**, seafront end of South Pattaya Rd. An exuberant in-house band pulls in a sizeable crowd to this large streetside lounge-style bar.

**Green Bottle**, adjacent to *Diana Inn*, Pattaya 2 Rd, Central Pattaya. A cosy, air-con, pub-style bar which has forged a studiously unsleazy atmosphere. Serves food.

**Hopf Brew House**, between sois 13/1 (Yamato) and 13/2 (Post Office), Pattaya Beach Rd, Central Pattaya. Cavernous air-con pub, designed like a German beer hall around an internal courtyard with a stage for the nightly live music. Attracts a youngish crowd, including vacationing couples, and serves bar snacks as well as beer.

**Kum Pun**, Soi 2, North Pattaya. Bar and restaurant known for its live bands who play nightly sets of authentic Thai folk music as well as soft rock.

**Mojo Club**, near Jomtien Complex, off Thanon Thep Prasit, North Jomtien. Laid-back bar run by a couple of jazz musicians, with live jazz and blues nightly.

**Shamrock**, Pattayaland 2 (Soi 13/4), South Pattaya. This British-run bar is a good place to catch local expat gossip. The manager sometimes entertains customers on his banjo, and his collection of folk-music tapes is also worth listening out for. On the edge of the gay district, but attracts a very mixed crowd.

**Shenanigans**, *Royal Garden Resort* hotel complex, Pattaya Beach/Pattaya 2 Rd, Central Pattaya. Irish pub that's a sister operation to the hugely popular outfit in Bangkok. Serves Guinness and Kilkenny Bitter every day of the week, enlivened by a timetable of different theme nights with appropriate food. The big screen shows major sports events, and there are nightly sets from a roster of live bands who start playing around 11pm.

**Wild Chicken**, the Pattaya 2 end of Soi 13/2 (Soi Post Office), South Pattaya. Attracts a friendly expat crowd, including the local Hash House Harriers. Discreet hostesses and amiable managers.

## Discos

Pattaya's **discos** tend to be pick-up joints with few frills, no admission charges, relatively inexpensive beer and a large number of unattached women hanging round the edges. The huge and sleazy *Marine Disco*, in the heart of "the strip", is the ultimate meat market, with its cramped upstairs dance floor encircled by ringside seats, and a more official boxing ring downstairs, starring prepubescent boys. The more hi-tech *Pattaya Palladium*, at the intersection of Soi 1 and Pattaya 2 Road in North Pattaya, boasts a more salubrious ambience, but is not exactly intimate – it's the biggest of its kind in Asia and is supposed to have a capacity of six thousand, with a troupe of 35 dancers to entertain them.

## Cabarets

Tour groups – and families – constitute the main audience at Pattaya's **transvestite cabarets**. Glamorous and highly professional, these shows are performed three times a night at three theatres in the resort: at Alcazar, opposite Soi 4 on Pattaya 2 Road in North Pattaya; at Tiffany's, north of Soi 1 on Pattaya 2 Road in North Pattaya; and also at Simon Cabaret on Beach Road in South Pattaya. Each theatre has a troupe of sixty or more transvestites who run through twenty musical-style numbers in fishnets and crinolines, ball gowns and leathers, against ever more lavish stage sets. All glitz and no raunch, the shows cost from B400.

## Listings

**Airlines** Bangkok Airways, 2nd Floor, *Royal Garden Plaza*, South Pattaya ☎ 038/411965; Thai Airways, inside the *Dusit Resort*, North Pattaya ☎ 038/429347.

**Cinemas** Central Cineplex, on the top floor of the Central Festival Centre on Pattaya 2 Rd in North Pattaya, has four English-language shows a day at each of its four screens. There's also a three-screen cinema on the top floor of *Royal Garden Plaza* in South Pattaya. Tickets from B70.

**Cookery classes** At the *Royal Cliff Beach Resort*, Royal Cliff Bay, 353 Thanon Pratamnak ☎ 038/250421, between South Pattaya and Jomtien. Held every Mon, Wed and Fri at 10am; B990.

**Emergencies** For all emergencies, call the tourist police on the free, 24hr phoneline ☎ 1699. Alternatively, contact the tourist police on Pattaya 2 Rd, just south of Soi 6, Central Pattaya ☎ 038/429371, or call in at the more central police station on Beach Rd, just south of Soi 9.

**Exchange** Numerous exchange counters and ATMs, particularly on Pattaya Beach Rd and Pattaya 2 Rd.

**Hospitals** The two most central private hospitals are the Pattaya International Hospital on Soi 4 ☎ 038/428374–5, and Pattaya Memorial Hospital on Central Pattaya Rd ☎ 038/429422–4. The Bangkok-Pattaya Hospital ☎ 038/427751–5 is on Thanon Sukhumvit, about 400m north of the intersection with North Pattaya Rd. The nearest divers' recompression chamber is at the Apakorn Kiatiwong Naval Hospital ☎ 038/601185 in Sattahip, 26km south of Pattaya; it's open 24hr a day.

**Immigration office** Opposite *Flipper Lodge* on Soi 8 (Mon–Fri 8.30am–4.30pm; ☎ 038/429409). Many travel agents offer cheap visa-renewal day-trips to Cambodia: check advertisements and local press for details.

**Internet access** At dozens of internet centres throughout the resort, including the very efficient, 24hr *Explorer Internet Café* , between sois 9 and 10 on Pattaya Beach Rd; Catnet at the small public CAT phone office on Soi 13/2.

**Mail** The post office is, not surprisingly, on Soi Post Office in Central Pattaya, though the road has now officially been re-signed as Soi 13/2.

**Telephones** The main CAT international telephone office is on South Pattaya Rd, just east of the junction with Pattaya 2 Rd, and there's a smaller, more central branch on Soi 13/2 in Central Pattaya. There are lots of private international call centres in the resort.

# Pattaya to Ko Samet

South of Pattaya, buses race along Highway 3 past the turn-off to the deep-sea fishing port of **Bang Saray**, before stopping to offload returning sailors at **Sattahip**, site of the Thai Navy headquarters. The few swimmable beaches along this stretch of shoreline are reserved for the exclusive use of holidaying sailors and their families. Though the nearby **U-Tapao** air base also belongs to the military, it is also used by Bangkok Airways – for details of their routes, see p.37.

Few farang travellers choose to stop for longer than they have to in the busy provincial capital of **RAYONG**, but it's a useful place for **bus connections**, particularly if you're travelling between the east coast and the northeast, or if you're trying to get to Ko Samet; Ban Phe, the ferry pier for Ko Samet, is served by frequent songthaews from Rayong bus station (see p.193 for details). Rayong is famous for producing the national condiment *nam plaa* – a sauce made from decomposed fish – and for the pineapples and durian grown in the provincial orchards, but there's nothing much for tourists here. The **TAT office** (☏038/655420, ⒻX655422, ⒺXtatry@infonews.co.th) for the Rayong region and Ko Samet is inconveniently located 7km east of Rayong town centre at 153/4 Thanon Sukhumvit (Highway 3), on the way to Ban Phe; any Ban Phe-bound bus or songthaew will drop you at its door.

In the unlikely event that you get stuck here overnight, there are three passable moderately priced **hotels** within walking distance of the bus terminal, a few hundred metres east along Thanon Sukhumvit, past the hospital. All three offer fan-cooled and air-conditioned rooms with attached bathroom; the least costly but dingiest rooms belong to the *Asia Hotel,* just north off Thanon Sukhumvit at no. 84 (☏038/611022; ➊–➌), otherwise try the *Rayong Otani* at no. 69 (☏038/611112; ➋–➎) or the nearby *Rayong Hotel* at no. 65/3 (☏038/611073; ➋–➍), both of them on the south side of the road. If you prefer a sea view, you could stay at one of the high-rise hotels or family bungalows along the **Rayong coast** that are finding increasing favour with Thai weekenders, despite the superiority of beaches elsewhere in the vicinity. Sandwiched between the seafront and the Rayong River estuary, a couple of kilometres southwest of Thanon Sukhumvit and the bus terminal, *Rayong Seaview* at 46 Beach Road (☏038/611364; ➏–➐) is the most moderately priced, while the *PMY Beach Hotel,* west along the shorefront at no. 147 (☏038/613002, ⒻX614887; ➑–➒) has a swimming pool, fitness centre and snooker club. The exclusive *Rayong Resort* (☏038/651000, ⒻX651007, ⓦwww.rayongresort.com; ➒) is much further east along the coast and occupies a nice spot on a headland just west of Ban Phe with sea views out to Ko Samet; facilities here include three shorefront swimming pools, tennis courts, table tennis and boat trips to Ko Samet.

# Ko Samet

Attracted by its proximity to Bangkok and its powdery white sand, backpackers, package tourists and Thai students flock to the island of **Ko Samet**, 80km southeast of Pattaya, whose former name, Ko Kaew Phitsadan, means "the island with sand of crushed crystal". Only 6km long, Ko Samet was declared a **national park** in 1981, but typically the ban on building has been ignored and there are now over thirty bungalow operations here. Inevitably, this has had a huge impact on the island's resources: the sea is no longer pristine, and you occasionally stumble across unsightly piles of rubbish. Though the authorities did try closing the island to overnight visitors in 1990, they have since come to a (controversial) agreement with the island's bungalow operators who now pay rent to the Royal Forestry Department.

Samet's beaches tend to be characterized by the type of **accommodation** you find there, though as the island gets increasingly upmarket, it is becoming more difficult to find a bungalow for under B300 a double in high season on any of the beaches. Ao Phrao, Ao Wong Duan and Hat Sai Kaew have the most upmarket places to stay, but all the other beaches still have at least

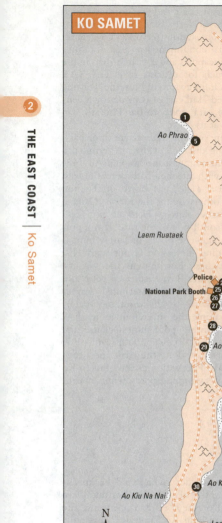

# KO SAMET

*Na Dan Pier*

Health Centre

Police

National Park Visitors' Centre

*Ao Phrao*

*Hat Sai Kaew*

*Ao Hin Kok*

*Ao Phai*

*Ao Tub Tim*

*Laem Ruataek*

*Ao Nuan*

*Pier*

*Ao Cho*

Police

National Park Booth

*Ao Wong Duan*

*Ao Thian*

*Ao Wai*

*Ao Kiu Na Nok*

*Ao Kiu Na Nai*

*Laem Khut*

*Ao Karang*

N

*Ko Chan*

0        1 km

| ACCOMMODATION | |
|---|---|
| Achalee | 17 |
| Ao Kiu Coral Beach | 30 |
| Ao Nuan | 21 |
| Ao Phai Hut | 13 |
| Ao Prao Resort | 1 |
| Ao Pudsa | 19 |
| Banana | 2 |
| Candlelight Beach | 28 |
| Coconut | 7 |
| Dome | 5 |
| Hat Sai Kaew Beach Resort | 6 |
| Jep's Inn | 12 |
| Laem Yai Resort | 4 |
| Lost Resort | 15 |
| Lung Dum Hut | 29 |
| Malibu Garden Resort | 24 |
| Naga | 10 |
| Pop Inn | 3 |
| Sai Kaew Villa | 8 |
| Samed Villa | 18 |
| Sea Breeze | 14 |
| Sea Horse | 25 |
| Silver Sand | 16 |
| Tarn Tawan | 23 |
| Tok's Little Hut | 11 |
| Tub Tim Resort | 20 |
| Vong Duan Resort | 26 |
| White Sand Resort | 9 |
| Wonderland | 22 |
| Wong Duan Villa | 27 |

a few budget-orientated bungalows, with the most accessible beaches – Ao Hin Kok, Ao Phai and Ao Tub Tim – being the most popular in this category. Typically you can expect to pay B150 for the simplest bamboo hut equipped only with a large, well-worn mattress, a blanket and a mosquito net; the same kind of huts with private bathrooms and electric fans cost B200–400. More upmarket bungalows are usually made of concrete and have good, tiled bathrooms; the most expensive have air-con, but prices also depend on whether or not you have an uninterrupted view of the sea. Samet has no fresh water, so water is trucked in from the mainland and should be used sparingly; most sets of bungalows offer at least a few huts with attached bathroom. Electricity in a few places is rationed for evening consumption only, but even these outfits have video shows after dark to help keep the beer flowing.

All beaches get packed on **weekends** and national holidays, so at these times you'd be sensible to take the first available room and if necessary change early the following day. You could also try phoning ahead to reserve a room, though not all bungalows accept bookings and it can be hard getting through in the first place as most places on Ko Samet still rely on satellite phones (code ☎01). At Songkhran (the Thai New Year, in April) it's said to be impossible to find a bungalow even on the most remote beaches, so it's probably worth altering your itinerary accordingly. Many bungalow managers raise their rates by sixty percent during peak periods and sometimes for weekenders as well: the rates quoted here are typical high-season rates. If all affordable accommodation is booked up, you can always **camp** – in accordance with national park rules, camping is permissible on any of the beaches, despite what you might be told.

Until a few years ago, Samet was considered to be malarial, but has now been pronounced safe. You'll still encounter plenty of **mosquitoes** at dusk though, so take lots of repellent; nets or screens are supplied by all bungalow operations and repellent is available from stalls and shops on the island.

### En route to the island: Ban Phe

The mainland departure-point for Ko Samet is the tiny fishing port of **BAN PHE**, about 200km from Bangkok. There are hourly direct **buses** from Bangkok's Eastern (Ekamai) Bus Terminal to the Ban Phe pier, departing between 5.30am and 5.30pm (some air-con services; 3hr), but if you miss those you can easily take one of the more frequent buses to **Rayong** (every 15min; 2hr 30min) and then change onto songthaews, which leave Rayong bus station about every thirty minutes and take half an hour to reach Ban Phe pier. Alternatively, you could take one of the **tourist minibuses** from Thanon Khao San to Ban Phe; prices for these do not include the boat fare and you should be prepared for some fairly crazed driving. From **Pattaya**, there are hardly any direct Ban Phe buses so you're probably best off taking a bus to Rayong (every 30min; 1hr 30min) and then one of the half-hourly songthaews. There are tourist minibuses from Pattaya as well, which can be booked through most hotels and cost B150 – be warned that the B50 boat ticket available as an add-on to the minibus ticket from Pattaya is for Ao Wong Duan, so if you want to go to one of the other beaches, wait and buy your boat ticket at Ban Phe. Coming by bus from points further east, such as **Chanthaburi** or **Trat** for example, you'll most likely be dropped at the Ban Phe junction on Highway 3, from where a songthaew or motorbike taxi will take you the remaining 5km to the pier.

If you get stuck with nothing to do between ferries, several places to check your **email** – a good idea here as internet access is very expensive on Ko Samet – can be found on and around Ban Phe's main pier-head, including a couple on the pier itself. There are a couple of **hotels** on the two-hundred-metre stretch of road between the main Saphaan Nuan Tip pier and the Ao Phrao (Saphaan Sri Ban Phe) pier. *TN Place* (②–④) has simple guest-house rooms with or without private bathroom; it's the cheaper and more traveller-oriented of the two.

It also has internet access and there's a restaurant next door. The nearby mid-range *Diamond Hotel* (☎038/651757; ❸–❹) has simple rooms with fan and more comfortable air-con ones with TV; you can check-in 24 hours a day, which could be useful.

## Boats to Ko Samet

Once in Ban Phe, you need to decide which beach you want and then choose your **boat** accordingly. Some boats are owned by individual resorts and ferry both pre-paid package tourists and fare-paying independent travellers; others make the crossing as soon as they have enough passengers (minimum eighteen people) or sufficient cargo to make it worth their while. In theory, boats to the two main piers on Ko Samet run hourly from 8am to 5pm during high season (Nov–Feb) and on national holidays, and every two hours at other times. In practice, many of the boats leave at the same time, so you may well end up waiting a couple of hours. Probably the best strategy is to get on the boat with the most people and buy your ticket on board rather than from one of the boat-specific booths on the pier-head. All boats charge the same fares.

The easiest place to get to on Ko Samet is **Na Dan pier** on the northeastern tip of the island, which is the most convenient arrival point for the beaches of Hat Sai Kaew, Ao Hin Kok, Ao Phai, Ao Tub Tim and Ao Nuan, and quite feasible for all the other beaches as well; songthaews meet the boats at Na Dan (see opposite) and will take you as far as Wong Duan, or you can walk to your chosen beach. Boats to Na Dan leave from Ban Phe's Saphaan Nuan Tip pier, opposite the 7-11 shop; they take thirty minutes to get to Samet and charge B40 one way.

---

### Leaving Ko Samet

Four **scheduled boats** leave Ko Samet's Na Dan pier every day, the first one at about 7am, the last at 5pm, and there are usually a few extra ones in between; times are posted at the pier, but if you have a plane to catch you should allow for boat delays. There are also regular departures from Ao Wong Duan, every two hours between 8.30am and 4.30pm and, in high season, you'll find at least one Ban Phe boat a day from Ao Cho and Ao Phrao.

Arriving at Ban Phe, you can pick up **buses** to Bangkok, Chanthaburi or Trat, or a songthaew to Rayong, from where buses to all these destinations, plus Pattaya and Si Racha, are far more frequent. The Ban Phe bus and songthaew stop is 400m east of the 7-11, though most buses and songthaews pass the pier-head and will pick up passengers there. If you're heading straight back to Bangkok's Thanon Khao San, to Don Muang airport or to Pattaya, your easiest (and most expensive) option is to buy a direct **minibus** ticket from one of Ko Samet's tour operators (there's at least one on every beach); these tickets don't include the boat fare, but departure times from Ban Phe are arranged to coincide with boat arrivals. You can also book tourist minibuses at the tour operators' offices in Ban Phe on the little soi beside the 7-11 shop, across from the main pier, though they may not always have room for last-minute bookings. Travelling **to Ko Chang**, it takes just two and a half hours by tourist minibus from Ban Phe to the Laem Ngop pier, though it's expensive at B250 (bookable at the *White Sand Resort* on Hat Sai Kaew); the alternative route by ordinary bus can take all day and often entails changing buses at Chanthaburi and then getting onto a Laem Ngop-bound songthaew in Trat, though it works out at half the price. Note that if you're going overland **to Cambodia** via Koh Kong near Trat and need to buy an advance visa (check with the embassy first to find out whether this is necessary), the *White Sand Resort* travel agent on Ko Samet can do this, avoiding the need for you to go back to Bangkok yourself; the service takes five days.

There are equally frequent boats to **Ao Wong Duan** (40min; B50), which is also convenient for the nearby beaches of Ao Cho and Ao Thian. Some boats go to Wong Duan direct from Ban Phe's Saphaan Nuan Tip pier, others stop at Na Dan first – it's often a question of how many passengers there are. Some of the bungalow resorts on the smaller beaches also run boats from Ban Phe direct to their beach – see the individual beach accounts below for details. Boats to **Ao Phrao** leave from a different pier, called Saphaan Sri Ban Phe pier, which is 200m west of the 7-11. The boat service is free to guests of the *Ao Phrao Resort,* or B90 return for non-guests; there are usually four boats a day, but call the resort on ☏ 038/616883 to check times.

### Island practicalities

Foreign visitors are charged the B200 national-park **entrance fee** on arrival (B100 for children under 14 or free for the under-3s), payable either at the checkpoint between the Na Dan pier and Hat Sai Kaew (where there is a national park visitor centre, with displays on Ko Samet's marine life) or at the booth near the Ao Wong Duan pier. There is a sporadic **songthaew** service on Ko Samet, but you may have to wait quite a while for your ride to fill up, and you shouldn't rely on the songthaews as a way to travel between beaches. Songthaews start at Na Dan pier and drive as far as Wong Duan, down the pot-holed track that runs along the centre of the island; fares are posted at Na Dan pier and range from B10 to Hat Sai Kaew (or B100 if you charter the songthaew) to B50 to Ao Kiu (B500 to charter). There are **motorbikes** for rent on every beach at a prohibitive B150 per hour, and a place next to *Sai Kaew Villa* on Hat Si Kaew rents out mountain bikes for B150 per day.

Ko Samet's **health centre** and **police station** are in Na Dan, and the island's **post office** is run by *Naga Bungalows* on Ao Hin Kok; they offer a poste restante service as well as basic postal facilities (see p.197 for details). You can make **international phone calls** at *Naga*, and at the bigger bungalow operations on every main beach; nearly all Ko Samet's phones are satellite phones so the charges are high, at around B100 per minute. Both *Naga* and *Sai Kaew Villa* on Hat Sai Kaew offer **internet access** by satellite phone, which is not surprisingly very expensive at around B7–10 per minute. The biggest bungalows also **change money**, though obviously rates are less favourable than on the mainland. In Na Dan and on Hat Sai Kaew, Ao Phai and Ao Wong Duan, small shops sell basic travellers' necessities, again at higher prices than in Ban Phe and Rayong.

## The beaches

Most of the islanders not associated with the tourist trade live in the **northeast** of the island, near Na Dan, where there are a few shops and foodstalls, as well as the island's only school, health centre and wat. Samet's best **beaches** are along the **east coast**, and this is where you'll find nearly all the bungalow resorts. A rough track connects some of them; otherwise it's a question of walking along the beach at low tide or over the low, rocky points at high water. Long stretches of the **west coast** are well-nigh inaccessible, though at intervals the coastal scrub has been cleared to make way for a track. The views from these clifftop clearings can be magnificent, particularly around sunset, but you can only safely descend to sea level at the bay up near the northwest headland. A few narrow tracks cross the island's forested central ridge to link the east and west coasts, but much of the **interior** is dense jungle, home of hornbills, gibbons and spectacular butterflies.

Samet has no decent coral reefs of its own, so you'll have to take a boat trip to the islands of Ko Kudi, Ko Thalu and Ko Mun, off the northeast coast, to get good **snorkelling** and **fishing**. Trips cost from B450 to B650 including equipment, and can be booked through at least one bungalow resort on every main beach. Some places also offer boat trips around Samet itself for about B400 for a full day. Despite the lack of great reefs, there are a couple of **dive operators** on Samet: Ploy Scuba (☎01/218 7636), next to *Sai Kaew Villa* on Hat Sai Kaew, offers introductory dives lasting one hour for B1200, or one day for B1600, and teaches the four-day open water course for B9500. Ao Prao Divers (☎038/616883, ✉aopraodivers@hotmail.com), based at *Ao Prao Resort* and with a branch at *Sea Breeze* on Ao Phai, is slightly more expensive, but has a big programme of dive trips and cruises and is PADI-certified.

## Hat Sai Kaew

Arriving at **Na Dan** pier, a ten-minute walk south along the track, past the health centre and school, brings you to **HAT SAI KAEW,** or Diamond Beach, named for its beautiful long stretch of luxuriant sand, so soft and clean it squeaks underfoot – a result, apparently, of its unusually high silicon content, which also makes it an excellent raw material for glass-making. Songthaews from Na Dan to Hat Sai Kaew cost B10 per person, or B100 when chartered.

The most popular – and congested – beach on Samet, this is the only part of the island where the beachfront is lined with bungalows, restaurants, beachwear stalls, deck chairs and parasols; the northern end is usually a lot more peaceful than the southern. Holidaying Thais and farangs flock here in pretty much equal numbers, especially at weekends and on public holidays, but big groups of day-tripping package tourists make stretches of the beach almost unbearable from around 11am to 4pm. At night, you have the option of enjoying a leisurely dinner at one of the big seafront seafood **restaurants**, watching videos at one of the bungalow cafés, hanging out at the beachside *Reggae Bar* or heading up the track that connects Hat Sai Kaew with the pier at Na Dan, where you'll find congenial little drinking dens such as *Roger's Vodka Bar* and the *Banana Bar*. *White Sand Resort* has a good **travel agent** which sells minibus tickets to Ko Chang and offers a Cambodian visa service, as well as doing all the usual day-trips and bus tickets. There is **internet access** at *Sai Kaew Villa* and a **dive shop** next door.

Much of the **accommodation** on Hat Sai Kaew is crammed uncomfortably close together. The best-value place on the beach is *Laem Yai Resort* (☎01/293 0208; ❹), whose decent, comfortable wooden bungalows occupy a pretty position under the Laem Yai headland at the nicest, far northern end of Hat Sai Kaew. Nearby the few simple huts at *Pop Inn* (❸) and *Banana* (☎01/218 5841; ❸) are set further back but also have access to the calmer stretch of the beach; they are the cheapest places on Hat Sai Kaew. The distinctive blue and white bungalows of *Hat Sai Kaew Beach Resort* are stylish and thoughtfully designed, which makes them the best in their price bracket (❽), with phones, TV and air-con in every room. The terraced bungalows at *Coconut* (☎01/294 6822; ❹–❼) are overpriced, though the detached air-conditioned bungalows are a lot more comfortable and may be worth splashing out for. A short walk south along the beach, the large and efficiently run *Sai Kaew Villa* (☎ & ℱ038/615852, Ⓦwww.saikaew.com; ❺–❽) comprises a dozen smart, clean rooms with fan or air-con in a hotel-like block, plus some prettier, more expensive bungalows; it also has internet access. The southern end of the beach is occupied by *White Sand Resort* (☎038/617195; ❹–❺) a huge complex of standard-issue bungalows set in a garden back from the shorefront; rooms here are unexciting but relatively well priced for this beach, and there's a choice between fan or air-con.

## Ao Hin Kok

Separated from Hat Sai Kaew by a low promontory on which sits a mermaid statue – a reference to Sunthorn Phu's early nineteenth-century poem, *Phra Abhai Mani* (see box on p.198) – **AO HIN KOK** is smaller and less cluttered than its neighbour. There are three bungalow outfits here, looking over the beach from the grassy slope on the far side of the track. **Songthaews** from Na Dan will drop you at Ao Hin Kok for B20 per person (or B150 when chartered), or you can walk here in about fifteen minutes.

Ao Hin Kok is a particularly good beach for food, with all three bungalows offering exceptional fare at their attached **restaurants**. *Naga* is especially recommended for its vegetarian dishes, its cocktails and its home-made bread and cakes; it also stages regular pool competitions and puts on fire-juggling shows. *Tok's Little Hut* is known for its seafood, and *Jep's Inn* serves up a fine menu of curries, seafood and travellers' fare at its tables on the beach, prettily decorated with fairy lights and given extra atmosphere by mellow music.

The English-run *Naga Bungalows* (☎01/353 2575; ❶–❸) has the cheapest **accommodation** on Ko Samet, offering a range of simple huts with mattresses on the floor, mosquito nets and shared facilities, with the price depending on whether you want a fan or air-con. It's extremely popular, and there's a pool table and a table-tennis table on the premises as well. Next door, *Tok's Little Hut* (☎01/218 1264; ❷–❸) offers slightly more comfortable bungalows, all with attached bathrooms. At the welcoming *Jep's Inn* (☎01/853 3121; ❸–❹) you have the option of staying in quite pleasant small bungalow blocks or in larger, more expensive detached wooden huts, all of them en-suite, but none with a sea view.

Ko Samet **post office** is run out of *Naga Bungalows* and offers a parcel packing, phone, fax and **internet** service as well as poste restante; letters are kept for three months and should be addressed c/o Poste Restante, Ko Samet Post Office, Naga Bungalows, Ko Samet.

## Ao Phai

Beach accommodation gets a little more upmarket around the next collection of rocks on the narrow but pleasant enough **AO PHAI**, where the bungalows tend to be well built and comfortable, and most have attractive tiled bathrooms. Facilities on Ao Phai include an outdoor bar and a minimarket, and *Sea Breeze* has a small library, sells boat trips and minibus tickets, rents out windsurfing equipment and offers overseas telephone and money-exchange facilities. **Songthaews** from Na Dan cost B20 per person to Ao Phai (or B150 when chartered), or you can walk it in twenty minutes.

The recommended *Ao Phai Hut* (☎01/353 2644; ❹–❺) occupies a lovely position on the rocky divide between Ao Phai and Hin Kok, and offers attractive, simply furnished **huts** which are nicely spaced in among the trees. All huts have attached bathrooms and some have air-con, though electricity is only available in the evenings. *Sea Breeze* (☎01/218 6397, ℻239 4780; ❸–❺) is the largest set of bungalows on the beach, offering inexpensive wooden huts, more solid concrete ones and bigger versions with air-con; they all have private bathrooms, but, as they're built up a sparsely wooded slope, none has a sea view. The adjacent *Silver Sand* (☎01/218 5195; ❸–❺) is good value for Ko Samet, offering decent, well-maintained bungalows with nice bathrooms, the price depending on distance from the sea (the cheapest ones are quite far back, with

Over thirty thousand lines long and written entirely in verse, the nineteenth-century romantic epic **Phra Abhai Mani** tells the story of a young prince and his adventures in a fantastical land peopled not only by giants and mermaids, but also by gorgeous women with whom he invariably falls in love. Seduced by an ogress who lives beneath the sea, and kept captive by her for several months, Phra Abhai Mani pines for dry land and eventually persuades a mermaid to help him escape. Naturally, the two fall in love, and decide to spend some time together on the near-by island of Ko Samet (hence the mermaid statue on Ao Hin Kok). But the prince soon tires of the mermaid's charms, and leaps aboard a passing ship in pursuit of another ill-fated affair, this time with a princess already engaged to someone else. And so it goes on.

Widely considered to be one of Thailand's greatest-ever poets, **Sunthorn Phu** (1786–1856) is said to have based much of his work on his own life, and the roman-tic escapades of *Phra Abhai Mani* are no exception. By all accounts, the man was a colourful character – a commoner alternately in and out of favour at Bangkok's Grand Palace, where he lived and worked for much of his life. The child of a bro-ken marriage, he was taken to the palace as a baby when his mother got a job as wet nurse to a young princess (his father had returned to his home town of Klaeng in Rayong province). His first brush with court officialdom came sometime before his twentieth birthday, when he was temporarily imprisoned for having an affair with a court lady. Soon pardoned, the couple married, and Sunthorn Phu was employed as the court poet. By the time Rama II ascended the throne in 1809, he was an established royal favourite, acting as literary aide to the king. However, he took to the bottle, was left by his wife and participated in a drunken fight that land-ed him in jail again. It was during this stint inside (estimated to be around 1821) that he started work on *Phra Abhai Mani*. The poem took twenty years to complete and was rented out in instalments to provide the poet with a modest income – nec-essary as royal patronage had ceased with the ascent to the throne of Rama III (1824–51), whose literary efforts Sunthorn Phu had once rashly criticized. Eventually, poverty forced the poet to become a monk, and he was only reinstated at court a few years before his death when Rama IV (1851–68) was crowned.

Aside from authoring several timeless romances, Sunthorn Phu is remembered as a significant **poetic innovator**. Up until the end of the eighteenth century, Thai poetry had been the almost exclusive domain of high-born courtiers and kings, written in an elevated Thai incomprehensible to most of the population, and con-cerned mainly with the moral Hindu epics the *Mahabarata* and the *Ramayana*. Sunthorn Phu changed all that by injecting huge doses of realism into his verses. He wrote of love triangles, thwarted romances and heartbreaking departures, and he also composed travel poems, or *nirat*, about his own journeys to well-known places in Thailand. Most crucially, he wrote them all in the common, easy-to-understand language of vernacular Thai. Not surprisingly, he's still much admired. In Bangkok, the centenary of his death was celebrated by the publication of sever-al new anthologies and translations of his work. And in the province of Rayong, he's the focus of a special memorial park, constructed, complete with statues of his most famous fictional characters, on the site of his father's home in Klaeng.

no view and some unsightly rubbish nearby), and whether or not you want air-con. The sturdy chalet-style bungalows at the well-appointed *Samed Villa* (℡01/494 8090, ℻945 5481; ❹–❺) are scenically sited along the rocks and up the slope behind the restaurant, so most have a sea view; they are all comfortably designed inside and the price depends on whether or not you want air-con. The cheapest huts on this part of the island are at *Achalee* (②—③), set behind *Samed Villa*, away from the beach; they're pretty scruffy but the pricier ones have private bathrooms.

## Ao Tub Tim

Also known as Ao Pudsa, **AO TUB TIM** is a small white-sand bay sandwiched between rocky points, partly shaded with palms and backed by a wooded slope. It feels secluded, but is only a short stroll from Ao Phai and the other beaches further north, so you get the best of both worlds. **Songthaews** will bring you here from Na Dan pier for B20 per person (or B150 when chartered), or you can walk it in about thirty minutes.

Of the two **bungalow** operations on the beach, *Tub Tim Resort* (Ⓣ & Ⓕ038/615041, Ⓦtubtimresort.hypermart.net; ④—⑦) offers the greatest choice of accommodation, from simple wooden huts through to big air-conditioned bungalows; prices also depend on proximity to the sea, though no hut is more than 200m away. Huts at the adjacent *Ao Pudsa* (Ⓣ01/239 5680; ③—④) are decent enough, with price depending on distance from the shore; the restaurant here occupies a nice site on the sand, with several tables fixed under the palm trees. *Ao Pudsa* also organizes boat trips, sells ferry tickets and has money-exchange facilities.

## Ao Nuan

Clamber up over the next headland (which gives you a panoramic take on the expanse of Hat Sai Kaew) to reach Samet's smallest beach, the secluded **AO NUAN**. The best way to get here from the pier is to take a **songthaew** from Na Dan for B20 per person (B150 when chartered).

The atmosphere here is relaxed and much less commercial than the other beaches, and the mellow restaurant of the friendly *Ao Nuan* has some of the best veggie food on the island. Because it's some way off the main track, the beach gets hardly any through traffic and so feels quiet and private. The huts are idiosyncratic (②—④), each built to a slightly different design (some circular, some A-frame, some thatched), and dotted across the slope that drops down to the bay; a few are built right on the beach. None of the huts has an attached bathroom, electricity is only available at night, and they all have mattresses on the floor and a mosquito net. Although not brilliant for swimming, the rocky shore reveals a good patch of sand when the tide withdraws, and the good beach at Ao Tub Tim is only five minutes' walk away.

## Ao Cho

A five-minute walk south along the track from Ao Nuan brings you to **AO CHO**, a fairly wide stretch of beach with just a couple of bungalow operations plus a pier, a minimarket and motorbikes for rent. Despite being long and partially shaded, this beach seems is less popular than the others, so it may be a good place to try if you want a low-key atmosphere, or if the bungalows on other beaches are packed out. There's some coral off the end of the pier, and you can rent snorkelling gear on the beach. It's also possible to arrange night-time trips on a squid boat, available through *Wonderland* for B5000 per boat (up to about twenty passengers). The easiest way to get to Ao Cho is to take a **boat** to Ao Wong Duan and then walk here, or you could take the normal boat to Na Dan and then hang around for a songthaew (B30). Alternatively call *Wonderland* the day before you arrive and they should send a boat to pick you up from Ban Phe (B50 per person).

*Wonderland* (☎ 01/943 9338; ❷–❺) has some of the cheapest **bungalows** on Ko Samet which, though small and basic and away from the shore, do have fans and private bathrooms; they also have lots of better bungalows with sea views and can organize snorkelling and fishing trips. Most of the bungalows at the Italian-managed *Tarn Tawan* (☎ 01/429 3298, Ⓦ www.kosamet.com; ❹–❺) also have a sea view; here the price depends on whether you go for a semi-detached unit with fan and private bathroom, or a larger, free-standing bungalow.

## Ao Wong Duan

The horseshoe bay of **AO WONG DUAN**, round the next headland, is dominated by mid-range and upmarket bungalow resorts with rather inflated prices. Few backpackers come here, but it is popular with older couples and with package tourists. Although the beach is fairly long and broad, it suffers revving jet-skis and an almost continual stream of day-trippers, and the shorefront is consequently fringed with a rash of beach bars and tourist shops. Both *Malibu* and *Sea Horse* have minimarts, motorbike rental, money exchange and overseas telephone services, and both places sell boat tickets and snorkelling trips. There's a national-park booth on the beach, where you must pay your B200 entry fee if alighting from a Ban Phe boat, and a police box. At least four direct **boats** a day should run from Na Dan to Wong Duan (B50); look for the *Malibu*, the *Sea Horse* and the *Wong Duan Resort* boats. Alternatively, take a boat to Na Dan, then a B30 ride in a songthaew (or a B200 taxi ride). Return boats depart every two hours between 8.30am and 4.30pm; if you're in a hurry you can charter a seven-person speedboat from the Wong Duan pier to Ban Phe for B1000.

The whitewashed concrete **bungalows** at *Malibu Garden Resort* (☎ 01/218 5345, Ⓔ samet@loxinfo.co.th; ❺–❼) are set round a shady tropical garden with a small swimming pool; the rooms are uninspiring but decent enough and come with fan or air-con and TV. Accommodation at the adjacent *Seahorse* (☎ 01/451 5184; ❻–❼) is currently the least good value on the beach in high season, though there are discounts of up to fifty percent from April through October. Rooms here are very plain and pricey considering there's no pool (though the beach is perfectly swimmable); the most expensive ones have air-con. *Vong Duan Resort* (☎ 038/651777, Ⓕ 651819; ❺–❻) is the best-value place to stay on the beach; its bungalows have character, are attractively designed inside and out (with or without air-con) and stand around a pretty tropical garden. Neighbouring *Wong Duan Villa* (☎ 038/652300, Ⓕ 651741; ❻–❼) also has nicely appointed bungalows, spacious, comfortably furnished and with big balconies, though the less expensive fan rooms seem overpriced.

## Ao Thian (Candlelight Beach)

Off nearly all beaten tracks, **AO THIAN** (also known as Candlelight Beach) is the best place to come if you want seclusion: though facilities are simple, prices are reasonable and the setting is quite lovely. Should you need provisions or distractions, Wong Duan is only a ten-minute walk away. Ao Thian's narrow white-sand bay is dotted with wave-smoothed rocks and partitioned by larger outcrops that create several distinct beaches; as it curves outwards to the south you get a great view of the east coast. Though occasional supply **boats** do travel from Ban Phe to Ao Thian, the most reliable route here is to get a boat to Wong Duan and then walk.

At the northern end, *Candlelight Beach* (☎ 01/218 6934; ❹–❺) has a dozen or so basic **huts** ranged along the shorefront slope and a few more along the coast itself; all have attached bathrooms, though they seem a little dilapidated. Right down at the other end of the beach is the much more interesting *Lung Dum*

*Hut* (☏01/458 8430; ❸–❹), where the thirty simple but idiosyncratic bungalows are all slightly different in design; the best are built right on the rocks with the sea just metres from the door. All huts have a private bathroom, fan and mosquito net, with electricity only available in the evenings; the price depends on the location. If you're looking for a romantic spot then this is a good choice; the staff are friendly and there are two little restaurants.

## Ao Kiu

You have to really like the solitary life to plump for Samet's most isolated beach, **AO KIU**, over an hour's walk south of Ao Thian through unadulterated wilderness – the track begins behind *Wong Duan Resort* and can be joined at the back of *Lung Dum Hut* at Ao Thian. It's actually two beaches: Ao Kiu Na Nok on the east coast and Ao Kiu Na Nai on the west, separated by a few hundred metres of scrub and coconut grove. The bungalows here belong to *Ao Kiu Coral Beach* (☏038/652561; ❸–❻), and most are set in among the palms on the east shore, although a couple look down on the tiny west-coast coral beach; you can also rent tents here for B100.

The most convenient way of **getting here** is by direct boat from the mainland; during high season at least one *Coral Beach* boat makes the run daily – call to check departure times. Songthaews here from Na Dan cost B50 per person or B500 to charter.

## Ao Phrao (Paradise Bay)

Across on the west coast, the rugged, rocky coastline only softens into beach once – at **AO PHRAO**, also known as Paradise Bay, on the northwestern stretch, some 4km north of Ao Kiu Na Nai. Ao Phrao gets nowhere near as many overnight visitors, but the beach is shady and not at all bad and, outside the weekends, you have lots of space to yourself. The most direct route from the east-coast beaches is via the inland **track** from behind *Sea Breeze* on Ao Phai, which takes about twenty minutes on foot, though the track from the back of *Tub Tim* on Ao Tub Tim will also get you there. Direct **boats** to Ao Phrao leave four times a day from Ban Phe's private Sri Ban Phe pier, and are free for guests of *Ao Phrao Resort*, or B90 return for non-guests. You can also get here by songthaew from Na Dan for B30 per person, or B200 on charter.

The best reason for coming to Ao Phrao is to stay at *Ao Prao Resort* (☏038/616883, ☏02/439 0352, ⓦwww.aopraoresort.com; ❽–❾), which offers the most stylish **accommodation** on the island, with comfortable wooden chalets set in a tropical flower garden that slopes down to the beach. All chalets have air-conditioning, TVs and balconies overlooking the sea; rooms are discounted on weekdays, but advance booking is advisable for any time of the week. There's a dive centre here (see p196), internet access, and an overseas phone service. The nicest of the handful of other options on Ao Phrao, none of which are budget-oriented, is *Dome* (☏01/218 7693, ☏038/652600; ❺–❼), whose bungalows are built up the side of a small slope and have sea views; some also have air-con.

# Chanthaburi

For over five hundred years, precious stones have drawn prospectors and traders to the provincial capital of **CHANTHABURI**, 80km east of Ban Phe, and it's this pivotal role within Thailand's most lucrative **gem-mining** area that makes it one of the most appealing of all the east-coast towns. Seventy percent of the country's gemstones are mined in the hills of Chanthaburi and Trat provinces, a fruitful source of sapphires and Thailand's only known vein of rubies. Since the fifteenth century, hopefuls of all nationalities have flocked here, particularly the Shans from Burma, the Chinese and the Cambodians, many of them establishing permanent homes in the town. The largest ethnic group, though, are Catholic refugees from Vietnam, vast numbers of whom arrived here in the wake of the recurrent waves of religious persecution between the eighteenth century and the late 1970s. The French, too, have left their mark: during their occupation of Chanthaburi from 1893 to 1905, when they held the town hostage against the fulfilment of a territorial treaty on the Lao border, they undertook the restoration and enlargement of the town's Christian cathedral.

This cultural diversity makes Chanthaburi an engaging place, even if there's less than a day's worth of sights here. Built on the wiggly west bank of the Maenam Chanthaburi, the town fans out westwards for a couple of kilometres, though the most interesting parts are close to the river, in the district where the Vietnamese families are concentrated. Here, along the soi running parallel

2

THE EAST COAST | Chanthaburi

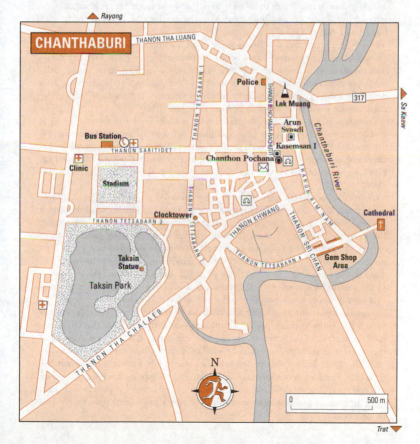

## Rubies and sapphires

As long ago as the fifteenth century, European travellers noted the abundance of precious stones in Chanthaburi and Trat, but the first **gem-mining rush** happened in 1857, when stories of farmers ploughing up cartloads of rubies and fishermen trawling precious stones from the sea bed brought in hundreds of prospectors from ruby-rich Burma. Before long they had been joined by Cambodians and Vietnamese, and then the British mine companies from Burma came over to organize the industry. By 1900, Sapphires and Rubies of Siam Ltd had bought up nearly all the mining fields in eastern Thailand, but it proved an unwise move, as most immigrant miners refused to work for the colonials and moved on elsewhere. When Thailand lost many of its best sapphire mines in a border dispute with Cambodia, the company decided to pull out, leaving the Chanthaburi fields once more to independent self-employed miners.

The next great transformation came half a century later, as a consequence of the upheavals in Burma, which until then had been the world's main supplier of **corundum** – the term for all crystalline forms of aluminium oxide, such as ruby and sapphire. In 1962 the Burmese effectively sealed their country against the outside world, ousting all foreign companies and ceasing all external trade. The Thai dealers promptly muscled in to fill the gap in the world corundum market, and rapidly achieved their current dominant status by forcing the government to ease import and export duties.

Locally produced stones account for a small fraction of the total trade in and around Chanthaburi, whose mines have now been exploited for so long that high-cost mechanical methods are the only viable way of getting at the rocks. Self-employed panhandlers have rushed to work on new veins in Cambodia, while Thai dealers pull the strings in Vietnam's embryonic industry and regularly buy up the entire annual production of some of Australia's gem fields.

Though artificially produced stones are now used where formerly only the genuine article would do – in the glasses of most high-quality watches for example – the demand for top-notch natural stones from jewellers and watchmakers is virtually limitless. In view of the profits to be made – an uncut 150-carat ruby sold for US$1.2 million in 1985 – it's inevitable that sharp practice should be commonplace.

Doctoring the classification of a stone is a common act of skulduggery. A low-quality rough stone from Africa might emerge from the cutter's workshop with a label identifying it as Burmese or Kashmiri, the top rank in the gem league. But perhaps the most prevalent form of fraud involves **heating the stones** to enhance their colour, a cosmetic operation recorded as long ago as the first century, when Pliny the Elder described the technique of enhancing the quality of agate by "cooking" it. Trace elements are what give corundums their colour – in the case of blue sapphires it's titanium and iron that create the hue. To convert a weakly coloured sapphire into an expensive stone, factories now pack the low-grade rocks with titanium and iron oxide, heat the lot to within a whisker of 2050°C – the melting point of sapphire – and thereby fuse the chemicals into the surface of the stone to produce an apparently flawless gem. As long as the cutter and polisher leave the new "skin" intact when they do their work, only an expert will be able to tell whether the highly priced end product is a sham. It takes a lot less effort to fool the gullible Westerners who reckon they can make a killing on the Chanthaburi market: tumble the red glass of a car taillight in a tub of gravel, and after an hour or two you've got a passable facsimile of a ruby.

to the river, the town presents a mixture of pastel-painted, colonial-style housefronts and traditional wooden shophouses, some with finely carved latticework.

Continuing south along this soi, you'll reach a footbridge on the other side of which stands Thailand's largest **cathedral**: the Church of the Immaculate Conception. There's thought to have been a church on this site ever since the first Christians arrived in town, though the present structure was revamped in French style in the late nineteenth century. West of the bridge, the **gem dealers' quarter** begins, where shopkeepers sit sifting through great mounds of tiny coloured stones, peering at them through microscopes and classifying them for resale. Some of these shops also cut, polish and set the stones: Chanthaburi is as respected a cutting centre as Bangkok, and Thai lapidaries are considered among the most skilled – not to mention most affordable – in the world. Most of Chanthaburi's market-trading is done on weekend mornings, when buyers from Bangkok descend in their hundreds to sit behind rented tables and haggle with local dealers.

Chanthaburi has a reputation for high-grade fruit too, notably durian, rambutan and mangosteen, all grown in the orchards around the town and sold in the daily **market**, a couple of blocks northwest of the gem quarter. Basketware products are also good buys here, mostly made by the Vietnamese.

West of the market and gem quarter, the landscaped **Taksin Park** is the town's recreation area and memorial to King Taksin of Thonburi, the general who reunited Thailand between 1767 and 1782 after the sacking of Ayutthaya by the Burmese. Chanthaburi was the last Burmese bastion on the east coast – when Taksin took the town he effectively regained control of the whole country. The park's heroic bronze statue of Taksin is featured on the back of the B20 note.

### Practicalities

Even if you're not planning a visit to Chanthaburi, you may find yourself stranded here for a couple of hours between **buses**, as this is a major interchange for east-coast services (some Rayong–Trat journeys require you to change here for example) and a handy terminus for buses to and from the northeast: eight daily buses make the scenic six-hour Chanthaburi–Sa Kaew–Khorat journey in both directions, with Sa Kaew being a useful interchange for buses to Aranyaprathet and the Cambodian border. Buses to and from all these places, as well as Bangkok's Eastern (Ekamai) and Northern (Mo Chit) stations, use the Chanthaburi **bus station** (☎039/311299) on Thanon Saritidet, about 750m northwest of the town centre and market. There are several **banks** with ATMs on Thanon Khwang.

The two best-located **accommodation** options are both near the river. The small and basic *Arun Svasdi* at 239 Thanon Sukha Phiban (☎039/311082; ❶–❷), down a soi off the eastern end of Thanon Saritidet, has quiet rooms with fan and bathroom and is in the heart of the Vietnamese part of town. Around the corner at 98/1 Thanon Benchama-Rachutit, the much larger *Kasemsan 1* (☎039/312340; ❷–❹) offers a choice between the sizeable, clean rooms with fan and bathroom on the noisy street side, and the similar but more expensive air-conditioned ones in the quieter section. The **restaurant** next door to *Kasemsan 1*, called *Chanthon Pochana* (no English sign), serves a range of standard rice and seafood dishes. Otherwise, check out the foodstalls in the market and along the riverside soi for Vietnamese spring rolls (*cha gio*) served with sweet sauce, and for the locally made Chanthaburi rice noodles (*kway tiaw Chanthaburi*).

# Trat and around

Most travellers who find themselves in and around the minor provincial capital of **Trat** are heading either for the island of **Ko Chang**, via the tiny fishing port of Laem Ngop, or for **Cambodia**, via the border at Ban Hat Lek. Trat itself has a certain charm, with its compact business district dominated by a traditional covered market, and its residential streets still lined with wooden houses. As the overland crossing into Cambodia gets increasingly popular, Trat will no doubt develop into more of a travellers' centre – new little inexpensive guest houses are already popping up all over the town. If you head out of the town, east along the coast road towards the Cambodian border, you'll travel through some exhilarating countryside before getting to the port of **Khlong Yai** and the border post at **Ban Hat Lek**; this route also passes the Khao Lan refugee camp museum, a testimony to one of the bleakest episodes of recent local history.

## Trat

The small and pleasantly unhurried market town of **TRAT**, 68km east of Chanthaburi, is the perfect place to stock up on essentials, change money, make long-distance telephone calls or extend your visa before striking out for the idylls of Ko Chang or the challenges of Cambodia.

Trat is served by lots of buses from Bangkok, including seven daily air-con government **buses** and at least half a dozen private tour buses from the Eastern (Ekamai) Bus Terminal (5–6hr), and three daily buses from the Northern (Mo Chit) Bus Terminal, which take about four hours. Trat also has useful bus connections with Ban Phe (for Ko Samet), Chanthaburi, Pattaya and Si Racha. All air-con buses, whether government or privately operated, drop passengers somewhere on the central four-hundred-metre stretch of Thanon Sukhumvit, at the relevant **bus office** as shown on the map opposite. Buses also depart from these different spots, where timetables for all Bangkok-bound services are clearly posted so you can easily see which company is running the next service. Non-air-con buses from Bangkok and other east-coast towns use the **regular bus station** near the *Thai Roong Roj Hotel*. If you're planning on travelling straight on **to Ko Chang** in the same day you should aim to get the 6am or 8.30am air-con bus here from Bangkok's Eastern Bus Terminal, though the 9am service might make it as well, so long as you're willing to charter a songthaew from Trat to the port at Laem Ngop. For details on transport to Ko Chang see p.213. An airport is due to open in Trat in 2003, and will be served by Bangkok Airways flights.

Trat's official **TAT** office is in Laem Ngop (see p.209), but any guest house will help you out with local information; alternatively, visit *Jean's Café* (see p.208) for a browse through the legendary travellers' comment books.

### Accommodation

**Guest houses** in Trat are small, friendly and inexpensive places, most of them very much traveller-oriented and run by well-informed local people who are used to providing up-to-date information on boats to Ko Chang and Cambodian border crossings. All the guest houses listed here are within ten minutes' walk of the bus and songthaew stops on Thanon Sukhumvit.

**Coco**, on the corner of Soi Yai Onn and Thanon Thoncharoen ☎039/530462. Run by an exceptionally friendly family who run a great restaurant downstairs, this place has very cheap and basic rooms with shared bathrooms. ❶

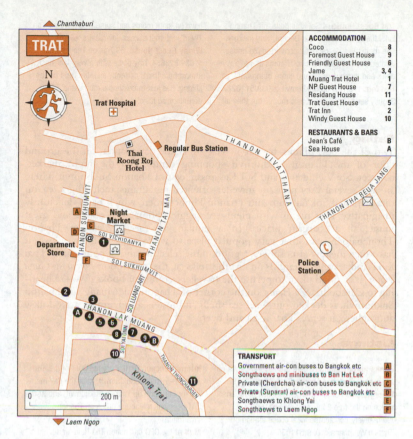

**ACCOMMODATION**

| | |
|---|---|
| Coco | 8 |
| Foremost Guest House | 9 |
| Friendly Guest House | 6 |
| Jame | 3, 4 |
| Muang Trat Hotel | 1 |
| NP Guest House | 7 |
| Residang House | 11 |
| Trat Guest House | 5 |
| Trat Inn | 2 |
| Windy Guest House | 10 |

**RESTAURANTS & BARS**

| | |
|---|---|
| Jean's Café | B |
| Sea House | A |

**TRANSPORT**

| | |
|---|---|
| Government air-con buses to Bangkok etc | A |
| Songthaews and minibuses to Ban Hat Lek | B |
| Private (Cherdchai) air-con buses to Bangkok etc | C |
| Private (Suparat) air-con buses to Bangkok etc | D |
| Songthaews to Khlong Yai | E |
| Songthaews to Laem Ngop | F |

**Foremost Guest House**, 49 Thanon Thoncharoen ☎039/511923. One of the longest-running guest houses in town; rooms here are basic and share a common bathroom, but there's a communal seating area downstairs and the very pleasant *Jean's Cafe* next door. The guest house is run by very well-informed people and offers lots of local information as well as a set of exceptionally useful travellers' comment books containing up-to-the-minute recommendations on Ko Chang and Cambodia (the books are available either at the guest house or at *Jean's Cafe*). Has B50 dorm beds. ❶

**Friendly Guest House**, 106–110 Thanon Lak Muang ☎039/524053. Rooms in the extended modern home of an exuberant family; all have windows and share bathrooms. ❶

**Jame**, 45/1 Thanon Lak Muang ☎039/530458. Very clean rooms of varying sizes, depending on how much you want to pay, all with shared bath.

Split between two houses on opposite sides of the road. ❶–❷

**Muang Trat Hotel**, 24 Soi Vichidanya ☎039/511091. On the edge of the night market, a typically basic and rather grubby town hotel, where the rather overpriced rooms are all en-suite and you can opt for air-con and TV if you want. ❸

**NP Guest House**, 10 Soi Yai Onn ☎039/512270. Friendly option, with simple but fair enough rooms with shared bathrooms; not all of them have windows. Plenty of information available from the manager. ❶

**Residang House**, 87/1–2 Thanon Thoncharoen ☎039/530103. The most comfortably appointed of all the guest houses in Trat, this place feels like a small hotel. Rooms are large and very clean and all have thick mattresses; bathrooms are shared. There are lockers downstairs and lots of local information. ❷

**Trat Guest House**, 4 Soi Khunpoka, off Thanon Lak Muang ☎039/511152. Decent, very inexpensive rooms in a characterful converted old house, located down a quiet little soi. Rooms all have windows and bamboo walls and share bathrooms. ❶

**Trat Inn**, 1–5 Thanon Sukhumvit ☎039/511028. Slightly seedy hotel with basic rooms, but they all have en-suite rooms and some also have air-con. There's internet access downstairs. ❶–❷

**Windy Guest House**, 63 Thanon Thoncharoen ☎039/523664. Tiny place with a very laid-back atmosphere that's perfectly situated right on the khlong. Has just three simple rooms and a B50 dormitory, so it's often full. ❶

## Eating

Two of the best **places to eat** in Trat are at the day market, on the ground floor of the Thanon Sukhumvit shopping centre, and the night market, between Soi Vichidanya and Soi Kasemsan, east of Thanon Sukhumvit. There are also several very pleasant traveller-oriented restaurants, including *Coco*, on the corner of Soi Yai Onn and Thanon Thoncharoen, which has a deliciously imaginative Thai menu with plenty of veggie options, real coffee and great music, all at bargain prices. In a similar vein, *Jean's Café* on Thanon Thoncharoen is another very popular place to while away an hour or two; it has a nice mellow atmosphere, a good music selection and of course tasty Thai food and travellers' fare. Run by the folks at the next-door *Foremost Guest House*, it's a good place to peruse the travellers' comment books if you're heading to Cambodia. *Sea House*, on the corner of Thanon Lak Muang and Thanon Sukhumvit, is decked out with sea shells and fosters an invitingly artsy-folksy atmosphere; it serves Thai food and beer.

## Listings

**Banks and exchange** There are several banks on the central stretch of Thanon Sukhumvit.

**Emergencies** For all emergencies, call the tourist police on the free 24hr phoneline ☎1699. Alternatively, contact the local police station off Thanon Vivatthana ☎039/511035.

**Hospital** Trat hospital ☎039/511986 is off Thanon Sukhumvit on the north edge of town.

**Immigration office** Located on the Trat–Laem Ngop road, 3km northeast of Laem Ngop pier (Mon–Fri 8.30am–4.30pm; ☎ 039/597215).

**Internet access** On the ground floor of the *Trat Inn* at 1–5 Thanon Sukhumvit, near the day market further north up Thanon Sukhumvit, and at the CAT overseas telephone office on Thanon Vivatthana.

**Mail** At the GPO on Thanon Tha Reua Jang.

**Telephones** The CAT overseas telephone office is on Thanon Vivatthana on the eastern edge of town (daily 7am–10pm).

## The road to the border

From Trat, the obvious land-based excursion is a trip as far as the Cambodian border. **Songthaews** to the small, thriving fishing port of Khlong Yai, 74km east, leave Trat about every thirty minutes from behind the shopping centre; they all travel via Khao Lan and take about an hour and a quarter. From Khlong Yai it's just a short journey on to Ban Hat Lek and the border.

The journey into this narrow tail of Thailand passes through some of the most enthralling countryside in the region, with sea views to the south and a continuous range of forested mountains to the north, pierced by a couple of waterfalls so mighty you can see them from the road. Midway to Khlong Yai, you might consider stopping off for an hour at the **Khao Lan refugee camp museum** (daily 8.30am–4pm; donation); ask the songthaew driver for "phipitapan Khao Lan" – though it's easy to spot because of the enormous Red Cross symbol outside. During the last few months of 1978, Cambodians started pouring across the Ban That mountains into eastern Thailand, desperate to escape the brutalities of Pol Pot's "Year Zero" mania and the violence that erupted with the Vietnamese invasion. Trat province received the heaviest influx of refugees, and Khao Lan became the largest of the six camps in Thailand, eventually comprising a hospital, an orphanage and an arts and crafts workshop as well as thousands of makeshift dwellings. In its nine years of operation, this Red Cross camp served as a temporary home to some 200,000 people. By the time it ceased operation in 1987, most of its refugees had been resettled, and Thailand's last Cambodian refugee camp was closed in April 1993.

Nothing now remains of the original Khao Lan camp: the museum is housed in a modern building close to the road, and the few other new structures on the site were purpose-built for the Thai soldiers stationed here. The contents of the museum are disappointingly sparse, offering only a sketchy historical and political context, spiced up with a few photos and a couple of waxwork tableaux of life in the camp. The overall tone of the place seems inappropriately ingratiating, with each exhibit presented more as a memorial to Queen Sirikit's gracious patronage of the camp (the queen is president of the Thai Red Cross and made several visits to the Khao Lan site) than as a testimony to the resilience of its displaced residents.

Forty kilometres to the south, **Khlong Yai** boasts a great setting, the town's long pier jutting way out to sea, partly flanked by rows of stilt houses that form a shelter for the fishing boats. It's a dramatic place to visit during rough weather, when the turbulent seas lash against the housefronts and the end of the pier disappears beneath low-lying storm clouds. There's little point venturing all the way on to **Ban Hat Lek** unless you're planning to cross into Cambodia (see box on p.210 for details).

## Laem Ngop

The departure point for Ko Chang and the outer islands is **LAEM NGOP**, 17km southwest of Trat and served by share-taxis (songthaews) every half-hour or so; rides can take anything from twenty to forty minutes, so leave plenty of time to catch the boat. The usual songthaew fare is B20 per person with a full load or about B30 with a minimum of eight people; if there aren't many passengers but everyone's in a hurry to catch the boat, there's sometimes a whip round to make up the difference. For details of **boat services** from here to Ko Chang, see p.213, and for boat services to the outer islands, see p.222.

If you do miss the boat or the seas are too rough to negotiate, it's no great hardship to be stuck in this tiny port, which consists of little more than a wooden pier, one main road and a small collection of traditional houses inhabited mainly by fisherfolk, many of whom are Muslim. If you happen to be in the area between January 17 and 21, it may be worth staying here for the festival commemorating the repulsing of French forces from Laem Ngop in 1941 and the loss of three Thai warships in the process.

Although it still retains its small-town atmosphere, Laem Ngop caters well to the Ko Chang tourist trade: there's a cluster of partisan **tourist information** booths around the main pier-head at which you can buy ferry tickets and reserve accommodation on the island – definitely worthwhile in peak season. There's also an official TAT office (daily 8.30am–4.30pm; ☎ & ℱ 039/597255) close by, which offers independent advice on the island and may be able to give

## Overland border crossings into Cambodia

There are currently two legal **border crossings** for tourists travelling to **Cambodia**: one at Ban Hat Lek, near the east-coast town of Trat, and the other at Aranyaprathet, midway between the east coast and Isaan. Recent reports claim that it is possible to buy a thirty-day Cambodian **visa on arrival** at both these points (it's worth checking the latest information with the Cambodian Embassy in Bangkok; see p.162), as well as at the airports in Phnom Penh and Siem Reap: you need US$20 and a photo for this. You may also want to bring a (real or fake) International Quarantine Booklet showing dates of your vaccinations, as border guards at both overland crossings have been known to (illegally) charge foreigners without vaccination cards a US$5 penalty fee.

If you're travelling nonstop from Bangkok to Cambodia, the fastest route is via Ban Hat Lek. If you don't fancy the overland route, you can **fly** with Bangkok Airways from Pattaya to Phnom Penh and from Bangkok to both Siem Reap and Phnom Penh; details are given in the relevant city accounts. Full details on **entering Thailand from Cambodia** are given in Basics on p.19, where you'll also find information on Thai visa requirements.

### Trat–Ban Hat Lek–Koh Kong–Sihanoukville

As Ban Hat Lek (on the Thai side) and Koh Kong (in Cambodia) are on opposite sides of the Dong Tong River estuary, crossing the border here involves taking at least one taxi-boat before you can board the scheduled public boat on to Sihanoukville. The first leg of the trip from Trat takes you to the Thai border post at **Ban Hat Lek**, 91km southeast of Trat (border open daily 7am–5pm). Share-taxis (songthaews) and air-con minibuses to Ban Hat Lek leave from Thanon Sukhumvit in central Trat and cost B100 per person. If you want to reach Sihanoukville in one day, you'll need to be at the minibus stop for about 4.30am, when drivers meet passengers off the overnight bus from Bangkok (departing the Eastern Bus Terminal at 11.30pm) and whisk them straight to Ban Hat Lek in time for the opening of the border at 7am. This gives you just enough time to catch the daily scheduled **boat** to **Sihanoukville** from the nearby town of **Koh Kong** across on the eastern bank of the estuary (sometimes referred to as Krong Koh Kong), which at the time of writing sets off at around 8am. To get to the Koh Kong pier, take a motorcycle or car taxi from the Ban Hat Lek immigration post to the west bank of the estuary (a 10min drive) and then a taxi-boat across to Koh Kong on the east bank.

you current boat times. You can **change money** at the Thai Farmers' Bank (usual banking hours), five minutes' walk back down the main road from the pier, or at the currency exchange booth on the pier, which has longer opening hours. There are several small **internet centres** on the road up to the pier and around the pier-head itself.

Your best bet for **accommodation** in Laem Ngop is the friendly and efficiently run *Chut Kaew* guest house (☎039/597088; ❷), close to the bank on the main road, and about seven minutes' walk from the pier. Besides simple rooms with shared bathrooms, it has plenty of information on Ko Chang (you can store luggage here while you're on the island) and rents bicycles to explore Laem Ngop. *Chut Kaew* also serves good travellers' **food**, and even if you're not staying in Laem Ngop it's worth getting an early songthaew from Trat and eating breakfast here before catching the first boat of the day to Ko Chang. There are a couple of large, scenically located restaurants on the pier-head too, where you can order anything from banana pancakes to seafood dinners; they're probably nicest at sunset though, after the crowds of ferry passengers have gone.

Shortly after leaving Koh Kong, the Sihanoukville boat makes a brief stop at **Pak Khlong** (aka Bak Kleng) at the western side of the river mouth, which can be reached directly from Ban Hat Lek. Doing so involves taking a taxi-boat across open sea all the way down to the mouth of the estuary, and is reportedly not very safe as the boats are old; if you want to take the risk, you can hire a taxi-boat from the pier near the Ban Hat Lek immigration post.

If you leave Trat later in the day and can't find transport all the way to Ban Hat Lek, take a songthaew to Khlong Yai, then change on to another songthaew or a motor-cycle taxi for the sixteen-kilometre ride to Ban Hat Lek. Once through immigration, follow the route described above to Koh Kong, where you can stay the night before catching the Sihanoukville boat the next morning.

For up-to-the minute details on routes, times and prices, check the travellers' comment books at Trat's *Foremost Guest House*, and for a thorough guide to Koh Kong and how to reach it from both sides of the border, visit ⓦkohkong.com/kohkong.

### Aranyaprathet–Poipet–Siem Reap

The other overland crossing into Cambodia is at **Poipet**, 4km east of the Thai town of **Aranyaprathet**. The border here is open daily from 7am to 5pm; once through the border, you have to face a gruelling eight- to twelve-hour journey in the back of a pick-up to cover the notoriously hellish 150km of potholed road between Poipet and Siem Reap. If you need a **hotel** in Aranyaprathet, try either the comfortable *Inter Hotel* on Thanon Chatasingh (ⓣ037/231291, ⓕ232352; ❹–❺), or the cheaper *Aran Garden II* at 110 Thanon Rat Uthit (❷–❸).

**From Bangkok**, the easiest way to get to Aranyaprathet is by **train**: there are two services a day, which take about six hours; you'll need to catch the one at 5.50am to ensure reaching the border before 5pm. Tuk-tuks will take you the 4km from the train station to the border post. Alternatively, take a **bus** from Bangkok's Northern (Mo Chit) Bus Terminal to Aranyaprathet (4 daily until 5.30pm; 4hr 30min), then a tuk-tuk from the bus station to the border. It's also possible to buy a **through ticket to Siem Reap** from Bangkok from almost any travel agent in Banglamphu for about B1600; transport is by minibus to the border and then by pick-up to Siem Reap. Travelling to Cambodia **from east-coast towns**, the easiest route is to take a bus from Chanthaburi to the town of **Sa Kaew**, 130km to the northeast, and then change onto a bus for the 55-kilometre ride east to Aranyaprathet.

# Ko Chang

The focal point of a national marine park archipelago of 52 islands, **Ko Chang** is Thailand's second-largest island (after Phuket) and is mainly characterized by a broad central spine of jungle-clad hills, the highest of which, Khao Salak Pet, tops 740m. Though it measures 30km north to south and 8km across, Ko Chang supports fewer than five thousand inhabitants, many of whom make their living from fishing and reside in the hamlets scattered around the fringes of the island. But it is the island's long, white-sand beaches that are now the main income-earner here, for Ko Chang is an increasingly mainstream desti-nation for foreign and domestic tourists alike.

Ko Chang's west coast has the prettiest **beaches** and is the most developed, with Hat Sai Khao (White Sand Beach) drawing the biggest crowds. The east coast is closer to the mainland and less exposed to storms, but has hardly any-where to stay. During **peak season**, accommodation on the west coast tends to fill up very quickly – and you'd be wise to avoid the island altogether on

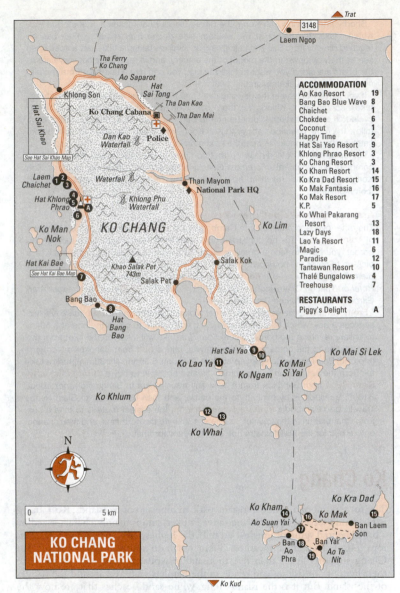

**ACCOMMODATION**

| | |
|---|---|
| Ao Kao Resort | 19 |
| Bang Bao Blue Wave | 8 |
| Chaichet | 1 |
| Chokdee | 6 |
| Coconut | 1 |
| Happy Time | 2 |
| Hat Sai Yao Resort | 9 |
| Khlong Phrao Resort | 3 |
| Ko Chang Resort | 3 |
| Ko Kham Resort | 14 |
| Ko Kra Dad Resort | 15 |
| Ko Mak Fantasia | 16 |
| Ko Mak Resort | 17 |
| K.P. | 5 |
| Ko Whai Pakarang Resort | 13 |
| Lazy Days | 18 |
| Lao Ya Resort | 11 |
| Magic | 6 |
| Paradise | 12 |
| Tantawan Resort | 10 |
| Thalé Bungalows | 4 |
| Treehouse | 7 |

**RESTAURANTS**

| | |
|---|---|
| Piggy's Delight | A |

KO CHANG
NATIONAL PARK

national holidays, when most places are booked out by groups of Thai students
– but it gets a lot quieter (and cheaper) from May to October, when fierce
storms batter the huts and can make the sea too rough to swim in.

A wide road runs almost all the way round the island, served by fairly frequent public **songthaews**; you can also rent motorbikes and mountain bikes
on most beaches, and should be able to arrange a motorbike taxi from the same
places if necessary. Only the southeastern and southwestern coasts remain

## Diving and snorkelling off Ko Chang

The **reefs** off Ko Chang are nowhere near as spectacular as Andaman coast dive sites, but they're decent enough and – a major advantage – not at all crowded. Local **dive sites** range from the beginners' reefs at the Southern Pinnacle, with lots of soft corals, anemones, myriad reef fish and the occasional moray eel at depths of 4–6m, to the more challenging 31-metre dive off Ko Rang, where you're likely to see snapper and possibly even a whale shark.

Just three **dive schools** currently operate out of Ko Chang. The longest running of the these is Sea Horse Diving at *Kai Bae Hut* on Hat Kai Bae (℡01/996 7147, ℮adidive@hotmail.com); PADI-certificated Eco Divers operates from the upmarket *Ban Pu Resort* on Hat Sai Khao (℡01/865 6408, ℗01/983 7127, ℮crispine75@hotmail.com); while a less formal dive centre runs out of one of the huts at *Bamboo Bungalow* (℡01/829 6721, ℮schmidti@tr.ksc.co.th), also on Hat Sai Khao. Waves permitting, the dive centres run trips to reefs off Ko Chang's more sheltered east coast during the **monsoon season** from June through September, though visibility is unlikely to be very rewarding during that period. Prices for dive trips should include two dives, transport and lunch, and in the range B1800–2400 depending on the operator and the destination; accompanying **snorkellers** generally pay B600–800 including lunch and equipment. All three dive centres also offer PADI **dive courses**: the two-day Scuba Diver averages B6500, the four-day Open Water B8500–10,000, and the two-day Advanced B7000–8000. The nearest **recompression chamber** is at the Apakorn Kiatiwong Naval Hospital in Sattahip (℡038/601185), 26km south of Pattaya. See p.67 in Basics for a general introduction to diving in Thailand and for advice as to what to look for in a dive centre.

inaccessible to vehicles. The island is now fully wired up for **electricity**, though a few bungalows ration their supply for evening consumption only. Many accommodation places are on the phone system, but as they use satellite **phones** (their numbers prefaced by the ℡01 code wherever you call from), it's not always possible to get through; some places can also be contacted via a land line on the mainland. **Internet access** on Hat Sai Khao and Hat Kai Bae is very expensive (B8 per minute) because it too relies on satellite phones, so you might want to get your emailing done in Trat or Laem Ngop before you hit the island. There are **money-exchange** facilities and small **shops** on Hat Sai Khao and Hat Kai Bae, including a couple of secondhand bookshops.

Though mosquitoes don't seem to be much in evidence, Ko Chang is one of the few areas of Thailand that's still considered to be **malarial**, so you may want to start taking your prophylactics before you get here, and bring repellent with you – refer to p.31 of Basics for more advice on this. Sand flies can be more of a problem on the southern beaches, but there's not a lot you can do about them except soothe your bites with calamine; apart from that, watch out for **jellyfish**, which plague the west coast in April and May, and for **snakes** sunbathing on the overgrown paths into the interior. Although there are a couple of **clinics** on Ko Chang, for anything serious you'll need to be taken to the hospital in Trat (see p.208).

### Travel practicalities

All **passenger boats** to Ko Chang depart from Laem Ngop (see p.209) and take 45 minutes to one hour to reach the island; **tickets** (B50) can be bought in Trat, at the Laem Ngop pier or on the boats themselves. During high season (Nov–April), boats should depart Laem Ngop every hour from 7am–5pm, though it's always worth checking in Trat first. Outside high season, weather permitting, boats leave every two hours from 9am–5pm. The boats arrive at

Tha Dan Kao on Ko Chang's northeast coast, from where **songthaews** (B30–50 per person) ferry passengers on to the main beaches. They should drop you outside your chosen bungalows; the more remote bungalows to the south of Hat Kai Bae sometimes send their own songthaew to meet the 3pm boats, but you'll still have to pay. From late October through to late May there's also one daily boat from Laem Ngop (at 3pm; B80) direct to *White Sand Beach Resort* on Hat Sai Khao.

If schedules run according to plan, it's possible to do the whole **Bangkok–Ko Chang** trip in a day by public transport, catching the 6am or 8.30am air-con bus from the Eastern (Ekamai) Bus Terminal, arriving in Trat by 2.30pm, and making the short connection to Laem Ngop in plenty of time for the 4pm boat; if you catch the 9am from Bangkok and arrive in Trat for 3.30pm, you should charter a songthaew right away and head speedily on to Laem Ngop. Budget tour operators in Bangkok run **tourist minibuses** from Thanon Khao San through to Laem Ngop (6hr) for B270; the big advantage of these is that you don't have to add on an extra couple of hours to get yourself through the early morning traffic jams between Thanon Khao San and the Eastern Bus Terminal, though the drivers of these minibuses are notoriously reckless.

If you have your own vehicle, you need to use one of the **car ferries** that operate between the Laem Ngop coast and Ao Saparot, on Ko Chang's northeast coast. There are two companies offering this service, from two different piers west of Laem Ngop, both clearly signposted off the Trat–Laem Ngop road; Ko Chang Ferry is at kilometre-stone 4 on Route 3156, while Ferry Ko Chang is at kilometre-stone 10. Both companies run five ferries a day in each direction between 7am and 5pm, charging B400 per car with driver, plus B30 per extra passenger; motorbikes cost B120 with driver. The journey takes 25 minutes. The vehicle ferries mean there may soon be a door-to-door service between Bangkok guest houses and Ko Chang bungalows, without the need to change on to the public ferry at Laem Ngop.

**Leaving Ko Chang**, boats run from Tha Dan Kao to an hourly timetable between 7am and 5pm in high season and to a two-hourly one between 9am and 5pm in low season. To get to Tha Dan Kao from Hat Sai Khao, simply stand on the main road and flag down a north-bound songthaew; from the other beaches, ask at your bungalows as there may be organized transport to your boat. Tickets for the daily **tourist minibuses** from Laem Ngop to Bangkok's Thanon Khao San (B270), Ban Phe (for Ko Samet; B220) and Pattaya (B300) are best bought from bungalows and tour agents on Ko Chang, but you should also be able to buy them once you've landed in Laem Ngop. Alternatively, hop on one of the public songthaews that meet the boat and make your onward travel arrangements in Trat.

## Hat Sai Khao (White Sand Beach)

Framed by a broad band of fine white sand at low tide, a fringe of casuarinas and palm trees and a backdrop of forested hills, **Hat Sai Khao** (White Sand Beach) is the island's longest beach and, some would argue, its prettiest too. It is also the busiest and most commercial, with over twenty different bungalow operations squashed in between the road and the shore, plus an increasing number of upmarket hotel-style developments – which inevitably detract from its loveliness. However, it's a lively and friendly place to be, with a regular Saturday-night disco on the central stretch of beach next to *Mac Bungalows* and several volleyball nets where players gather every evening at sunset. Should you prefer to be on the edge of the fray, there are several more isolated places to stay at the northern end of the beach, beyond *Yakah*, where each bungalow has its own sea view, there's hardly any passing pedestrian traffic and the road is out of earshot. Be warned, though, that there have been rumours of a dope-busting scam on Hat Sai Khao, whereby sellers inform the police straight away and then buyers are obliged to pay big fines. You should also be careful when swimming off Hat Sai Khao: currents are very strong here, so it's best to stay within your depth, particularly during low season when there may not be other swimmers around to help you out.

## Practicalities

**Songthaews** take about 25 minutes to drive from Tha Dan Kao to Hat Sai Khao. If you want the bungalows at *KC*, *Rock Sand* or *White Sand Beach Resort*, get off as soon as you see the sign for *Yakah*, and then walk along the beach. For bungalows further south, the songthaew should drop you right outside your chosen one. In high season there's also a daily **boat** from Laem Ngop direct to *White Sand Beach Resort*; see opposite for details.

You can rent **motorbikes** at several roadside stalls on Hat Sai Khao for B50 an hour or B350 a day – these prices are justified, apparently, because the road is poor and the demand high. The same places will act as a **taxi** service if you ask, charging about B60 for a ride to Khlong Phrao or B100 to Kai Bae, but you're better off waiting for a

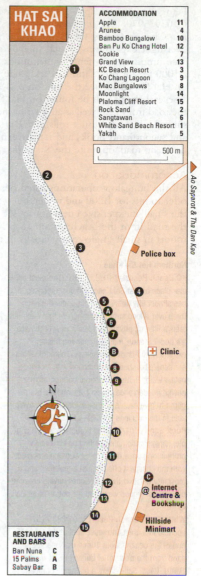

Ao Saparot & Tha Dan Kao

**ACCOMMODATION**

| | |
|---|---|
| Apple | 11 |
| Arunee | 4 |
| Bamboo Bungalow | 10 |
| Ban Pu Ko Chang Hotel | 12 |
| Cookie | 7 |
| Grand View | 13 |
| KC Beach Resort | 3 |
| Ko Chang Lagoon | 9 |
| Mac Bungalows | 8 |
| Moonlight | 14 |
| Ploama Cliff Resort | 15 |
| Rock Sand | 2 |
| Sangtawan | 6 |
| White Sand Beach Resort | 1 |
| Yakah | 5 |

0                    500 m

Police box

Clinic

N

Internet Centre & Bookshop

Hillside Minimart

**RESTAURANTS AND BARS**

| | |
|---|---|
| Ban Nuna | C |
| 15 Palms | A |
| Sabay Bar | B |

Laem Chaichet & Hat Khlong Phrao

songthaew to drive past: so long as the songthaew is heading that far anyway, you should be able to get to Hat Khlong Phrao for B20 and to Hat Kai Bae for B30.

Several bungalows run **snorkelling** and **fishing trips** to nearby islands, typically charging B250 per person for a three-hour outing, including equipment. Other places sell snorkelling trips to the islands of Ko Whai, Ko Mak and Ko

Rang organized by the Trat-based boat company Island Hopper (☎039/597060). *Sangtawan* bungalows runs day-long **jungle treks** through Ko Chang's forests for B250, while the folk at *Rock Sand* bungalows do overnight expeditions, which include a swim in a waterfall, forest walks and accommodation in tents or hammocks (B400 per person plus a share of the B1000 fee for the National Park guide). There are currently two **dive centres** on Hat Sai Khao (see the box on p.213 for details).

Several **shops** can be found on Hat Sai Khao, both on the beach and across the road from it: as well as all obvious necessities, including mosquito repellent, suntan lotion and toilet rolls, the *Ban Pu* minimarket complex also sells new and secondhand books and has **internet access** upstairs. There's a **clinic** on the main road, opposite the *Sabay Bar*.

## Accommodation

All the bungalow operations listed here are on the beach, and some of them offer rooms for B200 and under, but if they're full you may want to check out the small, inexpensive guest houses set among the shops and restaurants across the road from the beach: *Arunee*, *Ban Nuna*, *Tiger Hut* and *Jida* all offer simple rooms in small single-storey blocks in the ❷ category.

### Northern Hat Sai Khao

**KC Beach Resort** ☎ 01/833 1010. The most popular place on Hat Sai Khao, and deservedly so, *KC* has almost fifty huts strung out under the palm trees over a long stretch of beach so that each hut feels a little bit private and has a view of the sea. It's under friendly management and has an extremely laid-back atmosphere. The original huts are simple bamboo constructions with mosquito nets, electric lights and shared bathrooms; the newer wooden ones are en suite and are staggered to give each a sea view. Electricity is available in the evenings only. ❸–❹

**Rock Sand** ☎ 01/863 7611. Just seventeen simple, idiosyncratic huts perched up on a rocky promontory; price depends on size and amenities, with the cheapest offering just a mattress and a mosquito net, and the better ones having en-suite bathrooms, a good view, and the option of air-con. ❷–❺

**White Sand Beach Resort** ☎ 01/863 7737. Located in a quiet, attractive spot at the far north end of the beach (about 10min walk along the sand from the next set of bungalows at *Rock Sand*), *White Sand* offers a big range of nicely spaced huts, many of which are still only lit by paraffin lamps. Lots of huts have uninterrupted sea views, some have private bathrooms and a few have electricity as well; price depends on amenities and which of the three rows you're in. There's a restaurant here, but you have to walk a fair way to get a change of menu. The *White Sand* boat comes here once a day from late October through May, departing Laem Ngop at 3pm and costing B80. ❷–❹

### Central Hat Sai Khao

**Apple** ☎ 01/863 3398. Just a handful of good wooden bungalows, all with mosquito nets and electricity; a few have sea views, others have en-suite bathrooms. ❸–❹

**Bamboo Bungalow** ☎ 01/829 6721, ⓔ schmidti@tr.ksc.co.th. Many of the huts here are, not surprisingly, made of bamboo, and they all have mosquito nets and electricity. There's a small dive centre here too. The cheapest huts share bathrooms, though there are more solid huts with en-suite facilities. ❷–❸

**Ban Pu Ko Chang Hotel** ☎ 01/863 7314, ⓕ 983 7127, ⓔ banpu_kohchang@hotmail.com. The nicest upmarket accommodation on Hat Sai Khao, comprising a low-rise hotel block and spacious wooden bungalows with unusual, open-roofed bathrooms built around a pretty tropical garden and a small swimming pool. All rooms have sea view, air-con, TV and a veranda. There's internet access across the road and a dive centre in the hotel. ❽

**Cookie** ☎ 01/861 4327. Deservedly the most popular of the mid-range places on this beach, *Cookie* is the best in its price bracket on the central stretch of Hat Sai Khao. The smart bungalows all have small verandas, attached tiled bathrooms and electric fans, and are thoughtfully kitted out with clothes-hangers, pegs and towels. Huts are set very close together, but only those in the third row have no sea view; price depends on which row you're in. ❸–❹

**Ko Chang Lagoon** ☎01/863 1530. Large, resort-style two-storey hotel complex where all rooms are comfortably furnished with air-con, fridge and veranda. ❼

**Mac Bungalows** ☎01/864 6463. Sturdy wooden huts, all with veranda seating, good beds, fans and nice clean bathrooms; some have air-con. The pricier bungalows have sea views, but the huts are packed a little too close together to be worth the money. ❹–❼

**Yakah** ☎01/862 2795. This collection of basic, old-style bamboo huts is crowded together under the trees and furnished with mattresses and mosquito nets; some have beach views, others back onto the road. The pricier ones have attached bathrooms. ❷–❹

**Southern Hat Sai Khao**

**Grand View** (formerly *SunSai*) ☎01/863 7802. Efficiently run, child-friendly place with a big range of unusually well-spaced rooms set in a garden; there's a table-tennis table and dart board in the restaurant. Although the hotel garden drops down to a rocky part of the beach, the sandy bit is just a few steps away. The cheapest rooms share facilities but are close to the beach; mid-range places are en suite and located across the road from the beach; the most expensive ones are by the sea and have air-con and TV. ❷–❼

**Moonlight** ☎01/861 7672. Large, simple, en-suite bungalows widely spaced above a rocky part of the beach (though just a few metres from sand), most of them with sea view. It's a peaceful, unhurried place; the restaurant serves recommended barbecued seafood. ❸

**Plaloma Cliff Resort** ☎01/863 1305, ℻219 3867. Offers a big range of accommodation, from simple bamboo huts and sturdy bungalows on the lawn to plush air-con rooms in a hotel block with panoramic coastal views. As it's built on a rocky point there's no direct access to the sea from here, and the management can be a little off-hand. ❸–❼

## Eating and drinking

All the bungalow operations on Hat Sai Khao have **restaurants**, most of which offer very passable European food and standard Thai fare. Many of them do fish barbecues at night as well: the freshly caught barracuda, shark, tuna, king prawns, crab and squid are usually laid out on ice shavings for you to select yourself, and many places set out tables on the beach. Across the road from the beach, *Ban Nuna* makes a pleasant place for an evening meal: seating is Thai-style on cushions in a breezy open-sided *sala*, and the menu includes Thai curries, heaps of seafood dishes and pizzas. It's also well worth checking out *15 Palms*, where you can sit at tables right on the sand, enjoying real coffee and home-made bread as well as mid-priced English pies, pizzas and a good range of Thai food. After sundown, one of the most popular places on the beach is *Sabay Bar*, where you can either sit beside low tables on mats laid over the sand and work your way through the huge menu of cocktails, or take to the small dance-floor which pumps out European rave music till the early hours.

# Laem Chaichet and northern Hat Khlong Phrao

Four kilometres south along the tarmac road from southern Hat Sai Khao, **LAEM CHAICHET** is a small cape whose rocky headland curves round into a secluded casuarina-fringed bay to make an attractive and peaceful setting. There are currently just four bungalow operations on this little stretch of coast, and no shops as yet, but you can rent **motorbikes** (B60 per hour or B400 per day) and arrange boat trips here. **Songthaews** take about ten minutes to reach Laem Chaichet from Hat Sai Khao (B20), fifteen minutes from Hat Kai Bae, or 35 minutes from Tha Dan Kao. The access track from the main road leads straight to *Coconut Beach Bungalows* (☎01/949 3838; ❸–❽), which offers row upon row of **accommodation**, from simple wooden huts on the seafront with shared facilities, to mid-range huts and upmarket concrete versions with air-con and TV, a few of which have sea views. The six wooden bungalows on the edge of the *Coconut Beach* enclave belong to another branch of the same family and are rented out under the name *Coconut Restaurant* (T01/932 0519; ④); all are en suite and have sea views. *Coconut Restaurant* itself caters to guests at both sets of bungalows, serving travellers' fare, Thai standards plus regular seafood barbecues. If you follow the path 100m to the right of *Coconut Restaurant*, across a small khlong (with a bridge) and past the tiny boat harbour, you'll come to *Chaichet* (T01/862 3430; ②–⑦), prettily located on the headland and with a range of accommodation, from simple A-frame huts to bigger bungalows with bathrooms, fans and fine sea views, or rooms with air-con. If you don't mind staying away from the beach, the cheapest accommodation at Laem Chaichet is offered by *Happy Time* (②), which has a handful of ultra-basic bamboo huts right beside the main island road.

Ten minutes' walk south along the beach from *Coconut*, or a five-minute drive along the main road, brings you to the northern stretch of **HAT KHLONG PHRAO**. The beach here gets a fair bit of flotsam washed up, but is long and never gets crowded. The southern end is defined by quite a wide khlong (Khlong Phrao itself), which is only wadeable (up to your thighs) at low tide; if you want to get to the southern stretch of Hat Khlong Phrao on the other side of the khlong (see below), you're better off going via the road. There are two **accommodation** options on this northern stretch, both upmarket and neither that interesting. *Ko Chang Resort*, also known as *Rooks Ko Chang Resort* (T & F01/912 0738, W www.thaitrader.com/rooks; ⑧) has sixty rooms, most of them in bungalows and a few in a central block; all have air-con, TV and mini-bar, though they're not exactly in mint condition. During high season, guests at *Ko Chang Resort* can take a direct boat from the private Centrepoint pier in Laem Ngop, a few kilometres west of the regular pier; call to confirm times and availability. Five minutes' walk further south down the beach, the mid-range *Khlong Phrao Resort* (T01/830 0126, F039/597106; ⑤–⑧) is built round a seawater lagoon and offers slightly more reasonably priced rooms. The cheaper ones all have verandas from where you can cast fishing lines directly into the lagoon; the more expensive rooms have air-con, TVs and hot water. *Khlong Phrao Resort* can arrange snorkelling and fishing trips for guests.

## Khlong Phu waterfall and southern Hat Khlong Phrao

The road gets more potholed and bumpy south of the turn-off for the *Khlong Phrao Resort*. A couple of kilometres on, you'll see a sign for **Khlong Phu waterfall** (Nam Tok Khlong Phu), which is about 1500m east off the main road. The track to the falls is accessible on foot, mountain bike or motorbike; occasionally there's a guy on a motorbike waiting by the main road to ferry people up there, but most people come with their own wheels. The route fords the shallow khlong and cuts through pineapple fields and shady tropical forest before emerging at the falls. Some 20m high, Nam Tok Khlong Phu plunges into an invitingly clear pool defined by a ring of smooth rocks which are ideal for sunbathing.

Beyond the turn-off for the falls, the main road passes signs for *Thalé Bungalows* and then for *KP*; take either one of these signed tracks to get down to the southern stretch of **Hat Khlong Phrao** (a **songthaew** ride here from Hat Sai Khao costs B20–30). The beach here is very long, partially shaded by casuarinas and backed by a huge coconut grove. It has an appealingly mellow atmosphere and the beach invariably feels almost empty, which makes it one of the best places on Ko Chang to escape the crowds; as yet there are no shops or commercial outlets of any kind here other than the two bungalow operations, though there is a **clinic** and a fuel station on the main road, about 500m south of the *KP* access road, across from Wat Khlong Phrao. Like northern Hat Khlong Phrao, the beach here gets a fair bit of natural debris washed up along its sand, and the southern end is also cut off by a khlong, wider and deeper than the one at the northern end and only crossable by swimming.

Seven hundred metres off the main road, *KP* (☏01/863 5448; ❷–❹) is efficiently run by a former national–park ranger and his wife and is the more popular of the two **bungalow** outfits on this beach. The forty huts here are pretty simple, and come either with or without a fan and bathroom, but they are all attractively scattered through a coconut grove just a few steps from the beach. There's a nice restaurant here, as well as a bar shack further up the beach. The management rents out mountain bikes (B40 per hour or B200 per day), kayaks and windsurfers, and organizes snorkelling and fishing day-trips as well as a three-day sea-safari to Ko Kud (see p.223). *KP* is guaranteed to be open year-round and should be reserved well ahead for the· Christmas–New Year period. Ten minutes' walk up the beach, and separated from *KP* by an extensive coconut grove, *Thalé Bungalows* (☏01/926 3843; ❷) occupies the southern bank of the northern khlong and a fair length of the shorefront too. It offers some of the most basic bamboo huts on the island, with mattresses on the floors, shared bathrooms and no mosquito nets (it's probably worth buying your own from Trat if you plan to stay here). On the plus side, it does have electricity and has a certain romance, especially as it gets relatively few guests; the managers are friendly and serve meals.

South across the next khlong (again, impassable except by swimming) and round a headland, the main road runs past Wat Khlong Phrao and skirts the back of a couple more **bungalows** which, though officially also on Hat Khlong Phrao, are actually on a completely different little white-sand bay, which is palm-fringed and secluded. There are lots of options to choose from at *Magic* (☏01/861 4829; ❶–❼), which stands right on the beach, from very cheap no-frills bamboo huts at the bottom of the scale through to larger, more comfortable wood and stone bungalows with private facilities, sea views and the option of air-con. *Magic* rent out motorbikes (B80 per hour) and can arrange boat trips. The adjacent *Chokdee* (☏01/910 9052; ❷–❹) sits on a rocky promontory but of course has access to the sand in front of *Magic*; you can choose between huts with shared bathrooms or better en-suite ones with sea views. Five minutes' walk north from *Magic*, along the main road, the vegetarian **restaurant** and massage centre *Piggy's Delight* (Mon–Sat 4–10pm) gets rave reviews and makes a nice change from bungalow food.

## Hat Kai Bae

South of *Chokdee*, the road runs through a scenic swath of palm trees and past a few roadside restaurants and an internet centre (see p.220) before veering down to **HAT KAI BAE**, a couple of kilometres south along the coast. Though narrow, the beach here is overhung with trees and blessed with soft white sand and pale blue water – which would make a pretty scene if it were not for the unsightly piles of abandoned building rubble. Though almost all of the shorefront has been built on, the bungalows are mostly discreet bamboo and wood huts, nicely set among the palms and casuarinas. North of the access track, the shore becomes very rocky, loses the beach completely as it's dissected by a lagoon-like khlong and a shrimp farm, and then re-emerges as a sandy mangrove-fringed strand a bit further on. There are a couple of bungalows – *Coral* and *Nang Nual* – next to the khlong, which makes a surprisingly charming setting and feels not unlike staying in a small fishing village. But on the main part of Hat Kai Bae, the atmosphere lies somewhere between the good-time buzz on Hat Sai Khao and the solitary romance of southern Hat Khlong Phrao. Aside from a little pocket of commercialism around *Kai Bae Hut*, most of Kai Bae is peaceful and, above all, mellow. When the tide is in, people seem to spend their time swinging in hammocks that have been strung up on their verandas or making shell mobiles, and at night there are a handful of beach bar shacks for lounging in.

Big chunks of Kai Bae's beach completely disappear at high tide, so you might prefer to seek out the wider and more swimmable bay about twenty minutes' walk further south – just follow the road south from *Siam Bay* restaurant at the southernmost end of Kai Bae. If you carry on even further, the path takes you to so-called Lonely Beach, site of *Tree House*, thirty minutes' walk south of *Siam Bay*.

## Practicalities

Arriving by **songthaew** from Tha Dan Kao (50min; B50), you should ask to be dropped at your chosen bungalow. If not, you'll need to walk along the beach to your destination – it's less than fifteen minutes on foot from *Kai Bae Hut* to *Siam Bay* at the far southern end. Coming by songthaew from Hat Sai Khao, expect to pay B30 to *Kai Bae Hut*; the journey takes around 25 minutes. If you're on a motorbike, be prepared for the road to be in very poor condition – even washed away – in places.

All bungalows on Hat Kai Bae offer **snorkelling** outings to local reefs and islands from about B200 per person. Sea Horse Diving at *Kai Bae Hut* organizes **diving** trips in the area: see the box on p.213 for details. You can rent **motorbikes** at *Kai Bae Beach* (B60 per hour or B400 per day), and *Nang Nual* has **canoes** and boats for rent.

*Kai Bae Hut* has a well-stocked **minimart** that sells fishing tackle and snorkels as well as all the usual travellers' essentials. You can buy stamps and postcards at *Kai Bae Beach*, which also **changes money**, as does *Sea View*. There's a cluster of useful little businesses just east of the beach, on the stretch of main road opposite the access road to *Coral* and *Nang Nual*; here you'll find **internet access** at Kai Bae internet, a secondhand **bookshop** and a **clinic**.

## Accommodation and eating

All the Kai Bae bungalows have restaurants, but the best **food** on the beach is served up by *Coral* restaurant, which occupies a gorgeous breezy spot on the coral rocks north of the access road. The menu includes specialities like *som tam* and minced pork *larb*, as well as Thai curries and consistently good barbecued seafood. For a few relaxed **beers**, you could do worse than drop in at the ultra-laid-back *Comfortable Bar*, a few metres further north.

**Coral** ☎01/292 2562. Large concrete and wood bungalows built near the khlong on the coral rocks north of the access road, but only a 5min walk from a quiet stretch of sand. The bungalows are fairly simple but have bathrooms and fans. ❹

**Kai Bae Beach Bungalow** ☎01/862 8103. Popular, well-run outfit with lots of bungalows stretching over quite a big patch of the seafront and a restaurant at either end. Simple bamboo huts with shared facilities and comfortable wooden ones with fan and bathroom. ❸–❹

**Kai Bae Hut** ☎01/862 8426. Expensive place on the busiest part of Hat Kai Bae, next to the main access road. Wooden chalets with fan and bathroom, and concrete bungalows with air-con and TV. ❹–❽

**Nang Nual** ☎01/295 1348. Set beside the lagoon-like khlong just north of the access road, this place has no beach of its own. Offers simple huts of slit bamboo, all with en-suite bathrooms. ❸

**Porn** ☎01/864 1608. Laid-back, long-running travellers' hangout with a big range of simple bamboo bungalows (with and without bathrooms) set on the beach. There's an attractive shoreside eating area full of cushions and low tables, plus table-tennis and volleyball. ❶–❸

**Sea View Resort** ☎01/830 7529, ℗218 5055. The most upmarket place on the beach, *Sea View* is set in a tropical flower garden and has a table-tennis table under the palm trees, and a currency exchange desk. The wooden chalets here are hardly deluxe, but they all have private bathrooms and TVs, and some have air-con; rooms in the hotel block are slightly cheaper. Big discounts offered July–Sept. ❻–❼

**Siam Bay** ☎01/859 5529. Set right at the southern end of the beach, *Siam Bay* has a beautifully sited restaurant overlooking the rocks. The cheapest huts are simple bamboo ones set right on the beach, some with fan, bathroom and mosquito screens, others with shared facilities and mozzie nets. The sturdier concrete bungalows on the slope and by the beach are more expensive. ❷–❺

**Treehouse** A 30min walk south of Hat Kai Bae, or 10min by bike or songthaew, this German-Thai-managed place is set in its own little rocky bay known as Lonely Beach, and is an increasingly popular spot for getting away from the crowds. Huts are simple affairs mostly set on the rocks, and there's a fairly pricey restaurant. A regular taxi service runs here throughout the day from near *Kai Bae Hut*. Closed May–Sept. ❸

## Hat Bang Bao

From Kai Bae, the road gets rougher as it worms its way south through inland forest until it reaches Bang Bao fishing village and the isolated, sandy beach, **HAT BANG BAO**. During high season there's one daily boat here leaving from Laem Ngop at 3pm (2hr 30min; B120). Otherwise you can either try and persuade a songthaew to take you all the way, or walk from Hat Kai Bae in about three hours. From November through April you can stay on the beach at *Bang Bao Blue Wave* (☎01/439 0349; ❷–❹), which offers simple huts with or without attached bathrooms, and electricity in the evenings.

## The east coast

The east coast is not nearly as inviting as the west, and the few bungalows that used to operate on some of the beaches here seem to have been abandoned. The road runs south of the piers at Ao Saparot and Tha Dan Kao to **Than Mayom**, site of the national park office and national park bungalows, and then continues for another 4km before terminating at **Hat Salak Pet** on the south coast.

The southeast headland holds the best beach on this coast, **Hat Sai Yao** (also known as Long Beach), which is best reached by taking the 3pm Ko Whai boat from Laem Ngop during high season and asking to be dropped at Long Beach. Hat Sai Yao is excellent for swimming and has some coral close to shore. Depending on the sea conditions, some boats will take you directly into Hat Sai Yao, while others will drop you just around a small promontory close to *Tantawan Resort* (❷), an appealingly local, family-run place with just a dozen basic huts in a rocky spot that's good for fishing and just ten minutes' walk from the sands of Long Beach. For slightly better accommodation, follow the path westwards for ten minutes to the beachfront *Hat Sai Yao Resort* (☎039/511145 extn 218; ❶–❹), located on Long Beach itself, where large, simple huts are equipped with fans and electric lights. Both bungalows serve food.

## The outer islands

South of Ko Chang lies a whole cluster of **islands** of all different sizes, many of them now home to at least one set of tourist accommodation. All the islands are pretty much inaccessible during the rainy season, but from November to April the main islands – such as Ko Mak, Ko Kham and Ko Whai – are served by daily boats from Laem Ngop. For the latest information on boat times and weather conditions, ask at any guest house in Trat, or at the ticket offices near the pier in Laem Ngop.

### Ko Mak and Ko Kham

The island of **Ko Mak** (sometimes spelt "Maak") is the most visited and accessible of the outer islands. It lies off the south coast of Ko Chang, and boasts fine white-sand beaches along the south and west coasts; the rest of the sixteen-square-kilometre island is dominated by coconut and rubber plantations. The most recent population count, taken in 1995, put the number of residents at four hundred, most of whom either fish or work in the plantations. During the dry season, from November to April, there's one **boat** a day between the mainland and Ko Mak, leaving Laem Ngop at 3pm (3hr 30min; B170); the return boat leaves Ko Mak every morning at 8am. There are just a few **places to stay** on Ko Mak. One of the most popular is the British-run *Lazy Days* (📧 kohmak@hotmail.com; ❶–❸), which has nicely positioned teepees and bungalows (with and without private bathrooms) on a rather rocky stretch of beach on the southwest coast. The managers here organize dive trips to local reefs. Further down the coast, *Ao Kao Resort* (☎038/225263 or 01/457 6280, 📠039/597239; ❶–❺) is also recommended and has a range of nice huts amongst the palms with and without bathrooms. Near the pier on the northwest coast, *Ko Mak Resort* (☎02/3196714 or 01/219 1220, 📠02/3196715; ❺–❻) offers some of the largest and most comfortable bungalows on the island, while *Ko Mak Fantasia* (☎01/219 1220; ❶–❸), further up on the north coast, has simpler A-frame huts among the palm trees beside a narrow beach.

Miniature **Ko Kham** lies off the northern tip of Ko Mak, and has room for just one set of bungalows, *Ko Kham Resort* (☎039/538055 or 01/212 1814, 📠538054). Accommodation here is in twenty simple bamboo structures and meals at the resort restaurant are included in the price of B500 per person per day. There's little to do here except swim, sunbathe and enjoy being surrounded by sea. A daily **boat** sails from Laem Ngop to Ko Kham at 3pm (3hr; B170); the return boat leaves Ko Kham at around 8am daily.

## Ko Whai and Ko Lao Ya

The beaches on **Ko Whai**, which lies midway between Ko Chang and Ko Mak, tend to be rocky, which means that sunbathing here is not always so pleasurable, but the snorkelling is pretty good and the fishing is said to be rewarding here too. People who come here for the quiet are rarely disappointed.

There are currently two **places to stay** on the island: *Paradise* (☎039/597031; ❶–❷), which offers inexpensive bamboo huts on the western end of the island, and the more comfortable *Ko Whai Pakarang Resort*, sometimes known as *Coral Resort* (☎039/512581 or 01/945 4383; ❷–❹) which has forty bungalows across towards the eastern headland. **Boats** to Ko Whai depart Laem Ngop once a day at 3pm (Nov–April; 2hr 30min; B130).

Petite **Ko Lao Ya**, which sits just off Ko Chang's southeastern headland, is a package-tour island. Graced with pretty waters and white-sand beaches, it takes about two and a half hours to reach by tour boat from Laem Ngop. **Accommodation** at the *Lao Ya Resort* (☎039/531838) is in upmarket, air-conditioned bungalows and the all-inclusive price, for boat transfers, bungalow and three meals, is B1800 per person. Contact the resort for details and times of boats, which vary according to the number of tourists.

## Ko Kud

The second-largest island in the archipelago after Ko Chang, **Ko Kud** (also spelt Ko Kut and Ko Kood), south of Ko Mak, is known for its sparkling white sand and its exceptionally clear turquoise water. Accommodation here is in upmarket resorts and needs to be booked in advance: *Ko Kud Sai Kaeo* (☎ & Ⓕ039/511429; ❼) is located on Ao Ta Tin on the northwest coast, while across on the northeast coast at Ao Kluay you'll find the super-deluxe *Ko Kood Island Resort* (☎ & Ⓕ02/233 7276; ❾), and nearby *Kood Island Resort* (☎039/511145, Ⓕ02/398 2444; ❼–❾). The resorts only operate November to April, when the boat can make the five- or six-hour journey from Dan Kao pier, which is about 4km west of Trat town centre; you'll need to check schedules when you book your accommodation.

# Travel details

## Trains

**Aranyaprathet** to: Bangkok (2 daily; 5hr 20min–5hr 40min).

**Pattaya** to: Bangkok (1 daily; 3hr 45min); Si Racha (1 daily; 30min).

**Si Racha** to: Bangkok (1 daily; 3hr 15min); Pattaya (1 daily; 30min).

## Buses

**Aranyaprathet** to: Bangkok (4 daily; 4hr 30min).

**Ban Phe** to: Bangkok (12 daily; 3hr); Chanthaburi (6 daily; 1hr 30min); Rayong (every 30min; 30min); Trat (6 daily; 3hr).

**Chanthaburi** to: Bangkok (Eastern Bus Terminal; 18 daily; 4–5hr); Bangkok (Northern Bus Terminal; 3 daily; 3hr); Rayong (8 daily; 2hr); Sa Kaew (for Aranyaprathet; 8 daily; 3hr); Trat (every 1hr 30min; 1hr 30min).

**Pattaya** to: Bangkok (Don Muang airport, 3 daily; 2hr 30min); Bangkok (Eastern Bus Terminal; every 30min; 2–3hr 30min); Bangkok (Northern Bus Terminal; every 30min; 2–3hr); Chanthaburi (6 daily; 3hr); Rayong (every 30min; 1hr 30min); Trat (6 daily; 4hr 30min).

**Rayong** to: Bangkok (Eastern Bus Terminal; every 15min; 2hr 30min); Bangkok (Northern Bus Terminal; 2 daily; 2hr 30min); Ban Phe (for Ko Samet; every 30min; 30 min); Chanthaburi (8 daily; 2hr).

**Si Racha** to: Bangkok (every 30min; 2hr); Chanthaburi (6 daily; 3hr 30min); Pattaya (every 20min; 30min); Rayong (for Ban Phe and Ko Samet; 2hr); Trat (6 daily; 5hr).

**Trat** to: Bangkok (Eastern Bus Terminal; 13 daily; 5–6hr); Bangkok (Northern Bus Terminal; 3 daily; 4hr); Chanthaburi (every 1hr 30min; 1hr 30min); Pattaya (6 daily; 4hr 30min); Rayong (for Ko

Samet; 6 daily; 3hr 30min); Si Racha (6 daily; 5hr).

## Ferries

**Ban Phe** to: Ko Samet (4–18 daily; 30min).
**Laem Ngop** to: Ko Chang (5–10 daily; 45min–3hr); Ko Kham (Nov–April 1 daily; 3hr); Ko Mak (Nov–April 1 daily; 3hr 30min); Ko Whai (Nov–April 1 daily; 2hr 30min).
**Si Racha** to: Ko Si Chang (hourly; 40min).

## Flights

**U-Tapao** (Pattaya) to: Ko Samui (1 daily; 1hr); Phnom Penh (Cambodia; 1 daily; 1hr 10min).

# Southern Thailand:
# the Gulf coast

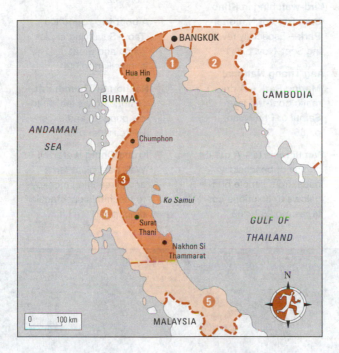

# CHAPTER 3

# Highlights

* **Phetchaburi** – Charming historic town, boasting several fine old working temples. p.229

* **Squid-pier hotels in Hua Hin** – Breezy, characterful rooms built on converted jetties. p.237

* **Bird-watching in Khao Sam Roi Yot National Park** – Especially rewarding Sept–Nov. p.241

* **Ang Thong National Marine Park** – A dramatic boat-trip from Samui or Pha Ngan. p.256

* **Samui resorts** – A great choice of beachside pads, from simple bungalows to luxurious cottages. pp.252–269.

* **Full moon at Hat Rin** – DIY beach parties draw ravers in their thousands. p.272

* **Ao Thong Nai Pan on Ko Pha Ngan** – Beautiful, secluded bay with good accommodation. p.277

* **A boat trip round Ko Tao** – Satisfying exploration and great snorkelling. p.000

* **Nakhon Si Thammarat** – Historic holy sites, shadow puppets and excellent cuisine. p.281

* **Krung Ching waterfall** – Walk past giant ferns and screeching monkeys to reach this spectacular drop. p.291

# Southern Thailand: the Gulf coast

The major part of southern Thailand's **Gulf coast**, gently undulating from Bangkok to Nakhon Si Thammarat, 750km away, is famed above all for the **Samui archipelago**, three small idyllic islands lying off the most prominent hump of the coastline. This is the country's most popular seaside venue for independent travellers, and a lazy stay in a Samui beachfront bungalow is so seductive a prospect that most people overlook the attractions of the mainland, where the sheltered sandy beaches and warm clear water rival the top sun spots in most countries. Added to that you'll find scenery dominated by forested mountains that rise abruptly behind the coastal strip, and a sprinkling of historic sights – notably the crumbling temples of ancient **Phetchaburi**. Though not a patch on the islands further south, the stretch of coast south of Phetchaburi, down to the traditional Thai resorts of **Cha-am** and **Hua Hin**, is handy for weekenders escaping the oppressive capital. In the early 1900s, the royal family "discovered" this stretch of the coast, making regular expeditions here to take the sea air and to go deer- and tiger-hunting in the inland jungle. It soon became a fashionable resort area for the lower echelons of Thai society, and Cha-am and Hua Hin

## Accommodation prices

Throughout this guide, guest houses, hotels and bungalows have been categorized according to the **price codes** given below. These categories represent the minimum you can expect to pay in the high season (roughly July, Aug & Nov–Feb) for a **double room**. If travelling on your own, expect to pay anything between sixty and one hundred percent of the rates quoted for a double room. Wherever a **price range** is indicated, this means that the establishment offers rooms with varying facilities – as explained in the write-up. Wherever an establishment also offers **dormitory beds**, the prices of these beds are given in the text, instead of being indicated by price code.

Remember that the top-whack hotels will add seven percent tax and a ten percent service charge to your bill – the price codes below are based on net rates after taxes have been added.

❶ under B150
❷ B150–250
❸ B250–400
❹ B400–600
❺ B600–900
❻ B900–1200
❼ B1200–1800
❽ B1800–3000
❾ B3000+

are now crammed with condos, high-rise hotels, bars and restaurants. There are no more tigers in the area, but nearby **Khao Sam Roi Yot National Park** is one of Thailand's most rewarding bird-watching spots. **Chumphon**, 150km further down the coast, has little to offer in its own right, but is the most convenient departure point for direct boats to Ko Tao.

Southeast of Chumphon lies **Ko Samui**, by far the most naturally beautiful of the islands, with its long white sand beaches and arching fringes of palm trees. The island's beauty has not gone unnoticed by tourist developers of course, but this at least means you can buy a little extra comfort if you've got the cash. In recent years the next island out, **Ko Pha Ngan**, has drawn increasing numbers of backpackers away from its neighbour: its bungalows are generally simpler and cost less than Ko Samui's, and it offers a few stunning beaches with a more laid-back atmosphere. **Hat Rin** is the distillation of all these features, with back-to-back white sands, relaxed resident hippies and t'ai chi classes – though after dusk it swings into action as Thailand's rave capital, a reputation cemented by its farang-thronged full moon parties. The furthest inhabited island of the archipelago, the small, rugged outcrop of **Ko Tao**, has taken off as a **scuba-diving** centre, but remains on the whole quieter and less sophisticated than Samui and Pha Ngan.

Tucked away beneath the islands, **Nakhon Si Thammarat**, the cultural capital of the south, is well worth a short detour from the main routes down the centre of the peninsula – it's a sophisticated city of grand old temples, delicious cuisine and distinctive handicrafts. With its small but significant Muslim population, and machine-gun dialect, Nakhon begins the transition into Thailand's deep south.

The **train** from Bangkok connects all the mainland towns, and **bus** services, along highways 4 (also known as the Phetkasem Highway, or, usually, Thanon Phetkasem when passing through towns) and 41, are frequent. Daily boats run to the islands from two jumping-off points: **Surat Thani**, 650km from Bangkok, has the best choice of routes, but the alternatives from **Chumphon** get you straight to the tranquillity of Ko Tao.

# Phetchaburi

Straddling the River Phet about 120km south of Bangkok, the provincial capital of **PHETCHABURI** (aka Phetburi) has been settled ever since the eleventh century, when the Khmers ruled the region, but only really got going six hundred years later, when it began to flourish as a trading post between the Andaman Sea ports and Burma and Ayutthaya. Despite periodic incursions from the Burmese, the town gained a reputation as a cultural centre – as the ornamentation of its older temples testifies – and after the new capital was established in Bangkok it became a favourite country retreat of Rama IV, who had a hilltop palace built here in the 1850s. Today the town's main claim to fame is as one of Thailand's finest sweet-making centres, the essential ingredient for its assortment of *khanom* being the sugar extracted from the sweet-sapped palms that cover Phetchaburi province. This being very much a cottage industry, modern Phetchaburi has lost relatively little of the ambience that so attracted Rama IV: the central riverside area is hemmed in by historic wats in varying states of disrepair, and wooden rather than concrete shophouses still line the river bank.

Despite the obvious attractions of its old quarter, Phetchaburi gets few overnight visitors as most people do it on a day-trip from Bangkok, Hua Hin or Cha-am – a reason in itself for bucking the trend. It's also possible to combine a day in Phetchaburi with an early morning expedition from Bangkok to the floating markets of Damnoen Saduak, 40km north; budget tour operators in the Thanon Khao San area offer this option as a day-trip package for about B500 per person.

### Arrival, information and transport

Arriving by **bus**, you are likely to be dropped in one of three places. The main station for **non-air-con buses** is on the southwest edge of Khao Wang, about thirty minutes' walk or a ten-minute songthaew ride from the town centre. However, non-air-con buses to and from **Cha-am and Hua Hin** use the small terminal in the town centre, just east of the market and one block south of Thanon Phongsuriya – less than ten minutes' walk from the Chomrut Bridge accommodation. The **air-con bus terminal** is also about ten minutes' walk from Chomrut Bridge, located near the post office just off Thanon Rajwithi. Phetchaburi **train station** is on the northern outskirts of town, not far from Khao Wang, about 1500m from the main area of sights.

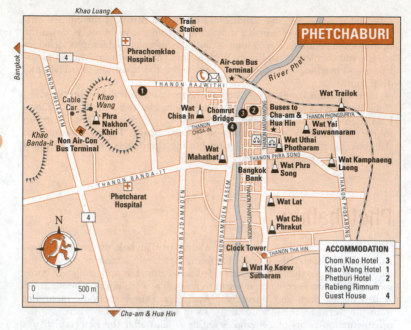

There is no TAT office in town, but *Rabieng Rimnum Guest House* is a good source of local **information**; they also offer **internet access** in the evenings, or you can check your email at the CAT **phone office** (daily 8am–8pm), which is next to the **GPO** on Thanon Rajwithi. The branch of Bangkok Bank 150m east of Wat Mahathat on Thanon Phra Song does **currency exchange** and has an ATM.

Phetchaburi's town centre might look compact, but to see the major temples in a day and have sufficient energy left for climbing Khao Wang and exploring the lesser sights, you might want to hire a **samlor** for a couple of hours (about B100 per hour) – also, samlor drivers have no qualms about riding through wat compounds, so you can get close-up views of the crumbling facades without getting out. Alternatively make use of the public **songthaews** which circulate round the town and charge B6, or **rent a motorbike** from *Rabieng Rimnum Guest House.*

## Accommodation

Most travellers **stay** at the *Rabieng Rimnum (Rim Nam) Guest House*, centrally located at 1 Thanon Chisa-in, on the southwest corner of Chomrut Bridge (☎032/425707, ☏410695; ➋). Occupying a century-old house next to the Phetburi River and, less appealingly, a noisy main road, the guest house offers half a dozen simple rooms with shared bathrooms, lots of local info, internet access and the best restaurant in town; they also rent motorbikes and organize overnight trips to a nearby national park for bird-watching and hiking. Less traveller-oriented, but quieter and cheaper, is the friendly *Chom Klao* hotel across on the northeast corner of Chomrut Bridge at 1–3 Thanon Phongsuriya (☎032/425398; ➊–➋); it's not signed in English, but is easily recognized by its pale blue doors and riverside location. Some of the rooms give out onto the riverside walkway and you can choose whether or not you want an en-suite bathroom. The other central option is the shabby *Phetburi Hotel*, at 39 Thanon Phongsuriya (☎032/425315; ❶). Across on the other side of town, near the base of Khao Wang, the slightly seedy *Khao Wang Hotel*, 174/1–3 Thanon Rajwithi (☎032/425167; ❷–❸), has both fan and air-con rooms, all with TV, but don't expect immaculate decor or furnishing.

## The Town

The pinnacles and rooftops of the town's thirty-odd wats are visible in every direction, but only a few are worth stopping off to investigate; the following description takes in the three most interesting, and can be done as a leisurely two-hour circular walk beginning from Chomrut Bridge.

Of all Phetchaburi's temples, the most attractive is the still-functioning seventeenth-century **Wat Yai Suwannaram** on Thanon Phongsuriya, about 700m east of Chomrut Bridge. The temple's fine old teak *sala* has elaborately carved doors, bearing a gash said to have been made by the Burmese in 1760 as they plundered their way towards Ayutthaya. Across from the *sala* and hidden behind high whitewashed walls stands the windowless Ayutthaya-style bot. The bot compound overlooks a pond, in the middle of which stands a small but well-preserved scripture library, or *ho trai*: such structures were built on stilts over water to prevent ants and other insects destroying the precious documents. Enter the walled compound from the south and make a clockwise tour of the cloisters filled with Buddha statues before entering the bot itself via the eastern doorway (if the door is locked, one of the monks will get the key for you). The bot is supported by intricately patterned red and gold pillars and contains a remarkable, if rather faded, set of murals, depicting Indra, Brahma and other lower-ranking divinities ranged in five rows of ascending importance. Once you've admired the interior, walk to the back of the bot, passing behind the central cluster of Buddha images, to find another Buddha image seated against the back wall: climb the steps in front of this image to get a close-up of the left foot, which for some reason was cast with six toes.

Fifteen minutes' walk east and then south of Wat Yai, the five tumbledown prangs of **Wat Kamphaeng Laeng** on Thanon Phra Song mark out Phetchaburi as the probable southernmost outpost of the Khmer empire. Built to enshrine Hindu deities and set out in a cruciform arrangement facing east, the laterite corncob-style prangs were later adapted for Buddhist use, as can be seen from the two which now house Buddha images. There has been some attempt to restore a few of the carvings and false balustraded windows, but these days worshippers congregate in the modern whitewashed wat behind these shrines, leaving the atmospheric and appealingly quaint collection of decaying prangs and casuarina topiary to chickens, stray dogs and the occasional tourist.

Continuing west along Thanon Phra Song from Wat Kamphaeng Laeng, across the river, you can see the prangs of Phetchaburi's most fully restored and important temple, **Wat Mahathat**, long before you reach them. Boasting the "Mahathat" title only since 1954, when the requisite Buddha relics were donated by the king, it was probably founded in the fourteenth century, but suffered badly at the hands of the Burmese. The five landmark prangs at its heart are adorned with stucco figures of mythical creatures, though these are nothing compared with those on the roofs of the main viharn and the bot. Instead of tapering off into the usual serpentine *chofa*, the gables are studded with miniature *thep* and *deva* figures (angels and gods), which add an almost mischievous vitality to the place. In a similar vein, a couple of gold-embossed crocodiles snarl above the entrance to the bot, and a caricature carving of a bespectacled man rubs shoulders with mythical giants in a relief around the base of the gold Buddha, housed in a separate mondop nearby.

Leaving Wat Mahathat, it's a five-minute walk north up Thanon Damnoen Kasem to Thanon Phongsuriya and another few minutes back to Chomrut Bridge, but if you have the time, backtrack a little and return via the **market**, which lines Thanon Matayawong and spills over into the alleyways on either side – there are enough stalls selling the locally famous *khanom* to make it worth your while.

### Khao Wang and Khao Banda-It

Dominating the western outskirts, about thirty minutes' walk from Wat Mahathat, stands Rama IV's palace, a stew of mid-nineteenth-century Thai and European styles scattered over the crest of the hill known as **Khao Wang**. During his day, the royal entourage would struggle its way up the steep brick path to the summit, but now there's a **cable car** (daily 8am–4pm; B50) which starts from the western flank of the hill off Highway 4, quite near the non-aircon bus terminal. To get to the base of the hill from the town centre, take a white local **songthaew** from Thanon Phongsuriya and ask for Khao Wang. If you want to walk to the summit, get off as soon as you see the pathway on the eastern flank of the hill, just across from the junction with Thanon Rajwithi; for the cable car, stay put until you've passed the last of the souvenir stalls on Highway 4, then walk south about 700m. If you do walk, you'll have to contend with the hundreds of opportunistic monkeys who hang out at the base of the hill and on the path up to the top.

Up top, the wooded hill is littered with wats, prangs, chedis, whitewashed gazebos and lots more, in an ill-assorted combination of architectural idioms – the prang-topped viharn, washed all over in burnt sienna, is possibly the ugliest religious building in the country. Whenever the king came on an excursion here, he stayed in the airy summer house, **Phra Nakhon Khiri** (daily 9am–4pm; B40), with its Mediterranean-style shutters and verandas. Now a museum, it houses a moderately interesting collection of ceramics, furniture and other artefacts given to the royal family by foreign friends. Besides being cool and breezy, Khao Wang also proved to be a good star-gazing spot, so Rama IV had an open-sided, glass-domed observatory built close to his sleeping quarters. The king's amateur astronomy was not an inconsequential recreation: in August 1868 he predicted a solar eclipse almost to the second, thereby quashing the centuries-old Thai fear that the sun was periodically swallowed by an omnipotent lion god.

If you've got energy to spare, the two cave wats out on the western edges of town make good time-fillers. **Khao Banda-it**, a couple of kilometres west of Khao Wang, comprises a series of stalactite caves filled with Buddha statues and a 200-year-old Ayutthaya-style meditation temple. A bizarre story goes with this wat, attempting to explain its design faults as an intentional whim. The money for the three wat buildings was given by a rich man and his two wealthy wives: the first wife donated the bot, the second wife gave the viharn and the husband stuck the chedi in the middle. The chedi, however, leans distinctly southwards towards the viharn, prompting local commentators to point this out as subtle public acknowledgement of the man's preferences. Five kilometres north of Khao Wang, the caves of **Khao Luang** have the distinction of being a favourite royal picnic spot, and have also been decorated with various Buddha images.

## Eating

Phetchaburi's best **restaurant** is the *Rabieng Rimnum (Rim Nam)*, which occupies a traditional wooden house beside the Chomrut Bridge, overlooking the Phetburi River; it's attached to the guest house of the same name but is open to non-guests as well. The restaurant boasts a long and interesting menu of inexpensive Thai dishes, from banana blossom salad to spicy crab soup, and is deservedly popular with local people. If you fancy sampling one of the local **sweet snacks**, such as *khanom maw kaeng* (sweet egg custard), you won't have to look far: almost half the shops in the town centre stock the stuff, as do many of the souvenir stalls crowding the base of Khao Wang, not to mention the day market on Thanon Matayawong.

# Cha-am and around

Forever in the shadow of its more famous neighbour Hua Hin, the beach resort of **CHA-AM**, 41km south of Phetchaburi, is burgeoning now as it picks up the overspill from Hua Hin and positions itself as a more sedate alternative. It used to be a typically Thai resort, with accommodation catering mainly to families and student groups from Bangkok and an emphasis on shorefront picnics rather than swimming and sunbathing, but that's beginning to change as the Europeans and expats move in, bringing with them jet-skis and minimarkets, travellers' accommodation and package-holiday high-rises. The most developed bit of Cha-am's coastal strip stretches about 3km along Thanon Rumachit (sometimes spelt Ruamjit), from the *Mark Land Hotel* in the north to the *Santisuk* bungalows in the south. The beach here is pleasantly shaded, though rather gritty and very narrow at high tide, and the water is perfectly swimmable if not pristine. During the week the pace of life in Cha-am is slow and peaceful, and it's easy to find a solitary spot under the casuarinas, particularly up at the northerly end of the beach – something that's rarely possible at weekends, when prices shoot up and traffic thickens considerably. Away from the seafront there's not all that much to do here, but there are several **golf-courses** within striking distance (see p.239) and buses shuttle between Cha-am and Hua Hin (25km south) every half-hour, taking just 35 minutes.

## Practicalities

Nearly all regular and air-con **buses** to and from Bangkok, Phetchaburi, Hua Hin, Chumphon and destinations further south stop in the town centre on Thanon Phetkasem (Highway 4), close to the junction with Thanon Narathip, 1km west of this beach. The **train station** (☏032/471159) is a few short blocks west of this junction. Thanon Narathip is the most useful of the side roads linking Thanon Phetkasem and the beachfront, and ends at a small seaside promenade and **tourist police** booth on Thanon Ruamchit, roughly halfway down the three-kilometre strip of beachfront development. To get down to the beach from Thanon Phetkasem, either walk or take a B20 motorbike taxi. Some private air-con buses to and from Bangkok use the depot at the little plaza on the beachfront Thanon Ruamchit, just south of the Ruamchit/Narathip junction.

Thanon Ruamchit is where you'll find most of the hotels and restaurants, as well as a few tourist-oriented businesses, including a small **post office** just south of *Scandy Resort*, a couple of places offering **internet access**, and several stalls where you can rent **motorbikes** as well as three-person pushbikes (B20). Cha-am's main business district occupies the small grid of streets west of Thanon Phetkasem, between the bus drop and the train station. Here you'll find the market, most of the shops, the **police station** (☏032/471323), the **GPO** and banks with **exchange** facilities and ATMs. The local **TAT** office (daily 8.30am–4.30pm; ☏032/471005, ✉tourism@np.a-net.net.th) is about 1km south of the centre on Highway 4.

## Accommodation

Most of the cheaper accommodation is concentrated in **central Cha-am**, set along the west side of beachfront Thanon Ruamchit; there are no hotels on the beach itself. All the Thanon Ruamchit hotels are described as being either north or south of the Narathip junction. The more expensive accommodation occupies the 25km of coastline **between Cha-am and Hua Hin**, where resorts are able to make the most of their extensive plots of land and enjoy what are in effect private beaches, though guests without transport have to rely on hotel shuttles or public buses to get to the shops and restaurants of Cha-am or Hua Hin. Many of the mid-market resorts in the Cha-am/Hua Hin strip are package-tour-orientated, but independent travellers can get reasonable **discounts** by booking online through almost any of the hotel finders listed in Basics on p.43; in addition, many hotels here give a fifteen to thirty percent discount from Sunday to Thursday.

### Central Cha-am

**Arunthip,** south of the Narathip junction at 263/40 Thanon Ruamchit ☏032/471503. In a shophouse block; reasonable enough fan and air-con rooms, some with sea-view balconies, above a street-level reception desk and restaurant. ❸–❹

**Happy Home**, north of the Narathip junction on Thanon Ruamchit ☏032/471393. Ten rather scruffy semi-detached bungalows in two facing rows, though they all have air-con and TV and are just a hop and a skip from the shore. ❹

**Kaen Chan Hotel**, north of the Narathip junction at 241/3 Thanon Ruamchit ☏032/471314, ☏471531. Mid-sized hotel with a sixth-floor swimming pool and rooms that are fairly good value, if unexciting, all featuring air-con, TV and distant sea view. ❺

**Mark Land Hotel**, north of the Narathip junction at 208/14 Thanon Ruamchit ☏032/433821, ☏433834. Recommended, good-value high-rise where the nicely appointed deluxe rooms all have a balcony, most of which afford a partial long-distance view of the sea. All rooms are equipped with air-con, TV and mini-bar, and there's a swimming pool and fitness room. ❼–❽

**Nirandorn Resort**, just north of the Narathip junction on Thanon Ruamchit ☏032/471893. Uninspired but adequate fan and air-con bungalows and hotel rooms. ❸–❹

**Santisuk**, south of the Narathip junction at 263 Thanon Ruamchit, beside the intersection with Thanon Racha Phli 2 ☏032/471212. The charming exterior of this collection of traditional-style cottages on stilts unfortunately belies very plain and shabby interiors. Accommodation is geared towards Thai family groups, with bungalows comprising two double bedrooms for a total price of B2000, though there are also a few double en-suite rooms in a larger stilt-house, with either fan or air-con. ❸–❹

**Scandy Resort**, north of the Narathip junction at 274/32–33 Thanon Ruamchit ☏ & ☏032/471926, ⓦwww.scandyresort.thethai.com. Small, mid-market guest house above a restaurant where the best rooms are huge, good value and have air-con, TV, balconies and good sea views. Also has a few cheaper fan rooms. Recommended. ❸–❹

### Between Cha-am and Hua Hin

**Beach Garden Hotel**, about 7km south of Cha-am at 949/21 Soi Suan Loi, off Thanon Phetkasem ☏032/471350, ☏471291. Set in a lush tropical garden that runs down to the sea, accommodation in this good-value resort is in either attractive, comfortably furnished cottages or a less characterful but smart hotel block. Has a swimming pool, games room, tennis courts, windsurfing and other watersports facilities. ❼–❽

**Dusit Resort and Polo Club**, 14km south of Cha-am and 9km north of Hua Hin at 1349 Thanon Phetkasem ☎032/520009, ℻520296, ⓦwww.dusit.com. One of the most luxurious and elegant spots on this stretch of coast, boasting five restaurants, a huge pool as well as a children's pool, all manner of sporting facilities – including a polo field, riding and sailing lessons and tennis courts – and cultural entertainments; there's an Avis car rental desk here too. ⑨

**Golden Sands**, about 9km south of Cha-am at 854/2 Thanon Burirom, off Thanon Phetkasem ☎032/471617, ℻471984. Standard upmarket rooms with private balconies and sea views in a 22-storey seaside block set in pleasantly landscaped gardens. There's a good pool and plenty of water-sports facilities. ⑧–⑨

**Regent Cha-am**, about 8km south of Cha-am at 849/21 Thanon Phetkasem ☎032/451240, ℻471491, ⓦwww.regent-chaam.com. Well-regarded upmarket resort set in appealing gardens that run down to a nice stretch of beach. Rooms are comfortably furnished; facilities include three swimming pools, squash and tennis courts and a fitness centre. ⑧–⑨

### Eating and drinking

The choice of **restaurants** in Cha-am is not a patch on the range you get in Hua Hin, but for a change from hotel food you might want to try the Mexican specials at *Chicken Coop*, signed off Thanon Narathip; or drop by the *Tipdharee*, next to *Scandy Resort*, which boasts a huge menu of mid-priced Thai dishes, including lots of seafood, curries and one-plate dishes. *Baan Plang Pub and Restaurant* on Thanon Narathip opens nightly from 7pm to 2am and stages **live music**, as does the *Jeep Pub*, located in the little enclave of bars and other businesses between *Scandy Resort* and *Kaen Chan Hotel*.

## Phra Ratchaniwet Marukhathaiyawan

Midway between Cha-am and Hua Hin lies the lustrous seaside palace of Rama VI, **Phra Ratchaniwet Marukhathaiyawan** (daily 8am–4pm; by donation), a rarely visited place despite the easy access; the half-hourly Cha-am–Hua Hin buses stop within a couple of kilometres' walk of the palace at the sign for Rama VI Camp – just follow the track through the army compound.

Designed by an Italian architect and completed in just sixteen days in 1923, the golden teak building was abandoned to the corrosive sea air after Rama VI's death in 1925. Restoration work began in the 1970s and today, most of the structure looks as it once did, a stylish composition of verandas and latticework painted in pastel shades of beige and blue, with an emphasis on cool simplicity. The spacious open hall in the north wing, hung with chandeliers and encircled by a first-floor balcony, was once used as a theatre, and the upstairs rooms, now furnished only with a few black-and-white portraits from the royal family photo album, were given over to royal attendants. The king stayed in the centre room, with the best sea view and access to the promenade, while the south wing (still not fully restored) contained the queen's apartments.

# Hua Hin

Thailand's oldest beach resort, **HUA HIN** used to be little more than an overgrown fishing village with one exceptionally grand hotel, but the arrival of mass tourism, high-rise hotels and farang-managed hostess bars have begun to make

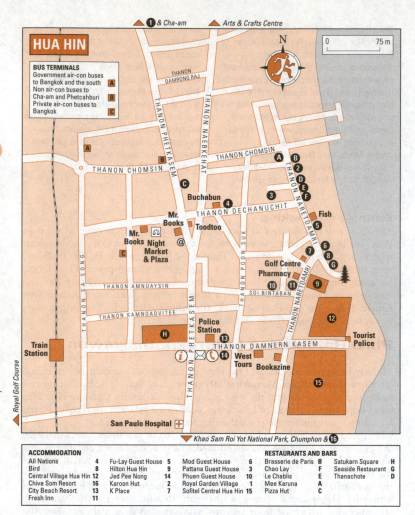

**HUA HIN**

**BUS TERMINALS**
Government air-con buses
to Bangkok and the south | **A**
Non air-con buses to
Cha-am and Phetcahburi | **B**
Private air-con buses to
Bangkok | **C**

THANON DAMRONG RAJ

THANON NAEBEKHAT

THANON PHETKASEM

THANON CHOMSIN

THANON CHOMSIN

Buchabun

Mr. Books

Mr. Books

Toodtoo

Night Market & Plaza

@

THANON DECHANUCHIT

THANON POON SUK

THANON NARETDAMRI

Fish

Golf Centre Pharmacy

SOI BINTABAN

THANON AMNUAYSIN

THANON SA SONG

THANON KAMNOADVITEE

THANON PHETKASEM

Police Station

Train Station

Royal Golf Course

San Paulo Hospital

West Tours

Bookazine

THANON DAMNERN KASEM

Tourist Police

Khao Sam Roi Yot National Park, Chumphon & 16

& Cha-am

Arts & Crafts Centre

N

0          75 m

| ACCOMMODATION | | | | RESTAURANTS AND BARS | | | |
|---|---|---|---|---|---|---|---|
| All Nations | 4 | Fu-Lay Guest House | 5 | Mod Guest House | 6 | Brasserie de Paris | B | Satukarn Square | H |
| Bird | 8 | Hilton Hua Hin | 9 | Pattana Guest House | 3 | Chao Lay | F | Seaside Restaurant | G |
| Central Village Hua Hin | 12 | Jed Pee Nong | 14 | Phuen Guest House | 10 | Le Chablis | E | Thanachote | D |
| Chiva Som Resort | 16 | Karoon Hut | 2 | Royal Garden Village | 1 | Mee Karuna | A | | |
| City Beach Resort | 13 | K Place | 7 | Sofitel Central Hua Hin | 15 | Pizza Hut | C | | |
| Fresh Inn | 11 | | | | | | | | |

a serious dent in its once idiosyncratic charm. With the far superior beaches of
Ko Samui, Krabi and Ko Samet so close at hand, there's little here to draw the
sunseeker, but it's nonetheless a convivial place in which to drink and enjoy fine
seafood and, if you can afford it, stay in the atmospheric former *Railway Hotel*.
In addition, the town makes a convenient base for day-trips to Khao Sam Roi
Yot National Park, 63km south, and there are half a dozen golf courses in the
area.

At the start of the twentieth century, **royalty** were Hua Hin's main visitors, but
the place became more widely popular in the 1920s, when the opening of the
Bangkok–Malaysia rail line made short excursions to the beach much more
viable. The Victorian-style *Railway Hotel* was built soon after to cater for the
leisured classes, and in 1926 Rama VII had his own summer palace, Klai Klangwon
(Far from Worries), erected at the northern end of the beach. It was here, ironi-
cally, that Rama VII was staying in 1932 when the coup was launched in Bangkok

against the system of absolute monarchy. The current king spends a lot of time here now, apparently preferring the sea breezes to the traffic fumes of the capital.

## Arrival, information and transport

Hua Hin is conveniently located on the Bangkok–Surat Thani rail line, but journeys tend to be slow (3hr 30min–4hr from Bangkok), and most of the trains arrive late in the afternoon or very early in the morning. The most conveniently timed train from Bangkok leaves Thonburi station at 7.20am. Hua Hin **train station** (☎032/511073) is at the west end of Thanon Damnern Kasem, about ten minutes' walk from the seafront.

Hua Hin's **bus** service is more useful. Non-air-con **Cha-am** and **Phetchaburi** buses arrive and depart every half-hour, using the terminal at the junction of Thanon Phetkasem and Thanon Chomsin, while government air-con buses to and from the Southern Bus Terminal in **Bangkok**, **Chumphon** and the south use the depot further west along Thanon Chomsin. The private air-con buses to southern destinations beyond Chumphon, such as **Phuket** (B680), **Krabi** (B700) and **Ko Samui** (B680 including ferry), all leave from town in the late evening; tickets should be booked through tour agents (see p.241). Bangkok Airways runs daily Bangkok–Hua Hin and Ko Samui-Hua Hin flights; the **airport** is about 5km north of town, beside the Phetkasem Highway, so you can flag down any south-bound bus into town or make use of the taxis that meet the flights.

The **tourist information** desk at the local government office (daily 8.30am–4.30pm; ☎032/532433), on the corner of Thanon Damnern Kasem and Thanon Phetkasem, offers advice on getting to Khao Sam Roi Yot National Park and sells bus tickets for southern destinations.

Hua Hin has plenty of samlors and motorbike taxis, but many tourists rent cars and motorbikes to explore the area by themselves. Avis (☎032/512021, ⓦwww.avis.com) have desks inside the *Hotel Sofitel*, and at the *Dusit Resort*, 9km north of Hua Hin (see p.235); several Hua Hin tour agencies also act as agents for Budget (ⓦwww.budget.co.th). The transport touts outside the *Hotel Sofitel* rent out 150cc bikes for around B200 a day.

## Accommodation

A night or two at the former *Railway Hotel* (now the *Sofitel*) is reason in itself to visit Hua Hin, but there are plenty of other **places to stay**, both in the luxury and the more budget-orientated categories. The most unusual guest houses are built on converted squid piers, with rooms strung out along wooden jetties so you can hear and feel the waves beneath you, even if you can't afford a room overlooking them. Rooms at jetty guest houses are fairly inexpensive, the only drawback being the rather strong aroma of seashore debris at low tide. Rates can drop significantly from Mondays to Thursdays, so don't be afraid to ask for a discount. Resorts beyond the northern fringes of Hua Hin, on the stretch of coast between Hua Hin and Cha-am, are described on pp.234–5.

### Inexpensive and moderate

**All Nations**, 10 Thanon Dechanuchit ☎032/512747, ⓔcybercafehuahin@hotmail.com. Large, comfortable and exceptionally spruce rooms, many of them with balconies and some with air-con. Bathrooms are shared between two rooms. Also has a nice roof terrace. ③–④

**Bird**, 31/2 Thanon Naretdamri ☎032/511630. A classic jetty guest house, with smallish but very clean, smart rooms set over the water, plus a nice breezy sea-view terrace at the end. All rooms have attached bathrooms, and some have air-con. Book ahead as it's very popular. ❸–❹

**Fresh Inn**, 132 Thanon Naretdamri ☎032/511389, ℱ532166. Small Italian-run hotel, with a friendly, cosy atmosphere; all rooms are spacious and comfortable, and have air-con, TV and hot water. ❺

**Fu-Lay Guest House**, 110/1 Thanon Naretdamri ☎032/513670, ℱ530320, ⓦwww.huahinguide.com/guesthouse/fulay. A beautifully appointed jetty guest house with a high standard of rooms, nice en-suite bathrooms, friendly staff, plus the characteristic breezy seating area set right over the water. The priciest ones have air-con and TV. Recommended. ❹–❺

**Jed Pee Nong**, 17 Thanon Damnern Kasem ☎032/512381, ℱ532063. This welcoming, though slightly shabby, low-rise hotel has a pool, which makes it decent value. The more expensive rooms have air-con and TV. ❺

**Karoon Hut**, 80 Thanon Naretdamri ☎032/530737. Friendly jetty guest house, with an open-air seating area at the end of the pier. The rooms, some with air-con, are simple but fine. ❹–❺

**K Place**, 116 Thanon Naretdamri ☎032/513908. Large, comfortable and well-appointed rooms, all with air-con and TV, make this small place a good-value mid-range option. ❺

**Mod Guest House**, 116 Thanon Naretdamri ☎032/512296. Jetty guest house with some good rooms (a few with air-con), others fairly basic but very cheap (for Hua Hin), plus an attractive seafront terrace-restaurant and seating area. Call ahead to secure a room. ❷–❹

**Pattana Guest House**, 52 Thanon Naretdamri ☎032/513393, ℱ530081, ✉huahinpattana@hotmail.com. Simple, inexpensive rooms in an appealingly traditional teak-wood house, quietly located at the end of a small soi. Some rooms have private bathrooms. ❸–❹

**Phuen Guest House**, Soi Bintaban (also spelt Binthabat) ☎032/512344. Traditional wooden house in a busy street of bars, crammed with lots of small, basic rooms, most en suite and a few with air-con. ❷–❸

## Expensive

**Central Village Hua Hin**, Thanon Damnern Kasem ☎032/512036, ℱ511014, ⓦwww.central group.com. Like its sister operation the *Sofitel*, the *Central Village*, comprised of 41 cream-painted wooden villas set in a seafront garden, has a distinctive old-fashioned charm,. All the villas have large verandas, and some have two rooms and an uninterrupted sea view, though they're not exactly the last word in contemporary luxury. There's a pool and a restaurant on the premises, and guests can also use the facilities at the *Sofitel* over the road. ❾

**Chiva Som International Health Resort**, south of Hua Hin at 73/4 Thanon Phetkasem ☎032/536536, ℱ511154, ⓦwww.chivasom.net. Internationally renowned super-deluxe spa and health resort with just 57 exclusive bungalows and hotel rooms set in tropical beachfront gardens. A whole range of health treatments on offer, from aqua-aerobics and traditional massage to cardiac rehabilitation and skin consultations. Recently voted the best spa resort in the world by readers of Condé Nast's *Traveller* magazine. All-inclusive room-and-treatment packages start at about $250 per person per day. ❾

**City Beach Resort**, 16 Thanon Damnern Kasem ☎032/512870, ℱ512448, ⓦwww.citybeach.co.th. Reasonably priced, centrally located high-rise hotel with comfortable, well-equipped rooms, all with air-con and TV and most enjoying a sea view from the balcony. Has a swimming pool and a couple of restaurants. ❽

**Hilton Hua Hin**, 33 Thanon Naretdamri ☎032/512879, ℱ511135, ⓦwww.hilton.com. Set bang in the centre of Hua Hin's beachfront, the *Hilton's* high-rise profile disfigures the local skyline, but the facilities are extensive and the views excellent. Has an impressive stepped swimming pool right on the seafront, and a pretty water garden. Rooms are comfortable though not exciting; rates start at B7000. ❾

**Hotel Sofitel Central Hua Hin**, 1 Thanon Damnern Kasem ☎032/512021, ℱ511014, ⓦwww.sofitel.com. The former *Railway Hotel* remains a classic of colonial-style architecture, with cool, high ceilings, heavy-bladed ceiling fans, polished wood panelling and wide sea-view balconies. All is much as it was in 1923, except for the swimming pools and tennis courts which were built especially for the filming of *The Killing Fields* – the *Railway Hotel* stood in as Phnom Penh's plushest hotel. Rates start at B5600; weekends get booked out several weeks in advance. ❾

**Royal Garden Village**, just north of Hua Hin at 43/1 Thanon Phetkasem ☎032/520250, ℱ520259, ⓦwww.royal-garden.com. Award-winning, atmospheric top-notch hotel comprising attractive traditional Thai-style pavilions set in fourteen acres of beachfront land. Has three restaurants, a free-form pool and its own stretch of beach. ❾

# The resort

The prettiest part of Hua Hin's five-kilometre-long **beach** is the patch in front of the *Sofitel*, where the sand is at its softest and whitest. North of here the shore is crowded with tables and chairs belonging to a string of small restaurant shacks, which is great if you're hungry but not ideal for solitary sunbathing; the beach then ends at a Chinese-style pagoda atop a flight of steps running down to Thanon Naretdamri. The coast to the north of the pagoda is dominated by the jetties and terraces of guest houses and seafood restaurants right up to the fishing pier, where the daily catch is still unloaded every morning. South of the *Sofitel*, upmarket hotels and condos overshadow nearly the whole run of beach down to Khao Takiab (Chopstick Hill), 8km further south.

Among the resort's myriad souvenir **shops**, Buchabun, at 22 Thanon Dechanuchit (Mon–Fri 5–10pm), stands out for its fine eclectic range of unusual antique arts and crafts collected from different parts of Thailand, and for its modern ceramics and other contemporary handicrafts. The Hua Hin Arts and Crafts Centre (daily 11am–10pm) at 18 Thanon Naeb Kehat, about 500m north of the junction with Thanon Chomsin, also sells antique and modern Thai paintings, woodcarvings and sculptures, and there are usually artists working on site too. Back in town at 27 Thanon Naretdamri, Fish is a small but alluring outlet selling gorgeous hand-made clothes in local cotton and silk fabrics. Plenty of other shops on and around Thanon Naretdamri sell beachwear and there are dozens of tailors here too. Other fun places to shop for clothes and souvenirs (after 6pm only) are the stalls at the night market on the west end of Thanon Dechanuchit, the more upmarket little shops in the Night Plaza that runs off it, and the collection of small shops selling good quality handicrafts, textiles and clothes among the restaurants in Satukarn Square at the Thanon Phetkasem/Thanon Damnern Kasem crossroads.

When you tire of eating, drinking and shopping, you can always make an **excursion** to Khao Sam Roi Yot National Park (described on p.241), either by renting a car or as part of a tour (see p.241 for details of tour operators). Most tour operators also sell day-trips to Pala-u Falls near the Burmese border, as well as to Phetchaburi (see p.229) and Bangkok. It's quite feasible to do Phetchaburi as a day-trip by public bus from Hua Hin, and even easier to visit the old summer palace of Phra Ratchaniwet Marukhathaiyawan, described on p.235.

## Golf courses

The Thai enthusiasm for **golf** began in Hua Hin in 1924, with the opening of the Royal Hua Hin Golf Club behind the train station, and now there are another five courses of international standard in the Hua Hin/Cha-am area. Visitors' green fees average B1200 on a weekday, B1800 on a weekend (though a couple are significantly cheaper), plus about B180 for a caddy. Some club houses also rent sets of clubs for B600, or you can ask at the Hua Hin Golf Centre (℡032/530119, ℻512085, ⊛www.huahingolf.com), on Thanon Naretdamri across from the *Hilton*, which sells and repairs clubs, stocks golfing accessories and organizes trips and packages to local golf courses.

The eighteen-hole Royal Hua Hin Golf Course (℡032/512475) is the most centrally located of the **courses**, easily reached on foot by simply crossing the railway tracks to the west side of Hua Hin Railway Station. To get to the other courses (all eighteen holes except where noted), you'll need to drive: the Palm Hills Golf Resort (℡032/520800) is just fifteen minutes' drive north of Hua

Hin, on the way to Cha-am; the Jack-Nicklaus designed Springfield Royal Country Club (☎ 032/471303) is a few kilometres further north, just to the south of Cha-am itself; and the 27-hole Imperial Lake View (☎ 032/520091) is on the northern side of Cha-am. Half an hour's drive west of Hua Hin is the Majestic Creek Country Club (☎ 032/520102); and 25 minutes' south of Hua Hin is the Bangkok Golf Milford (☎ 032/572437).

## Eating and drinking

Hua Hin is renowned for its **seafood**, and some of the best places to enjoy the local catch are the seafront restaurants along Thanon Naretdamri. Fish also features heavily at the **night market**, which sets up at sunset along the western end of Thanon Dechanuchit. For authentic European food, try any one of the farang-run bars and restaurants along Soi Bintaban or Thanon Damnern Kasem, where managers offer menus of pizzas and pasta, fish and chips, baked beans and German sausage. The biggest concentration of **bars** is along Soi Bintaban and around the back of the *Hilton* hotel; many of these places are so-called "bar-beers", with lots of seating round a large oval bar, and several hostesses dispensing beer and flirtation through the night.

**Brasserie de Paris**, 3 Thanon Naretdamri. Refined French restaurant that's known for its seafood and has an appealing terrace over the water. Specialities include crab Hua Hin, coquilles St Jacques and filet à la Provençal. Expensive.

**Chao Lay**, Thanon Naretdamri. Large and popular seafront restaurant specializing in quality seafood. Moderate.

**Le Chablis**, Thanon Naretdamri. Tasty and authentic French cuisine, plus some Thai dishes too. Moderate to expensive.

**Mee Karuna**, 26/1 Thanon Naretdamri. Upmarket restaurant, popular with Thai holidaymakers, which serves authentic, good quality Thai classics such as *tom yang kung*. Moderate to expensive.

**Satukarn Square**, at the Thanon Phetkasem/Damern Kasem junction. Every evening from around 6pm this tourist version of the more traditional night market becomes one of the most enjoyable places to be in Hua Hin. There are about twenty small restaurants in the partially open-air plaza (plus about the same number of handicraft shops) including specialist Italian, Indian, German and seafood outlets, all serving very reasonably priced food.

**Seaside Restaurant**, Thanon Naretdamri. Sample locally caught fish and seafood right on the seafront; worth the fairly steep rates. Moderate to expensive.

**Thanachote**, 11 Thanon Naretdamri. Atmospheric seafood restaurant, set on its own pier over the sea and serving exceptionally good fish dishes. Moderate.

## Listings

**Banks and exchange** There are currency, exchange counters all over the resort, especially on Thanon Damnern Kasem and Thanon Naretdamri; most of the main bank branches with ATMs are on Thanon Phetkasem.

**Books** Hua Hin is well stocked with English-language bookstores: there are two branches of Mr Books, one on Thanon Phetkasem and the other at the west end of Thanon Dechanuchit, plus a Bookazine opposite the *Hotel Sofitel*.

**Cookery classes** One-day courses (B990) can be arranged through the Buchabun handicrafts shop at 22 Thanon Dechanuchit (Mon–Fri 5–10pm; ☎ 032/547053); call to check when the next class is scheduled, or drop by the shop.

**Diving** No local reefs, but the bigger tour operators (see below) offer diving day-trips to Chumphon (see p.246) for B3000.

**Emergencies** For all emergencies, call the tourist police on the free, 24hr phoneline ☎ 1699, or contact them at their office opposite the *Sofitel* at the beachfront end of Thanon Damern Kasem ☎ 032/515995. The Hua Hin police station is further west on Damern Kasem ☎ 032/511027.

**Hospitals** The best private hospital in Hua Hin is the San Paulo, 222 Thanon Phetkasem ⓣ032/532576, south of the tourist information office. The government Thonburi Hua Hin Hospital is on the north edge of town at 17/155 Thanon Phetkasem ⓣ032/520900.

**Internet access** Available at several outlets in the resort, including on Thanon Phetkasem and at the CAT international phone office on Thanon Damnern Kasem.

**Mail** The GPO is on Thanon Damnern Kasem.

**Pharmacy** Several in the resort, including the exceptionally well-stocked Medihouse (daily 9am–10pm) opposite the *Hilton* on Thanon Naretdamri.

**Telephones** The CAT overseas telephone office (daily 8am–midnight) is on Thanon Damnern Kasem, next to the GPO.

**Tour operators** Both Toodtoo Tours, inside the Apilat Plaza on Thanon Phetkasem (ⓣ032/530553, ⓕ512209, ⓦwww.toodtoo.com), and Western Tours at 11 Thanon Damnern Kasem (ⓣ & ⓕ032/512560) sell bus and air tickets and do day-trips to the Sam Roi Yot National Park (B900 per person), Pala-u falls and diving excursions to Chumphon. Toodtoo rents out jeeps and 750cc bikes, and Western offers a car-plus-driver service.

# South to Chumphon

The 270-kilometre-long coastal strip between Hua Hin and Chumphon sees very few foreign tourists, though the beaches and birdlife of **Khao Sam Roi Yot National Park**, 63km south of Hua Hin, make a refreshing day-trip or even overnight stay. Less than 30km further south, the provincial capital of **Prachuap Khiri Khan** is famed for its seafood if not for its sand, but though it's a nice enough town there's nothing much to see there.

## Khao Sam Roi Yot National Park

With a name that translates as "The Mountain with Three Hundred Peaks", the magnificent **KHAO SAM ROI YOT NATIONAL PARK**, 63km south of Hua Hin, boasts a remarkable variety of terrain, vegetation and wildlife within its 98 square kilometres. The dramatic **limestone crags** after which it is named are indeed its dominant feature, looming up to 650m above the gulf waters and the forested interior, but perhaps more significant are the mud flats and freshwater marsh which attract and provide a breeding ground for thousands of migratory birds. **Bird-watching** is the major draw, but great caves, excellent trails through forest and along the coast and a couple of secluded beaches provide strong competition. Pick up a **park map** from Hua Hin's tourist information desk before you go – it's sketchy but better than nothing.

### Access and accommodation

Like most of Thailand's national parks, Khao Sam Roi Yot's chief drawback is also the secret of its appeal – it's very hard to visit by public transport. From Hua Hin, you need to take a local **bus** (every 20min; 40min) to **Pranburi** (23km) and then charter either a songthaew or a motorbike taxi (B150–250) to the park headquarters. But even once you're there, it's difficult to get about without wheels, as the sights, all accessible by park road, are spread all over the place – Hat Laem Sala and Tham Phraya Nakhon are 16km from HQ, Tham Sai is 8km, and the marsh at Rong Jai is 32km away. You can bypass the headquarters altogether and go directly to the beach at Laem Sala and the cave of Phraya Nakhon; from 6am to noon, hourly songthaews go from Pranburi market to the fishing village of **Bang Phu**, then it's a thirty-minute boat ride or a steep twenty- to thirty-minute trek from Bang Phu's temple – note that the last songthaew back leaves Bang Phu at 1pm.

Your best bet is to rent your own transport from Hua Hin, then follow Highway 4 south to Pranburi, turn left at Pranburi's main intersection and drive another 23km to the park checkpoint; carry on past the turn-off to Laem Sala, and continue 13km to the **park headquarters** and **visitor centre**, near the village of Khao Daeng. Alternatively, you could join a one-day **tour** from Hua Hin for about B900 (see p.241), though these tend to focus on the caves and beaches rather than the birds and animals.

The park's **accommodation** sites are around the headquarters and at Laem Sala; at both places it's a choice between camping, at B40 per person, or staying in one of the national park bungalows (B500–1000), which sleep up to twenty people. A more appealing option would be to stay a few kilometres outside the park entrance on the white-sand beach of Hat Phu Noi, where *Dolphin Bay Resort* (T 032/559333, F 559334, W www.explorethailand.com; ❻) offers air-con bungalows with sea views and a swimming pool, plus lots of excursions into the park, as well as dolphin-watching, sailing, snorkelling and fishing trips plus motorbike and car rental. To reach the resort, call to arrange transport from Hua Hin, or follow the above directions for the national park until you see the *Dolphin Bay* signs.

## The park

**Wildlife-spotting** is best begun from the **visitor centre**, which has easy access to the mud flats along the shore, and is the starting point for the park's two official **nature trails** – the "Horseshoe Trail", which takes in the forest habitats of monkeys, squirrels and songbirds, and the "Mangrove Trail", which leads through the swampy domiciles of crabs, mudskippers, monitor lizards and egrets (for more on mangrove habitats, see p.359). When hungry, the **long-tailed (crab-eating) macaque** hangs around the mangrove swamps, but is also quite often spotted near the park headquarters, along with the **dusky langur**, or leaf monkey (also known as the spectacled langur because of the distinctive white skin around its eyes); the nocturnal **slow loris** (very furry and brown, with a dark ring around each eye and a dark stripe along its back) is a lot shyer and rarely seen. The park's forested crags are home to the increasingly rare **serow** (a black ungulate that looks like a cross between a goat and an antelope), as well as hordes of monkeys. Eminently spottable are the small, tawny-brown **barking deer** and **palm civets**; **dolphins** are also sometimes seen off the coast.

The park hosts up to three hundred species of **bird**. Between September and November, the mud flats are thick with migratory shore birds from Siberia, China and northern Europe – some en route to destinations further south, others here for the duration. The freshwater marsh near the village of **Rong Jai** is a good place for observing **waders** and **songbirds**, and is one of only two places in the whole country where the **purple heron** breeds. It's worth picking up a photocopied "bird-watchers' guide" – and a pair of binoculars – from the visitor centre.

The park also has a number of trails leading to **caves**, **beaches** and **villages**, the most popular heading to the area around **Hat Laem Sala**, a sandy, casuarina-fringed bay shadowed by limestone cliffs (see above for access). Nearby, the huge, roofless **Tham Phraya Nakhon** is also quite a draw: it houses an elegant wooden pavilion constructed here by Rama V in 1890, and subsequent kings have left their signatures on the limestone walls. A three-hour trek from Phraya Nakhon, **Tham Sai** is a genuine dark and dank limestone cave, complete with stalactites, stalagmites and petrified waterfalls. The trek offers some fine coastal views, but a shorter alternative is the twenty-minute trail from **Khung Tanot** village (accessible by road), where you can rent a (very necessary) flashlight.

## Prachuap Khiri Khan

Between Hua Hin and Chumphon there's only one place that makes a decent way-station on the route south, and that's the provincial capital of **PRACHUAP KHIRI KHAN**, 90km beyond Hua Hin. Prachuap has attractive streets of brightly painted wooden houses and vibrant bougainvillea and hibiscus blossoms set out in a neat grid to the west of the not very interesting beach. The town is only 12km east of the Burmese border, and you can see the Burmese mountains clearly if you climb up the 417 steps the monkey-infested **Khao Chong Krajok** at the northern end of town.

Prachuap is on the main Southern Railway Line, with connections to Chumphon and Surat Thani in the south, and Hua Hin, Phetchaburi and Bangkok to the north. The **train station** is on the west edge of town at the western end of Thanon Kong Kiat, which runs eastwards down to the sea and the main pier. The **bus station**, which also runs services to Chumphon, Surat Thani, Hua Hin, Phetchaburi and Bangkok, is one block east of the train station and two blocks north, on Thanon Phitak Chat. For overnight stops, try the *Yutichai Hotel*, about 50m east of the train station at 115 Thanon Kong Kiat (⊤032/611055; ❶–❷), which has fan **rooms** with or without private bathroom, or the fairly similar *Inthira Hotel* (⊤032/611418; ❷), about 20m north around the corner and across from the inland night market (south of the bus station) at 118 Thanon Phitak Chat. At the better-appointed *Tesaban (Thaed Saban) Bungalows* (☎032/611204; ❸–❹), on Thanon Prachuap Khiri Khan just south of Khao Chong Krajok at the north end of the beach, you can choose between fan and air-con bungalows, most of which have good sea views. Prachuap has two exceptionally good **night markets**, one in the town centre on Thanon Phitak Chat and the other north of the pier on the seafront – both of them serve delicious fresh fish.

# Chumphon and around

South Thailand officially starts at **CHUMPHON**, where the main road splits into west- and east-coast branches, and inevitably the provincial capital saddles itself with the title "gateway to the south". Yet Chumphon has only recently begun to sell itself to tourists, an area of economic potential that assumed vital significance after November 1989, when Typhoon Gay – the worst typhoon to hit Thailand in recent decades – crashed into Chumphon province, killing hundreds of people and uprooting acres of banana, rubber and coconut plantations. With the mainstays of the region's economy in ruins, TAT and other government agencies began billing the beaches 12km east of town as a **diving** centre for the February to October season, when west-coast seas get too choppy. But although the nearby dive centre offers competitive prices and trips to unpolluted offshore reefs (see p.246), the town is simply not in the same league as neighbouring Ko Samui (see p.252). It's relaxed and friendly for sure, and not yet overrun with farangs, but the beaches are twenty minutes' drive out of

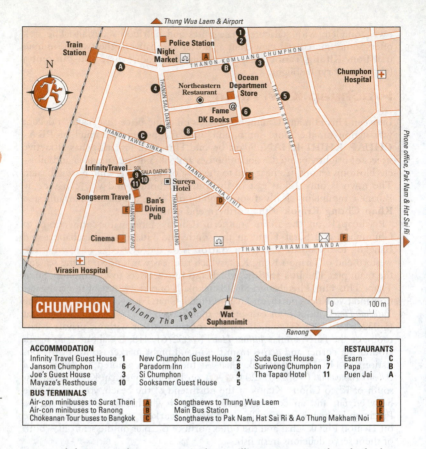

**CHUMPHON**

Khlong Tha Tapao

Ranong ▼

| ACCOMMODATION | | | | RESTAURANTS | |
|---|---|---|---|---|---|
| Infinity Travel Guest House | 1 | New Chumphon Guest House | 2 | Suda Guest House  9 | Esarn  C |
| Jansom Chumphon | 6 | Paradorm Inn | 8 | Suriwong Chumphon  7 | Papa  B |
| Joe's Guest House | 3 | Si Chumphon | 4 | Tha Tapao Hotel  11 | Puen Jai  A |
| Mayaze's Resthouse | 10 | Sooksamer Guest House | 5 | | |

**BUS TERMINALS**

Air-con minibuses to Surat Thani  A   Songthaews to Thung Wua Laem   D
Air-con minibuses to Ranong  B   Main Bus Station   E
Chokeanan Tour buses to Bangkok  C   Songthaews to Pak Nam, Hat Sai Ri & Ao Thung Makham Noi   F

town and the resorts there are seemingly unwilling to accommodate the budget visitor. For most travellers it is Chumphon's proximity to the island of **Ko Tao** that is the biggest draw, with three different boat services running out to the island every day, weather permitting. So it is that most backpackers stop by Chumphon for a night, take the boat to Ko Tao and spend another night here on their way back north; the town is well equipped to serve passers-through, offering clued-up travel agents, efficient transport links and plenty of internet cafés.

## Arrival and information

Chumphon is conveniently located on the Southern Railway Line and has several **trains** a day to and from Surat Thani and Hat Yai in the south and Hua Hin, Phetchaburi and Bangkok to the north. The train station (☎077/511103) is on the northwest edge of town, at the western end of Thanon Komluang Chumphon, less than ten minutes' walk from most guest houses and hotels. The main **bus terminal** (☎077/570294) is on Thanon Tha Tapao, within a few minutes' walk of many guest houses and travel agents; all non-air-con buses use this terminal, as do most air-con services including those to and from Bangkok, Phetchaburi, Hua Hin, Ranong, Phuket, Surat Thani and Hat Yai. There are also several private **air-con bus and minibus** services that leave from other parts of town: air-con minibuses to Surat Thani leave from Thanon Komluang Chumphon every half-hour; hourly air-con minibuses to Ranong leave from Thanon Tha Tapao; and Chokeanan Tour air-con buses to Bangkok (4 daily) leave from just off Thanon Pracha Uthit. There is an **airport** (☎077/591068) 35km north of town, which should be running Air Andaman **flights** to and from Bangkok and Phuket in the near future; check with any travel agent in town or contact the airline (☎02/2514905, ⓦwww.airandaman.com).

There are three different **boat services from Chumphon to Ko Tao**, all of which leave from the port area at Pak Nam, 14km southeast of Chumphon; tickets for all boats can be bought from travel agents and guest houses. The fastest but most stomach-churning option is the Numhasin (aka Nama Hamsin) **speed boat** (☎077/521755), which leaves at 7.30am (1hr 45min; B400); Numhasin provides free transfers from Chumphon guest houses, but the boat cannot run in windy weather. The **Songserm express boat** (☎077/503735) leaves at 7.30am every day from January through October (the seas are too rough in November and December) from Tha Yang pier (2hr 30min; B400 one-way, B750 return). A Songserm bus meets the morning trains arriving from Bangkok and takes passengers to their office in town, from where there's onward transport to the ferry at 7am; they will also pick up from guest houses in town. The **slow boat** (☎077/521615) departs at midnight from the Tha Reua Ko Tao pier (aka the Tha Thai and Seafood pier); services (6hr; B200) run in all but the very worst weather. To get to Tha Reua Ko Tao you'll need to take the taxi vans offered by guest houses, which leave town at about 10pm and cost B50 per person.

**Travel agents** in Chumphon are very accommodating to travellers' needs, and as well as Ko Tao boat tickets, they all sell bus, train and air tickets, and store luggage free of charge; some also offer free showers and video shows to travellers awaiting onward connections. The three best travel agents are all on Thanon Tha Tapao, within a few minutes' walk of the main bus station: Songserm Travel (☎077/506205) lets travellers kip down on the office floor while waiting for the boat and are open 24 hours; and both Infinity Travel (☎077/501937) and *Ban's Diving Pub* (☎077/570751) have internet access and a restaurant, and offer free showers and video shows to waiting travellers.

## Accommodation

As with most other Thai towns, Chumphon's **guest houses** are the friendliest places to stay, if not exactly the last word in comfort, and they're all geared up for travellers, with farang-friendly menus, bikes for hire and plenty of local information. The **hotels** in town are less pricey than those on the beaches, but nothing special.

Chumphon's guest houses are used to accommodating Ko Tao-bound travellers, so it's generally no problem to check into a room for half a day before catching the night boat. Most places will also store luggage for you until your return to the mainland.

**Infinity Travel**, check in through their office on Thanon Tha Tapao ☎077/501937. One of Chumphon's most clued-up travel agencies, *Infinity* has three rooms above its office on Thanon Tha Tapao, and another eight rooms in a characterful old wooden house on Soi 1, Thanon Komluang Chumphon. All rooms share bathrooms, and the old house has a nice seating area downstairs plus motorbike rental. ②

**Jansom Chumphon**, off Thanon Sala Daeng ☎077/502502, ⓕ502503. Chumphon's top hotel offers air-con, TV and all the usual trimmings, but is starting to look a little faded. ④–⑤

**Mayaze's Resthouse**, off Thanon Sala Daeng at 111/35 Soi 3 (aka Soi Bangkok Bank) ☎077/504452, ⓕ502217, ⓔmayazes@hotmail.com. Small, friendly guest house with comfortable fan and air-con rooms, all of which share bathrooms. Plenty of local information and free tea and coffee. ❸

**New Chumphon Guest House** (aka *Miao*), Soi 1, Thanon Komluang Chumphon ☎077/502900. Smallish rooms with shared facilities in a house on a quiet, residential soi. Nice outdoor seating area, and friendly clued-up staff. Price depends on the size of the room. ❷

**Paradorm Inn**, 180/12 Thanon Paradorm, east off Thanon Sala Daeng ☎077/511598, ℱ501112. The best value of the town's mid-range hotels: all rooms have air-con and TV, and there's a pool and restaurant. ❹

**Si Chumphon**, 127/22–24 Thanon Sala Daeng ☎077/511379. Very similar to neighbouring *Suriwong Chumphon*, with no ambience but reasonable rooms. Fan and air-con rooms available. ❷–❸

**Sooksamer Guest House**, 118/4 Thanon Suksumer ☎077/502430. Located on a peaceful street, this place is friendly and exceptionally cheap if a little ragged round the edges. Rooms in the traditional house are a bit box-like and share facilities, though the communal seating area is pleasant. ❶

**Suda Guest House**, off Thanon Sala Daeng on Soi 3 (aka Soi Bangkok Bank) ☎077/504366. Clean and well-maintained, with just three rooms with shared bathroom in the owner's own modern house, and the option of fan or air-con. Motorbikes for rent and breakfast on request. ❸

**Suriwong Chumphon**, 125/27–29 Thanon Sala Daeng ☎077/511397, ℱ502699. Large and characterless, but the rooms are clean and en suite and some have air-con. ❷–❸

**Tha Tapao Hotel**, 66/1 Thanon Tha Tapao ☎077/511479, ℱ502479. Unexciting mid-range hotel that's used to dealing with farang tourists, is convenient for the bus station, and has both fan and air-con rooms. ❸

## Beaches and islands

Chumphon's best beach is **THUNG WUA LAEM**, 12km north of town and served by frequent yellow songthaews from halfway down Thanon Pracha Uthit (B25). The long sandy stretch has a few bungalow resorts and a handful of seafood restaurants. *Chumphon Cabana* (☎077/560245, ℱ504442, ⓦ www.cabana.co.th; ❺–❽) offers a selection of well-appointed fan and air-con bungalows at the southern end of the beach, and also runs a **dive centre** (Jan–Sept only), featuring trips to nearby islands for B900 per diver and B500 per snorkeller, and offering NAUI-certificated five-day courses for B11,500. They provide free transport (3 daily) to the resort from their Chumphon office, which is next to Infinity Travel on Thanon Tha Tapao. Further up the beach, there's cheaper fan and air-con accommodation at *Seabeach Bungalow* (☎077/560115; ❸–❹).

If you're keen to go diving or snorkelling independently, then you should make for **HAT SAI RI**, 20km south of town and reached by frequent songthaews from Thanon Paramin Manda (B20). Though dirtier and busier than Thung Wua Laem, this is the best place to hire boats to the tiny offshore **islands**, some of the best of which are visible from the beach: it's well worth exploring the reefs around **Ko Mattra** and **Ko Rat** (the one with a profile like a half-submerged rhino), and although nearby **Ko Lang Ka Chiu** is out of bounds because of its birds'-nest collecting business (see box on p.379), it's permissible to dive in the surrounding waters. Further afield, about 18km offshore, the reefs and underwater caves around **Ko Ngam Yai** and **Ko Ngam Noi** are the usual destination of the *Chumphon Cabana* diving and snorkelling expeditions. To get to any of the above islands on your own, either negotiate directly with the fishermen on Hat Sai Ri or enlist the help of the amenable manager of *Sai Ri Lodge* (☎077/521212; ❻) at the southern end of the beach; a day's boat ride around all or some of these islands should cost about B2000 per ten-person boat (excluding any diving or snorkelling equipment). If you want to stay at the *Lodge*, you can choose between fan and air-con bungalows.

About 5km south of Hat Sai Ri, **Ao Thung Makham Noi** has become a popular spot with German tourists because of *MT Resort*, also known as *Mother Hut* (⊕077/558153, ⓕ558152; ➌), which offers appealing bungalows set among the palm trees beside the beach. There's a restaurant on the beach and you can organize snorkelling trips to Ko Thong Lang, just a few minutes off shore, as well as longer expeditions in squid boats. To get to Ao Thung Makham Noi, either take one of the songthaews from Thanon Paramin Manda or arrange transport through *Mayaze's Resthouse*.

### Eating

There are a couple of very good northeastern **restaurants** in town – the one next to the Ocean department store off Thanon Sala Daeng serves *kai yang*, *somtam* and sticky rice all day; the other, *Esarn* on Thanon Tawee Sinka, has basic Thai dishes in the daytime and northeastern fare in the evening. For freshly caught seafood, try the large, open-air *Papa* on Thanon Komluang Chumphon, or the similar *Puen Jai*, an upmarket garden restaurant across from the train station. After dark, the **night market** sets up along both sides of Thanon Komluang Chumphon and is a popular and enjoyable place to eat. For Western food, check out the breakfasts at *Paradorm Inn*; or the coffee bar on the third floor of the Ocean department store, which stocks ten different coffee blends; or the pizzas in the food centre on the same floor.

### Listings

**Banks and exchange** The main banks, with exchange counters and ATMs, are on Thanon Sala Daeng and Thanon Pracha Uthit.

**Books** A few English-language books and the *Bangkok Post* at DK Books opposite the *Jansom Chumphon* hotel.

**Emergencies** For all emergencies, call the tourist police on the free, 24hr phoneline ⊕1699, or contact the Chumphon police station on the north end of Thanon Sala Daeng ⊕077/511505.

**Hospitals** The government Chumphon Hospital (⊕077/503672) is on the northeast edge of town; the private Virasin Hospital (⊕077/503238) is in the southwest, on Thanon Paramin Manda.

**Internet access** Available at lots of places on Thanon Tha Tapao, including *Ban's Diving Pub* and Infinity Travel, as well as at Fame, opposite the *Jansom Thara* hotel.

**Mail** The GPO is on the southeastern edge of town, on Thanon Paramin Manda.

**Motorbike rental** For B150 per day from *Suda Guest House*, *New Chumphon Guest House* and Infinity Travel.

**Pharmacy** Several in the resort, including the exceptionally well-stocked Medihouse (daily 9am–10pm) opposite the *Hilton* on Thanon Naretdamri.

**Telephones** The main CAT overseas phone centre is on the far southeastern edge of town, several hundred metres east of the GPO on Thanon Paramin Manda: any Paramin Manda songthaew will drop you outside. The more central Fame, opposite the *Jansom Thara* hotel, also offers overseas phone and fax services.

# Chaiya and around

About 140km south of Chumphon, **CHAIYA** was the capital of southern Thailand under the Srivijayan empire, which fanned out from Sumatra between the eighth and thirteenth centuries. Today there's little to mark the passing of the Srivijayan civilization, but this small, sleepy town has gained new fame as the site of **Wat Suan Mokkh**, a progressively minded temple whose meditation retreats account for the bulk of Chaiya's farang visitors. Unless you're interested in one of the retreats, the town is best visited on a day-trip, either as a break in the journey south, or as an excursion from Surat Thani.

Chaiya is 3km from Highway 41, the main road down this section of the Gulf coast: **buses** from Chumphon to Surat Thani will drop you off on the highway, from where you can catch a motorbike taxi or walk into town; from Surat Thani's local bus station, hourly buses take an hour to reach Chaiya. Although the town lies on the main Southern Rail Line, most **trains** arrive in the middle of the night; only the evening trains from Bangkok are useful, getting you to Chaiya first thing in the morning.

### The Town

The main sight in Chaiya is **Wat Phra Boromathat** on the western side of town, where the ninth-century chedi – one of very few surviving examples of Srivijayan architecture – is said to contain relics of the Buddha himself. Hidden away behind the viharn in a pretty, red-tiled cloister, the chedi looks like an oversized wedding cake surrounded by an ornamental moat. Its unusual square tiers are spiked with smaller chedis and decorated with gilt, in a style similar to the temples of central Java.

The **National Museum** (Wed–Sun 9am–4pm; B10) on the eastern side of the temple is a disappointment. Although the Srivijaya period produced some of Thailand's finest sculpture, much of it discovered at Chaiya, the best pieces have been carted off to the National Museum in Bangkok. Replicas have been left in their stead, which are shown alongside fragments of some original statues and an exhibition of local handicrafts. The best remaining piece is a serene stone image of the Buddha from **Wat Kaeo**, an imposing chedi on the south side of town. Heading towards the centre from Wat Phra Boromathat, you can reach this chedi by taking the first paved road on the right, which brings you first to the brick remains of Wat Long, and then after 1km to Wat Kaeo, enclosed by a thick ring of trees. Here you can poke around the murky antechambers of the chedi, taking care not to trip over the various dismembered stone Buddhas that are lying around.

### Ban Phum Riang

If you've got some time on your hands, you could take one of the regular songthaews to **BAN PHUM RIANG**, 5km east of Chaiya, a Muslim crab-fishing village of wooden stilt houses clustered around a rickety mosque. The weavers here are famous for their original designs of silk and cotton; although the cottage industry is on the decline, you might still be able to pick up a bargain in the village's handful of shops.

### Wat Suan Mokkh

The forest temple of **Wat Suan Mokkh** (Garden of Liberation), 6km south of Chaiya on Highway 41, was founded by **Buddhadasa Bhikkhu**, southern Thailand's most revered monk until his death in 1993 at the age of 87. His back-to-basics philosophy, encompassing Christian, Zen and Taoist influences, lives on and continues to draw Thais from all over the country to the temple, as well as hundreds of farangs. It's not necessary to sign up for one of the wat's retreats to enjoy the temple, however – all buses from Chumphon and Chaiya to Surat Thani pass the wat, so it's easy to drop by for a quiet stroll through the wooded grounds.

The layout of the wat is centred on the Golden Hill: scrambling up between trees and monks' huts, you'll reach a hushed clearing on top of the hill which is the temple's holiest meeting-place, a simple open-air platform decorated with nothing more than a stone Buddha with the Wheel of Law. At the base of the hill, the outer walls of the Spiritual Theatre are lined with bas-reliefs, replicas of originals in India, which depict scenes from the life of the Buddha. Inside, every centimetre is covered with colourful didactic painting, executed by resident monks and visitors in a jumble of realistic and surrealistic styles.

### Meditation retreats

**Meditation retreats** are held by farang and Thai teachers over the first ten days of every month at the International Dharma Heritage, a purpose-built compound 1km from the main temple at Wat Suan Mokkh. Large numbers of farang travellers, both novices and experienced meditators, turn up for the retreats, which are intended as a challenging exercise in mental development – it's not an opportunity to relax and live at low cost for a few days. Conditions imitate the rigorous lifestyle of a *bhikkhu* (monk) as far as possible, each day beginning before dawn with meditation according to the Anapanasati method, which aims to achieve mindfulness by focusing on the breathing process. Although talks are given on Dharma (the doctrines of the Buddha – as interpreted by Buddhadasa Bhikkhu) and meditation technique, most of each day is spent practising Anapanasati in solitude. To aid concentration, participants maintain a rule of silence, broken only by daily chanting sessions, although supervisors are available for individual interviews if there are any questions or problems. Men and women are segregated into separate dormitory blocks and, like monks, are expected to help out with chores.

Each course has space for about one hundred people – turn up at the information desk in Wat Suan Mokkh by early afternoon on the last day of the month to enrol. The fee is B1200 per person, which includes two vegetarian meals a day and accommodation in simple cells. Bring a flashlight (or buy one outside the temple gates) and any other supplies you'll need for the ten days – participants are encouraged not to leave the premises during the retreat. For further information, go to ⓦwww.suanmokkh.org or contact TAT in Surat Thani.

# Surat Thani

Uninspiring **SURAT THANI**, 60km south of Chaiya, is generally worth visiting only as the jumping-off point for the Samui archipelago (see p.254, p.270 and p.281), though it might be worth a stay when the Chak Phra Festival (see box on p.251) is, or as a base for seeing the nearby historic town of Chaiya.

Strung along the south bank of the Tapi River, with a busy port for rubber and coconuts near the river mouth, the town is experiencing rapid economic growth and paralysing traffic jams. Its only worthwhile attraction is the **Monkey Training College** (daylight hours; from B300 per show; ⓣ077/227351), a thirty-minute trip out of town, where young monkeys are trained to pick coconuts from trees which are too tall for humans to reach. To get there, charter a songthaew, or take a local bus 6km east towards Kanchanadit and Don Sak and then walk the last 2km, following the signpost south from the main road. The serious business of the college is undoubtedly worthy – coconuts are the province's most important crop, providing a much-needed cash livelihood for small farmers – but the hour-long coconut-picking display that the owner, Somphon Saekhow, and his champion pig-tailed

Police Station

Tapi River

Ban Don
Pier

THANON TALAT LUANG

THANON BAN DON

Songserm
Travel

THANON BAN DON

THANON SI CHAIYA

Bank

Night
Market

THANON TONPOR

Seree
Hotel

Ban Don
Hotel

THANON NAMUANG

Samui
Tour

THANON TALADMAI

Talat Kaset I

Phantip Travel

THANON CHONKASEM

THANON THA THONG

0          200 m

N

**SURAT THANI**

Talat Kaset II

Cha
Thip 2

Vegetarian
Restaurant

Thai Airways

macaque put on for visitors may feel a little exploitative. At the end of the display, Khun Somphon will show you the stable at the back where the most laborious parts of the training take place. The three-month course costs the monkeys' owners B3000 per student, and graduates can farm up to one thousand coconuts a day.

## Practicalities

**Buses** to Surat Thani arrive at three different locations, two of which are on Thanon Taladmai in the centre of town, at Talat Kaset I on the north side of the road (local buses) and opposite at Talat Kaset II (many long-distance buses, including those from Phuket and Hat Yai). The new bus terminal, 2km southwest of the centre on the road towards Phunphin, handles services from Bangkok and a few other provinces. Arriving by **train** means arriving at **Phunphin**, 13km to the west, from where buses run into Surat Thani every ten minutes between 6am and 7pm, and share-taxis leave when full (B15 per person or about B90 to charter the whole car into town). It's also possible to buy express-boat and vehicle-ferry tickets to Ko Samui and Ko Pha Ngan from the train station, including a connecting bus to the relevant pier (Tha Thong, Don Sak or Khanom). If you're planning to leave by train, booking tickets at the reliable Phantip Travel, in front of Talat Kaset I at 293/6–8 Thanon Taladmai (☏077/272230 or 272906), will save an extra trip to Phunphin.

Phunphin and the bus stations are teeming with touts offering to escort you onto their employer's service to **Ko Samui** or **Ko Pha Ngan** – they're generally reliable but make sure you don't get talked onto the wrong boat. If you manage to avoid getting hustled, you can buy tickets direct from the boat operators: Songserm Travel, on Thanon Ban Don opposite the night-boat pier (☏077/285124–6), handles the express boats to Samui and Pha Ngan; Samui

## The Chak Phra Festival

At the start of the eleventh lunar month (September or October) the people of Surat Thani celebrate the end of Buddhist Lent with the **Chak Phra Festival** (Pulling the Buddha), which symbolizes the Buddha's return to earth after a monsoon season spent preaching to his mother in heaven. On the Tapi River, tugboats pull the town's principal Buddha image on a raft decorated with huge nagas, while on land sleigh-like floats bearing Buddha images and colourful flags and parasols are hauled across the countryside and through the streets. As the monks have been confined to their monasteries for three months, the end of Lent is also the time to give them generous offerings in the *kathin* ceremony, of which Surat Thani has its own version, called Thot Pha Pa, when the offerings are hung on tree branches planted in front of the houses before dawn. Longboat races, between teams from all over the south, are also held during the festival.

Tour, 326/12 Thanon Taladmai (☎077/282352), handles connecting buses for the vehicle ferries.

Arriving by **air**, you can take a B80 Songserm/Phantip minibus for the 27-kilometre journey south into Surat Thani, or a B280 combination ticket to Ko Samui; if you're flying out of Surat, you can catch the minibus from town to the airport at the Thai Airways office, south of the centre at 3/27–28 Thanon Karoonrat, off Thanon Chonkasem (☎077/272610 or 273710), or at the *Wangtai Hotel* (see below).

If you're coming from points south by **air-conditioned minibus** or **share-taxi**, you should be deposited at the door of your destination; when leaving Surat, minibus tickets can be booked at Phantip or the offices around Talat Kaset II; share-taxis also congregate at Talat Kaset II.

**TAT** has an office at the western end of town at 5 Thanon Taladmai (daily 8am–4pm; ☎077/288817–9, ✉tatsurat@samart.co.th), which stocks free, sketchy maps. Small **share-songthaews** buzz around town, charging around B10 per person.

### Accommodation and eating

Most budget **accommodation** in Surat Thani is noisy, grotty and overpriced – you'd probably be better off on a night boat to Ko Samui or Ko Pha Ngan. If you do get stuck here, head for the *Ban Don Hotel*, above a restaurant at 268/1 Thanon Namuang (☎077/272167; ❷), where clean rooms with fans and en-suite bathrooms are set back from the noise of the main road. A little upmarket but not as good value, *Seree Hotel*, 2/2–5 Thanon Tonpor (☎077/272279; ❸–❹), is also clean and quiet, with fan-cooled and air-con rooms. At the western end of town, *Wangtai Hotel*, 1 Thanon Taladmai (☎077/283020–39, ₣281007; ❻), was for a long time Surat Thani's only luxury option, and is still very good value with large, smart rooms around a swimming pool; its main challenger at the opposite end of town, the *Saowaluk Thani*, 99/99 Thanon Surat–Kanchanadit (☎077/213700–30, ₣213735; ❽), is more spacious and swankier, but twice the price.

For tasty, inexpensive Thai and Chinese **food** in large portions, head for the restaurant on the ground floor of the *Ban Don Hotel*. The night market between Thanon Si Chaiya and Thanon Ban Don displays an eye-catching range of dishes; a smaller offshoot by Ban Don pier offers less choice but is handy if you're taking a night boat. During the day, *Cha Thip 2* on the east side of Talat Kaset II bus station serves good dim sum and coffee, while one block east on

Thanon Tha Thong, an unnamed restaurant offers a wide selection of cheap and delicious tray food or fried dishes, mostly vegetarian though with some fish (look out for the yellow flags outside and a sign saying "vegetarian food"; closes 7pm). For more upmarket food, you could do a lot worse than the *Wangtai Hotel*, which at various restaurants and times of the day can offer buffet breakfasts, dim sum and tasty Thai and Western food, with friendly service and fierce air-conditioning.

# Ko Samui

An ever-widening cross-section of visitors, from globetrotting backpackers to suitcase-toting fortnighters, come to southern Thailand just for the beautiful beaches of **KO SAMUI**, 80km from Surat – and at 15km across and down, Samui is large enough to cope, except during the rush at Christmas and New Year. The paradisal sands and clear blue seas have kept their good looks, which are enhanced by a thick fringe of palm trees that gives a harvest of three million coconuts each month. However, development behind the beaches – which has brought the islanders far greater prosperity than the crop could ever provide – speeds along in a messy, haphazard fashion with little concern for the environment. A local bye-law limits new construction to the height of a coconut palm (usually about three storeys), but the island's latest hotel complexes bask in the shade of some suspiciously lofty trees, rumoured to have been brought in from northern Thailand.

For most visitors, the days are spent indulging in a few watersports or just lying on the beach waiting for the next drinks seller, hair braider or masseur to come along. For a day off the sand, you should not miss the almost supernatural beauty of the **Ang Thong National Marine Park**, which comprises many of the eighty islands in the Samui archipelago. A motorbike day-trip on the fifty-kilometre round-island road throws up plenty more gorgeous beaches, and night-time entertainment is provided by a huge number of beach bars, tawdry barbeers and clubs. Buffalo fighting, once a common sport on the island, is now generally restricted to special festivals such as Thai New Year; the practices and rituals are much the same as those of bullfighting in Hat Yai (see p.415).

The island's most appealing beaches, **Chaweng** and **Lamai**, have seen the heaviest development and are now the most expensive places to stay, while quieter beaches such as **Maenam** are generally less attractive. **Choeng Mon** in Samui's northeast corner makes a good compromise: the beaches are nothing to write home about but the views of the bay are, the seafront between the handful of upmarket hotels is comparatively undeveloped, and Chaweng's nightlife is within easy striking distance. **Accommodation** on the island is generally in bungalow resorts, from the basic to the very swish: at the lower end of the scale, there are very few places left for under B150, but nearly all bottom-end bungalows now have en-suite bathrooms and constant electricity; for the most upmarket places you can pay well over B3000 for the highest international standards. The price codes on the following pages are based on high-season rates, but out of season (roughly April–June, Oct & Nov) dramatic reductions are possible.

No particular **season** is best for coming to Ko Samui. The northeast monsoon blows heaviest in November, but can bring rain at any time between October and January, and sometimes makes the sea on the east coast too chop-

**KO SAMUI**

Ko Pha Ngan (Thong Sala) & Ko Tao ▲          ▲ Ko Pha Ngan (Hat Rin)

Ko Pha Ngan (Thong Sala) & Ko Tao

Surat Thani & Tha Thong

Don Sak & Khanom

Hat Thong Son

**Big Buddha**

Hat Choeng Mon

Hat Maenam

Hat Bophut

Hat Bangrak

Ban Tai

Ban Bang Po

Ban Maenam

4169

Ban Bophut

4171

4169

Ko Matlang

Ban Bang Makham

**Na Thon**

North Chaweng

**Tourist Police**

Ban Chaweng

Central Chaweng

**Immigration office**

Chaweng Noi

Khao Pom (635m)

Coral Cove

see 'Chaweng' map

Na Muang 2 Waterfall

4174

**Na Muang Waterfall**

see 'Lamai' map

Ban Lamai

4170

4169

Ban Thurian

Hat Lamai

Ban Taling Ngam

4173

Hin Yay & Hin Ta

Ao Phangka

Ban Hua Thanon

4170

N

Laem Hin Khom

Ban Thongkrut

Ban Thong Tanot

Ban Bangkao

Laem Set

Ko Taen

Ko Mad Sum

0          5 km

py for swimming. (The north coast is generally calm enough for swimming all year round.) January is often breezy, March and April are very hot, and between May and October the southwest monsoon blows mildly onto Samui's west coast and causes some rain.

**TAT** runs a small but helpful office (daily 8.30am–noon & 1–4.30pm; ☏077/420504, ✉tatsamui@samart.com), tucked away on an unnamed side road in Na Thon (north of the pier and inland from the post office). Another useful source of **information** is ⓦwww.sawadee.com, a website set up by a German based at Lamai, which allows, among other things, direct bookings at a range of hotels on the island.

Ko Samui has around a dozen **scuba-diving** companies, offering trips for qualified divers and a wide variety of courses throughout the year, and the only **decompression chamber** in this part of Thailand, at Bangrak. Although the coral gardens at the north end of Ang Thong National Marine Park offer good diving between October and April, most trips for experienced divers head for the waters around Ko Tao (see p.282), which contain the best sites in the region; a day's outing costs around B3000, though if you can make your own way to Ko Tao, you'll save money and have more time in the water. The range of courses is comparable to what's on offer at Ko Tao, though prices are generally higher. Established and reliable PADI Five-Star Dive Centres include Samui International Diving School (Ⓦ www.planet-scuba.net), which has its head office at the *Malibu Resort* towards the north end of Central Chaweng (Ⓣ 077/422386); and Easy Divers (Ⓦ www.thaidive.com), which has its head office opposite *Full Circle* on Chaweng (Ⓣ 077/413372–3).

### Getting to the island

The most obvious way of getting to Ko Samui is on a boat from the Surat Thani area. Services fluctuate according to demand and extra boats are often laid on in high season, but the longest-established ferry is the night boat which leaves Ban Don pier in **Surat Thani** itself for **Na Thon** – the main port on Samui – at 9pm every night (7–8hr); tickets (B150) are sold at the pier on the day of departure.

From **Tha Thong**, 5km east of Surat, one express boat a day, handled by Songserm Travel (see p.250) runs to Na Thon (2hr 30min); the B150 ticket includes bus transport from Surat or Phunphin train station to the pier. Vehicle ferries run seven times a day between **Don Sak** pier, 68km east of Surat, and Thong Yang, 8km south of Na Thon (1hr 30min; B55); to coincide with these boats, Samui Tour (see p.250) runs buses from Surat or Phunphin to Don Sak and from Thong Yang to Na Thon, costing B40 for ordinary buses, B50 for air-conditioned buses; similarly vehicle ferries operate from **Khanom**, 100km east of Surat (4 daily; 1hr 30min; B55), with coinciding air-con buses from Surat or Phunphin run by Songserm (B50). The total journey time using the vehicle ferries is much the same as on an express boat, and if the sea is turbulent, the shorter voyage can be a blessing.

**From Bangkok**, the State Railway, in association with Surat travel agency Phanthip, does train/bus/boat packages through to Ko Samui which cost almost exactly the same as organizing the parts independently – around B550 if you travel in a second-class bunk. Government-run overnight bus–boat packages from the Northern Terminal cost from B300, and are far preferable to some of the cheap deals offered by private companies on Thanon Khao San (from around B250), as the vehicles used on these latter services are often substandard and several thefts have been reported. At the top of the range, you can get to Ko Samui direct **by air** on Bangkok Airways (in Bangkok Ⓣ 02/229 3456; at Samui airport Ⓣ 077/422513); between twelve and fourteen flights a day leave Bangkok, and there are even daily flights from Phuket, Krabi, U-Tapao (near Pattaya) and Singapore. Air-con minibuses meet incoming flights (and connect with departures) at the **airport** in the northeastern tip of the island, charging B100 to Chaweng for example; the rustic terminal has a reservations desk for some of the island's moderate and expensive hotels, currency-exchange facilities, a post office with international telephones (daily 8am–8pm), restaurants, and a Budget car-rental branch (Ⓣ 077/427188, Ⓦ www.budget.co.th).

Finally, it's possible to hop to Ko Samui from **Ko Pha Ngan**: three express boats a day do the 45-minute trip from Thong Sala to Na Thon (B95), while two vehicle ferries cover the same route for the same price in 1hr 10min; from Hat Rin three passenger boats a day take an hour to reach Bangrak (B100). Between January and September, if there are enough takers and the weather's good enough, one boat a day starts at Thong Nai Pan, on Ko Pha Ngan's east coast, and calls at Hat Rin before crossing to Maenam.

### Island transport

**Songthaews**, which congregate at the car park between the two piers in Na Thon, cover a variety of set routes during the daytime, either heading off clockwise or anti–clockwise on Route 4169, to serve all the beaches; destinations are marked in English and fares for most journeys range from B20 to B45. In the evening, they tend to operate more like taxis and you'll have to negotiate a fare to get them to take you exactly where you want to go. Ko Samui now also sports a handful of **air-con taxis**, whose drivers hang out at the same car park and will ferry you to Chaweng for about B300.You can **rent a motorbike** from B150 in Na Thon, but it's hard to find a decent new bike in the capital, so it's probably safer, and more convenient, to rent at one of the main beaches – dozens are killed on Samui's roads each year, so proceed with caution.

## Na Thon

The island capital, **NA THON**, at the top of the long western coast, is a frenetic half-built town which most travellers use only as a service station before hitting the sand: although most of the main beaches now have post offices, currency-exchange facilities, supermarkets, travel agents and clinics, the biggest and best concentration of amenities is to be found here. The town's layout is simple: the two piers come to land at the promenade, Thanon Chonvithi, which is paralleled first by narrow Thanon Ang Thong, then by Thanon Taweeratpakdee, aka Route 4169, the round-island road; the main cross-street is Thanon Na Amphoe, just north of the piers.

### Practicalities

**Ferry agent** Songserm has its office on Thanon Chonvithi opposite the piers (℗077/421316–9), while tickets for the bus–ferry combination to Surat via Thong Yang and Don Sak can be bought from Samui Tour at The Bamboo House, south of the piers on Thanon Chonvithi. Bangkok Airways (℗077/422513) have an office next to Songserm's. Some of the **banks** have automatic teller machines, late-night opening and safe-deposit boxes; all the supermarkets and department stores are geared up for beachside needs. At the northern end of the promenade, there's a **post office** (Mon–Fri 8.30am–4.30pm, Sat & Sun 8.30am–noon) with poste restante and packing services and an IDD (international direct dialling) telephone service upstairs that's open daily from 8.30am to 9pm. Nathon Book Store, on Thanon Na Amphoe, is the best secondhand English-language **bookshop** in this part of Thailand.

For emergencies, the main police station is on Thanon Taweeratpakdee just north of Thanon Na Amphoe, or better still contact the **tourist police** (℗1699 or 077/421281 or 421441), who are based 1km south of town on Route 4169; private **clinics** operate on Thanon Ang Thong and Thanon Taweeratpakdee, while the less costly state **hospital** (℗077/421230–2 or 421399), 3km south of town off Route 4169, has recently been upgraded and is now preferable to the private hospitals on Chaweng. Tourist visas may be extended at the **immigration office**, also south of town, 2km down Route 4169 (Mon–Fri 8.30am–4.30pm; ℗077/421069). Finally, on a more soothing note, the Garden Home Health Center, 2km north along Route 4169 in Ban Bang Makham, dispenses some of the best **massages** (B150 per hr) and herbal **saunas** (B250) on the island, though note that it closes at sunset.

### Accommodation and eating

If you really need a **place to stay** in Na Thon, the best budget option is the *Seaview Guesthouse* which, though it fails to provide views of the sea, has quiet rooms at the rear; it's housed in a modern building at 67/15 Thanon Taweeratpakdee (☏077/236236; ❷). If you're on a slightly higher budget, head for *Jinta Residence* towards the south end of Thanon Chonvithi (☏077/420630-1, ⓕ420632, ⓦwww.tapee.com; ❸–❺), with smart, bright bungalows (some with en-suite hot-water bathrooms, air-con and TV) and its own **internet café** (B2 per min).

Several stalls and small cafés purvey inexpensive Thai **food** around the market on Thanon Taweeratpakdee and on Thanon Chonvithi (including a lively night market by the piers), and there are plenty of Western-orientated places clustered around the piers. Justifiably popular, especially for breakfast, is cheerful and inexpensive *RT (Roung Thong) Bakery*, with one branch opposite the piers and another on Thanon Taweeratpakdee, which supplies bread to bungalows and restaurants around the island and also serves Thai food. For lunch, head for the modern block of shops behind the large Samui Mart department store on Thanon Taweeratpakdee: here you can choose between *Zheng Teck*, a neat and simple Chinese-run veggie restaurant (daily 7am–3pm) which also sells vegetarian supplies, and *Yemeng*, a popular, well-run café serving duck or pork on rice.

## Ang Thong National Marine Park

Even if you don't get your buns off the beach for the rest of your stay, it's worth taking at least a day out to visit the beautiful **ANG THONG NATIONAL MARINE PARK**, a lush, dense group of 41 small islands strewn like dragon's teeth over the deep blue Gulf of Thailand, 31km west of Samui. Once a haven for pirate junks, then a Royal Thai Navy training base, the islands and their coral reefs, white sand beaches and virgin rainforest are now preserved under the aegis of the National Parks Department. Erosion of the soft limestone has dug caves and chiselled out fantastic shapes which are variously said to resemble seals, a rhinoceros, a Buddha image and even the temple complex at Angkor.

The surrounding waters are home to dolphins, wary of humans because local fishermen catch them for their meat, and *pla thu* (short-bodied mackerel), part of the national staple diet, which gather in huge numbers between February and April to spawn around the islands. On land, long-tailed macaques, leopard cats, common wild pig, sea otters, squirrels, monitor lizards and pythons are found, as well as dusky langurs which, because they have no natural enemies here, are unusually friendly and easy to spot. Around forty bird species have had confirmed sightings, including the white-rumped shama noted for its singing, the brahminy kite, black baza, little heron, Eurasian woodcock, several species of pigeon, kingfisher and wagtail, as well as common and hill mynah; island caves shelter swiftlets, whose homes are stolen for bird's nest soup (see box on p.379).

The largest land mass in the group is **Ko Wua Talab** (Sleeping Cow Island) where the park headquarters shelter in a hollow behind the small beach. From there it's a steep 430-metre climb (about 1hr return; bring walking sandals or shoes) to the island's peak to gawp at the panorama, which is especially fine at sunrise and sunset: in the distance, Ko Samui, Ko Pha Ngan and the mainland; nearer at hand, the jagged edges of the surrounding archipelago; and below the peak, a secret cove on the western side and an almost sheer drop to the clear blue sea to the east. Another climb from the beach at headquarters, only 200m but even harder going (allow 40min return), leads to Tham Buabok, a cave set high in the cliff-face. Some of the stalactites and stalagmites are said to resemble lotuses, hence the cave's appellation, "Waving Lotus". If you're visiting in

September, look out for the white, violet-dotted petals of **lady's slipper orchids**, which grow on the rocks and cliffs.

The feature which gives the park the name Ang Thong, meaning "Golden Bowl", and which was the inspiration for the setting of recent cult bestseller, *The Beach*, is a landlocked lake, 250m in diameter, on **Ko Mae Ko** to the north of Ko Wua Talab. A well-made path (allow 30min return) leads from the beach through natural rock tunnels to the rim of the cliff wall which encircles the lake, affording another stunning view of the archipelago and the shallow, blue-green water far below, which is connected to the sea by a natural underground tunnel.

### Practicalities

Apart from chartering your own boat at huge expense, the only way of **getting to Ang Thong** is on an organized day-trip; boats leave Na Thon every day at 8.30am, returning at 5.30pm. In between, there's a two-hour stop to explore Ko Wua Talab (just enough time to visit the viewpoint, the cave and have a quick swim, so don't dally), lunch on board the moored boat, some cruising through the archipelago, a visit to the viewpoint over the lake on Ko Mae Ko and a snorkelling stop (snorkel hire is an extra B50). Tickets cost B550 per person (including entry to the national park), available from Highway Travel (⊕077/421285 or 421290) by Na Thon pier and through agencies on Samui's main beaches. Similar trips run from Ban Bophut on Ko Samui (contact Air Sea Travel on ⊕077/422262–3, who also run speedboat trips to Ang Thong for B850) and from Thong Sala pier on Ko Pha Ngan, but less frequently; *Seaflower*, at Ao Chaophao on Ko Pha Ngan's west coast, does three-day "treks" (see p.278). It's also possible to combine a boat trip to Ang Thong with **kayaking** among the islands in the northern part of the park. The best operator of this kind of day-trip is Blue Stars, based near the *Green Mango* nightclub on Chaweng (⊕077/413231), which has English guides and charges B1800, including a light breakfast, lunch, kayaking and snorkelling.

If you want to **stay at Ko Wua Talab**, the National Parks Department maintains simple four- to fifteen-berth bungalows (B600–1500) at the headquarters. To book accommodation, contact the Ang Thong National Marine Park Headquarters (⊕077/420225), or the Forestry Department in Bangkok (see p.42). Camping is also possible in certain specified areas: if you bring your own tent, the charge is B50 per night, or two-person tents can be hired for B100 a night. If you do want to stay, you can go over on a boat-trip ticket – it's valid for a return on a later day. For getting around the archipelago from Ko Wua Talab, it's possible to charter a motor boat from the fishermen who live in the park; the best snorkelling, with the highest density and diversity of living coral, is off the west side of Ko Sam Sao or "Tripod Island", so named after its towering rocky arch. The limited canteen at park headquarters is open daily from 7am to 10pm.

## Maenam

The most westerly of the beaches on the north coast is **MAENAM**, 13km from Na Thon and now Samui's most popular destination for shoestring travellers. The exposed four-kilometre bay is not the island's prettiest, being more of a broad dent in the coastline, and the sloping beach is relatively narrow and coarse. But Maenam has the lowest rates for bed and board on the island, unspoilt views of fishing boats and Ko Pha Ngan, good swimming and – despite the recent opening of a luxury hotel – is the quietest of the major beaches. Jet-skis give way to windsurfing here (available from *Santiburi Dusit Resort* and on the beach just east of *Cleopatra's Palace*), and there's very little in the way of nightlife – though if you want to go on the razzle, there are late-night songthaews to and from Chaweng and Lamai. The main road is set back far from the beach among the trees, and runs through the sizeable fishing village of **Ban Maenam**, in the centre of the bay, one of the few places on Samui where there's more to life than tourism.

## Practicalities

Most visitors to Maenam **eat** in their hotel or resort restaurant, though a couple of unaffiliated places in Ban Maenam stand out. *Gallery Pizza* on the pier road (closes 8.30pm; ☎ 077/247420) dishes up delicious, authentic pizza to take away from a wood-fired oven. *Angela's Bakery* (closes 5.30pm), opposite the **police station** on the main through-road to the east of the pier, is a popular expat hangout, offering a wide choice of sandwiches, cakes and pies, plus a few other Western dishes and deli goods such as meats and cheeses to stock up on. Further east, beyond the access road to *Cleopatra's Palace*, is a **post office** with poste restante, while SK Travel, near *Gallery Pizza* on the pier road, provides **internet access** (B2 per min).

## Accommodation

As well as one or two upmarket resorts, Maenam has over twenty inexpensive bungalow complexes, most offering a spread of accommodation. There's little to choose between these places, although the best of the bunch are at the far eastern end of the bay.

**Axolotl Village**, not on Maenam itself, but 2km west at Ban Tai ☎ & ℱ 077/420017, ⓦ www.axolotlvillage.com. A peaceful, friendly place with Italian-German management, offering meditation and a variety of other courses. Clean, attractive bungalows, the more expensive with hot water and air-con, and an excellent Thai and Italian beachside restaurant. ❹–❼

**Cleopatra's Palace**, at the eastern end of the bay, 1km from the village ☎ 077/425486. A variety of clean wooden and concrete bungalows, all with fans and bathrooms, stand in a rather higgledy-piggledy, cramped compound; the Thai and Western food is recommended. ❷–❹

**Friendly** ☎ & ℱ 077/425484. About 500m east of *Cleopatra's Palace*. Easy-going place with helpful staff. All the bungalows are very clean and have their own bathrooms, though the place feels exposed, with no trees to provide shade. ❷–❹

**Home Bay**, at the far western end of Maenam ☎ 077/247214 or 247241, ℱ 247215. Has a grandiose-looking restaurant overlooking its own large stretch of untidy beach, tucked in beside a small cliff; sleeping options range from smart wooden bungalows with mosquito screens to big, concrete family cottages. ❸–❹

**Maenam Resort**, 500m west of the village ☎ 077/247286, ☎ & ℱ 425116. Just beyond *Santiburi Dusit Resort*. A moderately priced beach-front resort in tidy grounds, with a clean restaurant. The rooms and large bungalows, with verandas and air-con, offer good-value comfort. ❺–❻

**Naplarn Villa**, at the far western end, off the access road to *Home Bay* ☎ 077/247047. Good value if you don't mind a 5min walk to the beach: excellent food and clean, well-furnished, en-suite wooden bungalows with ceiling fans, mosquito screens and verandas, arrayed around a pleasant garden. ❷

**Rose**, next door to *Friendly* at the eastern end of the bay. Laid-back old-timer that has resisted the urge to upgrade: basic thatched-roofed wooden huts in a shady compound have mosquito nets and bathrooms but no fans, and the electricity still comes from a generator (lights out 11pm). ❷

**Santiburi Dusit Resort**, 500m west of the village ☎ 077/425031–8, ℱ 425040, ⓦ www.dusit.com. Luxury hotel in beautifully landscaped grounds spread around a huge freshwater swimming pool and stream. Accommodation is mostly in Thai-style villas, inspired by Rama IV's summer palace at Phetchaburi, each with a large bathroom and separate sitting area, furnished in luxurious traditional design. Facilities include watersports on the private stretch of beach, a health centre, an Avis car-rental desk, and an excellent "royal" cuisine restaurant, the *Sala Thai*. ❾

**Shangrilah**, west of *Maenam Resort*, served by the same access road ☎077/425189. A friendly place in a flower-strewn compound which sprawls onto the nicest, widest stretch of sand along

Maenam. Accommodation is in a variety of smart, well-maintained en-suite bungalows with verandas, decent furniture, mosquito screens and ceiling fans. The restaurant serves good Thai food. ❷–❹

**SR**, the far eastern end of the bay ☎01/891 8874. A quiet, welcoming place with a very good restaurant. Accommodation is in basic beachfront bamboo huts with bathrooms, verandas and chairs. ❷

# Bophut

The next bay east along from Maenam is **BOPHUT**, which has a similar look to Maenam but shows a marked difference in atmosphere and facilities. The quiet two-kilometre beach attracts a mix of young and old travellers, as well as families, and **Ban Bophut**, at the east end of the bay, is well geared to meet their needs with a bank currency-exchange booth, several scuba-diving outlets, a small bookstore, travel agents and supermarkets crammed into its two narrow streets. However, it mostly maintains a sleepy village feel, momentarily jostled when the speed boats to Ko Tao (see p.281) offload and pick up passengers. Many of the visitors here are French, whose culinary preferences are satisfied by a clutch of good Gallic-run restaurants on the beach road in Ban Bophut, most with fine views of the bay and Ko Pha Ngan from their terraces. The part of the beach which stretches from *Peace* to *World* bungalows, at the west end of the bay, is the nicest, but again the sand is slightly coarse by Samui's high standards.

Active pursuits are amply catered for, with jet-skis available just to the west of the village, kayaks at *Peace*, and sailboards, water-skiing and all sorts of other watersports near *Samui Palm Beach Resort*; Samui Go-kart, a **go-karting** track (daily 9am–9pm; ☎077/425097; from B300 for 10min) on the main road 1km west of the village, offers everyone the chance to let off steam without becoming another accident statistic on the roads of Samui.

## Accommodation

There's very little ultra-cheap accommodation left among Bophut's twenty or so resorts. Most establishments are well spaced out along the length of the beach, though a handful of places cluster together on the west side of Ban Bophut.

**Eddy's**, beyond *World*, at the far west end of Bophut back towards Maenam ☎077/245221, ☎245127, ✉Eddy_samui10@hotmail.com. Poor location on the main road, but only a 2min walk to the beach and good value for the facilities: large, stylish rooms with verandas, TVs, mini-bars and hot water (some rooms with air-con), helpful staff and a popular restaurant for Thai and Western food. ❻

**The Lodge**, towards the western end of the village ☎077/425337, ☎425336. Apartment-style block with immaculately clean and tastefully decorated modern rooms, all with balconies looking over the water, and boasting air-con, ceiling fan, fridge,

satellite TV, plus spacious bathrooms with tubs to soak in. There's a waterfront bar downstairs where you can get breakfast. ❼

**Peace**, at the mid-point of the beach ☎077/425357, ☎425343, ⊕www.kohsamui.net/peace. This large, well-run concern has shady and attractive lawned grounds, and being well away from the main road – and free of televisions – lives up to its name. Spotless bungalows, all with mosquito screens and their own bathroom, are brightly decorated and thoughtfully equipped; the larger ones, with hot water and air-con, are well suited to families. There's a small children's playground, a beautiful new pool with fountains and jacuzzi, and a beachside restaurant serving good Thai and European food. ④–⑦

**Samui Euphoria** ☏ 077/425100–6, ⓕ 425107, ⓦ www.samuieuphoria.com. Just to the east of *Peace*. A well-run, upmarket resort with several restaurants, watersports facilities and a large pool. In low-rise buildings, the rooms are spacious and smart, with plenty of traditional Thai decorative touches, and all come with TV, air-con, mini-bar and their own balconies, overlooking the manicured lawns or the beach. ⑨

**Samui Palm Beach Resort**, west of *Peace*, from which it's next door-but-two ☏ 077/425494 or 425495, ⓕ 425358, ⓔ spbhotel@samart.co.th.

Expensive but reasonable value, with frequent large discounts and American breakfast included in the price. Cottages are elegant – though a little frayed at the edges – with air-con, satellite TV, fridges and hints of southern Thai architecture, and there's an attractive swimming pool. ⑨

**Smile House**, across the road from *The Lodge*, at the western end of the village ☏ 077/425361, ⓕ 425239. Firmly in the moderate range, *Smile* has a reliable set of chalets grouped around a small, clean swimming pool. At the bottom end of the range you get a clean bathroom, mosquito screens and a fan; at the top, plenty of space, hot water and air-con. ④–⑦

# Bangrak

Beyond the sharp headland with its sweep of coral reefs lies **BANGRAK**, sometimes called Big Buddha Beach after the colossus which gazes sternly down on the sun worshippers from its island in the bay. The beach is no great shakes, especially during the northeast monsoon, when the sea retreats and leaves a slippery mud flat, but Bangrak still manages to attract the watersports crowd.

The **Big Buddha** is certainly big and works hard at being a tourist attraction, but is no beauty despite a recent face-lift. A short causeway at the eastern end of the bay leads across to a clump of souvenir shops and foodstalls in front of the temple, catering to day-tripping Thais as well as farangs. Ceremonial dragon-steps then bring you up to the covered terrace around the Big Buddha, from where there's a fine view of the sweeping north coast.

Bangrak's **bungalows** are squeezed together in a narrow, noisy strip between the road and the shore, underneath the airport flight path. The best of a disappointing bunch is *LA Resort* (☏ 077/425330; ③), a welcoming family-run place in a colourful garden, with clean and sturdy en-suite bungalows.

# The northeastern cape

After Bangrak comes the high-kicking boot of the **northeastern cape**, where quiet, rocky coves, overlooking Ko Pha Ngan and connected by sandy lanes, are fun to explore on a motorbike. Songthaews run along the paved road to the largest and most beautiful bay, **Choeng Mon**, whose white sandy beach is lined with casuarina trees which provide shade for the bungalows and upmarket resorts.

## Accommodation

Most of the accommodation on the northeastern cape is found around Choeng Mon. The tranquillity and prettiness of this bay have attracted two of Samui's most expensive hotels and a handful of bungalows and beach restaurants, but on the whole the shoreline is comparatively underdeveloped and laid-back.

**Boat House Hotel**, south side of Choeng Mon ☏ 077/425041–52, ⓕ 425460, ⓦ www.imperial hotels.com. Run by the reliable Imperial group, *Boat House* is named after the two-storey rice

barges which have been converted into suites in the grounds. It also offers luxury rooms in more prosaic modern buildings, often filled by package tours. Beyond the boat-shaped pool, the full gamut of watersports are drawn up on the sands.

**Choeng Mon Bungalows**, north of *Boat House* on Choeng Mon ⊤077/425372, ⓕ425219, ⓔsiriy-ong@samart.co.th. A shady compound with a good beachside restaurant, notable mostly for having the cheapest rooms on Choeng Mon – spartan wooden affairs with fans and en-suite showers – as well as top-of-the-range bungalows with air-con, mini-bars and hot-water bathrooms. ❷–❺

**Ô Soleil** ⊤ & ⓕ077/425232. Next door to *PS Villas*. A lovely, orderly place, with sturdy, pristine wooden bungalows. The most basic have fans and en-suite bathrooms, while the best have TV, mini-bar and air-con. ❸–❼

**PS Villas** ⊤077/425160, ⓕ425403. Next door to *White House*. Friendly place in large, beachfront grounds, offering a range of spacious, attractive fan-cooled or air-con bungalows with verandas and mosquito screens. ❸–❼

**The Tongsai Bay Cottages and Hotel**, north side of Choeng Mon ⊤077/425015–28, ⓕ425462,

ⓦwww.tongsaibay.co.th. Easy-going establishment with the unhurried air of a country club and excellent service. The luxurious hotel rooms and red-tiled cottages command beautiful views over the spacious, picturesque grounds, the private beach (with plenty of watersports), a vast salt-water swimming pool and the whole bay; most of them also sport second bathtubs on their secluded open-air terraces, so you don't miss out on the scenery while splashing about. The hotel's very fine restaurants include *Chef Chom's*, which specializes in improvising Thai dishes from the day's freshest ingredients, and there's a delightful health spa. ❾

**White House**, next door to *Choeng Mon Bungalows* ⊤077/245315–7, ⓕ245318, ⓦwww.whitehouse.kohsamui.net. Swiss-managed luxury hotel with narrow beach frontage and correspondingly cramped grounds around a small swimming pool and pretty courtyard garden. What it lacks in space it makes up for in style, with plants and beautiful traditional decor in the common areas and rooms. ❽

# Chaweng

For sheer natural beauty, none of the other beaches can match **CHAWENG**, with its broad, gently sloping strip of white sand sandwiched between the limpid blue sea and a line of palm trees. Such beauty has not escaped attention, which means, on the plus side, that Chaweng can provide just about anything the active beach bum demands, from thumping nightlife to ubiquitous and surprisingly diverse watersports. The negative angle is that the new developments are ever more expensive, building work behind the palm trees and repairs to the over-commercialized main drag are always in progress – and there's no certainty that it will look lovely when the bulldozers retreat.

The six-kilometre bay is framed between the small island of Ko Matlang at the north end and the 300-metre-high headland above Coral Cove in the south. From **Ko Matlang**, where the waters provide some colourful snorkelling, an often exposed coral reef slices southwest across to the mainland, marking out a shallow lagoon and **North Chaweng**. This S-shaped part of the beach has some ugly pockets of development, but at low tide it becomes a wide, inviting playground, and from October to January the reef shelters it from the worst of the northeast winds. South of the reef, the idyllic shoreline of **Central Chaweng** stretches for 2km in a dead-straight line, the ugly village of amenities on the parallel main drag largely concealed behind the treeline and the resorts. Around a low promontory is **Chaweng Noi**, a little curving beach in a rocky bay, which is comparatively quiet in its northern part, away from the road.

South of Chaweng, the road climbs and dips into **Coral Cove**, a tiny isolated beach of coarse sand hemmed in by high rocks, with some good coral for snorkelling. It's well worth making the trip to the *Beverly Hills Café*, towards the tip of the headland dividing Chaweng from Lamai, for a jaw-dropping view over Chaweng and Choeng Mon to the peaks of Ko Pha Ngan (and for some good, moderately priced food).

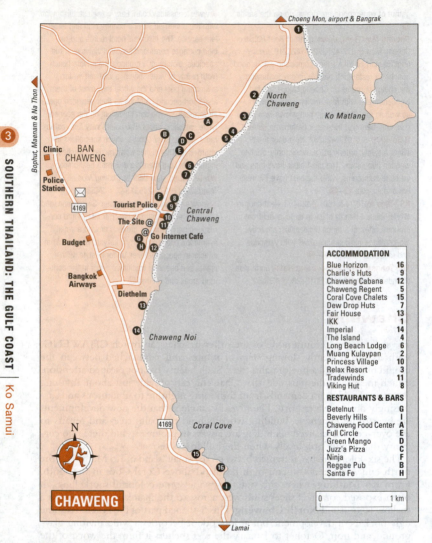

**CHAWENG**

*Choeng Mon, airport & Bangrak*

*Bophut, Maenam & Na Thon*

North Chaweng

*Ko Matlang*

Clinic
BAN
CHAWENG

Police
Station

Tourist Police

The Site @

Go Internet Café

Budget

Bangkok
Airways

Diethelm

*Central
Chaweng*

*Chaweng Noi*

N

*Coral Cove*

0                1 km

*Lamai*

| ACCOMMODATION | |
|---|---|
| Blue Horizon | 16 |
| Charlie's Huts | 9 |
| Chaweng Cabana | 12 |
| Chaweng Regent | 5 |
| Coral Cove Chalets | 15 |
| Dew Drop Huts | 7 |
| Fair House | 13 |
| IKK | 1 |
| Imperial | 14 |
| The Island | 4 |
| Long Beach Lodge | 6 |
| Muang Kulaypan | 2 |
| Princess Village | 10 |
| Relax Resort | 3 |
| Tradewinds | 11 |
| Viking Hut | 8 |

| RESTAURANTS & BARS | |
|---|---|
| Betelnut | G |
| Beverly Hills | I |
| Chaweng Food Center | A |
| Full Circle | E |
| Green Mango | D |
| Juzz'a Pizza | C |
| Ninja | F |
| Reggae Pub | B |
| Santa Fe | H |

## Practicalities

Small **banks** and **supermarkets** can be found at many locations along the main drag, as can **rental motorbikes** (from B150 a day) and **four-wheel drives** (from B800 a day); if reliability is your main priority, contact Budget in Ban Chaweng (☎077/427188, ⓦ www.budget.co.th; 4WD from around B1400 per day). Among dozens of places offering **internet access** are Go Internet Café, at the south end of Central Chaweng opposite the *Central Samui Beach Resort*; and The Site, a little to the north opposite *Tradewinds* (both B2 per min); while Diethelm (☎077/422320, ⓔ ditssum@samart.co.th), at the far south end of the beach road just before it joins Route 4169, is a reliable and knowledgeable – though expensive – **travel agent**. There's a **tourist police** booth in front of *Princess Village* in the heart of Central Chaweng. The original village of **Ban Chaweng**, 1km inland of Central Chaweng beach on the round-island road, has a **police station**, a **post office** with poste restante, a small **clinic** and a branch of Bangkok Airways (☎077/422512–8 or 420133).

## Accommodation

Over fifty **bungalow resorts** and **hotels** at Chaweng are squeezed into thin strips running back from the beachfront at right angles. In the inexpensive and moderate range, prices are generally over the odds, although a few places, all of them listed below, offer reasonable value. More and more expensive places are sprouting up all the time, offering sumptuous accommodation at top-whack prices.

### Inexpensive to moderate

**Blue Horizon**, above Coral Cove ☎077/422426, ℱ230293, ℮bluehorizon@samuitourism.com. One of several resorts clinging to the steep hillside, this is a friendly, well-ordered place, where some of the sturdy, balconied bungalows have air-con and hot water. **④**–**⑦**

**Charlie's Huts**, in the heart of Central Chaweng ☎077/422343 or 230285. Some of the cheapest accommodation options left on Chaweng are the wooden huts with shared bathrooms, mosquito nets and fans in the grassy compound here; en-suite and air-con bungalows also available, but no hot water in any of them. **②**–**⑤**

**Chaweng Cabana**, south end of Central Chaweng ☎077/422184, ℱ422377. Reliable, well-run option, for those who don't feel the need of a swimming pool with their luxuries; bungalows in a lush garden with bland but tasteful decor, some with air-con, cable TV and fridge. **⑥**–**⑨**

**Dew Drop Huts**, at the top end of Central Chaweng ☎077/422238, ℮jah_dub@hotmail.com. Secluded among dense trees, *Dew Drop* ignores the surrounding flash development to offer a friendly, laid-way-back ambience, old-fashioned primitive huts – now joined by some upgraded pads with air-con on the beach – plus herbal saunas and massages. **①**–**⑥**

**IKK**, around the point at the far north end of North Chaweng ☎077/422482–3. Comfortable en-suite bungalows on an unusually spacious and peaceful stretch of sand. **③**

**The Island**, in the middle of North Chaweng ☎077/230751–3, ℱ230942. A spread of well-designed accommodation with air-con and hot-water bathrooms encompassing concrete rooms at the back of the shady, orderly compound, as well as grand beachside cottages; there's also a good restaurant on the beach. **⑤**–**⑧**

**Long Beach Lodge**, towards the north end of Central Chaweng ☎ & ℱ077/422372. An unusually spacious and shady sandy compound, which may attract the beady eyes of developers. All the orderly, clean bungalows are a decent size and have fans and en-suite bathrooms; the larger, more expensive ones have hot water and air-con. **④**–**⑦**

**Relax Resort**, in the middle of North Chaweng ☎077/422280, ℱ422113. Friendly spot that lives up to its name, with a range of very clean and well-maintained fan-cooled and air-con rooms and chalets, all with en-suite hot-water bathrooms. **④**–**⑤**

**Viking Hut**, Central Chaweng ☎077/413304, ℮living99@loxinfo.co.th. A cheap, friendly place next door and similar to *Charlie's Huts*, with a little more shade. Good basic huts, some en suite. **②**–**④**

### Expensive

**Chaweng Regent**, at the bottom end of North Chaweng ☎077/422389–90, ℱ422222, ℮www.chawengregent.com. Elegant bungalows with all mod cons around lotus ponds and a pool, though conditions are a little cramped. **⑨**

**Coral Cove Chalets**, above Coral Cove ☎077/422260–1, ℱ422496, ℮www.kohsamui.net/ccc. Especially good-value and stylish place with bright, tasteful bungalows, each with balcony, TV and mini-bar, grouped around an attractive pool and jacuzzi. **⑧**

**Fair House**, north end of Chaweng Noi ☎077/422255–6, ℱ422373, ℮fairhouse@sawadee.com. A great location on a lovely stretch of beach, with extensive, lush gardens and two pools. The colourfully decorated bungalows are preferable to the large hotel rooms, which have good facilities but lack style. **⑨**

**Imperial**, on a small rise above Chaweng Noi ☎077/422020–36, ℱ422396–7, ⓦwww. imperialhotels.com. The longest-established luxury hotel on Samui is a grand but lively establishment with a Mediterranean feel, set in leafy grounds around two pools. ❾

**Muang Kulaypan**, North Chaweng ☎077/422305, ℱ230031, ℯkulaypan@sawadee.com. Original, stylish boutique hotel arrayed around a large, immaculate garden with a black-tiled swimming pool. Rooms – each with their own private balcony or garden – combine contemporary design with traditional Thai-style comforts. ❾

**Princess Village**, Central Chaweng ☎077/422216, ℱ422382,

ⓦwww.princess.kohsamui.net. Traditional Ayutthaya-style houses on stilts set in plenty of space around beautiful lotus ponds. Decorated with carved wooden panels, "axe" pillows and traditional cotton fabrics, which sit a little uneasily with the Western-style bathrooms, minibars and air-con. ❾

**Tradewinds**, next door to *Princess Village*, Central Chaweng ☎077/230602–4, ℱ231247, ℯtradewinds@sawadee.com. A cheerful, well-run place of characterful bungalows (all with air-con, hot water and mini-bar) with plenty of room to breathe in colourful tropical gardens. The resort specializes in sailing, with its own catamarans and yacht (instruction available). ❽

## Eating

It's hard to find good, reasonably priced **Thai food** here, but one place that's worth making a beeline for is the friendly and efficient beachside restaurant of *Relax Resort*. Avoid the curries in favour of the house speciality – seafood. Prawn cakes make a delicious starter, then choose your own ultra-fresh fish and have it weighed and cooked as you wish (red snapper in plum sauce is recommended). To go with it, there's a good selection of wine and draft Carlsberg at decent prices. Decent backstops are the *Chaweng Food Center*, 200m along the road to Ban Chaweng from North Chaweng, a day-and-night market of cheap and cheerful foodstalls that's popular with local workers; and *Ninja*, a very basic Thai restaurant near *Charlie's Huts* on Central Chaweng, that's unexceptional bar the fact that it stays open 24 hours. Moving upmarket, the *Budsaba Restaurant* at *Muang Kulaypan* fully justifies the journey: here you get to recline in your own open-sided beachfront hut, while tucking into unusual and excellent Thai dishes such as banana flower and shrimp salad.

For well-prepared **Western food**, especially if you're tired of the breakfast at your accommodation, head for the beachside restaurant at *The Island*. *Juzz'a Pizza* (daily 5pm–1am) does a lot more than its name (almost) suggests, with very good pizza, pasta and other Western fare, in surprisingly homely surroundings on the noisy lane leading to the *Green Mango*, at the north end of Central Chaweng. At the top end of the price range, *Betelnut* (☎077/413370, ⓦwww.thaisite.com/betelnut), down a small lane at the south end of Central Chaweng opposite the landmark *Central Samui Beach Resort*, is by far Samui's best restaurant, serving exceptional Californian-Thai **fusion food**. On the other side of the same lane, you can take a highly recommended **Thai cookery course**, or just buy some choice ingredients to take home with you, at the Samui Institute of Thai Culinary Arts (SITCA; ☎077/413172, ⓦwww.sitca.net).

## Drinking and nightlife

Avoiding the raucous bar-beers and English theme pubs on the main through road, the best place to **drink** is on the beach: at night dozens of resorts and dedicated bars lay out small tables and candles on the sand, especially towards the north end of Central Chaweng and on North Chaweng. Also on the beach, *Jah Dub* at *Dew Drop Huts* specializes in reggae, and holds parties in high season, usually on Tuesday and Friday nights.

Bang in the heart of Central Chaweng but set well back from the beach, *The Reggae Pub* is not just an unpretentious, good-time **nightclub**, but a venerable Samui institution, with a memorabilia shop, foodstalls, internet access and upstairs snooker tables. Chaweng's other long-standing dance venue, *Green Mango* at the north end of Central Chaweng, occupies a similarly huge shed which combines an industrial look with that of a tropical greenhouse, complete with fountain, fairy lights and ornamental garden. The title of Samui's best club, however, goes to *Full Circle*, a hip and stylish place with British DJs playing house music, done out in minimalist metal with splashes of primary colours; it's set amid a forest of bar-beers on North Chaweng (look out for flyers or ask about regular beach parties the club hosts at Hat Thong Son on the island's northeastern cape). Its sister club, *Santa Fe*, at the south end of Central Chaweng, has a Native American theme, with totem-like statues and a mosaic-decorated dance floor; it now caters mostly for Thais, with poppy "love" music (as they call it) and live bands, but is great fun nonetheless, and there are good pool tables if you need a break.

## Lamai

Samui's nightlife is most tawdry at **LAMAI** (though Chaweng is fast catching up these days): planeloads of European package tourists are kept happy here at go-go shows and dozens of open-air hostess bars, sinking buckets of booze while slumped in front of boxing videos. Running roughly north to south for 4km, the white palm-fringed beach is, fortunately, still a picture – though it doesn't quite match Chaweng – and it's possible to avoid the boozy mayhem by staying at the quiet extremities of the bay, where the backpackers' resorts have a definite edge over Chaweng's. At the northern end, the spur of land which hooks eastward into the sea is perhaps the prettiest spot: it has more rocks than sand, but the shallow sea behind the coral reef is protected from the high seas of November, December and January.

The action is concentrated into a farang toytown of bars and Western restaurants that has grown up behind the centre of the beach, packed cheek-by-jowl along the noisy, dusty rutted backroads. Crowded among them are supermarkets, clinics, banks and travel agents; jet-skis and water-skiing are available on the beach just south of *Lamai Inn 99*, level with the central crossroads.

The original village of **Ban Lamai**, set well back at the northern end, remains aloof from these goings-on, and its wat contains a small museum of ceramics, agricultural tools and other everyday objects. Most visitors get more of a buzz from **Hin Yay** (Grandmother Rock) and **Hin Ta** (Grandfather Rock), small rock formations on the bay's southern promontory, which never fail to raise a giggle with their resemblance to the male and female sexual organs. If the excitement gets too much for you, head for *The Spa Resort* (see p.267) at the far north end of the beach: its "Rejuvenation Menu" covers everything from colonic irrigation to healing clay facials, along with more traditional treatments such as Thai massage (B250 per hour) and herbal saunas (B250 per hour). In similar vein, but much more upmarket, is Tamarind Springs (℡077/230571 or 424436, ⓦwww.tamarindretreat.com), set in a beautiful, secluded coconut grove just north of *Spa Resort* off the main road; here a herbal sauna and two-hour Thai massage, for example, costs B1200.

### Practicalities

**Internet access** is provided at several places around the central crossroads and at Sawadee, next to the petrol station, on the road between *The Spa Resort* and Ban Lamai (B2/min; see also p.253).

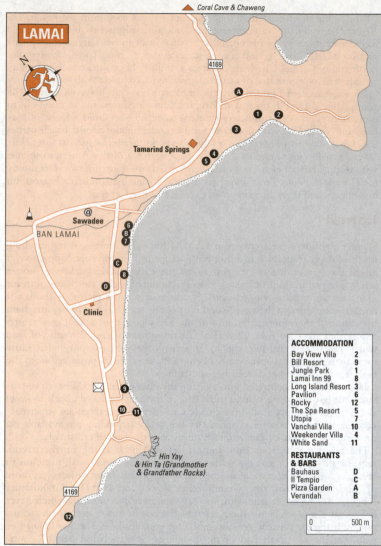

▲ Coral Cave & Chaweng

**LAMAI**

N

4169

A

1  2

3

**Tamarind Springs**

4

5

@
**Sawadee**

**BAN LAMAI**

6
B
7

C

8

D

**Clinic**

9

10  11

Hin Yay
& Hin Ta (Grandmother
& Grandfather Rocks)

4169

12

▼ Ban Hua Thanon & Na Thon

**ACCOMMODATION**

| | |
|---|---|
| Bay View Villa | 2 |
| Bill Resort | 9 |
| Jungle Park | 1 |
| Lamai Inn 99 | 8 |
| Long Island Resort | 3 |
| Pavilion | 6 |
| Rocky | 12 |
| The Spa Resort | 5 |
| Utopia | 7 |
| Vanchai Villa | 10 |
| Weekender Villa | 4 |
| White Sand | 11 |

**RESTAURANTS & BARS**

| | |
|---|---|
| Bauhaus | D |
| Il Tempio | C |
| Pizza Garden | A |
| Verandah | B |

0        500 m

3

SOUTHERN THAILAND: THE GULF COAST | Ko Samui

To tempt you away from your guest-house kitchen, there are several good
Italian **restaurants**, such as *Il Tempio*, a short way north of the tourist village's
main crossroads, and, a couple of hundred metres on, the German-run *Verandah*
at *Mui Bungalows*, which serves excellent, well-presented international and Thai
food. To work up an appetite, walk to the northern end of the bay where the
Austrian-run *Pizza Garden*, on the headland above *Jungle Park*, bakes great pizzas and baguettes, and serves good pastas and coffee.

Lamai's **nightlife** is all within spitting distance of the central crossroads.
Apart from the hostess bars, *Bauhaus* is the main draw, a barn-like entertain-

266

ment complex with pool, darts, a big screen showing satellite sport and a dance floor.

## Accommodation

Lamai's **accommodation** is generally less cramped and slightly better value than Chaweng's, though it presents far fewer choices at the top end of the market. The far southern end of the bay towards the Grandparent Rocks has the tightest concentration of budget bungalows.

**Bay View Villa**, on the bay's northern headland ☎ & ℱ 077/418429. Neat, stylish bungalows with verandas and en-suite bathrooms in an extensive, flower-bedecked compound. Offers a friendly welcome and great sunset views of the beach from the attractive restaurant. ❹

**Bill Resort**, at the far southern end of the bay ☎ 077/424403, ℱ 424286. An efficient and orderly setup, crammed into a fragrant, overgrown garden on a rocky stretch of beach and up the hill behind; clean bungalows with en-suite hot-water bathrooms, some with air-con. ❹–❼

**Jungle Park**, on the bay's northern headland ☎ 077/418034, ☎ & ℱ 077/424110. Next door to *Bay View Villa*. The shady compound with large swimming pool feels a little like a holiday camp but is reliable and well maintained; choose between rooms with fan and cold showers or spacious, sturdy bungalows with air-con and hot water. ❹–❻

**Lamai Inn 99**, on the beach by the tourist village's main crossroads ☎ 077/424212 or ☎ & ℱ 077/424427. A surprisingly spacious establishment, which offers a variety of bungalow styles and sizes, some with hot water and air-con. If you want to be near the throbbing heart of Lamai's nightlife, this is your place. ❹–❻

**Long Island Resort**, at the far north end of the beach ☎ 077/424202 or 418456, ℱ 424023, ⓦ www.sawadee.com/samui/longisland. A self-styled "boutique resort" with stylish but cosy bungalows (the cheapest with cold-water bathrooms, the priciest with air-con, cable TV and mini-bars), a decent-sized pool, a "mini spa" offering massages, steam and various other treatments, and a good Thai and Western restaurant serving up some interesting southern Thai dishes. ❹–❽

**Pavilion**, on the central stretch of Lamai, north of the crossroads ☎ 077/232083–6, ℱ 424029, ⓦ www.sawadee.com/samui/pavilion. Lamai's best upmarket choice, just far enough from the pubs and clubs to get some peace; the atmosphere is friendly and lively, and there's a good beachside

pool and restaurant. Most of the accommodation is in comfortable hotel rooms, but if your purse will stretch that far, go for one of the beachside cottages. ❽–❾

**Rocky**, beyond the headland, at the far southern end of the bay ☎ & ℱ 077/424326. Squeezes as much as it can into its beachside strip: a small swimming pool, a restaurant and a wide choice of rooms and bungalows, all with bathrooms, some with hot water and air-con. ❸–❺

**The Spa Resort**, at the far north end of the beach ☎ 077/230855, ℱ 424126, ⓦ www.spasamui.com Next to *Weekender Villa*. A wide variety of cosy, well-constructed rooms, decorated with shells and other bric-a-brac, though they're often full with people being rejuvenated (see p.265); delicious veggie and non-veggie food. ❸–❹

**Utopia**, on the central stretch of Lamai, north of the crossroads ☎ 077/233113, ℱ 233115, ⓔ jim_utopia@hotmail.com. Good-value, welcoming place on a narrow strip of land stuffed with flowers. The cheapest bungalows have mosquito screens, fans and en-suite bathrooms, while those at the top of the price range boast air-con and hot water. Good coffee and breakfasts, and plenty of free beach equipment. ❸–❺

**Vanchai Villa**, on the access road to *White Sand*, at the far southern end of the bay ☎ 077/424296. Quiet, family-run operation set back from the beach, offering a range of very clean, spacious bungalows with verandas among the palm trees, and excellent, cheap food. ❷–❹

**Weekender Villa**, between the main road and the beach to the east of Ban Lamai ☎ 077/424116. Despite its location this is a quiet spot; the staff are friendly and the large, en-suite wooden bungalows shelter in an airy coconut grove. ❷

**White Sand**, at the far southern end of the bay ☎ 077/424298. Long-established and laid-back budget place with around fifty simple beachside huts which attract plenty of long-term travellers. ❷

# The south and west coasts

Lacking the long beaches of the more famous resorts, the **south and west coasts** rely on a few charming, isolated spots with peaceful accommodation, which can usually only be reached by renting a motorbike or four-wheel drive. Heading south from Lamai, you come first to the Muslim fishing village at **Ban Hua Thanon** and then, about 3km south and well signposted off Route 4170, one of the island's most secluded hotels: originally founded as a private club on a quiet south-facing promontory, the *Laem Set Inn* (T077/424393, F424394, W www.laemset.com; ⑧–⑨) offers a wide range of elegant rooms and suites – some of them reassembled village houses – as well as an excellent restaurant, plenty of free watersports equipment and a scenically positioned swimming pool (open to non-guests who come for lunch).

The gentle but unspectacular coast beyond is lined with a good reef for snorkelling, which can be explored most easily from the fishing village of **Ban Bangkao**. Snorkellers rave about the coral around **Ko Mad Sum**, 4km offshore: an all-day tour from Ban Bangkao or the next village to the west, **Ban Thongkrut**, including mask, snorkel and lunch, will set you back around B350 per person. About 5km inland, near **Ban Thurian**, the **Na Muang falls** make a popular outing as they're not far off the round-island road (each of the two main falls has its own signposted kilometre-long paved access road off Route 4169). The lower fall splashes and sprays down a twenty-metre wall of rock into a large pool, while Na Muang 2 upstream is a more spectacular, shaded cascade but requires a bit of foot-slogging from the car park (about 15min uphill); alternatively you can walk up there from Na Muang 1, by taking the 1500-metre trail which begins 300m back along the access road from the lower fall. The self-styled "safari camp" at the Na Muang 2 car park offers thirty-minute **elephant rides**, taking in the falls, for B600 per person. The best budget place to stay hereabouts is the welcoming *Diamond Villa* (T077/424442; ❶–❹), in a secluded beachside coconut grove 1km west of Ban Bangkao, where you can choose either a wooden shack, with or without bathroom, or a smart concrete hut.

At the base of the west coast, **AO PHANGKA** (Emerald Cove) is a pretty horseshoe bay, sheltered by Laem Hin Khom, the high headland which forms Samui's southwestern tip, and by a coral reef which turns it into a placid paddling pool. The beach is poor and often littered with flotsam but, like the whole of the west coast, gives fine views of the tiny offshore islands of Ko Si Ko Ha – where birds' nests are harvested for the health-giving Chinese soup (see box on p.379) – with the sun setting over the larger Ang Thong archipelago behind. The best budget place to stay here is the laid-back *Seagull* on the north shore of the bay (T077/423091; ❷–❹), where a wide variety of clean bungalows, all with showers, is spread out on a flowery slope, and there's a good, if slow, restaurant. Across the headland on the south-facing shore of Laem Hin Khom and further upmarket, the quiet and welcoming *Coconut Villa* (T & F077/423151; ❸–❻) commands stunning views of Ko Mad Sum and its neighbouring islands; the fan-cooled or air-con bungalows all have en-suite bathrooms, the food is recommended, and there's an excellent swimming pool set in attractive gardens by the sea.

Further up the coast, the flat beaches are unexceptional but make a calm alternative when the northeast winds hit the other side of the island. In a gorgeous hillside setting near the village of the same name, *Baan Taling Ngam* (T077/423019–22, F423220, W www.meridien-samui.com; ❾), part of the international Meridien group, boasts a rather excessive total of seven swimming pools. The accommodation is in villas or balconied rooms on the resort's steep slopes, luxuriously decorated in traditional style. There's a spa and a Thai cooking school, and the hotel lays on the largest array of sports and watersports facilities on the island.

# Ko Pha Ngan

In recent years backpackers have tended to move over to Ko Samui's little sibling, **KO PHA NGAN**, 20km to the north, but the island still has a simple atmosphere, mostly because the lousy road system is an impediment to the developers. With a dense jungle covering its inland mountains and rugged granite outcrops along the coast, Pha Ngan lacks the huge, gently sweeping beaches for which Samui is famous, but it does have plenty of coral to explore and some beautiful, sheltered bays: **Hat Khuat** and **Hat Khom** on the north coast; **Thong Nai Pan** and half a dozen remote, virgin beaches on the east coast; and, on an isolated neck of land at the southeast corner, **Hat Rin**, a

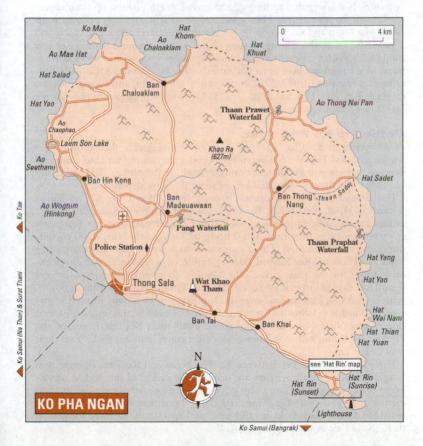

pilgrimage site for ravers. Most of Pha Ngan's development, however, has plonked itself along the less attractive south and west sides, linked by the only coastal roads on the island, which fan out from **Thong Sala**, the capital.

Pha Ngan's **bungalows** all now have running water and electricity (on the remoter beaches, only in the evenings and from individual generators), and most offer the choice of shared or en-suite bathrooms. There are no luxury hotels, and only a handful of places offer air-con. The two hundred or so resorts generally have more space to spread out than on Ko Samui, and the cost of living is lower; the prices given on the following pages are standard for most of the year, but in slack periods you'll be offered discounts, and at the very busiest times (especially in December and January) Pha Ngan's bungalow owners are canny enough to raise the stakes. As on Ko Samui, nearly all the bungalow resorts have inexpensive, traveller-orientated **restaurants**; at one or two of the cheapest resorts, however, where they make their money from food more than accommodation, owners have been known to kick out guests who don't eat at the in-house restaurant.

There's no TAT office on Ko Pha Ngan, but you might want to take a look at ⓦwww.kohphangan.com, a website with a miscellany of **information** about the island, set up by the owner of Phangan Batik in Thong Sala (see opposite). If you're going to be exploring, well worth picking up from supermarkets on the island is Visid Hongsombud's excellent, regularly updated **map** of Ko Pha Ngan and Ko Tao (B70; ⓦwww.thaiguidemap.com). The island isn't a great base for **scuba diving**: getting to the best sites around Ko Tao (see box on p.282) involves time-consuming and expensive voyages, and there aren't as many dive companies here as on Ko Samui or Ko Tao – of those that exist, Easy Divers on Hat Rin (☏077/375258, ⓦwww.thaidive.com) and Phangan Divers on Hat Rin and Hat Yao (☏077/375117, ⓦwww.phangandivers.com) are PADI Five-Star Centres.

### Getting to Ko Pha Ngan

Boat services to Ko Pha Ngan are even more changeable than those to Ko Samui and Ko Tao. Politicking for landing concessions, variable passenger demand and seasonal fluctuation combine to make the picture changeable and unreliable, but the services listed below seem the most dependable.

The slowest **ferry** from the Gulf coast leaves Ban Don pier in **Surat Thani** at 11pm every night for the ferry pier at Thong Sala (7hr; B200); tickets are available from the pier on the day of departure. One Songserm express boat a day runs from Tha Thong to Thong Sala (4hr; B200 including transport to the pier). Three express boats a day do the 45-minute trip from Na Thon on **Ko Samui** (B100), while two vehicle ferries cover the same route for the same price (1hr 10min). Two vehicle ferries a day sail from Don Sak, 68km east of Surat Thani, to Thong Sala (2hr 30min; B120), with connecting buses from Surat to Don Sak, run by Samui Tour (B50 air-con, B40 ordinary). Small boats also shuttle between Samui and the eastern side of Pha Ngan (see p.254), and speed boats from Bophut, Maenam and Nathon on Samui call in at Thong Sala after thirty minutes (B250) on their way to Ko Tao.

Three kinds of vessel run between Ko Pha Ngan and **Ko Tao**, though from roughly June to November they are occasionally cancelled due to bad weather. At least two speed boats a day cover the distance in 50min (B350), two express boats a day take 1hr 30min (B225), and one slow boat spends 3hr over it (B150). **From Bangkok**, bus and train packages similar to those for getting to Ko Samui are available (see p.254).

# Thong Sala and the south coast

Like the capital of Samui, **THONG SALA** is a port of entrance and little more, where the incoming ferries are met by touts sent to escort travellers to bungalows elsewhere on the island. In front of the pier, transport to the rest of the island (songthaews, jeeps and motorbike taxis) congregates by a dusty row of banks, travellers' restaurants, supermarkets, scuba-diving outfits and motorbike (from B150 a day) and jeep (B1000) rental places. If you go straight ahead from the pier, you can turn right onto the town's high street, a leafy mix of shops and houses that's ghostly and windswept at night. A short way down here you'll find laundries and, set back on the west side of the street, the multi-talented Phangan Batik (daily 10am–10pm; ☎077/377254, ⓦwww. kohphangan.com), which, besides selling batiks, rents out good-quality mountain bikes (B100 a day) and offers internet access (B100 per hr). Further on are a couple of clinics and, about 500m from the pier, the post office (Mon–Fri 8.30am–noon & 1–4.30pm, Sat 9am–noon). Thong Sala's sprinkling of travel agents can organize train and plane tickets, and visa extensions, and they sometimes put together trips to Ang Thong National Marine Park for B550 a head (see p.256). The island's hospital (☎077/377034) lies 3km north of town, on the inland road towards Mae Hat, while the police station (☎077/377114) is nearly 2km up the Ban Chaloaklam road.

In the vicinity of Thong Sala, an easy excursion can be made to the grandiosely termed Than Sadet–Ko Pha Ngan National Park, which contains **Pang waterfall**, Pha Ngan's biggest drop, and a stunning viewpoint overlooking the south and west of the island. The park lies 4km northeast of Thong Sala off the road to Chaloaklam – if you don't have a bike, take a Chaloaklam-bound songthaew as far as Ban Madeuawaan, and then it's a one-kilometre signposted walk east. A roughly circular trail has been laid out through the park, as mapped out by the signboard in the car park. The main fall – bouncing down in stages over the hard, grey stone – is a steep 250-metre walk up a forest path. The trail then continues for over 1km upriver beyond the falls, before skirting through thick rainforest to the viewpoint and back to the car park in a couple of hours.

The long, straight **south coast** is well served by songthaews and motorbike taxis from Thong Sala, and is lined with bungalows, especially around **Ban Khai**, to take the overspill from nearby Hat Rin. It's hard to recommend staying here, however: the beaches are mediocre by Thai standards, and the coral reef which hugs the length of the shoreline gets in the way of swimming.

On a quiet hillside above **Ban Tai**, 4km from Thong Sala, **Wat Khao Tham** holds ten-day meditation retreats most months of the year (B2900 per person to cover food; minimum age 20); the American and Australian teachers emphasize compassion and loving kindness as the basis of mental development. Only forty people can attend each retreat (they're especially heavily subscribed Dec–March), so it's best to pre-register; for further information, write to Wat Khao Tham, PO Box 18, Ko Pha Ngan, Surat Thani 84280, or go to ⓦwww.watkowtahm.org, where the schedule of retreats is posted.

If you need to **stay** around Thong Sala, walk 800m north out of town to *Siriphun* (☎077/377140, ☎377242; ❸–❺). The owner is helpful, the food very good and the bungalows are clean and well positioned along the beach; all have showers and mosquito screens on the windows, and an extra wad of baht buys air-con and one of the island's few bathtubs. Alternatively, *Charm Beach Resort*, a friendly, sprawling place only 1500m southeast of Thong Sala (☎077/377165 or 377412; ❶–❺), has a wide variety of decent bungalows and good Thai food.

The incongruous white high-rise overshadowing Thong Sala's pier is the *Pha Ngan Chai Hotel* (ⓣ & ⓕ077/377068; ➏), makes a fair stab at international-standard features, with air-conditioning, warm water, TVs, mini-bars and, in some rooms, sea-view balconies.

## Hat Rin

**HAT RIN** is now firmly established as the major **rave** venue in Southeast Asia, especially in the high season of December and January, but every month of the year people flock in for the full moon party (ⓦwww.thaisite.com/fullmoon-party) – something like *Apocalypse Now* without the war. There's a more sedate side to Hat Rin's alternative scene, too, with old- and new-age hippies packing out the t'ai chi, yoga and meditation classes, and helping consume the drugs that are readily available. Drug-related horror stories are common currency round here, and many of them are true: dodgy Ecstasy, MDMA omelettes, speed punch, diet pills, and special teas containing the local fungus, *hed khi kwai* (buffalo-shit mushrooms), put an average of two farangs a month into hospital for psychiatric treatment. The local authorities have started clamping down on the trade in earnest, setting up a permanent police box at Hat Rin, instigating regular roadblocks and bungalow searches, and drafting in scores of police (both uniformed and plain-clothes) on full-moon nights. It doesn't seem to have dampened the fun, only made travellers a lot more circumspect (the police's going rate for escaping a minor possession charge is a B50,000 "fine").

Hat Rin occupies the flat neck of Pha Ngan's southeast headland, which is so narrow that the resort comprises two back-to-back beaches, joined by transverse roads at the north and south ends. The eastern beach, usually referred to as **Sunrise**, or Hat Rin Nok (Outer Hat Rin), is what originally drew visitors here, a classic curve of fine white sand between two rocky slopes, where the swimming's good and there's even some coral at the southern end to explore. This is the centre of the action, with a solid line of beachside bars, restaurants and bungalows tucked under the palm trees. **Sunset** beach, or Hat Rin Noi (Inner Hat Rin), which for much of the year is littered with flotsam, looks ordinary by comparison but has plenty of quieter accommodation.

### Practicalities

The awkwardness of **getting to Hat Rin** in the past helped to maintain its individuality, but this is changing now that the road in from Ban Khai has been paved. Songthaews and motorbike taxis from Thong Sala now cover the steep roller-coaster route – take care if you're driving your own motorbike. The easiest approach of all, however, if you're coming from Ko Samui, or even Surat Thani, is by direct boat from Samui's north coast: three boats a day (currently 10.30am, 1pm & 4pm; B100) cross to Sunset beach from Bangrak in under an hour, and occasional longtails cover the Maenam–Hat Rin–Thong Nai Pan route.

The area behind and between the beaches – especially around what's known as Chicken Corner, where the southern transverse road meets the road along the back of Sunrise – is crammed with small shops and businesses: there are clinics, a post office (by Chicken Corner), secondhand bookstores, travel agents, motorbike rental places (from B150 a day), offices with expensive overseas phone facilities, bank currency-exchange booths, even a gym, tattooists and video-game arcades. Dozens of places offer **internet access**, but your best bet is probably *Bulan Cyber Café* (ⓣ077/375201, ⓔbulancybercafe@hotmail.com) off the southern transverse road towards the pier on Sunset.

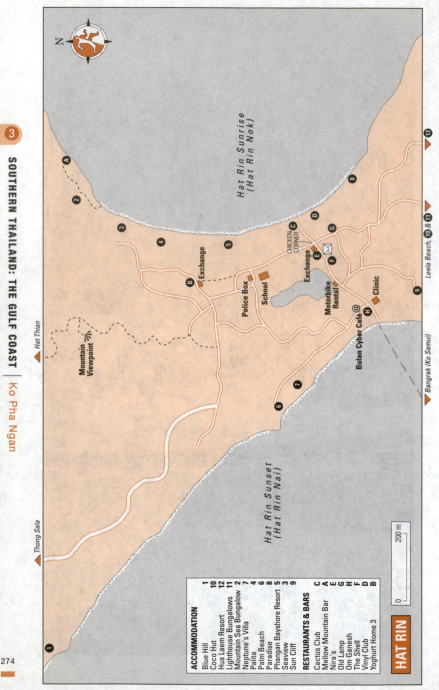

Thong Sala

Hat Thian

N

Mountain
Viewpoint

Hat Rin Sunrise
(Hat Rin Nok)

A

2

3

4

5

Exchange

B

Police Box

School

CHICKEN
CORNER

C

D

G

E

F

Exchange

Motorbike
Rental

Bulan Cyber Café @

H

Clinic

Leela Beach, 10 & 11

9

12

8

Bangrak (Ko Samui)

7

6

Hat Rin Sunset
(Hat Rin Nai)

0          200 m

ACCOMMODATION
Blue Hill                     1
Coco Hut                     10
Hua Laem Resort             12
Lighthouse Bungalows        11
Mountain Sea Bungalow        2
Neptune's Villa              7
Palita                       4
Palm Beach                   6
Paradise                     8
Phangan Bayshore Resort      5
Seaview                      3
Sun Cliff                    9

RESTAURANTS & BARS
Cactus Club                  C
Mellow Mountain Bar          A
Nira's                       E
Old Lamp                     G
Om Ganesh                    H
The Shell                    F
Vinyl Club                   D
Yoghurt Home 3               B

HAT RIN

## Accommodation

For most of the year, Hat Rin has enough bungalows to cope, but on **full-moon nights** as many as eight thousand revellers turn up. There's a little over three thousand rooms on the whole island, so your options are either to arrive early, to forget about sleep altogether or to hitch up with one of the many party boats (about B300 per person) organized by guest houses and restaurants on Ko Samui, especially on Bangrak and Bophut, which usually leave at 9pm and return around dawn. Even at other times, staying on **Sunrise** is often expensive and noisy, though a few places can be recommended. On **Sunset**, the twenty or more resorts are laid out in orderly rows, and are especially quiet and inexpensive between June and September.

**Blue Hill**, at the far northern end of Sunset, a 20min walk from Chicken Corner. Quiet spot run by a friendly, laid-back couple, with slighly ramshackle en-suite bungalows, good, cheap food in generous portions, and great views of the sunset and across to Samui. Catch a songthaew or motorbike taxi to *Bird Bungalows*, then walk northwest for 5min along the beach. ❷

**Coco Hut**, Leela Beach, out towards the lighthouse on the west side of the headland ☏ 077/375369, ⓦ www.cocohut.com. On a clean, quiet stretch of beach, about a 20min walk from Chicken Corner along a well-signposted route, these newly built bungalows are roomy and bright; internet access is available. The owners were building a 24-room guest-house extension next door at the time of writing. ❻

**Hua Laem Resort**, about 1km south along the coast from Sunrise ☏ 077/375222. Reached by following signs from Chicken Corner which take you along a well-maintained cliffside walk, offering stunning views across the whole of Hat Rin Sunrise below. Set in a charming, secluded spot, rooms are basic but in good order and clean (some have private balconies); the owners are friendly and obliging and the panoramic restaurant offers good, cheap food. ❷

**Lighthouse Bungalows**, on the far southwestern tip of the headland ⓔ Lighthouse_bg@hotmail.com. A 30min walk from Chicken Corner, the last section along a rickety wooden walkway over the rocky shoreline, which can be a bit disconcerting at night. At this friendly haven, wooden bungalows, sturdily built to withstand the wind and backed by trail-filled jungle, either share bathrooms or have their own. The restaurant food is varied and tasty. ❶–❸

**Mountain Sea Bungalow**, at the quieter northern end of Sunrise. A great spot, bungalows rising up on the rocks at the end of the beach, with verandas to take in the views. Set in the very

peaceful, shady garden, all have bathrooms and fans. ❸

**Neptune's Villa**, near the small promontory at the centre of Sunset ☏ 01/956 3575. A popular, laid-back place in grassy, shady grounds giving onto the beach. Rooms are basic but cheap – pay extra if you want a Western-style toilet. ❷–❸

**Palita**, at the northern end of Sunrise ☏ 077/375170, ⓔ palitas9@hotmail.com. Clean, well-run place with en-suite bungalows (some aircon) giving on to the beach, and large, simple, better-value huts (some with their own bathrooms) among the coconut palms behind. The food gets rave reviews. ❶–❻

**Palm Beach**, on and around the tiny head at the centre of Sunset ☏ 077/375240. This place is typical of the establishments here, but offers a little more room as it spreads over the headland. In a peaceful setting, the clean, sturdy wooden bungalows, most of them fronting the sand, either share bathrooms or have their own. ❷–❸

**Paradise**, spread over the far southern end of Sunrise and up the slope behind ☏ 077/375244. Well-established place, with a good restaurant – the original full moon party began here, and it's still a party focus once a month. All bungalows are en suite and some of the cheaper hillside options offer fine views over the bay from their verandas. ❸–❺

**Phangan Bayshore Resort**, on the middle of Sunrise ☏ 077/ 375227, ⓕ 375226. An upmarket, well-ordered place, though staff seem somewhat jaded and service is brusque. Big bungalows with spacious verandas, some with air-con, are set on a green lawn, shaded with palms. ❺–❻

**Seaview**, at the quieter northern end of Sunrise ☏ 077/375160. On a big plot of shady land, this clean, orderly place is a similar setup to *Palita* next door. Simple, en-suite huts at the back, posher bungalows (some air-con) beachside. ❸–❻

**Sun Cliff**, high up on the tree-lined slope above the south end of Sunset ☎077/375134. Friendly place with great views of the south coast and Ko Samui, and a wide range of bright, well-maintained bungalows, some with large balconies, fridges, hot water and air-con. ❷–❻

## Eating and nightlife

As well as good simple Thai fare at some of the bungalows, Hat Rin sports an unnerving choice of world **foods** for somewhere so remote, and vegetarians are unusually well provided for. All-day breakfasts of croissants, cakes and good coffee at *Nira's* bakery café near Chicken Corner are especially popular (the bakery shop stays open 24hr), as well as at *Yoghurt Home 3* behind the north end of Sunrise, which offers home-made yoghurt in many combinations, as well as newspapers and generous servings of veggie food. Also worth seeking out are comparative old-timer *The Shell* on the southern transverse, for reasonably priced pasta; *Om Ganesh*, an excellent Indian restaurant on the same street with cheerful service, whether eat-in or delivered to your bungalow (☎077/375123); and *The Old Lamp*, just south of Chicken Corner, where simple but delicious Western and Thai food is served at relaxing low tables.

**Nightlife** normally centres around the bars and clubs at the south end of Sunrise – notably the *Cactus Club* for pop/handbag rave and the *Vinyl Club* for heavy trance – which pump out music onto their indoor dance-floors and low-slung beach tables. Up the hill behind the southern end of Sunrise, the *Back Yard* nightclub makes a good alternative venue, with a large balcony area overlooking the beach; this is where the full moon party continues into the next day and beyond. For somewhere to chill, head for *Mellow Mountain Bar*, which occupies a great position up in the rocks on the north side of Sunrise beyond *Seaview Bungalows*, and has an eclectic play-list, from drum 'n' bass to ambient. On full-moon night itself, *Paradise* styles itself as the party host, but the mayhem spreads along most of Sunrise, fuelled by hastily erected drinks stalls and sound systems.

## The east coast

North of Hat Rin, the rocky, exposed **east coast** stretches as far as Ao Thong Nai Pan, the only centre of development. No roads run along this coast, only a rough, steep, fifteen-kilometre trail, which starts from Hat Rin's northern transverse road (signposted) and runs reasonably close to the shore, occasionally dipping down into pristine sandy coves with a smattering of bungalows. In season (roughly Jan–Sept), if the weather's good enough, boats run to the east coast beaches (occasionally as far as Hat Khuat) from Hat Rin, some of them starting from Thong Sala or Maenam on Ko Samui, or you can arrange a boat on Sunrise if you're staying at one of the bungalows up the coast (B50 per head to *The Sanctuary*, for example). A few of the resorts on Sunrise, such as *Paradise*, organize occasional boat trips with snorkelling and fishing up this coast (typically B300 a head including dinner); otherwise you can splash out on chartering your own longtail (around B1500 to Thong Nai Pan and back).

About ninety minutes up the trail, **HAT THIAN**, a shady bay that's good for snorkelling, has established a reputation as a quiet alternative to Hat Rin. Accommodation is available at the friendly *Haad Tien Resort* (contact *Yoghurt Home 3* in Hat Rin, ☎01/229 3919, for further details, or go to ⓦwww.haadtien-resort.com; ❷), with well-built en-suite wooden bungalows on the slope above the beach; and at the even mellower *Sanctuary* (in Bangkok ☎02/551 9082, ⓦwww.kohphangan.com/sanctuary; ❸–❺), which offers a wider range of en-suite bungalows, as well as dorm accommodation (B60), and good vegetarian fare and seafood, and hosts courses in yoga, meditation, massage and the like.

Steep, desolate **HAT SADET**, 12km up the trail from Hat Rin, has a handful of basic bungalow operations, sited here because of their proximity to **Thaan Sadet**, a boulder-strewn brook which runs out into the sea. The spot was popularized by various kings of Thailand who came here to walk, swim and vandalize the huge boulders by carving their initials on them. A rough road has been bulldozed through the woods above and parallel to Thaan Sadet to connect with the equally rough track from Thong Sala to Ao Thong Nai Pan.

**AO THONG NAI PAN** is a beautiful, semicircular bay backed by steep, green hills, which looks as if it's been bitten out of the island's northeast corner, leaving a tall hump of land dividing the bay into two parts. The southern half has the better sand and a hamlet which now sports a few farang bars and shops; the northern half is quieter, disturbed only by the little bit of surf which squeezes in. Both halves are sheltered and deep enough for swimming, and there's good snorkelling around the central headland and along the outer rim of the bay's southern half. A bumpy nightmare of a dirt road winds its way for 12km over the steep mountains from Ban Tai on the south coast to Thong Nai Pan. Jeeps connect with incoming and outgoing boats at Thong Sala every day, but if there's heavy rain they don't chance it.

Half a dozen resorts line the southern half of the bay, where the friendly *Pingjun* (☎077/299004; ❶–❸) has a range of large, en-suite bungalows with verandas and hammocks on a broad stretch of beach. But with most of the northern beach to themselves, *Star Huts I* and *II* (☎077/299005 or 01/219 1136; ❶–❸) get the nod as Thong Nai Pan's best budget choice: very clean, well-maintained bungalows, with en-suite or shared bathrooms, line the sand, and the friendly owners dish up good food, have canoes for rent and can provide information about local walks. The steep slopes of the central outcrop make a beautiful setting for *Panviman* (☎077/238544, ⓕ238543, ⓦwww. kohphangan.com/panviman; ❼–❽), Ko Pha Ngan's only attempt at a luxury resort, with pricey fan-cooled or air-conditioned cottages and hotel-style rooms. For non-guests it's worth making the climb up here for the view from the restaurant perched over the cliff edge.

## The north coast

The village of **BAN CHALOAKLAM**, on the largest bay on the **north coast**, has long been a famous R&R spot for fishermen from all over the Gulf of Thailand, with sometimes as many as a hundred trawlers littering the broad and sheltered bay. Nowadays it is also a low-key tourist destination, as it can easily be reached from Thong Sala, 10km away, by songthaew or motorbike taxi along the island's best road. Facilities include travel agencies, motorbike rental, clinics, international phone and internet services and scuba outfits. The best bit of beach is at **Hat Khom**, a tiny cove dramatically tucked in under the headland to the east, with a secluded strip of white sand and good coral for snorkelling. For **accommodation**, try *Fanta* (☎077/374065; ❷–❸) at the eastern end of Ban Chaloaklam, on a wide spread of beach backed by casuarinas with clean, en-suite bungalows and good food. Or walk out to friendly *Coral Bay* (☎01/677 7241; ❶–❹), which has plenty of space and great views on the grassy promontory dividing Hat Khom from the rest of Ao Chaloaklam. The sturdy bungalows range from simple affairs with mosquito nets and shared bathrooms to large pads with funky bathrooms built into the rock; snorkelling equipment is available to make the most of Hat Khom's reef.

If the sea is not too rough, longtail boats run three times a day for most of the year from Ban Chaloaklam to secluded **HAT KHUAT** (Bottle Beach), the best of the beaches on the north coast, sitting between steep hills in a perfect cup of a bay; you could also walk there along a testing trail from Hat Khom in around ninety minutes. The four friendly resorts here are all owned by the same extended family, so there's little to choose between them. The original is *Bottle Beach* (☎01/229 4762; **❶–❸**), which has smart beachfront bungalows, tightly packed huts behind and highly recommended food.

## The west coast

Pha Ngan's **west coast** has attracted about the same amount of development as the forgettable south coast, but the landscape here is more attractive and varied, broken up into a series of long sandy inlets with good sunset views over the islands to the west; most of the bays, however, are sheltered by reefs which can keep the sea too shallow for a decent swim, especially between April and October. The roads from Thong Sala as far up as Hat Yao are in decent condition, but routes beyond that as far as Ao Mae Hat (which is best reached from Ban Chaloaklam on the north coast), especially the side roads down to Hat Salad, have not as yet been similarly upgraded, and are testing if you're on a bike. Motorbike taxis run as far as Hat Yao; songthaews, jeeps or even boats cover the rest.

The first bay north of Thong Sala, Ao Wogtum (aka Hinkong), yawns wide across a featureless expanse which turns into a mud flat when the sea retreats behind the reef barrier at low tide. The nondescript bay of **AO SEETHANU** beyond is home to the excellent *Loy Fah* (☎077/377319 or 01/979 2050; **❶–❹**), a well-run place which commands good views from its perch on top of Seethanu's steep southern cape, and offers decent snorkelling and swimming from the rocks; lodgings range from simple huts with mosquito nets and showers, to concrete cottages with verandas and chairs.

Continuing north, there's a surprise in store in the shape of **Laem Son Lake**, a beautiful, tranquil stretch of clear water cordoned by pines which spread down to the nearby beach. Under the shade of the pines, the rudimentary en-suite huts of *Bovy Resort* (**❶**) can only be recommended for their beachfront peace and quiet. *Seethanu Bungalows* (☎077/274106 for the phone booth outside the restaurant, ✉seetanubungalow@hotmail.com; **❷–❻**), actually round the next headland on the small bay of **AO CHAOPHAO**, is a lively spot with a popular restaurant; sturdy, characterful wooden bungalows (all en-suite) are arrayed around a slightly messy garden, with the more expensive options by the beach. Next door, *Seaflower* (**❶–❸**) is quieter and more congenial, set in a well-tended garden: bungalows with their own bathrooms vary in price according to their size and how far you have to roll out of bed to land on the beach, and the veggie and meaty food is excellent. If you're feeling adventurous, ask the owner about the occasional three-day longtail-boat treks to Ang Thong National Marine Park (see p.256), which involve snorkelling, caving, catching your own seafood, and sleeping in hammocks or rough shelters (B1800 per person). Two doors away, friendly *Haad Chao Phao* (**❷**) is also recommended: in a shady garden, the ten clean and well-kept en-suite bungalows (all with mosquito nets and verandas) lead down to an attractive patch of beach.

Beyond Chaophao, livelier **HAT YAO** offers a long, gently curved beach, a diving outfit and a nonstop line of bungalows, with a swankier resort under construction towards its north end. Good bets here are *Ibiza* (☎01/229 4721; **❷**), with smart, airy en-suite bungalows in a spacious garden, and the friendly

Bay View (☏01/229 4780; **❶**–**❹**), which offers good food and views from a wide range of bungalows on the quiet northern headland. The only bay to the north of that, **HAT SALAD**, is probably the best of the bunch: it's pretty and quiet, with good snorkelling off the northern tip. *My Way* and *Salad Hut* (both **❶**–**❷**) are relaxing places for chilling out here, featuring primitive bungalows with shared or en-suite bathrooms, and recommended, though moderately expensive, food.

On the island's northwest corner, **AO MAE HAT** is good for swimming and snorkelling among the coral which lines the sand causeway to the tiny islet of Ko Maa. The bay, which is most easily reached by the road west from Ban Chaloaklam, also supports several decent bungalow resorts, including *Island View Cabana* (☏077/377144; **❶**–**❸**), a popular place with a well-positioned, thatch-roofed restaurant, snooker tables and a variety of well-designed bungalows shaded by casuarina trees.

# Ko Tao

**KO TAO** (Turtle Island) is so named because its outline resembles a turtle nose-diving towards Ko Pha Ngan, 40km to the south. The rugged shell of the turtle, to the east, is crenellated with secluded coves where one or two bungalows hide among the rocks. On the western side, the turtle's underbelly is a long curve of classic beach, facing Ko Nang Yuan, a beautiful Y-shaped group of islands offshore, also known as Ko Hang Tao (Turtle's Tail Island). The 21 square kilometres of granite in between is topped by dense forest on the higher slopes and dotted with huge boulders that look as if they await some Easter Island sculptor. It's fun to spend a couple of days exploring the network of rough trails, after which you'll probably know all 750 of the island's inhabitants. Ko Tao is now best known as a venue for **scuba diving**, with most companies at Mae Hat, the main village and arrival point; see the box on p.282 for further details.

The island is the last and most remote of the archipelago which continues the line of Surat Thani's mountains into the sea. There were over ninety sets of **bungalows** at the latest count (still not enough at times during the peak season from December to March, when travellers occasionally have to sleep on the beach until a hut becomes free) concentrated along the west and south sides. Some still provide the bare minimum, with plain mattresses for beds, mosquito nets and shared bathrooms, but most places can now offer en-suite bathrooms and a few comforts, and there are even a few air-con chalets knocking around. Electricity still comes from private generators, usually evenings only, with few kept running 24 hours a day. If you're just **arriving**, it might be a good idea to go with one of the touts who meet the ferries at Mae Hat, with pickup or boat on hand, since at least you'll know their bungalows aren't full or closed – the former is possible from December to March, the latter from June to August; failing that, call ahead as even the remotest bungalows now have mobile phones. Some resorts with attached scuba-diving operations have been known to refuse guests who don't sign up for diving trips or courses; on the other hand, some of the bigger dive companies now have their own functional lodgings, staying at which is often included in the price of a dive course.

**Food** can be a little pricey and limited in range because most of it is brought across on the ferry boats. As is the case on Ko Pha Ngan, at some of

Chumphon ◄

Ko Pha Ngan, Ko Samui & Surat Thani ◄

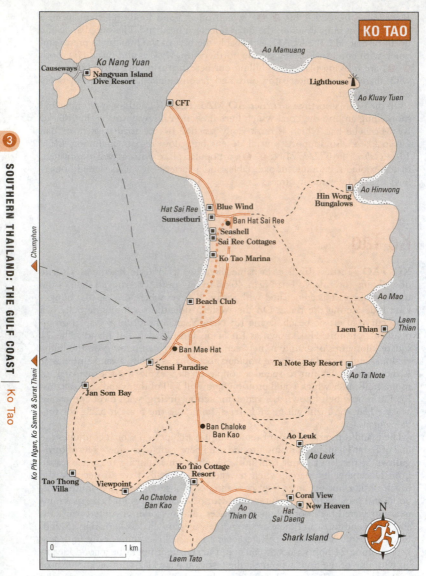

**KO TAO**

the cheapest resorts, where they make their money from food more than accommodation, owners have been known to kick out guests who don't eat at the in-house restaurant.

The **weather** is much the same as on Pha Ngan and Samui, but being that bit further off the mainland, Ko Tao feels the effect of the southwest monsoon more: June to October can have strong winds and rain, with a lot of debris blown onto the windward coasts.

## Getting to Ko Tao

There are three different boat services **from Chumphon** to Ko Tao: the Numhasin **speed boat** (departs daily in fine weather only at 7.30am; 1hr 45min; B400); the **Songserm express boat** (departs daily from January through October at 7.30am; 2hr 30min; B400); and the **slow boat** (departs daily in all but the very worst weather at midnight; 6hr; B200). **Tickets** for all boats can be bought in Chumphon at any guest house or travel agent, all of whom provide transport to the port and some of whom also offer free showering facilities and video shows between connections; see the Chumphon account on p.245 for full details.

Three kinds of vessel run between Thong Sala on **Ko Pha Ngan** and Ko Tao: at least two speed boats a day (50min; B350), two express boats a day (1hr 30min; B225) and one slow boat (3hr; B150). The speed boats originate at Bophut, Maenam and Na Thon on **Ko Samui** (total journey time to Ko Tao 1hr 30min; B450–550). There's also a night boat from **Surat Thani**, departing at 11pm (9hr; B400).

These services fluctuate according to demand and so on, and in high season extra boats may appear. All voyages to and from Ko Tao are also at the mercy of the weather, especially between June and November; plenty of travellers have missed onward connections through being stranded on the island, so it's best not to plan to visit at the end of your holiday.

## Island transport

You can **get around** easily enough on foot, but there are roads of sorts now to most of the resorts, though some are still four-wheel drive only; motorbike taxis and pickups (B20–50 per person, more for 4WD), and even rental mopeds (B150–200 a day), are available in Mae Hat. Mountain **bikes** can be rented for around B100 per day from the island's all-purpose fixer, Mr J, with outlets just north of Mae Hat by the school and at Ao Chaloke Ban Kao behind *Buddha View Dive Resort*. **Longtail-boat taxis** are available at Mae Hat or through your bungalow, or you could splash out on your own **round-island boat tour**, allowing you to explore the coastline fully with stops for snorkelling and swimming, including a visit to Ko Nang Yuan (about B1500 for the boat for the day); alternatively you could hook up with a group tour, again through your resort or at Mae Hat (usually about 5hr; B250–300 a head).

# The west coast and Ko Nang Yuan

All boats to the island dock at **MAE HAT**, a small, lively village with a few seafront restaurants, clinics, a Krung Thai Bank currency-exchange booth (daily 9am–3pm; cash advances on credit cards available) and a post office in one of the larger supermarkets (daily 8.30am–10pm), with phone, currency-exchange and poste restante facilities. Worth singling out among the **eating and drinking** options here are the *Swiss Bakery*, 100m straight ahead from the pier up the hill, serving good coffee and a wide range of pastries and savouries, including delicious croissants; and *Whitening*, a cool restaurant, bar and nightclub, 200m south of the pier overlooking the bay, which dishes up interesting and tasty Thai and Western food.

## South of Mae Hat

For somewhere good to stay on the southern edge of Mae Hat, try *Sensi Paradise Resort* (☎077/456244, ℱ456245), which has taken over the former *Coral Beach Resort* and now sprawls over the lower slopes of the headland to

## Scuba diving off Ko Tao

Some of the best **dive sites** in Thailand are found around Ko Tao. The island is blessed with outstandingly clear (visibility up to 35m) and deep water relatively close to shore, and provides near-perfect conditions for a wide range of coral species. On top of that, there's a kaleidoscopic array of marine life, and you may be lucky enough to encounter whale sharks, barracudas, leatherback turtles and pilot whales. Diving is possible at any time of the year, with sheltered sites on one or other side of the island in any season – the changeover from southwest to northeast monsoon in November is the worst time, while visibility is best from April to July, in September (usually best of all) and October.

To meet demand, Ko Tao has about thirty **dive companies**, nearly all of them based at Mae Hat, Hat Sai Ree or Ao Chaloke Ban Kao. The companies have by agreement set fixed prices across the island: by far the most popular course, PADI's four-day "Openwater" for beginners, costs B7800 at the time of writing; one-day introductions to diving are also available for B1500, as is the full menu of PADI courses, up to "Dive Master"; for qualified divers, one dive costs B800, a ten-dive package B5500, with fifteen percent discounts if you bring your own gear. Some of the companies, including Easy Divers, will take **snorkellers** along on their dive trips, providing good-quality snorkel, mask and fin sets for B300 a day.

With no distinction in price, other factors come into play when **choosing a company** in such a competitive market. Make sure that the gear and the boat are well maintained and check out the kind of instruction and whether you get on with the instructors. Companies often throw in your accommodation for the duration of an Openwater course, but ask exactly how long it's for (3 or 4 nights), where it is and what it's like; some will also throw in a free fun dive at the end of the course; free snacks and drinking water should be provided on the boat. PADI Five-Star Dive Centres, all of which are committed to looking after the environment, involving maintaining their own dive sites as well as taking part in regular, organized clean-ups around the island, include Scuba Junction on Hat Sai Ree ⓦwww.scuba -junction.com, Big Blue at Mae Hat ☏077/456050, ⓦwww.bigbluediving.com, Easy Divers at Mae Hat ☏077/456010, ⓦwww.thaidive.com and on Ko Nang Yuan (see

the south of the village. It offers some of the best upmarket accommodation on the island, with well-designed, air-con wooden cottages, including some large family units, in pretty, flower-covered sloping grounds (**❾**), as well as cheaper bungalows with shared bathrooms (**❸**); five minutes beyond the edge of the property, there's a sandy, palm-sheltered cove for secluded sunbathing and swimming.

In this direction, also handy for the village (15min walk) is *Jan Som Bay* (☏077/502502–10; **❹**), a characterful place overlooking a beautiful rocky beach, with snorkels and fins to rent. In traditional Thai style, the large wooden chalets have only shutters on the windows and slits under the roof to catch the breeze (bed nets rather than screens keep the mosquitoes off), as well as large verandas with deckchairs and tables.

A good way further down the coast (40min walk from Mae Hat or B50 in a taxi-boat), *Tao Thong Villa* (☏077/456078; **❶**) offers plenty of shady seclusion and good snorkelling and swimming. Sturdy bungalows with decent mosquito nets are dotted around a rocky outcrop and the slope behind, with a breezy restaurant on the small, sandy isthmus in between.

### North of Mae Hat

Five minutes' walk north of Mae Hat, sheltering on the south side of a small promontory, the quiet and friendly *Beach Club* caters to a wide range of budg-

p.284), and Planet Scuba at Mae Hat and next to *Sai Ree Cottages* on Hat Sai Ree ℡01/229 4336, Ⓦ www.planet-scuba.net.

## Main dive sites

**Ko Nang Yuan**. Perfect for beginners and good for snorkelling; hard coral, sponges and granite boulders.

**White Rock (Hin Khao)**. Sarcophyton leather coral turns the granite boulders here white when seen from the surface; also wire, antipatharian and colourful soft corals, and gorgonian sea fans. Plenty of fish, including titan triggerfish.

**Shark Island**. Large granite boulders with acropora, wire and bushy antipatharian corals, sea whips, gorgonian sea fans and barrel sponges. Reef fish include angelfish, parrotfish and groupers; occasional whale sharks.

**Hinwong Pinnacle**. Generally for experienced divers, often with strong currents. Similar scenery to White Rock, over a larger area, with beautiful soft coral at 30m depth. A wide range of fish, including blue-spotted fantail stingrays and large groupers.

**Chumphon** or **Northwest Pinnacle**. A granite pinnacle, over 30m in depth, its top covered in anemones, with the possibility of exceptional visibility. Barrel sponges, tree and antipatharian corals at deeper levels; a wide variety of fish, in large numbers, attract local fishermen; occasional whale sharks and huge groupers.

**Southwest Pinnacle**. Probably the top site in terms of visibility, scenery and marine life. A huge pyramid-like pinnacle rising to 6m below the surface, its upper part covered in anemones, with smaller pinnacles around; at lower levels, granite boulders, barrel sponges, sea whips, bushy antipatharian and tree corals. Big groupers and snappers; occasionally, large stingrays, leopard and sand sharks, swordfish, finback whales and whale sharks.

**Sail Rock (Hin Bai)**. Visibility of up to 25m, and a ten-metre-deep underwater chimney. Antipatharian corals, both bushes and whips, and carpets of anemones. Large groupers, snappers and fusiliers, bright blue-ringed angelfish, curious batfish and juvenile clown sweetlips; occasional whale sharks.

ets (℡ and Ⓕ 077/456222, Ⓔ beachclub@kohtao.com; ❸−❼): choose between clean, en-suite thatched huts, some with verandas on the beach, and smart concrete chalets with cold-water bathrooms, fridges and fans or air-conditioning; **windsurfers** can be rented here for B300–400 per hour.

Beyond the promontory, you'll find **Hat Sai Ree**, Ko Tao's only long beach. The strip of white sand stretches for 2km in a gentle curve, backed by a smattering of coconut palms. Over twenty bungalow resorts have set up shop here, and a small village, **BAN HAT SAI REE**, with bars, supermarkets, a clinic and a bakery, has evolved at its northern end. Towards the midpoint of the beach, twenty minutes' walk from Mae Hat, *Ko Tao Marina* (℡077/456173, Ⓕ456213, Ⓔ kohtaomarina@hotmail.com; ❸−❻) is a well-maintained, family-run operation that offers small bungalows with mosquito nets, fans and their own bathrooms, or larger, swankier affairs with mosquito screens, and a good beachside restaurant. In another shady, flower-strewn garden a couple of doors up, *Sai Ree Cottages* (℡077/456126; ❶−❷) has primitive huts and sturdy en-suite bungalows by the beach, and serves excellent grub; a branch of Planet Scuba behind the cottages rents out two-person **sea kayaks** at B400 per half-day or B700 per day. The spacious, tidy compound next door belongs to *Seashell Resort* (℡077/456271 or 01/229 4621), a friendly, well-run place under the tall palm trees; it offers internet access as well as very smart, sturdy bungalows, with en-suite showers and mosquito screens, either with fans (**3**) or with air-con and baths (**6**). A hundred metres or so further up the beach by the village is the new *Sunsetburi Resort* (℡077/456266, ℉377801; **7**), Ko Tao's most upmarket lodgings, with its own large swimming pool and air-con, hot water and mini-bars in smart, modern concrete cottages.

*Blue Wind* (℡077/456116, ⒺBluewind_wa@yahoo.com), next door but one, is another good choice here: the smart, well-kept bungalows are scattered about a shady compound, and the very good beachside restaurant serves up home-made breads, croissants and cakes, as well as Western and Thai meals. The track north of the village ends beyond the beach at secluded *CFT* (**1–4**) on the rocky northwest flank of the island, which offers cheap shacks or en-suite bungalows, and excellent food; there's no beach here, but the views over to Ko Nang Yuan are something else.

## Ko Nang Yuan

One kilometre off the northwest of Ko Tao, **KO NANG YUAN**, a close-knit group of three tiny islands encircled by a ring of easily accessible coral, provides the most spectacular beach scenery in these parts, thanks to the causeway of fine white sand which joins up the islands. Longtail boats scheduled for day-trippers leave Mae Hat and Hat Sai Ree in the morning, returning in the late afternoon (B60 return). A boat also meets incoming and outgoing ferries at Mae Hat, for people staying at the *Nangyuan Island Dive Resort* (℡077/456088–91 or 01/229 5212, ℉077/456093, Ⓦwww.nangyuan.com; **7–9**), which makes the most of its beautiful location, its swanky fan and air-con bungalows spreading over all three islands. Rules to protect the environment here include banning visitors from bringing cans and plastic bottles with them; one of Thailand's foremost diving operations, Easy Divers, works out of the resort.

## The east and south coasts

The sheltered inlets of the **east coast**, most of them containing one or two sets of bungalows, can be reached by boat or four-wheel drive. The most northerly inhabitation here is at **Ao Hinwong**, a deeply recessed bay strewn with large boulders, which has a particularly remote, almost desolate air. Nevertheless, *Hin Wong Bungalows* (℡01/229 4810; **3**) is welcoming and provides good, basic accommodation on a steep, grassy slope above the rocks. In the middle of the coast, the dramatic tiered promontory of **Laem Thian** shelters a tiny beach and a colourful reef on its south side. With the headland to itself, *Laem Thian* (℡01/229 4478; **1–3**) offers simple rooms or comfy bungalows, decent food and a secluded, castaway feel. Laem Thian's coral reef stretches down towards **Ao Ta Note**, a horseshoe inlet sprinkled with boulders and plenty of coarse sand, with the best snorkelling just north of the bay's mouth. The pick of the handful of resorts here is *Ta Note Bay Dive Resort* (℡01/970 4703; **2–5**), whose well-designed wooden bungalows, set among thick bougainvillea, range from simple affairs with mosquito nets, shared bathrooms and no fans, to en-suite chalets with large verandas and views out towards Ko Pha Ngan and Ko Samui; snorkelling equipment and kayaks are available to rent. The last bay carved out of the turtle's shell, **Ao Leuk**, has a well-recessed rocky beach and deep water for swimming and snorkelling. The simple en-suite huts at *Ao Leuk Resort* (**2**) are a bit ramshackle, but they're cheap and enjoy plenty of space and shade in a palm grove.

The **southeast corner** of the island sticks out in a long, thin mole of land, which shelters the sandy beach (Hat Sai Daeng) on one side if the wind's coming from the northeast, or the rocky cove on the other side if it's blowing from the southwest. Straddling the headland is *New Heaven* (℡01/981 2762; ❸), a laid-back, well-equipped place with a good kitchen; its pleasantly idiosyncratic en-suite bungalows enjoy plenty of elbow room and good views. The only other resort on Hat Sai Daeng is the less characterful, but adequate *Coral View* (℡01/970 0378 or 970 2280; ❸–❹), with a choice between concrete and wooden bungalows on the slope behind the beach and a breezy, elevated restaurant.

The **south coast** is sheltered from the worst of both monsoons, and consequently **Ao Chaloke Ban Kao** has seen a fair amount of development, with several dive resorts taking advantage of the large, sheltered bay. *Buddha View Dive Resort* – which even has its own swimming pool for training divers – rents out one-person (B250/B400 per half-day/full day) and two-person (B400/B700) **kayaks**. Two accommodation options stand out from the crowd here. Run by a friendly, young bunch and home to Big Bubble Diving, *Viewpoint Bungalows* (℡ & ℻01/210 2207, ℮bigbubble@hotmail.com; ❶–❸) sprawl along the western side of the bay; the well-built, clean bungalows have shared or en-suite bathrooms, the best of them with verandas overlooking the sunset from the headland. *Ko Tao Cottage Resort* (℡ & ℻077/456133 or 456198, ℮divektc@samart.co.th; ❹–❻) is one of the island's few stabs at institutionalized luxury and worth a splurge, especially if you're considering scuba diving with its diving school. The cottages, which have verandas, ceiling fans and plain, smart decor (some with sea views and mini-bars), are ranged around a shady garden and restaurant by the beach.

# Nakhon Si Thammarat and around

**NAKHON SI THAMMARAT**, the south's second-largest town, occupies a blind spot in the eyes of most tourists, whose focus is fixed on Ko Samui, 100km to the north. Its neglect is unfortunate, for it's an absorbing place, though a bit short on accommodation and other facilities. The south's major pilgrimage site and home to a huge military base, Nakhon is relaxed, self-confident and sophisticated, well known for its excellent cuisine and traditional handicrafts. The stores on Thanon Thachang are especially good for local nielloware (*kruang tom*), household items and jewellery elegantly patterned in gold or silver on black, and *yan lipao*, sturdy basketware made from intricately woven fern stems of different colours. Nakhon is also the best place in the country to see how Thai shadow plays work, at Suchart Subsin's workshop.

The town is recorded under the name of Ligor (or Lakhon), the capital of the kingdom of Lankasuka, as early as the second century, and classical dance-drama, *lakhon*, is supposed to have been developed here. Well placed for trade with China and southern India, Nakhon was the point through which the Theravada form of Buddhism was imported from Sri Lanka and spread to Sukhothai, the capital of the new Thai state, in the thirteenth century.

Known as *muang phra*, the "city of monks", Nakhon is still the religious capital of the south, and the main centre for **festivals**. The most important of these are the **Tamboon Deuan Sip**, held during the waning of the moon in the tenth lunar month (either September or October), and the **Hae Pha Khun That**, which is held twice a year, on Maha Puja (February full moon – see also p.59) and on Visakha Puja (May full moon – see p.59). The purpose of the former is to pay homage to dead relatives and friends; it is believed that during this fifteen-day period all *pret* – ancestors who have been damned to hell – are allowed out to visit the world, and so their relatives perform a merit-making ceremony in the temples, presenting offerings from the first harvest to ease their suffering. A huge ten-day fair takes place at Sri Nakharin park (on the north side of town towards the airport) at this time, as well as processions, shadow plays and other theatrical performances. The Hae Pha Khun That also attracts people from all over the south, to pay homage to the relics of the Buddha at Wat Mahathat. The ceremonial centrepiece of this festival is the Pha Phra Bot, a strip of yellow cloth many hundreds of metres long, which is carried in a spectacular procession around the chedi.

## The Town

The **town plan** is simple, but puzzling at first sight: it runs in a straight line for 7km from north to south and is rarely more than a few hundred metres wide, a layout originally dictated by the availability of fresh water. The modern centre for businesses and shops sits at the north end around the train station, with the main day market (to the east of the station on Thanon Pak Nakhon) in this food-conscious city displaying a particularly fascinating array of produce that's best around 8 or 9am. To the south, centred on the elegant, traditional mosque on Thanon Karom, lies the old Muslim quarter; south again is the start of the old city walls, of which few remains can be seen, and the historic centre, with the town's main places of interest now set in a leafy residential area.

### Wat Mahathat

Missing out **Wat Mahathat** would be like going to Rome and not visiting St Peter's, for the Buddha relics in the vast chedi make this the south's most

important shrine. Inside the temple cloisters, which have their main entrance facing Thanon Ratchadamnoen about 2km south of the modern centre, the courtyard looks like a surreal ornamental garden, with row upon row of small-er chedis, spiked like bayonets, each surrounded by a box hedge and all in the shadow of the main chedi, the **Phra Boromathat**. This huge, stubby Sri Lankan bell supports a slender, ringed spire, which is in turn topped by a shiny pinnacle said to be covered in 600kg of gold leaf. According to the chronicles, relics of the Buddha were brought here from Sri Lanka two thousand years ago by an Indian prince and princess and enshrined in a chedi. It's undergone plen-ty of face-lifts since: an earlier Srivijayan version, a model of which stands at one corner, is encased in the present twelfth-century chedi. The most recent restoration work, funded by donations from all over Thailand, rescued it from collapse, although it still seems to be leaning dangerously to the southeast. Worshippers head for the north side's vast enclosed stairway, framed by lions and giants, which they liberally decorate with gold leaf to add to the shrine's radiance and gain some merit. In the left-hand shrine at the foot of the stairs here, look out for some fine stuccoes of the life of the Buddha.

The **Viharn Kien Museum** (hours irregular, but usually daily 8.30am–noon & 1–4pm), which extends north from the chedi, is an Aladdin's cave of bric-a-brac, said to house fifty thousand artefacts donated by worshippers, ranging from ships made out of seashells to gold and silver models of the Bodhi Tree. At the entrance to the museum, you'll pass the Phra Puay, an image of the Buddha giving a gesture of reassurance. Women pray to the image when they want to have children, and the lucky ones return to give thanks and to leave photos of their chubby progeny.

Outside the cloister to the south is the eighteenth-century **Viharn Luang**, raised on elegant slanting columns, a beautiful example of Ayutthayan

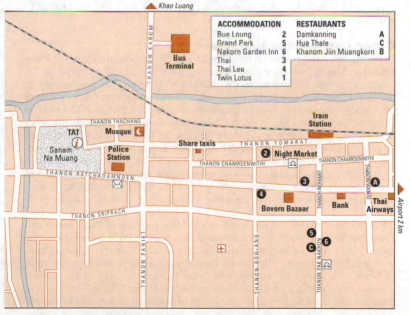

architecture. The interior is austere at ground level, but the red coffered ceiling shines with carved and gilded stars and lotus blooms. Elsewhere in the spacious grounds, cheerful, inexpensive stalls peddle local handicrafts such as shadow puppets, bronze and basketware.

### The National Museum

A few minutes' walk south again from Wat Mahathat, the **National Museum** (Wed–Sun 9am–noon & 1–4.30pm; B30) houses a small but diverse collection, mostly of artefacts from southern Thailand. In the prehistory room downstairs, look out for the two impressive ceremonial bronze kettledrums, dating from the fifth century BC and topped with chunky frogs (the local frogs are said to be the biggest in Thailand and a prized delicacy). Next door are some interesting Hindu finds and many characteristic Buddha images made in imitation of the Phra Buddha Sihing at the city hall, the most revered image in southern Thailand. Among the collections of ceramics and household articles upstairs, you can't miss the seat panel from Rama V's barge, a dazzling example of the nielloware for which Nakhon is famous – the delicate animals and landscapes have been etched onto a layer of gold which covers the silver base, and then picked out by inlaying a black alloy into the background.

### The shadow puppet workshop

The best possible introduction to *nang thalung*, southern Thailand's **shadow puppet theatre**, is to head for 110/18 Soi 3, Thanon Si Thammasok, ten minutes' walk east of Wat Mahathat (☏075/346394): here Suchart Subsin, one of the south's leading exponents of *nang thalung*, and his son have opened up their workshop to the public, and, for a small fee (usually around B50), they'll show you a few scenes from a shadow play in the small open-air theatre. You can also see the intricate process of making the leather puppets and can buy the finished products as souvenirs: puppets sold here are of much better quality and design than those usually found on southern Thailand's souvenir stalls.

### Other shrines and temples

In the chapel of the provincial office on Thanon Ratchadamnoen sits the **Phra Buddha Sihing**, which according to legend was magically created in Sri Lanka in the second century. In the thirteenth century it was sent by ship to the king of Sukhothai, but the vessel sank and the image miraculously floated on a plank to Nakhon. Two other images, one in the National Museum in Bangkok, one in Wat Phra Singh in Chiang Mai, claim to be the authentic Phra Buddha Sihing, but none of the three is in the Sri Lankan style, so they are all probably derived from a lost original. Although similar to the other two in size and shape, the image in Nakhon has a style unique to this area, distinguished by the heavily pleated flap of its robe over the left shoulder, a beaky nose and harsh features, which sit uneasily on the short, corpulent body. The image's plumpness has given the style the name *khanom tom* – "banana and rice pudding".

You're bound to pass the small, red-roofed Hindu shrines of **Phra Isuan** and **Phra Narai** on Thanon Ratchadamnoen, legacies of Nakhon's ancient commercial links with India (hours irregular, but usually Mon–Fri 8.30am–4pm, with a break for lunch). The former houses a lingam, a phallic representation of Shiva worshipped by women who want to conceive, and in its grounds there's a ritual swing, a smaller version of the Sao Ching Cha at Wat Suthat in Bangkok; the latter shelters a life-size image of Narai, an incarnation of Vishnu.

## Shadow puppets

Found throughout southern Asia, **shadow puppets** are one of the oldest forms of theatre, featuring in Buddhist literature as early as 400 BC. The art form seems to have come from India, via Java, to Thailand, where it's called *nang*, meaning "hide": the puppets are made from the skins of water buffalo or cows, which are softened in water, then pounded until almost transparent, before being carved and coloured to represent the characters of the play. The puppets are then manipulated on sticks in front of a bright light, to project their image onto a large white screen, while the story is narrated to the audience.

The grander version of the art, **nang yai** – "big hide", so called because the figures are life-size – deals only with the *Ramayana* story. It's known to have been part of the entertainment at official ceremonies in the Ayutthayan period, but has now almost died out. The more populist version, **nang thalung** – *thalung* is probably a shortening of the town name, Phatthalung (which is just down the road from Nakhon), where this version of the art form is said to have originated – is also in decline now: performances are generally limited to temple festivals, marriages and ordinations, lasting usually from 9pm to dawn. As well as working the sixty-centimetre-high *nang thalung* puppets, the puppet master narrates the story, impersonates the characters, chants and cracks jokes to the accompaniment of flutes, fiddles and percussion instruments. Not surprisingly, in view of this virtuoso semi-improvised display, puppet masters are esteemed as possessed geniuses by their public.

At big festivals, companies often perform the *Ramayana*, sometimes in competition with each other; at smaller events they put on more down-to-earth stories, with stock characters such as the jokers Yor Thong, an angry man with a pot belly and a sword, and Kaew Kop, a man with a frog's head. Yogi, a wizard and teacher, is thought to protect the puppet master and his company from evil spirits with his magic, so he is always the first puppet on at the beginning of every performance.

In an attempt to halt their decline as a form of popular entertainment, the puppet companies are now incorporating modern instruments and characters in modern dress into their shows, and are boosting the love element in their stories. They're fighting a battle they can't win against television and cinemas, although at least the debt owed to shadow puppets has been acknowledged – *nang* has become the Thai word for "movie".

The Brahmin community based at these shrines supplies astrologers to the royal court and priests for the Ploughing Ceremony, held every May in Bangkok.

## Practicalities

Nakhon's **bus terminal** and **train station** are both centrally placed, and even the **airport** is only 2km north of the centre, served by air-con minibus to and from the Thai Airways office at 1612 Thanon Ratchadamnoen (075/342491 or 343874). **Share-taxis** congregate towards the south end of Thanon Yomarat. For getting around Nakhon, small blue **share-songthaews** ply up and down Thanon Ratchadamnoen for B5 a ride.

**TAT** has an office in a restored 1920s government officers' club on Sanam Na Muang (daily 8.30am–4.30pm; 075/346515–6, tatnakon@nrt.cscoms.com), which also covers the provinces of Trang and Phatthalung. The main **post office** (Mon–Fri 8.30am–4.30pm), nearby on Thanon Ratchadamnoen opposite the police station, has an **international phone office** upstairs which is open 24 hours a day.

## Accommodation

Though most of Nakhon's **hotels** are dingy and soulless, there are enough exceptions to get by.

**Bue Loung Hotel**, 1487/19 Soi Luang Muang, Thanon Chamroenwithi ☎ 075/341518, ℱ 343418. Central but reasonably quiet; gets the thumbs-up from visiting businessmen, with a choice of fan or air-con in double or twin rooms. ❷–❸

**Grand Park Hotel**, 1204/79 Thanon Pak Nakhon ☎ 075/317666–73, ℱ 317674. If you're looking for something more upmarket in the centre of town, this newly established place is worth considering – it's large, stylish and bright, and staff are cheery and attentive. ❺

**Nakorn Garden Inn**, 1/4 Thanon Pak Nakhon ☎ 075/313333, ℱ 342926. A rustic but sophisticated haven in a three-storey red-brick building overlooking a tree-shaded yard. Large, smart rooms come with air-con, hot water, cable TV and mini-bars. The best moderately priced option in town. ❹

**Thai Hotel**, 1375 Thanon Ratchadamnoen ☎ 075/341509, ℱ 344858. Formerly top of the range in Nakhon, this large institutional high-rise can still offer clean, reliable, fan-cooled and air-con rooms, though staff can be surly, not to say rude. ❸–❹

**Thai Lee Hotel**, 1130 Thanon Ratchadamnoen ☎ 075/356948. For rock-bottom accommodation, the plain and basic rooms here aren't a bad deal (it's worth asking for a room at the back of the hotel to escape the noise of the main street). ❶

**Twin Lotus**, about 3km southeast of the centre at 97/8 Thanon Patanakarn Kukwang ☎ 075/323777, ℱ 323821. Gets pride of place in Nakhon – though not location; sports five restaurants, a swimming pool and a health club. ❻

## Eating and drinking

Nakhon is a great place for inexpensive **food**. Most famous, and justifiably so, is the lunchtime-only *Khanom Jiin Muangkorn* on Thanon Panyom near Wat Mahathat: the rough-and-ready outdoor restaurant dishes up one of the local specialities, *khanom jiin*, noodles topped with hot, sweet or fishy sauce served with *pak ruam*, a platter of crispy raw vegetables. Also boasting rock-bottom prices for lunch is *Krua Nakhon* in the Bovorn Bazaar on Thanon Ratchadamnoen, a big, rustic pavilion with good *khanom jiin* and other local dishes: *kaeng som*, a mild yellow curry; *kaeng tai plaa*, fish stomach curry; and various *khanom wan*, coconut milk puddings.

Also in Bovorn Bazaar, *Hao Coffee* is a good spot for Thai or Western breakfast or lunch, with a wide selection of coffees, including Thai filter coffee, to wash it down. It's a busy, friendly place, modelled on an old Chinese-style coffee shop, packed full of ageing violins, clocks and other antiques. If you're not in the mood for nostalgic charm, head for the shiny, air-con *Ligor Bakery*, at the entrance to the Bovorn Bazaar, which offers plenty of cakes, decent Western-style breakfasts and good coffees.

The busy night market on Thanon Chamroenwithi near the *Bue Loung Hotel* is great for inexpensive food, such as *yam plaa meuk* and *yam kung*, and people-watching. In the old Muslim quarter, many stalls near the corner of Thanon Karom and Thanon Yomarat sell good Muslim food, such as *roti* (sweet pancake – also available at stalls in and around the night market) and chicken with curried rice.

The best of Nakhon's more conventional **restaurants** is *Hua Thale*, on Thanon Pak Nakhon opposite the *Nakorn Garden Inn* (daily 4–10pm), renowned among locals for its excellent, inexpensive seafood. Run by a friendly Thai who lived in Los Angeles for many years and who will take your order (no English menu), it's plain and very clean, with the day's catch displayed out front and relaxing patio tables out the back. Recommended dishes include whole baked fish and *hoy meng pho op mordin*, large green mussels in a delicious herb soup containing lemon grass, basil and mint. On the corner of Thanon Watkid and Thanon Ratchadamnoen, *Damkanning* is a decent fallback, one of many affordable, popular restaurants with pavement tables in the area.

If you're looking for somewhere to **drink**, head for *99% Rock*, a wooden open-air bar in the Bovorn Bazaar that's popular with Nakhon's sprinkling of expats, or to Thanon Watkid, where a group of congenial bars with names like *Lucky Light* and *Marine Pub* offer live music.

# Khao Luang National Park

Rising to the west of Nakhon Si Thammarat and temptingly visible from all over town, is 1835-metre-high **Khao Luang**, southern Thailand's highest mountain. A huge national park encompasses Khao Luang's jagged green peaks, beautiful streams with numerous waterfalls, tropical rainforest and fruit orchards, as well as the source of the Tapi River, one of the peninsula's main waterways, which flows into the Gulf of Thailand at Surat Thani. **Fauna** here includes macaques, musk deer, civets, binturongs, as well as more difficult to see Malayan tapirs and serows, plus over two hundred bird species. There's an astonishing diversity of **flora** too, notably rhododendrons and begonias, dense mosses, ferns and lichens, plus more than three hundred species of both ground-growing and epiphytic orchids, some of which are unique to the park. The best time to visit is after the rainy season, from January onwards, when there should still be a decent flow in the waterfalls, but the trails will be dry and the leeches not so bad. However, the park's most distinguishing feature for visitors is probably its difficulty of access: main roads run around the 570-square-kilometre park with spurs into some of the waterfalls, but there are no roads across the park and very sparse public transport along the spur roads. Only **Krung Ching waterfall**, one of Thailand's most spectacular, which features on the back of one-thousand-baht notes, really justifies the hassle of getting there.

Before heading off to Khao Luang, be sure to drop into Nakhon's TAT office for a useful park **brochure**, with a sketch map and sketchy details of the walking routes to Krung Ching waterfall and to the peak itself (for the latter, which begins at Ban Khiriwong on the southeast side of the park and involves at least one night camping on the mountain, ask at TAT about the possibility of hiring local guides). Irregular **songthaews** on the main roads around the park and to Ban Khiriwong congregate on and around Thanon Chamroenwithi near the *Bue Loung Hotel* in Nakhon. The only **rental transport** available in town are pricey air-conditioned minibuses from Muang Korn Travel, 1242/67 Thanon Boh-Ang (☎075/356574; B1500 per day); otherwise you might try doing a deal with a share-taxi driver at the bottom of Thanon Yomarat to take you to the park.

### Park headquarters and Kharom waterfall

**Park headquarters** (B200 admission) lie 33km west of Nakhon, 3km off Highway 4015 to Chawang, on the south side of the mountain; songthaews will usually drop you at the turning off the highway, though you might find one that will leg it up the very steep access road to HQ. Around 300m beyond, **Kharom waterfall** is very popular with Thai picnickers at weekends but its extensive rocky cascades are a little disappointing – and not a patch on Krung Ching. If you need them, four-person bungalows are available at HQ (B300), and it's possible to camp with your own tent.

## Krung Ching

A trip to **Krung Ching**, a nine-tier waterfall on the north side of the park, makes for a highly satisfying day out, with a mostly paved nature trail taking you through dense, steamy jungle to the most beautiful, third tier. The easiest way to **get there** from Nakhon with your own transport is to head north on Highway 401 towards Surat Thani, turning west at Tha Sala onto Highway 4140, then north again at Ban Nopphitam onto Highway 4186, before heading south from Ban Huai Phan on Highway 4188, the spur road to Ban Phitham and the Krung Ching park office, a total journey of about 70km. Songthaews will get you from Nakhon to Ban Huai Phan in about an hour, but you'd then have to hitch the last 13km. Four-person bungalows are available at the park office (B300), as well as tents (B100); camping is free if you bring your own. There's a sporadically open canteen, and an informal shop selling snacks and drinks.

The shady four-kilometre **trail** to the dramatic main fall is very steep in parts, so you should allow four hours at least there and back. On the way you'll pass giant ferns, including a variety known as *maha sadam*, the largest fern in the world, gnarled banyan trees, forests of mangosteen and beautiful, thick stands of bamboo. You're bound to see beautifully coloured birds and insects, but you may well only hear macaques and other mammals. At the end, a long, stepped descent brings you down to a perfectly positioned wooden platform with fantastic views of the forty-metre fall; here you can see how, shrouded in thick spray, it earns its Thai name, Naan Fon Saen Ha, meaning "heavy rain".

## Sichon

The coast north from Nakhon is dotted with small, Thai-orientated beach resorts, none of which can match the Ko Samui archipelago, lurking in the Gulf beyond, for looks or facilities. However, if you're searching for a quiet, low-key antidote to Samui's Western-style commercialism, the most interesting of these resorts, **SICHON**, might be just the place for you.

Buses and share taxis make the 65-kilometre journey north from Nakhon along the Surat Thani road to Talat Sichon, as the town's unpromising modern centre, with a few facilities such as banks and plenty of motorcycle taxis, is known. This half-hearted built-up area sprawls lazily eastwards for 3km to Pak Nam Sichon, a lively and scenic fishing port at the mouth of the eponymous river. Here, when they're not fishing in the bay, brightly coloured boats of all sizes draw up at the docks, backed by low-slung traditional wooden shophouses, the angular hills around Khanom beyond and, in the far distance, Ko Samui. About 1km south of the river mouth **Hat Sichon** (aka Hat Hin Ngarm) begins, a pretty crescent bay of shelving white sand, ending in a tree-tufted, rocky promontory. The beach is home to the best-value accommodation option in the area, *Prasarnsuk Villa* (T 075/335561–2, F 335562; ❸–❼), a neatly organized, welcoming place with a good, popular restaurant that stretches to a few tables and umbrellas on the beach. Amid spacious lawns, trees and flowers, bungalows range from decent, fan-cooled, en-suite affairs with verandas to "VIP" suites with air-con, hot water and TV. The next beach south, **Hat Piti**, is not quite so attractive, a long, straight, deserted stretch of white sand backed by palm trees. But if you want a few more facilities, this is where to come: *Piti Resort* (T or F 075/335301–4; ❼), 2km south of *Prasarnsuk*, can offer a small swimming pool, an entertainment club and a tastefully designed beachside restaurant, as well as hot water, air-con and cable TV in all bungalows.

# Travel details

## Trains

**Cha-am** to: Bangkok (12 daily; 3hr 10min–3hr 50min); Chumphon (10 daily; 4–5hr); Hua Hin (11 daily; 25min); Surat Thani (7 daily; 7hr 10min–8hr 25min).

**Chumphon** to: Bangkok (12 daily; 7hr–9hr 30min); Hua Hin (12 daily; 3hr 30min–5hr); Surat Thani (10 daily; 2hr 15min–4hr).

**Nakhon Si Thammarat** to: Bangkok (2 daily; 15hr).

**Hua Hin** to: Bangkok (12 daily; 15hr); Chumphon (10 daily; 3hr 30min–5hr 20min); Surat Thani (10 daily; 5hr 40min–8hr).

**Phetchaburi** to: Bangkok (8 daily; 2hr 45min–3hr 45min); Cha-am (12 daily; 35min); Chumphon (10 daily; 4hr 30min–6hr 30min); Hua Hin (12 daily; 1hr); Surat Thani (9 daily; 6hr 45min–9hr).

**Surat Thani** to: Bangkok (10 daily; 9–12hr); Butterworth (Malaysia; 1 daily; 11hr); Hat Yai (5 daily; 4–5hr); Nakhon Si Thammarat (2 daily; 3hr 30min); Phatthalung (5 daily; 3–4hr); Sungai Kolok (2 daily; 9hr); Trang (2 daily; 4hr); Yala (4 daily; 6–8hr).

## Buses

**Cha-am** to: Bangkok (every 40min; 2hr 45min–3hr 15min); Chumphon (every 2hr; 4hr 10min–5hr 10min); Hua Hin (every 30min; 35min); Phetchaburi (every 30 min; 50min).

**Chumphon** to: Bangkok (12 daily; 6hr 30min–9hr); Hat Yai (4 daily; 7hr 30min); Hua Hin (every 40min; 3hr 30min–4hr 30min); Phuket (3 daily; 7hr); Ranong (hourly; 2hr); Surat Thani (every 30min; 2hr 45min).

**Hua Hin** to: Bangkok (every 40min; 3hr 30min); Cha-am (every 30min; 35min); Chumphon (every 40min; 3hr 30min–4hr 30min); Phetchaburi (every 30min; 1hr 30min); Pranburi (every 20min; 40min).

**Ko Samui** to: Bangkok (Southern Terminal; 3 daily; 15hr).

**Nakhon Si Thammarat** to: Bangkok (Southern Terminal; 10 daily; 12hr); Hat Yai (every 30min; 3hr); Ko Samui (1 daily; 5hr); Krabi (5 daily; 3hr); Phatthalung (every 30min; 3hr); Phuket (every 30min; 6–7hr); Songkhla (every 30min; 3hr); Surat Thani (every 20min; 3hr); Trang (1 daily; 3hr).

**Phetchaburi** to: Bangkok (every 30min; 2hr); Cha-am (every 30 min; 50min); Chumphon (about every 2hr; 5hr–6hr); Hua Hin (every 30 min; 1hr 30min).

**Surat Thani** to: Bangkok (Southern Terminal; 7 daily; 11hr); Chaiya (hourly; 1hr); Chumphon (every 30min; 2hr 45min); Hat Yai (9 daily; 5hr–6hr 15min); Krabi (hourly; 4hr); Nakhon Si Thammarat (every 20min; 3hr); Narathiwat (2 daily; 7hr); Phuket (20 daily; 4hr 30min–6hr); Phunphin (every 10min; 30min); Ranong (17 daily; 4hr); Trang (2 daily; 3hr).

## Ferries

**Chumphon** to: Ko Tao (3 daily; 1hr 40min–6hr).

**Don Sak** to: Ko Samui (7 daily; 1hr 30min); Ko Pha Ngan (2 daily; 2hr 30min).

**Khanom** to: Ko Samui (4 daily; 1hr 30min).

**Ko Pha Ngan** to: Ko Samui (8 daily; 45min–1hr); Ko Tao (5 daily; 50min–3hr).

**Surat Thani** to: Ko Pha Ngan (1 nightly; 7hr); Ko Samui (1 nightly; 7hr).

**Tha Thong** to: Ko Pha Ngan (1 daily; 4hr); Ko Samui (1 daily; 2hr 30min).

## Flights

**Hua Hin** to: Bangkok (1 daily; 30min); Ko Samui (1 daily; 1hr).

**Ko Samui** to: Bangkok (12–14 daily; 1hr 20min); Krabi (1 daily; 40min); Phuket (2 daily; 50min); Singapore (1 daily; 1hr 20min); U-Tapao, near Pattaya (1 daily; 1hr).

**Nakhon Si Thammarat** to: Bangkok (1–2 daily; 1hr 15min).

**Surat Thani** to: Bangkok (2 daily; 1hr 10min).

# Southern Thailand: the Andaman coast

# CHAPTER 4

# Highlights

✳ **Khao Sok National Park** – Sleep in a treehouse and wake to the sound of hooting gibbons. p.309

✳ **Ko Similan** – Remote chain of islands with some of the best diving in the world. p.317

✳ **Reefs and wrecks** – Dive Thailand's finest underwater sights from Phuket (p.322), Ao Nang (p.365) or Ko Phi Phi (p.372).

✳ **The Vegetarian Festival** – Awesome public acts of self-mortification on parade in Phuket. p.327

✳ **Northwest Phuket** – Quiet, affordable beaches at Hat Mai Khao (p.330), Hat Nai Thon (p.333) and Hat Kamala. p.334

✳ **Sea-canoeing along the Krabi coastline** – The perfect way to explore the region's myriad mangrove swamps and secret lagoons. p.361

✳ **Rock-climbing on Laem Phra Nang** – Get a bird's eye view of fabulous coastal scenery. p.363

✳ **Ao Phra-Ae** – Ko Lanta's loveliest white-sand beach. p.386

✳ **Ko Jum** – Tiny island where there's nothing to do but chill out. p.389

# Southern Thailand: the Andaman coast

A s Highway 4 switches from the east flank of the Thailand peninsula to the **Andaman coast** it enters a markedly different country: nourished by rain nearly all the year round, the vegetation down here is lushly tropical, with forests reaching up to 80m in height, and massive rubber and coconut plantations replacing the rice and sugar-cane fields of central Thailand. In this region's heartland the drama of the landscape is enhanced by sheer limestone crags, topographical hallmarks that spike every horizon and make for stunning views from the road. Even more spectacular – and the main crowd-puller – is the Andaman Sea itself: translucent turquoise and so clear in some places that you can see to a depth of 30m, it harbours the country's largest **coral reefs** and is far and away the top diving area in Thailand.

Unlike the Gulf coast, the Andaman coast is hit by the **southwest monsoon** from May to October, when the rain and high seas render some of the outer islands inaccessible. However, conditions aren't generally severe enough to ruin a holiday on the other islands, while the occasional mainland cloudburst is offset by the advantages of notably less expensive and crowded accommodation.

## Accommodation prices

Throughout this guide, guest houses, hotels and bungalows have been categorized according to the **price codes** given below. These categories represent the minimum you can expect to pay in the high season (roughly July, Aug & Nov–Feb) for a **double room**. If travelling on your own, expect to pay anything between sixty and one hundred percent of the rates quoted for a double room. Wherever a **price range** is indicated, this means that the establishment offers rooms with varying facilities – as explained in the write-up. Wherever an establishment also offers **dormitory beds**, the prices of these beds are given in the text, instead of being indicated by price code.

Remember that the top-whack hotels will add seven percent tax and a ten percent service charge to your bill – the price codes below are based on net rates after taxes have been added.

| | | |
|---|---|---|
| ① under B150 | ④ B400–600 | ⑦ B1200–1800 |
| ② B150–250 | ⑤ B600–900 | ⑧ B1800–3000 |
| ③ B250–400 | ⑥ B900–1200 | ⑨ B3000+ |

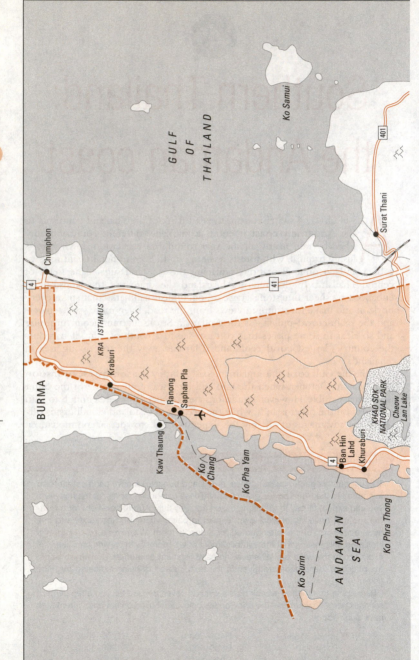

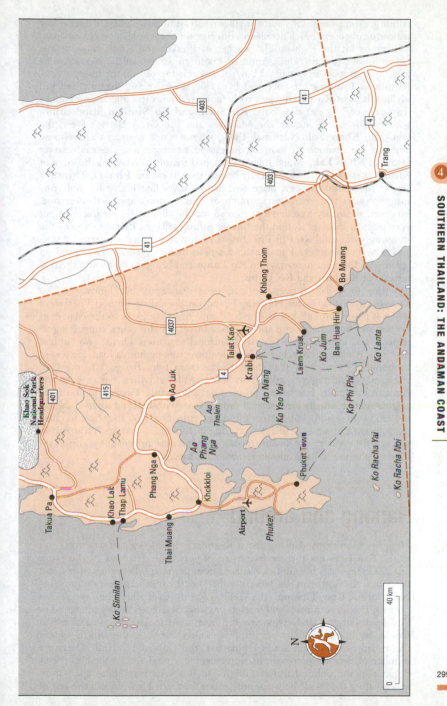

Trang

403

41

4

403

41

Bo Muang

Khlong Thom

Ban Hua Hin

4037

Ko Jum

Talat Kao

Laem Kruat

Ko Lanta

Krabi

Ao Nang

4

Ao Yao Yai

Khao Sok
National Park
Headquarters

415

Ao Luk

Ko Phi Phi

401

Ao
Thalen

Ko Yao Yai

Ao
Phang Nga

Phuket Town

Phang Nga

Ko Racha Yai

Khokkloi

Takua Pa

Khao Lak
Thap Lamu

Airport

Ko Racha Noi

Thai Muang

Phuket

Ko Similan

N

40 km

0

Although some bungalows at the smaller resorts shut down entirely during low season, nearly every beach detailed in this chapter keeps at least one place open.

Eager to hit the high-profile beaches of Phuket and Krabi, most people either fly over the first three-hundred-kilometre stretch of the west coast or pass through it on an overnight bus, thereby missing out on the lushly forested hills of **Ranong** province and bypassing several gems: the tiny and still idyllic island of **Ko Chang** (not to be confused with its larger, more famous namesake off the east coast); the **Ko Surin** and **Ko Similan** island chains, whose reefs rate alongside the Maldives and the Great Barrier Reef; the enjoyable **Khao Sok National Park**, where you can stay in a treehouse beneath the shadows of looming limestone outcrops; and the mid-market resort of **Khao Lak**, which hugs the rugged mainland coast on the edge of Khao Lak National Park. Tourism begins in earnest on **Phuket**, Thailand's largest island and the best place to learn to dive. The high-rises and consumerist gloss that characterize much of Phuket don't appeal to everyone, however, and many travellers opt instead for the slightly less mainstream but very popular beaches around the former fishing village of **Krabi**. Nearby the stunningly beautiful **Ko Phi Phi** attracts a lot of attention considering its size, and is beginning to crack under the strain, so many travellers have moved on again, searching out hideaways on **Ko Lanta** and bringing custom to the tiny retreats of **Ko Jum** and **Ko Bubu**.

Getting to Andaman coast destinations is made easy by Highway 4, also known as the Phetkasem Highway – and usually called Thanon Phetkasem when it passes through towns. The road runs from Bangkok to the Malaysian border, and frequent air-con and ordinary **buses** ply this route, connecting all major – and most minor – mainland tourist destinations. There is no rail line down the Andaman coast, but as the numerous cross-peninsula roads are served by frequent buses, many travellers take the **train** from Bangkok to the Gulf coast, enjoy the region's splendours for a while and then nip over to the Andaman coast by bus before proceeding southwards. **Ferries** to the most popular islands usually leave several times a day (with reduced services during the monsoon season), but for more remote destinations you may have to charter your own or wait for islanders' trading boats to pick you up. Alternatively, you can **fly** direct to the Andaman coast: there's a busy international airport on Phuket, plus useful local ones in Krabi and Ranong.

# Ranong and around

Highway 4 hits the Andaman coast at **Kraburi**, where a signpost welcomes you to the **Kra Isthmus**, the narrowest part of peninsular Thailand. At this point just 22km separates the Gulf of Thailand from the inlet where the River Chan flows into the Andaman Sea, west of which lies the southernmost tip of mainland Burma, **Kaw Thaung** (aka Victoria Point). Ever since the seventeenth century, Thai governments and foreign investors have been keenly interested in this slender strip of land, envisaging the creation of an Asian Suez canal which would cut some 1500km off shipping routes between the Indian Ocean (Andaman Sea) and the South China Sea (the Gulf of Thailand). Despite a number of detailed proposals, no agreement has yet been reached, not least because of the political implications of such a waterway: quite apart from accentuating the divide between prosperous southern Thailand and the rest of the country, it would vastly reduce Singapore's role in the international shipping industry.

Seventy kilometres south of the isthmus, the channel widens out at the provincial capital of **Ranong**, which thrives on its proximity to Burma. Thai tourists have been coming here for years, to savour the health-giving properties of the local spring water, but foreign holidaymakers have only recently discovered that Ranong is a useful departure-point for the delightful nearby islands of **Ko Chang** and **Ko Pha Yam**. The other reason to stop off in Ranong is to make a day-trip to the Burmese town of Kaw Thaung and acquire a new thirty-day Thai tourist visa into the bargain – an option that's popular with Phuket expats.

Ranong is the capital of Thailand's wettest province, which soaks up over 5000mm of rain every year – a fact you'll undoubtedly experience first-hand if you linger in the region. The landscape to the south of Ranong town is particularly lush, and any journey along Highway 4 will whizz you between densely forested hills to the east and mangrove swamps, rubber plantations and casuarina groves to the west; much of this coastal strip is preserved as **Laem Son National Park**. The hillsides are streaked with waterfalls which are, of course, seen to their best advantage during the rainy season, though the effect is striking at almost any time of year.

## The Town

Despite – or perhaps because – it's the wettest town in the whole country, **RANONG** has an enjoyable buzz and enthusiastic energy about it, fuelled in great part by the apparently amiable mix of Burmese, Thai, Chinese and Malay inhabitants. Many town-centre businesses promote their wares in curly Burmese script, and there's lots of pleasure to be had from simply enjoying the different faces and styles of dress. As with most border areas, however, there's also a flourishing illegal trade operating out of Ranong – in amphetamines, guns and labour apparently – though the closest you're likely to get to these activities is reading about them in the *Bangkok Post*.

The **geothermal springs** so favoured by Thai tourists are the focus of diminutive Raksawarin Park just off Thanon Phetkasem, ten minutes' walk north of the bus terminal or 1km southeast of the town centre – take songthaew #2 from the central Thanon Ruangrat or a motorbike taxi. You can't submerge yourself in the water here, but you can buy eggs to boil in the sulphurous 65°C water, or paddle in the cooler pools that have been siphoned off from the main springs. Picnickers throng here at weekends, but to properly appreciate the springs you need to soak in them: *Jansom Thara Hotel*, five minutes' walk away, channels the mineral waters into its public bath (B100 for non-guests).

If you haven't had already had enough of water features, you could make a trip out of town to the impressive **Nam Tok Ngao**, an enormous waterfall 12km south of Ranong, which cascades almost all the way down the eastern hillside in full view of Highway 4. Any south-bound bus will drop you there.

## Practicalities

Bangkok Airways operates four weekly **flights** between Bangkok and Ranong, which arrive at the **airport** 20km south of Ranong on Highway 4; taxis meet the flights, or you can walk out of the airport on to Highway 4 and flag down any north-bound bus. Air tickets can be bought from the tours desk at the

*Jansom Thara* hotel (see below). All west-coast buses travelling between Bangkok or Chumphon and Takua Pa, Phuket or Krabi stop briefly at Ranong's **bus station** on Highway 4 (Thanon Phetkasem), 1500m southeast of the centre; coming from Surat Thani and Khao Sok, you'll probably need to change buses at Takua Pa. Several city **songthaews** serve Ranong bus station, including one that runs to the hotels, day market and nearby songthaew depot on Thanon Ruangrat, and another that shuttles between the bus station and the port area at Saphan Pla 5km to the southwest, where you pick up boats to Kaw Thaung in Burma and to Ko Chang and Ko Pha Yam; another songthaew runs direct from the market on Thanon Ruangrat to the Saphan Pla port area. Many songthaews have their destinations written in English on the side, and most charge B7–10 per ride. There is no official **tourist information** in town, but several hotels carry detailed advertisements for bungalows on Ko Chang and Ko Pha Yam, and you can book some island bungalows through the *Chaong Thong* restaurant (see opposite), whose English-speaking staff are very helpful.

Marking the town centre, Thanon Ruangrat is where you'll find the handful of budget hotels and traveller-oriented restaurants, as well as the day and night **markets**, a small **post office** (at the northern end), half a dozen places offering **internet access** (most of them north of the *Sin Tawee* hotel), and at the southern end, a Bangkok Bank with an ATM and an **exchange** counter. Thanon Ruangrat runs approximately northwest–southeast and at its southern end is crossed by Thanon Tha Muang, where the CAT **international phone office** (Mon–Fri 8am–8pm, Sat & Sun 8.30am–4.30pm), also with internet access, is located about 200m to the east of the Ruangrat junction. English-language books and newspapers are stocked at the **bookstore** diagonally across the road from the *Chaong Thong*. The Thonburi-Ranong **hospital** (T077/834214) is at 41/142 Thanon Tha Muang. Ranong's **immigration office** is 5km out of town in Saphan Pla; for details on how to extend or renew your visa here see pp.303–304.

## Accommodation

Most travellers linger in Ranong for just one night, and the town's budget Thai-Chinese **hotels** don't exactly encourage you to prolong your stay. The most popular is the decidedly average *Sin Tawee* at 81/1 Thanon Ruangrat (T077/811213; ❷–❸), which offers cheap and simple en-suite fan and air-con rooms about 100m north of the day market and songthaew depot. Equally uninspired, but decent enough, the *Asia Hotel* (T077/811113; ❷–❺) is at 39/9 Thanon Ruangrat, about 70m south of the market, and easily recognized by its pale blue colour scheme inside and out; staff speak English, the rooms are large, and you can choose between fan or air-con rooms. About 600m north up Thanon Ruangrat from the market, across from the branch post office, the *Boat Restaurant* rents out a few rooms at cheap prices (❷). With its mineral baths, jacuzzis and range of upmarket rooms, *Jansom Thara Hotel* (T077/811510, F821821; ❻–❾), located about 1200m east of the town centre, near the hot springs and bus station at 2/10 Thanon Phetkasem, used to be the town's best accommodation; it's now been superseded by the more modern chain hotel the *Royal Princess*, slightly more centrally located off the west arm of Thanon Tha Muang (T077/835240, F835238, W www.royalprincess.com; ❽), which also has jacuzzis with spa water, and a swimming pool.

## Eating and drinking

Ranong's ethnic diversity ensures an ample range of **eating** options, and a stroll up Thanon Ruangrat will take you past Muslim foodstalls and Chinese pastry shops as well as a small but typically Thai night market. Deservedly the most popular travellers' restaurant is *Chaong Thong*, 8–10 Thanon Ruangrat (Mon–Sat 6am–9.30pm), across from the *Asia Hotel* and south a bit, next to the Bangkok Bank; here you can choose from a long and varied selection of inexpensive dishes that includes Spanish omelette, shrimp curry and lemon-grass tea, as well as lots of veggie options and hearty breakfasts. About 100m north of the *Sin Tawee* hotel, the very cheap *Veetiang* boasts a long menu covering all manner of seafood cooked to myriad Thai and Chinese recipes, as well as standard over-rice dishes. Another 200m north up Thanon Ruangrat, across from the post office and next to the cinema, a small café serves vegetarian food every day until 6pm. A few metres north of the veggie place, at 301 Thanon Ruangrat, the *Sir Dol Pub* opens nightly at 7pm for pool, live music, beer and snacks.

## Kaw Thaung (Ko Song)

The southernmost tip of Burma – known as Kaw Thaung in Burmese, Ko Song in Thai, and Victoria Point when it was a British colony – lies just a few kilometres west of Ranong across the River Chan estuary, and is easily reached from the Thai side of the border. So long as you follow the procedures detailed below, it's quite straightforward for foreign tourists to **enter Burma** at this point, and nipping across the border and back is a fairly popular way of getting a new thirty-day Thai tourist visa, but if you already have a sixty-day visa and are looking for another month, it's faster and a little cheaper (B500 plus two photos) to extend your existing visa at the Thai immigration office in Saphan Pla (see below) and avoid going into Burma at all – which also means you are not giving your money to the Burmese military regime.

Having said that, although there's nothing much to do in **KAW THAUNG** itself, it's an enjoyable focus for a trip out of Ranong, and sufficiently different from Thai towns to merit an hour or two's visit. Alighting at the quay, the market and tiny town centre lie before you, while over to your right, about twenty minutes' walk away, you can see an eye-catching hilltop pagoda, surmounted by a huge reclining Buddha and a ring of smaller ones. Once you've explored the covered market behind the quay and picked your way through the piles of tin trunks and sacks of rice that crowd the surrounding streets, it's fun to take a coffee break in one of the typically Burmese quayside pastry shops before negotiating a ride in a boat back to Saphan Pla; Thai money is perfectly acceptable in Kaw Thaung. There are also a couple of seafood restaurants on the quay, as well as the decent enough *Honey Bee Hotel* (❺) should you want to stay over.

### Practicalities

Longtail boats to Kaw Thaung leave from **SAPHAN PLA**, Ranong's fishing port and harbour, which is about 5km southwest of the town centre and served by regular songthaews from Ranong's Thanon Ruangrat and bus station (20min; B7). All non-Thais must first get a Thai exit stamp before boarding a boat to Kaw Thaung, so get out of the songthaew at the Thai **immigration office** (daily 8.30am–4.30pm) on the outskirts of Saphan Pla: the office is clearly signed on the right, across the road from the Thai Farmers Bank. Boat boys usually hover outside the office to try and secure your custom, so once you've got your stamp you can either accompany them (in which case you'll probably end up chartering the boat) or just continue walking down the road for about fifteen minutes until you reach the PTT petrol station, where you should turn down to the right to find a quayside thick with longtails. There's another small quay a few hundred metres further up the quayside, but the PTT one is busier.

**Longtails** leave for Kaw Thaung when they have enough custom: the fare should be B50 per person in an already crowded boat, or B150 one-way to charter the whole boat. The crossing takes about thirty minutes, but the long-tails have to stop en route at a tiny island containing the **Burmese immigration** office, where you buy your Burmese visa: US$5 (or B300) for a one-to three-day pass, or US$36 for thirty days. For stays of over a day you also need to change US dollars into Foreign Exchange Certificates (FECs): $50 for two to three days, or $300 for a month's stay. Legally, you are not allowed to travel beyond Kaw Thaung unless you have already bought a proper visa from a Burmese embassy (see p.19) to supplement the Kaw Thaung passes. If you do have a visa, you can fly to Rangoon from the airport 7km north of Kaw Thaung, but road travel from here to Rangoon is currently forbidden to foreigners.

If you're simply making the trip to get a new Thai visa you can take the boat straight back to Saphan Pla from the immigration island, though Kaw Thaung is just a few minutes' boat ride further on. If you do visit Kaw Thaung, when you return to Saphan Pla your boat will stop at the Burmese immigration island to collect your passport; once back on Thai soil you must return to the Thai immigration office to get your new Thai thirty-day tourist visa before catching a songthaew back to Ranong.

## Ko Chang

Not to be confused with the much larger island of Ko Chang on Thailand's east coast (see p.211), Ranong's **KO CHANG** is a forested little island about 5km offshore, with less than perfect beaches but a charmingly low-key, friendly and laid-back atmosphere. The beaches are connected by tracks through the trees; there are no cars and only sporadic, self-generated supplies of electricity. With *Eden Bungalows* at one end and *Paradise Bungalows* at the other, you begin to get the picture, which for once doesn't stretch the imagination too far. The pace of life on Ko Chang is very slow, the emphasis strongly on kicking back and chilling out – bring your own hammock and you'll fit right in.

Many of the islanders live in the small **village** behind the long pier that juts out from the middle of Ao Yai, just north of the shallow khlong. Partially hidden amongst the trees beside the beach is the village wat and monks' quarters, with a sign that asks tourists to dress modestly when in the area and not to swim or sunbathe in front of it. The 800-metre-long stretch of **beach** that runs north from the pier is the most attractive on the island, with yellow and grey sand that swirls together in leopardskin-like patterns and has a texture so soft that it squeaks. This part of the beach is nice and wide even at high tide, and especially popular with kids. The beach that runs south of the pier and the khlong is less impressive: it's very narrow at high tide, but when the water goes out you have to walk a longish distance to find any depth. Southern Ao Yai, which begins just beyond the rocky divide occupied by *Ko Chang Resort*, has greyish sand but is fine for swimming.

Nearly all the bungalows on Ko Chang **close** down from June through October when the island is subjected to very heavy rain; many bungalow staff relocate to the mainland for this period, so you should phone ahead if you want to stay here then.

## Practicalities

Longtail **boats** to Ko Chang leave from Ranong's port area, **Saphan Pla** (as do boats to Ko Pha Yam, see p.306), which is about 5km southwest of the town centre and served by regular **songthaews** from Thanon Ruangrat and the bus station (20min; B7). When the songthaew stops at the toll-booth entry to Saphan Pla you'll see a PTT petrol station to the right (which is the landmark for boats to Kaw Thaung in Burma) and a small soi on the left; turn down the left-hand soi (there are a couple of faded Ko Chang bungalow signs on the wall here) and follow it as it twists its way down to the water about 400m further on. At the waterfront you'll see a couple of small restaurants, including the Burmese-run *Quick Stop*, where you can find out when the next boat to the island is due to depart (the current timetable is also available at *Chaong Thong* restaurant in Ranong) and while away the time over a cup of Burmese tea.

At time of writing there was one scheduled daily boat **departure** at 10am, and usually another one in the early afternoon, but if there are more than six in your party, you can probably charter your own boat almost immediately; the journey takes about an hour and costs B100 per person. Tell the boatman which bungalow you want and he'll drop you as close as possible (though you'll probably have to wade in); if you haven't decided on one, you won't have to walk for long from wherever you get dropped. Very few boats travel to Ko Chang during the rainy months of June through October, and those that do drop passengers on Ko Chang's east coast, a three-kilometre walk from Ao Yai. During the tourist season, there's at least one boat a day from Ko Chang **back to Saphan Pla**, generally in the morning between about 7am and 9am – ask at your bungalows the day before. Any songthaew will take you back from Saphan Pla to Ranong, but if you want to go directly to the bus station be sure to catch a blue-coloured one.

To date there is no commercial activity at all on Ko Chang, save for one small beach **stall** at *Golden Bee* selling a few basic necessities, and a dive operator who runs his business from a hut just north of *Cashew Resort*. **Overseas phone calls** can be made at *Golden Bee* and *Cashew Resort*.

## Accommodation

Most of the **bungalow** operations are simple bamboo affairs, comprising just a dozen huts and a small restaurant each. Though they nearly all have their own generators, it's a good idea to bring a torch as many bungalow managers bow to customers' preference to stick to candles and paraffin lamps.

**Cashew Resort**, north of the pier on central Ao Yai ☎01/229 6667. The longest-running set of bungalows on the island, and also the largest, this place is located among the cashew trees and has simple wooden huts with shared bathrooms, as well as more solid en-suite versions with glass windows. Has more of a busy atmosphere than the other bungalows on Ao Yai. ❶–❷

**Chang Tong**, south of the pier on central Ao Yai ☎077/833820. Simple, very clean wood and bamboo bungalows, well spaced in two rows. All have mosquito nets and some have bathrooms. ❶–❷

**Eden Bungalows**, north of the pier on central Ao Yai. Widely spaced and nicely secluded bungalows amongst the trees at the far north end of Ao Yai. ❶–❷

**Full Moon**, southern Ao Yai. Sturdy wooden bungalows along the beachfront, with or without private bathroom. ❶–❷

**Golden Bee**, south of the pier on central Ao Yai ☎077/844485. Ultra-simple huts set among the palm trees near the pier. All huts have a mattress on the floor, and some have attached bathrooms. ❶–❷

**Hornbill**, north around two headlands from Ao Yai. Simple, unobtrusive bungalows built amongst the trees behind their own little gold-sand bay, just a few minutes' walk north of *Ko Chang Contex*, and within easy reach of Ao Yai. Lives up to its name, as majestic black and white hornbills are a common sight here. ❶ – ❷

**Ko Chang Contex**, north around the headland from Ao Yai. Located in its own peaceful little bay a short walk north of Ao Yai, the handful of huts here is scattered across the rocks above the beach, with just the resident black-and-white hornbills for company. ❶ – ❷

**Ko Chang Resort**, southern Ao Yai ⓔ sound_of_sea@lycos.com. Occupying a fabulous spot high on the rocks, the newer and sturdier en-suite wooden bungalows here have fine sea views from their balconies and are simply but thoughtfully designed inside. The older ones share bathrooms. There's a stylish restaurant with low tables, cushions and a similarly engaging panorama, and the swimmable beach is just a couple of minutes' scramble to the south. ❷

**Lae Tawan**, south around the headland from southern Ao Yai. Basic huts in their own small bay,

with or without bathroom. Twenty minutes' walk from Ao Yai, with great sunset views. ❶ – ❷

**Paradise**, southern Ao Yai. Very popular, laid-back place, with some huts overlooking the rocks and others ranged up the bank at the back, looking down onto the beach. Some are en suite. ❶ – ❷

**Sabay Jai**, south of the pier on central Ao Yai. Friendly little place with a restaurant and just eight bungalows, some semi-detached, others freestanding and en-suite. ❶ – ❷

**Sunset Bungalows**, north of the pier on central Ao Yai. Set in a rather dark grove of cashew-nut trees on the edge of the beach, comprising decent huts with or without attached bathrooms. ❶ – ❷

**Tadang Bay**, southern Ao Yai. Set up on the headland at the far southern end of Ao Yai, the huts here enjoy nice long views of the whole bay. The price depends on the size of the hut; all share bathrooms. ❶

## Ko Pha Yam

The tiny island of **KO PHA YAM** offers fine white-sand beaches and coral reefs and is home to around a hundred islanders, most of whom make a living by growing cashew nuts. It's a touch more developed than Ko Chang, having vehicle-worthy tracks and a few vehicles that use them, but it's still a peaceful place. Most islanders live in the fishing village on the northeast coast, where there's a pier and a temple as well as a couple of foodstalls and a phone office. From November through May there's at least one **boat** a day from Ranong's port area, Saphan Pla, to Ko Pha Yam, departing at 2pm and taking two hours to reach the east coast (B100) or about three hours for west-coast destinations (B150); see p.303 for details of how to get to the Saphan Pla pier from Ranong. The boat returns from the island's west coast at 7am, passing the east coast at about 8am. Boats are less regular during the rainy season, from June through October, and many bungalows close up, so call ahead during this period to check first and arrange transport.

The nicest beach on the island is the 2.5-kilometre-long **Ao Yai** on the southwest coast, where the sand is soft and blindingly white and there's snorkelling off the little rocky outcrop at the end of the bay. The sunsets are quite spectacular here too. Towards the southern end of the beach, *Ao Yai Bungalows* (☎077/821753; ❷) has a handful of nice wooden bungalows with attached bathrooms and offers discounts for stays of a week or more; it's open year-round. Nearby *Bamboo* (☎01/273 3437; ❷) has huts of a similar standard, also en suite. Further up on the northwest coast, on **Ko Kwai** beach, *Vijit* (☎077/834082; ❷) offers clean wooden en-suite bungalows set in a garden and surrounded by trees; you can walk from here to the village on the east coast in about 45 minutes. Across on the east coast, the dozen basic bungalows of *Ko Pha Yam Resort* (☎077/812297; ❸ – ❺) are scattered among a cashew plantation on the edge of the beach.

# Ko Surin and around

The coastal town of **Khuraburi**, 110km south of Ranong on Highway 4, is the closest (though not necessarily the most convenient) departure point for the magnificent national park island chain of **Ko Surin**, a group of five small islands around 60km offshore, just inside Thai waters. Also accessible from Khuraburi is the island of **Ko Phra Thong**, said to be exceptionally rewarding for birdwatching and boasting a popular eco-resort.

## Ko Surin

The spectacular shallow reefs around **KO SURIN** offer some of the best snorkelling and diving on the Andaman coast. The most beautiful and easily explored of the reefs are those surrounding the two main islands in the group, Ko Surin Nua (north) and Ko Surin Tai (south), which are separated only by a narrow channel. **SURIN NUA**, slightly the larger at about 5km across, holds the national park headquarters, visitor centre and park bungalows on its southwest coast. The water is so clear here, and the reefs so close to the surface, that you can make out a forest of sea anemones while sitting in a boat just 10m from the park headquarters' beach. Visibility off the east and west coasts of both islands stretches to a depth of 40m.

Across the channel, **SURIN TAI** is the long-established home of a community of *chao ley* (see p.308) who divide their time between boat-building and fishing. Every April, as part of the Songkhran New Year festivities, hundreds of *chao ley* from nearby islands (including those in Burmese waters) congregate here to celebrate with a ceremony involving, among other rites, the release into the sea of several hundred turtles, which are a symbol of longevity and especially precious to Thai and Chinese people.

### Practicalities

Because the islands are so far out at sea, Ko Surin is effectively out of bounds during the monsoon season, when the sixty-kilometre trip becomes a potentially suicidal undertaking. During the rest of the year, getting to Ko Surin can be both time-consuming and expensive. The easiest way to reach the islands is to join an organized live-aboard **dive trip** with one of the dive operators in Khao Lak (see box on p.315) or Phuket (see box on p.322), which usually also feature other remote reefs such as Richelieu Rock or the Burma Banks, and cost from B16,000–20,000 for four days all inclusive with at least eight dives.

If you're determined to see the islands independently, you could try to catch one of the **national park boats** that sail at least once a week from November through April from the Khuraburi pier at Ban Hin Lahd, about 8km north of Khuraburi town. To get to the pier, get off the bus at kilometre-stone 110 on Highway 4 (ask the driver for Ko Surin) and then take a motorcycle taxi down to the pier. The boats take from three to five hours and cost B1000 return; ask at the national park office near the pier-head (℡076/491378) for details. It's also possible to charter your own fishing boat from the pier for around B6000 a day (journey time 4–5hr): unless you speak fluent Thai the best way to arrange this is by calling the national park office. Once you're on the islands, you can **charter a longtail** to explore the coasts: a four-hour cruise is priced at around B500.

Sometimes called sea gypsies, the **chao ley** or *chao nam* ("people of the sea" or "water people") have been living off the seas around the west coast of the Malay peninsula for hundreds of years. Some still pursue a traditional nomadic existence, living in self-contained houseboats known as **kabang**, but many have now made permanent homes in Andaman coast settlements in Thailand and Malaysia.

Dark-skinned and sometimes with an auburn tinge to their hair, the sea gypsies are thought to be Austronesian or Malay in **origin**, and their migration probably first started west and then north from the Riau-Lingga archipelago, which lies between Singapore and Sumatra. It's estimated that around five thousand *chao ley* now live off the coasts of the Andaman Sea, divided into five groups, with distinct lifestyles and dialects.

Of the different groups, the **Urak Lawoy**, who have settled on Ko Lipe in Ko Tarutao National Park (see p.413) and in Phuket (see p.348), are the most integrated into Thai society. They are known as *Mai Thai*, or "New Thai", and many have found work on coconut plantations or as fishermen. Other groups continue in the more traditional *chao ley* **occupations** of hunting for pearls and sea shells on the ocean floor, attaching stones to their waists to dive to depths of 60m with only an air-hose connecting them to the surface; sometimes they fish in this way too, taking down enormous nets into which they herd the fish as they walk along the sea bed. Their agility and courage make them good birds'-nesters as well (see box on p.379), enabling them to harvest the tiny nests of sea swifts from nooks and crannies hundreds of metres high inside caves along the Andaman coast.

The **Moken** of Thailand's Ko Surin islands and Burma's Mergui archipelago are the most traditional of the *chao ley* communities and still lead remote, itinerant lives. They own no land or property, but are dependent on fresh water and beaches to collect shells and sea slugs to sell to Thai traders. They have extensive knowledge of the plants that grow in the remaining jungles on Thailand's west-coast islands, using eighty different species for food alone, and thirty for medicinal purposes.

The sea gypsies are **animists**, with a strong connection both to the natural spirits of island and sea and to their own ancestral spirits. On some beaches they set up totem poles as a contact point between the spirits, their ancestors and their shaman. The sea gypsies have a rich **musical heritage** too. The Moken do not use any instruments as such, making do with found objects for percussion; the Urak Lawoy on the other hand, due to their closer proximity to the Thai and Malay cultures, are excellent violin- and drum-players. During community entertainments, the male musicians form a semicircle around the old women, who dance and sing about the sea, the jungle and their families.

**Building a new boat** is the ultimate expression of what it is to be a *chao ley*, and every newly married couple has a *kabang* built for them. But the complex art of constructing a seaworthy home from a single tree trunk, and the way of life it represents, is disappearing. In Thailand, where **assimilation** is actively promoted by the government, the truly nomadic flotillas have become increasingly marginalized, and the number of undeveloped islands they can visit unhindered gets smaller year by year. On Phuket, the Urak Lawoy villages have become sightseeing attractions, where busloads of tourists trade cute photo poses for coins and sweets, setting in motion a dangerous cycle of dependency. In Burma, the continued political instability and repression has further restricted their mobility, and there is a real danger of getting arrested and even forced into slave labour – nothing short of hell on earth especially for a people whose lives have always been determined by the waves and the wind.

### Accommodation and eating

As boats to the islands tend to leave very early in the morning, you'll probably have to spend at least one night in a **Khuraburi hotel**. The fairly basic *Rungtawan* (**②**) is next to the bus stop for the pier, at kilometre-stone 110 on Highway 4, or there are newer and more salubrious bungalows at *Thararin River Hut Resort* (**③–④**) a couple of kilometres out of town. Alternatively, try the attractively designed wooden chalets at *Khuraburi Greenview Resort* (**☎** & **ⓕ** 076/421360; **⑦–⑧**) which all have air-con, TV and use of the swimming pool and are located 12km south of Khuraburi, alongside Highway 4.

For accommodation on Ko Surin, you have the choice of renting one of the expensive six-person national park **bungalows** on Surin Nua (B1200, but deals for couples may be negotiable), settling for a dorm bed (B100) in the nearby longhouse or opting for a B100 two-person national park tent. Accommodation gets very booked up at weekends and on public holidays, so it's worth reserving a bed in advance by calling **☎** 076/491378. Otherwise, you can camp in your own tent in the vicinity of the park buildings. Unless you take your own **food** to the islands, you'll be restricted to the three set meals a day served at the restaurant on Surin Nua for B300 (vegetarian and other special meals can be supplied if requested in advance).

## Ko Phra Thong

One kilometre off the Khuraburi coast, **KO PHRA THONG** (Golden Buddha Island) is home to an eco-resort, the *Golden Buddha Beach Resort* (**☎** 01/230 4744, **ⓕ** 02/863 1301, **ⓔ** sandler@mozart.inet.co.th) which, as well as renting out kayaks and running a turtle sanctuary, also hosts yoga retreats. Its bungalows have mosquito nets and open-air bathrooms, and are set among the trees beside the main beach, which is 7km long and blessed with fine white sand. The resort is run by a company called Lost Horizons (**ⓦ** www.losthorizonsasia.com), which charges B1200 per person per day to stay here, including all meals; they arrange transport from Ranong or Khuraburi if contacted in advance.

# Khao Sok National Park

Forty kilometres south of Khuraburi, Highway 4 reaches the junction town of **Takua Pa**. Highway 401, which cuts east from here, is the route taken by most Surat Thani-bound buses from Phuket and Krabi, and it's a spectacular journey across the mountains that stretch the length of the peninsula, a landscape of limestone crags and jungle, scarred only by the road. Most of what you see belongs to **KHAO SOK NATIONAL PARK**, a tiny part of which – entered 40km east of Takua Pa – is set aside for overnight stays. Although the park is an increasingly popular destination for day-trippers from Khao Lak and Phuket, it definitely merits a good 48 hours: waking up to the sound of hooting gibbons and the sight of thick white mist curling around the karst formations is an experience not quickly forgotten, and there are plenty of opportunities for hikes and overnight treks into the jungle.

### Access and accommodation

The park entrance is located at kilometre-stone 109, less than an hour by **bus** from Takua Pa, ninety minutes from Khao Lak, or two hours from Surat Thani.

Buses run at least every ninety minutes in both directions; ask to be let off at the park and you'll be met by a knot of competing guest-house staff waiting to give you a free lift to their accommodation, the furthest of which is 3km from the main road. Coming by bus from Bangkok, Hua Hin or Chumphon, take a Surat Thani-bound bus, but ask to be dropped off at the junction with the Takua Pa road, about 20km before Surat Thani, and then change onto a Takua Pa bus. Onward bus connections are frequent and guest-house staff will ferry you back to the main road. Most guest houses also offer a taxi service for a maximum of three people to Khao Lak (B1200), Surat Thani (B1400) and Phuket (B2000).

## Accommodation

Despite the area being a national park, a cluster of appealing jungle **guest houses** has grown up along tracks to the south and east of the national park visitor centre and trail-heads: most are simple wood or bamboo huts set peacefully among the trees or beneath the limestone karsts. They all have restaurants and can arrange trekking guides as well. The longest-running and most peaceful guest houses are situated down a side track that branches off the north–south track from the main road to the visitor centre and runs alongside the river; the newer ones are located along the main north–south track. All guest houses serve food, and there are a couple of small restaurants along the main north–south track, as well two tiny minimarkets where you can buy essentials and change money.

**Art's Riverview Jungle Lodge**, about 800m east along the side track ⓟ076/421613. Efficiently run place comprising half-a-dozen wooden cabins (price depends on size and location) and three treehouses in a tropical garden located right next to a good swimming hole. It's popular with backpackers' tour groups, so advance booking is recommended. ❸–❺

**Bamboo House**, about 150m east along the side track. One of the first guest houses in the park and run by members of the park warden's family, this place offers simple bamboo huts with attached bathroom as well as sturdier but less atmospheric concrete ones. ❶–❺

**Bamboo 2**, beside the river, on the main track, about 1200m from the main road. Characterless concrete bungalows overlooking the river, though they might be worth the money if you're looking for an insect-proof option. ❸

**Freedom House**, on the main track, about 1km from the main road ⓣ & ⓟ077/214974, ⓣ01/979 2765, ⓔthaitour_surat@hotmail.com. Australian-managed place comprising a handful of big bamboo houses raised unusually high on stilts, with verandas that look straight into a patch of jungle. Standard simply furnished accommodation, with en-suite bathrooms. ❷

**Garden Huts**, on the main track, about 900m from the main road. Set well away from the main track

and prettily located beside a small pond surrounded by wild flowers, the half-dozen bungalows here are simple bamboo affairs with attached bathrooms, mosquito nets, fans and electricity, and nice views of the karsts. Run by a friendly, enthusiastic family. ❷

**Khao Sok Jungle Huts**, on the main track, about 1100m from the main road. Tall bamboo huts on stilts with long views out towards the karsts. Price depends on the size of the hut and on proximity to the track (some are pretty close); they all have attached bathrooms. ❶–❷

**Nung House**, about 200m east along the side track. Small, friendly place with just nine huts run by the park warden's son and his family. Choose between simple bamboo constructions with en-suite facilities, concrete bungalows, and treehouses. Their restaurant serves good food. ❶–❸

**Our Jungle House**, on a branch track off the side track ⓟ076/421706, ⓔour_jungle_house@hotmail.com. The most romantically located of Khao Sok's guest houses is set in a secluded riverside spot beneath the limestone cliffs, about fifteen minutes' walk on from *Nung House*, along the left-hand fork in the track. Here you can choose between beautifully situated treehouses, private cabins by the river, and rooms in the main house. All accommodation has its own bathroom, but there's no electricity in the cabins and treehouses, so candles are provided. ❸–❺

**Treetops River Huts**, on the main track, about 1400m from the main road ⓣ 077/299150, ⓕ 285987. Located beside the river, very close to the visitor centre and trailheads, with a choice of accommodation ranging from simple bamboo huts with bathrooms through to en-suite wood or stone ones. Comfortable but has a busier feel than many, partly because it's popular with small tour groups. ❷–❺

## The park

The B200 national park **entrance fee** (B100 for kids) is payable at the checkpoint close to the visitor centre and is valid for three days – you'll need to pay this in addition to the fees for any guided treks or tours. Several trails radiate from the park headquarters and visitor centre, some of them more popular and easier to follow than others, but all quite feasible as day-trips. The **visitor centre** (daily 8am–4pm) sells a small sketch map of the park and trails, as well as the recommended **guide book** to the park, *Waterfalls and Gibbon Calls* by Thom Henley (B250), which includes lots of background information on the flora and fauna of Khao Sok as well as a full description of all the things to look out for on the interpretative trail (see below). If you don't buy the book, you might want to spend a few minutes looking at the exhibition inside the visitor centre, which also gives interesting details, in English and Thai, on Khao Sok's highlights.

When choosing your trail, consult the sketch map and the noticeboard at the trailheads, and then check with one of the rangers to make sure it's still accessible – rangers sometimes decommission trails if they get eroded or overgrown, or if animals and birds in the vicinity need to be shielded from too much human contact. Also, be prepared to remain alert to the course of your trail, as broken trail markers are now rarely replaced because of cuts to the park's budget. Take plenty of water as Khao Sok is notoriously sticky and humid.

Eight of the park's nine current **trails** follow the same route for the first 5km. This route heads directly west of the park headquarters and follows the course of the Sok river; it is clearly signed as leading to trails #1–8. The first 3.5km of the route is marked with numbered signposts which refer to the **interpretative trail** described in *Waterfalls and Gibbon Calls*. The interpretative trail takes about ninety minutes one way and though not exciting in itself (a broad, road-like track most of the way) is made a lot more interesting if you refer to the descriptions in the book.

Most people carry on after the end of the interpretative trail, following signs for trail #1, which takes you to **Ton Gloy waterfall**. Nine kilometres from headquarters (allow 3hr each way), the falls flow year-round and tumble into a pool that's good for swimming. En route to Ton Gloy, you'll pass signs for other attractions including **Bang Leap Nam waterfall** (trail #4, 4.5km from headquarters), which is a straightforward hike; and **Tan Sawan waterfall** (trail #3, 9km from headquarters), a more difficult route that includes a wade along the river bed for the final kilometre and should not be attempted during the rainy season.

The other very popular trail is #9 to **Sip-et Chan waterfall**, which shoots off north from the park headquarters and follows the course of the Bang Laen river. Though the falls are only 4km from headquarters, the trail can be difficult to follow and involves a fair bit of climbing plus half a dozen river crossings. You should allow three hours each way, and take plenty of water and some food. With eleven tiers, the falls are a quite spectacular sight; on the way you should hear the hooting calls of white-handed gibbons at the tops of the tallest trees, and may get to see a helmeted hornbill flying overhead.

## Guided treks and tours

Longer **guided treks** into the jungle interior can be arranged through most of Khao Sok's guest houses, but if your accommodation doesn't come up with the goods try either *Freedom House*, *Nung House*, *Bamboo House* or *Treetops*. Note that all prices listed below are exclusive of the three-day national park pass, which costs B200 per person.

For B300–400 per person, you can join a trek along the main park trails (usually to Ton Gloy waterfall or Sip-et Chan falls) or to a nearby cave, but the most interesting treks start from **Cheow Lan lake**, which is studded with spectacular karst formations, with three impressive caves near the access trail; it's about an hour's drive from the accommodation area and is only open to guided treks. A typical day-trip to the lake (B1000–1200) includes a boat ride and swim, with a possible fishing option too, plus a trek to one of the nearby caves – one of which has a river running through it, so you may have to swim in parts. This is quite an adventurous outing: when not straining your neck to observe the gibbons in the treetops, you'll be wading through rivers and keeping an eye out for hungry leeches. Overnight trips to the lake generally cover the same ground and feature either camping in the jungle (B1800) or accommodation at the national park raft house on the lake (B2200); the more expensive version, run through *Freedom House*, adds on a trek to a waterfall, a night safari and night fishing (B2500).

Most guest houses also do **night safaris** along the main park trails, at around B300 for two hours or B500 for four hours, when you're fairly certain to see civets and might be lucky enough to see some of the park's rarer inhabitants, like elephants, tigers, clouded leopards and pony-sized black and white tapirs.

The **Sok river** that runs through the park and alongside many of the guest houses is fun for swimming in and inner-tubing down; tubes can be hired at *Bamboo House*. You can also go on a guided canoe trip down the river: a two-hour, ten-kilometre canoe ride costs B600–800 per person and can be arranged through *Bamboo House*. Many guest houses can also arrange **elephant rides** (2hr; B800) and trips to a rather uninteresting local cave temple (B300).

If you're in a hurry, consider organizing an overnight trekking expedition to Khao Sok through a **tour agent** in Khao Lak, Krabi or Phuket. A two-day trip including transport, raft-house accommodation, guided trekking and a night safari costs around B4800 per adult or B2800 per child; refer to the relevant town accounts for details. Santana in Phuket (☎076/294220, ⓕ340360, ⓦwww.santanphuket.com) can also arrange overnight kayaking trips in Khao Sok.

# Khao Lak and Bang Niang

Fringed by casuarina, palm and mangrove trees, the scenic strip of bronze-coloured beach at **KHAO LAK**, 30km south of Takua Pa, makes a reasonably appealing destination in its own right, though its main role is as a departure point for **diving trips** to Ko Similan (see p.317) and Ko Surin (see p.307). There's no real village to speak of at Khao Lak: most of the accommodation is down on the beach, about 500m west of Highway 4 on the other side of a rubber plantation, and the main road itself is lined with small restaurants, dive operators, several little shopping plazas and a few guest houses. During the monsoon, the crashing waves and squelchy mud can make Khao Lak seem

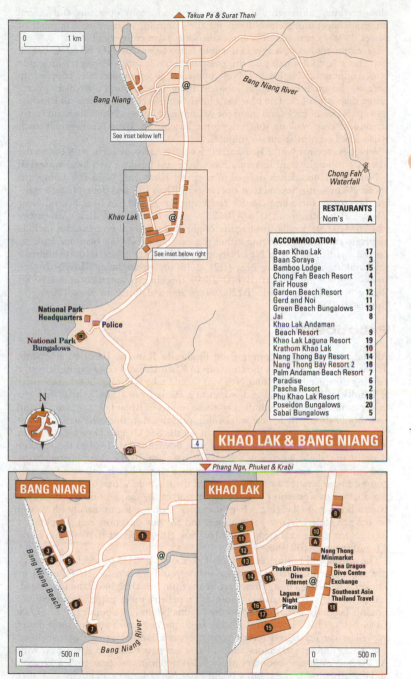

Takua Pa & Surat Thani

0        1 km

Bang Niang

Bang Niang River

@

See inset below left

Chong Fah Waterfall

Khao Lak

@

See inset below right

**RESTAURANTS**

Nom's                    A

**ACCOMMODATION**

| | |
|---|---|
| Baan Khao Lak | 17 |
| Baan Soraya | 3 |
| Bamboo Lodge | 15 |
| Chong Fah Beach Resort | 4 |
| Fair House | 1 |
| Garden Beach Resort | 12 |
| Gerd and Noi | 11 |
| Green Beach Bungalows | 13 |
| Jai | 8 |
| Khao Lak Andaman | |
| Beach Resort | 9 |
| Khao Lak Laguna Resort | 19 |
| Krathom Khao Lak | 10 |
| Nang Thong Bay Resort | 14 |
| Nang Thong Bay Resort 2 | 16 |
| Palm Andaman Beach Resort | 7 |
| Paradise | 6 |
| Pascha Resort | 2 |
| Phu Khao Lak Resort | 18 |
| Poseidon Bungalows | 20 |
| Sabai Bungalows | 5 |

**National Park Headquarters**

**Police**

**National Park Bungalows**

N

20

4

**KHAO LAK & BANG NIANG**

Phang Nga, Phuket & Krabi

**BANG NIANG**

Bang Niang Beach

Bang Niang River

2

1

3

4    5

@

6

7

0        500 m

**KHAO LAK**

8

9

11

12

13

14    15

16

17

19

10

A

Nang Thong Minimarket

Sea Dragon Dive Centre

Phuket Divers Dive Internet @

Exchange

Southeast Asia Thailand Travel

Laguna Night Plaza

18

0        500 m

almost wintry; although all dive operators, most tour operators and several bungalow operations close down for the duration, an increasing number of places do stay open and offer huge discounts as an enticement.

Development has now spread north of Khao Lak to **BANG NIANG** beach, two and a half kilometres up the coast and accessed by a kilometre-long side track running off Highway 4. New upmarket accommodation is popping up here all the time, but for the moment Bang Niang is still a smaller, quieter resort than Khao Lak. The beach is a lovely long stretch of golden sand, for the most part free of rocks and good for swimming between November and April. If you just keep walking south along the beach from Bang Niang you'll reach Khao Lak beach in about 45 minutes.

Whichever resort you're based at, once you've had your fill of trips out to the islands, you might want to rent a motorbike and head off to a local **waterfall** – Nam Tok Chongfah is only 5km north of Khao Lak, Nam Tok Lumphi is about 20km south. Several tour operators in Khao Lak and Bang Niang organize **day-tours**, including *Bamboo Lodge* and Jungle and Sea Tour, behind *Nang Thong Bay Resort* (☎076/420625), and Eco Khao Lak Adventure (☎076/420224), inside the Laguna Night Plaza. Typical programmes include elephant-riding and canoeing either just outside Khao Sok National Park, or on the coast in Si Phang Nga National Park (B2000 adults/B1000 children); sea-kayaking in Ao Phang Nga (B2150/1500); overnight in Khao Sok with trekking and a night safari (B4800/2800); trekking to waterfalls in nearby Sri Phang Nga National Park (B1200/600); and a day-trip to Kaw Thaung in Burma (B2000/1000).

## Practicalities

All the regular **buses** running from Phuket to Ranong, Takua Pa and Surat Thani, and vice versa, pass the turn-offs to Khao Lak and Bang Niang; if you're coming from Krabi or Phang Nga you should take a Phuket-bound bus as far as **Khokkloi** bus terminal and switch to a Takua Pa or Ranong bus. Most bus drivers will be familiar with the big-name resorts in Khao Lak and Bang Niang and should drop you as near as possible; otherwise, for most Khao Lak beach hotels you should get off as soon as you see the Sea Dragon Dive Center, from where it's a five-hundred-metre walk west down the side road to the sea. For Bang Niang, alight when you see a cluster of signs for the Bang Niang resorts and either walk the kilometre down the road to the beach, following the relevant signs, or arrange a motorbike taxi at the roadside. When it comes to moving on, it's just a question of hopping on one of the frequent north- or southbound buses and changing where necessary (hotel staff can usually fill you in on bus schedules). Many guest houses and all tour operators can arrange taxi services for up to four people to Khao Sok (B900), Krabi (B1600) and Surat Thani ferry pier (B2100).

The **shops** and businesses in Khao Lak should be able to meet your everyday requirements, but for anything major you'll need to go to Takua Pa or Phuket. The Nang Thong minimart, across from Sea Dragon on the main road, stocks travellers' essentials like mosquito repellent, toilet paper, sunscreen and English-language newspapers, and the Laguna Night Plaza beside the *Khao Lak Laguna Resort* has a bookstore, clothes boutique, restaurant and souvenir outlet as well as car rental and several tour operators. Dotted along the main road you'll also find several tailors' shops. There are two **banks** in Khao Lak, with ATMs and exchange counters (daily 8.30am–6pm): one next to Sea Dragon and the other inside the Laguna Night Plaza. Several places on Highway 4 offer

## Dive operators in Khao Lak

Though Khao Lak has charms enough of its own to keep you happy for a few days, most travellers are drawn here because of the **diving and snorkelling trips** to the Similan islands (see p.317) and beyond. These trips are extremely popular and don't leave every day so you should try to book them in advance. Normal live-aboard boats take around four or five hours to reach the Similans from Khao Lak, but some dive operators also use speedboats for day-trippers – these only take a couple of hours, but aren't recommended for anyone prone to seasickness. The diving season runs from November through April, though if you're in the area a couple of weeks either side of this period it may be worth enquiring about dive trips on the off-chance.

**Kon-Tiki**, inside the Laguna Night Plaza ⊕076/420208, ⊕420120, ⊛www.kontiki-khaolak.com. Swiss-run PADI Five-Star Instructor Development Centre, with another branch in Phuket. They use a speed boat for their one-day dive trips to the Similans (B3500), but also do two- and three-day live-aboards (around B9000 and B13,000), with accompanying snorkellers welcomed at about forty percent discount. Also run courses for kids aged 7–11 (B700), as well as one- and two-day Discover Scuba courses on the Similans (B4500/6500).

**Phuket Divers**, beside Highway 4 in central Khao Lak, and in front of *Gerd and Noi* on the beach ⊕076/420628, ⊛www.phuketdivers.com. Three-day trips on a comfortable live-aboard boat to the Similans for B14,000, or B16,500 for a four-day expedition to the Similans, Surin islands and Richelieu Rock. Snorkellers welcome on both for a reduced price. Four-day Open water PADI dive courses can be done in Khao Lak for B8000 or added to above dive trips for B7000.

**Poseidon**, at *Poseidon Bungalows*, 7km south of central Khao Lak, near the village of Lam Kaen (see p.317) ⊕076/443258, ⊛www.similantour.nu. Highly recommended three-day live-aboard snorkelling trips to the Similans (B5500); can arrange dives for accompanying divers if requested. Current departures are twice weekly on Tuesdays and Fridays.

**Sea Dragon Dive Center**, beside Highway 4 in central Khao Lak, also bookable through *Paradise* in Bang Niang ⊕076/420420, ⊕420418, ⊛www.seadragondivecenter.com. The longest-running Khao Lak dive operator is managed by experienced and safety-conscious farangs, has a good reputation and is highly recommended. They have three live-aboard boats, and prices range from B9000 for a two-day trip to the Similans with six dives, to B16,000 for a four-day expedition with fourteen dives on the Similans, Surin islands, Ko Bon, Ko Tachai and Richelieu Rock. Snorkellers can accompany some trips at one-third off the price. Aside from live-aboards you can also do one-day local dives for B1300–1800. All their PADI dive courses can be done in Khao Lak – one-day Discover Scuba around B1700, or four-day Openwater for B8000 – and some can be also be done while on one of the above dive trips.

**internet** access, as does *Bamboo Lodge* down by the beach. South–East Asia Thailand Travel (⊕076/420611) sells international and domestic air tickets, arranges train tickets, organizes tours and can arrange accommodation if necessary; for day-trip operators, see opposite. *Green Beach* rents **mountain bikes**, Eco Khao Lak Adventure (⊕076/420224) in the Laguna Night Plaza has **motorbikes** (B250/day) and mountain bikes (B150) for rent and is an outlet for Budget **car rental** (⊛www.budget.co.th). There's a **clinic** at *Krathom Thai* every evening from 4.30pm–9.30pm.

Bang Niang is less commercial, but has a small cluster of businesses beside Highway 4 at the turn-off to the beach, where you'll find a tour operator, internet access and an informal taxi service.

## Accommodation and eating

The standard of **accommodation** in Khao Lak and Bang Niang is high, but rates are pricey (there's little under B550) and the trend is upmarket, with several places already building swimming pools; it's certainly not a budget travellers' resort. Unless otherwise stated, all accommodation occupies beachfront land, and generally you'll be staying in bungalows rather than rooms in a block. Accommodation in all categories is best reserved ahead as the resort is very popular with mid-market German and Swedish travellers as well as tourists on eco-packages. Those places that stay open during the rainy season, from May through October, usually offer discounts of up to fifty percent on the rates quoted below.

All the bungalow resorts in Khao Lak and Bang Niang have **restaurants**, and these are always popular: those at *Nang Thong Bay Resort* and *Jai* stand out. There are a few little dedicated restaurants along the roadside in Khao Lak, including the very inexpensive *Nom's*, which emphasizes home-style cooking and serves noodle and rice dishes as well as plenty of fresh seafood. At the other end of the spectrum, *Old Siam*, inside the Laguna Night Plaza, boasts a more refined, mid-priced menu featuring delicious fish cakes, *tom yam kung* and the like.

### Khao Lak

**Baan Khao Lak** ☎ 076/420199, ℻ 420198. Upmarket collection of 28 bungalows set in a garden around a shorefront swimming pool. ❽

**Bamboo Lodge** ☎ 076/420625. One of the cheaper options, with just half a dozen en-suite bungalows set back from the shore in a bamboo grove. ❹

**Garden Beach Resort** ☎ 076/420121, ℻ 420129. Lots of rather uninspiring but reasonably priced whitewashed concrete bungalows, all with fan. Those on the beachfront cost more. Closed mid-May to mid-Oct. ❸–❺.

**Gerd and Noi**, also known as *Khao Lak Bungalows* ☎ 076/420145, ℻ 420144. Large, nicely furnished villas with huge glass windows that look out on to the tropical shorefront garden. All rooms have fans; price depends on the location. ❺–❻

**Green Beach Bungalows** ☎ 076/420043, ℻ 420047. Forty fan and air-con bungalows set around a small khlong, each with a balcony, woven bamboo walls and mosquito screens. Rents mountain bikes. Open all year with forty percent discounts May–Oct. ❺–❻

**Jai** ☎ 076/420390. Friendly family-run place offering the cheapest accommodation in Khao Lak, comprising simple old-style bamboo bungalows furnished with mozzie nets and bathrooms, set close to the main road and some distance from the beach. There's a good restaurant here too. ❷

**Khao Lak Andaman Beach Resort** ☎ 076/420136, ℻ 420134. Thirty huge bungalows,

all smartly outfitted and good value. There are a few fan-cooled ones but most have air-con; price depends on closeness to the sea. Recommended. ❺–❼

**Khao Lak Laguna Resort** ☎ 076/420200, ℻ 076/431297, ℮ khaolak2@png.a-net.net.th. The pick of the crop in Khao Lak, where guests stay in tasteful, traditional *sala*-style villas, equipped with fan or air-con, mini-bar and hot water. There's a swimming pool and a restaurant in the attractively landscaped beachfront grounds and a small shopping plaza beside the road. Very popular, so reserve ahead. Open all year; fifty percent discount May–Oct. ❾

**Krathom Khao Lak** ☎ 076/420149, ℻ 431226, ℮ krathom@hotmail.com. Nine comfortably furnished wood and thatch bungalows scattered among the trees some way back from the main road, with no beach access. Run by the local doctor's family and open all year. There's a restaurant and small bar here too. ❹

**Nang Thong Bay Resort** ☎ & ℻ 01/229 2181. Efficiently run, popular place that offers a range of very clean, smartly maintained bungalows, all with fans and attached bathrooms; the most expensive ones are set in a garden that leads right down to the water, the cheaper ones are set in another garden on the other side of the track. The restaurant serves good but pricey food and has a book exchange. Open all year, with a fifty discount in low season. ❹–❻

**Nang Thong Bay Resort 2** ☎ 076/420078, ℻ 420080. Three dozen bungalows comfortably furnished to a similarly high standard as at its sister resort. The cheapest ones have fan and bathroom; the pricier accommodation has air-con and a fridge. Reserve ahead. Open all year. ④–⑦

**Phu Khao Lak Resort** ☎076/420141, ℻420140. Diagonally across the main road from the *Laguna*, the spotlessly clean concrete bungalows at this family-run place sit prettily amid a coconut plantation. They're among the cheapest in the resort, though they're a bit of a walk from the beach. Price depends on the size of the bungalow. ③–④

**Poseidon Bungalows** ☎076/443258, Ⓦwww.similantour.nu. Seven kilometres south of central Khao Lak, on a wild and rocky shore surrounded by jungle and rubber plantations, this Swedish-Thai-run guest house is a lovely place to hang out for a few days and it's also a long-established organizer of snorkelling expeditions to the Similan islands (see below). The smaller, cheaper bungalows share facilities, while the more expensive en-suite ones are larger and more comfortable; there's a good restaurant here too. To get here, ask to be dropped off the bus at the village of Lam Kaen (between kilometre-stone markers 53 and 54), from where it's a 1km walk or B40 motorbike-taxi ride to the bungalows. Motorbikes are available for rent. Closed May–October. ③–⑤

## Bang Niang

**Baan Soraya** ☎076/420192, ℮baan_soraya@phang-nga.net. Just half a dozen very attractive bungalows, with stylish furnishings, hot water and some air-con; a mere hop and a skip from the sea, though only one bungalow actually enjoys a proper sea view. Run by a Dutch-Thai couple. Closed May–Oct. Recommended. ⑤–⑦

**Chong Fah Beach Resort** ☎076/420056, ℻420055, ℮chongfah@usa.net. The original hotel on Bang Niang beach, but poorly laid out, so that

the small blocks of rooms overlook each other rather than the sea. Interiors are very comfortable though, some rooms have air-con, and the place is efficiently run. ⑤–⑧

**Fair House**, beside Highway 4, just north of the turn-off to the beach, ☎076/420394. A handful of concrete bungalows widely spaced in a garden set back from the main road, but a good kilometre's walk from the beach. ④

**Palm Andaman Beach Resort** ☎076/420185, ℻420189, ℮palm_as1@hotmail.com. A rather stylish and relatively good-value outfit, whose very spacious air-con bungalows are attractively designed and have unusual open-air bathrooms. ⑧

**Paradise** ☎076/420184. One of the most popular places on Bang Niang, chiefly because it offers simple, old-style bamboo huts, rather than the concrete versions favoured by most resorts in this area. The huts all have fans, mosquito nets and bathrooms and are set in a palm grove that runs right down the shore; price depends on size and proximity to the beach. You can book Sea Dragon dive trips and courses here, rent motorbikes and organize local tours. From May through Oct you should phone ahead to check whether they're open. ③–⑤

**Pascha Resort** ☎076/420280, ℻420282, ℮pascha43@hotmail.com. Tastefully designed teak-wood bungalows, each one furnished in traditional Thai style and equipped with air-con, TV and mini-bar; a swimming pool is planned. Across a track from the beach. ⑦

**Sabai Bungalows** ☎076/420142. Run by the same people as *Gerd and Noi* on Khao Lak, *Sabai* offers the cheapest accommodation in Bang Niang, with ten bamboo bungalows set in a garden beside a track, less than 100m from the beach. Rooms have fans and good bathrooms. ③

# Ko Similan

Rated by *Skin Diver* magazine as one of the world's top ten spots for both above-water and underwater beauty, the nine islands that make up the **KO SIMILAN** national park are among the most exciting **diving** destinations in Thailand. Massive granite boulders set magnificently against turquoise waters give the islands their distinctive character, but it's the thirty-metre visibility that draws the divers. The underwater scenery is nothing short of overwhelming here: the reefs teem with a host of coral fish, from the long-nosed butterfly fish to the black-, yellow- and white-striped angel fish, and the ubiquitous purple and turquoise parrot fish, which nibble so incessantly at the coral. A little further offshore, magnificent mauve and burgundy crown-of-thorns starfish stalk the sea bed, gobbling chunks of coral as they go – and out here you'll also see turtles, manta rays, moray eels, jacks, reef sharks, sea snakes, red grouper and quite possibly white-tip sharks, barracuda, giant lobster and enormous tuna.

The **islands** lie 64km off the mainland and are numbered from nine at the northern end of the chain to one at the southern end. In descending order, they are: Ko Bon (number nine), Ko Ba Ngu, Ko Similan, Ko Payoo, Ko Miang (actually two islands, numbers five and four, known collectively as Ko Miang), Ko Pahyan, Ko Pahyang and Ko Hu Yong. Only islands number eight (Ko Ba Ngu) and number four (Ko Miang) are inhabited, with the national park head-quarters and accommodation located on the latter; some tour groups are also allowed to camp on island number eight. Ko Similan is the largest island in the chain, blessed with a beautiful, fine white-sand bay and impressive boulders; Ko Hu Yong has an exceptionally long white-sand bay and is used by **turtles** for egg-laying (see box on p.331) from November to February.

As well as suffering from indigenous predators and from the repercussions of El Niño in the 1990s, the Similan reefs have also been damaged in places by anchors and by the local practice of using dynamite in fishing. National parks authorities have recently responded by taking drastic action to protect this pre-cious region, banning fishermen from the island chain (to vociferous and at times violent protest), enforcing strict regulations for tourist boats, and, at the time of writing, closing off islands one, two and three to all visitors. The whole Similan chain is closed to all visitors from May through October, when high seas make it almost impossible to reach anyway.

## Practicalities

Ko Similan is not really a destination for the independent traveller, but if you have your own diving gear and want to do it on your own, you should head down to **Thap Lamu pier**, which is signed off Highway 4 about 8km south of central Khao Lak. A company called Met Sine Tourist, based at the Thap Lamu pier (☎ & ℻ 076/443276), runs day-trips by speedboat from here to the Similans (B2100), which depart every day during the season at 8.30am, take two hours and can also be used by independent travellers wanting to stay on the island for a few days. It's also possible to buy one-way tickets to island num-ber four on the daily Songserm speedboat which leaves Phuket every morn-ing at 8.30am from December through April, takes approximately ninety min-utes and cost B700 each way.

Limited **accommodation** is available on Ko Miang, in the shape of nation-al park bungalows (B600 for four beds) and tents (B150), and there's an expen-sive restaurant here too. It's definitely worth booking your accommodation in advance with the national parks office on the Thap Lamu pier (☎076/411913–4), as the place can get crowded with tour groups, especially on weekends and holidays. There's no drinking water available outside Ko Miang, and campfires are prohibited on all the islands. Inter-island shuttles, the only way of getting from place to place, are expensive, at B250 per person per trip.

### Organized snorkelling and diving tours

It's far simpler to do what most people do and join an organized **tour** (Nov–May only). Most travel agents in Phuket sell snorkelling **day-trips** to Ko Similan for B2300–3000, which either go by boat all the way from Phuket to the Similans or travel first to Thap Lamu by bus and then take a speedboat;

either way the whole journey takes around three hours. Kon-Tiki in Khao Lak (see box on p.315) also does one-day dive trips to the Similans (B3500).

The more rewarding option would be to do an **overnight** trip to the islands. Met Sine in Thap Lamu (☎ & ⓕ 076/443276) runs two- and three-day Similan packages (B3200/4000), which include accommodation on Ko Miang and snorkelling equipment, while many dive companies sell two- to four-day all-inclusive live-aboard trips. Most live-aboard boats take four to five hours to reach Ko Similan from Khao Lak or Phuket. The cheapest, most informal tours are run out of Khao Lak, where prices average B9000 for a two-day live-aboard **diving** trip or B16,000 for four days, with about a forty percent discount for accompanying snorkellers; a three-day dedicated **snorkelling** trip costs B5300; for full details see box on p.315. Most of the Phuket-based dive operators (see p.322) only offer four-day live-aboards to the Similans (also featuring Richlieu Rock and a couple of other sites) for US$550–600; some trips are open to accompanying snorkellers at a slight discount.

4

SOUTHERN THAILAND: THE ANDAMAN COAST | Phuket

# Phuket

Thailand's largest island and a province in its own right, **Phuket** (pronounced "Poo-ket") has been a well-off region since the nineteenth century, when Chinese merchants got in on its tin-mining and sea-borne trade, before turning to the rubber industry. Phuket remains the wealthiest province in Thailand, with the highest per-capita income, but what mints the money nowadays is **tourism**: with an annual influx that tops one million, Phuket ranks second in popularity only to Pattaya, and the package-tour traffic has wrought its usual transformations. Thoughtless tourist developments have scarred much of the island, particularly along the west coast, and the trend on all the beaches is upmarket, with very few budget possibilities. As mainstream resorts go, however, those on Phuket are just about the best in Thailand, offering a huge range of **watersports** and magnificent **diving** facilities to make the most of the clear and sparkling sea. Remoter parts of the island are still attractive, too, particularly the interior: a fertile, hilly expanse dominated by rubber and pineapple plantations and interspersed with wild tropical vegetation.

Phuket's capital, Muang Phuket or **Phuket town**, lies on the southeast coast, 42km south of the Sarasin Bridge linking the island to the mainland. Most people pass straight through the town on their way to the beaches on the **west coast**, where three big resorts corner the bulk of the trade: high-rise **Ao Patong**, the most developed and expensive, with a nightlife verging on the seedy; the slightly nicer **Ao Karon**; and adjacent **Ao Kata**, the smallest and least spoilt of the trio. If you're really looking for peace and quiet you should turn instead to some of the beaches on the far northwest coast, such as the twelve-kilometre-long national park beach of **Hat Mai Khao**, its more developed neighbour **Hat Nai Yang** or the delightful little bays of **Hat Nai Thon** and **Hat Kamala**. Most of the other west-coast beaches have been taken over by one or two upmarket hotels, specifically **Hat Nai Harn**, **Hat Surin** and

319

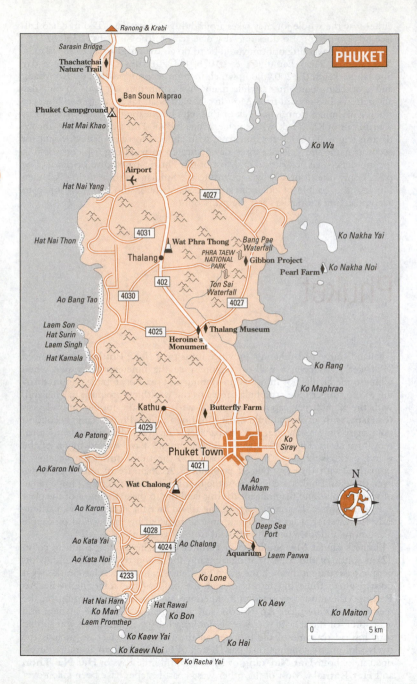

Ranong & Krabi

Sarasin Bridge
Thachatchai
Nature Trail

Ban Soun Maprao

Phuket Campground

Hat Mai Khao

Ko Wa

4

Airport

Hat Nai Yang

4027

Ko Nakha Yai

4031

Hat Nai Thon

Wat Phra Thong

Bang Pae
Waterfall

PHRA TAEW
NATIONAL
PARK

Gibbon Project

Pearl Farm

Ko Nakha Noi

Thalang

402

Ton Sai
Waterfall

Ao Bang Tao

4030

4027

Laem Son
Hat Surin
Laem Singh

4025

Thalang Museum

Heroine's
Monument

Hat Kamala

Ko Rang

Ko Maphrao

Kathu

Butterfly Farm

4029

Ao Patong

Phuket Town

Ko
Siray

Ao Karon Noi

4021

Ao
Makham

Wat Chalong

Ao Karon

N

4028

Deep Sea
Port

Ao Kata Yai

4024

Ao Chalong

Ao Kata Noi

Aquarium

Laem Panwa

4233

Ko Lone

Hat Nai Harn
Ko Man
Laem Promthep

Hat Rawai
Ko Bon

Ko Aew

Ko Maiton

Ko Kaew Yai

0          5 km

Ko Kaew Noi

Ko Hai

Ko Racha Yai

SOUTHERN THAILAND: THE ANDAMAN COAST | Phuket

**Ao Bang Tao**. In complete contrast, the south and east coasts hold one of Thailand's largest seafaring *chao ley* communities (see p.308), but the beaches along these shores have nothing to offer tourists, having been polluted and generally disfigured by the island's tin-mining industry.

There's an excellent **website** about Phuket Ⓦ www.phuket.com, which has numerous links to Phuket tour operators and businesses and is particularly good for discounted accommodation on the island.

## Getting to the island

Quite a few airlines operate direct **international flights** to Phuket, so if you're starting your Thailand trip in the south, it may be worth flying straight here or via another Asian city rather than having to make connections via Bangkok. Bangkok Airways also does a tempting thrice-daily shuttle between Phuket and Siem Reap in Cambodia.

Given that bus journeys from Bangkok are so long and tedious, you might want to consider taking a **domestic flight** from the capital – or elsewhere – to Phuket. Thai Airways runs seventeen flights a day between Phuket and Bangkok, and also links the island with Hat Yai daily; Bangkok Airways does two daily runs between Phuket and Ko Samui, and the Phuket-based airline Air Andaman flies daily to Krabi, Surat Thani and Nakhon Si Thammarat, and is intending to extend its service to include Chumphon and Ranong.

**Phuket International Airport** (Ⓣ076/327230) is located on the northwest coast of the island, 32km northwest of Phuket town. There is currently no reliable public transport system from the airport to the beaches, so you are more or less obliged to take a **taxi** to your chosen destination. These cost about B400–600 to the main west-coast beaches of Ao Patong, Ao Karon and Ao Kata, or about B300 to Phuket town. You can **rent cars** direct from the airport: both Avis (Ⓣ076/327358, Ⓦ www.avisthailand.com) and Budget (Ⓣ076/205396, Ⓦ www.budget.co.th) have desks in the arrivals area, and there's a **left-luggage** service at the airport too.

The cheapest way of **getting to the airport** is by Tour Royal Limousine, which charges B80 per person. Unfortunately their office and pick-up point is inconveniently located at 55/3 Thanon Vichitsongkhram (Ⓣ076/222062), 4km west of Phuket town centre. Limousine minivans depart from here at 6.30am and then hourly from 7am to 6pm and take about 45 minutes. Not surprisingly, most people take taxis instead, and nearly all hotels on Patong, Karon and Kata offer a taxi service to the airport for B400–600; the trip takes about an hour. The domestic **departure tax** of B30 is included in the price of the air ticket, but for international departures you will be charged B500 at check-in. Contact details for the Phuket offices of international and domestic airlines are given on p.328.

## By bus

All direct **air-con buses** from Bangkok's Southern Bus Terminal make the journey overnight, leaving at approximately half-hourly intervals between 5.30pm and 7pm and arriving about fourteen hours later. Most air-con buses from Phuket to Bangkok also make the journey overnight, though there are a few departures during the morning. There is no train service to Phuket, but if you can't face taking the bus all the way from Bangkok, a more comfortable (and less nerve-wracking) alternative would be to book an overnight sleeper train to Surat Thani, about 290km east of Phuket, and take a bus from there to Phuket (about six hours). There are fourteen buses a day between **Surat Thani** and Phuket, all travelling via **Khao Sok**, **Takua Pa** and **Khao Lak**; and six

## Diving and snorkelling off Phuket

The reefs and islands within sailing distance of Phuket rate among the most spectacular in the world, and the desire to dive off the Andaman coast draws hordes of visitors to the resort. This is where you'll find Thailand's largest concentration of **dive centres**, offering some of the best-value certificated courses and trips in the country. All the dive centres listed below offer PADI- and/or NAUI-certificated diving courses and have qualified instructors and dive-masters; we have highlighted those centres that are accredited PADI Five-Star Centres (the Instructor Development Centres are one step higher than the Five-Star Centres); see p.67 for details. Nonetheless, you should still try to get recommendations from other divers before signing up with any dive centre, however highly starred. Always check the equipment and staff credentials carefully and try to get first-hand recommendations from other divers. You should also check that the dive centre is a member of Hyperbaric Services Thailand (HST), which runs Phuket's **recompression chamber**, located at 233 Thanon Song Roi Phi on Ao Patong (☎076/342518). The recompression chamber is available free to member organizations and their customers; non-members need to put down a deposit of B100,000 before they can get treated. All dive centres rent **equipment**, and many of them sell essential items too; for the full range, visit Dive Supply, at 189 Thanon Song Roi Phi on Ao Patong (daily 9.30am–7pm; ☎076/342511).

A half- or one-day introductory **diving course** averages B1500–2000, and a four-day Openwater course costs between B5000–9500, usually including equipment. The price of **day-trips** to local reefs depends on the distance to the dive site, and the operator, but generally falls between B2000–3500, including at least two dives, all equipment and food. Nearly all dive centres also offer **live-aboard** cruises: a typical four-day live-aboard trip to Ko Similan (see p.317) and Ko Surin (see p.307) costs US$500 including at least eight dives, all equipment and full board.

**Snorkellers** are usually welcome to join divers' day-trips (about B1000) and can sometimes go on live-aboard cruises at slightly reduced rates. In addition, all travel agents sell mass-market day-trips to Ko Phi Phi, which include snorkelling stops at Phi Phi Le and Phi Phi Don, an hour's snorkelling (mask, fins and snorkel provided) and a seafood lunch. Transport is on large boats belonging to the main local ferry companies, with prices averaging B1100, or B750 for children. Most of these companies also offer day-trips to Ko Similan, for B2300–3000, depending on the speed of the boat; some companies use boats from Phuket which take three hours, while other companies bus passengers to Thap Lamu and then use speedboats, which also takes around three hours in total.

### Dive centres

All the centres listed below offer a variety of itineraries and cruises, with schedules depending on weather conditions and the number of divers. Check out the Phuket Island Access website (🌐 www.phuketcom.co.th/diving/guide.htm) for links to Phuket dive operators and for some fine underwater pictures.

### Ao Patong

**Fantasea Divers**, next to *Holiday Inn* at the southern end of Patong ☎076/340088, 🅕 340309, 🌐 www.fantasea.net.

**Holiday Diving Club**, at *Patong Beach Hotel*, south of Soi Bangla ☎076/341235, 🅕 340998, 🅔 seawalk@phuket-ksc.co.th.

**Santana**, 6 Thanon Sawatdirak ☎076/294220, 🅕 340360, 🌐 www.santanaphuket .com. Five-Star PADI Instructor Development Centre.

**South East Asia Divers**, 62 Thanon Thavee Wong ☎076/344022, 🅕 342530, 🌐 www.phuketdive.net. Five-Star PADI Instructor Development Centre.

#### Ao Karon/Ao Kata

**Andaman Scuba**, 114/24 Thanon Taina on the Kata/Karon headland ☏076/331006, ℱ330591, ☒www.andamanscuba.com.

**Dive Asia**, 12/10 Thanon Patak, north Karon ☏076/396199; Kata/Karon headland ☏076/330598, ℱ284033, ☒www.diveasia.com. Five-Star PADI Instructor Development Centre.

**Kon-Tiki**, c/o *Karon Villa*, central Karon ☏076/396312, ℱ396313, ☒www.kon-tiki-diving.com. Five-Star PADI Dive Centre.

**Marina Divers**, next to *Marina Cottages* at 120/2 Thanon Patak ☏076/330272, ℱ330998, ☒www.marinadivers.com. Five-Star PADI Instructor Development Centre.

## Andaman coast dive sites

The major dive sites visited from Andaman coast resorts are listed below. In these waters you'll find a stunning variety of coral and a multitude of fish species, including sharks, oysters, puffer fish, stingrays, groupers, lion fish, moray eels and more. For more information on marine life see the colour section on "Underwater Thailand" in the Introduction; for detailed ratings and descriptions of Andaman coast dive sites, consult the handbook *Diving in Thailand*, by Collin Piprell and Ashley J. Boyd (Asia Books).

**Anemone Reef**, about 22km east of Phuket. Submerged reef of soft coral and masses of sea anemones that starts about 5m deep. Lots of fish, including leopard sharks, tuna and barracuda. Usually combined with a dive at nearby Shark Point.

**Burma Banks**, about 250km northwest of Phuket. A series of submerged "banks", well away from any land mass and very close to the Burmese border. Visibility up to 25m.

**Hin Daeng and Hin Muang**, 26km southwest of Ko Rok Nok, near Ko Lanta (see box on p.382). Hin Daeng is a highly recommended reef wall, with visibility up to 30m. One hundred metres away, Hin Muang also drops to 50m and is a good place for encountering stingrays, manta rays, whale sharks and silvertip sharks. Visibility up to 50m.

**King Cruiser**, near Shark Point, between Phuket and Ko Phi Phi. Dubbed the Thai Tanic, this has become a wreck dive as of May 1997, when a tourist ferry sank on its way to Ko Phi Phi. Visibility up to 20m.

**Ko Phi Phi**, 48km east of Ao Chalong. Visibility up to 30m. Spectacular drop-offs; good chance of seeing whale sharks. See p.372.

**Ko Racha Noi** and **Ko Racha Yai**, about 33km and 28km south of Ao Chalong respectively. Visibility up to 40m. Racha Yai is good for beginners and for snorkellers; at the more challenging Racha Noi there's a good chance of seeing manta rays, eagle rays and whale sharks.

**Ko Rok Nok** and **Ko Rok Nai**, 100km southeast of Ao Chalong, south of Ko Lanta (see p.382). Visibility up to 18m.

**Ko Similan**, 96km northwest of Phuket. One of the world's top ten diving spots. Visibility up to 30m. Leopard sharks, whale sharks and manta rays, plus caves and gorges. See p.317.

**Ko Surin**, 174km northwest of Phuket. Shallow reefs particularly good for snorkelling; see p.307.

**Richelieu Rock**, just east of Ko Surin. A sunken pinnacle that's famous for its manta rays and whale sharks.

**Shark Point (Hin Mu Sang)**, 24km east of Laem Panwa. Protected as a marine sanctuary. Visibility up to 10m. Notable for soft corals, sea fans and leopard sharks. Often combined with the King Cruiser dive and/or Anemone Reef.

private minibuses a day from Phuket to Surat Thani, which leave from opposite the *Montri Hotel* on Thanon Montri. Takua Pa is a useful interchange for local services to Khuraburi and Ranong, though there are four direct buses a day between **Ranong** and Phuket. As for points further south: seventeen buses a day run between **Krabi** and Phuket, via **Phang Nga**, and there are also frequent services to and from **Trang**, **Nakhon Si Thammarat** and **Hat Yai**.

Nearly all buses to and from Phuket use the **bus station** (☎076/211977) at the eastern end of Thanon Phang Nga in Phuket town, from where it's a ten-minute walk or a short tuk-tuk ride to the town's central hotel area, and slightly further to the departure-point for the beaches in front of the fruit and vegetable market on Thanon Ranong.

### By boat

If you're coming to Phuket **from Ko Phi Phi** or **Ko Lanta**, the quickest and most scenic option is to take the **boat**. During peak season, up to four ferries a day make the trip to and from Ko Phi Phi, taking between ninety minutes and two and a half hours and docking at the deep-sea port on Phuket's southeast coast; during low season, there's at least one ferry a day in both directions. Travellers from Ko Lanta have to change boats on Ko Phi Phi. Minibuses meet the ferries in Phuket and charge B100 per person for transfers to Phuket town and the major west-coast beaches, or B150 to the airport.

### Island transport

Although the best west-coast beaches are connected by road, to get from one beach to another by **public transport** you nearly always have to go back into Phuket town; songthaews run regularly throughout the day from Thanon Ranong in the town centre and cost between B15 and B25 from town to the coast. **Tuk-tuks** do travel directly between major beaches, but charge at least B120 a ride. However, almost everyone on Phuket rides **motorbikes** (some of which would be more accurately described as mopeds), and you might consider saving time, money and aggravation by doing likewise. All the main resorts rent out motorbikes for B200–250 per day (be sure to ask for a helmet as well, as the compulsory helmet law is strictly enforced on Phuket); alternatively, rent a **jeep** for B800–1200. Be aware though that traffic accidents are legion on Phuket, especially for bikers: there were reportedly 179 motorcycle fatalities on Phuket in 1999 alone.

# Phuket town

Though it has plentiful hotels and restaurants, **PHUKET TOWN** (Muang Phuket) stands distinct from the tailor-made tourist settlements along the beaches as a place geared primarily towards its residents. Most visitors hang about just long enough to jump on a beach-bound songthaew, but you may find yourself returning for a welcome dose of real life; Phuket town has an enjoyably authentic market and some of the best handicraft shops on the island. If you're on a tight budget, the town is worth considering as a base, as accommodation and food come a little less expensive, and you can get out to all the beaches with relative ease. Bear in mind, though, that the town offers little in

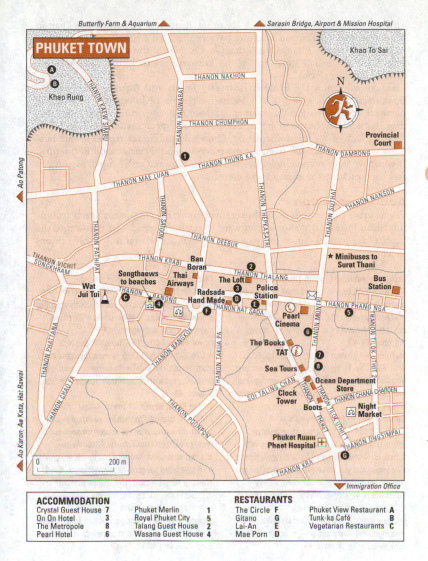

**PHUKET TOWN**

Butterfly Farm & Aquarium

Sarasin Bridge, Airport & Mission Hospital

Khao To Sai

Khao Rung

THANON YAOWARAT

THANON NAKHON

THANON CHUMPHON

THANON KAEW SIMBU

Provincial Court

THANON DAMRONG

THANON THUNG KA

THANON MAE LUAN

THANON SUTHAT

THANON NANSON

THANON SATON

THANON THEPKASATRI

THANON DEEBUK

Minibuses to Surat Thani

THANON VICHIT SONGKHRAM

THANON KRABI

Ban Boran

THANON PATHIPAT

Songthaews to beaches

Thai Airways

THANON THALANG

Bus Station

Wat Jui Tui

THANON RANONG

The Loft

Radsada Hand Made

Police Station

THANON PHANG NGA

THANON RAT SADA

Pearl Cinema

THANON TLOK UTHIT

THANON PHATTANA

THANON BANGKOK

The Books

TAT

THANON MONTRI

THANON TAKUA PA

Sea Tours

Ocean Department Store

Ao Karon Ao Kata, Hat Rawai

THANON CHAO FA

THANON PHONPON

SOI TALING CHAN

Clock Tower

Boots

THANON CHANA CHAROEN

THANON TLOK UTHIT

THANON THEP

Night Market

Phuket Ruam Phaet Hospital

THANON ONGSIMPAI

THANON KRA

0   200 m

Immigration Office

**ACCOMMODATION**

| | | | |
|---|---|---|---|
| Crystal Guest House | 7 | Phuket Merlin | 1 |
| On On Hotel | 3 | Royal Phuket City | 5 |
| The Metropole | 8 | Talang Guest House | 2 |
| Pearl Hotel | 6 | Wasana Guest House | 4 |

**RESTAURANTS**

| | | | |
|---|---|---|---|
| The Circle | F | Phuket View Restaurant | A |
| Gitano | G | Tunk-ka Café | B |
| Lai-An | E | Vegetarian Restaurants | C |
| Mae Porn | D | | |

the way of nightlife, and as public transport to and from the more lively beaches stops at dusk, you'll have to either rent your own wheels or spend a lot of money on tuk-tuks.

Aside from a manically bustling market on Thanon Ranong there's not a great deal to see, though a two-hour wander around the streets will take you past several faded **colonial-style residences** built by Chinese merchants at the turn of the century. Recognizable by their doors and shutters painted in pastel pinks, blues and greens, a string of these elegant old mansions lines Thanon Talang: the carved lintels and brightly painted shutters of the building next door to the Chinese temple are definitely worth an upward glance. You'll find relics of other historical buildings on Thanon Yaowarat, and on Thanon Ranong (where the Thai Airways office is a fine example), Thanon Phang Nga (the *On On Hotel*) and Thanon Damrong, where the town hall stood in for the US embassy in Phnom Penh in the film *The Killing Fields*.

Kids usually enjoy the **Phuket Butterfly Farm and Aquarium** (*Faam Phi Seua*; daily 9am–5.30pm; B200), located a couple of kilometres beyond the northern end of Thanon Yaowarat at 71/6 Soi Paneang in Ban Sam Kong, but though there are heaps of butterflies of various species, and a few reef fish, there's a lack of specific information. There's no public **transport** to the butterfly farm, but a tuk-tuk from the town centre should cost around B80 return. If you have your own vehicle, follow Thanon Yaowarat as far north as you can and then pick up the signs for the farm.

## Accommodation

Few tourists choose to stay in Phuket town, preferring to opt for beach accommodation instead. But should you want to buck the trend – or if you find the beaches are packed out or too expensive – there are several reasonable options in all categories.

**Crystal Guest House**, 41/16 Thanon Montri ☎076/222774. One of several good, clean guest houses in the town centre; all rooms have attached bathroom, the more expensive have air-con, hot water and TV as well. internet access in the lobby. ❸–❹

**Metropole**, 1 Thanon Montri ☎076/215050, ☏215990. One of the largest hotels in town, and popular with package tourists and businesspeople. Rooms are comfortably equipped if not particularly stylish. ❽

**On On Hotel**, 19 Thanon Phang Nga ☎076/211154. This attractive, colonial-style 1920s building is a long-running favourite with travellers. Rooms are basic but adequate; they're all en suite and you can choose between fan and air-con. internet access in the lobby. ❷–❸

**Pearl Hotel**, 42 Thanon Montri ☎076/211044, ☏212911. Upper-mid-range hotel favoured by package tourists; facilities include a rooftop restaurant and swimming pool, which make it reasonable value for its class. ❼

**Phuket Merlin**, 158/1 Thanon Yaowarat ☎076/212866, ☏216429. Former top-class hotel that now aims mid-market, with decently equipped rooms, all furnished with air-con and TV, plus a swimming pool and nightclub. ❼

**Royal Phuket City**, 154 Thanon Phang Nga ☎076/233333, ☏233335, ⊛www.royalphuketcity.com. Huge chain hotel, with swimming pool, gym, business centre and comfortable rooms. The best in town. ❽–❾

**Talang Guest House**, 37 Thanon Talang ☎076/214225, ✉talanggh@phuket.ksc.co.th. Large fan and air-con rooms in an old wooden house in one of Phuket's most traditional streets. All rooms have attached bathrooms, and soap and towels are provided. A little faded but good value nonetheless. ❸–❹

**Wasana Guest House**, 159 Thanon Ranong ☎076/211754, ☏225424. Friendly, traveller-oriented guest house that's right next to the departure-point for Patong and Karon songthaews. The rooms, all en-suite and some with air-con, are good value for Phuket. ❷–❺

## Eating and drinking

For authentically inexpensive and tasty Thai **food**, hit any one of the noodle shops along Rat Sada or Takua Pa roads, or check out the curries, soups and stews at the no-frills food centre on the top floor of the Thanon Montri Ocean department store (10am–10pm). Alternatively, there's always the night market which materializes around the square off Thanon Tilok Uthit 1 every evening at about 6pm. Foodstalls are also set up at night opposite the TAT office on Thanon Phuket, but the prices here are inflated because of the English-language menu.

**The Circle**, beside the roundabout on Thanon Rat Sada. Conveniently located a couple of blocks east of the songthaew stop, and open-fronted for maximum street-view, this place is ideal for a coffee and a snack, serving cappuccinos, real coffees (including hill-tribe blends from north Thailand), fabulous cakes, plus a few hot dishes.

**Gitano**, opposite *McDonalds* at 14 Thanon Ongsimpai. Lively, Columbian-managed music café that serves Californian and Thai dishes plus a range of cocktails. Stages regular special events including live music and comedy shows. Nightly 6pm–2am.

**Lai-An**, 58 Thanon Rat Sada. Large, busy, air-con Chinese restaurant offering a huge array of moderately priced dishes, including some Thai standards.

**Mae Porn**, 50–52 Thanon Phang Nga. Popular and very reasonably priced seafood restaurant serving typical Thai and Chinese dishes.

**Phuket View Restaurant**, on Thanon Kaew Simbu near the top of Khao Rung, the wooded hill on the northwestern outskirts of town. Middle-class Phuketians drive up to this slightly formal, mid-priced restaurant for outdoor seafood with a view. Bring mosquito repellent.

**Tunk-ka Café**, just above *Phuket View* on Thanon Kaew Simbu near the top of Khao Rung. Renowned for its (moderately priced) seafood, mixed grills, iced coffees and panoramic views.

**Vegetarian Restaurants**, Thanon Ranong. Two canteen-style restaurants side by side, staffed by volunteers from the nearby Wat Jui Tui Chinese temple. Most dishes are made with meat substitutes (usually soya), so the menu lists such delights as roast duck curry. It's a friendly place and very cheap. Opens for breakfast and lunch only.

## Shopping

Phuket town has the best **bookshop** on the island: The Books (daily 11am–9.30pm), near the TAT office on Thanon Phuket, stocks a phenomenal range of English-language books about Thailand, plus a few shelves of coffee-table books and modern novels. Ban Boran, at 51 Thanon Yaowarat, specializes

### Ngan Kin Jeh: the vegetarian festival

For nine days every October or November, at the start of the ninth lunar month, the streets of Phuket are enlivened by **Ngan Kin Jeh** – the Vegetarian Festival – which culminates in the unnerving spectacle of men and women parading about with steel rods through their cheeks and tongues. The festival marks the beginning of **Taoist Lent**, a month-long period of purification observed by devout Chinese all over the world, but celebrated most ostentatiously in Phuket, by devotees of the island's five Chinese temples. After six days' abstention from meat, alcohol and sex, the white-clad worshippers flock to their local temple, where drum rhythms help induce a trance state in which they become possessed by spirits. As proof of their new-found transcendance of the physical world they skewer themselves with any available sharp instrument – fishing rods and car wing-mirrors have done service in the past – before walking over red-hot coals or up ladders of swords as further testament to their otherworldliness. In the meantime there's much singing and dancing and almost continuous firework displays, with the grandest festivities held at Wat Jui Tui on Thanon Ranong in Phuket town.

The ceremony dates back to the mid-nineteenth century, when a travelling Chinese opera company turned up on the island to entertain emigrant Chinese working in the tin mines. They had been there almost a year when suddenly the whole troupe – together – with a number of the miners came down with a life-endangering fever. Realizing that they'd neglected their gods somewhat, the actors performed expiatory rites which soon effected a cure for most of the sufferers. The festival has been held ever since, though the self-mortification rites are a later modification, possibly of Hindu origin.

## Day-trips and other activities

There are heaps of things to do on Phuket, from deep-sea fishing to rock climbing, cookery courses to mountain-bike tours. Tour agents on all the main beaches will be only too happy to fix you up with your activity of choice, or you can arrange it yourself by calling the relevant numbers. Transport from your hotel is usually included in the price of a day-trip. For details of dive operators in Phuket, see pp.322–323.

### Activities

**Bungy-jumping** Catapult yourself off a 54-metre tower and look down over Ao Patong at Tarzan's Jungle Bungy Jump on Soi Sunset ☏01/464 1581.

**Elephant trekking** Too many treks to list, but every tour agent sells at least one. Treks last up to two hours, cost about B750 (kids B450) and follow a path through forest close to the beach. Some companies such as Siam Safari ☏076/280116 and the almost identical Island Safari ☏076/280858 offer combination programmes (around B1350/950 adults/children) featuring, for example, canoeing, a "jeep safari" and a monkey show as well as elephant riding.

**Golf** Phuket has four eighteen-hole courses open to the public: the Banyan Tree Club on Hat Bang Tao ☏076/324350, the Blue Canyon Country Club near Hat Nai Yang ☏076/327440; the Phuket Century Club in Kathu ☏076/321329, and the Phuket Golf and Country Club, also in Kathu ☏076/321038. Eighteen holes range from B2200 to 3500, with club rental B300–500 and caddies B200. You can arrange golf packages through Golf Phuket (☏076/280461, ⊕www.golfphuket.com) or Phuket Golf Service ☏076/321278.

**Horse riding** Ride along jungle trails and sandy beaches with Laguna Riding Club ☏076/324199 on Hat Bang Tao, or Phuket Riding Club in Rawai ☏076/288213.

**Paintball and shooting** At Phuket Shooting Range, on the Kata/Karon road (daily 9am–6pm; ☏076/381667).

**Rock climbing** Practise your climbing skills on the fifteen-metre-high Quest Rock Climbing Tower on Hat Bang Tao ☏076/324062 before heading out to the real rock faces in Krabi (see p.363).

**Thai cookery courses** Half-day courses featuring a choice of half a dozen different menus, plus fruit-carving and lunch or dinner at the Supachai Thai Cookery School, 101/14 Moo Ban Irawadee (the bypass) just outside Phuket town (☏076/355291,

in **clothes** made from the handspun cotton of north and northeast Thailand; some of the fabric is exquisite, and they have some interesting designs too. Along the same road you'll find several **antiques** shops, displaying furniture and artefacts from the north and northeast, as well as pieces from Burma. Housed in a fine old colonial building at 36 Thanon Talang, The Loft (closed Sundays) also specializes in classy Asian **artefacts** and antiques, including Chinese, Korean and Japanese furniture, Vietnamese and Burmese antiques, Laotian textiles and Tibetan rugs. It's a fine place for a browse, and the temporary exhibitions of modern art displayed in the art gallery upstairs are generally worth a look too. For cheaper, good-quality Thai **handicrafts**, check out Radsada Hand Made, which sells textiles, carved wooden textile hangers, mango- and coconut-wood vases and bowls, silver jewellery and hill-tribe trinkets.

## Listings

**Airlines** Air Andaman, at the airport ☏076/351374; Air Lanka c/o Phuket Centre Tour, 27 Thanon Rat Sada ☏076/212892; American Airlines, 156/13 Thanon Phang Nga

@www.phuketdir.com/supachai; B1500–2700 including transport); and every Saturday and Sunday at *The Boathouse* hotel on Kata beach (☎076/330015, @www.theboathousephuket.com; B2400).

## Days out

**Deep sea fishing** Day-trips and overnight charters in custom-built boats from Andaman Hooker ☎076/282036, An Angling Experience ☎076/283270 and Phuket Sport Fishing Centre ☎076/214713; less strenuous freshwater line-casting at Phuket Fishing Park near the Heroine's Monument, off Highway 402 ☎076/239391.

**Mountain-bike tours** Graded routes around the island, through forests and to beaches; bike rental included in the price: Andaman Trails ☎076/235098, Asian Adventures ☎076/341799 and Phang Nga Discovery ☎076/340636.

**Sea canoeing** One and two-day self-paddling expeditions in sea kayaks around the limestone karsts of Phang Nga bay (see p.350) or through the jungles of Khao Sok (see p.309) for around B2700 per person per day: Santana ☎076/294220, @www.santanaphuket.com, Sea Canoe Thailand ☎076/212252, @www.seacanoe.com and Sea Cave Canoe ☎076/210434, @www.seacavecanoe.com

## Nights out

**Phuket Fantasea** ☎076/271222. Enjoyable spectacular that's staged at the Fantasea entertainments complex just inland of Hat Kamala. The 75-minute show is a slick, hi-tech fusion of high-wire trapeze acts, acrobatics, pyrotechnics, illusionists, comedy and traditional dance – plus a depressing baby elephant circus. Transport is included in the steep ticket price (B1000/700 adults/children), with an optional pre-show dinner (B400). The show starts at 9pm every night except Tuesday; tickets can be bought through any tour operator.

**Phuket Simon Cabaret** ☎076/342011. Famous extravaganza in which a troupe of gorgeously feminine transvestites perform song-and-dance numbers, attired in outrageously flamboyant costumes. It's all very Hollywood – a little bit risqué but not at all sleazy, so the show is popular with tour groups and families. The cabarets are staged twice a night, and tickets can be bought from any tour agent for B500; agents should provide free transport to the theatre which is south of Patong, on the road to Karon.

☎076/232511; Bangkok Airways, 158/2–3 Thanon Yaowarat ☎076/225033; China Airlines, at the airport ☎076/327099; Dragon Air, 37/52 Thanon Montri ☎076/215734; Emirates, as Air Lanka; EVA Air, as Air Lanka; Iberia, as American Airlines; Korean Airlines c/o Crown Family Tour, *Phuket Merlin Hotel*, Thanon Yaowarat ☎076/234775; Lauda Air c/o LTU Asia Tours ☎076/327432; Malaysia Airlines 1/8 Thanon Thungka ☎076/216675; Silk Air/Singapore Airlines, 183 Thanon Phang Nga ☎076/213895; Thai Airways, 78 Thanon Ranong (☎076/212499).

**American Express**, c/o Sea Tours, 95/4 Thanon Phuket (☎076/218417, ℱ216979; Mon–Fri 8.30am–5pm, Sat 8.30am–noon). Refunds on lost traveller's cheques are usually available here within the hour, and staff keep poste restante letters and faxes for at least a month.

**Banks and exchange** All the main banks have branches on Phang Nga or Rat Sada roads, with adjacent exchange facilities open till at least 7pm and ATMs dispensing cash around the clock.

**Hospitals** The private Mission Hospital (aka Phuket Adventist Hospital), about 1km north of TAT on Thanon Thepkasatri (☎076/212386, emergencies 211173), has Phuket's best and most expensive facilities, including private rooms and an emergency department; Phuket International Hospital (☎076/249400, emergencies 210935), on the airport bypass road just outside Phuket town, is a new hospital with good facilities, an emergency department and an ambulance service. Also in town are Bangkok Phuket Hospital at 2/1

Thanon Hongyok Utis ☎ 076/254425, and Wachira Phuket Hospital on Thanon Yaowarat ☎ 076/211114.

**Immigration office** At the southern end of Thanon Phuket, near Ao Makham ☎ 076/212108; Mon–Fri 8.30am–4.30pm.

**internet access** At *Crystal Guest House*, 41/16 Thanon Montri; and *On On Hotel*, 19 Thanon Phang Nga; there's Catnet public internet access at the phone office on Thanon Phang Nga.

**Mail** The GPO is on Thanon Montri. Poste restante should be addressed c/o GPO Thanon Montri, Phuket 83000 and can be collected Mon–Fri

8.30am–4.30pm, Sat 8.30am–3.30pm.

**Pharmacy** There's a branch of Boots on Thanon Tilok Uthit 1.

**TAT** 73–75 Thanon Phuket (daily 8.30am–4.30pm ☎ 076/212213, ℮ 213582, ℮ tathkt@phuket.ksc.co.th).

**Telephones** For international calls use the CAT phone office on Thanon Phang Nga (daily 8am–midnight).

**Tourist Police** 24hr help available on ☎ 1699, or contact the police station on the corner of Thanon Phang Nga and Thanon Thepkasatri ☎ 076/355015.

# Around the island

This account of the island starts at the top of Phuket's most appealing coast and follows an anti-clockwise route around the perimeter, through the chief tourist centres. The west coast boasts a series of long sandy beaches punctuated by sheer rocky headlands, unprotected from the monsoons and consequently quite rough and windswept from May to October, but nevertheless heavily developed and packed with Phuket's best hotels and facilities. Shadowed by the mainland, the east coast is much more sheltered and thus makes a convenient docking point for ships, but is hopeless for swimming and sunbathing. The interior remains fairly untouched either by industry or by the tourist trade, and can make a refreshing break from the beaches.

## Hat Mai Khao

Phuket's northwest coast kicks off with the island's longest and least-visited beach, the twelve-kilometre **HAT MAI KHAO**, which starts a couple of kilometres north of the airport and 34km northwest of Phuket town, and remains almost completely unsullied by any touristic enticements, with to date just a couple of discreet budget accommodations hidden behind a sandbank at the back of the shore. Together with Hat Nai Yang immediately to the south (see p.332), Hat Mai Khao constitutes **Sirinath National Park**, chiefly because giant marine turtles come ashore here between October and February to lay their eggs (see box on p.331). Mai Khao is also a prime habitat of a much-revered but non-protected species – the sea grasshopper or sea louse, a tiny crustacean that's considered a great delicacy. While you're at Mai Khao, you might want to make a trip to the Thachatchai Nature Trail, which also comes under the protection of the Sirinath National Park, but is actually on Phuket's northeast coast, very close to the Sarasin Bridge and about 8km north from the Hat Mai Khao accommodation; it's described on p.349.

If you're looking for peace, solitude and 12km of soft sand to yourself, then the Hat Mai Khao **accommodation** is for you. The two places to stay here, both run by members of the same family and both serving food, occupy adjacent plots at the back of the beach that are only accessible by a 1500-metre track. *Phuket Camp Ground* (☎ 01/676 4318, ℮ www.phuketdir/campground .com) rents out tents (B200) which you can either set up near their small

Thailand is home to four species of **marine turtle**: the green, the leatherback, the Olive Ridley and the hawksbill; the loggerhead turtle also once swam in Thai waters, until the constant plundering of its eggs rendered it locally extinct. Of the remaining four species, the **green turtle** is the commonest, a mottled brown creature named not for its appearance but for the colour of the soup made from its flesh. Adults weigh up to 180kg and are herbivorous, subsisting on sea grass, mangrove leaves and algae. The **leatherback**, encased in a distinctive ridged shell, is the world's largest turtle, weighing in at between 250kg and 550kg; it eats nothing but jellyfish. The small **Olive Ridley** weighs up to 50kg and feeds mainly on shrimps and crabs. Named for its peculiar beak-like mouth, the **hawksbill** is prized for its spectacular carapace (the sale of which was banned by CITES in 1992); it weighs up to 75kg and lives off a type of sea sponge.

The survival of the remaining four species is by no means assured – prized for their meat, their shells and their eggs, and the frequent victims of trawler nets, all types of marine turtle are now **endangered species**. The worldwide population of female turtles is thought to be as small as 70,000 to 75,000, and only around fifty percent of hatchlings reach adulthood. As a result, several of the Thai beaches most favoured by egg-laying turtles have been protected as **marine parks**, and some equipped with special hatcheries. The breeding season usually starts in October or November and lasts until February, and the astonishing egg-laying ritual can be witnessed, under national park rangers' supervision, on Phuket's Hat Mai Khao (see p.330), Ko Surin Tai (p.307, and Ko Tarutao (p.410).

Broody female turtles of all species always return to the beach on which they were born to lay their **eggs**, often travelling hundreds of kilometres to get there – no mean feat, considering that females can wait anything from twenty to fifty years before reproducing. Once *in situ*, the turtles lurk in the water and wait for a cloudy night before wending their laborious way onto and up the beach: at 180kg, the green turtles have a hard enough time, but the 550kg leatherbacks endure an almost impossible uphill struggle. Choosing a spot well above the high-tide mark, each turtle digs a deep nest in the sand into which she lays ninety or more eggs; she then packs the hole with the displaced sand and returns to sea. Tears often stream down the turtle's face at this point, but they're a means of flushing out sand from the eyes and nostrils, not a manifestation of grief.

Many females come back to land three or four times during the nesting season, laying a new batch of ninety-plus at every sitting. Incubation of each batch takes from fifty to sixty days, and the temperature of the sand during this period determines the sex of the hatchling: warm sand results in females, cooler sand in males. When the **baby turtles** finally emerge from their eggshells, they immediately and instinctively head seawards, guided both by the moonlight on the water – which is why any artificial light, such as flashlight beams or camera flashes, can disorientate them – and by the downward gradient of the beach.

restaurant or move down onto the beach a few metres away beyond the sandbank. On the other side of a small shrimp-breeding pond, *Mai Khao Beach Bungalows* (☎01/895 1233, ⓕ076/206205, ⓔbmaikhao_beach@hotmail.com; ❷–❹) has just a few bungalows with fan and en-suite bathrooms as well as a handful of tiny, tent-like A-frame huts with mattresses, mosquito nets and shared bathrooms.

The easiest way to get to Hat Mai Khao is by long-distance **bus**. All buses travelling between Phuket town bus station and any mainland town (eg Krabi, Phang Nga, Khao Lak, Surat Thani) take Highway 402 to get on or off the island: just ask to be dropped in Ban Soun Maprao, a road junction just north of kilometre-stone 37. (If coming directly here from the mainland you'll waste a good couple of hours if you go into town and then come back out again.) Five songthaews a day also travel this far up Highway 402, but buses are faster and more frequent. From the bus drop, walk 1km down the minor road until you reach a signed track off to the west, which you should follow for 1500m to reach the accommodation and the beach; there's unlikely to be anymotorbike taxis to transport you, but you might get lucky. Travelling to Hat Mai Khao from the airport, is only a three-kilometre-ride in a metered taxi.

## Hat Nai Yang

Despite also being part of the Sirinath National Park – and location of the national park headquarters – the long curved sweep of **HAT NAI YANG**, 5km south of Hat Mai Khao and 30km north of Phuket town, has become fairly developed, albeit in a relatively low-key way, with around thirty open-air restaurant-shacks and small bars set up along the beachfront road and the track that runs off it, and a small tourist village of tour operators, transport rental outlets, minimarkets, an internet centre and the inevitable tailors. For the moment though, the developments are fairly unobtrusive and the beach is a pleasant place to while away a few hours, ideally around lunch- or dinner-time when you can browse the restaurant menus at leisure – barbecued seafood and wood-fired pizzas are the local specialities. Eating out here in the shade of the feathery casuarina trees that run the length of the bay is a hugely popular Sunday pastime with local Thai families; to avoid the crowds, come during the week. Should you feel a little more energetic, the beach is fairly clean and fine for swimming, and there's a reasonable, shallow **reef** about 1km offshore (10min by longtail boat) from the national park headquarters, which are a fifteen-minute walk north of the tourist village. If you're staying here and have your own transport, you could make a trip to the Thachatchai Nature Trail (see p.349).

### Practicalities

**Accommodation** is pleasingly limited on Hat Nai Yang. The cheapest and most peaceful place to stay is at the national park bungalows (T076/327407; 3–5), prettily set out under the trees on a very quiet stretch of beach fifteen minutes' walk north from the tourist village. Two-person bungalows are basic but en-suite, their price depending on the size of the hut; they must be booked in advance. Tents are also available for B300 and can be pitched anywhere you like; if you bring your own you must first get permission from the park headquarters or visitor centre (both daily 8.30am–4.30pm). *Nai Yang Beach Resort* (T076/328300, F328333, E nai-yang@phuket.ksc.co.th; 5–7) in the heart of the tourist village has a range of comfortable, mid-market bungalows set in a spacious garden on the inland side of the beachfront road, and offers a choice between fan and air-con. Just to the north is the less appealing *Crown Nai Yang Suite Hotel* (T076/327420, F327322, W www.phuket.com/crown-naiyang; 8–9) which has some strangely dark bedroom suites, including fully equipped kitchens, and pricier but nicer ones, all set around a swimming pool; it's used by airline crews. Best of the lot is the elegant and luxurious *Pearl Village* (T076/327006,

ⓕ 327338,ⓦ www.phuket.com/pearlvillage; ➒) where hotel rooms and pretty cottages are set in gorgeously landscaped tropical gardens that run down to the southern end of the beachfront road; facilities here include a swimming pool and tennis courts.

Hat Nai Yang is just 2km south of the **airport**, so a taxi ride down to the beach shouldn't cost much. An infrequent **songthaew** service (B30; 1hr 45min) runs between Phuket town and Hat Nai Yang via the airport, but a better public transport option might be to take any long-distance **bus** running to or from the mainland (they all use Highway 402) and get off at the turn-off to the airport. From here it should be easy to flag down a tuk-tuk, metered taxi or motorcycle taxi to Hat Nai Yang. A tuk-tuk from Phuket town to Hat Nai Yang costs around B300. There are plenty of transport touts in Nai Yang to help with return or onward journeys.

## Hat Nai Thon

The next bay south down the coast from Hat Nai Yang is the small but perfectly formed **Hat Nai Thon**, one of the least commercialized beaches on the island. The 500-metre-long gold-sand bay is shaded by casuarinas and surrounded by fields and plantations of coconut, banana, pineapple and rubber trees, all set against a distant backdrop of hills. The access road off Highway 402 winds through this landscape, passing a few villages en route before reaching the shore, and to date there are just three formal places to stay at the beach, plus a couple of homes with rooms for rent, one dive operator, a few jeeps for hire and a restaurant attached to each hotel. There's good snorkelling at reefs that are easily reached by longtail, but otherwise you'll have to make your own entertainment. The best way to get to Nai Thon is to take one of the half-hourly **songthaews** (B20; 1hr 30min) from Phuket town to Ao Bang Tao, the next resort south down the coast, and then hire a taxi, which could cost as much as B150.

At the northern end of the shorefront road, across the road from the sea, *Phuket Naithon Resort* (ⓣ 076/205233, ⓕ 205214; ➏–➐) offers big, apartment-style **rooms** in terraced bungalows with the choice between (genuine) mountain views or (less interesting) sea views, and the option of air-con, balcony and TV. About 100m south down the road, *Naithon Beach Resort* (ⓣ 076/205379, ⓕ 205381; ⓔ naithonbeachresort@hotmail.com; ➐–➑), set in a small garden across the road from the beach, has wooden fan and air-con bungalows with more character but lesser views. The nearby *Tien Sen* restaurant (ⓣ 076/205260; ➎) has rooms upstairs, at the cheapest rates in Nai Thon, though it's worth paying a bit more here to get the rooms with air-con and a sea view.

## Ao Bang Tao

The eight-kilometre-long **AO BANG TAO** is effectively the private beach of the upmarket *Laguna Resort*, an "integrated resort" comprising five luxury hotels set in extensive landscaped grounds around a series of lagoons. There's free transport between the hotels, and for a small fee all *Laguna* guests can use facilities at any one of the five hotels – which include fifteen swimming pools, thirty restaurants, several children's clubs, a couple of spas and countless sporting facilities ranging from tennis courts to riding stables, windsurfers, and hobie-cats to badminton courts. There's also the eighteen-hole Banyan Tree golf course, the Quest Laguna outdoor sports centre and a kids' activity centre called Camp Laguna, with activities for 8- to 18-year-olds ranging from abseiling and rock climbing to team games and arts and crafts workshops. Not surprisingly the *Laguna* hotels are exceptionally popular with families, though beware of the undertow off the coast here, which confines many guests to the hotel pools. Half-hourly **songthaews** (B20; 1hr 15min) cover the 24km from Phuket town to Ao Bang Tao; taxis cost about B200 for the same journey. There are reputable **car-rental** desks at all the hotels, as well as small shopping arcades.

### Accommodation

All *Laguna Phuket* **hotels** are in the top price bracket: the *Allamanda* has the cheapest rooms with high-season rates from US$150, and the *Banyan Tree Phuket* is the most exclusive option on the beach with rates starting at US$400; the cheapest rooms at the other three hotels average $285. The above quoted rates are generally discounted a little if you book via the *Laguna Phuket* website (Ⓦ www.lagunaphuket.com), and rates drop by up to fifty percent during the low season from May to October.

**Allamanda** ⓣ076/324359, ⓕ324360. Consciously family-oriented hotel comprising 235 apartment-style suites – all with a kitchenette – set round the edge of a lagoon and the fringes of the golf course. There are some special children's suites, three children's pools and a babysitting service. ❾

**Banyan Tree Phuket** ⓣ076/324374, ⓕ324375. The most sumptuous and exclusive of the *Laguna* hotels, with a select 108 villas, all gorgeously furnished and outfitted with private gardens and outdoor sunken baths. Also on site are the award-winning Banyan Tree spa and the eighteen-hole Banyan Tree golf course. ❾

**Dusit Laguna** ⓣ076/324320, ⓕ324174. Located between two lagoons, all rooms here have private balconies with good views. Facilities include a spa, a couple of swimming pools and a club for kids aged 4 to 12. ❾

**Laguna Beach Resort** ⓣ076/324352, ⓕ324353. Another family-oriented hotel, with a big water park, lots of sports facilities, Camp Laguna activities for children, plus luxury five-star rooms in the low-rise hotel wings. ❾

**Sheraton Grande Laguna** ⓣ076/324101, ⓕ324108. Built on its own island in the middle of one of the lagoons, with five-star rooms, nine bars and restaurants and conference facilities. ❾

## Hat Surin (Ao Pansea)

The favourite haunt of royalty and Hollywood stars, dainty little **HAT SURIN** (also sometimes known as **Ao Pansea**) occupies the bay south of Ao Bang Tao, beyond Laem Son cape. Nearly always a peaceful spot, it boasts Phuket's most indulgent resort, the *Amanpuri* (ⓣ076/324333, ⓕ324100, Ⓦ www.phuket.com/amanpuri; ❾), part of the super-exclusive, Hong Kong-based Aman chain, where luxuries include a personal attendant, a private Thai-style pavilion and unlimited use of the black marble swimming pool; rates start at US$500. Also here are the delightful traditional-style thatched villas at *The Chedi* (formerly *The Pansea*; ⓣ076/324017, ⓕ324252, Ⓦ www.chedi-phuket .com; ❾) whose published prices start at a slightly more reasonable US$295. Songthaews travel the 24km between Phuket town and Hat Surin approximately every half-hour and cost B25.

## Hat Kamala and Laem Singh

A small, characterful tourist development has grown up along the shorefront of **HAT KAMALA**, sandwiched between the beach and the inland Muslim village of Ban Kamala, about 200m west of the main Patong–Surin road and 26km northwest of Phuket town. With cheerfully painted houses, no high-rises or big hotels and an emphasis on garden compounds and rooms for rent, Hat Kamala has an almost Mediterranean ambience and is one of the most appealingly low-key resorts on Phuket. Aside from the accommodation, the little tourist village, which is clustered either side of Thanon Rim Had (also spelt Rim Hat), has several restaurants and bars, transport rental, internet access, a minimarket, a health centre, a post office and a tour operator. For anything else you'll need to head south around the headland to Ao Patong, just a few kilometres away. The Phuket Fantasea entertainments complex (see box on p.329) is about 1km northeast of Hat Kamala on the main Patong–Surin road. If you look closely you'll see that the shorefront land across the road from the Fantasea is actually a Muslim cemetery – the grass is dotted with small shards of rock indicating the burial plots. A few hundred metres north of the cemetery, a couple of steep paths lead west off the main road and down to **Laem Singh** cape, a pretty little sandy cove that's a picturesque combination of turquoise water and smooth granite boulders; it's nice for swimming and very secluded. The easiest way to get to Hat Kamala is by songthaew from Phuket town (every 30min, 1hr 15min; B25).

## Accommodation and eating

Hat Kamala is popular with long-stay tourists, and many of the **hotels** offer rooms with kitchenettes; on the whole, prices here are reasonable for Phuket. A few of the hotels have **restaurants**, most notably the *Two Chefs* seafood restaurant at *Papa Crab Guest House*, and there are several independent restaurants along Thanon Rim Had as well, most of which, like *Roberta* and *Charoen Seafood*, emphasize seafood, the local speciality.

**Benjamin Resort**, 83 Thanon Rim Had, opposite the school at the southerly end of the beachfront road, ☎ & ⓕ 076/325739. Set right on the beach, nearly all thirty rooms in this hotel have fine sea views from their balconies, as well as air-con, TV and a fridge. Lacks the character of some of the others but good value. ⑤

**Bird Beach Bungalow**, central seafront road at 73/3 Thanon Rim Had ☎ & ⓕ 076/279669. Popular, long-running place with well-furnished bungalows set around a courtyard. Rooms are a bit dark but comfortable and reasonable value, with a choice of fan or air-con. ⑤

**Kamala Beach Estate** ☎ 076/270756, ⓕ 324115, ⓦ www.phuket.com/kamala/beach. Stunningly located on Hat Kamala's far southern headland and set around a swimming pool in tropical gardens, this place offers luxury serviced apartments for rent and is favoured by long-term and repeat guests. ⑨

**Malinee House**, 75/4 Thanon Rim Had ☎ 076/324094, ⓕ 279465, ⓔ malineehouse@hotmail.com. Very friendly, traveller-oriented guest house with internet access and the Jackie Lee tour operator downstairs, and large, comfortably

furnished fan and air-con rooms upstairs, all of them with balconies. Good value and recommended. ④–⑤

**Papa Crab Guest House**, southerly end of the seafront road at 93/5 Thanon Rim Had ☎ & ⓕ 076/324315. Exceptionally stylish decor in this three-storey block of rooms above the Swedish-managed *Two Chefs* restaurant. Striking mango-coloured paintwork, rattan furnishings and the option of fan or air-con rooms. Try to get a room on the top floor if possible. ⑤

**Phuket Kamala Resort**, northern end of the seafront road at 74/8 Thanon Rim Had ☎ 076/324396, ⓕ 324399, ⓔ kamalaresort@hotmail.com. Efficiently run hotel with forty rooms in air-con bungalows set either round the swimming pool or in the garden to the rear. All rooms have TVs and some also have a kitchenette. There's a restaurant and tour desk here too. ⑦

**Seaside Inn**, central seafront at 88/6 Thanon Rim Had ☎ & ⓕ 076/270894. Two dozen nice bungalows ranged around a pretty garden across the road from the seafront. All rooms have air-con, TV and kitchenette. ⑦

# Ao Patong

The most popular and developed of all Phuket's beaches, **AO PATONG** – 5km south of Ao Kamala and 15km west of Phuket town – is where the action is: the broad, three-kilometre-long beach offers good sand and plenty of shade beneath the casuarinas and parasols, plus the densest concentration of top hotels, restaurants and bars and the island's biggest choice of watersports and diving centres. On the downside, a congestion of high-rise hotels, tour agents and souvenir shops disfigures the beachfront, and limpet-like touts are everywhere. Signs are that things can only get worse: "entertainment plazas" are mushrooming all over Patong, each one packed with hostess bars and strip joints that make this the most active scene between Bangkok and Hat Yai, attracting an increasing number of single Western men. Before long, this might be a second Pattaya.

Already close to saturation point, Patong just keeps on growing outwards and upwards, which can make it hard to orientate yourself. But essentially, the resort is strung out along the two main roads – **Thavee Wong** and **Raja Uthit/Song Roi Phi,** that run parallel to the beachfront, spilling over into a network of connecting sois which in turn have spawned numerous pedestrian-only "plazas". It's along the two major thoroughfares that you'll find most of the accommodation, while the two landmark sois connecting them have become established entertainment zones: **Soi Bangla** and its offshoots throb away at the heart of the nightlife district, while the more sedate **Soi Post Office** is dominated by tailors' shops and small cafés and restaurants.

## Practicalities

**Songthaews** to Patong leave Phuket town's Thanon Ranong approximately every fifteen minutes between 6am and 6pm and take about twenty minutes. They approach the resort from the northeast, driving south along Thanon Thavee Wong as far as the *Patong Merlin*, where they usually wait for a while to pick up passengers for the return trip to Phuket town. A **tuk-tuk** from Patong to Ao Karon will probably set you back about B200. SMT/National **car rental** (☏076/340608) has a desk inside the *Holiday Inn*, or you can hire jeeps or motorbikes from the transport touts who hang out along Thanon Thavee Wong.

Most of the **tour agents** and **dive operators** have offices on the southern stretch of Thanon Thavee Wong: see the box on pp.328–9 for a roundup of available day-trips and activities, and the box on pp.322–3 for diving details. There are private **internet** centres every few hundred metres on all the main roads in the resort, which charge much less than the business centres in the top hotels. The **police station** is on Thanon Thavee Wong, across from the west end of Soi Bangla.

## Accommodation

**Moderately priced** accommodation on Patong is poor value by usual Thai standards. Because demand is so great, rudimentary facilities cost twice as much here as they would even in Bangkok, and during high season it's almost impossible to find a vacant room for less than B600. Some of the best-value mid-range places are at the far northern end of Thanon Raja Uthit, beneath the hill road that brings everyone in from town; because this part of Patong is a 750-metre walk from the central shopping, eating and entertainment area (though only 100m from the sea itself), prices are noticeably lower, and rooms and bungalows larger into the bargain. In general, Patong's **upmarket** hotels are better value, and many occupy prime beachfront sites on Thavee Wong. Officially, the beach itself is a building-free zone, but a sizeable knot of developments has

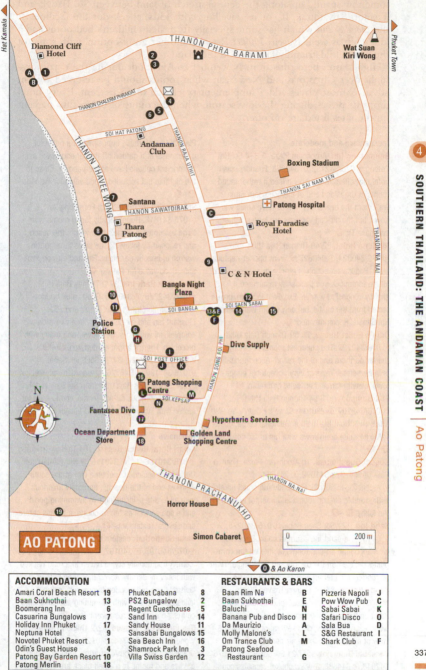

## AO PATONG

**ACCOMMODATION**

| | | | |
|---|---|---|---|
| Amari Coral Beach Resort | 19 | Phuket Cabana | 8 |
| Baan Sukhothai | 13 | PS2 Bungalow | 2 |
| Boomerang Inn | 6 | Regent Guesthouse | 5 |
| Casuarina Bungalows | 7 | Sand Inn | 14 |
| Holiday Inn Phuket | 17 | Sandy House | 11 |
| Neptuna Hotel | 9 | Sansabai Bungalows | 15 |
| Novotel Phuket Resort | 1 | Sea Beach Inn | 16 |
| Odin's Guest House | 4 | Shamrock Park Inn | 3 |
| Patong Bay Garden Resort | 10 | Villa Swiss Garden | 12 |
| Patong Merlin | 18 | | |

**RESTAURANTS & BARS**

| | | | |
|---|---|---|---|
| Baan Rim Na | B | Pizzeria Napoli | J |
| Baan Sukhothai | E | Pow Wow Pub | C |
| Baluchi | N | Sabai Sabai | K |
| Banana Pub and Disco | H | Safari Disco | O |
| Da Maurizio | A | Sala Bua | D |
| Molly Malone's | L | S&G Restaurant | I |
| Om Trance Club | M | Shark Club | F |
| Patong Seafood Restaurant | G | | |

somehow sprung up along the central stretch of sand between Soi Bangla and Thanon Sawatdirak. If you're travelling with **kids**, check-out the facilities at the *Holiday Inn* which has some specially furnished children's bedrooms and a kids' club as well; *Novotel Phuket Resort* is another good option, with some of the most child-friendly facilities on the island.

High season here runs from November to April, but during the crazy fortnight over Christmas and New Year, when rooms should be reserved well in advance, most places add a supplementary charge of 25 percent. Every hotel drops its prices during the low season, when discounts of up to fifty percent on the rates listed are on offer.

### Inexpensive and moderate

**Boomerang Inn**, Aroonsom Plaza, 5/3–4 Soi Hat Patong ☎ 076/342182, ⊕ 342868. Friendly small hotel that offers reasonably priced if rather faded rooms at the inland end of the soi, about 5min walk from the beach. Fan rooms have small windows, but the air-con versions are larger, lighter and have TV. ⑤

**Neptuna Hotel**, 82/49 Thanon Raja Uthit ☎ 076/340824, ⊕ 340627, ⓦ www.phuket-neptuna .com. Popular collection of air-con bungalows with all the trimmings in a pleasantly manicured if slightly congested garden. Excellent location, protected from the bustle, but only 200m walk from Soi Bangla. Recommended. ⑦

**Odin's Guest House**, 78/59 Thanon Raja Uthit ☎ 076/340732. The cheapest rooms in Patong, at the far northern end of the resort. Accommodation is in two-storey rows of very acceptable bungalows, all with fan and en-suite bathroom. ③

**PS2 Bungalow**, 78/54 Thanon Raja Uthit ☎ 076/342207, ⊕ 290034. Close by *Odin's*, so also a fair walk from the main attractions. Large, good-value en-suite bungalows with fan or air-con. ④–⑥

**Regent Guesthouse**, 70 Aroonsom Plaza, Thanon Raja Uthit ☎ 076/341099, ⊕ 341664, ⓔ regent@e-mail.in.th. Efficiently run small hotel with sizeable air-con rooms and internet access in the lobby. ⑥–⑦

**Sand Inn**, 171 Soi Saen Sabai ☎ 076/340275, ⊕ 341519, ⓔ sand-inn@samart.co.th. Spotless, well-appointed air-con rooms, a little on the compact side, east off the bar-packed Soi Bangla. TV in all rooms and internet access downstairs. ⑦

**Sandy House**, 87/14 Thanon Thavee Wong ☎ 076/340458, ⓔ sandyhse@phuket.ksc.co.th. Right on the beach; two good but pricey rooms with beachfront view, plus several others with no view at all. All rooms have air-con. ⑦–⑧

**Sansabai Bungalows**, 17/21 Soi Saensabai ☎ 076/ 342948, ⊕ 344888, ⓦ www.phuket-sansabai.com.

Plain but comfortable bungalows in a peaceful green oasis of a garden off the far end of the soi; the priciest options have air-con and TV. Close to the nightlife but secluded. Good value for Patong. ⑥–⑦

**Sea Beach Inn**, 90/1–2 Soi Permpong 2 ☎ & ⊕ 076/341616. Huge, slightly faded rooms with large balconies, a stone's throw from the beach and reached by following the signs through the warren of beachwear stalls. Fan and air-con available. Good value for Patong. ⑤

**Shamrock Park Inn**, 17/2 Thanon Raja Uthit ☎ 076/342275, ⊕ 340990. Good value budget-oriented option that's near *Odin's* and *PS2*. Pleasant fan and air-con rooms in a two-storey complex, all with en-suite shower and many with balconies. There's a roof garden, too. ④–⑤

**Villa Swiss Garden**, 84/24 Soi Saen Sabai ☎ 076/341120, ⊕ 340726, ⓔ vsgarden@phuket.ksc .co.th. East across Raja Uthit from Soi Bangla, this place has enormous air-con rooms, comfortably furnished with TV, fridge and ghetto-blaster. ⑥

### Expensive

**Amari Coral Beach Resort**, 104 Thanon Traitrang ☎ 076/340106–14, ⊕ 340115, ⓦ www.amari.com. Occupies a secluded spot on a cliff at the southernmost end of the beach; supremely luxurious with all facilities, including two swimming pools and a spa as well as tennis courts, a fitness centre and several restaurants. ⑨

**Baan Sukhothai**, eastern end of Soi Bangla ☎ 076/340195, ⊕ 340197, ⓦ www.baan-sukhothai .com. A traditionally styled haven in a road packed with tacky modernity. Accommodation here is in lavishly done-out wooden bungalows, set in a landscaped garden with swimming pool and tennis courts. An excellent restaurant, too. ⑨

**Casuarina Bungalows**, 92/2 Thanon Thavee Wong ☎ 076/341197, ⊕ 340123, ⓦ www.phuketdir.com/casuarina. Individual bungalows and rooms in a small block are set attractively in tree-covered grounds just across the road from the sea, in the least congested part of the resort. Swimming pool and sauna. ⑧–⑨

**Holiday Inn Phuket**, 86/11 Thanon Thavee Wong ☎076/340608, ℱ340435, ⓦwww.phuket.com/holidayinn. Recommended upmarket option that offers very smart rooms while retaining a relaxed and informal atmosphere. Large pool and three restaurants, and an interesting programme of daily activities. Also has some kidsuites – bedrooms designed for children – and a kids' club. ⑨

**Novotel Phuket Resort**, Thanon Kalim Beach ☎076/342777, ℱ342168. Smart, comfortable chain hotel set on the hillside at the quieter, northern end of the beach. Set in landscaped tropical gardens and offering fine views. Facilities include three restaurants and a multilevel swimming pool. Especially good for families as it offers heaps of sporting activities and runs a free kids' club with games, videos and craft-making. Free for under 16s sharing their parents' room. ⑨

**Patong Bay Garden Resort**, 33 Thanon Thavee Wong ☎076/340297, ℱ340560, ⓔpatongbay@email.in.th. Small hotel set right on the beach, with many rooms having French windows that literally open out onto the (rather crowded) sand and others that give out onto the courtyard swimming pool. Rooms are comfortable and well equipped, with air-con and TV. ⑨

**Patong Merlin**, 99/2 Thanon Thavee Wong ☎076/340037, ℱ340394, ⓦwww.merlinphuket.com. Huge hotel at the southern end of the road, with four hundred top-quality rooms and three swimming pools. Popular with tour groups. ⑨

**Phuket Cabana**, 94 Thanon Thavee Wong ☎076/340138, ℱ340178, ⓦwww.impiana.com. Gorgeous collection of very tastefully designed bungalows, all equipped with air-con, TV and fridge, and set around a garden swimming pool. Right on the beach and definitely the choice option in its price bracket. ⑨

## Eating

Western–orientated cafés squashed in among the high–rises and shops are popular for daytime snacks, with Italian food and seafood big favourites. Prices are fairly high however, and there's not always quality to match. One place where you can be sure of a cheap feed is at the **night market** that sets up after dark along Thanon Raja Uthit, between Soi Bangla and Soi Sai Nam Yen.

**Baan Rim Na**, far northern end of Thanon Thavee Wong ☎076/340789. Popular, elegant, traditional Thai restaurant, beautifully sited in a teak building overlooking the bay. Specializes in classic Thai dishes and unusual contemporary cuisines. Advance booking advised. Expensive.

**Baan Sukhothai**, hotel restaurant at the eastern end of Soi Bangla. Elegant upmarket restaurant, particularly recommended for its fine "Royal Thai" dishes. Expensive.

**Baluchi**, inside the *Horizon Beach Hotel* on Soi Kepsap. Perhaps the best Indian restaurant in the resort, specializing in North Indian cuisine and tandoori dishes. Moderate to expensive.

**Da Maurizio**, far northern end of Thanon Thavee Wong ☎076/344709. Superior Italian restaurant in a stunning location set on the rocks overlooking the sea. Authentic pasta and antipastos, and a good wine list. Reservations advisable. Expensive.

**Patong Seafood Restaurant**, on the central stretch of Thanon Thavee Wong. A deservedly popular, open-air restaurant which serves all manner of locally caught fish and seafood, particularly

Phuket lobster, cooked to Thai, Chinese and Western recipes. Moderate.

**Pizzeria Napoli**, Soi Post Office. Recommended Italian place, serving traditional wood-fired pizzas and home-made pasta. Moderate.

**Roma de Mauro c Franco**, 89/15 Soi Post Office. Fresh pasta served amid checked tablecloths, candles and an intimate ambience. Inexpensive to moderate.

**Sabai Sabai**, Soi Post Office. Family-run place serving the usual Thai and European dishes, as well as hearty American breakfasts and mixed grills. Inexpensive.

**Sala Bua**, Thanon Thavee Wong. Fabulously stylish, breezy, beach-view restaurant attached to the equally glamorous *Phuket Cabana* hotel. The innovative Pacific Rim menu includes ravioli stuffed with mud crabs and rock-lobster omelette. Expensive but worth it.

**S&G Restaurant**, Soi Post Office. The selection of real coffees and cappuccinos make this a good choice for breakfast. Inexpensive.

### Nightlife and entertainment

Much of Patong's **nightlife** is packed into the strip of neon-lit open-air "bar-beers" along Soi Bangla and the tiny sois that lead off it, where a burgeoning number of go-go bars (some of them advertising "couples welcome") add a seedier aspect to the zone. The bars and clubs listed below are the best of the more salubrious options. The **gay** entertainment district is mainly concentrated around the network of small sois and dozens of bar-beers in front of *Paradise Hotel* on Thanon Raja Uthit. If you're looking for something else to do with yourself or your kids in the evening, you could always try the **House of Horror** theme park on Thanon Prachanukho at the southern edge of Patong (daily 5pm–2am; B400), where an old hospital has been converted into sixteen horror chambers, each inspired by a different horror movie and populated by role-playing actors to get you spooked; you can also eat here at the *Graveyard Restaurant*, where kids get a free meal if accompanying adults. Alternatively, check out the nearby transvestite **Simon Cabaret**, or the spectacular show at **Phuket Fantasea**, both described in the box on p.329.

**Banana Pub and Disco**, 124 Thanon Thavee Wong. Very popular, very central upstairs disco and street-level bar attracting a mixed clientele of Thais, expats and tourists. Live music. Nightly 9pm–2am.

**Molly Malone's**, near *KFC* on the corner of the Patong Shopping Centre at 69 Thanon Thavee Wong. As you'd expect, the resort's original Irish pub dishes out draught Guinness and Kilkenny beer, dishes out bar food and entertains drinkers with an Irish band every night. Has a nice beer garden too. Daily 11am–2am.

**Om Trance Club**, Soi Kepsap. Psychedelic decor to go with the house and garage music. Nightly 9pm–2am.

**Safari Disco**, just beyond the southern edge of Patong, between Simon Cabaret and the *Le Meridien* beach at 28 Thanon Siriat. Decked out to look like a jungle theme park, complete with waterfalls, this is one of the most popular dance venues on Phuket, with two bands playing nightly from around 9pm; the music fuses disco beats from the 1980s with more recent techno sets. There's a restaurant here too. Shuts at 3am.

**Shark Club**, Thanon Song Roi Phi. Huge glitzy disco in the heart of the action, with laser-beam light shows and thumping sound systems. Nightly 9pm–2am.

## Ao Karon

Twenty kilometres southwest of Phuket town, **AO KARON** is only about 5km south from Patong, but a lot less congested. With the help of a healthy scattering of café-bars, restaurants and relatively inexpensive guest houses, Ao Karon generally tempts the younger couples and mid-budget backpackers away from its increasingly manic neighbour. Although the central stretch of beachfront is dominated by large-capacity hotels, the beach itself is completely free of developments, and elsewhere you'll find mainly low-rise guest houses and bungalows, some of them set around gardens, interspersed with stretches of undeveloped grassland.

While long and sandy, the **beach** offers very little in the way of shade; south of the *Phuket Arcadia* it feels quite exposed because of the road that runs right alongside it, and it almost disappears at high tide. That said, it's a popular place to swim, and local entrepreneurs rent out parasols and deckchairs on some stretches. Be warned that the **undertow** off Ao Karon is treacherously strong during the monsoon season from May to October, so you should heed the warning signs and flags and ask for local advice – fatalities are not uncommon. For the rest of the year, there's plenty of scope for

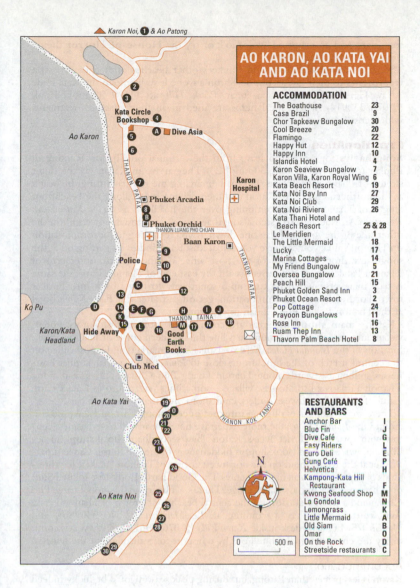

Karon Noi, **1** & Ao Patong

## AO KARON, AO KATA YAI AND AO KATA NOI

Ao Karon

Kata Circle Bookshop

Dive Asia

Karon Hospital

Phuket Arcadia

Phuket Orchid

Baan Karon

Police

Ko Pu

Karon/Kata Headland

Hide Away

Good Earth Books

Club Med

Ao Kata Yai

Ao Kata Noi

THANON PATAK

THANON LUANG PHO CHUAN

SOI BANGLA

THANON TAINA

THANON PATAK

THANON KOK TANOD

N

0    500 m

### ACCOMMODATION

| | |
|---|---|
| The Boathouse | 23 |
| Casa Brazil | 9 |
| Chor Tapkeaw Bungalow | 30 |
| Cool Breeze | 20 |
| Flamingo | 22 |
| Happy Hut | 12 |
| Happy Inn | 10 |
| Islandia Hotel | 4 |
| Karon Seaview Bungalow | 7 |
| Karon Villa, Karon Royal Wing | 6 |
| Kata Beach Resort | 19 |
| Kata Noi Bay Inn | 27 |
| Kata Noi Club | 29 |
| Kata Noi Riviera | 26 |
| Kata Thani Hotel and Beach Resort | 25 & 28 |
| Le Meridien | 1 |
| The Little Mermaid | 18 |
| Lucky | 17 |
| Marina Cottages | 14 |
| My Friend Bungalow | 5 |
| Oversea Bungalow | 21 |
| Peach Hill | 15 |
| Phuket Golden Sand Inn | 3 |
| Phuket Ocean Resort | 2 |
| Pop Cottage | 24 |
| Prayoon Bungalows | 11 |
| Rose Inn | 16 |
| Ruam Thep Inn | 13 |
| Thavorn Palm Beach Hotel | 8 |

### RESTAURANTS AND BARS

| | |
|---|---|
| Anchor Bar | I |
| Blue Fin | J |
| Dive Café | G |
| Easy Riders | L |
| Euro Deli | E |
| Gung Café | P |
| Helvetica | H |
| Kampong-Kata Hill Restaurant | F |
| Kwong Seafood Shop | M |
| La Gondola | N |
| Lemongrass | K |
| Little Mermaid | A |
| Old Siam | B |
| Omar | D |
| On the Rock | D |
| Streetside restaurants | C |

**4**

SOUTHERN THAILAND: THE ANDAMAN COAST | Ao Karon

**watersports** here; windsurfing is good all year round, and the reefs around the tiny island of Ko Pu, just off the headland separating Karon from neighbouring Ao Kata Yai to the south, make for enjoyable snorkelling. The tiny bay just north of Ao Karon – known as Karon Noi or Relax Bay – is almost exclusively patronized by guests of the swanky *Le Meridien* hotel, but non-guests are quite welcome to swim and sunbathe here. For inland entertainment, you could do a round at Dino Park **mini-golf** (daily 10am–midnight; B200), next to *Marina Cottages* on the Kata/Karon headland, which is part of a pseudo-prehistoric theme park comprising a dino burger bar, a dino

341

restaurant and an erupting "volcano"; or try the **House of Horror** theme park on Patong (see p.340).

Some of the posher hotels on Phuket's other beaches offer expensive **spa treatments** to their guests, but on Karon anyone is welcome to the Kata Hide Away Herbal Aromatic Spa, near *Peach Hill* at 116/9 Thanon Patak (T 076/330914), where local herbs are used in all their massage treatments which cost B400–950.

### Practicalities

**Songthaews** for Ao Karon leave from the terminal on Thanon Ranong in Phuket town (every 20min; 30min; B20). They arrive in Karon via the outer stretch of Thanon Patak (the ring road encircling the resort), hitting the beach at the northern end of Ao Karon and then driving south along the beachfront length of Thanon Patak, continuing over the headland as far as *Kata Beach Resort* on Ao Kata Yai. To catch a songthaew back into town, just stand on the other side of the road and flag one down. If you're aiming for accommodation on Thanon Taina, you can save yourself at least ten minutes by getting off at the songthaew drop just north of the post office on the eastern, outer arm of Thanon Patak, where it intersects with the east end of Thanon Taina; the same is true in reverse when picking up a songthaew to travel back into Phuket town. For Soi Bangla accommodation, get off just after the *Baan Karon* hotel at the Thanon Luang Pho Chuan intersection.

Karon's main **shopping** areas are confined to four smallish knots: hotels, restaurants, dive shops and minimarts line the northern curve of Thanon Patak, location of the *Islandia Hotel*; there are banks, supermarkets and a post office on the central stretch of the beachfront, close to *Phuket Arcadia*, with similar businesses spilling eastwards along Thanon Luang Pho Chuan; and spread along Thanon Taina is a little tourist village – sometimes referred to as Kata Centre – full of tailors, beachwear outlets, craft shops, minimarts and café-bars.

There are several places offering **internet access** along Thanon Patak, and also around the *Islandia Hotel*; the more expensive hotels nearly all have business centres with (pricey) internet access. Karon's best secondhand **bookshop** (sometimes known as Karon Bookshop) is hidden away inside the Karon Circle supermarket at the roundabout on the northwest corner of Thanon Patak; it has thousands of paperbacks in all literary genres. The Good Earth Bookstore (closed Sun) on Thanon Taina has a smaller range. There's a **clinic** on Thanon Luang Pho Chuan and a **police station** on the central beachfront stretch of Thanon Patak. Avis **rental cars** has a counter at *Le Meridien* (T 076/340480), and National/SMT has a desk inside *Karon Villa* (T 076/396139, W www.avis.com); or try the cheaper vehicles hired out by transport touts throughout the resort.

### Accommodation

Karon is less pricey than Patong, but during peak season you'd be lucky indeed to find any **accommodation** in the ❷ category, with most places only dropping their rates below ❸ on weekdays during the monsoon season. One of the best places to search for budget hotels is on the Karon/Kata headland, particularly along Thanon Taina, which bisects the road to Kata Yai. Not only are most guest houses here significantly less expensive than those on Karon proper, they're also convenient for bars, restaurants and shops, and yet less than ten minutes' walk from the beach. Soi Bangla, which runs south off Thanon Luang Pho Chuan, can also be a fruitful place to look.

High season here runs from November to April, but you'll almost certainly be charged an extra 25 percent over the Christmas and New Year fortnight when everything gets booked up weeks in advance. During the low season, expect to get discounts of up to fifty percent on the rates given below.

### Inexpensive and moderate

**Casa Brazil**, 127/14 Soi Bangla, which runs south off Thanon Luang Pho Chuan ☎ 076/396317, ⓦ www.phukethomestay.com. Unusually stylish little hotel, designed in Santa Fe style, with adobe-look walls and funky decor and furnishings. The 21 rooms are comfortable and all have air-con. ❼

**Happy Hut**, up a hill at the southern end of Karon ☎ 076/330230. One of the last remaining old-style bungalows on Phuket – and one of the cheapest. Pleasantly located in a grassy dip some 300m from the beach, with simple wooden huts all furnished with a bathroom and mosquito net; the price depends on the hut's size. Has a nice atmosphere. Recommended. ❷–❹

**Happy Inn**, Soi Bangla ☎ 076/396260. Nice assortment of smart bungalows in a small garden that occupies a surprisingly peaceful spot. Price depends on the size of the bungalow and whether it has air-con. Recommended. ❸–❺

**Karon Seaview Bungalow**, 36/9 Thanon Patak ☎ 076/396798, ⓕ 396799. Slightly grotty fan and air-con bungalows with attached bathroom, ranged either side of a tree-lined walkway just across the road from the beach in this central area. Reasonably priced considering the location. ❸–❹

**The Little Mermaid**, 94/25 Thanon Taina ☎ 076/330730, ⓕ 330733. Exceptionally good bungalow rooms, all with air-con, TV and comfortable furnishings, set round a swimming pool. Also some cheaper, city-style fan and air-con rooms in the central hotel block. Advance booking essential. ❸–❺

**Lucky**, 110/44–45 Thanon Taina ☎ 076/330572. Inexpensive place offering good, bright en-suite rooms in a low-rise block (the best ones have balconies) and some rather plain semi-detached bungalows on land further back. ❸

**My Friend Bungalow**, 36/6 Thanon Patak ☎ 076/396344, ⓕ 396161, ⓔ baumlers@phuket-internet.co.th. Popular collection of fifty rather musty-smelling bungalows – the air-con versions are a bit more appealing – set back from the road in the northern central beach area. There's a streetside bar and restaurant. ❹–❺

**Peach Hill**, 113 Thanon Patak ☎ 076/330603, ⓕ 330895, ⓔ peachill@phuket.ksc.co.th. Popular and stylish mid-range place, perfectly located on a hill between the Thanon Taina bars and the beach. Some rooms are in the hotel wing and others are in private bungalows set in the garden. All rooms have air-con and TV, and there are three pools. Recommended; booking ahead is essential. ❻

**Phuket Golden Sand Inn**, northern end of Ao Karon ☎ 076/396493, ⓕ 396117, ⓔ golsands@phuket.ksc.co.th. Medium-sized hotel, one of the least costly of its kind, with good-value fan or air-con bungalows, plus pricier rooms in the central block. Popular and friendly. ❻–❽

**Phuket Ocean Resort**, behind the lagoon at the far northern end of Karon ☎ 076/396599, ⓕ 396470, ⓦ www.phuket-ocean.com. Good, unpretentious hotel ranged up a slope and offering large rooms, all with air-con and balconies: price depends on whether you want a sea view or not. Three swimming pools and internet access in the lobby. ❽

**Prayoon Bungalows**, up a gentle rise on Soi Bangla. Friendly, family-run place with just seven smart bungalows ranged across a grassy slope a little way off the beach. ❺

**Rose Inn**, Thanon Taina ☎ 076/330582. Rooms here are a bit dark, but not bad for the price and area. Only 5min walk from Karon beach. All rooms with bathroom, some with air-con. ❹

**Ruam Thep Inn**, far southern end of beachfront Thanon Patak ☎ 076/330281. Forty very good, fully equipped air-con bungalows, just 20m from the beach. Superbly situated restaurant terrace jutting out over the sea. ❽

### Expensive

**Karon Villa, Karon Royal Wing**, 36/4 Thanon Patak ☎ 076/396139, ⓕ 396122, ⓦ www.karonvilla .com. The most attractive place on Ao Karon: a self-contained village in the central beach area. Bungalows built to several different designs stand in lovely gardens, with even more luxurious accommodation provided in the main "Royal Wing" building. Numerous restaurants and bars, plus a pool and fitness club. ❾

**Le Meridien**, on Karon Noi (also known as Relax Bay), north Karon ☎ 076/340480, ⓕ 340479, ⓔ meridien@phuket.ksc.co.th. Has the tiny bay all to itself; facilities include nine restaurants, a huge lake-style swimming pool (with islands), a spa, squash and tennis courts and private woods. A good place for kids, with special activities arranged every day for under-14s. Thai cookery classes also available. ❾

**Marina Cottages**, 120 Thanon Patak, far south-ern end of Ao Karon, on the Karon/Kata headland ⊺076/330625, ℗330516, ⓦwww.marina-cot-tage.com. Full range of luxurious cottages in a gorgeous tropical garden that leads right down to the beach. Convenient for bars and restaurants. Advance booking recommended. ⑨

**Thavorn Palm Beach Hotel**, 128/10 Thanon Patak, in the central beach area ⊺076/381034, ℗396090, ⓦwww.thavornpalmbeach.com. Top-quality high-rise accommodation in this large chain hotel, set in exuberantly landscaped gardens interlaced with five free-form pools and four chil-dren's pools. Also has tennis courts and several restaurants. Rates from $240. ⑨

## Eating

Many of Karon's more reasonably priced **restaurants** and bars are sprin-kled along Thanon Taina on the Karon/Kata headland, though for the cheapest and most authentic Thai food you can't beat the hot-food carts that dish out noodle soup, satay and fried bananas on Thanon Taina throughout the day; there's also a very cheap local-food kitchen tucked away in a house next to the *Easy Riders* bar on Thanon Taina. Another very enjoyable place to eat is at the string of five open-fronted streetside restau-rants just north of the *Ruam Thep Inn* on Thanon Patak. The food here is pretty inexpensive and ranges from king prawns to burgers and *matsaman* curries to spaghetti.

**Dive Café**, Thanon Taina. Popular, cheap and cheerful restaurant serving a good choice of authentic Thai curries – yellow, green and *mat-saman* in various permutations – plus plenty of seafood. Inexpensive.

**Euro Deli**, across from *Marina Cottages* on Thanon Patak. Real coffee, fresh brioches, crois-sants and Danish pastries make this a good if pricey place to start the day.

**Helvetica**, Thanon Taina. Swiss-run restaurant that serves especially good breakfasts, including a basket of different home-made breads, muesli and *rösti*.

**Kampong-Kata Hill Restaurant**, Thanon Taina. Occupies a superb position on a steep slope just off the main road, its winding, flower-lined walk-way lit up with fairylights after dark. As you'd expect, the food is fairly high-class, too, with quali-ty Thai dishes a speciality. Moderate to expensive.

**Kwong Seafood Shop**, Thanon Taina. Very popu-lar for its array of freshly caught fish and seafood which can be barbecued or cooked to order. Moderate.

**La Gondola**, Thanon Taina. Authentic Italian cui-sine and exceptionally good pizzas. Expensive.

**Lemongrass**, Kata/Karon headland. Pleasant place with classy touches that specializes in good-quality Thai food (mainly curries, noodles and seafood) at reasonable prices; the shrimp curry is especially delicious. Moderate to expensive.

**Little Mermaid**, northern curve of Thanon Patak. Scandinavian joint that seems to be the most pop-ular place in Karon for noon-time breakfasts. Their rye breads and foreign cheeses are tasty but expensive. Moderate.

**Old Siam**, in front of the *Thavorn Palm Beach Hotel*, Thanon Patak ⊺076/396090. Large but fair-ly elegant teak-wood restaurant with indoor and outdoor dining areas; renowned for its traditional Royal Northern Thai cuisine. Stages classical Thai dance (Wed & Sat) and can feel overly touristy. Call for free transport here. Moderate to expensive.

**On the Rock**, in the grounds of *Marina Cottages*, Kata/Karon headland. Open-air seafood restaurant situated right on the rocks overlooking Ao Karon. Recommended. Moderate.

## Drinking and nightlife

Most of the Thanon Taina **bars** are small, genial places, usually with just a hand-ful of tables, a reasonable selection of beers and bar snacks, and a pool table; *Blue Fin* and *Anchor Bar* are both recommended, but there are plenty of others. Though there are as yet no go-go bars on Karon, the Patong bar scene has made inroads into the resort, and there are little clusters of bar-beers with hostess serv-ice around the *Islandia Hotel* on the northern curve of Thanon Patak and around the *Thavorn Palm Beach* in the central beachfront. For non-alcoholic entertainment, try the nearby transvestite **Simon Cabaret** or the spectacular show at **Phuket Fantasea** both of which are described in the box on p.329.

# Ao Kata Yai and Ao Kata Noi

Tree-lined and peaceful, **AO KATA YAI** (Big Kata Bay) is only a few minutes' drive around the headland from Karon (17km from Phuket town), but both prettier and safer for swimming thanks to the protective rocky promontories at either end. The northern stretch of Kata Yai is completely given over to the unobtrusive buildings of the *Club Med* resort, and then it's a lengthy trek down to the rest of the accommodation at the southern end, where you'll also find the restaurants, bars, minimarkets, tour operators and transport rental outlets. A headland at the southernmost point divides Ao Kata Yai from the much smaller **AO KATA NOI** (Little Kata Bay), which is an attractive little gold-sand bay, very popular and so quite crowded with parasols and deckchairs. Kata Noi has its own small cluster of businesses including a minimarket, several restaurants and bars, transport rental and even a tailor's shop.

Most **songthaews** from Phuket go first to Karon, then drive south past *Club Med* and terminate at *Kata Beach Resort* on the headland between Kata Yai and Kata Noi. To get to Kata Noi, continue walking over the hill for about ten minutes, or take a tuk-tuk for about B100. A tuk-tuk from Kata Yai to Karon should cost you about the same. There are plenty of transport touts offering jeeps and motorbikes for rent.

## Accommodation and eating

There is no budget **accommodation** on Kata Yai, and only a couple of places on Kata Noi with rooms for under B600. On Kata Yai, the **restaurant** of choice is *The Boathouse Wine and Grill*, which has a famously extensive wine list and an exquisite and extremely expensive menu of Thai and Western delicacies, and runs Thai cooking classes every Saturday and Sunday for B2400. Also managed by *The Boathouse* hotel is the less formal but still fairly pricey *Gung Café,* with beachfront seating and a menu that includes a range of Thai dishes as well as seafood and rock lobster ("*gung*"). For a nice change from the ubiquitous seafood, check out the Indian and Muslim dishes at *Omar* near *Cool Breeze* in Kata Yai, or the wood-fired pizzas at *Flamingo*.

### Kata Yai

**The Boathouse**, 2/2 Thanon Patak ☎076/330015, ☎330561, ⊛www. theboathousephuket.com. Exclusive and very pricey beachfront boutique hotel with just 36 elegantly furnished rooms and a reputation for classy service. Room rates from B7400. **⑨**

**Cool Breeze**, 5/5 Thanon Patak ☎076/330484, ☎330173. Sixteen appealing bungalows set up the hillside, above the streetside restaurant. The best ones have sea views; choose between fan and air-con. **⑤–⑦**

**Flamingo**, 5/19 Thanon Patak ☎076/330776, ☎330814, ⊛www.flamingo-resort.com. Dozens of prettily positioned bungalows built among the trees on a steep incline above the pale pink restaurant and bar. Fan or air-con bungalows

available; most have verandas and some have sea views. **⑤–⑥**

**Kata Beach Resort**, 5/2 Thanon Patak ☎076/330530, ☎330128, ⊛www.katagroup.com. Huge high-rise hotel with grounds that run down to the white-sand beach. Has a big swimming pool, a kids' pool and lots of watersports facilities; popular with families. **⑨**

**Oversea Bungalow** 5/6 Thanon Patak ☎ & ☎076/284155. Nine large bungalows ranged up a hillside and accessed by a series of steep stairways. Some offer long-distance sea views; all have air-con. Fifty-percent discount May–Oct. **⑦**

**Pop Cottage**, on the southern fringes of Kata Yai at 2/12 Thanon Patak ☎076/330181, ☎330794, ⊛www.phuket-popcottage.com. This mid-sized hotel on a hill a few minutes' walk from the beach has pleasant enough air-con rooms, some with long-range sea views. There's a large pool plus, for the kids, a separate games room and another pool. ⑦–⑨

## Kata Noi

**Chor Tapkeaw Bungalow**, 4/13 Thanon Patak ⓣ 076/330433, Ⓕ 330435. The best of Kata Noi's cheaper options, whose spacious and fairly comfortably furnished bungalows are ranged up the hillside at the far southern end of the road; the verandas give good sea views and the restaurant is right on the beach. Book ahead as there are only 24 rooms and it's very popular. ⑥

**Kata Noi Bay Inn**, 4/16 Thanon Patak ⓣ 076/330570, Ⓕ 333308, Ⓔ katanoi_bayinn@hotmail.com. Small, friendly little hotel attached to a seafood restaurant, offering good-value rooms with balconies and, in some cases, a distant sea view. Fan and air-con available. ④–⑥

**Kata Noi Club**, 3/25 Thanon Patak ⓣ 076/284025, Ⓕ 330194, Ⓔ katanoi_club@yahoo.com. Has some rather spartan bungalows at the far southern end of the beachfront road, as well as a few better, pricier air-con ones. ⑤–⑦

**Kata Noi Riviera**, 3/21 Thanon Patak ⓣ 076/330726, Ⓕ 330294. Rooms here feel uninspired and rather box-like but they are the least expensive on this beach. The priciest ones have air-con. ④–⑦

**Kata Thani Hotel and Beach Resort**, 3/24 Thanon Patak ⓣ 076/330124, Ⓕ 330426, ⓦ www.phuket.com/katathani. The biggest outfit on Kata Noi, occupying about half the beachfront and a good chunk of land 200m further down the road as well. Rooms here come in various degrees of luxury, but all feature air-con, use of the four swimming pools, tennis courts and kids' playground; there are restaurants, a dive shop and a shopping plaza on the premises too. Rates from B6300. ⑨

# Hat Nai Harn and Laem Promthep

Around the next headland south from Kata Noi, **HAT NAI HARN** – 18km southwest of Phuket town – is generally considered to be one of the loveliest beaches on the island, given character by a sparkling saltwater lagoon and dominated by the luxurious hotel, the *Phuket Yacht Club*.

Follow the coastal road 2km south and you'll get to a small bay which has coral reefs very close to the shore, though the currents are strong and the sewage pipes uncomfortably close. A further 1km on, you reach the southernmost tip of Phuket at the sheer headland of **Laem Promthep**. Wild and rugged, jutting out into the deep blue of the Andaman Sea, the cape is one of the island's top beauty spots: at sunset, busloads of tour groups get shipped in to admire the scenery – and just to ensure you don't miss the spectacle, a list of year-round sunset times is posted at the viewpoint. Several reefs lie just off the cape, but it's safer to snorkel from a boat rather than negotiate the rocky shore.

## Practicalities

**Songthaews** from Phuket (every 30min; B25) bypass Laem Promthep and follow the direct inland road between Nai Harn and Hat Rawai instead, so you may have to do the lengthy climb round the promontory on foot. It's a popular spot though, so it should be easy enough to hitch.

The internationally acclaimed *Le Royal Meridien Phuket Yacht Club* (ⓣ 076/381156, Ⓕ 381164, ⓦ www.phuket-yachtclub.com) is one of the most exclusive **hotels** on the whole island, offering superb rooms and exquisite service for a published price of $440 a night, but with huge discounts available online. For more moderately priced accommodation, head a little further round the headland to the minuscule Ao Sane, where *Jungle Beach Resort* (ⓣ 076/381108, Ⓕ 381542; ⑦–⑨) offers 44 comfortable air-con bungalows and a swimming pool.

# Hat Rawai and its islands

The eastern side of Laem Promthep curves round into **HAT RAWAI**, Phuket's southernmost beach and the first to be exploited for tourist purposes. Twenty-five years on, the developers have moved to the softer sands of Kata and Karon and returned Rawai to its former inhabitants, the *chao ley*. A few bungalow outfits still operate here, but most visitors come either to eat seafood with Phuket's townspeople in one of the open-air seafood restaurants on the beachfront, or to hire a longtail out to the **islands** offshore. Of these, Ko Khai Nok, Ko Hai (aka Coral Island), Ko Racha Yai and Ko Racha Noi are good for snorkelling and diving – the visibility and variety of the reefs around **Ko Racha** in particular compare with those off Ko Similan further up the Andaman coast, and make a popular destination for Phuket's diving centres (see box on pp.322–3).

Hat Rawai boasts an idiosyncratic monument in the shape of the *Henry Wagner*, a very ordinary twelve-metre longtail boat set back from the road just west of the pier. In June 1987, five disabled men set off in this boat to pioneer a course across the Isthmus of Kra, and in just six weeks they navigated the rivers connecting the Andaman Sea to the Gulf of Thailand, without the aid of accurate charts. The captain and inspiration behind the enterprise was the late Tristan Jones, a Welsh-born 64-year-old amputee, veteran adventurer and campaigner for the disabled, who told the story of the trip in his book, *To Venture Further*.

## Practicalities

**Songthaews** from Phuket town pass through Rawai (B20) on their way to and from Nai Harn. Longtail **boats** to the islands are easily chartered from Rawai; for a maximum of eight people, a boat to Ko Racha Yai (1hr) should cost around B2000 for a day-trip, including snorkelling time and return transport, or around B1000 for a simple transfer to Ko Racha Yai. Longtails to Ko Hai are cheaper at around B800 for a half-day snorkelling charter, or a bit less for a single journey to the island.

Unless you're keen on desolate beaches, Rawai makes a pretty dismal place to stay, but if you're just waiting for a boat out to one of the islands you could try the **bungalows** at *Porn Sri* (076/381264, 288043; ❹–❻). Accommodation on nearby islands is much more appealing: on **Ko Racha Yai** you can stay at *Ban Raya Resort* (076/354682, 224439, www.phuket.com/banraya; ❼–❽) which has fan and air-con bungalows scattered through a palm grove on a headland, within a few minutes' walk of several lovely beaches. On **Ko Hai** there's *Coral Island Resort* (076/281060, 381957, www.phuket.com /coralisland; ❽–❾) with 64 bungalows and a pool set in lush tropical gardens and within easy reach of several beautiful white-sand beaches. Day-trippers are not allowed onto tiny little **Ko Maiton**, which is home to the very exclusive *Maiton Island Resort* (076/214954, 214959, www.phuket.com/maiton; ❾), whose luxurious traditional-style villas all have direct access to a blindingly white sand beach; rates start at B10,800.

# The east coast

Tin mines and docks take up a lot of Phuket's east coast, which is thus neither scenic nor swimmable. East of Rawai, the sizeable offshore island of **Ko Lone** protects the broad sweep of **Ao Chalong**, where many a Chinese fortune was made from the huge quantities of tin mined in the bay. Ao Chalong tapers off eastwards into **Laem Panwa**, at the tip of which you'll find the **Phuket Aquarium** (daily 10am–4pm; B20), 10km south of Phuket town and accessible by frequent songthaews. Run by the island's Marine Research Centre, it makes a poor substitute for a day's snorkelling, but not a bad primer for what you might see on a reef. The research centre is also involved in the protection of marine turtles (see box on p.331); there's a hatchery on the premises, although it's out of bounds to casual visitors.

Around the other side of Laem Panwa, the island's main port of **Ao Makham** is dominated by a smelting and refining plant, bordered to the north by **Ko Siray** (aka Ko Sire), just about qualifying as an island because of the narrow canal that separates it from Phuket. Tour buses always stop off here to spy on Phuket's largest and longest-established *chao ley* community, an example of exploitative tourism at its worst. For more on the *chao ley* see p.308.

## The interior

If you have your own transport, exploring the lush, verdant **interior** makes a good antidote to lying on scorched beaches. All the tiny backroads – some too small to figure on tourist maps – eventually link up with the arteries connecting Phuket town with the beaches, and the minor routes south of Hat Nai Yang are especially picturesque, passing through monsoon forest which once in a while opens out into spiky pineapple fields or regimentally ordered **rubber plantations**. Thailand's first rubber trees were planted in Trang in 1901, and Phuket's sandy soil proved to be especially well suited to the crop. All over the island you'll see cream-coloured sheets of latex hanging out to dry on bamboo racks in front of villagers' houses.

North of Karon, Phuket's minor roads eventually swing back to the central Highway 402, also known as Thanon Thepkasatri after the landmark monument that stands on a roundabout 12km north of Phuket town. This **Heroines' Monument** commemorates the repulse of the Burmese army by the widow of the governor of Phuket and her sister in 1785: the two women rallied the island's womenfolk who, legend has it, cut their hair short and rolled up banana leaves to look like musket barrels to frighten the Burmese away. All songthaews to Hat Surin and Hat Nai Yang pass the monument (as does all mainland-bound traffic), and this is where you should alight for **Thalang Museum** (Wed–Sun 8.30am–4pm; B20), five minutes' walk east of here on Route 4027. Phuket's only museum, it has a few interesting exhibits on the local tin and rubber industries, as well as some colourful folkloric history and photos of the masochistic feats of the Vegetarian Festival (see box on p.327). If you continue along Route 4207 you'll eventually reach the Gibbon Rehabilitation Project, described below.

Eight kilometres north of the Heroines' Monument, just beyond the crossroads in the small town of **Thalang**, stands **Wat Phra Thong**, one of Phuket's most revered temples on account of the power of the Buddha statue it enshrines. The solid gold image is half-buried and no one dares dig it up for fear of a curse that has struck down excavators in the past. After the wat was built around the statue, the image was encased in plaster to deter would-be robbers.

### Phra Taew National Park

The road east of the Thalang intersection takes you to the visitor centre of **Phra Taew National Park**, 3km away. Several paths cross this small hilly enclave, leading you through the forest habitat of macaques and wild boar, but the most popular features of the park are the Gibbon Rehabilitation Project and the Ton Sai and Bang Pae waterfalls, which combine well as a day-trip. The

Gibbon Project is located about 10km northeast of the Heroines' Monument, off Route 4207. **Songthaews** from Phuket town, more frequent in the morning, will take you most of the way: ask to dropped off at Bang Pae (a 40min drive from town) and then follow the signed track for about 1km to get to the project centre. You can get drinks and snacks at the foodstall next to the Rehabilitation Centre, and the route to the waterfalls is signed from here.

## The Gibbon Rehabilitation Project

Phuket's forests used once to resound with the whooping calls of indigenous white-handed lar gibbons, but because these primates make such cute and charismatic pets there is now not a single wild gibbon at large on the island. The situation has become so dire that the lar is now an endangered species, and in 1992 it became illegal in Thailand to keep them as pets, to sell them or to kill them. Despite this, you'll come across a good number of pet gibbons on Phuket, kept in chains by bar and hotel owners as entertainment for their customers or as sidewalk photo opportunities for gullible tourists. The **Gibbon Rehabilitation Centre** (daily 10am–4pm, last tour at 3.15pm; donation; ⓣ076/260491, ⓕ260492, ⓔgibbon@poboxes.com) aims to reverse this state of affairs, first by rescuing as many pet gibbons as they can, and then by resocializing and re-educating them for the wild before finally releasing them back into the forests. It is apparently not unusual for gibbons to be severely traumatized by their experience as pets. To begin with the young gibbons will have been taken forcibly from their mothers – who most likely would have been shot – and then they may have been taunted or even abused by their owners; in addition many "bar babies" never learn how to use their arms – a catastrophe for a wild lar who can swing through the trees at up to 30km per hour. Not surprisingly, the therapy takes a long time – to date only one gibbon has been reintroduced to the forests, and that's to an uninhabited island in Phang Nga bay.

Visitors are welcome at the project, which is centred in the forests of Phra Taew National Park, close to Bang Pae waterfall, but because the whole point of the rehab project is to minimize the gibbons' contact with humans, you can only admire the creatures from afar. There's a small exhibition here on the aims of the project, and the well-informed volunteer guides will fill you in on the details of each case and on the idiosyncratic habits of the lar gibbon (see Contexts on p.448 for more about Thailand's primates). Should you want to become a project volunteer yourself, you can fax or email the project centre.

## Bang Pae and Ton Sai waterfalls

If you follow the track along the river from the Gibbon Project, you'll soon arrive at **Bang Pae waterfall**, a popular picnic and bathing spot, ten to fifteen minutes' walk away. Continue on the track for another 2.8km (about 1hr 30min on foot) and you should reach **Ton Sai waterfall**: though not a difficult climb, it is quite steep in places and can be rough underfoot, so take plenty of water and wear decent shoes. There are plenty of opportunities for cool dips in the river en route. Once at Ton Sai you can either walk back down to the Phra Taew National Park access road and try to hitch a ride back home, or return the way you came.

# Thachatchai Nature Trail

Forty-one kilometres north of the Thalang intersection, just 700m south of the Sarasin Bridge exit to the mainland, a sign east off Highway 402 brings you to the **Thachatchai Nature Trail**, part of the Sirinath National Park (which also covers the west-coast beaches of Hat Mai Khao and Hat Nai Yang). Although probably not worth a special trip, the trail does combine nicely with a visit to Hat Mai Khao (see p.330) or Hat Nai Yang (see p.332) – and it's free. Any bus running between Phuket town and the mainland will drop you at the sign (it's across the road from the old headquarters of the Sirinath National Park, now moved to Hat Nai Yang), just be sure to get off before you cross the bridge. There's a visitor centre at the trailhead where you can pick up a leaflet, and a drinks stall next door.

The six-hundred-metre trail runs along a raised wooden walkway that loops through a patch of coastal mangrove swamp. Informative English-language interpretive boards are set at regular intervals to show you what **flora and fauna** to look and listen out for: you can't fail to spot the swarms of fiddler crabs scuttling about in the sand and mud around the roots of the mangrove trees, and with a little patience you might also notice a few of the crabs which you may already have encountered elsewhere, as they're the ones that give the distinctive taste to the green papaya salad, *som tam*. The "bok-bok" sound that you can hear above the roar of the distant highway is the sound the mangrove-dwelling shrimps make when they snap their pincers as they feed. For more on mangroves, see box on p.359.

# Ko Phi Phi and the Krabi coast

East around the mainland coast from Phuket's Sarasin Bridge, the limestone pinnacles that so dominate the landscape of southern Thailand suddenly begin to pepper the sea as well, making **Ao Phang Nga** one of the most fascinating bays in the country. Most travellers, however, head straight for the hub of the region at **Krabi**, springboard for the spectacular mainland beaches of **Laem Phra Nang** and the even more stunning – and very popular – **Ko Phi Phi**. If it's tropical paradise minus the crowds that you're after, opt instead for the sizeable but more peaceful **Ko Lanta Yai** or the smaller **Ko Jum**.

All the major islands are served by frequent **ferries** from Krabi except during the rainy season (May–Oct), when convoluted routes via other mainland ports are sometimes possible. Buses and songthaews connect all mainland spots whatever the weather, and you can rent motorbikes in Krabi.

# Ao Phang Nga

Protected from the ravages of the Andaman Sea by Phuket, **AO PHANG NGA** has a seascape both bizarre and beautiful. Covering some four hundred

square kilometres of coast between Phuket and Krabi, the mangrove–lined bay is littered with limestone karst formations up to 300m in height, jungle–clad and craggily profiled. The bay is thought to have been formed about twelve thousand years ago when a dramatic rise in sea level flooded the summits of mountain ranges which over millions of years had been eroded by an acidic mixture of atmospheric carbon dioxide and rainwater. The best of the most affordable ways of seeing the bay is to join an **organized tour** from the town of **Phang Nga** – you can go from Phuket or Krabi, but the Phuket boats are relatively expensive and generally too big to manoeuvre in the more interesting areas, and Krabi tours go via Phang Nga anyway.

## Phang Nga

All buses from Phuket and Takua Pa to Krabi pass through nondescript little **PHANG NGA** about midway along their routes, dropping passengers at the bus station (T076/412014) on Thanon Phetkasem. If you want to go straight to the bay, change onto a songthaew bound for **Tha Don**; the pier is 9km to the south. There's no official **tourist information**, but the staff at Sayan Tour inside the bus station compound are helpful and will store your baggage for a few hours; they also sell bus and boat tickets for onward journeys to Krabi, Ko Phi Phi, Ko Lanta and Ko Samui. Phang Nga has hourly **buses** to Phuket and Krabi, and four air-con departures a day to Surat Thani, with the 11.30am departure timed to link up with the Ko Samui boat, getting you to the island at 5pm. If you're heading to or from Khao Lak or points further north up the west coast, you'll probably find it faster to get a bus to Khokkloi and then change.

All Phang Nga's hotels are within a 250-metre radius of the bus station, which is itself towards the northern end of this long, thin town. This is also where you'll find the main **banks**, with exchange counters and ATMs. Most other municipal facilities are further south down Thanon Phetkasem: the **police station** (T076/412975) and immigration office (T076/412011) are about 500m south of the bus station, off Soi Thungchedi, the **telephone office** is another 100m south of them, and **Phang Nga Hospital** (T076/412034) and the **post office** are over 2km south of the bus station.

### Accommodation and eating

Phang Nga's best budget **hotels** are all within 100m of each other, two on each side of Thanon Phetkasem. *Ratanapong Hotel* at no. 111 (T076/411247; ❶–❸) gets the most custom, offering the cheapest fan rooms plus some with air-con, and an informal restaurant on street level; the similar *Thawisuk Hotel* at no. 77 (T076/412100; ❷) has large, clean rooms and a rooftop terrace. Mid-way between these two hotels, the recently built *Phang Nga Guest House* (T076/144358, F430333, Ephang-ngainn@png.co.th; ❷–❸) has exceptionally clean and comfortable rooms, some with en-suite bathrooms and air-con. Rooms at the *Muang Tong* (T076/411132; ❶–❸) on the other side of the road at no. 128 are en suite and pretty standard, with the choice between fan and air-con; the hotel also runs budget tours of the bay. The most upmarket accommodation in town is at *Phang Nga Inn* (T076/411963, F430333, Ephang-ngainn@png.co.th; ❹–❼), which is clearly signed to the left of the bus station, about 250m away at 2/2 Soi Lohakji just off the town's main road; it's the former family home of the people who also run the *Phang Nga Guest House*, and the 17 rooms here are all very attractively furnished and equipped with air-con and TV, the price depending on the size of the room. Down at Tha Don pier, the *Phang Nga Bay Resort* (☎076/412067, 🖷412070; ➐–➑) boasts a swimming pool and good facilities, but has disappointing views considering the bayside location.

For **eating**, check out the *Phing Kan Restaurant* under the *Ratanapong Hotel*, where you can choose from a variety of noodle and rice standards detailed on the English-language menu. The well-established streetside restaurant nearby also has an English menu and a large selection of rice, noodle and fish dishes. Otherwise, plenty of noodle stalls line Thanon Phetkasem day and night.

### Tours of the bay

The most popular budget tours are the **longtail-boat trips** operated by the long-established Sayan Tour (☎076/430348, 🖃sayuntour@hotmail.com), housed in an office inside the bus station (see opposite). Similar ones are organized from adjacent bus station offices by Mr Kaen Tour (☎076/430619) and James Bond Tour (☎076/413471), and by Mr Hassim at the *Muang Tong Hotel* across the road (☎ 076/412132). All offer half-day tours (daily at 8am & 2pm; 3–4hr) costing B200 per person (minimum four people), as well as full-day extensions which last until 4pm and cost B500 including lunch. (Take the 8am tour to avoid seeing the bay at its most crowded.) The tours leave from the tour operators' offices, but will pick up from the town's hotels if booked in advance; people staying at Tha Don, the departure-point for trips around Ao Phang Nga, can join the tours at the pier.

All tour operators also offer the chance to **stay** overnight on **Ko Panyi**. This can be tacked onto the half- or full-day tour for an extra B250; dinner, accommodation, and morning coffee are included in the price. Sayan Tour also offers overnight stays on the private Ko Yang Dang (aka Elephant Island), where you can swim and go canoeing; alternatively a couple of hours' canoeing can be added to the standard tour for B400.

If you have the money, the most rewarding way to see the bay is by **sea canoe**. Several companies in Phuket and Khao Lak now offer this activity, in which you paddle round the bay in two-person kayaks, exploring the hidden lagoons (*hongs*) inside the karst outcrops (see box on p.361), and observing the seabirds, kingfishers and crab-eating macaques that haunt the mangrove-fringed shores – without the constant roar of an engine to scare them away. Most outings also include snorkelling and swimming time, plus lunch on a deserted beach somewhere; some companies offer overnight trips with the chance to paddle into *hongs* after dark, and the longest-running operator, Sea Canoe, does expeditions lasting up to a fortnight. Everyone gets full paddling instruction and English-speaking guides should always be to hand; some companies have big support boats as well. Prices range from around B2200 (kids B1500) per person per day out of Khao Lak (see p.314) to B2700 (B1350) from Phuket (see box on p.329).

### The bay

On tours, the standard itinerary follows a circular or figure-of-eight route around the bay, passing extraordinary karst silhouettes that change character with the shifting light – in the eerie glow of an early-morning mist it can be a breathtaking experience. Many of the formations have nicknames suggested by their weird outlines – like **Khao Machu**, which translates as "Pekinese Rock", and **Khao Tapu**, or Nail Rock. Others have titles derived from other attributes – **Tham Nak** (Naga Cave) gets its name from the serpentine stalagmites inside; and a close inspection of **Khao Kien** (Painting Rock) reveals a cliff wall decorated with paintings of elephants, monkeys, fish, crabs and hunting weapons, believed to be between three thousand and five thousand years old.

Ao Phang Nga's most celebrated feature, however, earned its tag from a movie: the cleft **Khao Ping Gan** (Leaning Rock) is better known as **James Bond Island**, after doubling as Scaramanga's hideaway in *The Man With the Golden Gun*. Every boat stops off here and the rock crawls with trinket vendors.

From Khao Ping Gan most of the boats return to the mainland via the eye-catching settlement of **Ko Panyi**, a Muslim village built almost entirely on stilts around the rock that supports the mosque. Nearly all boat tours stop here for lunch, so the island's become little more than a tourists' shopping and eating arcade. You're best off avoiding the expensive and noisy seafood restaurants out front, and heading towards the islanders' foodstalls around the mosque. The overnight tours, which include an evening meal and dormitory-style accommodation on the island, offer a more tranquil experience and a chance to watch the sun set and rise over the bay, though there's little to do in the intervening hours and you're confined to the village until a boat picks you up after breakfast.

At some point on your trip you should pass several small brick **kilns** on the edge of a mangrove swamp – once used for producing charcoal from mangrove wood – before being ferried beneath **Tham Lod**, a photogenic archway roofed with stalactites and opening onto spectacular limestone and mangrove vistas.

# Krabi

The compact little fishing town of **KRABI** is both provincial capital and major hub for onward travel to some of the region's most popular islands, including Ko Phi Phi, Ko Lanta and the Laem Phra Nang beaches. So efficient are the transport links that you don't really need to stop here, but it's an attractive spot, strung out along the west bank of the Krabi estuary, with mangrove-lined shorelines to the east, a harbour filled with rickety old fishing vessels and looming limestone outcrops on every horizon. The main Thanon Utrakit runs north–south along the estuary, veering slightly inland just north of the Tha Reua Chao Fa (Chao Fa pier) and forming the eastern perimeter of the tiny town centre. There are plenty of guest houses, so it's possible to base yourself here and make day-trips to the Krabi beaches (see p.360), 45 minutes' ride away by boat or songthaew, though most people prefer to stay at the beaches. Krabi is at its busiest during high season from November through February, a period which officially begins with the annual Andaman Festival, a week of festivities featuring parades, outdoor concerts, fishing contests, a funfair and lots of street stalls that climaxes at Loy Krathong, the nationwide festival celebrated in late October or early November.

## Arrival, transport and information

There are at least two daily Thai and/or Bangkok Airways **flights** between Bangkok and Krabi; Andaman Air shuttles between Phuket and Krabi three times a day. Diminutive Krabi **airport** (⊤075/691940) is 18km east of town,

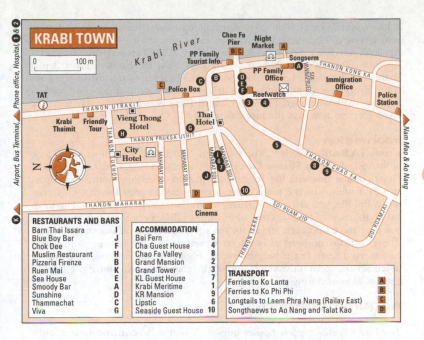

**KRABI TOWN**

0    100 m

Krabi River

Chao Fa Pier

Night Market

PP Family Tourist Info.

Songserm

THANON KONG KA

PP Family Office

Immigration Office

Police Box

Reefwatch

Police Station

TAT

THANON UTRAKIT

Krabi Thaimit

Friendly Tour

Vieng Thong Hotel

THANON PRUKSA UTHIT

Thai Hotel

THANON SUKHON

City Hotel

MAHARAT SOI 8

MAHARAT SOI 6

MAHARAT SOI 4

MAHARAT SOI 2

THANON MAHARAT

Cinema

THANON CHAO FA

THANON ISSARA

SOI RUAM JID

SOI RUAM JIO

Nam Mao & Ao Nang

Airport, Bus Terminal,

Phone office, Hospital, 1 & 2

**RESTAURANTS AND BARS**
| | |
|---|---|
| Barn Thai Issara | I |
| Blue Boy Bar | J |
| Chok Dee | F |
| Muslim Restaurant | H |
| Pizzeria Firenze | B |
| Ruen Mai | K |
| Sea House | E |
| Smoody Bar | A |
| Sunshine | D |
| Thammachat | C |
| Viva | G |

**ACCOMMODATION**
| | |
|---|---|
| Bai Fern | 5 |
| Cha Guest House | 4 |
| Chao Fa Valley | 8 |
| Grand Mansion | 2 |
| Grand Tower | 3 |
| KL Guest House | 7 |
| Krabi Meritime | 1 |
| KR Mansion | 9 |
| Lipstic | 6 |
| Seaside Guest House | 10 |

**TRANSPORT**
| | |
|---|---|
| Ferries to Ko Lanta | A |
| Ferries to Ko Phi Phi | B |
| Longtails to Laem Phra Nang (Railay East) | C |
| Songthaews to Ao Nang and Talat Kao | D |

just off Highway 4. Thai Airways minibuses transport passengers from the airport into town for B60, though these seem often to be commandeered by tour groups, so you may end up getting a taxi for B300 to Krabi or B500 to Ao Nang (maximum four passengers). Budget **car rental** have a desk in the airport arrivals area (075/620028, www.budget.co.th), as do National/SMT (075/691939, smtcar@samart.co.th).

Direct air-con and VIP **buses** from Bangkok leave the Southern Bus Terminal at staggered intervals between 6.30pm and 8pm and take at least twelve hours. Air-con buses run hourly to and from Surat Thani, so if you're travelling from Bangkok, you could take an overnight **train** to Surat Thani and then pick up a Krabi bus. There are also hourly buses to and from Phuket via Phang Nga; if travelling to or from Khao Sok or Khao Lak you may have to change buses at Khokkloi. Only a few buses drop their passengers in central Krabi: most pull in at the **bus terminal** 5km north of town in the village of Talat Kao, which stands at the intersection of Thanon Utrakit and Highway 4. From here there's a frequent songthaew service to Krabi's Thanon Maharat.

When it comes to moving on from Krabi, you can buy combination bus and train tickets **to Bangkok** via Surat Thani (2 daily; 16hr; B600–850) from any travel agent; these firms also sell tickets on private buses, minibuses and boats to **Ko Samui** (2 daily; 6hr; B300–370), **Ko Pha Ngan** (2 daily; 6hr; B400), Bangkok's **Thanon Khao San** (daily; 14hr; B450–550), **Penang** (2 daily; 6hr; B400) and **Langkawi** (daily; 12hr; B550).

Two companies, Songserm and PP Family, run **ferries** from Krabi to Ko Phi Phi and to Ko Lanta; both companies use the two Chao Fa **piers**, and both have offices on nearby Thanon Kong Ka. There's nothing to choose between the two, whose prices and journey times are identical, but the timetables are different: PP Family runs year-round ferries **to Ko Phi Phi** at 10.30am and

2.30pm, and from December to April adds an extra 9am service; Songserm runs ferries at 11am and 3pm with an extra 9am service from December to April. All ferries from Krabi to Ko Phi Phi cost B200. Ferries **to Ko Lanta** via Ko Jum only run from November through May: PP Family's boats depart Krabi at 10.30am and 1.30pm, and Songserm's boat leaves at 8am; the trip costs B200. Every tour agent in town sells tickets for both companies or you can buy them on the boat. Longtail boats for **Laem Phra Nang** (45 min; B70) use the Chao Fa piers as well as the pier closer to TAT.

## Information

Krabi's **TAT office** (daily 8.30am–4.30pm, ☎ 075/612740) is housed in a lone whitewashed hut on Thanon Utrakit at the northern edge of the town centre. Don't confuse this with the Tourist Information office run by the ferry operator PP Family, which is more conveniently located beside the pier for ferries to Ko Phi Phi; you can get information here, but it may be partisan. The town has no shortage of **tour agents**, all of whom will be only too happy to sell you bus, boat and train tickets and to fix you up with a room on one of the islands. There's actually no need to buy ferry tickets in advance as none of the boats has reserved seats, but it may be worth booking your first night's island or beach accommodation through one of these agents, as Ko Phi Phi especially gets packed out during peak season.

## Accommodation

The least expensive guest houses offer rock-bottom **accommodation**, often cramped and windowless but perfectly adequate for one night: if all those listed are full, head for the pierside stretch of Thanon Kong Ka, where several tour operators advertise rooms for rent in the ➋ category.

**Bai Fern**, a 5min walk west from the pier along Thanon Chao Fa ☎ 075/630339. Sizeable, well-maintained rooms in a three-storey block that's away from the main fray; some rooms have private bathrooms and all have a balcony. ➋–➌

**Cha Guest House**, opposite the post office on Thanon Utrakit ☎ 075/621125, ⓦ www.thaisouth.com/cha. Long-standing traveller-oriented place with good rooms in bungalows set round a garden compound behind Krabi's most clued-up internet centre. Room rates depend on size and whether you want a private bathroom. Recommended. ➋–➌

**Chao Fa Valley**, a 7min walk west from the pier along Thanon Chao Fa ☎ 075/612499. Spacious en-suite bungalows arranged around a pretty flower garden with an appealingly calm atmosphere. Price depends on the size of the bungalow. ➋–➌

**Grand Mansion**, a 12min walk north up Thanon Utrakit from the pier ☎ 075/611371, ⓕ 611372. Though a little way from the town centre, this is the most convenient of Krabi's more comfortable hotels. The best rooms have air-con, hot water and TV. ➍–➎

**Grand Tower Hotel**, at the corner of Thanon Utrakit and Thanon Chao Fa ☎ 075/621456, ⓕ 611741. Central and deservedly popular, this is a very comfortable travellers' hotel with clean, nicely furnished and well-maintained rooms, all of them en suite and some with TV and air-con. internet access downstairs. Better than many pricier hotels in town. Recommended. ➌–➍

**KL Guest House**, Soi 2, Thanon Maharat ☎ 075/612511. No-frills, budget option; all rooms have a fan and shared bathroom, but the cheaper ones have no window. ➊–➋

**KR Mansion**, a 10min walk west from the pier along Thanon Chao Fa ☎ 075/612761, ⓕ 612545, ⓔ krmansion@hotmail.com. Popular travellers' haunt with clean and well-kept rooms, some with attached bathroom. Lots of traveller's information, a nice rooftop bar and a good restaurant. Also offer internet access, book exchange and bicycle rental. ➋–➎

**Krabi Meritime**, 2km north of town off Thanon Utrakit ☎ 075/620028, ⓕ 612992, ⓔ krabi@asianet.co.th. Beautifully located luxury hotel, set beside the limestone karsts and mangroves of the Krabi River. Rooms are attractive and have fine views, there's a big pool, a spa, a kids' games room and babysitting service. Good value for its class; thirty percent discounts May–Oct. ⑧

**Lipstic**, 20–22 Soi 2, Thanon Maharat ☎075/612392, ⓔkayanchalee@hotmail.com. Good budget choice tucked away off the street

with nice clean rooms, many with windows but none with private bathroom. ②

**Seaside Guesthouse**, 8–10 Thanon Maharat ☎075/630530, ⓕ630529. Windowless cells with shared bathrooms; clean enough. internet access downstairs. ②

# Eating and drinking

Krabi has plenty of traveller-oriented restaurants, the best of which are detailed below, but for a truly inexpensive Thai meal, head for the riverside **night market**, which sets up around the pier-head every evening from about 6pm.

**Barn Thai Issara**, Soi 2, Thanon Maharat. Expensive home-made pizzas, fresh pasta dishes, Indian and Mexican food plus some unusual sourdough sandwiches.

**Blue Boy Bar**, Soi 4, Thanon Maharat. Downtown bar staging live music to help wash down the beer.

**Chok Dee, Sea House and Sunshine**, Thanon Kong Ka. Three independently run little restaurants next to each other on the road down to the pier, all deservedly popular, serving standard Thai and Western dishes, inexpensive set breakfasts, real coffee, curries and burgers. Service is friendly and relaxed.

**Krabi Meritime**, 2km north of the town centre off Thanon Utrakit. Fabulous views from the sky lounge on the eighth floor at Krabi's poshest hotel – a great place for a sundowner as you're admiring the riverine landscape of karsts and mangrove swamps.

**Muslim Restaurant**, Thanon Pruksa Uthit. Cheap and filling *rotis* (flat fried breads) served with a choice of curry sauces.

**Pizzeria Firenze**, Thanon Kong Ka. Authentic Italian dishes, including pizzas, pastas, sandwiches and ice creams. Tasty but pricey.

**Ruen Mai**, about 2km north of the town centre on Thanon Maharat. Popular with locals and well regarded, this typical garden restaurant is worth making the effort to get to, not least for the change from the more touristed options in the town centre. It serves a mid-priced menu of quality Thai dishes, including lots of seafood and *tom yam*.

**Smoody Bar**, Thanon Kong Ka. Nightly live music and reasonably priced beer on the waterfront at the edge of the night market.

**Tamarind Tree**, restaurant attached to *KR Mansion* on Thanon Chao Fa. Does a full range of slap-up organic and macrobiotic Thai and Western fare at reasonable prices. It's well worth coming here before sunset to soak up the distant mountain views from the separate rooftop bar (open 4pm–1am) and work your way through the cocktail menu.

**Thammachat**, Thanon Kong Ka. Boasts the best and most adventurous mid-priced menu in town, which is particularly strong on unusual Thai and vegetarian dishes. The veggie *hoh mok* (baked bean-curd omelette with basil and lemon grass) is highly recommended.

# Listings

**Airlines** The Thai Airways office is just outside the *Krabi Meritime Hotel* on Thanon Utrakit ☎075/622440; for flights with other carriers contact any Krabi tour operator.

**Banks and exchange** All major banks have branches on Thanon Utrakit with exchange counters and ATMs.

**Car rental** At Krabi airport (see p.355), and through some guest houses and tour companies, including Friendly Tour at 173 Thanon Utrakit

☎075/612558, ⓔkrabifriendly@hotmail.com; and Krabi Thaimit at 177 Thanon Utrakit ☎075/632054, ⓦwww.asiatravel.com/thailand/krabicarrent; both rent jeeps for B1200 per 24hr and cars for B1500, including full insurance.

**Cookery classes** Available at the Krabi Thai Cookery School, just off the Krabi–Ao Nang road (10am–3pm; B1000 including transport; ☎01/396 5237, ⓔkrabicookeryschool@hotmail.com), and bookable through any tour operator.

**Dive centre** Although there are dive centres at all the Krabi beaches, it's possible to organize trips and courses from Krabi town through the British-run Reefwatch Worldwide Dive Operator, 48 Thanon Utrakit ☏ 075/632650, ⊛ www.reefwatch-worldwide.com. They charge B7900 for the four-day Openwater course and run dive trips to local sites (see p.323) for B1400–2400, generally in a longtail boat.

**Hospitals** Krabi Hospital is about 1km north of the town centre at 325 Thanon Utrakit ☏ 075/611226.

**Immigration office** On Thanon Utrakit (Mon–Fri 8.30am–4.30pm; ☏ 075/611097).

**internet access** At nearly every Krabi guest house; *Cha Guest House*, opposite the post office on Thanon

Utrakit has the most terminals. Catnet internet access at the phone office on Thanon Utrakit.

**Mail** The GPO is on Thanon Montri. Poste restante should be addressed c/o GPO and can be collected Mon–Fri 8.30am–4.30pm, Sat 8.30am–3.30pm.

**Motorbike rental** Through some guest houses and tour companies for about B250 per day.

**Police** 24hr help available on ☏ 1699, or contact the police station at the southern end of Thanon Utrakit ☏ 075/611222.

**Telephones** For international calls use the CAT phone office about 2km north of the town centre on Thanon Utrakit (Mon–Fri 8am–8pm, Sat & Sun 8.30am–4.30pm), which is easily reached on any songthaew heading up that road, or on foot.

## Day-trips from Krabi

With time on your hands you'll soon exhaust the possibilities in Krabi, but there are a few trips to make out of town apart from the popular excursions to Laem Phra Nang (p.361), Hat Nopparat Thara (see p.368), Ao Phang Nga (see p.350) and Ko Phi Phi (see p.369). Alternatively, you could join one of the numerous **organized tours** sold by every Krabi travel agent, for example the tours of four or five islands which take in the reefs and beaches around Laem Phra Nang, or the hikes through the national park near Khlong Thom, home of the rare Gurney's pitta; because tour agencies sell the same basic itineraries, prices are kept competitive.

### The mangroves

Longtail-boat tours of the **mangrove swamps** that infest the Krabi River estuary are an increasingly popular activity and can be organized directly with the boatmen who hang around Krabi's two piers (about B300 per hour for up to six people) or through most tour operators (average B500 per person for three hours). All mangrove tours give you a chance to get a close-up view of typical mangrove flora and fauna (see box opposite), and most will stop off at a couple of riverside caves on the way. The most famous features on the usual mangrove itinerary are the twin limestone outcrops known as **Khao Kanab Nam**, which rise a hundred metres above the water from opposite sides of the Krabi River near the *Krabi Meritime Hotel* and are so distinctive that they've become the symbol of Krabi. One of the twin karsts hides caves which can be easily explored – many skeletons have been found here over the centuries, thought to be those of immigrants who got stranded by a flood before reaching the mainland.

Even more fun than taking a longtail tour of the mangroves is a self-paddle **kayaking** tour of the mangroves and *hong*s, hidden lagoons found further north up the coast. Every tour operator in Krabi sells these outings; see the box on p.361 for itineraries and prices.

### Wat Tham Seua

Beautifully set amid limestone cliffs 12km northeast of Krabi, the tropical forest of **Wat Tham Seua** (Tiger Cave Temple) can be reached by taking a red songthaew from Thanon Utrakit (20min; B8), and then walking 2km down the

## Life in a mangrove swamp

**Mangrove swamps** are at their creepiest at low tide, when their aerial roots are fully exposed to form gnarled and knotted archways above the muddy banks. Not only are these roots essential parts of the tree's breathing apparatus, they also reclaim land for future mangroves, trapping and accumulating water-borne debris into which the metre-long mangrove seedlings can fall. In this way, mangrove swamps also fulfil a vital ecological function: stabilizing shifting mud and protecting coastlines from erosion and the impact of tropical storms.

Mangrove swamp mud harbours some interesting creatures too, like the instantly recognizable **fiddler crab**, named after the male's single outsized reddish claw, which it brandishes for communication and defence purposes – the claw is so powerful it could open a can of baked beans. If you keep your eyes peeled you should be able to make out a few **mudskippers**; these specially adapted fish can absorb atmospheric oxygen through their skins as long as they keep their outsides damp, which is why they spend so much time slithering around in the sludge. As you'd imagine from the name, on land they move in tiny hops by flicking their tails, aided by their extra-strong pectoral fins. Of the bigger creatures who patrol the mangrove swamps in search of food, you might well come across **kingfishers** and white-bellied **sea eagles**, but you'd be very lucky indeed to encounter the rare crab-eating macaque. For more on mangrove ecosystems see Contexts, p.448.

To date, the Krabi mangroves have escaped the **environmentally damaging** attentions of the prawn-farming industry that has so damaged the swamps around Kanchanaburi (see "Environmental Issues" in Contexts, p.451, for more on this). But mangrove wood from this area has been used to make commercial charcoal, and on any boat trip around the Krabi coastline you'll almost certainly pass the remains of old tiny brick kilns near cleared patches of swamp.

signed track. As this is a working monastery, signs request that visitors wear respectable dress (no shorts or singlets for men or women), so bear this in mind before you leave town.

The temple's main **bot** – on your left under the cliff overhang – might come as a bit of a shock: alongside portraits of the abbot, a renowned teacher of Vipassana meditation, close-up photos of human entrails and internal organs are on display – reminders of the impermanence of the body. Any skulls and skeletons you might come across in the compound serve the same educational purpose. The most interesting part of Wat Tham Seua lies beyond the bot, reached by following the path past the nuns' quarters until you get to a couple of steep **staircases** up the 600-metre-high cliffside. The first staircase is long (1272 steps) and very steep, and takes about an hour to climb, but the vista from the summit is quite spectacular, affording fabulous karst views over the limestone outcrops and out to the islands beyond. There's a small shrine and a few monks' cells hidden among the trees at the top. The second staircase, next to the large statue of the Chinese fertility goddess Kuan Im, takes you on a less arduous route down into a deep dell encircled by high limestone walls. Here the monks have built themselves self-sufficient meditation cells, linked by paths through the lush ravine: if you continue along the main path you'll eventually find yourself back where you began, at the foot of the staircase. The valley is home to squirrels and monkeys as well as a pair of remarkable trees with overground **buttress roots** over 10m high. Triangular buttress roots are quite a common sight in tropical forests such as this, where the overhead canopy is so dense that it blocks out most of the sunlight, starving the soil of the nutrients necessary to sustain such enormous trees and rendering subterranean roots ineffective; these lateral extensions to the trunk both absorb foodstuff from the forest floor, in the form of fallen leaves and fungi, and act as the tree's anchor.

### Susaan Hoi

Thais make a big deal out of **Susaan Hoi** (Shell Cemetery), 17km west around the coast from Krabi, but it's hard to get very excited about a shoreline of metre-long 40-centimetre-thick beige-coloured rocks that could easily be mistaken for concrete slabs. Nevertheless, the facts of their formation are impressive: these stones are 75 million years old and made entirely from compressed shell fossils. You get a distant view of them from any longtail boat travelling between Krabi and Ao Phra Nang; for a closer look take any of the frequent Ao Nang-bound songthaews from Thanon Utrakit.

# Krabi beaches

Although the mainland beach areas west of Krabi can't compete with the local islands for underwater life, the stunning headland of **Laem Phra Nang** is accessible only by boat, so staying on one of its three beaches can feel like being on an island, albeit a crowded and potentially rather claustrophobic one. In contrast, a road runs right along the **Ao Nang** beachfront, which has enabled a burgeoning but likeable resort to thrive around its rather unexceptional beach. The next bay to the west, **Hat Nopparat Thara,** is long and unadulterated and has some appealingly solitary places to stay at its western end. Snorkelling conditions deteriorate at all Krabi beaches during the rainy season from May through October, so prices at all accommodation drops by up to fifty percent for this period, though a few places close down for the duration.

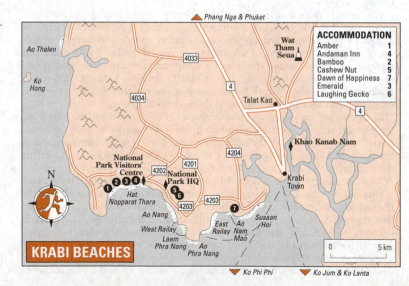

## Sea-kayaking in the Krabi area

By far the most rewarding way of exploring the glories of the Krabi coastline is by sea kayak. Paddling silently and stealthily into the eerie mangrove swamps and secret lagoons, or *hongs,* hidden inside the limestone karsts is an awesome experience and gives you close-up views of birds, animals and plants that would be impossible in a roaring longtail.

Hongs are the *pièce de résistance* of south Thailand's coastline – invisible to any passing vessel, these secret tidal lagoons can only be accessed at certain tides in canoes and boats small enough to travel along the narrow tunnels that lead into the karst's central pool. Once inside a *hong* you are completely enclosed by a ring of cliff faces hung with strange plants which nourish a local population of flying foxes and monkeys and support an ecosystem that's remained unchanged for millennia. Like the karsts themselves, the *hongs* have taken millions of years to form, the softer limestone hollowed out from above by the wind and the rain, and from the side by the pounding waves. Eventually, when the two hollows met, the heart of the karst was able to fill with water via the wave-eroded passageway at sea level, creating a lagoon. At high water these tunnels are filled and so impassable to any human, but when the tide recedes – for about fifty minutes every six hours – some tunnels do become passable to kayaks, enabling people to navigate into the mysterious *hong* at the heart of the karst.

Many companies take tourists kayaking around the karsts and mangrove swamps along the Krabi coastline, to impressive spots such as Ao Thalen (aka Ao Talin or Talan), about 25km northwest of Krabi town, where you paddle out to the *hongs* and beaches of Ko Hong and Ko Bileh. Another 25km north up the Krabi coast, the Ban Bor Tor (aka Ban Bho Tho) area of Ao Luk bay is famous as much for its caves as for its mangroves and karst landscape, and is another popular destination for kayak trips. The most famous cave up here is Tham Lod, with a long tunnel hung with stalagmites and stalactites and an entrance that's obscured by vines. The walls of nearby Tham Phi Hua Toe display around a hundred prehistoric cave-paintings as well as some interestingly twisted stalactite formations. Most Ao Luk tours also feature a visit to the inland botanical gardens of Than Bokkharani, 1km south of Ao Luk. Called Than Bok for short, the tiny park is a glade of emerald pools, grottoes and waterfalls enclosed in a ring of lush forest; if you want to see them independently, catch an Ao Luk songthaew from Krabi (1hr) and then walk down to the gardens.

Kayaking trips to any of the above destinations usually cost about B1200–1700 for a full day or B700–900 for half a day. Timing is obviously crucial in the exploration of these *hongs,* so sea-kayaking tour operators have to arrange their itinerary day by day to coincide with the tide. They can be arranged through any tour operator in Krabi town, Laem Phra Nang or Ao Nang, or directly with reputable kayaking operators such as Sea Canoe (☎075/637170, ⊛www.seacanoe.com) and Sea Kayak Krabi (☎075/630270). Sea Canoe also does longer trips of up to a fortnight, including the one-nighter based at their island camp (B7500 per person). All kayaking tours are priced for self-paddling, and tour leaders should give you full kayaking instruction; if asked, most tour operators can arrange for someone else to paddle you around for an extra B300.

# Laem Phra Nang and Ao Nam Mao

Seen from the close quarters of a longtail boat, the combination of sheer limestone cliffs, pure white sand and emerald waters at **LAEM PHRA NANG** is spectacular – and would be even more so without the hundreds of other admirers gathered on its beaches. Almost every centimetre of buildable land on the cape has now been taken over by bungalows, but at least high-rises don't feature yet, and much of the construction is hidden among coconut palms or set amid prettily landscaped gardens. The headland has three beaches within ten minutes' walk of each other: **Ao Phra Nang** graces the southwestern edge, and is flanked by **east and west Railay**. The scene here is laid-back, but by no means comatose; it's as popular with backpackers as it is with couples on short breaks, and the accommodation and entertainment facilities reflect this. It's also a major rock-climbing centre, both for beginners and experienced climbers, many of whom hang out here for months at a time while ticking off the three hundred different routes. Even if you don't want to stay, it's worth coming for the day to gawp at the scenery and scramble down into the lushly vegetated area around the cape's enclosed lagoon. Just about visible from east Railay but only accessible from it by a ten-minute longtail ride, **Ao Nam Mao** feels secluded and is the site of just one mid-priced eco-resort.

### The beaches

Set against a magnificent backdrop of cliffs and palms, diminutive **AO PHRA NANG** (aka Hat Tham Phra Nang) is the loveliest spot on the cape, attracting sunbathers to its luxuriously soft sand and snorkellers to the reefs some 200m offshore. Of the three beaches, it alone has no bungalows visible from the shore, just a couple of makeshift beachfront café-bars. Screened from the beach is just one luxury resort, with the sole means of direct access to Ao Phra Nang, but non-guests can walk there from east Railay in under ten minutes, following the resort's hedge until it gives onto a walkway which winds under the lip of the karst to the beach.

The beach and cape are named after a princess (*phra nang* means "revered lady"), whom the local fisherfolk believe lives here and controls the fertility of the sea. If you walk past the entrance to **Tham Phra Nang** (Princess Cave), hollowed out of the huge karst outcrop at the eastern edge of the bay, you'll see a host of red-tipped wooden phalluses stacked as offerings to her, by way of insurance for large catches. The numerous passageways and rocks around the cave are fun to clamber over, but getting down into **Sa Phra Nang** (Princess Lagoon) is more of a challenge. Buried deep inside the same rock, the lagoon is accessible only via a steep 45-minute descent that starts at the "resting spot" halfway along the walkway connecting the east edge of Ao Phra Nang with east Railay. After an initial ten-minute clamber, negotiated with the help of ropes, the path forks: go left for a panoramic view over the east and west bays of Hat Railay, or right for the lagoon. (For the strong-armed, there's the third option of hauling yourself up ropes to the top of the cliff for a bird's-eye view.) Taking the right-hand fork, you'll pass through the tropical dell dubbed "big tree valley" before eventually descending to the murky lagoon. The muddy banks have spawned a lagoonside gallery of clay models fashioned by visitors. The exterior face of Sa Phra Nang is popular with novice rock climbers, and courses are held here throughout the day during the dry season; see below for details.

Sometimes known as Sunset Beach, **WEST RAILAY** comes a close second to Ao Phra Nang, with similarly impressive karst scenery, crystal-clear water and a much longer stretch of good sand. There's some shade here too, and you only have to walk a few hundred metres to get beyond the longtails and the beachfront diners' line of vision. For more seclusion and an absence of longtails, wade or swim the few hundred metres to the lovely, uncrowded beach around the headland to the immediate north of west Railay (beyond the compound of the private time-share outfit, the *Railay Beach Club*).

The least attractive of the cape's beaches, **EAST RAILAY** (also sometimes known as Nam Mao, but not to be confused with the better known Ao Nam

Mao immediately to the east) is not suitable for swimming because of its fairly dense mangrove growth, a tide that goes out for miles and a bay that's busy with incoming longtails. Still, there's a greater concentration of inexpensive bungalows here, and none is more than ten minutes' walk from the much cleaner sands of west Railay and Ao Phra Nang. To get to east Railay from Ao Phra Nang, follow the walkway from the eastern edge; from west Railay walk through the *Railay Bay* or *Sand Sea* bungalow compounds.

**AO NAM MAO** is more suitable for swimming than east Railay though the tide here also runs out a long way and the sand is nothing like as deluxe as on west Railay. It's much less congested though, and you can walk to the Susaan Hoi shell cemetery in about twenty minutes.

### Diving, climbing and kayaking

All bungalows on Laem Phra Nang organize **snorkelling trips** (B250–400 including equipment) to the nearby islands of Hua Kwan and Ko Poda, and some offer two-night trips to Bamboo Island (B2000). From October through May, Phra Nang Divers, located next to *Railay Village* on west Railay (T & F 075/637064, W www.pndivers.com) runs one-day **diving trips** to nearby islands (B1800–2700), and two- and three-day live-aboards for B9000 and B15,500; they also offer a range of PADI-certificated diving courses (B9500 for the four-day Openwater). The most popular period for diving is January through March when it's worth reserving ahead if you're on a tight schedule. The nearest **recompression chamber** is on Ao Patong in Phuket (see p.322).

Given the topography, there's huge potential for **rock climbing**, abseiling and caving at Laem Phra Nang. There are some three hundred bolted sport-climbing routes on the cape, ranging in difficulty from 5a–8c, and no shortage of places where you can rent equipment and hire guides and instructors. Two of the longest-established climbing outfits are King Climbers (T 075/637125, F 612914, W www.railay.com/railay/climbing/climbing_intro.shtml), located at the back of the *Ya Ya* compound on east Railay, and Tex Climbing at the edge of *Railay Bay* (T 075/631509, F 621186, E texrock@loxinfo.co.th). It's a good idea to check with other tourists before choosing a climbing guide, as operators' safety standards vary. All the climbing centres rent out equipment (B1000 per day for two people) and offer a range of climbing **courses** and expeditions. A typical half-day introduction for novice climbers costs B800, a one-day climbing outing is B1500, and for B5000 you get a three-day course which should leave you experienced enough to strike out on your own. If you're already self-sufficient, you might want to get hold of the *Route Guide* to the Laem Phra Nang climbs, written by the guys at King Climbers and available from most of the climbing shops.

Limestone cliffs and mangrove swamps also make great landscapes for **kayaking**, and several places on east and west Railay rent them out for B100-150 per hour, with discounts for half- and full-day rental. Some places also offer kayaking tours of spectacular Ao Luk and Ko Hong (see p.361) for B850–900.

### Practicalities

Laem Phra Nang is only accessible by **boat** from Krabi town, Ao Nang, Ao Nam Mao and Ko Phi Phi. Longtail boats to Laem Phra Nang depart from various spots along the **Krabi** riverfront and from Chao Fa pier (45min; B70), leaving throughout the day as soon as they fill up. There are usually several different boatmen touting for custom at the same time, but as they each need a minimum of six passengers (the maximum load is fourteen), it's often more efficient to make your own group of six before committing to one particular boatmen. Depending on the tide, all Krabi boats land on or off east Railay, so you'll probably have to wade; from east Railay it's easy to cut across to west Railay along any of the through-tracks. Krabi boats do run during the rainy season, but it's a nerve-wracking experience so you're advised to go via Ao Nang instead. **Ao Nang** is much closer to Laem Phra Nang, and longtails run from the beachfront here to west Railay (10min; B40) year-round. During high season there's one direct boat a day between Laem Phra Nang and **Ko Phi Phi**. The easiest way of getting to **Ao Nam Mao** is by songthaew: all Krabi–Ao Nang songthaews pass the resort's entrance (every 10min; B20). Demand for boats between Ao Nam Mao and Laem Phra Nang is small, but if you don't mind waiting an hour or so you should be able to get a longtail between the two for about B40 (10min).

The three big bungalow operations on west Railay all have tour agencies and shops selling beach gear and postcards. You can **change money** at nearly all the bungalow operations on the cape, but rates can be up to ten percent lower than at the Krabi banks. There is (slow and expensive) **internet access** at *Ya Ya* on east Railay, an **overseas phone** service at *SandSea* and *Railay Village*, a **clinic** in the *Railay Bay* compound, mid-way along the access track between east and west Railay, and a small **bookshop** stocked with new and secondhand books at *Railay Village*.

## Accommodation and eating

Aside from the opulent *Rayavadee Premier* resort, **accommodation** on the headland is of a fairly uniform standard which tends to be more expensive and less good value than equivalent options on the mainland. The places on east Railay are more budget-orientated than those on west Railay, but most bungalows offer a range of choices, priced to reflect flimsiness of hut or nature of view, though bear in mind that no room on the cape is more than 200m from the sea. To get a decent room at a decent price during high season, it's essential to arrive on the beaches as early in the morning as possible and, if necessary, to hang around waiting for people to check out. Prices listed below are for high season, but rates can drop up to fifty percent from May to October.

All the bungalow operations have **restaurants** where food is generally pricey and unremarkable. Evening entertainment consists either of watching the restaurant videos – most places have twice-nightly screenings – or patronizing one of the relaxed beachfront **bars**, like *Rapala* and *Last Bar*, both near *Diamond 2* bungalows on east Railay. Rock-climbers tend to gravitate towards the *Sunset Bar* on west Railay, where there's fire-juggling most nights.

### Ao Phra Nang

**Rayavadee Premier**, on Ao Phra Nang, right at the tip of the cape ☎075/620740, ℱ620630, ⒲www.rayavadee.com. Set in a beautifully landscaped compound bordering all three beaches, and the only place with direct access to Ao Phra Nang, this exclusive resort is an unobtrusively designed small village of supremely elegant two-storey pavilions costing a staggering B23,000 a night. The lack of beachfront accommodation is more than compensated for by a swimming pool with sea view. ⑨

### West Railay

**Railay Bay** ☎ & ℱ075/622330. A huge range of accommodation on land that runs down to both east and west Railay. The cheapest rooms are in small fan-cooled huts while the top-end bungalows are thoughtfully designed and have sea-view verandas and air-con. Some of the lower-priced huts are closer to east than west Railay. ④–⑧

**Railay Village** ☎075/622578, ℱ622579. Attractive fan and air-con bungalows occupying landscaped grounds in between the two beaches, with nowhere more than 300m from the west Railay shore. Efficiently run and nicely maintained; recommended. ⑤–⑧

**SandSea** ⓣ 075/622167, ⓕ 622168. Comfortable bungalows with fan and bathroom, plus deluxe air-con versions with big windows and nice furniture. All accommodation is set around a lovely tropical garden, and the place feels peaceful and secluded from the fray. Recommended. ⑥–⑧

### East Railay

**Coco Bungalow**, in the centre of the beach ⓣ 01/228 4258. The cheapest accommodation on the cape, comprising basic but pleasant enough en-suite bamboo huts in a small garden compound. Always fills up fast. ①

**Diamond Cave Bungalows**, at the far eastern end of the beach ⓣ 075/622589, ⓕ 622590. Huge range of rooms, mostly in detached bungalows, impressively located beside several karsts, including Diamond Cave itself. Rooms are plainly but comfortably furnished, some have air-con and TV, and the cheapest ones, which have shared bathrooms, are rented out to climbers at good monthly rates. ⑤–⑦

**Diamond 2**, at the far eastern end of the beach ⓣ 075/622591. Just a handful of ultra-basic, no-frills bamboo huts crammed into a small area at the far end of the beach. The cheaper rooms share facilities. ②

**Sunrise Bay Bungalows**, towards the western (Laem Phra Nang) end of the beach ⓣ 075/622591. Forty small concrete huts with private bathrooms; price depends on proximity to the beachfront. ④–⑤

**Viewpoint**, at the far eastern end of east Railay ⓣ 075/622587. Set up above the shore, which means that many of the bungalows enjoy good bay-views from the large picture windows; some rooms in a hotel block are also available. The terrace restaurant affords great vistas of the mangrove and karst-dotted seascape too, and is worth a visit from non-guests. ④–⑥

**Ya Ya Bungalows** in the centre of the beach ⓣ 075/622750. Dozens of huts and three-storey wooden towers jammed into a small area make this place seem a bit claustrophobic and leave the ground-floor rooms rather dark. All rooms have private facilities and some have air-con. ③–⑥

### Ao Nam Mao

**Dawn of Happiness**, Ao Nam Mao ⓣ 01/895 2101, ⓕ 075/612914. A peaceful, self-styled eco-resort comprising just a handful of characterful rustic bungalows with bamboo walls, mosquito nets and cold-water showers. They run lots of soft-adventure tours to local spots, including snorkelling and kayaking, and overnight trips to Bamboo Island and to Khao Sok. Open all year, with forty percent discounts in low season. ⑤–⑥

# Ao Nang

Now that Laem Phra Nang is full to bursting point, **AO NANG** (sometimes confusingly signed as Ao Phra Nang), a couple of bays further north up the coast, has blossomed into quite a lively resort. Though it lacks the cape's fine beaches, some people find it a friendlier and less claustrophobic place than Laem Phra Nang. A road runs right alongside a big chunk of Ao Nang's narrow shore, with the resort area stretching back over 1km along both arms of Highway 4203, but you only need to walk down the track that runs to the south of *Ao Nang Villa* to get to a much prettier and quieter part of the beach; better still, swim or wade around the small headland at the southernmost tip to find yourself on another long bay of fine gold sand. A half-hour walk in the other direction takes you to the unadulterated sands of Hat Nopparat Thara, or it's an impressive ten-minute boat ride from the Ao Nang shore to the beaches of Laem Phra Nang. In short, from wherever you stand, the expansive seaward view of crystal-clear water dotted with limestone monoliths remains pretty awesome.

## Diving, snorkelling and kayaking

About ten **dive shops** operate out of Ao Nang, with offices on the beach road and up Route 4203, including Ao Nang Divers at *Krabi Seaview*

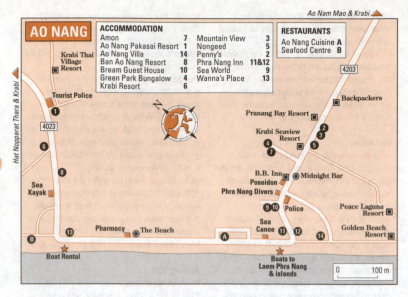

**ACCOMMODATION**
| | | | | |
|---|---|---|---|---|
| Amon | 7 | Mountain View | 3 | |
| Ao Nang Pakasai Resort | 1 | Nongeed | 5 | |
| Ao Nang Villa | 14 | Penny's | | |
| Ban Ao Nang Resort | 8 | Phra Nang Inn | 11&12 | |
| Bream Guest House | 10 | Sea World | 9 | |
| Green Park Bungalow | 4 | Wanna's Place | 13 | |
| Krabi Resort | 6 | | | |

**RESTAURANTS**
Ao Nang Cuisine **A**
Seafood Centre **B**

Krabi Thai Village Resort

Ao Nam Mao & Krabi

Tourist Police

Backpackers

Pranang Bay Resort

Krabi Seaview Resort

Sea Kayak

B.B. Inn
Poseidon
Phra Nang Divers
Midnight Bar

Police

Peace Laguna Resort

Pharmacy    The Beach

Sea Canoe

Golden Beach Resort

Boat Rental

Boats to Laem Phra Nang & islands

0          100 m

(☎075/637242, ⓦwww.krabi-seaview.com), Calypso (☎075/637056), Coral Diving at *Krabi Resort* (☎075/637465), Phra Nang Divers (☎ & Ⓕ075/637064, ⓦwww.pndivers.com), and Poseidon (☎075/637263). Most one-day **dive trips** head for the area round Ko Phi Phi (see p.372) and include dives at Shark Point and the "King Cruiser" wreck dive (see p.323 for descriptions) for B2000–2400 including two tanks, or B900 for snorkellers. Two dives in the Ao Nang area – at Ko Poda and Ko Yawasam – average B1800 (B500–700 for snorkellers) or B1400 if you opt to go in a longtail rather than a dive boat. PADI dive courses start at B1800 for the introductory day, or B9000 for the Openwater. The nearest **recompression chamber** is run by Hyperbaric Services Thailand and is located on Ao Patong in Phuket (see p.322); check to see that your dive operator is insured to use it.

It's quite common to arrange your own **snorkelling trips** with the longtail boatmen who congregate on the Ao Nang beachfront: a typical price would be B200 per person for a four- or five-hour snorkelling trip to Ko Poda and other nearby islets. Alternatively, all Ao Nang tour agents sell snorkelling and swimming day-trips such as those advertised as "four-island" tours. Most dive shops rent mask, snorkel and fins for about B150 the set.

Several tour agents in Ao Nang offer **kayaking** expeditions, including the longest-established and highly reputable SeaCanoe (☎075/637170, ⓦwww.seacanoe.com), which has an office on the beachfront road, and Seakayak Krabi (☎075/630270) which is based opposite the *Ban Ao Nang* hotel. For around B1700 they take you on self-paddle trips through the mangrove swamps and caves of Ao Luk or Ao Thalen, just south of Ao Phang Nga. See the box on p.361 for more on kayaking in the Krabi area. Some outlets also rent kayaks by the hour, at B100–150 per hour.

### Practicalities

Access to Ao Nang is easy, as **songthaews** run from Krabi regularly throughout the day, taking about 45 minutes (every 10min from 6am–6.30pm, every

30min from 6.30pm–10.30pm; B20), and there are frequent longtail **boats** shuttling back and forth to west Railay on Laem Phra Nang (10min; B40). From November to May, a daily boat connects Ao Nang with Ko Phi Phi Don (1hr). There are plenty of facilities on Ao Nang, including official **money exchange** counters, lots of **internet** centres, several minimarkets, a proliferation of beachwear stalls, numerous tour operators and dive shops (see p.365), and the inevitable tailors' shops. The local **tourist police** are based next to the *Pakasai Resort* (☏075/637208). Most guest houses rent out **motorbikes** for B120–200 per 24 hours, and tour operators rent out jeeps for B1200/day. There's a *muay Thai* **boxing** stadium 1km west out of Ao Nang, near the *Laughing Gecko* guest house on Hat Nopparat Thara (see p.369), which stages regular bouts in high season; check local flyers for details.

## Accommodation and eating

The tourist season at Ao Nang is short, so the high-season **hotel** prices listed below only apply from late November through February; if you're planning on coming here in January, the busiest month, you should definitely book your accommodation in advance. Outside high season, rates can drop by up to fifty percent, making early November and March the best-value time to stay here (being neither wet, nor crowded, nor expensive). Although **budget accommodation** may at first glance appear thin on the ground at Ao Nang, several budget and moderate places do exist, the best of them a few hundred metres north of the seafront, along Route 4203.

As for **eating**, *Ao Nang Cuisine*, on the beachfront road, has a good reputation for authentic, quality Thai seafood dishes, or try *Ao Nang Seafood*, in among the cluster of little bars and restaurants sometimes referred to as the Seafood Centre at the western end of the beachfront road, where you get very good fish dishes plus an uninterrupted view of the waves.

### Inexpensive and moderate

**Amon**, on Route 4203 ☏ 075/637695. The en-suite concrete row-houses here have neither views nor atmosphere but come at a good price. ❸

**Bream Guest House**, on Route 4203 ☏ 075/637555, ✉ bream-prapa@hotmail.com. Urban-style guest house offering some of the cheapest rooms in the resort, all with shared bathroom. ❸

**Green Park Bungalow**, on Route 4203 ☏ 075/637300. Friendly family-run place set in a shady grove of trees and offering bamboo huts with verandas and private bathrooms or more expensive concrete versions. Recommended budget option. ❷–❹

**Mountain View**, on Route 4203 ☏ 01/637294. Reasonably priced en-suite bungalows under a limestone cliff. ❹

**Nongeed**, on Route 4203 ☏ 075/637237. Range of rooms with the nicest and priciest on the upper floor, blessed with great karst views and air-con. The better downstairs rooms have TVs to compensate for the lack of outlook. Good value for Ao Nang. ❸–❺

**Penny's**, on Route 4203 ☏ 075/637295, ☏ 637468, ✉ johneyre@loxinfo.co.th. Friendly, family-run place offering very clean, comfortable rooms with or without bathroom and/or air-con. Located in a small block right under a limestone cliff, so there are magnificent views from the rooftop sun terrace. Discounts of up to fifty percent in low season. ❹–❼

**Sea World**, on Route 4203 ☏ 075/637388. Very good, well-priced rooms with bathroom, balcony and great views, with or without air-con; a few of the cheapest rooms share bathrooms. internet access downstairs. Very popular so try to reserve ahead. ❷–❺

**Wanna's Place and Ao Nang Beach Bungalow**, central beachfront road ☏ 075/637322, ☏ www.wannasplace.com. This two-in-one operation is the most affordable of the few beachfront places and offers nice enough, if rather plain, fan and air-con bungalows around a garden with a swimming pool. It's very popular so worth reserving ahead. ❺–❻

### Expensive

**Ao Nang Pakasai Resort**, on the road to Hat Nopparat Thara ☏ 075/637777, ☏ 637637,

@apakasai@loxinfo.co.th. Run by the same group as the *Krabi Meritime* in Krabi, this stylish resort is equally luxurious, with accommodation scattered up the hillside in landscaped grounds giving fine bay views. The rooms are beautifully furnished and there's a scenically located swimming pool, table tennis, games room and bicycle hire. Not suitable for guests with mobility difficulties. Rates from B5000. ❾

**Ao Nang Villa**, just off the beach ☏ & ℻075/637270. A relatively upmarket resort-style operation with attractive air-con bungalows and sea-view hotel rooms just off the beach. All rooms have air-con, TV and use of the pool. ❽

**Ban Ao Nang Resort**, opposite *Krabi Resort* on the road to Hat Nopparat Thara ☏075/637072,

℻637070, @baonan@loxinfo.co.th. A low-rise establishment just 2min walk from the sea; there's a pool here and the air-con rooms are comfortably furnished. ❽

**Krabi Resort**, just north of the main beachfront, on the road to Hat Nopparat Thara ☏075/637030, ℻637051. Set in a large tropical garden in a tiny bay; one of the poshest places on Ao Nang with both top-notch bungalows and rooms in a low-rise hotel. ❾

**Phra Nang Inn**, on the main beachfront ☏075/637130, ℻637134, @phranang@loxinfo.co.th. Elegant wooden hotel with spacious, well-equipped rooms and a small swimming pool. Big discounts May–Oct. ❽–❾

## Hat Nopparat Thara

Follow the road northwest past *Krabi Resort* for about 1km and you come to the **eastern** end of two-kilometre-long **Hat Nopparat Thara**. Invariably almost deserted, this beach is part of the national marine park that encompasses Ko Phi Phi, with the park headquarters about two-thirds of the way along and the **visitor centre** another kilometre further on, beyond the T-junction. At low tide it's almost impossible to swim here, but the sands are enlivened by millions of starfish and thousands of hermit crabs, and you can walk out to the small offshore island if you tire of the supine life. There's some development on the inland side of the beachfront road here, with signs of more to come, so the distance between eastern beach accommodation and the restaurants and shops of Ao Nang is set to decrease.

The **western** stretch of Hat Nopparat Thara feels like a different beach as it's separated from the visitor centre and eastern Hat Nopparat Thara by a khlong, and can only be reached by the longtails which depart from the national park pier, Tha Hat Nopparat Thara (the 4WD track to the beach is private). Sometimes known as Hat Ton Son, western Hat Nopparat Thara currently has just four bungalow operations sharing the long swathe of peaceful casuarina- and palm-shaded shoreline, and is a great place to escape the crowds and commerce of other Krabi beaches. The views of the karst islands are magnificent – and you can walk to some of the nearer ones at low tide, though swimming here is just as tide-dependent as on eastern Hat Nopparat Thara. All the bungalow outfits here can arrange snorkelling trips to nearby islands, and *Andaman Inn* offers quite a range of day-trips inland.

### Practicalities

All Krabi–Ao Nang **songthaews** go via the national park visitor centre (for the pier and boats to the western beach) and all travel the length of eastern Hat Nopparat Thara as well. The fare is B20 from Krabi (30min) or B10 from Ao Nang (10–15min). **Longtails** from Tha Hat Nopparat Thara leave for the western beach when full and will either drop you beside the closest set of bungalows, *Andaman Inn* (B10), from where you can walk to the accommodation of your choice, or at high tide they'll take you further up the beach if asked (B20–30).

As for **accommodation**, most of the western beach **bungalows** have electricity in the evenings only, and most close for the rainy season from May through October. You are quite free to camp anywhere on the beach, though on the eastern beach there's very little shelter, and the road is visible along most of it. All accommodation places on both beaches serve **food**, and there are a few hot-food and snack stalls near the national park bungalows.

## Eastern Hat Nopparat Thara

**Cashew Nut**, 200m down a track from the main beachfront road. Fairly comfortable, sturdy concrete bungalows with fan and bathroom. ➍

**Laughing Gecko**, 200m down a track from the main beachfront road. En-suite, simply equipped bamboo huts managed by a friendly family. ➋

**National Park Bungalows**, beside the visitor centre and pier at the western end of the eastern beach ☎075/637159. Just a handful of spartan bungalows sleeping two, or four-person tents for hire at B200. ➌

## Western Hat Nopparat Thara

**Amber Bungalows**, westernmost end of the beach, about 700m walk from the khlong ☎01/894 8761, amberandaman@hotmail.com. A very quiet spot, this welcoming Thai-French-run place has just nine spacious bamboo bungalows with mosquito nets and private bathrooms, each

enjoying a good sea view from the large verandas. In low season, call to check whether it's open. ➋–➌

**Andaman Inn**, 100m west of the khlong ☎01/956 1173. The most commercial and popular place on the western beach, with a huge range of huts, from very simple affairs with shared bathrooms to large en-suite versions. Does day-trips and snorkelling tours. ➊–➌

**Bamboo**, between *Emerald* and *Amber* ☎01/892 2532. The simplest and most *laissez faire* of the places on the beach, offering very basic bamboo huts, with or without private showers, and lamplight in the evenings. Closed April to mid–Nov. ➊–➋

**Emerald Bungalows**, next to *Andaman Inn* ☎01/956 2566, ✆075/631119. Offers the most comfortable accommodation on the beach, in big, brightly painted and nicely furnished wooden bungalows, all with sea views, private bathroom and fan. Runs boat trips to nearby islands at B1500 for up to eight people. Closed May–Aug. ➏

# Ko Phi Phi

Now well established as one of southern Thailand's most popular destinations, the two islands known as **KO PHI PHI** lie 40km south of Krabi and 48km east of southern Phuket, encircled by water so clear that you can see almost to the sea bed from the surface, easily making out the splayed leaves of cabbage coral and the distinctively yellow-striped tiger fish from the boat as you approach the islands. The action is concentrated on the larger **Ko Phi Phi Don**, packed with bungalow operations and tourist enterprises serving the burgeoning ranks of divers, snorkellers and sybarites who just come to slump on the long white beaches. No less stunning is the uninhabited sister island of **Ko Phi Phi Leh**, whose sheer cliff-faces get national marine park protection on account of the lucrative bird's nest business (see box on p.379).

Inevitably, both islands have started to suffer the negative consequences of their outstanding beauty. Some of the beaches are now littered with plastic bottles and cigarette ends, and Phi Phi Don seems to be permanently under construction, with building rubble disfiguring the interior and piles of stinking rubbish left rotting behind the ranks of bungalows. This problem has worsened since Phi Phi Leh gained worldwide attention when it was used as the film location for the movie *The Beach*, with businesses on Phi Phi Don capitalizing

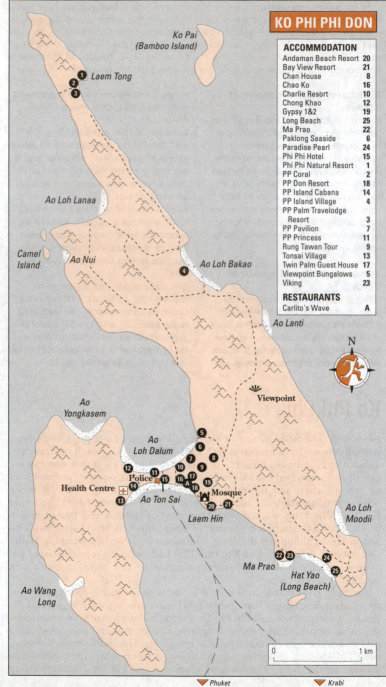

KO PHI PHI DON

**ACCOMMODATION**

| | |
|---|---|
| Andaman Beach Resort | 20 |
| Bay View Resort | 21 |
| Chan House | 8 |
| Chao Ko | 16 |
| Charlie Resort | 10 |
| Chong Khao | 12 |
| Gypsy 1&2 | 19 |
| Long Beach | 25 |
| Ma Prao | 22 |
| Paklong Seaside | 6 |
| Paradise Pearl | 24 |
| Phi Phi Hotel | 15 |
| Phi Phi Natural Resort | 1 |
| PP Coral | 2 |
| PP Don Resort | 18 |
| PP Island Cabana | 14 |
| PP Island Village | 4 |
| PP Palm Travelodge Resort | 3 |
| PP Pavilion | 7 |
| PP Princess | 11 |
| Rung Tawan Tour | 9 |
| Tonsai Village | 13 |
| Twin Palm Guest House | 17 |
| Viewpoint Bungalows | 5 |
| Viking | 23 |

**RESTAURANTS**

| | |
|---|---|
| Carlito's Wave | A |

Ko Pai
(Bamboo Island)

Laem Tong

Ao Loh Lanaa

Camel
Island

Ao Nui

Ao Loh Bakao

Ao Lanti

N

Viewpoint

Ao
Yongkasem

Ao
Loh Dalum

Police

Health Centre

Ao Ton Sai

Mosque

Laem Hin

Ao Loh
Moodii

Ma Prao

Hat Yao
(Long Beach)

Ao Wang
Long

0          1 km

Phuket          Krabi

mercilessly on the islands' increasing popularity, resulting in some of the worst-value accommodation in the whole of Thailand and a less than welcoming atmosphere. There are exceptions of course, but be warned that many tourists find Phi Phi a disappointment.

### Getting to the islands

During peak season, **ferries** to Ko Phi Phi Don run at least four times daily **from Krabi** and up to six times a day from **Phuket**; ticket prices depend on the speed and comfort of the boat, though be warned that the glassed-in air-con ferries can be far stuffier and more fume-ridden than the open-sided ones. Buying a return ticket offers no advantages and can sometimes be limiting, as some ferries won't take tickets issued by other companies. In the rainy season the service from both Krabi and Phuket is reduced to once or twice daily. From November to May, there are also daily boats to Phi Phi Don from **Ao Nang** and **Ko Lanta Yai**. The only way you can get to Phi Phi Leh is by long-tail from Phi Phi Don or as part of a tour.

Because of the accommodation situation, you might prefer to see Phi Phi on a **day-trip**: tour agents in Phuket, Ao Nang, Krabi town and Ko Lanta all organize snorkelling excursions to Phi Phi Don and Phi Phi Leh, with prices starting from around B1100 including lunch and snorkelling equipment, or B750 for under-12s. Alternatively, you could organize your own outing to Phi Phi Don on the scheduled ferries: the return boat to Ko Lanta leaves Phi Phi Don at 2pm, while the last boats to Krabi and Phuket leave at around 3.30pm.

**Onward transport** from Phi Phi can be arranged through any of the numerous tour agents in Ton Sai village – they can fix pretty much anything from domestic flights to boat, bus and train tickets.

## Ko Phi Phi Don

**KO PHI PHI DON** would itself be two islands were it not for the tenuous palm-fringed isthmus that connects the hilly expanses to east and west, separating the stunningly symmetrical double bays of Ao Ton Sai to the south and Ao Loh Dalum to the north. So steep is the smaller western half that the tiny population lives in isolated clusters across the slopes of the densely vegetated eastern stretch, while the tourist bungalows stick mainly to the intervening sandy flats, with a few developments on the beaches fringing the cliffs east and north of the isthmus.

All boats dock at **Ao Ton Sai**, the busiest bay on the island. From here you can catch a longtail to any of the other beaches or walk – there are a couple of short motorbike tracks but no roads on Phi Phi Don, just a series of paths across the steep and at times rugged interior, at points affording superb views over the bays. **Accommodation** on Phi Phi Don ranges from the exclusive to the ramshackle, but in the "budget" and mid-market categories you could end up paying as much as three times what you'd pay on the mainland. The prices listed below are for high season, which runs from October to April, but most bungalow operators slap on a thirty to fifty percent surcharge during the ridiculously hectic Christmas and New Year period; reservations are absolutely essential over this holiday fortnight, and are strongly recommended throughout high season. From May to September you should be able to negotiate up to fifty percent off the prices listed below. The commercial heart of the island is Ton Sai village, which has all sorts of tourist-oriented **facilities** including exchange counters, internet access, international telephone centres, postal services and lots of small shops.

## Diving, snorkelling, kayaking and rock climbing on Ko Phi Phi

More accessible than Ko Similan and Ko Surin, Ko Phi Phi and its neighbouring islands rate very high on the list of Andaman coast diving and snorkelling spots, offering depths of up to 35m, visibility touching 30m, and the possibility of seeing white-tip sharks, moray eels and stingrays. At uninhabited Ko Pai (or Bamboo Island), off the northeast coast of Phi Phi Don, much of the reef lies close to the surface, and gives you a chance of seeing the occasional turtle and possibly the odd silver- and black-striped banded sea snake – which is poisonous but rarely aggressive. At the adjacent Ko Yung (or Mosquito Island), the offshore reef plunges into a steep-sided and spectacular drop. Off the west coast of Phi Phi Don, Ao Yongkasame also has good reefs, as do the tranquil waters at Ao Maya on the west coast of Phi Phi Leh. For a description of the other local top sites, see p.323.

Dive centres on Phuket (see p.322), Ao Nang (p.365) and Laem Phra Nang (p.363) run daily excursions here, and there are also about twenty centres on Phi Phi itself. The biggest concentration is in Ton Sai village, where there are over a dozen competing outfits, so prices are cheap and some operators cut corners; because of this it's very important to check your operator's credentials and equipment and to try and talk to other divers about their experiences. Note that the cheaper dive trips are usually by longtail boat rather than the much more comfortable, better-equipped proper dive boats: ask to see a photo of your boat before booking. Many dive centres on Phi Phi sell American-made dive equipment, and they all rent equipment too. Recommended Ton Sai operators include the PADI Five-Star Instructor Development Centres Barrakuda (☎ & ⊕075/620698, ⊛www.barakuda.com), Moskito (☎01/229 1361, ⊕076/217106, ⊛www.moskitodiving.com) and Viking Divers (☎01/970 3644, ⊛www.vikingdiversthailand.com). There are also small dive centres on Hat Yao, Ao Loh Bakao and Laem Tong. Average prices for day-trips including two tanks and lunch are: B1800 for local reefs off Phi Phi Leh; B2600 for the King Cruiser wreck; or B3600 for Hin Daeng and Hin Muang (by speedboat). Excalibur Liveaboards (⊛www.thailand-liveaboard.com), which currently runs out of Moskito, organizes live-aboard trips direct from Phi Phi to the Similans (about US$650 for four days) and Burma (US$1100, six days). Dive courses on Phi Phi cost B2500 for an introductory one-day session, B10,000 for the certificated four-day Openwater course, and

## Ao Ton Sai

The constantly expanding village at **AO TON SAI** is now a full-blown low-rise holiday resort, and it's the liveliest – if not exactly the pleasantest – place to stay on the island. Backpacker-oriented shops, tour operators, restaurants and dive centres line the main track that parallels the beachfront and runs east as far as *Chao Ko* bungalows, while every available inch of land between the Ao Ton Sai shoreline and the resorts on Ao Loh Dalum is crammed with more makeshift stalls, tin-shack guest houses, beach bars, massage shops and cafés. If you can ignore the building debris at every turn, the constant hum of overworked generators and the pervasive whiff of sewage, it can be quite a fun place to hang out for a few hours; if not, head up the coast as fast as you can. All the main services are here, including two **exchange** counters run by national banks (daily 7am–10pm), a licensed post office, international telephone call centres and scores of little places offering **internet access**, where rates are higher than on the mainland but not outrageous. The island's **health centre** is at the western end of Ton Sai, in the compound of the *PP Island Cabana*, and there's a **police** box at the pier and another one next to the *Apache Bar* on the track to Laem Hin.

The **beach** itself is most attractive at the western end, under the limestone karsts, but even this stretch gets unbearably crowded in the middle of the day

B8000 for a two-day Advanced course. If you're short on time, email ahead to reserve a place on a dive course or live-aboard trip. The nearest **recompression chamber** is run by Hyperbaric Services Thailand and is located on Ao Patong in Phuket (see p.322); check to see that your dive operator is insured to use it.

Nearly all the tour operators and bungalow operations on Phi Phi Don organize day and half-day **snorkelling** trips. Prices range from B400–600 for a day-trip including lunch and snorkelling gear, with the price depending on the size of the boat and number of participants. In the case of snorkelling, the longtails that run from Ko Phi Phi are better than the larger fishing boats and the Phuket cruise ships, which are so popular you can rarely see the fish for the swimmers. Many dive operators will take accompanying snorkellers on their one-day dives for about B500.

The limestone cliffs and secluded bays of the Phi Phi islands make perfect **kayaking** territory, as the lagoons and palm-fringed coasts are much better appreciated in silence than over the roar of a longtail or cruise ship. If you rent a kayak for a whole day you can incorporate sunbathing and snorkelling breaks on small unpopulated bays nearby. Lots of tour operators in the village rent out kayaks at B150–300 per hour or B800–1000 per day, depending on size and quality, and there are also kayaks for rent on Hat Yao. Seafun Watersports at *PP Princess* on Ao Loh Dalum (℡01/897 2256, ℻075/612188, ℮sea_fun@hotmail.com) offers guided kayaking tours to Phi Phi Leh and Bamboo Island for B1000, including lunch, snorkelling gear and longtail transfer. They also teach **windsurfing** (B300 per hour or B700 half a day) and offer a variety of interesting **sailing trips** including a one-day tour of local islands (B1800), and trips around Ao Phang Nga ($75 per day) or to Langkawi in Malaysia ($75 per day), lasting several days; the overnight trips need to be booked in advance.

Phi Phi's topography is also a gift for **rock-climbers** and several places in the village offer climbing instruction and equipment rental, including Hang Out Rock Climbing (℮suthida@hotmail.com), located close to *Carlito's Wave* on the track to Laem Hin. They charge B1000 for up to three climbs, with full instruction and equipment. The main climbing area is a small beach just to the west of Ao Ton Sai, and includes the Ton Sai Tower and the Drinking Wall, with heights of 15m and 30m.

when it plays host to hundreds of day-trippers who snorkel just off-shore and then eat lunch on the beach. The central part of the bay is far too busy with ferries and longtails to even consider swimming in, but the eastern stretch, in front of *Chao Ko*, is a little quieter.

## Accommodation

Most of Ton Sai's **accommodation** is packed between the Ao Ton Sai and Ao Loh Dalum beaches, and at the foot of the hills to the east and west. The cheapest places are the ever-growing number of small guest houses stuffed cheek-by-jowl into extremely rickety shacks that look like a significant fire hazard and are very poor value for money.

**Chan House**, beside the path to the viewpoint on the northeast edge of the village. Welcoming staff but low-grade en-suite rooms in this small, simply designed block. ❹

**Chao Ko**, 10min walk east of the pier at the edge of the village ℡075/611313. Fills up fast because it's both close to the village action and more qui-

etly located on the less congested fringes. Standard concrete bungalows, all with private bathroom and some with air-con and partial sea view. ❹–❽

**Chong Khao Bungalows**, behind *Tonsai Village* and *PP Cabana*, at the western end of the village ℡01/894 8786. Set in a coconut grove, this place

feels peaceful, homely and spacious, and is just 200m from the beach at Ao Loh Dalum. There's a range of en-suite huts, from the ultra-basic to the fairly comfortable. ③ –⑤

**Phi Phi Hotel**, 50m north (inland) from the pier ☎ 075/620599 ℱ 611233. Low-rise hotel with smart rooms, each equipped with air-con, TV, phone and mini-bar; some have sea view. ⑧ –⑨

**PP Island Cabana**, just west (left) of the pier ☎ 075/620634, ℱ 612132, ⓦ www.phiphicabana -hotel.com. Cute mid-range bungalows set in a shorefront garden, plus more upmarket air-con rooms in the central hotel block. Swimming pool and restaurant on the premises. ⑦ –⑨

**Rung Tawan Tour**, in the heart of the inland village ☎ 01/895 2395. Friendly place with

very basic but bearable rooms in a rickety shack, all with bathrooms and most with a view of next door's wall. internet access down-stairs. ④

**Tonsai Village**, the far western end of the beach ☎ & ℱ 075/612434. Located under a cliff at the far end of the beach, these nicely appointed bun-galows are kitted out with air-con, TV and comfort-able furnishings, though they're a bit dark and close together. ⑧

**Twin Palm Guest House**, north of *Mama's* restaurant in the thick of the inland scrum ☎ 01/958 8753, ℯ twinpalm@phiphithailand.com. Scrapes by with a handful of dark Bangkok-style en-suite guest-house rooms, plus some slightly nicer bungalows. ④ –⑦

## Eating and drinking

Ton Sai is by far the best place to eat on the island – there are dozens of lit-tle **restaurants** in the village, ranging from bakeries to Muslim foodstalls, but the biggest crowd-puller is the seafood. At night almost every restaurant displays the day's catch, and huge barracuda, red snapper and sharks lie temptingly alongside crabs and lobsters. New restaurants spring up as old ones fold, but French-run *Mama's*, on the main track from the pier, is a long-standing favourite for seafood and good cakes; *Le Grand Bleu*, also on the main track, is another recommended French place, serving classy and expensive menus of the day. *Lemongrass*, next to the post office on one of the side tracks, serves only Thai food on its lengthy, mid-priced menu that includes mussels, red and green curries and some decent veggie options. Less expensive but just as tasty are the typically Thai curry-and-rice shops at the heart of the village, and there are always lots of hawkers flogging *rotis* and fried bananas from their hand-carts. The best places for breakfast are the two **bakeries** on opposite sides of the main track, where you're served real cof-fee to go with the huge selection of croissants, Danish pastries, home-made breads, cakes and cookies.

Small **bars** proliferate here too, adorned with hand-painted signboards and throbbing to the usual Bob Marley and Euro-pop standards. *Carlito's Wave*, next to *Chao Ko* on the eastern edge of the village, is a popular seafront joint with a big cocktails menu and laid-back atmosphere; further east along the track, *Apache Bar* is a huge multi-tiered bar and dance-floor which holds reg-ular parties (check locally posted flyers) and has a long happy hour. In the heart of the village, *Reggae Bar* stages nightly bouts of Thai boxing for its cus-tomers.

## Laem Hin

East along the coast from *Chao Ko*, about ten minutes' walk from the pier, is the promontory known as **Laem Hin**, beyond which is a small stretch of beach that's quieter than Ao Ton Sai and better for swimming. Bungalows cover the Laem Hin promontory and beach, and they're popular places to stay, being in easy reach of the restaurants and nightlife at Ao Ton Sai – a ten- to fifteen-minute walk that's feasible day or night – while feeling a little less claustro-phobic and hectic.

**Andaman Beach Resort**, east of *PP Don Chukit* ℡075/621427. Large choice of fairly comfortable bungalows set on a grassy area running down to the sea. The sea-view ones in the front row have air-con and are the most expensive, but they're right beside the main track and subject to the roar of passing longtails; the cheapest places are poorly designed rooms in row-houses at the back of the compound. ❺–❽

**Bay View Resort**, far eastern end of Laem Hin beach ℡ & ℗075/621223. Nicely furnished air-con bungalows occupying a superb position high on the cliffside, their massive windows affording unbeatable views. Good value considering the competition. ❽

**Gypsy 1**, inland, down the track between the mosque and *PP Don* ℡01/229 1674. Clean, pleasant, good-value concrete bungalows, all with attached bathroom; set round a lawn about 150m north of the water. Recommended. ❹

**Gypsy 2**, 100m north along the track from *Gypsy 1*. Unadorned grey concrete huts run by relatives of the people at *Gypsy 1*. ❹

**PP Don Chukit Resort**, just east of the promontory ℡01/894 2511. Uninspired collection of mid-range air-con bungalows, plus some overpriced fan rooms in single-storey blocks. ❺–❼

## Ao Loh Dalum

Though less attractive than Hat Yao, **AO LOH DALUM** is a much quieter place for swimming and sunbathing than Ao Ton Sai, yet the bungalows here are only five or ten minutes' walk from Ton Sai's restaurants and nightlife. The bungalows' seafront bars on Loh Dalum are also popular and genial places to hang out. The main drawback here is that the tide goes out for miles, leaving you with a long trek over sodden sand before you can get a decent dip. Loh Dalum's mid-range and upmarket **bungalows**, are some of the most attractive on the island; they have good facilities too, including watersports equipment for hire at *PP Pavilion* and *PP Princess*.

The **viewpoint** which overlooks the far eastern edge of the beach affords a magnificent wraparound panorama of both Ao Loh Dalum and Ao Ton Sai: photographers slog up the steep half-hour climb for sunset shots of the two bays, but early morning is an equally good time to go, as the café at the summit serves simple breakfasts as well as cold drinks. To get there, follow the track inland (south) from beside *Paklong Seaside* and then branch off to your left (eastwards) near the water treatment plant. From the viewpoint you can descend the rocky and at times almost sheer path to **Ao Lanti**, a tiny bay on the east coast with choppy surf and a couple of resident *chao ley*. Theoretically, it should also be possible to reach the northeastern bay of Ao Loh Bakao (see p.378) by a path from near the viewpoint, but the two-kilometre route is unsignposted and overgrown.

**Charlie Resort**, in the middle of the beach ℡ & ℗075/620615. Mid-range place with relatively good-value fan-cooled bungalows, each one with its own tiny garden area out front; price depends on proximity to the seafront. Lively bar and restaurant on the beach. ❹–❻

**Paklong Seaside**, easternmost end of the beach ℡01/958 6371. Comfortable guest house right on the shore, with a handful of decent fan-cooled rooms in a small wooden building; price depends on the size of the room. ❹–❼

**PP Pavilion**, eastern end of the beach ℡075/620677, ℗620633, ℮pavilion@phiphithailand.com. Attractive upmarket wooden chalets, nicely spaced over the beachfront grounds. Fan and air-con available. ❼–❽

**PP Princess**, at the westernmost end of the beach, 300m north of the Ton Sai pier ℡075/622079, ℗612188, ℗www.ppprincess.com. Offers the plushest and most tastefully designed accommodation on the island: comfortably furnished wooden chalets with big windows, verandas, air-con, TV and mini-bar. They have an eco-friendly waste-disposal system too. Price depends on proximity to shorefront. ❽–❾

**Viewpoint Bungalows**, up the cliffside at the far eastern end of the beach ℡ & ℗ 075/622351. Strung out across the hillside, these attractive but pricey bungalows boast great views out over the bay. The most expensive have air-con and TV. ❼–❽

## Hat Yao

With its deluxe sand and large reefs packed with polychromatic marine life just 20m offshore, **HAT YAO** (Long Beach) is the best of Phi Phi's main beaches. It's also the most crowded, with hundreds of sunbathers pitching up on the gorgeous sand every day and throngs of day-trippers making things even worse at lunchtime. Unperturbed by all the attention, shoals of golden butterfly fish, turquoise and purple parrot fish and hooped angel fish continue to scour Hat Yao's coral for food, escorted by brigades of small cleaner fish who live off the parasites trapped in the scales of larger species. For the best of the coral and the biggest reef in the vicinity, you should make for the submerged rock known as **Hin Pae** off the southern end of Hat Yao – novice divers get ferried out there by boat, but if you're a strong swimmer you can easily reach it from the beach. The Scuba Hut dive shop at *Long Beach* runs day-trips to local reefs and rents out diving and snorkelling equipment.

Longtail **boats** do the ten-minute shuttle between Hat Yao and Ao Ton Sai from about 8am to 8pm, but it's also possible to **walk** between the two in half an hour. At low tide you can get to Hat Yao along the shore, though this involves quite a bit of clambering over smooth wet rocks – not ideal when wearing a heavy rucksack, nor after a night spent trawling the bars of Ton Sai village (take a torch). The alternative route takes you over the hillside via the steps up from *Bay View Resort* on Laem Hin – with side tracks running off to the bays holding *Pirate*, *Ma Prao* and *Viking* – and then finally dropping down to Hat Yao. When returning, follow the path up into the trees from behind one of the last *Paradise Pearl* bungalows at the far western end of Hat Yao, and continue as far as you can along the track. You'll need to dip down to the shore briefly at *Ma Prao*, before finally coming down to sea level at *Bay View* on Laem Hin. Several other **paths** connect Hat Yao to the beaches of Ao Loh Dalum to the north and the tiny bay of Loh Moodii to the northeast: the trails start behind the last of the *Long Beach Bungalows*.

### Accommodation

The most attractive of Hat Yao's **accommodation** is tucked away in a little cove west of Hat Yao itself, with easy access via a rocky path. The small, secluded and friendly Belgian-run *Ma Prao* (T075/622486; ❶–❹) has a good selection of 32 simple wood and bamboo bungalows ranged across the hillside overlooking the sea, and a pleasant eating area out front. The cheapest huts share bathrooms, but some have a terrace; the more expensive options have private bathrooms, fans and decks. There's a small dive operation here, you can rent kayaks, and the kitchen produces a long and varied menu that includes eighty different cocktails and home-made yoghurt. Not surprisingly, it's a popular place, so call the day before to secure a room, or check in somewhere else and put yourself on the waiting list. Just around the rocks in the next tiny cove to the east sit the seven ultra-basic bamboo huts belonging to *Viking* (❷), Phi Phi's last remaining homage to the typical Asian beach experience: rudimentary facilities, laid-back staff and inexpensive rates.

Of the two bungalow operations on Hat Yao, most budget travellers head first for *Long Beach Bungalows* (T075/612410; ❸–❹), which covers the eastern half of the beach. Some of the cheapest huts here are on the verge of collapse – and the proximity of rubbish dumps makes them no more enticing – but the newer, more expensive huts are better value, and most of these have private bathrooms. The larger, better-maintained bungalows at *Paradise Pearl* (T & F075/622100; ❹–❻) are decently spaced along the western half of the beach; all have attached bathrooms and some are very comfortably furnished. Prices mainly reflect proximity to the sea, though none is more than 20m from the water; front-row residents get the worst of the noise from incoming longtails.

### Ao Loh Bakao and Laem Tong

Far removed from the hustle of Ao Ton Sai and its environs, a few exclusive resorts have effectively bought up the secluded northern beaches of Phi Phi Don. This is primarily package-holiday territory – you're unlikely to find a room free if you turn up unannounced – and it's difficult and expensive to get to the other parts of the island, so you should choose your hotel with care. There are no regular boats here from Ao Ton Sai, but longtail boats will take you for about B200; the trip takes around an hour to Ao Loh Bakao and a further half-hour north to Laem Tong. To charter a return boat at night, you're looking at B1000 for a round trip including waiting time.

Just over halfway up the coast, the eighty plush, fan-cooled and air-conditioned chalets on stilts at *Phi Phi Island Village* (T 076/215014, F 214918; 9) have the beach of **Ao Loh Bakao** all to themselves; the bungalows are designed in traditional Thai style and there's a pool in the gardens. At the northernmost tip, **Laem Tong** has three upmarket resorts on its shores and views across to nearby Bamboo Island and Mosquito Island. The beautifully designed *Phi Phi Palm Beach Travelodge Resort* (T 01/676 7316, F 076/215090, W www.phiphi-palmbeach.com; 9; room rates start at B6500) is a popular honeymoon spot, and a lovely location for anyone looking for a quiet, comfortable break: all bungalows are air-conditioned and there's a swimming pool, outdoor jacuzzi, dive centre and tennis courts here as well as batik and cookery courses and trips to local islands. The rustic wooden cabins at *PP Coral Resort* (T 076/211348, F 215455, W www.ppcoral.com; 8–9) are a little less deluxe – and a little more affordable – but the sense of seclusion is slightly marred by the daily arrival of lunching day-trippers. The furthest north is *Phi Phi Natural Resort* (T 075/613010, F 613000, W www.phiphinatural.com; 7–9), with stylish, reasonable-value chalets scattered around the tropical shorefront garden, plus a swimming pool and a terrace restaurant offering fine sea views; snorkelling, fishing and dive trips are all available here.

## Ko Phi Phi Leh

More rugged than its twin Ko Phi Phi Don, and a quarter the size, **KO PHI PHI LEH** is home only to the **sea swift**, whose valuable nests are gathered by intrepid *chao ley* for export to specialist Chinese restaurants all over the world. Tourists descend on the island not only to see the nest-collecting caves but also to snorkel off its sheltered bays and to admire the very spot where *The Beach* was filmed; the anchoring of tourist and fishing boats has damaged much of the coral in the most beautiful reefs. Most snorkelling trips out of Phi Phi Don include Phi Phi Leh, which is only twenty minutes south of Ao Ton Sai, but you can also get there by hiring a longtail from Ao Ton Sai or Hat Yao (B500–700 per six-person boat). If you do charter your own boat, go either very early or very late in the day, to beat the tour-group rush. Alternatively, why not try paddling yourself in and out of the quiet bays in a kayak – see box on p.382 for details.

Most idyllic of all the bays in the area is **Ao Maya** on the southwest coast, where the water is still and very clear and the coral extremely varied – a perfect snorkelling spot and a feature of most day-trips. Unfortunately the discarded lunch boxes and water bottles of day-trippers now threaten the health of the marine life in **Ao Phi Leh**, an almost completely enclosed east-coast

## Bird's nesting

Prized for its aphrodisiac and energizing qualities, **bird's-nest soup** is such a delicacy in Taiwan, Singapore and Hong Kong that ludicrous sums of money change hands for a dish whose basic ingredients are tiny twigs glued together with bird's spit. Collecting these nests is a lucrative but life-endangering business: sea swifts (known as edible nest swiftlets) build their nests in rock crevices hundreds of metres above sea level, often on sheer cliff-faces or in cavernous hollowed-out karst. **Nest-building** begins in January and the harvesting season usually lasts from February to May, during which time the female swiftlet builds three nests on the same spot, none of them more than 12cm across, by secreting an unbroken thread of saliva which she winds round as if making a coil pot. **Gatherers** will only steal the first two nests made by each bird, prising them off the cave walls with special metal forks. Gathering the nests demands faultless agility and balance, skills that seem to come naturally to the *chao ley*, whose six-man teams bring about four hundred nests down the perilous bamboo scaffolds each day, weighing about 4kg in total. At a market rate of B20,000–50,000 per kilo, so much money is at stake that a government franchise must be granted before any collecting commences, and armed guards often protect the sites at night. The *chao ley* themselves seek spiritual protection from the dangers of the job by making offerings to the spirits of the cliff or cave at the beginning of the season; in the Viking Cave, they place buffalo flesh, horns and tail at the foot of one of the stalagmites.

lagoon of breathtakingly turquoise water. Not far from the cove, the **Viking Cave** gets its misleading name from the scratchy wall-paintings of Chinese junks inside, but more interesting than these 400-year-old graffiti is the **bird's-nesting** that goes on here: rickety bamboo scaffolding extends hundreds of metres up to the roof of the cave, where the harvesters spend the day scraping the tiny sea-swift nests off the rockface.

# Ko Lanta Yai

Although **KO LANTA YAI** can't compete with Phi Phi's stupendous scenery, the 25-kilometre-long island does offer plenty of fine sandy beaches and safe seas and is actually a much friendlier place to stay, not least because – despite a booming tourist industry – it still feels like it belongs to its twenty thousand residents (something which can't be said of Ko Phi Phi, Phuket or Ko Samui), the majority of whom are mixed-blood Muslim descendants of Malaysian and *chao ley* peoples. Aside from fishing, many of the islanders support themselves by cultivating the land between the beaches and the forested ridges that dominate the central and eastern parts of Lanta Yai; the others work mainly in the tourist industry, most of which is still run by local families. Traditional *chao ley* rituals are celebrated on Ko Lanta twice a year, when ceremonial boats are set afloat on the full moon nights in June and November (see p.308 for more on the *chao ley*).

The local *chao ley* name for the island is *Pulao Satak*, "Island of Long Beaches", an apt description of the string of silken **beaches** along the western coast, each separated by rocky points and strung out at quite wide intervals. The northernmost one, Hat Khlong Dao, is developed almost to full capacity,

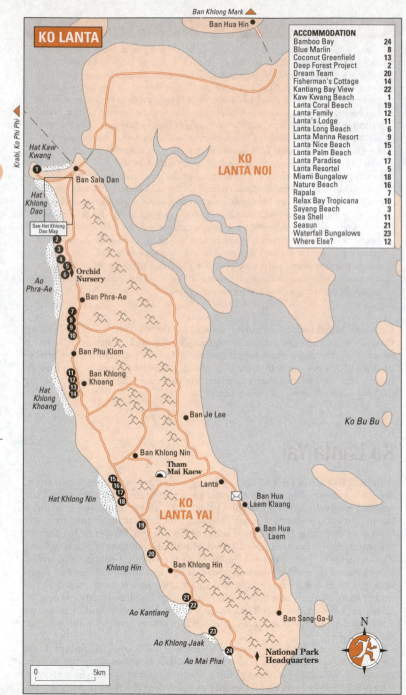

**KO LANTA**

Ban Khlong Mark ▲
Ban Hua Hin ●

Krabi, Ko Phi Phi ▲

Hat Kaw Kwang

KO LANTA NOI

① Ban Sala Dan

Hat Khlong Dao

See Hat Khlong Dao Map

② ③ ④ ⑤ ⑥ Orchid Nursery

Ao Phra-Ae

Ban Phra-Ae ●

⑦ ⑧ ⑨ ⑩

Ban Phu Klom ●

⑪ ⑫ Ban Khlong Khoang
⑬ ⑭

Hat Khlong Khoang

Ban Je Lee ●

Ko Bu Bu

Ban Khlong Nin ●

Tham Mai Kaew ●

⑮ ⑯ ⑰ ⑱ Lanta ●
Hat Khlong Nin
Ban Hua Laem Klaang ●

⑲
Ban Hua Laem ●

KO LANTA YAI

⑳ Ban Khlong Hin ●
Khlong Hin

㉑ ㉒
Ao Kantiang
Ban Sang-Ga-U ●

㉓
Ao Khlong Jaak

㉔
Ao Mai Phai
National Park Headquarters ▲

N

0        5km

**ACCOMMODATION**

| | |
|---|---|
| Bamboo Bay | 24 |
| Blue Marlin | 8 |
| Coconut Greenfield | 13 |
| Deep Forest Project | 2 |
| Dream Team | 20 |
| Fisherman's Cottage | 14 |
| Kantiang Bay View | 22 |
| Kaw Kwang Beach | 1 |
| Lanta Coral Beach | 19 |
| Lanta Family | 12 |
| Lanta's Lodge | 11 |
| Lanta Long Beach | 6 |
| Lanta Marina Resort | 9 |
| Lanta Nice Beach | 15 |
| Lanta Palm Beach | 4 |
| Lanta Paradise | 17 |
| Lanta Resortel | 5 |
| Miami Bungalow | 18 |
| Nature Beach | 16 |
| Rapala | 7 |
| Relax Bay Tropicana | 10 |
| Sayang Beach | 3 |
| Sea Shell | 11 |
| Seasun | 21 |
| Waterfall Bungalows | 23 |
| Where Else? | 12 |

but deserted spots are not hard to find further south and they nearly all offer luxuriously soft sand and clear water. All the bungalow outfits advertise snorkelling trips to the reefs off Ko Lanta's myriad satellite islands, and diving is also a popular and rewarding activity; Ko Lanta's mangrove-fringed east coast is unsuitable for swimming but ideal for kayaking.

Ko Lanta is extremely popular during **high season** (Nov–Feb), when it's well worth either booking your first night's accommodation in advance or taking up the suggestions of the bungalow touts who ride the boats from the mainland. **Accommodation pricing** on Ko Lanta is extremely flexible and alters according to the number of tourists on the island: it's not uncommon, for example, for bungalow rates to triple in the thirty-day period from mid-November to mid-December, while between May and October rates are vastly discounted. The price range shown in our Ko Lanta accommodation listings are for the beginning and end of high season (generally Nov & March–April). All bungalows increase their rates for the peak months of December and January; most places double their prices for this period, the exceptions being many of the cheapest (**❶**–**❸**) places which can triple or even quadruple their prices, and the most expensive places (**❼** and **❽**) which usually "only" add around twenty percent. The island is much quieter during the **rainy season** (May–Oct), when the seas become too rough for boats to travel here from Krabi and the shores suffer from a fair bit of water-borne debris. A number of the more remote bungalow operations close down during this period, but most of the bungalows on the main beaches stay open, and many are willing to discount their rates too.

### Getting to the island
From November to May two daily **ferries** run from Krabi to Ban Sala Dan on the northern tip of Ko Lanta Yai, and there's at least one ferry a day between Ko Phi Phi and Ban Sala Dan. Bungalow touts always meet the boats at Ban Sala Dan and transport you to the beach of your choice. During the rest of the year (the rainy season), you'll need to arrange **minivan** transport from Krabi with one of the tour agencies, which costs the same and takes about the same time if not a bit longer. The minivans take the **overland route**, going via Ban Hua Hin on the mainland, from where they drive onto a small ferry, get taken across to Ban Khlong Mark on Ko Lanta Noi, drive across to Lanta Noi's northwest tip, take another ferry over the channel to Ko Lanta Yai (every 20 min from 7am–9pm; 20min; B50 per car) and then drive down to whichever beach you've decided to stay on. This is also the route used year-round by transport operators from Trang and by anyone bringing their own vehicle on to the island: if you do come with your own wheels, be warned that Lanta's roads are far from perfect and in the south degenerate into extremely rough tracks.

When it comes to **moving on** from Ko Lanta, every tour operator in Ban Sala Dan and almost every bungalow outfit on the island can sell you onward transport to Krabi (three boats daily from November to May, two at 8am and the last at 1pm; B200) and Ko Phi Phi (daily from November to May at 8am; B200), as well as minibus tickets to Trang, onward bus from Trang or Krabi to Surat Thani or Hat Yai, and flights from Krabi or Trang airports.

### Island practicalities
Though a road runs the entire length of Ko Lanta Yai's west coast, becoming quite rough just after Hat Khlong Nin and finally grinding to a bumpy halt at

## Diving, snorkelling, kayaking and day-trips on Ko Lanta

Ko Lanta is a significant diving centre, with local reefs a lot quieter and more pristine than the ones round Phi Phi and Phuket, and an excellent place for seeing whale sharks. The diving season runs from November to April or mid-May, with all the dive centres running expeditions and diving courses during this period; outside these months the seas are too rough to travel on.

Some of Lanta's best **dive sites** are located between Ko Lanta and Ko Phi Phi, including the soft coral at **Hin Bidah**, where you get lots of leopard sharks, barracuda and tuna. West and south of Lanta, the **Ko Ha** island group offers four different dives on each of its five islands, including steep drop-offs and caves. Much further south, about four hours' boat ride, there's a fifty-metre wall at spectacular **Hin Daeng** and **Hin Muang**, plus a good chance of seeing tuna, jacks, silvertip sharks, manta rays and even whale sharks. See the descriptions of Andaman coast dive sites on p.323 for more on some of these reefs. A typical **day-trip** to some of these reefs costs B2200–3000 including equipment rental and two tanks (B600–800 for snorkellers), but all dive centres offer discounts if you do three consecutive one-day dives. For an overnight expedition to local islands with accommodation either on the boat or on one of the islands, and four tanks, you pay about B6000. Diving **courses** average out at B11,000 for the four-day Openwater course, or B7500–8000 for the two-day Advanced course.

Nearly all Ko Lanta **dive centres** have their headquarters in the village of Ban Sala Dan, and many also have branch offices on the beaches. Some of the best include the reputable and long-established Ko Lanta Diving Centre/Ko Lanta Tauchschule, on Ban Sala Dan's seafront road (T & F075/612969, Wwww.kohlantadivingcenter.com), run by prolific dive author and photographer Christian Mietz; British-run The Dive Zone (T075/684056, Wwww.thedivezone.com), which also has a branch at *Golden Bay* on Hat Khlong Dao; and the German-run Atlantis (T075/68 40 81, F612914, Wwww.top-com.com/atlantis), which also has a branch on Hat Khlong Dao. The nearest **recompression chamber** is located on Ao Patong in Phuket (see p.322); check to see that your dive operator is insured to use it.

### Snorkelling

All tour operators and bungalow outfits also sell tickets for the large-scale outings in big boats that can hold around a hundred passengers: these go to three or four

the far southern tip, **transport** between the beaches is quite difficult as there's no regular songthaew service on the island. Once you're established on your beach you have either to hire a motorbike from your accommodation (about B40 per hour, B250 per day; B500 per day for a big trail bike), or cadge a lift with the bungalow operators when they go and meet the boats at Ban Sala Dan. Tour operators in Ban Sala Dan also rent jeeps (B1200 per day) as well as bikes. You can usually arrange a **motorbike taxi** in Ban Sala Dan to take you back to your bungalow (B20–30 from the village to Hat Khlong Dao, B30–40 to Ao Phra-ae), or you might be able to hitch a ride, though if you're staying on Hat Khlong Dao it's an easy half-hour walk to the village.

Most bungalows will **change money**, though you'll get the best rates at the bank in Ban Sala Dan. **Telephone** lines were laid on the island in 2001, so many businesses now have T075 numbers, though some are still using satellite phones with T01 codes; many bungalows offer international telephone services for guests. **internet** centres are popping up all over the place; there's a reliable one on the southern edge of Ban Sala Dan.

islands off the Trang coast (see pp.403–407 for island descriptions), usually including the enclosed emerald lagoon on the island of **Ko Mook** (aka Ko Muk), nearby **Ko Hai** (aka Ko Ngai) and **Ko Kradan**; they cost B650 per person including snorkelling gear and lunch. The twin islands of **Ko Rok Nok** and **Ko Rok Nai**, which are further south still at 47km from Ko Lanta, are another top destination but can only be reached by small speedboat, which takes just an hour to get there and costs B1200. Some bungalow operators offer private longtail-boat tours to the reefs off the **Ko Ha** island group (about two hours' boat ride from Lanta), with snorkelling or fishing as requested: Ko Lanta Tour at *Lanta Villa* on Hat Khlong Dao charges B3000 for a four-person boat including fishing and/or snorkelling gear.

### Kayaking
The north coast of Ko Lanta Noi, around Ban Rapu, is rich in mangroves and caves which makes it fun to explore by **kayak**. Kayaking outings can be arranged from Ban Sala Dan tour operators for B1300 per person including transport, lunch and kayak.

### Day-trips
Ko Lanta's biggest inland attraction is the **Tham Mai Kaew caves**, located in the heart of the island, and signposted from the west-coast road at Hat Khlong Nin. There are myriad chambers here, some of which you can only just crawl into, and they boast stalactites and interesting rock formations as well as a creepy cave pool and the inevitable bats. To properly explore the cave system you need to bring your own torch, and you need a guide: the Muslim family that live close to the caves act as caretakers and guides and give two-hour tours for B50 per person. The **waterfall** inland from Ao Khlong Jaak is another fairly popular spot, and can be reached from the bay by walking along the course of the stream for about two hours; alternatively join one of the numerous tours that combine visits to the caves and the waterfall in a half-day-trip for about B300, or B600 with a ninety-minute **elephant ride** thrown in. South Nature Travel tour operator in Ban Sala Dan also offers full-day tours of Ko Lanta for around B1300 (kids B950), which includes kayaking and snorkelling as well as a visit to a rubber plantation and to the **Lanta Orchid Nursery**. Located inland from Ao Phra-ae, near *Lanta Resortel*, the nursery includes an exhibition on orchid-farming (open Nov to mid-April daily; B30, children B20).

# Ban Sala Dan

During high season, direct boats from Krabi and Phi Phi arrive at Lanta's main settlement, the Muslim fishing port and village of **BAN SALA DAN**, located on the northernmost tip of Ko Lanta Yai. It's essentially a T-junction village, with about three dozen shops and businesses within easy walking distance of each other. Though many of these cater for tourists, the village has a low-key atmosphere, and fishing is still a significant income-earner. Several minimarkets sell essentials like mosquito repellent and sunscreen, as well as new and secondhand books, beachwear and postcards. There's a Siam City bank with currency **exchange** and a Visa cash advance service (Mon–Fri 8.30am–3.30pm), several places offering **internet** access, a **police** booth and a **health centre**, though for anything serious you'll need to go to Krabi or Phuket. Ban Sala Dan is the best place on the island to arrange a **diving** course or expedition and also has half-a-dozen tour operators offering all manner of **day-trips** (see box above for a guide to diving and day-tripping destinations), as well as bike and jeep rental and boat, bus, train and air tickets.

While you're in the village, it's well worth stopping for a breezy meal at one of the **restaurants** whose dining area juts out on a shaded jetty right over the water, giving enjoyable views of the fishing boats and Ko Lanta Noi. Both *Seaside* and the nearby *Sea View* have good, very inexpensive menus offering authentic Thai dishes from chicken and cashews to fish fried with chilli or garlic.

## Hat Khlong Dao

Lanta Yai's longest and most popular beach is **HAT KHLONG DAO**, the northernmost of the west-coast beaches, about half an hour's walk from Ban Sala Dan, or 2–3km by road. The sand here is soft and golden, palms and casuarinas shade parts of the shore, the sunsets can be magnificent, and the whole is framed by a dramatic hilly backdrop. Not surprisingly, this is where you'll find the densest collection of bungalows on the island, but though most of the shorefront land has been developed, none encroaches on the sand itself and development is relatively discreet. The northern curve of Hat Khlong Dao juts out into a rocky promontory known as **Laem Kaw Kwang** (Deer Neck Cape), whose north-facing shore, **Hat Kaw Kwang**, is mainly characterized by mud flats and mangroves and is home to a *chao ley* settlement.

There's a tiny minimart next to *Lom Thaleh* at the southern end of Hat Khlong Dao, and dive shops at several of the bungalows; for anything else you'll need to go to Ban Sala Dan. The nicest way to walk to the village (about 30min from *Golden Bay*) is to head to the deer neck at the northern curve of the beach, and then take a right along the mostly shaded track which leads from *Kaw Kwang Bungalows* to the road into Ban Sala Dan.

All the bungalows have **restaurants** serving travellers' fare and standard Thai dishes, and at night they're lit up with fairy lights and low lanterns, which lends a nice mellow atmosphere to the evenings and makes a welcome change from the neon frenzy at other resorts. Most restaurants also offer fresh seafood at night, where you choose your specimen and the cooking method and are

**HAT KHLONG DAO**

Ban Sala Dan

N

0    200 m

**RESTAURANTS**

Danny's A
Flower Power Bar C
Otto B

**ACCOMMODATION**

Andaman Lanta Resort 17
Diamond Sand Palace 7
Golden Bay Cottages 6
Hans 5
Kaw Kwang Bungalows 1
Khlong Dao
  Beach Bungalows 12
Laguna Beach Club 3
Lanta Bee Garden 16
Lanta Garden Home 14
Lanta Island Resort 10
Lanta Noble House 2
Lanta Sand 15
Lanta Sea House 11
Lanta Villa 9
Lom Taleh 13
Southern Lanta Resort 8
Sun, Fun & Sea 4

BAN
KHLONG DAO

Ao Phra-ae

charged by its weight: the seafood barbecues at *Lanta Villa* are popular and enjoyable. *Hans*, towards the northern end of the beach, is highly recommended for its German-style fillet steaks, as well as its creamy coconut curries and barbecued meats. At the far southern end of the beach, past *Lanta Garden Home*, *Danny's* specializes in extravagant seafood barbecues, but also offers a good selection of fiery Thai soups, curries, and Mexican enchiladas. Further south still, at the end of the beach, *Otto* is another enjoyable place to sample similar fare before idling away the rest of the evening at the mellow *Flower Power Bar* next door.

## Accommodation

There's a pretty good choice of **accommodation** on Khlong Dao: none of the bungalows in the places listed below is more than 100m from the sea, and they all have private bathrooms.

**Andaman Lanta Resort** ⊤075/684200, Ⓕ684203, ⓦwww.lanta.de/andamanlanta. The poshest place on the beach, with poolside bungalows as well as rooms in a hotel block with big balconies, air-con and TV; there's a kids' playground and a table tennis room too. It's worth paying the extra for a sea view. ❼–❽

**Diamond Sand Palace** ⊤075/621135. Sizeable and well-furnished bungalows with fan or air-con set in facing rows. None has a sea view, but all are just a few metres from the shore. ❹–❺

**Golden Bay Cottages** ⊤01/229 1879, ⓦwww.ko-lanta.com/hotels/goldenbay.htm. Occupies a good spot in the northern part of the bay, and offers comfortable, nicely spaced and relatively good-value accommodation, from basic bamboo huts at the back of the compound to cheerful, nicely furnished concrete bungalows, most with partial sea view. ❶–❷

**Hans** ⊤01/606 2258. Range of huts in an attractive garden, from simple bamboo ones with mosquito nets through to better-furnished wooden versions with screened windows. ❷–❹

**Kaw Kwang Beach Bungalow**, northernmost end of Khlong Dao on the deer neck itself ⊤01/228 4106, Ⓕ075/621373. Set in a beachfront garden in a nice secluded position about 10min walk away from the other bungalows on this beach, this place offers simple bamboo huts with mosquito nets; bigger, more comfortable bungalows; and some deluxe air-con ones with uninterrupted sea views and TVs. ❶–❻

**Khlong Dao Beach Bungalows** ⊤01/228 3740. Clean, smart bungalows at relatively reasonable rates. ❹

**Laguna Beach Club** ⊤075/611572, Ⓔlagunabeachclub@hotmail.com. Has some simple bamboo-walled huts plus some stone and wooden ones, all fairly comfortable. There's a dive centre here too. ❸–❹

**Lanta Bee Garden** ⊤01/606 6344. Just ten nice clean bungalows, all with fan and a decent bathroom and some with sea view. ❸–❹

**Lanta Garden Home**. Friendly, family-run place offering a range of large, basic but well maintained old-style bamboo huts, nearly all with sea view. ❷–❸

**Lanta Island Resort**, central stretch of the beach ⊤075/621524, Ⓕ622485, Ⓔsiambeka@mail.cscoms.com. Large, efficiently run operation, popular with package tours; offers day-trips, phone service and either fan or air-con rooms. Though the bungalows are spacious and attractively furnished, there are rows and rows of them packed into too small a space, which makes it feel rather claustrophobic. ❷–❻

**Lanta Noble House** ⊤075/684096, Ⓔlantanoblehouse@hotmail.com. Swiss-run place where the welcoming bungalows have big glass windows and bath tubs. ❹

**Lanta Sand** ⊤01/476 6446. A dozen simple but cosy little bamboo huts, all with good beds and sea views. Recommended. ❷

**Lanta Sea House**, southern end of the beach ⊤075/684073, Ⓕ684113, Ⓔlantaseahouse@hotmail.com. Selection of comfortable wooden chalet-style bungalows prettily set round a seafront garden; most have a sea view and the priciest ones have air-con too. ❷–❻

**Lanta Villa**, middle of the beach ⊤ & Ⓕ075/620629, ⓦwww.ko-lanta.com/hotels/lantavilla.htm. Big collection of comfortably furnished, decent-sized wooden bungalows, set in a garden running back from the shore, many with air-con and TV, and some with sea view. Also has internet access and a good restaurant. ❹–❺

**Lom Taleh**, southern end of the beach ☎ 01/228 3720. Handful of comfortably furnished bungalows widely spaced in a seafront garden. ❹

**Southern Lanta Resort** ☎ & ℻ 075/684174, ℮ southlt@cscoms.com. One of the poshest places on the beach, offering nice air-con bungalows set around a swimming pool, some of them with sea views. Popular with families. ❼

**Sun Fun & Sea** ☎ 01/787 1208, ⓦ www.thailandbungalow.ch. Eleven prettily furnished bungalows scattered around a garden, all with fan and hot water. ❺

# Ao Phra-ae (Long Beach)

A couple of kilometres south of Khlong Dao, **AO PHRA-AE** (also known as **Long Beach**) boasts a beautiful long strip of peaceful white sand, with calm, crystal-clear water and an exceptionally peaceful ambience. Many of the bungalows here are very pleasant places to stay, set discreetly among the palm trees and for the most part some way away from their next-door neighbour, making Ao Phra-ae perhaps the best beach on the island for anyone seeking a quiet few days and good swimming. The main stretch of the beach is divided by a shallow, easily wadeable khlong, with bungalows to north and south of it. South of the main beach, there are a couple of other places to stay, set in their own little bays between rocky points. All bungalows on Ao Phra-ae rent out **motorbikes** for around B250 a day and organize boat trips for snorkelling and fishing.

## Accommodation and eating

Unless otherwise stated, all the **bungalows** listed below should be open year-round. The *Sanctuary* **restaurant** next to *Rapala* serves recommended Indian dal and seafood noodles, and the kitchen at *Sayang Beach Resort* has a tandoori oven, so they serve Indian as well as Thai food. There are also a few restaurants on the stretch of round-island road that runs through the inland village of Ban Phra-ae, including the popular *Earth*, which plays dance music and has a bar.

**Blue Marlin** ☎ 01/600 5702. Located in a palm grove at the far southern end of the main beach, the twenty huts here are simple and fairly inexpensive, with bamboo walls, concrete floors and mosquito nets; price depends on size and view. ❶–❷

**Deep Forest Project** ☎ 01/464 4643. Basic, inexpensive huts at the northernmost end of the beach, all equipped with mosquito net, fan and en-suite bathroom. ❶–❷

**Lanta Marina Resort** ℮ lantamarina@hotmail.com. Around the southern headland from the main stretch of Ao Phra-ae, close to a rocky point, this place is very well run and deservedly popular. The seventy traditional-style bungalows all face the sea and are thoughtfully designed. Some are two-storeyed A-frames with beds on the upstairs platform and coral-floored bathrooms down below; others are a more standard design. A friendly, low-key place. Recommended. ❶–❺

**Lanta Palm Beach** ☎ 01/606 5433. A lovely place to stay, with its good-value bamboo huts spread out in a coconut grove north of the khlong, most with full view of the sea, and equipped with mattresses, attached bathrooms and mosquito nets. The pricier ones have huge verandas and garden bathrooms, or you can pitch a tent here for B50. Deservedly popular. Recommended. ❶–❷

**Lanta Resortel** ☎ 01/476 3349. Just south of the khlong, this is the most commercial and upmarket place on the beach, with fifty comfortably furnished but fairly characterless air-con bungalows ranged in rows. ❼–❾

**Rapala** ☎ 01/228 4562, ℮ rapala-longbeach @hotmail.com. Located towards the southern end of the main beach, the idiosyncratically designed hexagonal huts here are nicely set round the seafront garden and comfortably furnished with decent beds and attached bathrooms. Price depends on the location of the bungalow. Usually closed in the rainy season. ❸–❹

**Relax Bay Tropicana** ☎01/228 4213, ⓦwww.ko-lanta.com/hotels/relaxbay.htm. Set in its own tiny bay south around the next rocky point from *Lanta Marina*, this place has some fairly standard concrete bungalows as well as a few tastefully simple bamboo and rattan bungalows, most with big verandas and open-air bathrooms. ⑤

**Sayang Beach Resort** ☎075/612138, ⓦwww.lanta.de/sayang. Small and friendly place occupying expansive grounds with huts nicely spaced among the palm trees. All bungalows are built with natural materials and have decent bathrooms; price depends on location and size. ⑤–⑦

# Hat Khlong Khoang

The lovely long beach at **HAT KHLONG KHOANG**, 2km south of *Relax Bay Tropicana*, is peppered with rocks and only really swimmable at high tide. That said, it's quite rewarding for snorkelling and has some very laid-back bungalow operations, mostly set in shorefront coconut groves and fostering an appealingly low-key atmosphere.

## Accommodation

**Coconut Greenfield** ☎01/228/4602, ⓦwww.kolanta.net/coconutgreenfield. Memorably friendly place with good facilities, a laid-back atmosphere, twenty comfortable bungalow, and tents for rent at B80 a double. Also has a pool table, mini-golf, a small minimarket and a regular programme of traditional festivities, plus the beachfront *Robin Hood Bar.* Recommended. ②–⑤

**Fisherman's Cottage** ☎01/476 1529, ⓔfishermanscottage@hotmail.com. This quiet, low-key place at the southern end of the beach has just half-a-dozen bungalows, each with big glass windows, mosquito nets and decent bathrooms. ②

**Lanta Family** Ten large and well-kept bungalows ranged under the palm trees; mosquito nets supplied on request. ②–③

**Lanta's Lodge** ☎01/228 4378. Thirty sizeable, if a little spartan, wooden bungalows, some with aircon; the price depends on their proximity to the shorefront. Closed May–Oct. ②–④

**Sea Shell** Just three bungalows run by a Dutch-Thai couple; nicely furnished and with good bathrooms. ②–③

**Where Else?** As you might expect from the name, this has a relaxed, laid-back atmosphere and consists of just fifteen bamboo and coconut-wood bungalows, with attached coral-floored bathrooms. ②

# Hat Khlong Nin to Khlong Hin

A further 5km on, the long, sandy stretch of **Hat Khlong Nin** is very good for swimming, though three of the four bungalow operations here are clustered together in a rather claustrophobic knot at the centre of the shore. You can walk the 3km to the Tham Mai Kaew caves from Khlong Nin in about an hour. *Miami Bungalow* rents **motorbikes** for B250 per day and has an international phone service.

All the **bungalows** on Hat Khlong Nin are open all year. Built on its own at the far northern end of the beach, *Lanta Nice Beach Resort* (☎075/629062; ①–③) does its name justice, being located on a broad swathe of sandy beach and offering twenty spacious concrete bungalows, many with sea views. The twenty sky-blue concrete bungalows at *Nature Beach Bungalow* (☎01/397 4184; ③–④) lack character inside, but are run by a friendly local family. Next door, at the long-running *Lanta Paradise* (☎01/607 5114; ①–③), you can choose between old bamboo huts and big, smart, concrete bungalows which are packed rather uncomfortably close together but feel spacious inside. The accommodation at neighbouring *Miami Bungalow* (☎01/228 4506; ①–④)

ranges from simple wooden huts with fans to larger concrete versions, some with air-con and sea view.

Just over a kilometre south of Hat Khlong Nin, the road passes diminutive **Khlong Nam Jun**, a tiny cove that's rocky in parts but enjoys a swimmable beach and just one set of bungalows, *Lanta Coral Beach* (T 01/228 4326; ④–⑤; closed May–Oct). The seventeen good-sized concrete huts here are scattered among the palms (some of which are hung with hammocks) and have fans and well-appointed bathrooms. It's a quiet place, away from the crowds but not too remote.

The bungalows at *Dream Team* (T 01/228 4184, W www.ko-lanta.com/hotels /dreamteam.htm; ①–⑤) have the next rocky headland known as **Khlong Hin** all to themselves and, though this beach is hopeless for swimming, there's a good sandy stretch just fifteen minutes' walk to the north. The bungalows are set in a pretty, cultivated flower garden and they range from ultra-basic to air-conditioned luxury; the mid-range ones are reasonably priced and quite comfortable. There's a good restaurant here too, with fine sea views.

## Ao Kantiang, Ao Khlong Jaak and Ao Mai Pai

Three kilometres south of Khlong Hin, the secluded, almost remote fishing cove of **Ao Kantiang** boasts an impressively curved sweep of long, sandy bay backed by wild, jungle-clad hillsides whose resident monkeys occasionally pop down to seaside. The beach is good for swimming, and snorkelling and fishing trips are easily arranged from the bungalow outfits here. Right on the shore, *SeaSun* (①–②) offers inexpensive bamboo huts; the sixteen bamboo bungalows at neighbouring *Kantiang Bay View Resort* (T 01/606 3546; ②–⑤) are set in two facing rows and furnished with fan and bathroom.

The road gets worse and worse as you head south from Ao Kantiang, eventually degenerating into a track that leads to the isolated little **Ao Khlong Jaak**, site of the exceptionally popular *Waterfall Bungalows* (T 01/228 4014, F 075/612084, W www.waterfallbaybeach.com; ③–⑤). The 23 huts here are simple but stylish, many with split-level accommodation in the roof and bathrooms downstairs; the huts nearer the sea are more expensive, as are those with air-con. It's a friendly, clued-in retreat and offers day-trips to the islands and the nearby national park, as well as pretty good food. Advance booking is essential and the place is open year-round.

An abysmal coastal track continues for 3km south of *Waterfall*, affording good sea views, passing a quiet sandy beach and then coming to a halt at the lighthouse. Few drivers will offer to bring you down here, however much you pay them, but if you like the quiet, solitary life it might be worth making the trip in order to stay at *Bamboo Bay* bungalows (②–④) at the pretty cove of **Ao Mai Pai**; the bamboo huts here are simple, but have large verandas and electricity in the evenings, and it's just an hour's boat ride to some nice snorkelling islands.

# Ko Bubu and Ko Jum

Now that Ko Lanta is firmly registered on the beaten track, tourists in search of a more Robinson Crusoe-style haven have pushed on to a couple of other nearby islands. The minuscule **Ko Bubu**, only 7km off Lanta Yai's east coast, is the preserve of just one bungalow outfit, but in contrast to many one-resort islands, this is not an exclusive upmarket operation. The same is true of **Ko Jum**, which is slightly larger than Phi Phi Don but nevertheless offers only three accommodation options.

## Ko Bubu

With a radius of not much more than 500m, wooded **KO BUBU** has room for just thirty bungalows at *Bubu Bungalows* (T01/228 4510; ③–⑤; closed May–Oct), plus a few tents for rent at B150 a double. The island is twenty minutes' chartered longtail ride (B100) from the small town of **Lanta** on Ko Lanta Yai's east coast and can also be reached direct **from Krabi** by following the rainy-season route for Ko Lanta Yai and taking a longtail from Bo Muang for B150. Most of Krabi's tour agents (see p.356) will book you in for the Ko Bubu bungalow resort and can organize through transport from Krabi.

## Ko Jum (Ko Pu)

Situated halfway between Krabi and Ko Lanta Yai, **KO JUM** (also known as **Ko Pu**) is the sort of laid-back and simple spot that people come to for a couple of days, then can't bring themselves to leave. Its mangrove-fringed east coast holds two of the island's three fishing villages – Ban Ko Pu sits on the northeast tip and Ban Ko Jum, complete with it own beachfront school, is down on the southeast tip – while across on the sandy west coast there are a couple of small bungalow operations to the south of the third village, Ban Ting Lai. Much of the north is made inaccessible by the breastbone of forested hills, whose highest peak (395m) is Khao Ko Pu, and the ten-kilometre track that connects the north and south of the island runs around its northeastern flank. There's little to do here except hunt for shells, stroll the kilometre across the island to buy snacks in Ban Ko Jum or roast on the beach and then plunge into the sea. Sandflies can be quite a problem on Ko Jum, so bring plenty of insect repellent, and some bite-cream too in case it doesn't work.

The 35 smart wood and concrete **bungalows** of the long-running *Joy Bungalows* (T01/229 1502; ②–⑤) are comfortably equipped with balconies, beds and nets, and the bamboo huts are simple but fine enough. Close by *Joy*, *New Bungalow* (①–③) has just fifteen basic bamboo huts plus a couple of tree-houses; their fish dinners are recommended. If you get sick of bungalow food, try the inexpensive and authentic Thai food at *Rimthang* on the track into Ban Ko Jum, or *Mama Cooking*, in Ban Ko Jum itself.

Both bungalows send **longtails** out to meet the Krabi–Ko Lanta ferries as they pass the west coast (1hr 30min from Krabi or about 45min from Ko Lanta). In the rainy season they sometimes organize a daily songthaew and longtail to cover the alternative mainland route, which runs from Krabi via the pier at **Laem Kruat**, 40km southeast, from where the boat takes you out to Ko Jum's east coast – ask any Krabi tour operator for songthaew departure times.

# Travel details

## Buses

**Khao Lak** to: Khao Sok (every 90min; 1hr 30min); Phuket (11 daily; 2hr 30min); Ranong (8 daily; 2hr 30min–3hr); Surat Thani (every 90min; 3hr 30min); Takua Pa (every 40min; 30min).

**Khao Sok** to: Khao Lak (every 90min; 1hr 30min); Surat Thani (every 90min; 2hr); Takua Pa (every 90min; 50min).

**Krabi** to: Bangkok (9 daily; 12–14hr); Hat Yai (13 daily; 4–5hr); Nakhon Si Thammarat (9 daily;

4

3–4hr); Penang (2 daily; 6hr); Phang Nga (17 daily; 1hr 30min–2hr); Phuket (17 daily; 3–5hr); Ranong (3 daily; 4hr); Satun (2 daily; 5hr); Surat Thani (hourly; 4hr); Takua Pa (4 daily; 3hr 30min–4hr 30min); Trang (14 daily; 3hr).

**Phang Nga** to: Bangkok (4 daily; 11hr–12hr 30min); Krabi (hourly; 1hr 30min–2hr); Phuket (hourly; 1hr 30min–2hr 30min); Surat Thani (4 daily; 4hr).

**Phuket** to: Bangkok (at least 10 daily; 14–16hr); Hat Yai (12 daily; 6–8hr); Khao Lak (14 daily; 2hr); Khao Sok (14 daily; 3–4hr); Krabi (17 daily; 3–4hr); Nakhon Si Thammarat (at least 7 daily; 7–8hr); Phang Nga (17 daily; 2hr 30min); Phattalung (2 daily; 6–7hr); Ranong (4 daily; 5–6hr); Satun (2 daily; 7hr); Sungai Kolok (2 daily; 11hr); Surat Thani (20 daily; 4hr 30min–6hr); Takua Pa (14 daily; 2hr 30min–3hr); Trang (22 daily; 5–6hr).

**Ranong** to: Bangkok (7 daily; 9–10hr); Chumphon (every 90min; 2hr); Khuraburi (8 daily; 2hr); Phuket (8 daily; 5–6hr); Takua Pa (8 daily; 2hr 30min–3hr).

**Takua Pa** to: Bangkok (10 daily; 12–13hr); Krabi (4 daily; 3hr 30min–4hr 30min); Phuket (every 40min; 3hr); Ranong (8 daily; 2hr 30min–3hr); Surat Thani (11 daily; 3hr).

## Ferries

**Ko Phi Phi Don** to: Ao Nang (Nov–May 1 daily); Ko Lanta Yai (Nov–May 2 daily; 1hr 30min); Krabi (4–6 daily; 1hr 30min–2hr); Phuket (Nov–May up to 4 daily; 1hr 30min–2hr 30min).

**Krabi** to: Ko Jum (1hr 30min); Ko Lanta Yai (Nov–May 2 daily; 2hr 30min); Ko Phi Phi Don (4–6 daily; 1hr 30min–2hr).

**Phuket** to: Ko Phi Phi Don (2–6 daily; 1hr 30min–2hr 30min); Ko Similan (Dec–May daily; 1hr 30min).

**Ranong** to: Ko Chang (Nov–May 1–2 daily; 1hr); Ko Pha Yam (Nov–May 1 daily; 1–2hr).

**Thap Lamu (Khao Lak)** to: Ko Similan (Nov–May 1 daily; 2hr).

## Flights

**Krabi** to: Bangkok (2 daily; 65min); Phuket (3 daily; 30min).

**Phuket** to: Bangkok (17 daily; 1hr 25min); Hat Yai (1–2 daily; 45min); Ko Samui (2 daily; 50min); Krabi (3 daily; 30min); Nakhon Si Thammarat (daily; 40min); Siem Reap (Cambodia; 3 daily; 2hr 20min); Surat Thani (daily; 40min).

**Ranong** to: Bangkok (4 weekly; 1hr 20min).

# The deep south

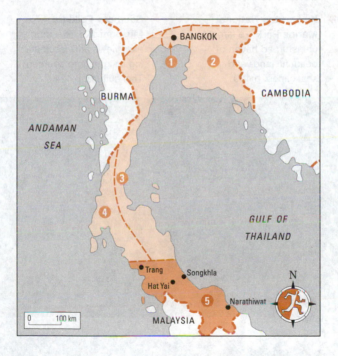

# CHAPTER 5

# Highlights

* **Thale Noi Waterbird Park** – Boating on this fascinating inland lake isn't just for bird-watchers. p.398

* **Ko Mook** – best of the Trang islands, with laid-back beach resorts and the stunning Emerald Cave. p.404

* **Ko Tarutao National Marine Park** – a largely undisturbed haven of beautiful land- and seascapes. p.409

* **Thale Ban National Park** – waterfalls, caves, noisy, sweaty jungle – and solitude. p.408

* **Songkhla** – sand-and-see all-rounder, with diverting sights, great accommodation and restaurants, and miles of beach. p.419

* **Southern Folklore Museum, Ko Yo** – stunning views and fascinating insights into southern Thai culture. p.424

# 5

# The deep south

The frontier between Thailand and Malaysia carves across the peninsula six degrees north of the equator, but the cultures of the two countries shade into each other much further north. According to official divisions, the southern Thais – the *thai pak tai* – begin around Chumphon, and as you move further down the peninsula you see ever more sarongs, yashmaks and towering mosques, and hear with increasing frequency a staccato dialect that baffles many Thais. In **Trang**, **Phatthalung** and **Songkhla** provinces, the Muslim population is generally accepted as being Thai, but the inhabitants of the four southernmost provinces – **Satun**, **Pattani**, **Yala** and **Narathiwat** – are ethnically more akin to the Malays: most of the 1,500,000 followers of Islam here speak Yawi, an old Malay dialect. To add to the ethnic confusion, the deep south has a large urban population of Chinese, whose comparative wealth makes them stand out sharply from the Muslim farmers and fishermen.

On a journey south, the first thing you might be tempted by is an atmospheric boat trip through the **Thale Noi Waterbird Park** near Phatthalung. The easiest route after that is to hop across to the great natural beauty of the **west coast**, with its sheer limestone outcrops, pristine sands and fish-laden coral stretching down to the Malaysian border. The spread of tourism outwards from Phuket is slowly inching its way south to the idyllic islands around

## Accommodation prices

Throughout this guide, guest houses, hotels and bungalows have been categorized according to the **price codes** given below. These categories represent the minimum you can expect to pay in the high season (roughly July, Aug & Nov–Feb) for a **double room**. If travelling on your own, expect to pay anything between sixty and one hundred percent of the rates quoted for a double room. Wherever a **price range** is indicated, this means that the establishment offers rooms with varying facilities – as explained in the write-up. Wherever an establishment also offers **dormitory beds**, the prices of these beds are given in the text, instead of being indicated by price code.

Remember that the top-whack hotels will add seven percent tax and a ten percent service charge to your bill – the price codes below are based on net rates after taxes have been added.

| | | |
|---|---|---|
| ❶ under B150 | ❹ B400–600 | ❼ B1200–1800 |
| ❷ B150–250 | ❺ B600–900 | ❽ B1800–3000 |
| ❸ B250–400 | ❻ B900–1200 | ❾ B3000+ |

Krabi
Nakhon & Surat
Nakhon
Thale Noi Waterbird Park
Ban Thale Noi
Ranot
Trang River
Lam Pam
Thale Luang
Phatthalung
Sikao
Khu Khut Waterbird Park
Ko Hai
Ban Pak Meng
Trang
Khao Ron (1350m)
Ko Cheuak
Ko Mook
Kantang
Ban Chao Mai
Ko Kradan
Ko Libong
Palian
Thale Sap
Songkhla
Ko Yo
Rattaphum
Ko Sukorn
Thung Wa
Ko Lao Lieng
Ko Phetra
Hat Yai
Chana
ANDAMAN SEA
Langu
Pak Bara
Ao Noon
Ko Bulon Lae
Ban Khwan Sator
Wang Prachan
THALE BAN NATIONAL PARK
Chalung
Nathawi
Ko Tarutao
KO TARUTAO NATIONAL MARINE PARK
Satun
Padang Besar
Sadao
Ko Rawi
Ko Adang
Thammalang
Kangar
Ko Lipe
Kuah
Langkawi Island
Kuala Perlis
MALAYSIA
Alor Setar
N
0
50 km
Butterworth (for Penang)
4
41
408
404
43
407
416
406


**Trang**, but for the time being at least these remain more or less unscathed, and further south in the spectacular **Ko Tarutao National Park**, you'll usually still have the beaches all to yourself.

On the less attractive **east** side of the peninsula, you'll probably pass through the ugly, modern city of **Hat Yai** at some stage, as it's the transport capital for the south and for connections to Malaysia, but a far more sympathetic place to stay is the old town of **Songkhla**, half an hour away on the seashore. The

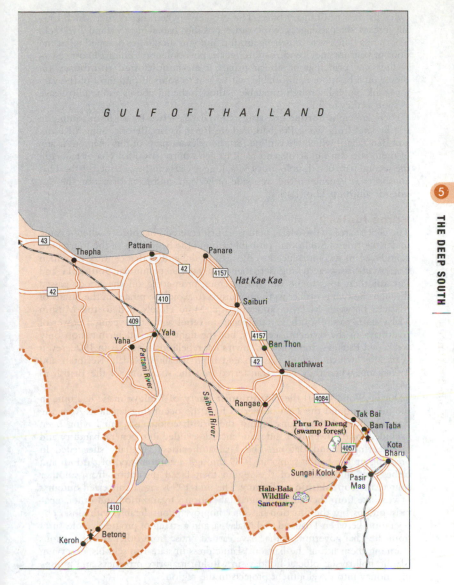

GULF OF THAILAND

43 — Thepha — Pattani — Panare
42 — 4157 — *Hat Kae Kae*
42 — 410 — Saiburi
409 — Yala — 4157 — Ban Thon
Yaha — *Pattani River* — 42 — Narathiwat
*Saiburi River* — Rangae — 4084 — Tak Bai
**Phru To Daeng** **(swamp forest)** — Ban Taha
4057 — Kota Bharu
Sungai Kolok — Pasir Mas
**Hala-Bala** **Wildlife** **Sanctuary**
410
Keroh — Betong

region southeast of here is where you'll experience Malay Muslim culture at its purest, though with the exception of **Narathiwat**, a pleasant stopover on the journey south to the border, it has little to offer the visitor.

As well as the usual bus services and the rail line, which forks at Hat Yai to Butterworth and Kuala Lumpur on the Malaysian west coast and Sungai Kolok on the eastern border, the deep south is the territory of **share-taxis** – sometimes grand old 1950s Mercs, which connect all the major towns for about twice the fare of ordinary buses. The cars leave when they're full, which usually means six passengers, with, quite possibly, babes-in-arms and livestock. They are a quick way of getting around and you should get dropped off at the door of your journey's end. A more recent phenomenon, run on almost exactly the same principles at similar prices, is **air-conditioned minibuses**; on these you'll be more comfortable, with a seat to yourself, and most of the various ranks publish a rough timetable – though the minibuses also tend to leave as soon as they're full.

There are eight **border crossings** to Malaysia – two by sea from Satun, the rest by land from Wang Prachan, Padang Besar, Sadao, Betong, Sungai Kolok, and Ban Taba – which are outlined in the relevant parts of this chapter. At any of them you can nip across and back to get a thirty-day Thai visa or to begin the second part of a double-entry visa; longer visas can be obtained at the Thai consulates at Penang on the west side of Malaysia and Kota Bharu on the east side (details on p.22 of Basics).

## Some history

The central area of the Malay peninsula first entered Thai history when it came under the rule of Sukhothai, probably around the beginning of the fourteenth century. Islam was introduced to the area by the end of that century, by which time Ayutthaya was taking a firmer grip on the peninsula. **Songkhla** and **Pattani** then rose to be the major cities, prospering on the goods passed through the two ports across the peninsula to avoid the pirates in the Straits of Malacca between Malaysia and Sumatra. More closely tied to the Muslim Malay states to the south, Pattani began to **rebel** against the central power of Ayutthaya in the sixteenth century, but the fight for self-determination only weakened Pattani's strength. The town's last rebellious fling was in 1902, seven years after which Pattani was isolated from its allies, Kedah, Kelantan and Trengganu, when they were transferred into the suzerainty of the British in Malaysia.

During World War II the **Communist Party of Malaya** made its home in the jungle around the Thai border to fight the occupying Japanese. After the war they turned their guns against the British colonialists, but having been excluded from power after independence, descended into general banditry and racketeering around Betong. The Thai authorities eventually succeeded in breaking up the bandit gangs in 1989 through a combination of pardons and bribes, but the stability of the region then faced disruption from another source, a rise in **Islamic militancy**. The mid-1990s saw a concerted outburst of violence from the Pattani United Liberation Organization and other separatist groups, but the situation has since improved considerably, with closer cooperation between Thailand and Malaysia, and a string of progressive measures from the Thai government that have earned praise from other Islamic nations – among them lifting the ban on Islamic dress in state-run schools, observing Islamic holidays as official holidays in Muslim majority provinces and pumping money into development projects in the region.

# Phatthalung and around

Halfway between Nakhon and Hat Yai, the hot, dusty town of **PHATTHALUNG** is worth a stop only if you're tempted by a boat trip through the nearby Thale Noi Waterbird Park, its beautiful watery landscape rich in exotic birds and vegetation. Although its setting among limestone outcrops is dramatic, the town itself is drab and unwelcoming: its only claims to fame are *nang thalung*, the Thai shadow puppet theatre to which it probably gave its name (see box on p.289), and bandits, though it has cleaned up its act in recent years.

If you've time to kill before or after a visit to the waterbird park, head for **Khao Hua Taek** or "Broken-Headed Mountain", the limestone outcrop with a dent in its peak which rises abruptly out of the west end of the centre. **Wat Kuha Sawan**, on the east side, has been built around a large, cool cave in the base of the outcrop, where a crude Buddha image is sheltered by a model of the bodhi tree hung with delicate brass leaves. Climb the concrete steps to the right of the cave, then follow the path to the left to reach the summit, where you'll get a good view over Phatthalung and the surrounding rice fields. To the east, you'll also be able to see **Khao Ok Taloo**, "Broken-Hearted Mountain", so called because of the natural tunnel through its peak: according to legend, Hua Taek and Ok Taloo were the wife and the mistress of a third mountain to the north, **Khao Muang**, over whom they had a fierce fight, leaving them with these wounds.

If a visit to Khao Hua Taek still leaves you with time on your hands, you could make a short trip out of town towards the resort of Lam Pam, half an hour away to the northeast: take one of the frequent songthaews from the rail crossing on Thanon Ramet. About 6km out on the right-hand side, stop off at the 200-year-old bot of **Wat Wang** to see a series of elegant and dynamic murals depicting the life of the Buddha – ask a monk for the key to the formidable cloisters which surround it. Two former **governor's palaces**, appealing examples of traditional southern Thai architecture, overlook a picturesque canal 200m beyond Wat Wang on the same side of the road. Nearer to the road, the "old" residence, Wang Khao, which dates from the middle of the nineteenth century, is built entirely of wood on inward-sloping stilts, a design whose tensile properties mean that it can be held together with tongue-and-groove joints rather than nails. In the so-called "new palace", Wang Mai, built in 1889 with a raised stone courtyard around a large tree, look out for the intricate traditional carvings on the main house, especially the "sunrise" gable, sometimes called the "crest of a monk's robe" because it resembles the edge of the robe gathered into pleats by a monk's hand. At **Lam Pam** itself there's nothing to do but eat and drink at minimal cost, while relaxing in a deckchair on the shady banks of the Thale Luang, the lagoon adjoining Thale Noi (see p.398).

## Practicalities

Phatthalung is served by frequent **buses** from north and south and from Trang, 57km to the west, and is on the major rail line, which crosses the main street, Thanon Ramet, in the centre of town. Most buses stop near the **train station**, which is on the north side of Thanon Ramet; through buses only stop at the junction of highways 4 and 41, to the west, leaving a short songthaew hop into town.

Out of a poor selection of **hotels**, the best value is the friendly *Thai Hotel*, at 14 Thanon Disara Sakarin, behind the Bangkok Bank on Thanon Ramet (☏074/611636; ❷–❸); rooms with attached bathrooms and a choice of fan or air-conditioning are clean and reasonably quiet. *Koo Hoo*, at 9 Thanon Prachabamrung (parallel to and south of Ramet), is an excellent, moderately priced **restaurant** – try the chicken with lemon sauce on a bed of fried seaweed, or the delicious giant tiger prawns.

**Thale Noi Waterbird Park** isn't just for bird-spotters – even the most recalcitrant city-dweller can appreciate boating through the bizarre fresh-water habitat formed at the head of the huge lagoon that spills into the sea at Songkhla. Here, in the "Little Sea" (*thale noi*), the distinction between land and water breaks down: the lake is dotted with low, marshy islands, and much of the intervening shallow water is so thickly covered with water vines, lotus pads and reeds that it looks like a field. But the real delight of this area is the hundreds of thousands of birds which breed here – brown teals, loping purple herons, white cattle egrets and nearly two hundred other species. Most are migratory, arriving here from January onwards from as far away as Siberia – March and April provide the widest variety of birds, whereas from October to December you'll spot just a small range of native species. Early morning and late afternoon are the best times to come, when the heat is less searing and when, in the absence of hunters and fishermen, more birds are visible.

To get from Phatthalung to **BAN THALE NOI**, the village on the western shore, take one of the frequent **songthaews** (1hr) from Thanon Nivas, which runs north off Thanon Ramet near the station. If you're coming from Nakhon or points further north by bus, you can save yourself a trip into Phatthalung by getting out at **Ban Chai Khlong**, 15km from Ban Thale Noi, and waiting for a songthaew there. **Longtail boats** can be hired at the pier in the village: for around B300 (depending on the number of people in your party), the boat-man will give you a two-hour trip around the lake. If you want to get a dawn start, stay in one of the few national park **bungalows** built over the lake (donation required; book at least fifteen days in advance on ☎075/685230).

# Trang province

Trang town, 60km west of Phatthalung, is fast developing as a popular jumping-off point for backpackers, drawn south from the crowded sands of Krabi to the pristine **beaches and islands** of the Trang coast. Its islands sport only a couple of bungalow outfits each, though some of these have moved upmarket in recent years and it won't be long before resorts multiply and prices rise. **Inland**, too, tourism is developing, and several outfits in Trang town now offer white-water rafting, kayaking and trekking excursions. So popular is the area becoming that it even has its own website: the excellent ⓦ www.trangonline.com has plenty of well-presented information on attractions, tours and accommodation in the region, and allows online bookings.

## Trang town

The town of **TRANG** (aka Taptieng), which prospers on rubber, oil palms, fish-eries and – increasingly – tourism, is a sociable place whose wide, clean streets are dotted with crumbling, wooden-shuttered houses. In the evening, restaurant tables sprawl onto the main Thanon Rama VI and Thanon Wisetkul, and dur-ing the day, many of the town's Chinese inhabitants hang out in the cafés, drink-ing the local filtered coffee. Trang's Chinese population makes the **Vegetarian Festival** at the beginning of October almost as frenetic as Phuket's (see box on p.327) – and for veggie travellers it's an opportunity to feast at the stalls set up

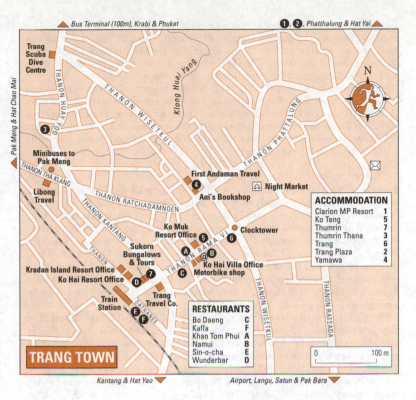

Bus Terminal (100m), Krabi & Phuket

**1**, **2**, Phatthalung & Hat Yai

Trang
Scuba
Dive
Centre

THANON HUAY YOD

Klong Huay Yang

THANON WISETKUL

THANON PHATTALUNG

Pak Meng & Hat Chao Mai

**3**

Minibuses to
Pak Meng

THANON THA KLANG

Libong
Travel

THANON RATCHADAMNOEN

THANON KANTANG

First Andaman Travel

**4**

Night Market

Ani's Bookshop

Ko Muk
Resort Office

**5**

THANON RAMA VI

**6** Clocktower

Sukorn
Bungalows
& Tours

**A**

**@** **B**

Ko Hai Villa Office

**C** Motorbike shop

Kradan Island Resort Office

Ko Hai Resort Office

**7**

**D**

THANON WISETKUL

THANON RATSADA

Train
Station

**E**

**F**

SATHANEE

Trang
Travel Co.

**RESTAURANTS**
| | |
|---|---|
| Bo Daeng | C |
| Kaffa | F |
| Khao Tom Phui | A |
| Namui | B |
| Sin-o-cha | E |
| Wunderbar | D |

**ACCOMMODATION**
| | |
|---|---|
| Clarion MP Resort | 1 |
| Ko Teng | 5 |
| Thumrin | 7 |
| Thumrin Thana | 3 |
| Trang | 6 |
| Trang Plaza | 2 |
| Yamawa | 4 |

**TRANG TOWN**

0          100 m

Kantang & Hat Yao

Airport, Langu, Satun & Pak Bara

around the temples. Getting there is easy, as Trang is ninety minutes from Phatthalung and well served by buses from all the surrounding provinces.

## Practicalities

There are daily Thai Airways **flights** (around B2300 one way) between Bangkok and Trang **airport**, which is connected to Trang town by B30 air-conditioned minibuses, operated by Trang Travel Company (see p.400). Two overnight **trains** from the capital run down a branch of the southern line to Trang, stopping at the station at the western end of Thanon Rama VI. Most **buses** arrive at the terminal on Thanon Huay Yod, to the north of the centre; buses from Satun and Palian stop on Thanon Ratsada, which runs south from the eastern end of Thanon Rama VI. **Air-conditioned minibuses** for Hat Yai are based on Thanon Huay Yod near the main bus terminal; those for Nakhon Si Thammarat are found on Thanon Klong Huai Yang, off Thanon Wisetkul about 200m from the clocktower; and those for Ko Lanta leave from the offices of several travel agents around town who handle bookings for them, including Sukorn Beach Bungalows and Tours (see p.400). This agency also operate minibuses to Pak Bara in high season (roughly Nov–May); at other times of year you have to take a bus to Langu and then a songthaew.

There's an excellent **bookshop**, Ani's, round the corner from the *Yamawa Bed and Breakfast* at 285 Thanon Ratchadamnoen; it stocks a wide range of books in English and other languages, as well as souvenirs from Trang province. The owners are a good source of information on the area, and also have a couple of **motorbikes**, which they rent out for B150 per day. There's a greater choice available from the motorbike shop at 44 Thanon Rama VI (B200 per day), as well as air-conditioned vans, with driver, for B1700 per day. On Thanon Sathanee, both the Trang Travel Company at no. 99 (T075/219598–9, F211290, Etrangtravel@hotmail.com) and Sukorn Beach Bungalows and Tours at no. 22 (T & F075/211457, Wwww.sukorn-island-trang.com) can arrange **car hire**, with driver, at similar rates. For self-drive car rental, contact Avis (T075/691941, Etst@avisthailand.com), who have plans to open a branch at Trang airport. You can connect to the **internet** at 116 Thanon Rama VI (daily 8am–10.30pm; B1 per minute), and at the Trang Travel Company (daily 8am–8pm; B2 per minute).

## Accommodation

**Hotels** in Trang are concentrated along Thanon Rama VI and Thanon Wisetkul. The town's outstanding **budget** choice is the *Yamawa Bed and Breakfast* at 94 Thanon Wisetkul (T075/216617; ❷), a gem of a guest house whose six large rooms, with shared bathrooms, are spread over three floors, beautifully decorated throughout and festooned with plants; rates include breakfast. There's a restaurant on the ground floor, as well as a leafy roof terrace. The friendly Thai-Belgian family who run the guest house also organize treks in the Trang area. If you can't get a room here, a second best is the *Ko Teng Hotel* at 77–79 Thanon Rama VI (T075/218622; ❷), a little rough around the edges, but friendly enough and with en-suite rooms that are large and clean.

The pick of the **moderate** range, *Trang Hotel*, 134/2–5 Thanon Wisetkul, at the junction with Thanon Rama VI overlooking the clocktower (T075/218944, F218451; ❹), has large, comfortable twin rooms with air-conditioning, hot water and television. *Thumrin Hotel*, on Rama VI near the station (T075/211014, F218057; ❹), used to be the town's only deluxe option, but is now looking down-at-heel, having been decisively usurped by no fewer than three **luxury** hotels: the *Trang Plaza*, 2km east of the centre at 132 Thanon Phattalung (T075/226902–10, F226901; ❻); the *Clarion MP Resort Hotel*, a little further out on the same road (T075/214230–45, F211177, Wwww.mpresort.com; ❼); and the *Thumrin Thana*, 1km north of the train station at 69/8 Thanon Thana (T075/211211, Wwww.thumrin.co.th; ❽); note that hefty discounts are often available at all three hotels.

## Eating and drinking

Trang's **food** comes into its own in the early evenings, when the excellent night market opens for business; it's around the back of the city hall, just off Thanon Rama VI, 100m north of the clocktower. Try the *khanom jiin*, soft noodles topped with hot, sweet or fishy sauces and eaten with crispy greens. *Khao Tom Phui*, 1/11 Thanon Rama VI (open from 5pm), is a very popular and reasonable pavement restaurant on the north side of the street. For something posher, head for *Namui* on the opposite side at no. 130, a large, clean institution specializing in good seafood; ignore the unprepossessing interior and head straight through the restaurant to the creeper-covered patio and outdoor seating at the back. An even nicer setting can be found at the *Riverside* restaurant, a boat permanently moored on the Trang River, 5km from the centre of town; you need to take a tuk-tuk there and back, but it's worth the extra effort for the breezy location and great Thai food.

There are several good places to sample Trang's **café** society. Diagonally opposite *Thumrin Hotel* on Thanon Rama VI, *Bo Daeng* serves the ubiquitous *kopii* (filtered coffee) with *patongkoh* (Chinese doughnuts) and *ahaan det diap*, plates of assorted tasty titbits such as spring rolls, baby corn and sausage. For a daytime coffee fix and Western-style cakes, head for *Sin-o-cha*, next to the station at 25/25–26 Thanon Sathanee, or the equally popular *Kaffa*, a few doors along at no. 25/47. Trang even boasts a farang **bar**, pandering to its small expat community and growing population of tourists: *Wunderbar*, at the bottom end of Rama VI near the station, offers a wide selection of drinks, Thai food, burgers, pizzas and other Western favourites.

## Around Trang

From Ban Pak Meng, 40km due west of Trang town, to the mouth of the Trang River runs a thirty-kilometre stretch of lovely **beaches**, broken only by dramatic limestone outcrops which are pitted with explorable caves. Air-conditioned minibuses run from Trang to Pak Meng in the north, and via Hat Yao to Ban Chao Mai in the south, but if you want to explore the whole coastline, you'll need to rent or hire a motorbike, car or taxi in Trang.

Much nicer than the mainland beaches – and more geared towards foreign tourists – are the fantastic **islands** off the coast, most notable among them Hai, Mook and Kradan. Blessed with blinding white beaches, great coral and amazing marine life, these have managed, despite increasing popularity, to cling on to that illusory desert-island atmosphere which better-known places like Phuket and Samui lost long ago. The situation is changing fast, however: prices have risen in line with the number of tourists, accommodation is often fully booked at peak times and many resorts that were previously open in high season only (Nov–May) are now opening year round – though in practice many remain inaccessible out of season due to treacherous seas. We give details of opening seasons in the individual island accounts below, but it's sensible to phone ahead – either to the place you want to stay, or to its office in Trang town or Bangkok – to check on opening months, vacancies and transport. In addition to some public ferry services, there are boat services which many resorts run in the morning; at other times the resort you're interested in may well be willing to despatch a longtail to pick you up.

Besides the specific resort offices (detailed below in the island accounts), there are a couple of **travel agencies in Trang** which offer a wider range of services. The Trang Travel Company (see opposite) can provide information on, and make reservations at, any of the places on the islands, or if you just fancy a day exploring the islands, can organize a **boat trip** (mid-Oct to mid-May only) to Ko Mook, Ko Hai and Ko Cheuak ("Robe Island", so named after its limestone folds) for B600 per person including packed lunch; snorkelling gear can be rented (B30 per day) and the boat will drop you off at one of the islands if you wish. The well-organized Sukorn Beach Bungalows and Tours (see opposite) offer a similar range of services – accommodation booking, boat trips and car rental – in addition to running their own bungalow outfit on Ko Sukorn. The friendly Thai-Dutch owners are a great source of information on the area, and their office makes a good first stop in town. They can also book you onto any of the white-water rafting, canoeing and trekking trips run by Libong Travel (see p.402).

To do some **scuba-diving** off the Trang coast, contact Trang Scuba Dive Centre at 59/33–34 Thanon Huay Yod (℡075/222189, ℻222194, ℮trangscuba@thumrin.co.th); they offer day-trips to Ko Mook, Ko Hai and Ko Kradan for B2000–2500 per person, or can organize longer trips of up to a week (staying aboard or at one of the island resorts). Ko Hai also has its own dive shop, Rainbow Divers (see p.404).

Away from the beach, **inland** Trang Province has plenty to offer too. Outdoor pursuits have mushroomed in the last few years, and several operators now offer **trekking**, **white-water rafting** or **canoeing** excursions, most taking in some of the myriad caves and waterfalls which are scattered though the province. One of the longest established operators is Libong Travel, 59/1 Thanon Tha Klang (ⓣ075/222929 or 01/606 8530, ⓕ214676), opposite the minibus stand for Pak Meng; they offer a fairly typical spread of trips, including white-water rafting (B850 day-trip), canoeing through the mangroves near Ban Chao Mai and the caves along the Trang coast (B750 day-trip), and a three-day jungle trek up to the 1200-metre peak of nearby Mount Rutu (B1700). They also offer a day-trip to Thale Noi Waterbird Park near Phatthalung for B650 (see p.398), as well as island tours.

## The coast: Pak Meng to Ban Chao Mai

Although it has a fine outlook to the headlands and islands to the west, the beach at **PAK MENG** is not the most attractive on the coast, a rather muddy strip of sand truncated at its northern end by a busy pier and to the south by a newly constructed promenade and sea wall. If it's just a day at the beach you're after, you're much better off continuing further south down the coast to Hat Yong Ling or Hat Yao. Getting to Pak Meng takes about an hour on one of the air-conditioned **minibuses** that leave when full (roughly hourly; B50) from Thanon Tha Klang, the northwesterly continuation of Thanon Ratchadamnoen in Trang. The nicest place **to stay** is the *Lay Trang Resort*, a stone's throw from the pier (ⓣ075/274027–8, ⓦ www.laytrang.com; ⑤); its smart brick air-conditioned bungalows, ranged around a large, peaceful garden, come with balconies and spacious hot-water bathrooms. The owners can organize longtail day-trips to Ko Mook, Ko Hai and Ko Kradan for B550 a head including lunch. There's a pleasant, reasonably priced **restaurant** attached – the seafood dishes are particularly good – and there are plenty of foodstalls and simple eateries lining the back of the beach.

A paved road heads south from Pak Meng, passing, after 7km, the turning for the headquarters of the **Hat Chao Mai National Park** (entry B200) at Hat Chang Lang. The park covers 230 square kilometres, including the islands of Mook and Kradan and the entire stretch of coastline from Pak Meng down to Ban Chai Mai. The headquarters have limited information available in English, but there are some eight-berth **bungalows** available to rent (B500 each), or for B200 a night, two-person tents can be pitched under the casuarina trees at the back of the sandy beach. You'll need to bring your own food unless you're prepared to retrace your steps a couple of kilometres north along the coast road to the *Chang Lang Resort* (ⓣ075/291008–9, ⓕ291008; ④), a decent bungalow outfit with attached restaurant, set back from the beach just off the main road – if you do eat here, try the oysters, for which Hat Chang Lang is famous. Primarily aimed at Thai weekenders, the pleasant resort has well-built concrete bungalows, some air-conditioned, and all with mosquito screens, en-suite bathrooms and their own verandas. The run-down concrete rooms at the nearby *Seasand Resort* (④) should be given a wide berth.

Four kilometres south of Hat Chang Lang is **Hat Yong Ling**, an attractive convex beach with a large cave which you can swim into at high tide or walk into at low tide. You'll need to pay the national park entrance fee and bring a picnic as there are no food or drink stalls, but the reward is a quiet, pristine strip of sand with crystal-clear waters, probably the nicest along this stretch of coast. Immediately beyond comes **Hat Yao** (Long Beach), also known as Hat Chao Mai, which runs in a broad five-kilometre white-sand strip, backed by casuarina trees and some simple restaurants. In a scenic spot at the southern end of the beach, *Sinchai's Chaomai Resort* (T01/396 4838; ①–③) is very relaxed and friendly, and offers a choice between simple huts with mosquito nets, and rooms in sturdy wooden or concrete bungalows; two-person tents are also available for B50 per night. The laid-back owners can rustle up tasty Thai meals, there's a small English-language library, and fishing and snorkelling tours can be arranged on request.

A short walk away from *Sinchai's* is the Muslim village of **BAN CHAO MAI**, a straggle of simple thatched houses on stilts, which exists on fishing, especially for crabs. Hourly air-conditioned **minibuses** from Trang via Hat Yao reach Ban Chao Mai in about an hour (B100). By the harbour, the distinctive green tin-roofed *Had Yao Nature Resort* (T01/894 6936, ⓔnatureresorts@thai-land.com; ②–⑤) is an official YHA **hostel** – clean, friendly and efficiently run by a young Thai brother and sister, who are very clued up about eco-tourism in the area and recycle all their rubbish (they also own the *Libong Nature Beach Resort*, covered on p.406, and can arrange transport there). Dorm beds in the large house cost B100, and there are also some fan-cooled rooms with shared bath, as well as nicer self-contained bungalows with tables, chairs and their own balcony over the canal. The attached vegetarian restaurant serves up excellent grub. **Bikes** – an excellent means of transport for the nearby beaches – can be rented at the hostel for B100 per day, and there are also some **kayaks** available for exploring the mangrove swamps on the canal running behind the village (B200–300 per day). The owners organize kayak trips (B300 per person) to Tham Chao Mai, a nearby cave which is large enough to enter by boat; inside are impressively huge rock pillars and a natural theatre, its stage framed by rock curtains.

## Ko Hai

Of all the Trang islands, **KO HAI** (aka Ko Ngai), 16km southwest of Pak Meng, is the most developed, though it's still pretty low-key. The island's action, such as it is, centres on the east coast: three resorts, and an unobtrusive *chao ley* (see p.308) hamlet, enjoy a dreamy panorama of jagged limestone outcrops, whose crags glow pink and blue against the setting sun, stretching across the sea to the mainland behind. A two-kilometre-long beach of fine, white sand has a gentle slope that's ideal for swimming, and there's some good snorkelling in the shallow water off the southeast tip – though be careful of sea urchins and the sharp stag coral. For the best snorkelling in the region you can rent a longtail on Ko Hai (half-day B600) to get to Ko Cheuak, Ko Maa and Ko Waen, just off Ko Hai to the east, where you can swim into caverns and explore a fantastic variety of multicoloured soft and hard coral. All three resorts on Ko Hai run excursions to Ko Mook's Emerald Cave.

Ko Hai's **resorts** are theoretically **open year round**, with prices dropping slightly in the low season, but bear in mind that out of season the sea is often too rough for boats to cross. When they're running, **boats** leave Pak Meng for the one-hour voyage at 10.30am, charging B150 one way; if you miss the boat, longtails can be chartered for B400. The cheapest of the island's resorts, *Ko Hai Villa* (T01/677 0319; Trang office at 112 Thanon Rama VI, T075/210496; ④–⑤) has the beach much to itself. Simple, well-organized bamboo bungalows on a nice grassy plot boast verandas, small toilets and mosquito nets, or you could opt for a newer concrete bungalow or room in a concrete longhouse. The more upmarket *Ko Hai Resort* (T075/211045; Trang office at 205 Thanon Sathanee, T075/210317, F227092; Bangkok reservations T02/316 3577, F316 7916; ⑤–⑧) occupies a sandy cove by the island's jetty; besides a good restaurant, it has a spread of rooms ranging from fan-cooled en-suite huts on the rocks to air-conditioned beachside bungalows with wooden verandas and spacious bathrooms. The resort also has a well-organized **dive shop**: the German-run Rainbow Divers (@rainbowtau@aol.com) offers day-trips around Ko Hai, Ko Rok and the nearby islands (two tanks and lunch US$50–60), as well as PADI certification (4–5 days; around US$300). Operated by the same company as *Ko Hai Resort*, the *Ko Hai Fantasy Resort* (T075/216339, W www.kohngai.com; Trang office details and Bangkok reservations as for *Ko Hai Resort*; ❽), 1km north of its sister resort on a secluded stretch of beach, is swankier still, with foot spas outside each bungalow to wash away the sand before you step inside. Its thirty pastel-coloured bungalows are set in a pretty garden under coconut palms, some right on the beach, and there's a good restaurant too.

## Ko Mook

**KO MOOK**, about 8km southeast of Ko Hai, offers some of the best budget accommodation on the Trang islands, though at time of writing the resorts here were open in high season only. The island supports a comparatively busy fishing village on its east coast, but its main source of renown is **Tham Morakhot**, the stunning "Emerald Cave" on the west coast, which can only be visited by boat but shouldn't be missed. An eighty-metre swim through the cave – 10m or so of which is in pitch darkness – brings you to an inland beach of powdery sand open to the sky, at the base of a spectacular natural chimney whose walls are coated with dripping vegetation. Unless you're a nervous swimmer, avoid the organized tours on bigger boats offered by some of the resorts on nearby islands, and charter your own longtail instead: you won't get lifejackets and torches, but the boatman will swim through the cave with you and – if you're lucky – you'll avoid the tours and get the inland beach all to yourself, an experience not to be forgotten.

The peaceful **Hat Farang**, south of Tham Morakhot and a thirty-minute walk west from the island village, is by far the best beach on Ko Mook, with gently shelving white sand, crystal-clear water that's good for swimming and snorkelling, and beautiful sunsets. To get to Hat Farang from the mainland, either charter a longtail from Pak Meng direct to the beach (B400), or take the midday **ferry** from Kuantunku Pier (8km south from Pak Meng, connected by regular B40 minibus) to the island village, and then a motorbike taxi across (B30). The nicest of the three **bungalow** outfits here is *Charlie's* (T01/476 0478; ❷), with simple bamboo huts and spacious well-ventilated two-man tents set right on the beach under the coconut palms. It has a spotlessly clean shower block, and a simple open-air restaurant serving Western snacks alongside the tasty Thai dishes. **Motorbikes** can be rented here to explore the island (B200 per day), and there's also some snorkelling gear available (B100 per day); a longtail charter to the Emerald Cave will set you back B300 per boat. If *Charlie's* is full, the simple bamboo huts and basic mattress-on-floor rooms at the *Hat Farang* (T075/224475 in Trang after 7pm; ❷–❸) are a good second choice, set 50m or so back from the beach in a grassy plot and run by a friendly Thai woman. At the rocky, northern end of the beach, the *Sawatdee's* bamboo huts (book through *Wunderbar* in Trang – see p.401; ❸) are a little dilapidated, but compensate with uninterrupted sea views.

The beaches on the eastern side of the island are disappointing, often reduced to dirty mud flats when the tide goes out. On this coast just north of the village is the *Ko Mook Resort* (T075/212613; Trang office at 45 Thanon Rama VI, T & F075/214441; ❸–❺); arrayed here on shady slopes around a decent restaurant are basic bungalows (with fans, mosquito screens and shared bathrooms) as well as big bamboo and wood versions with verandas and private bathrooms. Their office in Trang can arrange transport here by car and boat, departing from their office at 11.30am every day in season (B150 per person); otherwise longtails can be chartered at Pak Meng for around B300, or there's the midday ferry from Kuantunku. The resort runs free boat transport every day to nicer beaches around Ko Mook, and can also organize snorkelling trips to nearby islands.

## Ko Kradan

About 6km to the southwest of Ko Mook, **KO KRADAN** is the remotest of the inhabited islands off Trang, and one of the most beautiful. An unimaginatively designed complex on the east coast, *Kradan Island Resort* (Trang office at 66/10 Thanon Sathanee, ☎ & ℻075/211391; Bangkok reservations ☎02/391 6091; ❺–❻) is Ko Kradan's only sign of life, offering reasonable **bungalows** with bathrooms, fans and mosquito-screened windows overlooking the beach, as well as cheaper accommodation in four-room wooden longhouses. The friendly staff speak good English and can arrange fishing trips and longtail tours of the surrounding islands and the Emerald Cave. You can swim at the long, narrow beach of steeply sloping, powdery sand in front of the resort – complete with its own coral reef – or at Sunset Beach, in a small bay ten minutes' walk away on the other side of the island. There's more good snorkelling among a great variety of hard coral in the clear waters off the island's northeastern tip, while the waters off the southwest of the island are a popular spot for **windsurfing**; the resort rents out windsurfers if you want to give it a go. To get there, phone the resort's Trang office in advance to be picked up at Pak Meng for the ninety-minute voyage (B600 for the boat); the resort is officially **open all year**, but often inaccessible due to bad weather conditions.

## Ko Libong

The largest of the Trang islands, **KO LIBONG**, lies 10km southeast of Ko Mook, opposite Ban Chao Mai on the mainland. Less visited than its northern neighbours, it's known mostly for its wildlife, although it has its fair share of golden beaches too. Libong is one of the most significant remaining refuges in Thailand of the **dugong** (also known as the manatee), a large marine mammal which feeds on sea grasses growing on the sea floor – the sea-grass meadow around Libong is reckoned to be the largest in Southeast Asia. Sadly, dugongs are now an endangered species, traditionally hunted for their blubber (used as fuel) and meat, and increasingly affected by fishing practices such as scooping, and by coastal pollution which destroys their source of food. The dugong has now been adopted as one of fifteen "reserved animals" of Thailand and is the official mascot of Trang province, but it remains to be seen how effective methods of conservation will be, especially with tourist interest in the dugong growing all the time – one Trang venture is proposing guaranteed-sighting money-back tours, tracking the normally elusive animals down by sonar.

Libong is also well known for its migratory **bird life**, which stops off here on its way south from Siberia, drawn by the island's food-rich mud flats (now protected by the Libong Archipelago Sanctuary, which covers the eastern third of the island). For those seriously interested in ornithology, the best time to come is during March and April, when you can expect to see crab plovers, great knots, Eurasian curlews, bar-tailed godwits, brown-winged kingfishers, masked finfoots and even the rare black-necked stork, not seen elsewhere on the Thai–Malay peninsula. Both of the island's resorts can arrange longtail charters with local fishermen (B800 per boat) out to the Juhol Cape, the prime viewing point on the island; late afternoon is best, when the bird life is more active.

## Practicalities

**Ferries** depart daily year-round at 3pm from **Kantang** (reached by regular B40 minibus from Thanon Kantang near Trang's train station), arriving one hour later at Ban Hin Kao, Ko Libong's main settlement; from here motorbike taxis (B40) transport you across to Ban Lan Khao and the island's two resorts. Alternatively, the *Had Yao Nature Resort* in Ban Chao Mai offers a direct transfer to the *Libong Nature Beach Resort* for B100 per person.

Situated on the long, thin strip of golden sand which runs along the southwestern coast, both of Ko Libong's **resorts** are **open all year**. The beach is pretty enough, though at low tide the sea retreats for hundreds of metres, exposing rock pools that are great for splashing about in but not so good for a dip. The newly opened *Libong Nature Beach Resort* (☎01/894 6936; Bangkok reservations ☎02/378 1428 or 378 1550; or book through *Had Yao Nature Resort* – see p.403; ℮natureresorts@thailand.com; ❸–❺) is the nicer of the two, run by the same brother-and-sister team who operate the *Had Yao Nature Resort* on the mainland. Its simple bamboo huts and neat brick en-suite bungalows with cheerful green tin roofs are set slightly back from a secluded stretch of beach, a ten-minute walk south of the fishing village of Ban Lan Khao; there's a good restaurant attached too. Motorbikes are available to rent (B400 per day), and the helpful owners can also organize snorkelling, seakayaking, fishing and boat trips to nearby islands. Dugong-spotting excursions are also available; you're unlikely to see the animals themselves, but you can sometimes spot their feeding trails, 2–3m long, in the sea grass below. At *Libong Beach Resort* (☎075/281160; Trang office at 18/2 Moo 6 Tambon Bankuan, ☎075/225205, ℮libongbeach@hotmail.com; ❸–❹), on the opposite, northern, side of Ban Lan Khao, a little closer to the clutter of the village, simple wooden bungalows on stilts come with or without bathroom, and there's also a reasonable restaurant.

## Ko Sukorn

A good way south of the other Trang islands, low-lying **KO SUKORN** lacks the white-sand beaches and beautiful coral of its neighbours but makes up for it with its friendly inhabitants, laid-back ambience and one excellent resort; for a glimpse of how island villagers – mainly fishermen and rubber farmers – live and work, this is the place to come.

The lush interior of the island is mainly given over to rubber plantations, interspersed with rice paddies, banana and coconut palms; there's a fringe of mangroves on the northern coast near the pier, while the island's main **beach** – 500m of gently shelving brown sand, backed by coconut palms – runs along the southwestern shore. It's here you'll find the excellent *Sukorn Beach Bungalows* (☎01/228 3668; Trang office at 22 Thanon Sathanee, ☎075/211457, ⓦwww.sukorn-island-trang.com; ❸–❹), one of the few Trang resorts that's reliably open and accessible all year round (discounts of up to sixty percent are available in low season). The clued-up Thai-Dutch duo who run the place are keen to keep the resort low-key and work with the local islanders as much as possible, something that's reflected in the friendly welcome you get all over the island. Nicely decorated concrete and thatch bungalows and longhouses – all spotlessly clean and with en-suite bathrooms – are set around a lush garden dotted with deckchairs (prices vary with distance from the beach) and there's an excellent well-priced **restaurant**.

Boat excursions from the resort range from **fishing trips** (with baskets – for squid and crab – in the morning, with nets in the evening, and with rods all day) to **snorkelling trips** out to Ko Phetra, Ko Lao Lien and Ko Takieng (all part of the Ko Phetra National Marine Park; see p.414). The latter run in high season only, when the sea is calm enough; at other times of year you're restricted to the island itself, though there's plenty to occupy you. At thirty square kilometres, it's a good size for exploring, and the resort has both motorbikes (half-day B175) and mountain bikes (half-day B85) for rent, as well as a handy map which marks all the sights, including the crab market (daily at 11am), the village health centre (where you can get a massage) and a viewpoint – at 150m up, the island's highest point – which you can climb in the dry season.

A songthaew-and-boat **transfer to the island** (B70 per person) leaves the resort's office in Trang daily at 11.30am and takes a couple of hours. Leaving the island, there's no need to return to the mainland; *Sukorn Beach Bungalows* can organize **longtail-boat transfers** to any of the other Trang islands, as well as to Ko Bulon Lae (see p.414). The resort can also arrange to pick you up from these islands if you call ahead.

# Satun province

Satun province, which lies south of Trang and flush against the Malaysian border, provides the first glimpse of Thailand for many travellers on their way up through the Thai-Malay peninsula. The sleepy provincial capital, **Satun**, offers few attractions for the visitor, but makes a good base for the nearby **Thale Ban National Park**, with its caves, waterfalls and luxuriant jungle. The province's main attraction, however, is the **Ko Tarutao National Marine Park**, one of the loveliest beach destinations in Thailand, with pristine stretches of sand and a fantastic array of marine life. North of the national park, the tiny islands of the **Ko Phetra National Marine Park** are much less visited, with the exception of **Ko Bulon Lae**, which has a good selection of privately run bungalows along its long and beautiful beach.

## Satun

Nestling in the last wedge of Thailand's west coast, remote **SATUN** is served by just one road, Highway 406, which approaches the town through forbidding karst outcrops. Set in a green valley bordered by limestone hills, the town is leafy and relaxing but not especially interesting: the boat services to and from Malaysia are the main reason for farangs to come here, though some use the town as an approach to Thale Ban National Park (see p.408).

Frequent **buses** depart from Thanon Ratsada in Trang, and regular buses also come here from Hat Yai and from Phatthalung – if you don't get a direct bus from Phatthalung to Satun, you can easily change at **Rattaphum**, on the junction of highways 4 and 406. Buses arrive at the terminal on Thanon Satun Thani, the main road into town; share-taxis and air-con minibuses are based 400m southwest of the bus terminal around the junction of Thanon Saman Pradit (the main east–west thoroughfare) and Thanon Buriwanit, which runs parallel to Thanon Satun Thani. There's **internet access** at Satun CyberNet, 136 Thanon Satun Thani (daily 9am–10pm; B30 per hour).

From Satun, it's possible to travel into Malaysia by songthaew or longtail boat. Songthaews leave every thirty minutes from opposite the *Rian Thong* hotel, heading to the Malaysian border via Wang Prachan in the Thale Ban National Park. The border checkpoint lies 2km beyond the park headquarters, and share-taxis wait at Bukit Kayu Hitam on the other side to ferry you south to Alor Setar or Penang.

From Thammalang pier, 10km south of Satun at the mouth of the river, longtail boats leave when full on regular trips (daily 8am–3pm; 30min; B100 per person) to Kuala Perlis on Malaysia's northwest tip, from where there are plentiful transport connections down the west coast. Four ferry boats a day are scheduled to cross to the Malaysian island of Langkawi from Thammalang (currently departing at 8.30am, 10am, 1.30pm & 4pm; 50min); buy tickets (B180) from the town's main travel agent, Satun Travel and Ferry Service, opposite the *Pinnacle Wangmai Hotel* at 45/16 Thanon Satun Thani (☎074/711453, ✆721959), and check on departures, as they are sometimes cancelled if there are too few takers. Frequent songthaews (B20) and motorbike taxis (B100) run to Thammalang from the junction of Thanon Saman Pradit and Thanon Buriwanit, taking around thirty minutes. If you are entering Thailand by sea from Malaysia, be sure to report to the immigration office at Thammalang pier to have your passport stamped, otherwise you may have problems on your eventual departure from Thailand.

By the town pier, *Rian Thong*, 4 Thanon Saman Pradit (☎074/711036; ❷), is the best budget **hotel** in Satun; the owners are friendly, and some of the clean, well-furnished rooms overlook the canal. *Farm Gai* (☎074/730812; ❶), more or less in open country ten minutes' west of the centre (take a motorbike taxi; B20), is run by a Swiss who was once a pioneering bungalow-builder on Ko Samui. The comfortable, well-designed huts and rooms sit in a quiet, somewhat overgrown garden; the family prefers guests who will stay for a while to sample Thai country life, but don't insist on it. In complete contrast, *Pinnacle Wangmai Hotel*, out towards the bus depot at 43 Thanon Satun Thani (☎074/711607–8, ✆722162, ⓦwww.pinnaclehotels.com/satun.html; ❺), is a typical "deluxe" hotel with air-conditioned rooms in a modern concrete building; similar but more central is the newer *Sinkiat Thani*, 50 Thanon Buriwanit (☎074/721055–8, ✆721059; ❺), where large bedrooms offer good views over the surrounding countryside. For **food**, try *Yim Yim* on Thanon Saman Pradit by the Chinese temple, a clean and popular restaurant which serves good, simple Chinese food from 6pm onwards. A good daytime option for ice creams and moderately priced Thai food is the air-conditioned *Time Restaurant*, next door to the *Pinnacle Wangmai Hotel* on Thanon Satun Thani.

If you're thinking of visiting the Ko Tarutao National Marine Park, it's worth checking whether Satun Travel and Ferry Service (see box above) have reinstated their weekend boat service to Ko Lipe; this was dropped due to lack of demand, but may well start up again as the park becomes more popular. With a journey time of just under two hours, it's a good, quick route to the island.

## Thale Ban National Park

Spread over rainforested mountains along the Malaysian border, **THALE BAN NATIONAL PARK** is a pristine nature reserve which shelters a breathtaking variety of wildlife: from tapirs, Malayan sun bears and clouded leopards, to butterflies, which proliferate in March, and unusual birds such as bat hawks, booted eagles and flamboyant argus pheasants. Unfortunately for naturalists and casual visitors alike, few trails have been marked out through the jungle, but the lush, peaceful setting and the views and bathing pools of the Yaroy waterfall are enough to justify the trip.

**From Satun**, half-hourly songthaews leave from opposite *Rian Thong* hotel, passing through the village of **Wang Prachan** and reaching Thale Ban **headquarters** (☎074/797073), 2km further on, in an hour. **From Hat Yai**, share-taxis (B70) leave from opposite the post office north of the train station and take you straight through to the park headquarters.

Hemmed in by steep, verdant hills and spangled with red water lilies, the **lake** by the headquarters is central to the story that gives the park its name. Local legend tells how a villager once put his *ban* (headscarf) on a tree stump to have a rest; this caused a landslide, the lake appeared from nowhere, and he, the stump and the *ban* tumbled into it. The water is now surrounded by thirteen **bungalows** (B500–1000 per night depending on size), for which lower rates can be negotiated when business is slow. A **campsite** (B20 per person per night) with showers and toilets and a decent open-air **canteen** also overlook the lake.

One of the easiest trips from park headquarters brings you to **Tham Tondin**, a low, sweaty stalactite cave which gradually slopes down for 800m to deep water. It's about 2km north of headquarters back along the road to Khwan Sator – look out for the wooden sign in Thai, on the west side of the main road just north of kilometre-stone 18, then climb 30m up the slope to see the tiny entrance at your feet. If you time your visit so that you emerge just before dusk, you'll see hundreds of bats streaming out of the hole for the night. It's best to consult the detailed map at headquarters before you visit the cave, and you'll need a flashlight.

A more compelling jaunt, though, is to **Yaroy waterfall** – bring swimming gear for the pools above the main fall. Take the main road north from the headquarters through the narrow, idyllic valley for 6km (beyond the village of Wang Prachan) and follow the sign to the right. After 700m, you'll find the main, lower fall set in screeching jungle. Climbing the path on the left side, you reach what seems like the top, with fine views of the steep, green peaks to the west. However, there's more: further up the stream are a series of gorgeous shady pools, where you can bathe and shower under the six-metre falls.

The most interesting **jungle walk** heads northeast from the headquarters, then west, approaching Yaroy waterfall from above after 16km. The trail, often steep and arduous, is marked with yellow distance markers on trees every 500m, with more frequent orange tape around trees, but these tapes are sometimes pulled down by animals or people – someone at headquarters might be free to guide you for a small fee. If you set out early and at a decent pace, it's possible to complete the walk and get back from Yaroy waterfall to headquarters in a day (a minimum of about 8hr) or, if you're fully equipped, you could overnight at one of three marked **camping** areas by small streams near the trail. Along the way, you'll be rewarded with magnificent views that on a clear day stretch as far as the islands of Tarutao and Langkawi, you'll pass old elephant passages and mating playgrounds of argus pheasants, and you'll be unlucky not to spot at least boars, gibbons and bats.

## Ko Tarutao National Marine Park

The unspoilt **KO TARUTAO NATIONAL MARINE PARK** is probably the most beautiful of all Thailand's accessible beach destinations. Occupying 1400 square kilometres of the Andaman Sea, the park covers 51 mostly uninhabited islands, of which three – Ko Tarutao, Ko Adang and Ko Lipe – are easy

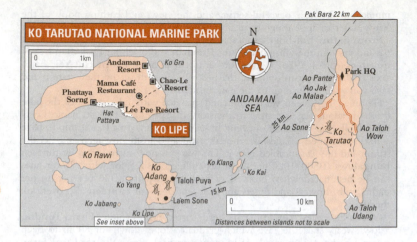

KO TARUTAO NATIONAL MARINE PARK

Pak Bara 22 km ▲

N

0    1km

Andaman
Resort            ○ Ko Gra

Mama Café
Restaurant         ■ Chao-Le
                      Resort
Phattaya
Sorng     ■
          ○  ■
Hat      Lée Pae Resort
Pattaya

KO LIPE

ANDAMAN
SEA

Ao Pante        ▲ Park HQ
Ao Jak
Ao Malae

25 km   Ao Sone

Ko
Tarutao   Ao Taloh
            Wow

Ko Rawi

Ko
Adang
         ● Taloh Puya
Ko Yang
              Ko Klang   ○ Ko Kai

Ko Jabang ○
          ● Laem Sone
       Ko Lipe

15 km

0                    10 km

Ao Taloh
Udang

See inset above    Distances between islands not to scale

to reach from the mainland port of **Pak Bara** and offer accommodation for
visitors. The area's forests and seas support an incredible variety of **fauna**: langurs, crab-eating macaques and wild pigs are common on the islands, which
also shelter several unique subspecies of squirrel, tree shrew and lesser mouse
deer; among the hundred-plus bird species found here, reef egrets and hornbills are regularly seen, while white-bellied sea eagles, frigate birds and pied
imperial pigeons are more rarely encountered; and the park is the habitat of
about 25 percent of the world's fish species, as well as marine mammals such as
the dugong, sperm whale and dolphins. The islands are also an important site
for **turtle egg-laying** (see box on p.331): Olive Ridley, green, hawksbill and
leatherback turtles lay their eggs on Ko Tarutao's sands between September and
April, green turtles on Ko Adang from September to December; park rangers
try to keep an eye on the nests and are generally happy to share the information with visitors. The park's delicate environment can bear the current level
of tourism, but will be disastrously disturbed if proposals to set up regular boat
connections with the highly developed Malaysian resort on Langkawi island,
8km from Ko Tarutao, are acted upon.

The park is officially **closed** to tourists from mid-May to mid-November
(the exact dates vary from year to year), when storms can make the sea passage
hazardous, and even in the open season, especially at its beginning or end, boats
won't leave if conditions are bad or there aren't enough passengers to break
even. On the other hand, private operators do still operate boat services to the
islands out of season if there's enough demand, and while the park amenities
on Tarutao and Adang islands remain closed outside the official months, the
private bungalow concerns on Ko Lipe generally open their doors before the
official season starts and remain open after it closes. Furthermore, as the Tarutao
archipelago increases in popularity, it's possible that the entire park may begin
to open year-round in the next few years – call the **Pak Bara visitor centre**
(℡074/781285) for the latest.

You should have no problem finding somewhere to stay except at the three
New Years (Thai, Chinese and Western), when it's best to book ahead in
Bangkok (see p.42). Outside of Ko Lipe, the west coast of Ko Tarutao has the
best facilities in the park. The *Traveler's Adventure Handbook* to Tarutao is a must-
buy at B40, though sometimes out of print – try Pak Bara's visitor centre (they

publish it) or the one at Ao Pante on Ko Tarutao. **Snorkelling gear** can be rented at either visitor centre or on Ko Adang for B50 per day, and is widely available from the private bungalow outfits on Ko Lipe. In recent years, several **diving** operations have started up in the Tarutao area; the best diving is to be found west of Ko Tarutao around Ko Klang, Ko Adang, Ko Rawi and Ko Dong, where encounters with whale and reef sharks, dolphins, stingrays and turtles are common. One of the longest-established operators is the Canadian-run Sabye Sports, 6 Soi 1, Thanon Prachayindee, Hat Yai (℡074/233288 or 01/897 8725 in Hat Yai, ℡01/230 8195 on Ko Lipe, ⓦwww.stgt.com/sabye /home.htm); also very reliable is the American-run Starfish Scuba, 166 Thanon Phattalung, Songkhla (℡074/321943 or 01/896 9319, ⓦwww.starfishscuba .com). For watery adventures above the surface, Paddle Asia, 93/6 Soi Samakit 2, Phuket (℡076/254742, ⓦwww.paddleasia.com), organizes small-group **sea-kayaking** trips around the Tarutao islands, costing US$100–150 per person per day.

## En route to Tarutao and Bulon Lae: Pak Bara

**From Trang**, Sukorn Beach Bungalows and Tours (see p.406) runs regular direct minibuses to **PAK BARA** in high season; at other times you'll need to take a Satun-bound bus (2hr 30min) or a share-taxi (1hr 30min) to the inland town of **Langu** and change there to a red songthaew for the ten-kilometre hop to the port. Frequent buses and taxis **from Satun** make the fifty-kilometre trip to Langu. Coming **from Hat Yai**, you're best off catching one of the air-conditioned minibuses (B60; 2hr) which leave every hour from an office on Thanon Prachathipat and take you all the way through to Pak Bara pier.

In season, **ferries** leave Pak Bara at 10.30am and 3pm daily for the ninety-minute voyage to Ao Pante on Ko Tarutao (B300 return); the 10.30am boat then continues on to Ko Adang (B800 return from Pak Bara), 40km west of Ko Tarutao, from where it's just a short longtail hop (B50) over to Ko Lipe. The Tarutao–Adang leg can take anything from two hours upwards, depending on the sea conditions. Coming back, boats leave Ko Adang at 9am, calling in at Ko Tarutao before returning to Pak Bara; there's also an additional 9am sailing from Ko Tarutao.

These ferries are supplemented by boats run by **private operators**, which set off regardless of the official season if there's enough demand and the sea conditions are safe; they charge the same as the ferries and leave when there's a full complement of passengers (generally in the early afternoon). If you're thinking of visiting the Tarutao islands out of season, it's best to call ahead to check if boats are running; Adang Sea Tours (℡074/781268 or 01/609 2604) is one of the most reliable operators, or you could try Udom Tour (℡01/963 6916 or 01/897 4755), Araya Travel (℡074/781212 or 01/306 0213) or Andrew Tour (℡074/781159 or 01/276 7866). All these operators have offices on the road leading up to Pak Bara pier; Araya Travel also offers **internet access**.

Simple **accommodation** is available in Pak Bara for people who miss the boats. The best choice is the friendly *Diamond Beach* (℡074/783138; ❷–❸), 500m before the pier, which offers well-kept bamboo A-frames and simpler concrete huts in a shady compound by the beach, and serves good food. Slightly cheaper – and closer to the pier – is the *Bara Guesthouse* (℡074/783068 or 01/478 6258; ❶–❷), which has some basic and rather dingy mattress-on-floor rooms as well as much nicer en-suite ones looking onto a small courtyard. At the time of writing, there were **no currency–exchange** facilities in Pak Bara or on the Tarutao islands, so you may well need to change money before you arrive.

## Ko Tarutao

The largest of the national park's islands, **KO TARUTAO** offers the greatest natural variety: mountains covered in semi-evergreen rainforest rise steeply to a high point of 700m; limestone caves and mangrove swamps dot the shoreline; and the west coast is lined with perfect beaches for most of its 26-kilometre length. The last of these is also where you'll find the park's best facilities for visitors outside Ko Lipe.

Boats dock at **Ao Pante**, on the northwestern side of the island, where the admission fee (B200) is collected and where the **park headquarters** is situated. Here you'll find the only shop on the island, selling basic supplies, as well as a visitor centre, a well-stocked library and a simple restaurant. The **bungalows** (from B300 per bungalow sleeping six), which are spread over a large, quiet park behind the beach, are for the main part national park standard issue with cold-water bathrooms, but there are also a couple of newer two- or three-person bungalows with air-conditioning (B750–1500 per bungalow) as well as some basic mattress-on-floor four-person rooms in **bamboo longhouses**, sharing bathrooms (B400 per room, or B100 per person). No mosquito nets are provided here, so come with your own or bring plenty of mosquito repellent. Two-person **tents** can be rented for B200 a night; campers with their own gear are charged B20 per person per night.

Behind the settlement, the steep, half-hour climb to **To-Boo cliff** is a must, especially at sunset, for the view of the surrounding islands and the crocodile's-head cape at the north end of the bay. A fun one-hour boat trip (B40 per person; contact the visitor centre to book) can also be made near Ao Pante, up the canal which leads 2km inland from the pier, through the lush leaves and dense roots of a bird-filled mangrove swamp, to the entrance to **Crocodile Cave** – where you're unlikely to see any of the big snappers, reported sightings being highly dubious.

A half-hour walk south from Ao Pante brings you to the two quiet bays of **Ao Jak** and **Ao Malae**, fringed by coconut palms and filled with fine white sand. Behind the house at the south end of Ao Malae, a road leads over the headland to **Ao Sone** (a 2hr walk from Ao Pante), where a pretty freshwater stream runs past the ranger station at the north end of the bay, making this a good place for peaceful camping. A favourite egg-laying site for sea turtles, the main part of the bay is a three-kilometre sweep of flawless sand, with a ninety-minute trail leading up to a waterfall in the middle and a mangrove swamp at the far south end.

On the east side of the island, **Ao Taloh Wow** is a rocky bay with a ranger station, connected to Ao Pante by a twelve-kilometre road through old rubber plantations and evergreen forest. If you have a tent, you might want to set off along the overgrown, five-hour trail beyond Taloh Wow, which cuts through the forest to **Ao Taloh Udang**, a sandy bay on the south side where you can set up camp. Here the remnants of a penal colony for political prisoners are just visible: the plotters of two failed coup attempts were imprisoned here in the 1930s before returning to high government posts. The ordinary convicts, who used to be imprisoned at Ao Taloh Wow, had a much harsher time, and during World War II, when supplies from the mainland dried up, prisoners and guards ganged together to turn to piracy. Pirates and smugglers still occasionally hide out in the Tarutao archipelago, but the main problem now is illegal trawlers fishing in national park waters.

## Ko Adang

At **KO ADANG**, a wild, rugged island covered in tropical rainforest, the boat pulls in at the **Laem Sone** park station on the southern shore, where the beach is steep and narrow and backed by a thick canopy of pines. As at Ao Pante, there are rooms in **bamboo longhouses** (B400 per room sleeping four, or B100 per person), sharing bathrooms; two–person **tents** can be rented (B200 a night), or campers can pitch their own tents for B20 per person per night. There's a **restaurant** here, though it's a bit pricey and only does a limited range of food.

The half-hour climb to **Sha–do** cliff on the steep slope above Laem Sone gives good views over the sand spit of the harbour and Ko Lipe to the south. About 2km west along the coast from the park station, the small beach is lined with coconut palms and an abandoned customs house, behind which a twenty-minute trail leads to the small **Pirate Waterfall**. For more ambitious explorations, the park handbook recommends "**snork-hiking**", an amphibious method of reaching distant attractions. Up the east coast, you can make such a day-trip to **Rattana waterfall**, 3km from the park station, and to the *chao ley* (see p.308) village of **Taloh Puya**, 1km further on, which has a fine coral reef directly offshore and a nice beach to the north.

## Ko Lipe

**KO LIPE**, 2km south of Adang, makes a busy contrast to the other islands. A small, flat triangle, it's covered in coconut plantations and inhabited by *chao ley*, with shops, a school and a health centre in the village on the eastern side. By rights, such a settlement should not be allowed within the national park boundaries, but the *chao ley* on Lipe are well entrenched: Satun's governor forced the community to move here from Ko Lanta between the world wars, to reinforce the island's Thai character and prevent the British rulers of Malaya from laying claim to it. Relations with park rangers have been strained in the past, but the park authority is working on a scheme to demarcate village and national park areas, which will hopefully go some way towards both resolving the tensions and preserving some of the island's natural beauty.

There are several **bungalow** outfits on the island, mostly operated by enterprising newcomers from the mainland rather than the indigenous *chao ley*. None is outstanding, but the best choices can be found on **Hat Pattaya**, a crescent of white sand 1km from the village on the south side of the island; this is also the prettiest beach on Ko Lipe, and has a good offshore reef to explore too. At the western end of the beach, the Italian–run *Phattaya Sorng* (②–④) has a lovely location: basic but clean bamboo huts, all with attached cold-water bathrooms and mosquito nets, are strung out behind the beach or up on the steep hillside, with the nicest of all perched high up on the rocks and accessed by precarious bamboo ladders. There's an excellent cosy restaurant – the most popular on the island – and fishing and snorkelling trips can be arranged if you want to visit the coral reefs around Ko Jabang and Ko Yang, on the west side of Adang. For paddling about around Lipe, sea **canoes** can be rented for B600 per day. The beach's other resort, the *Lee Pae Resort* (☎074/712181 or 01/896 5491; ③–⑤), has more facilities but less charm: its 75 bungalows range from pleasant concrete cottages with fan, screens and en-suite bathroom, to basic bamboo huts with mosquito nets and a mattress on the floor.

Over on the other side of the island, there are a couple more options on the beach in front of the village: the *Chao-Le Resort* (☎074/729201; ②–⑤) offers neat concrete en-suite bungalows and cheaper wooden huts in a sandy, scrubby compound under the pine trees, while the *Andaman Resort* (☎074/729200;

413

**❸–❹**) has bungalows of a similar standard in a more secluded spot away from the clutter of the village. *Andaman Resort* also has some two-person tents to rent for B100 per night, or you can pitch your own for B30. The beach on this side of the island is nowhere near as nice as Hat Pattaya, though there's rewarding water and a beautiful coral reef around tiny **Ko Gra**, 200m out to sea from the village.

Midway along the path that connects the two beaches, the pretty garden of the *Mama Cafe Restaurant*, owned and run by a friendly *chao ley* family, is a nice place to stop for a simple lunch of fried fish and rice, or go there for breakfast and sample its "*chao ley* pastries", tiny pancakes that come in eighteen different flavours.

## Ko Phetra National Marine Park

The thirty tiny islands of the **KO PHETRA NATIONAL MARINE PARK**, which sprinkle the sea between the Trang islands to the north and the Tarutao islands to the south, are for the most part inaccessible to tourists – with the notable exception of **Ko Bulon Lae** which, though it offically falls under the auspices of the park, has been allowed to develop much as it likes. A handful of the other islands can be visited on day-trips – there's fantastic snorkelling and diving, particularly around some of the more remote islands; Starfish Scuba (see p.411) organizes live-aboard **diving** excursions in the park.

The **park headquarters** (daily 8am–4.30pm; ☎074/783008) is on the mainland at Ao Noon, 4km south of Pak Bara (take a motorbike taxi); the staff here speak very little English, but they do have some leaflets on the park, and can advise on accommodation in **Ko Lidi**, one of the more accessible islands. Just 5km from the mainland (charter a longtail from Ao Noon for the 15min journey; B500), the quiet beaches of Ko Lidi are mainly popular with groups of Thai tourists; there are some simple eight-person tents (B300) available for visitors, but you'll need to bring your own mats, bedding and food. To the northwest, the steep limestone crags of **Ko Khao Yai** (charter a longtail) jut up from the water in fantastic gothic shapes; the lack of fresh water here means there's nowhere to stay, but there are some good coral reefs surrounding the island. The best snorkelling, however, is to be had at the more remote islands dotted around **Ko Phetra**, 40km or so from park headquarters just over the border in Trang province. These islands, with their small sandy coves and undisturbed reefs, are most easily and enjoyably reached through the excellent day-trips (Nov–May only) organized by *Sukorn Beach Bungalows* on nearby Ko Sukorn (see p.406). Ko Phetra itself, the main island of the group, is generally off-limits – there's big money in the birds' nests found here (see box on p.379) and concessions are jealously guarded – but trips take in the neighbouring islands of **Lao Lien** and **Takieng**, and it's even possible to camp overnight on the latter.

### Ko Bulon Lae

The scenery at tiny **KO BULON LAE**, 20km west of Pak Bara, isn't as beautiful as that found elsewhere along Andaman coast, but it's not at all bad: a two-kilometre strip of fine white sand runs the length of the casuarina-lined east coast, while *chao ley* fishermen make their ramshackle homes in the tight coves of the western fringe. A reef of curiously shaped hard coral closely parallels the eastern beach, while **White Rock** to the south of the island has beautifully coloured soft coral and equally dazzling fish. **Snorkelling** gear, as well as boats for day-trips to White Rock and surrounding islands (B1000 per boat seating up to eight people), can be rented at *Pansand*, the island's largest and best **resort** (☎01/397 0802, ℮pansand@cscoms.com; ❻–❼), where accommodation ranges from neat little bamboo huts to swanky clapboard cottages with bathrooms, fans and mosquito screens on the windows. On the beach side of the spacious, shady grounds, there's a sociable restaurant serving up good seafood and other Thai dishes. To book a room here or find out about boats in the off-season, contact the resort directly or First Andaman Travel at 82–84 Thanon Wisetkul in Trang (☎075/218035, ℱ211010). There are two other options on the island, both of which have fans and mosquito nets in all bungalows: nearby *Moloney* (❷–❹), which offers a choice of en-suite or shared bathroom; and, ten minutes' walk away in Ao Phangka Yai on the north coast, *Phangka Bay Resort*, with well-designed, en-suite bungalows (❸–❹) and a good restaurant.

**Ferries** for Ko Bulon Lae leave Pak Bara daily at 2pm (1hr 30min; B300 return), returning from the island at 9am the following day. They're scheduled to run roughly from November to April, but sometimes set off in the low season. In addition, private operators will generally stop off at Ko Bulon Lae on their way to Ko Tarutao if there is enough demand, or you can charter a long-tail (B1500 for up to five people).

# Hat Yai

**HAT YAI**, the transport axis of the region, was given a dose of instant American-style modernization in the 1950s, since when it's commercially usurped its own provincial capital, Songkhla. The resulting concrete mess, reminiscent of Bangkok without the interesting bits, attracts over a million tourists a year, nearly all of them Malaysians and Singaporeans who nip across the border to shop and get laid. If the concrete and the sleaze turn you off a protracted stay, remember that Songkhla (see p.419) is only 25km away.

Hat Yai is one of the south's major centres for **bullfighting**, which in its Thai version involves bull tussling with bull, the winner being the one which forces the other to retreat. Fights can last anything from a few seconds to half an hour, in which case the frantic betting of the audience becomes more interesting than the deadlock in the ring. Every weekend, day-long competitions, beginning between 9 and 10am, are held at various points around the south. Admission is usually B600–700 for the whole day, and it's best to get there in the early afternoon as the big fights, involving betting of up to one million baht, are lower down the card. It's worth checking with TAT for the latest information but, at the time of writing, the most convenient events are at Noen Khum Thong, 10km out of Hat Yai on the way to the airport, on the first Saturday of the month (charter a songthaew to get there); and on the fourth Saturday of the month at Ban Nam Krajai, 200m south of the Ko Yo intersection on the Hat Yai–Songkhla road (catch a bus towards Songkhla).

## Practicalities

On any extended tour of the south you are bound to end up in Hat Yai, and you may as well take the opportunity to call in at the **TAT** office for Songkhla and Satun provinces at 1/1 Soi 2, Thanon Niphat Uthit 3 (daily 8.30am–4.30pm; ☎074/243747, ℱ245986, ℮tatsgkhl@tat.or.th). The **tourist police** have an office at Thanon Sripoovanart on the south side of town

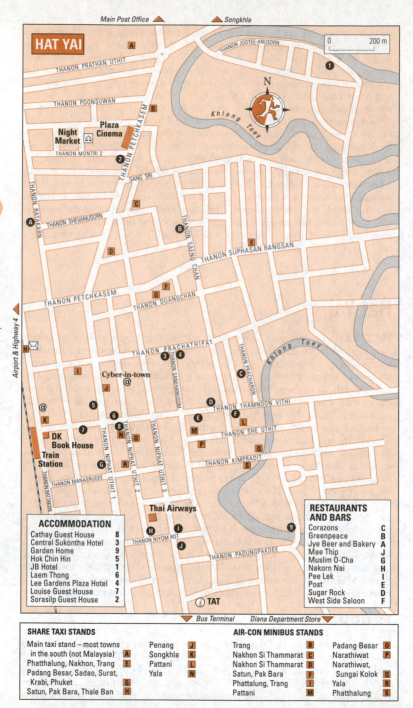

# HAT YAI

*Main Post Office*  ▲  ▲ *Songkhla*

THANON JOOTEE-ANUSORN

0    200 m

A

THANON PRATHAN UTHIT

THANON POONSUWAN

B

Khlong Toey

N

**Night Market**  **Plaza Cinema**

2

THANON MONTRI 2

THANON PETCHKASEM

SANG SRI

C

THANON SHEVANUSORN

A

THANON BATAKAN

D

B

THANON SAENG CHAN

E

THANON SUPHASAN RANGSAN

F

THANON PETCHKASEM

G

THANON DUANGCHAN

THANON PRACHATHIPAT

3  4

THANON SANEHANUSORM

C

THANON PRACHARON

Khlong Toey

**Cyber-in-town**
@

I

J

D

THANON THAMNOON VITHI

E

F  L

5

6

8

THANON NIPHAT UTHIT 1

N

O

THANON NIPHAT UTHIT 2

THANON NIPHAT UTHIT 3

M

P

THANON SHE UTHIT

7

@

K

**DK Book House**

**Train Station**

G

R

THANON KIMPRADIT

Q

S

THANON MANASRUDEE

THANON BATAKAN

**Thai Airways**

H

I

THANON NIYOM ROT

J

9

THANON PADUNGPAKDEE

ℹ **TAT**

**Airport & Highway 4** ◄
H ✉

## ACCOMMODATION

| | |
|---|---|
| Cathay Guest House | 8 |
| Central Sukontha Hotel | 3 |
| Garden Home | 9 |
| Hok Chin Hin | 5 |
| JB Hotel | 1 |
| Laem Thong | 6 |
| Lee Gardens Plaza Hotel | 4 |
| Louise Guest House | 7 |
| Sorasilp Guest House | 2 |

## RESTAURANTS AND BARS

| | |
|---|---|
| Corazons | C |
| Greenpeace | B |
| Jye Beer and Bakery | A |
| Mae Thip | J |
| Muslim O-Cha | G |
| Nakorn Nai | H |
| Pee Lek | I |
| Post | E |
| Sugar Rock | D |
| West Side Saloon | F |

▼ *Bus Terminal*    *Diana Department Store* ▼

## SHARE TAXI STANDS

| | |
|---|---|
| Main taxi stand – most towns in the south (not Malaysia) | A |
| Phatthalung, Nakhon, Trang | E |
| Padang Besar, Sadao, Surat, Krabi, Phuket | G |
| Satun, Pak Bara, Thale Ban | H |
| Penang | J |
| Songkhla | K |
| Pattani | L |
| Yala | N |

## AIR-CON MINIBUS STANDS

| | | | |
|---|---|---|---|
| Trang | B | Padang Besar | O |
| Nakhon Si Thammarat | C | Narathiwat | P |
| Nakhon Si Thammarat | D | Narathiwat, | |
| Satun, Pak Bara | F | Sungai Kolok | Q |
| Phattalung, Trang | I | Yala | R |
| Pattani | M | Phatthalung | S |

Hat Yai is only 50km from the border with **Malaysia**. The fastest way of getting across (5–6hr) is to take a **share-taxi** to Penang (where you can renew your visa at the Thai consulate); taxis depart every morning for about B250. Tickets for the more comfortable and slightly less expensive **air-conditioned minibuses** to Penang (B220) can be bought at Hat Yai travel agents, such as Cathy Tour at 93 Thanon Niphat Uthit 2 (☎074/235044), or Golden Way, 132 Thanon Niphat Uthit 3 (☎074/233917). Both these agents also handle minibuses to Sungai Kolok (3hr; B170), Alor Setar (3hr; B230) and Butterworth (5hr; B230), and VIP buses to Kuala Lumpur (12hr; B350) and Singapore (18hr; B550). The least expensive but most time-consuming method is to catch a **bus** to Padang Besar (every 15min; 1hr 40min), walk 800m across the border and take a share-taxi to Kuala Perlis (30min) or Alor Setar (1hr) – avoid the obvious route straight down Highway 4 to Sadao, because there's a long stretch between the opposing border posts which there's no inexpensive way of covering.

Most comfortable are the **trains**, though they're not very frequent: two a day run from Hat Yai to Sungai Kolok on the east-coast border, and one a day heads to Butterworth (for the ferry to Penang or trains on to Kuala Lumpur) via the frontier at Padang Besar.

(☎074/246733), and the **immigration office** is on Thanon Petchkasem (☎074/243019). The three central Niphat Uthit roads are known locally as *sai neung, sai sawng* and *sai saam*.

If you're leap-frogging into the deep south via Hat Yai **airport** you'll arrive 12km from town, then be shuttled into the centre by shared minibus (B50) or taxi (B240) straight to your destination; there are regular minibuses back to the airport from the Thai Airways office at 190/6 Thanon Niphat Uthit 2 (☎074/234238) – the schedule is displayed outside. The smooth passage of Malaysian and Singaporean dirty-weekenders is facilitated by regular flights between Hat Yai and Johor Bahru, Kuala Lumpur, Kota Kinabalu, Kuching and Miri (all operated by Malaysia Airlines), and Singapore (Thai Airways).

The **train station** is on the west side of the centre at the end of Thanon Thamnoon Vithi, and contains a useful left-luggage office (daily 6am–6pm; B10 per piece per day); the **bus terminal** is far to the southeast of town on Thanon Kanchanawanit, leaving you with a songthaew ride to the centre, but most buses make a stop at the Plaza Cinema on Thanon Petchkasem, on the north side of the centre. **Share-taxis** and **air-conditioned minibuses** should drop you off at your destination; for departure, they have a number of different ranks around town (marked on the map opposite) according to where you want to go. Both Avis (☎074/352239, ✉hdy@avisthailand.com) and Budget (☎074/239033–4, ✉brachy6@budget.co.th) have **car-rental** desks at the *Central Sukontha* hotel (see p.418), with daily rates starting from around B1400 for a jeep; Avis has another desk at the airport (☎074/227259).

There's central **internet access** opposite the station at 4/4 Thanon Rattakan (daily 9.30am–8.30pm; B25 per hour), and at the swish Cyber-in-town, 56 Thanon Niphat Uthit 2 (Mon–Fri 10am–10pm, Sat 9am–10pm & Sun 9am–4pm; B40 per hour) – the latter has drinks and snacks available. DK Book House, just by the station at 2/4–5 Thanon Thamnoon Vithi, is a good **bookshop** with a small but reasonably priced selection of English-language titles.

The helpful Cathy Tour (see box above) can **book flights** as well as bus tickets, and also runs private minibus services to many popular tourist destinations. C & P Tour, 129/1 Thanon Niphat Uthit 3 (☎074/233388, ✉232243) offers an unusual minibus **tour** to **Khao Namkhang**, 80km south of Hat Yai near Sadao, to see the complex of tunnels here, an erstwhile hideout of the Communist Party of Malaya (see also p.396 & p.428).

## Accommodation

Hat Yai has a huge range of **hotels**, none of them very good value and most worked by prostitutes, though a few in the budget range are geared to travellers.

**Cathay Guest House**, 93 Thanon Niphat Uthit 2 ☎074/243815, ☏354104. This friendly place is falling apart, but the fittings are reasonably clean; the café acts as a sociable meeting-place (and shows Western movies nightly), and the information board and guest comment books are guidebooks in themselves. Dorm beds B90. ②

**Central Sukontha Hotel**, 3 Thanon Sanehanusom ☎074/352222, ☏352223, ✉sukontha@hatdyai.loxinfo.co.th. Luxury hotel in a handy central location next to the Central Department Store. Offers great views over the city from its two top-notch restaurants and coffee bar. ⑧

**Garden Home**, southeast of the centre at 51/2 Thanon Hoi Mook ☎074/236047, ☏224444. This pastiche of a grand mansion built around a plant-filled courtyard offers very good value; the large bedrooms show some sense of decor and boast a good range of facilities (air-con, hot water, TV and mini-bar). ⑤

**Hok Chin Hin**, 87 Thanon Niphat Uthit 1 ☎074/243258, ☏350131. The best of many cheap Chinese hotels around the three central Niphat Uthit roads. Offers rooms with en-suite bathrooms and ceiling fans or air-con above a café serving noodle soups and other simple fare. ②–③

**JB Hotel**, 99 Thanon Jootee-Anusorn ☎074/234300–18, ☏234328, ⒲www.jb-hotel.com. Hat Yai's best hotel furnishes quite enough luxury to justify the price – among the highlights are a large swimming pool, a top-class Chinese restaurant and the *Jazz Bistro*, a civilized place for Thai and Western fare or just a drink. ⑧

**Laem Thong**, 46 Thanon Thamnoon Vithi ☎074/352301, ☏237574, ✉laemthong99@hotmail.com. Large and efficient Chinese-run place, with a choice of fan-cooled or air-con rooms, most with hot water. ②–④

**Lee Gardens Plaza Hotel**, 29 Thanon Prachatipat ☎074/261111, ☏353555. Upmarket option with great views of the city from its comfortable rooms. Facilities include a pool and jacuzzi. ⑥

**Louise Guest House**, by the train station at 21–23 Thanon Thamnoon Vithi ☎074/220966. Clean and very friendly Chinese-run place, with much the same facilities as the larger, more impersonal *Laem Thong*, though the fan-cooled rooms here are a little overpriced. ③–④

**Sorasilp Guest House**, 251/7–8 Thanon Petchkasem ☎074/232635. On the upper floors of a modern building beside the Plaza Cinema. Friendly and clean, though a little noisy. ②

## Eating, drinking and nightlife

Hat Yai's **restaurants**, a selection of which are listed below, offer a choice of Thai, Chinese, Muslim and Western food, while the sprawling **night market**, behind the Plaza Cinema on Thanon Montri 2, has something for everyone: seafood and beer, Thai curries, deep-fried chicken and the Muslim speciality *khao neua daeng*, tender cured beef in a sweet red sauce.

For a quiet **drink**, head for *Sugar Rock*, 114 Thanon Thamnoon Vithi, a pleasant café-bar with low-volume Western music. More lively are *West Side Saloon*, on the same road at no. 135/5, and *Corazons Latin Pub and Restaurant*, at 41 Thanon Pracharom – both are extremely popular nightspots, with excellent house bands that cover everything from Thai country music and "songs for life" to 1970s disco. To get away from it all, the five mini-theatres at Diana department store, on Thanon Sripoovanart on the south side of the centre, show Western **movies** with English soundtracks.

**Greenpeace Restaurant**, 50 Thanon Saeng Chan. Comes as a pleasant surprise in Hat Yai, with its leafy patio overlooking a quiet road; it's popular with local expats and offers a good menu of Thai and Western food. Open from 5pm.

**Jye Beer and Bakery**, Thanon Ratakarn. Good for a bit of a splurge – they do posh Thai and American food in a cosy, rustic atmosphere.

**Mae Thip**, 187/4 Niphat Uthit 3. Good reliable Thai place, popular with locals; also does a few Malay dishes, including satay.

**Muslim O-Cha**, 117 Niphat Uthit 1. A simple, clean restaurant which serves small portions of curried chicken and rice, and other inexpensive Muslim dishes. Daily until 8.30pm.

**Nakorn Nai**, 166/7 Niphat Uthit 2. Cool and comfortable, this is a reasonable place for all-day breakfasts, Western food and some interesting Thai dishes.

**Pee Lek 59**, 185/4 Niphat Uthit 3, at the junction with Thanon Niyom Rot. This welcoming place gets the thumbs-up for moderately priced Thai-style seafood – try *gataa rawn*, a sizzling dish of mixed marine life.

**Post**, Thanon Thamnoon Vithi. Popular with farangs, this comfy, spacious restaurant-bar has a large Western menu and shows nonstop music videos.

# Songkhla and around

Known as the "big town of two seas" because it sits on a north–pointing peninsula between the Gulf of Thailand and the **Thale Sap** lagoon, **SONGKHLA** provides a sharp contrast to Hat Yai. A small, sophisticated provincial capital, it retains many historic buildings – such as the elegant Wat Matchimawat and the Chinese mansion that now houses the National Museum – and its broad, quiet streets are planted with soothing greenery. With some fine restaurants and excellent accommodation, and its proximity to the wonderful Southern Folklore Museum at Ko Yo, Songkhla makes a stimulating place in which to hole up for a few days.

The settlement was originally sited on the north side of the mouth of the Thale Sap, where a deepwater port has now been built, and flourished as a **trading port** from the eighth century onwards. The shift across the water came after 1769, when a Chinese merchant named Yieng Hao was granted permission by the Thai ruler, Taksin, to collect swallows' nests from Ko Si Ko Ha – now part of Khu Khut Waterbird Park. Having made a packet from selling them for their culinary and medicinal properties, he was made governor of Songkhla by Taksin and established the city on its present site. For seven generations the **Na Songkhla dynasty** he founded kept the governorship in the family, overseeing the construction of many of the buildings you see today. The town is now an unhurried administrative centre, which maintains a strong central Thai feel – most of the province's Muslim population live in the hinterland.

## The Town

The town which the Na Songkhlas built has expanded to fill the headland, and makes a great place for strolling around. The western side, where the town first developed, shelters a fishing port which presents a vivid, smelly scene in the mornings. Two abrupt hills – **Khao Tung Kuan** and the smaller **Khao Noi** – border the north side of the centre, while in the heart of town lie the main tourist attractions, the **National Museum** and the extravagantly decorated **Wat Matchimawat**. Sitting on the fringe of town at the southern end of Hat Samila – the 8km of beach along the eastern shore – **Khao Saen** is an impoverished but vibrant fishing village, whose multicoloured boats provide

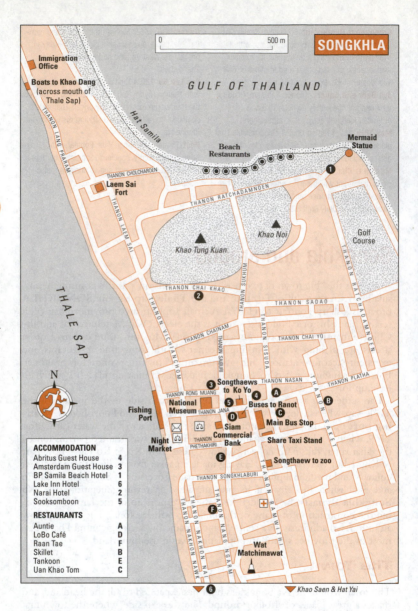

**SONGKHLA**

GULF OF THAILAND

Immigration Office

Boats to Khao Dang (across mouth of Thale Sap)

Hat Samila

Mermaid Statue

Beach Restaurants

❶

THANON LANG PHRAAM

Laem Sai Fort

THANON CHOLCHAROEN

THANON RATCHADAMNOEN

Khao Noi

Golf Course

Khao Tung Kuan

THANON LAEM SAI

THANON CHAI KHAO

THANON SUKHUM

❷

THALE SAP

THANON VICHIANCHOM

THANON CHAINAM

THANON SAIBURI

THANON SADAO

THANON SISUDA

THANON CHAI YO

N

THANON RONG MUANG

❸ Songthaews to Ko Yo

THANON NASAN

❹ Ⓐ

THANON PLATHA

Ⓑ

Fishing Port

National Museum

THANON JANA

Ⓖ Buses to Ranot

Ⓒ Main Bus Stop

THANON RATCHADAMNOEN

Night Market

THANON PHETHAKHIRI

Siam Commercial Bank

Share Taxi Stand

THANON SAKET

Ⓔ

Songthaew to zoo

THANON SONGKHLABURI

THANON BAMWITHII

THANON NAKHON NAWK

THANON NANG NGARM

Ⓕ

✚

Wat Matchimawat

❻

Khao Saen & Hat Yai

**ACCOMMODATION**

| | |
|---|---|
| Abritus Guest House | 4 |
| Amsterdam Guest House | 3 |
| BP Samila Beach Hotel | 1 |
| Lake Inn Hotel | 6 |
| Narai Hotel | 2 |
| Sooksomboon | 5 |

**RESTAURANTS**

| | |
|---|---|
| Auntie | A |
| LoBo Café | D |
| Raan Tae | F |
| Skillet | B |
| Tankoon | E |
| Uan Khao Tom | C |

0          500 m

Songkhla's most hackneyed postcard image. If you're about on a Sunday, don't miss the hectic **morning market** – the largest in southeast Thailand – which fills the streets around Songkhla's main bus stop.

### Khao Tung Kuan, Laem Sai Fort and Hat Samila

420

To get your bearings, climb up **Khao Tung Kuan** at the northwestern end of town; unfortunately the hill has become something of a hangout for local drug addicts, so it's safest to avoid it in the early morning and the evening, especially if you're on your own. From Thanon Laem Sai, on the western side of the hill, steps rise past simple monks' huts which surround what looks like a red-brick Wendy house – Rama V ordered the pavilion to be built at the height of his westernization programme, but the local artisans clearly couldn't get their heads round the monarch's conception. From the chedi at the top of the hill, you can look south over the town and the fishing port, and west over the Thale Sap to the island of Ko Yo. On the eastern side of the hill, down on the road that runs between Khao Tung Kuan and Khao Noi, you'll often see people turning up in the late afternoon to feed fruit to the macaque monkeys that live on the two hills.

Further up Thanon Laem Sai, you can visit **Laem Sai Fort**, with its low walls and cannon, which was built by the French in the seventeenth century, when they held favour with the kings of Ayutthaya. Just beyond lies palm-fringed **Hat Samila**; its famous **mermaid statue**, the symbol of the town, lies a few hundred metres east along the beach in front of the *BP Samila Beach Hotel*.

## Songkhla National Museum

The **Songkhla National Museum** (Wed–Sun 9am–noon & 1–4pm; B30) on Thanon Jana, the main east–west street, is worth a visit for its architecture alone. Built in 1878 in south Chinese style and recently renovated to its original condition, this graceful mansion was first the residence of the governor of Songkhla and Nakhon, then the city hall, and later the local poorhouse before being converted into a museum in the 1970s. Its best side faces the garden at the back: from here you can see how the ornamental staircases and the roof were constructed in shapely curves to disorientate straight-flying evil spirits.

A jumble of folk exhibits, such as masks for the *manohra* (the southern Thai dance-drama) and agricultural implements, are strewn around the garden, while inside the wildly diverse collection includes well-preserved examples of Ban Chiang pottery, early Hindu statues and Mahayana Buddhist images from the Srivijaya period, and a selection of beautiful Chinese ceramics. Upstairs everything is upstaged by overblown Chinese and Thai furniture, all lacquer and mother-of-pearl and bas-relief carving.

## Wat Matchimawat

From the museum, you can explore the atmospheric old streets of Nakhon Nai and Nakhon Nawk, which show European influence in their colonnaded pavements and crumbling stucco, on your way south to **Wat Matchimawat**, a grand, attention-grabbing affair set in ornamental grounds on Thanon Saiburi. What stands out most of all is the bot, a florid mixture of Chinese and Thai styles, which was apparently modelled on Wat Phra Kaeo in Bangkok. Fetching stone bas-reliefs decorate the low walls around the bot, depicting leafy scenes from the *Romance of the Three Kingdoms*, a Chinese historical novel which served as a handbook of manners and morals in the middle of the nineteenth century, when the temple was built. Every centimetre of the lofty interior is covered with colourful *Jataka* murals, telling of the previous lives of the Buddha, mixed in with vivacious tableaux of nineteenth-century Songkhla life. The bot is usually locked, but you can get the key from the adjacent informal museum (daily, irregular hours), which is filled with ceramics, votive tablets, stuffed animals and other clutter.

## Khao Saen

To see the best of the Muslim shanty village of **Khao Saen**, set against a rocky headland on the southern edge of Songkhla's tide of development, visit in the

late afternoon, when the boisterous fish market is in full swing (except Fri). Songthaews from Thanon Platha make the trip in fifteen minutes. The crowded, rotting shacks of the village make a bleak contrast with the objects for which Khao Saen is most celebrated – its decorated prawn-fishing vessels. Drawn up in rows on the beach, these immaculate small boats have dragon prows wrapped in lucky garlands and hulls brightly painted with flags and intricate artwork. These pictures, which mostly depict mosques and idyllic landscapes, are the work of an artist at Saiburi, further down the coast (see p.431), and cost each fisherman a month's income.

## Practicalities

Most **buses** arrive at the major junction of Thanon Ramwithi with Jana and Platha roads. People usually come here straight from Hat Yai, 25km southwest, but buses also run direct from Nakhon. **Taxis** for these towns and places further afield congregate on the south side of the main bus stop, just off Thanon Ramwithi. If the heat gets to you as you stroll around town, catch one of the **songthaews** (B5–10 per person) or motorbike taxis (B10–20) which cruise the streets. **Mountain bikes** can be rented at the *Amsterdam Guest House* for B100 per day, and they also have some motorbikes available (B200 per day), useful for getting to Songkhla zoo and Ko Yo. *LoBo Café* can also arrange motorbike and car rental (B200/B800 per day respectively).

There are several places for **internet access** around town, including Dot Com (Mon–Sat 8am–10pm, Sun 9am–10pm; B40 per hour), next door to the *Abritus Guest House*, and E-Milk, 72 Thanon Saiburi (daily 11am–9pm; same price); the latter also sells coffee, fruit shakes, pizza and waffles. Several **banks** with ATMs can be found in the centre, including Siam Commercial Bank on Thanon Saiburi. The **post office** is on Thanon Nakhon Nai. Songkhla's **immigration office** is at 1/65 Thanon Lang Praram (Mon–Fri 8.30am–4.30pm; ☎074/313480).

### Accommodation

Budget travellers are spoilt for choice when it comes to **places to stay** in Songkhla, with a couple of excellent guest houses. For more luxury, the recently refurbished *BP Samila Beach* provides all the creature comforts.

**Abritus Guest House**, 28/16 Thanon Ramwithi ☎074/326047, ⓔ abritus_th@yahoo.com. Scores high on friendliness; the Bulgarian family who run the place are especially welcoming, and a mine of information on the town. Huge clean rooms with shared bathrooms are set above a popular café which dishes up great breakfasts – including German bread and filter coffee – as well as salads, omelettes and Bulgarian meatballs. ❷

**Amsterdam Guest House**, at 15/3 Thanon Rong Muang on the north side of the museum ☎074/314890. Of Songkhla's budget places to stay, this homely vine-covered place is best geared up to backpackers. The rooms, with shared bathrooms, are bright and clean; there's cable TV, lots of handy brochures, an English-language library and a relaxed downstairs seating area

that's well equipped with comfy sofas monopolized by dozing cats. Outside is a small shady patio, and next door an excellent little restaurant serves up beer and toasties alongside the delicious Thai dishes. ❷

**BP Samila Beach Hotel**, 8 Thanon Ratchadamnoen ☎074/440222, ⓕ 440442. The best hotel in town, with outdoor swimming pools, a herb steamroom and the beach right on its doorstep; rooms come with sea or "mountain" view. ❻–❼

**Lake Inn Hotel**, 301 Thanon Nakhon Nawk ☎074/321441–2, ⓕ 321044. Good hotel 500m south of the centre close by the Thale Sap lagoon; half of the tastefully furnished rooms face the lake and there's a good ground-floor restaurant, also with views of the water. ❺

**Narai Hotel**, 14 Thanon Chai Khao
ⓣ074/311078. Another friendly place situated in a
quiet, rambling wooden house at the foot of Doi
Tung Kuan. Good value; the cheapest of the budget
options in Songkhla. ❷

**Sooksomboon 2**, 18 Thanon Saiburi
ⓣ074/323809–10, ⓕ321406. Comfortable air-con
rooms, all with hot-water bathrooms, at this good-
value, centrally located hotel. ❹

### Eating and drinking

A good spot for **breakfast** is the cosy *LoBo Café* at 10/1 Thanon Jana, which
offers a huge list of pancakes alongside the usual Western breakfasts. For daytime eating, pull up a deck chair and relax at the shaded beach **restaurants**
which congregate at the northern end of Thanon Sukhum and at the east
end of Thanon Platha; or saunter down to the quiet and clean *Tankoon
Restaurant*, 25/1 Thanon Saiburi (closes 8.30pm), where you can relax with a
beer and some tasty Thai fodder in its peaceful leafy interior; the attached
**coffee shop**, *Coffeebucks*, serves delicious iced coffee. Songkhla's most
famous restaurant, *Raan Tae*, at 85 Thanon Nang Ngarm, is spotlessly clean
and justly popular, serving especially good seafood – but it's closed between
2pm and 5pm, and after 8pm. Also specializing in seafood, as well as the rice
porridge of its name, is *Uan Khao Tom*, Talat Rot Fai, where you can relax
outdoors on a quiet street under fairy lights (opens 6pm). The **night
market**, south of the post office on Thanon Nakhon Nai, is the place for
budget-conscious travellers.

A ghetto of Westernized **bars** and restaurants on Saket, Sisuda and Sadao
roads caters to the good ole boys who work on the offshore oil rigs: places such
as the *Skillet* ("vittles and stuff"), on Thanon Saket near Platha, and *Auntie*,
62/1 Thanon Sisuda, are open until midnight and serve good American-style
food and ice-cold beers, at a price.

## Around Songkhla

The excellent **Southern Folklore Museum** on Ko Yo is the biggest draw
outside Songkhla; a visit there is best combined with lunch at one of the
island's renowned seafood restaurants. Slightly further afield, the **Khu Khut
Waterbird Park** is similar to, though not as impressive as, Thale Noi (see
p.398) near Phatthalung, but if you're not planning to visit Phatthalung, it's
worth coming here on a day-trip.

### Ko Yo

**KO YO**, the small island in the Thale Sap to the west of Songkhla, has long
been a destination for day-trippers, and the road link with the land on both
sides of the lagoon has accelerated the transformation of **Ban Nok** – the
island's main settlement – into a souvenir market. Here you'll find durian cakes,
an amazing variety of dried and treated seafood, and the high-quality fabrics –
mostly cotton, but sometimes with small amounts of silk woven in – for which
Ko Yo is famous; if you're around in the morning, you can fork left off the main
road in the village to watch the weavers at work in their houses.

The best way of getting there **from Songkhla** is by songthaew (B10), which
set off at regular intervals from Thanon Jana, opposite the *LoBo Café*.
Alternatively, take one of the frequent Ranot-bound buses (every 30min; B5),
which depart from the same street and take half an hour to get to Ko Yo, before
continuing to Khu Khut Waterbird Park. If you're coming **from Hat Yai**,
there's no need to go into Songkhla first: take a Songkhla-bound bus or

minibus but get off on the edge of the suburbs at the junction with Highway 408, and catch a songthaew or bus across the bridge to Ko Yo.

The chief appeal of Ko Yo is the **Southern Folklore Museum** (daily 8.30am–5pm; B50), which sprawls over the hillside on the northern tip of Ko Yo just before the northern bridge. Affording stunning views over the water to Songkhla and of the fishing villages on the western side of the island, the park is strewn with all kinds of boats and wooden reproductions of traditional southern houses, in which the collections are neatly set out. The exhibits inside, such as the shadow-puppet paraphernalia and the *kris* – long knives with intricately carved handles and sheaths – show the strong influences of Malaysia and Indonesia on southern Thailand. Also on show are the elaborate dance costumes for the *manohra*, but probably the most fascinating objects are the *lek kood*, or coconut scrapers, which are set into seat-blocks carved into an offbeat variety of shapes – rabbits, elephants, phalluses, beauty queens. The museum's **shop** has the island's finest selection of fabrics, and there's a pleasant **café** with great views over the museum rooftops to the fishing villages below. Better still are the panoramas from the top of the **viewing tower** in the museum courtyard.

Ko Yo is renowned for its excellent seafood **restaurants**. One hundred metres south of the museum, a short slip road leads up to the popular *Suan Kaeo*, in a breezy spot overlooking the Thale Sap and Songkhla – try *hor mok thalay*, mixed fresh seafood in a chilli and coconut sauce. Alternatively, follow the access road to the museum west around the island for 200m to reach a couple of simpler places right on the water's edge – *Ko Kaeng* and *Ko Tong* – both with great seafood.

### Khu Khut Waterbird Park

About 40km up Highway 408 from Songkhla, a left turn by the police station leads after 2km to the headquarters of **Khu Khut Waterbird Park**, a conservation area on the Thale Luang where over 140 species of mostly migratory birds are found. Ranot-bound buses only drop you off at the junction, from where you can take a motorbike taxi (B20) to reach the park. The best time of year to visit is from January to March, and the birds are at their most active in the early morning and late afternoon. A longtail trip to view the birds costs B200 for an hour, while for B400 you get a two-hour jaunt across the shallow lake, weaving between water reeds and crayfish traps, to **Ko Si Ko Ha**, the dramatic limestone islands where birds' nests (see box on p.379) are gathered for Chinese gourmets. However, you won't be able to set foot on the islands as the concession-holders jealously guard their hugely profitable business from spies and thieves.

### Songkhla Zoo

Songkhla's newest attraction, **Songkhla zoo** (daily 9am–6pm; B30), is situated some 15km south of the city on Highway 408, the Songkhla–Nathawi road. It's a huge place, spread over eleven square kilometres of hills, so making your way around it can be rather tiring – though the benefit of the elevation is the great view it gives back over Songkhla and Ko Yo. As yet the zoo is rather sparsely populated with animals, but it's growing fast, and plans in the future to become a breeding centre for tapirs. The easiest way to get here is to hire a motorbike from the *Amsterdam Guest House* or *LoBo Café* in Songkhla (see p.423); this gives the added benefit of a means of transport around the zoo itself (for an additional B10 entry fee). Alternatively, take a Chana-bound songthaew from Thanon Ramwithi (B10).

# Pattani

**PATTANI**, the traditional centre of the Muslim south, is a rather forbidding town, but presents a fascinating cultural clash embodied by the discord between its polychrome Chinese temples and the remains of its sixteenth-century mosque. Founded around the beginning of the fifteenth century, not long after the introduction of Islam to the area, Pattani soon became an important port for trade in the Gulf of Thailand. The port eventually declined when the river silted up and became no longer easily navigable, but the industry and fisheries which in recent years have been established around the town have turned it into a busy, though rather ugly, commercial centre.

From the time of its founding, Pattani owed allegiance to the Thai kings at Ayutthaya, and after the capital was moved to Bangkok the city-state was fully integrated into Thailand. However, having close ties with fellow Islamic states to the south, it has always chafed against the central power – the separatist Pattani United Liberation Organization originated here – though in recent years a more positive relationship has developed. Pattani is also home to a sizeable Chinese community, whose rivalry with Islam is enshrined in the town's most famous legend. In the 1570s a certain Lim Toh Khiem, a notorious Chinese pirate, married a local woman and was converted to Islam. To show his conviction in his new faith, he began building a mosque – at which point, legend has it, his sister Lim Ko Niaw sailed from China to persuade him to renounce Islam and return to his homeland. When her mission failed she hanged herself from the nearest cashew-nut tree, which was later carved into a statue of her, preserved at the **San Jao Lim Ko Niaw**. The shrine, located on Thanon Arnoaru (a side street off the northern stretch of Thanon Yarang, the main north–south street), is gaudy and dimly lit, groaning with rich offerings and grimy with the soot of endless joss sticks; the doll-like image of Lim Ko Niaw is its centrepiece. During the annual Lim Ko Niaw festival, held in the mini-stadium opposite in the middle of the third lunar month (usually March), the image is carried through a raging bonfire by entranced devotees, who by this and other masochistic feats seek to prove their purity to their heroine goddess.

Lim Ko Niaw's suicide put a curse on her brother's mosque, the **Masjid Kreu Se**, which confounded his and his successors' attempts to finish it. Located 5km east of town towards Narathiwat, the roofless brick shell has an unofficial Muslim guard stationed near the entrance to prevent non-Muslims from walking onto the holy ruins. Next door to the mosque the Chinese have built an ostentatious shrine around the horseshoe burial mound of Lim Ko Niaw. The mosque can be visited by songthaew or bus from Thanon Ramkomud, the eastern continuation of Thanon Rudee, whose intersection with Thanon Yarang marks the centre of town.

## Practicalities

Facilities for visitors are very limited, though at a pinch the town can be visited on a long day-trip from Hat Yai or as a break in the journey south; the **bus station** is towards the south end of Thanon Yarang, and share-taxis and minibuses are clustered a kilometre or so north on the same road. The pick of a pitiful choice of budget **hotels** in Pattani is the central *Palace*, on Thanon Preeda, between Thanon Pipit and Thanon Rudee (☎073/349711; **②–③**), which has reasonably clean fan-cooled and air-conditioned rooms. Those who can afford it are much better off upgrading to the luxury *CS Pattani*, 299 Moo 4, Thanon Nongchik, on the western outskirts of town (☎073/335093–4; **⑦**). There's good, though pricey,

THE DEEP SOUTH | Pattani

Chinese **food** at the *London Restaurant* at 89/5 Thanon Yarang; cheaper and just as tasty is the fare at the busy night market on the north side of Thanon Pipit.

# South to Yala and the border

From Pattani, Highway 410 heads due south to **Yala**, a dull but efficient town 43km across the coastal plain, then on for 140km through the mountains to **Betong**, the most southerly point on the Thai–Malaysian border. This makes a quiet, scenic route into Malaysia but otherwise has little to offer.

## Yala

**YALA** is the business and education centre of the Muslim border provinces, a town of tree-lined boulevards that's won awards as the cleanest town in Thailand. An uninspiring place, its liveliest time is during the **ASEAN Barred Ground Dove Festival**, usually in the first weekend of March, when hundreds of competitors flock here from all over Southeast Asia. The breeding of luck-bringing Java doves is an obsession among the Muslim population of the south, where most houses have a bird cage outside and many villages feature fields of metal poles six to eight metres tall on which to hang the cages during the competition season, which is normally March and April. The birds are judged on the pitch, melody and volume of their cooing and on their appearance; the most musical specimens change hands for as much as two million baht at the Yala jamboree.

Though staunchly Islamic (the town is home to the largest mosque in Thailand), Yala attracts busloads of Buddhist pilgrims, who come to revere the 25-metre-long reclining Buddha at **Wat Khuhaphimuk** (aka Wat Na Tham), 8km out of town on the road to Yaha and Hat Yai. The image's aura of holiness comes from its atmospheric setting in a broad, dank cave, and from its great age: it's said to have been constructed (and the temple founded) by a king of Palembang (Sumatra), some time around the end of the eighth century. To get there, take a bus from behind the *Thepvimarn* hotel, which will leave you with a five-hundred-metre walk south to the temple.

### Practicalities

The **train station**, opposite which share-taxis and air-conditioned minibuses congregate, is on the northeast side of the centre. **Buses** from Pattani stop on Thanon Sirorot, north of the station and east of the tracks; those from Hat Yai stop 500m southwest on the same road. The best budget place to **stay** is *Thepvimarn* at 31 Thanon Sribumrung (☏073/212400 or 211655; ❷–❹), which has large, clean fan-cooled and air-conditioned rooms; if you're coming from the train station, it's the first left off Thanon Pipitpakdee. The luxury *Yala Rama Hotel* is on the same road at no. 21 (☏073/212815; ❻). For an evening **meal** of simple, reasonable seafood, try the popular *Tara Seafood Restaurant* at the corner of Thanon Sribumrung and Thanon Pipitpakdee.

## Betong

Perched on the tip of a narrow tongue of land reaching into Malaysia, the small town of **BETONG** is only worth considering if you're heading out of the country – it's notorious for its fog, and most of Betong's visitors come across the border for shopping and brothel-creeping. The mountains and thick jungle surrounding the town proved a perfect hiding ground for the headquarters of the **Communist Party of Malaya**, whose hidden underground camp of **Pitya Mit**, just 20km from Betong on the Yala road, survived undetected for almost twenty years under the noses of their enemies. Around 180 communists lived in the complex of **tunnels**, built over three months in 1976 – 10m deep and over 1km long – before peacefully giving themselves up in a 1989 settlement with the Thai government. Today the tunnels are open to the public, with several of the old communists acting as guides. The camp is open daily, but you'll need your own transport to get there. Several such tunnel complexes lie dotted around the south of Thailand; another, larger, one was recently opened to tourists at **Khao Namkhang** (see p.417 for details of a tour there from Hat Yai).

The mountainous route from Yala to Betong is largely the preserve of share-taxis and air-conditioned minibuses, which cover the ground in three hours, as the one sluggish bus a day takes around six hours. From here you can **cross the border** by taxi to Keroh in Malaysia, which gives access to Sungai Petani and the west coast.

# Narathiwat and around

The coastal region between Pattani and the Malaysian border is one of the least developed areas of the deep south, although the main town of the region, **Narathiwat**, is slowly coming up in the world, with a brand-new regional tourist office and airport terminal both opening in the last few years. Increasingly popular with travellers stopping off on their way to or from the border, Narathiwat's an easy-going place in which to soak up the atmosphere for a couple of days, with a decent range of hotels and restaurants. It also offers the opportunity of a day at the beach (though if you're after a more protracted beach stay, you're better off on the other side of the Thai peninsula) and an excursion to the beautiful **Wat Chonthara Sing He**, 30km to the south in Tak Bai. Its most famous sight, however, the **Phra Buddha Taksin Mingmongkon**, touted near and far as the largest seated Buddha in Thailand, impresses only by virtue of its vital statistics (it's 24m high, 17m knee to knee).

Off the coast, tiny **Ko Losin**, 100km northeast of Narathiwat, is unremarkable but for the superb **diving** it offers on the coral-encrusted rock beneath the surface – some of the best in Thailand. Visibility is generally excellent, and much of the reef and its inhabitants – blacktip reef sharks, giant manta rays, whale sharks and turtles – can be viewed between 5m and 20m down. Divemaster, 100/63 Ladprao Soi 18, Thanon Ladprao, Bangkok (⊕02/512 1664, Ⓦwww.divemaster.net), and Songkhla's Starfish Scuba (see p.411) both run live-aboard charters to the island between June and September.

## Narathiwat town

**NARATHIWAT** is set on the west bank of the slowly curving Bang Nara River, at the mouth of which, just five minutes' walk north of the centre, sits a shanty fishing village fronted by *korlae* boats (see p.431). It's worth getting up early on a Friday morning for the bustling, colourful **market** which sprawls over the north end of Thanon Puphapugdee (the main river-bank road). Local batiks are sold here, as well as all kinds of food, including the local fish sauce,

**nam budu**: all around the region you'll see hundreds of concrete and ceramic pots laid out along the roadside containing the fermenting fish that goes to make the sauce – it takes a year or so before the sauce can be bottled and sold.

Just beyond the fishing village, peaceful deckchair restaurants overlook Hat Narathat, a beach too dangerous for swimming. Fortunately, the best **beach** in the area, boulder-strewn **Ao Manao**, 3km south towards Tak Bai, then 3km left down a paved side road, is within easy reach by motorbike taxi. Known as Lemon Bay due to the long, gentle curve of its coastline, this beautiful stretch is lined with trees and dotted with seafood restaurants.

Narathiwat's annual **Khong Dee Muang Nara** festival takes place in September every year, coinciding with the royal family's one-month visit to the nearby Taksin Ratchaniwet palace (see p.432); the festival involves *korlae* boat racing along the river and a dove-cooing contest.

## Practicalities

Narathiwat's two main streets run from north to south: Thanon Puphapugdee and the inland Thanon Pichit Bamrung, where most **buses** make a stop to the south of the clocktower – though the bus terminal is on the southwest side of town. **Air-conditioned minibuses** for Pattani are based at the corner of Thanon Puphapugdee and Thanon Vejitchaiboon, those for Hat Yai at the corner of Thanon Pichit Bamrung and Thanon Jamroonara, and for Sungai Kolok and Ban Taba at 308/5 Thanon Pichit Bamrung; **share-taxis** for Hat Yai, Pattani and Yala hang around further north on the same road. The **airport**, served by Thai Airways' minibuses (B50), lies 12km north of town. **Trains** on the line to Sungai Kolok stop at **Tanyongmat**, a half-hour songthaew ride from the centre.

Narathiwat's **TAT** office (daily 8.30am–4.30pm; ⊤ 073/516144, Ⓕ 522412, Ⓔ tatnara@tat.or.th), which has responsibility for Narathiwat, Yala and Pattani provinces, is inconveniently situated a couple of kilometres out of town on the Tak Bai road (take a motorbike taxi). The friendly office has a few English-

---

### Crossing into Malaysia near Narathiwat

You can cross to Malaysia southeast of Narathiwat at either of two frontier posts, both of which are well connected to **Kota Bharu**, the nearest town on the other side. Frequent songthaews and buses from Narathiwat make the ninety-minute trip to the riverside frontier post of **Ban Taba**, a village 5km beyond Tak Bai with a couple of mediocre hotels in case you're really stuck. From here a ferry (B6) shuttles across to the Malaysian town of Pengalan Kubur, which has frequent taxis and buses to Kota Bharu.

If you're coming from points north of Narathiwat, transport connections are likely to draw you inland to **Sungai Kolok**, a seedy brothel town popular with Malaysian weekenders. The longer-established of the border posts, Sungai Kolok is the end of the rail line from Bangkok, its station in the northern part of town a mere 800m west of the frontier bridge; motorbike taxis and samlors cover the ground if you can't face the walk. Hat Yai and Narathiwat air-conditioned minibuses are based opposite the station, and most buses stop to set down or pick up there, too. From Rantau Panjang on the other side, frequent taxis and buses head for Kota Bharu. There should be no reason for you to stay in Kolok, but if you need a **hotel**, the best of the town's many budget places is the *Thanee*, at 4/1 Thanon Cheunmanka (⊤ 073/611241; ❷–❸), five minutes' walk south from the train station down Thanon Charoenkhet (turn right at the *Merlin Hotel*); like most of Kolok's hotels, it doubles as a brothel, but the rooms, some with air-conditioning, are clean enough and the staff reasonably helpful.

language brochures, but a much better source of information on the town and its surroundings is the excellent *Baan Burong Riverside Guest House*; downstairs is a **travel agency** which can book plane, bus, minibus and train tickets, and arranges **visa runs** to the Thai consulate in Kota Bharu (transport costs B1500 per person). There's an **internet** shop (daily 9am–10pm; B30 per hour) next door to the *Royal Princess* hotel on Thanon Pichit Bamrung.

### Accommodation and eating

One of the best places to **stay** in Narathiwat is the *Baan Burong Riverside Guest House* at 399 Thanon Puphapugdee (☎073/511027, ⑤512001, ⓔnatini @chaiyo.com; ③–④). Situated in a 60-year-old Sino-Portuguese house in a central location overlooking the river, the guest house is nicely decorated and spotlessly clean, with just three air-conditioned rooms sharing hot-water bathrooms, and a living room with satellite TV, a small book collection and free tea and coffee. Guests have free use of bicycles and kayaks (for non-guests, bicycles are B50 per day, kayaks B50 per hour), and **motorbike rental** (B250 per day) and **car hire** with driver (B1800 per day) can also be arranged – useful for exploring the nearby coast. The helpful and friendly owner, Natini, can also organize a variety of activities, including Thai cooking courses (B200–400), batik-making (B350) and goat-milking (B150), as well as an exhaustive range of **tours**, everything from overnight fishing trips in nearby Saiburi (B1500 for boat), to morning hikes in Phru To Daeng, Thailand's last remaining swamp forest (B450), and two-day eco-tours of the Hala Bala tropical rainforest wildlife sanctuary, where ten of the world's twelve species of hornbill can be found.

Much cheaper than the *Baan Burong*, but nowhere near as nice, is the *Narathiwat Hotel*, which occupies a characterful wooden building on the same street at no. 341 (☎073/511063; ①); the rooms on the upper level are reserved for foreign tourists and are clean enough, if rather basic. On a cross street towards the north end of town, the friendly and comfortable *Tanyong Hotel* at 16/1 Thanon Sopapisai (☎073/511477–9, ⑤511834; ④–⑤) is highly recommended for a splurge, with some cheaper fan rooms available. Narathiwat's best hotel is the luxury *Royal Princess*, 228 Thanon Pichit Bamrung (☎073/515041–50, ⑤515040, ⓦwww.royalprincess.com; ⑦), which offers a swimming pool and other smart international-standard amenities; it's generally booked solid in September when the royal family and their entourage decamp to Taksin Ratchaniwet.

The top **restaurant** in town is the swish *Mankornthong* at 433 Thanon Puphapugdee, with a floating platform at the back; the seafood is pricey but very good. Much simpler, and considerably cheaper, is the spotlessly clean Muslim restaurant *Chesenik* on Thanon Sopapisai, which specializes in *kai korlae* (chicken in a mild thick curry gravy). This dish can be found in its more traditional form – grilled on sticks – in the small **night market** opposite the *Royal Princess Hotel*, where you can also snack on excellent *roti*. Some distance out of town at 1/3 Thanon Rangae–Mukka, the idyllic *Baan Suan Gasoh Garden Restaurant* is worth the journey for its delicious, reasonably priced Thai food and lush garden setting; call ahead on ☎073/521700 or 511027 for a free pickup from your hotel.

## The coast: Saiburi to Panare

From Narathiwat, a minor road (Route 4157) stretches all the way north up the coast to Panare – with a brief detour inland just before Saiburi – passing dozens of tiny Muslim fishing villages, protected from the winds that batter the coast during the monsoon by sturdy palm-frond windbreaks. It's a picturesque route, with goats and sheep straying onto the road and fish laid out to dry on racks by the roadside. The **beaches** that line much of this coastline are pretty enough, but cater mainly to Thai day-trippers; accommodation, where it exists at all, tends to be basic and rather seedy, while the beaches themselves can be blighted with litter from the omnipresent snack stalls. Note too that this is a fervently Muslim area, so women should cover up with a T-shirt on the beach. That said, a trip to one of the beaches listed below makes a pleasant day out, and during the week you'll have the added benefit of them all to yourself. The best way to reach them is to rent a **motorbike** or, if there's a small group of you, a chauffeured **car** from the *Baan Burong Riverside Guest House* in Narithiwat (see p.430); this will also give you freedom to take in a few other sights around the town. Alternatively, regular **songthaews** head all the way up the coast to Panare.

**SAIBURI**, 50km from Narathiwat on the bus route to Pattani, is a relaxing, leafy town sprinkled with evidence of its former importance as a trading port – ancient Chinese shophouses, dilapidated wooden mansions and the brick shell of a 400-year-old mosque, Masjid Khao, preserved in landscaped gardens. About 2km from the centre, across the Saiburi River and behind the fishing port, the quiet, tree-lined beach of **Hat Wasukri** is served by a handful of restaurants and the uninspiring *Muang Sai Resort* (☎073/411318; ❸), the town's only accommodation, whose dilapidated concrete bungalows are equipped with fans and bathrooms. The beach is the venue for the town's annual fishing competition, held every May.

The best of this area, however, lies further north towards **Panare**. The remote riverside village of **Ban Pasey Yawo** (Ban Bon), 2km up the road, is renowned as one of the best centres for the manufacture of **korlae** boats, the beautifully decorated smacks used by Muslim fishermen all along this coast, and visitors are welcome to watch the craftsmen at work in the shade of the village's coconut plantation. The intricacy and extent of their decoration is what makes these boats unique – floral motifs and pastoral scenes cover every centimetre, from the bird-of-paradise figurehead to the *singtoh* lion god at the stern, thought to protect the fishermen from the spirits of the sea. Each boat is entirely hand-made, takes four months to complete and sells for over B60,000, although B1000–3000 replicas are produced as a sideline.

About 15km further up towards Panare, you'll come to a turning (no English sign) for **Hat Kae Kae**, an idyllic seaside hamlet among shady palm trees, which gets its onomatopoeic name from the sound the sea makes when it hits the smooth boulders on the small, steeply sloping beach. If you're coming by songthaew, ask to be let off at Hat Kae Kae and you'll be left with a five-hundred-metre walk over a low rocky rise to reach the seashore, backed by some simple foodstalls.

# Wat Chonthara Sing He and Taksin Ratchaniwet

South of Narathiwat, one of the finest bots in Thailand lies about 30km down the coast in **TAK BAI**. Standing in a sandy, tree-shaded compound by the river, the bot at **Wat Chonthara Sing He** (aka Wat Chon) was built in the middle of the last century, as an emblem of Thai sovereignty to prove that Narathiwat was an integral part of Thailand, at a time when the British were claiming the area as part of Malaya. The building's brightly coloured fifteen-tiered roof exemplifies the fashion for curvaceous Chinese styles, here mixed with typical southern Thai features, such as the spiky white nagas, to produce an elegant, dynamic structure. Ask a monk for the key and look at the lively, well-preserved murals which completely cover the interior, portraying bawdy love scenes as well as typical details of southern life: bull- and goat-fighting, and men dressed in turbans and long sarongs.

The wat can be visited either as an easy day-trip from Narathiwat or on your way to the border – frequent buses bound for Sungai Kolok or buses and songthaews for Ban Taba pass through the small town. About 7km into the hour-long trip, you can't miss the **Taksin Ratchaniwet palace**, which stands on a wooded hill overlooking the sea. It is possible to visit the grounds when the king is not in residence (generally Oct–Aug daily 9am–4pm; free), but you'll need your own transport to get round the extensive grounds, and the excursion is only of real interest to devotees of the royal family. If you do make the trip, look out for the **gold-leaf vine** in the grounds; the velvety leaves of this highly prized plant, which is native only to the area around Narathiwat, turn an iridescent pink, then gold, then silver, each year from September to November. Other provinces have attempted to cash in on the vine's money-spinning appeal by planting it in other areas of Thailand – only to find that the leaves remain resolutely green all year round.

## Travel details

### Trains

**Hat Yai** to: Bangkok (5 daily; 16hr); Butterworth (Malaysia; 1 daily; 5hr 30min); Padang Besar (1 daily; 1hr 40min); Phatthalung (10 daily; 1–2hr); Sungai Kolok (2 daily; 3hr 30min); Surat Thani (8 daily; 4hr–6hr 30min); Yala (9 daily; 1hr 30min–3hr).

**Phatthalung** to: Bangkok (5 daily; 13hr 30min–16hr 30min); Hat Yai (10 daily; 1–2hr).

**Sungai Kolok** to: Bangkok (2 daily; 20hr); Hat Yai (2 daily; 3hr 30min–5hr); Nakhon Si Thammarat (1 daily; 9hr 40min); Phatthalung (5 daily; 5–7hr); Surat Thani (3 daily; 9–12hr); Yala (8 daily; 1hr 45min–2hr 30min).

**Trang** to: Bangkok (2 daily; around 16hr).

**Yala** to: Bangkok (4 daily; 18–20hr); Hat Yai (9 daily; 1hr 30min–3hr).

### Buses

**Hat Yai** to: Bangkok (every 30min; 13hr); Chumphon (5 daily; 8hr 15min); Ko Samui (1 daily; 6hr 30min); Krabi (2 daily; 4–5hr); Nakhon (every 30min; 3–4hr); Narathiwat (5 daily; 3–4hr); Padang Besar (every 10min; 1hr 40min); Pak Bara (3 daily; 2hr 30min); Pattani (13 daily; 1hr 45min–2hr 40min); Phatthalung (16 daily; 1hr 50min); Phuket (13 daily; 7–9hr); Satun (every 15min; 1hr 30min); Songkhla (every 10min; 30min); Sungai Kolok (2 daily; 5hr); Surat Thani (9 daily; 5hr–6hr 15min); Trang (every 30min; 3–4hr); Yala (every 30min; 2–3hr).

**Narathiwat** to: Ban Taba (every 30min; 1hr 30min); Bangkok (3 daily; 17hr); Pattani (hourly;

1–2hr); Sungai Kolok (every 30min; 1–2hr); Tak Bai (every 30min; 1hr).

**Pattani** to: Bangkok (3 daily; 16hr).

**Phatthalung** to: Bangkok (4 daily; 13hr).

**Satun** to: Bangkok (2 daily; 16hr); Trang (every 30min; 3hr).

**Songkhla** to: Chana (every 30min; 30min); Hat Yai (every 10min; 30min); Nakhon Si Thammarat (every 30min; 3hr); Ranot (every 30min; 1–2hr).

**Sungai Kolok** to: Bangkok (3 daily; 18–20hr); Hat Yai (5 daily; 4hr); Narathiwat (hourly; 1–2hr); Pattani (4 daily; 2–3hr); Surat Thani (3 daily; 9–10hr); Tak Bai (hourly; 30min); Yala (hourly; 3hr).

**Trang** to: Bangkok (8 daily; 14hr); Krabi (hourly; 2hr); Nakhon Si Thammarat (hourly; 2–3hr); Phatthalung (hourly; 1hr); Phuket (hourly; 4hr 30min); Satun (every 30min; 3hr).

**Yala** to: Bangkok (4 daily; 19hr); Betong (1 daily; 6hr); Hat Yai (every 30min; 2–3hr); Pattani (every 45min; 45min).

### Flights

**Hat Yai** to: Bangkok (6 daily; 1hr 30min); Johor Bahru (Malaysia; 3 weekly via KL; 6hr); Kota Kinabalu (Malaysia; 3 weekly via KL; 7hr); Kuala Lumpur (Malaysia; 3 weekly; 1hr); Kuching (Malaysia; 3 weekly via KL; 7hr); Phuket (1–2 daily; 1hr); Singapore (1 daily; 1hr 35min).

**Narathiwat** to: Bangkok (1 daily; 3hr); Phuket (1 daily; 1hr).

**Trang** to: Bangkok (1 or 2 daily; 1hr 30min).

# contexts

# contexts

History ................................................................435

Religion: Thai Buddhism ....................................442

The coastal environment.....................................447

Books ..................................................................452

Language .............................................................457

Glossary ..............................................................461

CONTEXTS

# History

Thailand's history is long and complex and what follows is only a brief account of the major events in the country's past. For more detailed coverage, get hold of a copy of David Wyatt's *Thailand* (see p.453).

## Early history

The region's first distinctive civilization, **Dvaravati**, was established around two thousand years ago by an Austroasiatic-speaking people known as the Mon. One of its mainstays was Theravada Buddhism, which had been introduced to Thailand during the second or third century BC by Indian missionaries. In the eighth century, peninsular Thailand to the south of Dvaravati came under the control of the **Srivijaya** empire, a Mahayana Buddhist state centred on Sumatra, which had strong ties with India.

From the ninth century onwards, both Dvaravati and Srivijaya Thailand succumbed to invading **Khmers** from Cambodia, who took control of north-eastern, central and peninsular Thailand. They ruled from Angkor and left dozens of spectacular temple complexes throughout the region. By the thirteenth century, however, the Khmers had overreached themselves and were in no position to resist the onslaught of a vibrant new force in Southeast Asia, the Thais.

The earliest traceable history of the **Thai people** picks them up in southern China around the fifth century AD, when they were squeezed by Chinese and Vietnamese expansionism into sparsely inhabited northeastern Laos. Their first significant entry into what is now Thailand seems to have happened in the north, where, some time after the seventh century, the Thais formed a state known as Yonok. Theravada Buddhism spread to Yonok via Dvaravati around the end of the tenth century, which served not only to unify the Thais themselves, but also to link them to the wider community of Buddhists.

By the end of the twelfth century, they formed the majority of the population in Thailand, then under the control of the Khmer empire. The Khmers' main outpost, at Lopburi, was by this time regarded as the administrative capital of a land called "Syam".

## Sukhothai and Ayutthaya

Some time around 1238, Thais in the upper Chao Phraya valley captured the main Khmer outpost in the region at **Sukhothai** and established a kingdom there. When the young Ramkhamhaeng came to the throne around 1278, he seized control of much of the Chao Phraya valley, and over the next twenty years gained the submission of most of Thailand under a complex tribute system.

Although the empire of Sukhothai extended Thai control over a vast area, its greatest contribution to the Thais' development was at home, in cultural and political matters. A famous inscription by Ramkhamhaeng, now housed in the Bangkok National Museum, describes a prosperous era of benevolent rule, and it is generally agreed that Ramkhamhaeng ruled justly according to Theravada Buddhist doctrine. A further sign of the Thais' growing self-confidence was the invention of a new script to make their tonal language understood by the non-Thai inhabitants of the land.

After the death of Ramkhamhaeng around 1299, however, his empire quickly fell apart, and **Ayutthaya** became the capital of the Thai empire. Soon after founding the city in 1351, the ambitious king Ramathibodi united the principalities of the lower Chao Phraya valley, which had formed the western provinces of the Khmer empire. When he recruited his bureaucracy from the urban elite of Lopburi, Ramathibodi set the style of government at Ayutthaya, elements of which persist to the present day. The elaborate etiquette, language and rituals of Angkor were adopted, and, most importantly, so was the concept of the ruler as *devaraja* (divine king).

The site chosen by Ramathibodi for an international port was the best in the region, and so began Ayutthaya's rise to prosperity, based on exploiting the upswing in trade in the middle of the fourteenth century along the routes between India and China. By 1540, the Kingdom of Ayutthaya had grown to cover most of the area of modern-day Thailand. Despite a 1568 invasion by the Burmese, which led to twenty years of foreign rule, Ayutthaya made a spectacular comeback, and in the seventeenth century its foreign trade boomed. In 1511, the Portuguese had become the first Western power to trade with Ayutthaya, while a treaty with Spain in 1598 was followed by similar agreements with Holland and England in 1608 and 1612 respectively. European merchants flocked to Thailand, not only to buy Thai products, but also for the Chinese and Japanese goods on sale there.

In the mid-eighteenth century, however, the rumbling in the Burmese jungle to the north began to make itself heard again. After an unsuccessful siege in 1760, February 1766 saw the **Burmese** descend upon the city for the last time. The Thais held out for over a year but, finally, in April 1767, the city was taken. The Burmese savagely razed everything to the ground, led off tens of thousands of prisoners to Burma and abandoned the city to the jungle.

## From Taksin to Rama III

Out of this lawless mess emerged **Phraya Taksin**, a charismatic general, who was crowned king in December 1768 at his new capital of **Thonburi**, on the opposite bank of the river from modern-day Bangkok. Within two years, he had restored all of Ayutthaya's territories and, by the end of the next decade, had brought Cambodia and much of Laos into a huge new empire.

However, by 1779 all was not well with the king. Taksin was becoming increasingly irrational and sadistic, and in March 1782 he was ousted in a coup. Chao Phraya Chakri, Taksin's military commander, was invited to take power and had Taksin executed.

With the support of the Ayutthayan aristocracy, Chakri – reigning as **Rama I** (1782–1809) – set about consolidating the Thai kingdom. His first act was to move the capital across the river to what we know as Bangkok, on the more defensible east bank. Borrowing from the layout of Ayutthaya, he built a new royal palace and impressive monasteries in the area of Ratanakosin within a defensive ring of two (later expanded to three) canals. In the palace temple, Wat Phra Kaeo, he enshrined the talismanic Emerald Buddha, which he had snatched during his campaigns in Laos. Trade with China revived, and the style of government was put on a more modern footing: while retaining many of the features of a *devaraja*, he shared more responsibility with his courtiers, as a first among equals.

The peaceful accession of Rama I's son as **Rama II** (1809–24) signalled the establishment of the Chakri dynasty, which is still in place today. This Second Reign is best remembered as a fertile period for Thai literature; indeed, Rama II himself is renowned as one of the great Thai poets.

By the reign of **Rama III** (1824–51), the Thais were starting to get alarmed by British colonialism in the region. In 1826, Rama III was obliged to sign the Burney Treaty, a limited trade agreement with the British, by which the Thais won some political security in return for reducing their taxes on goods passing through Bangkok.

## Mongkut and Chulalongkorn

Rama IV, more commonly known as **Mongkut** (1851–68), had been a Buddhist monk for 27 years when he succeeded his brother. But far from leading a cloistered life, Mongkut had travelled widely throughout Thailand, and had taken an interest in Western learning, studying English, Latin and the sciences.

Realizing that Thailand would be unable to resist the military might of the British, the king reduced import and export taxes, allowed British subjects to live and own land in Thailand and granted them freedom of trade under the Bowring Treaty. Within a decade, similar agreements had been signed with France, the United States and a score of other nations. Thus, by skilful diplomacy the king avoided a close relationship with just one power, which could easily have led to Thailand's annexation.

Mongkut's son, **Chulalongkorn**, took the throne as Rama V (1868–1910) at the age of only fifteen, but was well prepared by an excellent education which mixed traditional Thai and modern Western elements – provided by Mrs Anna Leonowens, subject of *The King and I*. One of his first acts was to scrap the custom by which subjects were required to prostrate themselves in the presence of the king. In the 1880s, he began to restructure the government to meet the country's needs, setting up a host of departments – for education, public health, the army and the like – and bringing in scores of foreign advisors to help with everything from foreign affairs to rail lines.

Throughout this period, however, the Western powers maintained their pressure on the region. The most serious threat to Thai sovereignty was the Franco–Siamese Crisis of 1893, which culminated in the French sending gunboats up the Chao Phraya River to Bangkok. Flouting numerous international laws, France claimed control over Laos and made other outrageous demands, which Chulalongkorn had no option but to agree to. During the course of his reign, the country was obliged to cede almost half of its territory, and forewent huge sums of tax revenue in order to preserve its independence; but by Chulalongkorn's death in 1910, the frontiers were fixed as they are today.

## The end of absolute monarchy and World War II

Chulalongkorn was succeeded by a flamboyant, British-educated prince, **Vajiravudh** (Rama VI, 1910–25) and by the time the young and inexperienced **Prajadhipok** – seventy-sixth child of Chulalongkorn – was catapulted to the throne as Rama VII (1925–35), Vajiravudh's extravagance had created severe financial problems, which were exacerbated by the onset of the Great Depression.

On June 24, 1932, a small group of middle-ranking officials, dissatisfied with the injustices of monarchical government and led by a lawyer, Pridi Phanomyong, and an army major, Luang Phibunsongkhram (Phibun), staged a coup with only a handful of troops. Prajadhipok weakly submitted to the conspirators, and a hundred and fifty years of **absolute monarchy** in Bangkok came to a sudden end. The king was sidelined to a position of symbolic significance, and in 1935 he abdicated in favour of his ten-year-old nephew, Ananda, then a schoolboy living in Switzerland.

**Phibun** emerged as prime minister after the decisive elections of 1938, and a year later officially renamed the country Thailand ("Land of the Free") – Siam, it was argued, was a name bestowed by external forces, and the new title made it clear that the country belonged to the Thais rather than the economically dominant Chinese.

The Thais were dragged into **World War II** on December 8, 1941, when, almost at the same time as the assault on Pearl Harbour, the Japanese invaded the east coast of peninsular Thailand, with their sights set on Singapore to the south. The Thais at first resisted fiercely, but realizing that the position was hopeless, Phibun quickly ordered a ceasefire.

The Thai government concluded a military alliance with Japan and declared war against the United States and Great Britain in January 1942, probably in the belief that the Japanese would win. However, the Thai minister in Washington, Seni Pramoj, refused to deliver the declaration of war against the US, and, in cooperation with the Americans, began organizing a resistance movement called Seri Thai. Pridi Phanomyong, now acting as regent to the young king, secretly coordinated the movement, smuggling in American agents and housing them in Bangkok. By 1944, Japan's defeat looked likely, and in July, Phibun, who had been most closely associated with them, was forced to resign by the National Assembly.

## Postwar upheavals

With the fading of the military, the election of January 1946 was for the first time contested by organized political parties, resulting in Pridi becoming prime minister. A new constitution was drafted, and the outlook for democratic, civilian government seemed bright. Hopes were shattered, however, on June 9, 1946, when King Ananda was found dead in his bed, with a bullet wound in his forehead. Three palace servants were hurriedly tried and executed, but the murder has never been satisfactorily explained. Pridi resigned as prime minister, and in April 1948, Phibun, playing on the threat of communism, took over the premiership again.

As **communism** developed its hold in the region with the takeover of China in 1949 and the French defeat in Indochina in 1954, the US increasingly viewed Thailand as a bulwark against the red menace. Between 1951 and 1957, when its annual state budget was only about $200 million a year, Thailand received a total of $149 million in American economic aid and $222 million in military aid.

Phibun narrowly won a general election in 1957, but only by blatant vote-rigging and coercion. After vehement public outcry, General Sarit, the commander-in-chief of the army, overthrew the new government in September the same year. Believing that Thailand would prosper best under a unifying authority, Sarit set about re-establishing the monarchy as the head of the social hierarchy and the source of legitimacy for the government. Ananda's successor, **Bhumibol** (Rama IX), was pushed into an active role, while Sarit ruthlessly silenced critics and pressed ahead with a plan for economic development.

## The Vietnam War and the democracy movement

Sarit died in 1963, whereupon the military succession passed to General Thanom. His most pressing problem was the **Vietnam War**. The Thais, with the backing of the US, quietly began to conduct military operations in Laos, to which North Vietnam and China responded by supporting anti-government insurgency in Thailand. By 1968, around 45,000 US military personnel were on Thai soil, which became the base for US bombing raids against North Vietnam and Laos. The effects of the American presence were profound. The economy swelled with dollars, and hundreds of thousands of Thais became reliant on the Americans for a living, with a consequent proliferation of prostitution – centred on Bangkok's infamous Patpong district – and corruption. Moreover, the sudden exposure to Western culture led many to question traditional Thai values and the political status quo.

Poor farmers in particular were becoming increasingly disillusioned with their lot, and many turned against the Bangkok government. At the end of 1964, the Communist Party of Thailand and other groups formed a broad left coalition which soon had the support of several thousand insurgents in remote areas of the northeast and the north. By 1967, a separate threat had arisen in southern Thailand, involving Muslim dissidents and the Chinese-dominated Communist Party of Malaysia.

Thanom was now facing a major security crisis, and in November 1971 he imposed repressive **military rule**. In response, student demonstrations began in June 1973, and in October as many as 500,000 people turned out at Thammasat University in Bangkok to demand a new constitution. Clashes with the police ensued but elements in the army, backed by King Bhumibol, prevented Thanom from crushing the protest with troops. On October 14, 1973, Thanom was forced to resign.

In a new climate of openness, Kukrit Pramoj formed a coalition of seventeen elected parties and secured a promise of US withdrawal from Thailand, but his government was riven with feuding. In October 1976, the students demonstrated again, protesting against the return of Thanom to Bangkok. This time there was no restraint: supported by elements of the military and the government, the police and reactionary students launched a massive assault on Thammasat University. On October 6, hundreds of students were brutally beaten, scores were lynched and some even burnt alive; the military took control and suspended the constitution.

## Premocracy

Soon after, the military-appointed prime minister, Thanin Kraivichien, forced dissidents to undergo anti-communist indoctrination, but his measures seem to have been too repressive even for the military, who forced him to resign in October 1977. General Kriangsak Chomanand took over, and began to break up the insurgency with shrewd offers of amnesty. He in turn was displaced in February 1980 by General Prem Tinsulanonda, backed by a broad parliamentary coalition.

Untainted by corruption, Prem achieved widespread support, including that of the monarchy. Overseeing a period of rapid economic growth, Prem maintained the premiership until 1988, with a unique mixture of dictatorship and democracy sometimes called **Premocracy**: although never standing for parliament himself, Prem was asked by the legislature after every election to become prime minister. He eventually stepped down because, he said, it was time for the country's leader to be chosen from among its elected representatives.

## The 1992 demonstrations

The new prime minister was indeed an elected MP, Chatichai Choonhavan. He pursued a vigorous policy of economic development, but this fostered widespread corruption. Following an economic downturn and Chatichai's attempts to downgrade the political role of the military, the armed forces staged a bloodless coup on February 23, 1991, led by Supreme Commander Sunthorn and General Suchinda, the army commander-in-chief, who became premier.

When Suchinda reneged on promises to make democratic amendments to the constitution, hundreds of thousands of ordinary Thais poured onto the streets around Bangkok's Democracy Monument in **mass demonstrations** between May 17 and 20, 1992. Suchinda brutally crushed the protests, leaving hundreds dead or injured, but was then forced to resign when King Bhumibol expressed his disapproval in a ticking-off that was broadcast on world television.

## Chuan, Banharn and Chavalit

In the elections on September 13, 1992, the Democrat Party, led by **Chuan Leekpai**, a noted upholder of democracy and the rule of law, gained the largest number of parliamentary seats. Despite many successes through a period of continued economic growth, he was able to hold onto power only until July 1995, when he was forced to call new elections.

Chart Thai and its leader, **Banharn Silpa-archa**, emerged victorious, but allegations of corruption soon followed – Banharn was nicknamed "the walking ATM" by the press for his vote-buying reputation – and in the following year he was obliged to dissolve parliament. In November 1996, **General Chavalit Yongchaiyudh**, leader of the New Aspiration Party (NAP), just won what was dubbed as the most corrupt election in Thai history, with an estimated 25 million baht spent on vote-buying in rural areas.

## The economic crisis

At the start of Chavalit's premiership, the Thai **economy** was already on shaky ground. In February 1997, foreign-exchange dealers began to mount speculative attacks on the baht, alarmed at the size of Thailand's private foreign debt – 250 billion baht in the unproductive property sector alone, much of it accrued through the proliferation of prestigious skyscrapers in Bangkok. The government valiantly defended the pegged exchange rate, spending $23 billion of the country's formerly healthy foreign-exchange reserves, but at the beginning of July was forced to give up the ghost – the baht was floated and soon went into free-fall.

Blaming its traditional allies, the Americans, for neglecting their obligations, Thailand sought help from Japan; Tokyo suggested the IMF, who in August 1997 put together a rescue package for Thailand of $17 billion. Among the conditions of the package, the Thai government was to slash the national budget, control inflation and open up financial institutions to foreign ownership.

Chavalit's performance in the face of the crisis was viewed as inept, and in November, he was succeeded by Chuan Leekpai, who took up what was widely seen as a poisoned chalice for his second term.

## Chuan's second term – and Thaksin

Chuan immediately took a hard line to try to restore confidence: he followed the IMF's advice, which involved maintaining cripplingly high interest rates to protect the baht, and pledged to reform the financial system. Although this played well abroad, at home the government encountered increasing hostility. Unemployment had doubled to 2 million by mid-1998 and there were frequent public protests against the IMF. By the end of 1998, however, Chuan's tough stance was paying off, with the baht stabilizing at just under 40 to the US dollar, and interest rates and inflation starting to fall. Foreign investors slowly began returning to Thailand, and by October 1999 Chuan was confident enough to announce that he was forgoing almost $4 billion of the IMF's planned $17 billion rescue package.

The year 2000 was dominated by the build-up to the **general election**, which was eventually held in January 2001. It was to be the first such vote under the 1997 constitution, which was intended to take the traditionally crucial role of money, especially for vote-buying, out of politics. However, this election coincided with the emergence of a major new party, **Thai Rak Thai** (Thai Loves Thai), formed by one of Thailand's wealthiest men, telecoms tycoon **Thaksin Shinawatra**. As expected, Thaksin achieved a sweeping victory, entering into a coalition with Chart Thai and New Aspiration and thus controlling 325 seats out of a possible 500. But instead of a move towards greater democracy, as envisioned by the new constitution, Thaksin's new government seemed to represent a full-blown merger between politics and big business, concentrating economic power in even fewer hands.

However, in September 1999, the **National Counter-Corruption Commission** had announced an investigation into Thaksin's affairs, citing a failure to disclose fully his business interests when he joined Chavalit's 1997 government. The NCCC also wanted to know how members of Thaksin's household – including his maid, nanny, driver and security guard – came to hold over one billion baht's worth of stock in his businesses. At the time of writing it remains to be seen whether Thaksin will escape this corruption indictment against him, which if upheld by the Constitutional Court could see him kicked out of office.

As this book went to press, it was announced that Thaksin had been cleared of the charges by a narrow margin of 8–7 in the Constitutional Court.

# Religion: Thai Buddhism

Over ninety percent of Thais consider themselves Theravada Buddhists, followers of the teachings of a holy man usually referred to as the Buddha
(Enlightened One), though more precisely known as Gautama Buddha to distinguish him from three lesser-known Buddhas who preceded him, and from
the fifth and final Buddha who is predicted to arrive in the year 4457 AD.
Theravada Buddhism is one of the two main schools of Buddhism practised
in Asia, and in Thailand it has absorbed an eclectic assortment of animist and
Hindu elements into its beliefs as well. The other ten percent of Thailand's
population comprises Mahayana Buddhists, Muslims, Hindus, Sikhs and
Christians.

## The Buddha: his life and beliefs

Buddhists believe that Gautama Buddha was the five-hundredth incarnation of
a single being: the stories of these five hundred lives, collectively known as the
**Jataka**, provide the inspiration for much Thai art. (Hindus also accept Gautama
Buddha into their pantheon, perceiving him as the ninth manifestation of their
god Vishnu.)

In his last incarnation he was born in Nepal as **Prince Gautama
Siddhartha** in either the sixth or seventh century BC, the son of a king and
his hitherto barren wife, who finally became pregnant only after having a
dream that a white elephant had entered her womb. At the time of his birth
astrologers predicted that Gautama was to become universally respected, either
as a worldly king or as a spiritual saviour, depending on which way of life he
pursued. Much preferring the former idea, the prince's father forbade anyone
to let the boy out of the palace grounds, and took it upon himself to educate
Gautama in all aspects of the high life. Statues of the Buddha with elongated
earlobes refer to this pampered existence, when he would have worn heavy
precious stones in his ears.

The prince married and became a father, but at the age of 29 he flouted his
father's authority and sneaked out into the world beyond the palace. On this
fateful trip he encountered successively an old man, a sick man, a corpse and a
hermit, and thus for the first time was made aware that pain and suffering were
intrinsic to human life. Contemplation seemed the only means of discovering
why this should be so, and Gautama decided to leave the palace and become a
**Hindu ascetic**.

For six or seven years he wandered the countryside leading a life of self-
denial and self-mortification, but failed to come any closer to the answer.
Eventually concluding that the best course of action must be to follow a
"Middle Way" – neither indulgent nor over-ascetic – Gautama sat down
beneath the famous riverside bodhi tree at **Bodh Gaya** in India, facing the rising sun, to meditate until he achieved enlightenment. For 49 days he sat cross-
legged in the "lotus position", contemplating the causes of suffering and
wrestling with temptations that materialized to distract him. Most of these
were sent by **Mara**, the Evil One, who was finally subdued when Gautama
summoned the earth goddess **Mae Toranee** by pointing the fingers of his
right hand at the ground – the gesture known as *Bhumisparsa Mudra*, which has
been immortalized by hundreds of Thai sculptors. Mae Toranee wrung torrents
of water from her hair and engulfed Mara's demonic emissaries in a flood, an

episode that also features in several sculptures and paintings, most famously in the statue in Bangkok's Sanam Luang.

Temptations dealt with, Gautama soon came to attain **enlightenment** and so become a Buddha. As the place of his enlightenment, the **bodhi tree** (or bo tree) has assumed special significance for Buddhists: not only does it appear in many Buddhist paintings and a few sculptures, but there's often a real bodhi tree (*ficus religiosa*) planted in temple compounds as well. Furthermore, the bot is nearly always built facing either a body of water or facing east (preferably both).

The Buddha preached his **first sermon** in a deer park in India, where he characterized his *Dharma* (doctrine) as a wheel. From this episode comes the early Buddhist symbol the **Dharmachakra**, known as the Wheel of Law, Wheel of Doctrine or Wheel of Life, which is often accompanied by a statue of a deer. Thais celebrate this first sermon and many other important events in the Buddha's life with public holidays and festivals, see Basics, p.59.

For the next forty-odd years the Buddha travelled the region converting non-believers and performing miracles. He also went back to his father's palace where he was temporarily reunited with his wife and child: the Khon Kaen museum houses a particularly lovely carving of this event.

The Buddha "died" at the age of eighty on the banks of a river at Kusinari in India – an event often dated to 543 BC, which is why the Thai calendar is 543 years out of synch with the Western one, so that the year 2004 AD becomes 2547 BE (Buddhist Era). Lying on his side, propping up his head on his hand, the Buddha passed into **Nirvana** (giving rise to another classic pose, the Reclining Buddha), the unimaginable state of nothingness which knows no suffering and from which there is no reincarnation.

## Buddhist doctrine

After the Buddha entered Nirvana, his **doctrine** spread relatively quickly across India, and probably was first promulgated in Thailand in about the third century BC. His teachings, the *Tripitaka*, were written down in the Pali language – a derivative of Sanskrit – in a form that became known as Theravada or "The Doctrine of the Elders".

As taught by the Buddha, **Theravada Buddhism** built on the Hindu theory of perpetual reincarnation in the pursuit of perfection, introducing the notion of life as a cycle of suffering which could only be transcended by enlightened beings able to free themselves from earthly ties and enter into the blissful state of Nirvana. For the well-behaved but unenlightened Buddhist, each reincarnation marks a move up a vague kind of ladder, with animals at the bottom, women figuring lower down than men, and monks coming at the top – a hierarchy complicated by the very pragmatic notion that the more comfortable your lifestyle the higher your spiritual status.

The Buddhist has no hope of enlightenment without acceptance of the **four noble truths**. In encapsulated form, these hold that desire is the root cause of all suffering and can be extinguished only by following the eightfold path or Middle Way. This **Middle Way** is essentially a highly moral mode of life that includes all the usual virtues like compassion, respect and moderation, and eschews vices such as self-indulgence and anti-social behaviour. But the key to it all is an acknowledgement that the physical world is impermanent and ever-changing, and that all things – including the self – are therefore not worth craving. Only by pursuing a condition of complete **detachment** can humans transcend earthly suffering.

By the beginning of the first millennium, a new movement called **Mahayana** (Great Vehicle) had emerged within the Theravada school, attempting to make Buddhism more accessible by introducing a Hindu-style pantheon of *bodhisattva* or Buddhist saints who, although they had achieved enlightenment, nevertheless postponed entering Nirvana in order to inspire the populace. Mahayana Buddhism subsequently spread north into China, Korea, Vietnam and Japan, also entering southern Thailand via the Srivijayan empire around the eighth century and parts of Khmer Cambodia in about the eleventh century. Meanwhile Theravada Buddhism (which the Mahayanists disparagingly renamed "Hinayana" or "Lesser Vehicle") established itself most significantly in Sri Lanka, northern and central Thailand and Burma.

## The monkhood

In Thailand it's the duty of the 200,000-strong **Sangha** (monkhood) to set an example to the Theravada Buddhist community by living a life as close to the Middle Way as possible and by preaching the *Dharma* to the people. A monk's life is governed by 227 strict rules that include celibacy and the rejection of all personal possessions except gifts.

Each day begins with an alms round in the neighbourhood so that the laity can donate food and thereby gain themselves merit (see p.445), and then is chiefly spent in meditation, chanting, teaching and study. The stricter of the Thai Sangha's two main sects, the **Thammayutika**, places strong emphasis on scholarship and meditation, but the much larger and longer-established **Mahanikai** sect encourages monks to pursue wider activities within the community. Always the most respected members of any community, monks act as teachers, counsellors and arbiters in local disputes and, in rural areas, they often become spokesmen for villagers' rights, particularly on environmental and land ownership issues. Although some Thai women become nuns, they belong to no official order and aren't respected as much as the monks.

Monkhood doesn't have to be for life: a man may leave the Sangha three times without stigma and in fact every Thai male (including royalty) is expected to **enter the monkhood** for a short period at some point in his life, ideally between leaving school and marrying, as a rite of passage into adulthood. So ingrained into the social system is this practice that nearly all Thai companies grant their employees paid leave for their time as a monk. The most popular time for temporary ordination is the three-month Buddhist retreat period – **Pansa**, sometimes referred to as "Buddhist Lent" – which begins in July and lasts for the duration of the rainy season. (The monks' confinement is said to originate from the earliest years of Buddhist history, when farmers complained that perambulating monks were squashing their sprouting rice crops.) **Ordination ceremonies** take place in almost every wat at this time and make spectacular scenes, with the shaven-headed novice usually clad entirely in white and carried about on friends' or relatives' shoulders, or even on elephants. The boys' parents donate money, food and necessities such as washing powder and mosquito repellent, processing around the temple compound with their gifts, often joined by dancers or travelling players hired for the occasion.

### Monks in contemporary society

In recent years, some monks have extended their role as village spokesmen to become influential activists: those of Wat Phai Lom near Bangkok have established the country's largest breeding colony of Asian open-billed storks for example. However, the increasing involvement of many monks in the secular world has not met with unanimous approval.

Less heroic, and far more disappointing to the laity, are those monks who **flout the precepts** of the Sangha by succumbing to the temptations of a consumer society, flaunting Raybans, Rolexes and Mercedes (in some cases actually bought with temple funds), chain-smoking and flirting, even making pocket money from predicting lottery results and practising faith healing. With so much national pride and integrity riding on the sanctity of the Sangha, any whiff of a deeper scandal is bound to strike deep into the national psyche, and everyone was shocked when a young monk confessed to robbing and then murdering a British tourist in 1995. Since then Thai monks have been involved in an unprecedented litany of crimes, including several rapes and murders, and there's been an embarrassment of exposés of corrupt, high-ranking abbots caught carousing in disreputable bars, drug-dealing and even gun-running. This has prompted a stream of editorials on the state of the Sangha and the collapse of spiritual values at the heart of Thai society. The inclusivity of the monkhood – which is open to just about any male who wants to join – has been highlighted as a particularly vulnerable aspect, not least because donning saffron robes has always been an accepted way for criminals, reformed or otherwise, to repent of their past deeds. Interestingly, back in the late 1980s, the influential monk, Phra Bodhirak, was unceremoniously defrocked after criticizing what he saw as a tide of decadence infecting Thai Buddhism and advocating an all-round purification of the Sangha. He now preaches from his breakaway Santi Asoke sect headquarters on the outskirts of Bangkok, but his ascetic code of behaviour is not sanctioned by the more worldly figures of the Sangha Supreme Council.

## Buddhist practice

In practice most Thai Buddhists aim only to be **reborn** higher up the incarnation scale rather than to set their sights on the ultimate goal of Nirvana. The rank of the reincarnation is directly related to the good and bad actions performed in the previous life, which accumulate to determine one's **karma** or destiny – hence the Thai obsession with "making merit".

**Merit-making** (*tham bun*) can be done in all sorts of ways, from giving a monk his breakfast to attending a Buddhist service or donating money to the neighbourhood temple, and most festivals are essentially communal merit-making opportunities. For a Thai man, temporary ordination is a very important way of accruing merit not only for himself but also for his mother and sisters – wealthier citizens might take things a step further by commissioning the casting of a Buddha statue or even paying for the building of a wat. One of the more bizarre but common merit-making activities involves **releasing caged birds**: worshippers buy one or more tiny finches from vendors at wat compounds and, by liberating them from their cage, prove their Buddhist compassion towards all living things. The fact that the birds were free until netted earlier that morning doesn't seem to detract from the ritual at all. In riverside and seaside wats, birds are sometimes replaced by fish or even baby turtles.

## Spirits and non-Buddhist deities

The complicated history of the area now known as Thailand has, not surprisingly, made Thai Buddhism a strangely syncretic faith. While regular Buddhist merit-making insures a Thai for the next life, there are certain **Hindu gods**

**and animist spirits** that most Thais also cultivate for help with more immediate problems. Sophisticated Bangkokians and illiterate farmers alike find no inconsistency in these apparently incompatible practices, and as often as not it's a Buddhist monk who is called in to exorcize a malevolent spirit. Even the Buddhist King Bhumibol employs Brahmin priests and astrologers to determine auspicious days and officiate at certain royal ceremonies and, like his royal predecessors of the Chakri dynasty, he also associates himself with the Hindu god Vishnu by assuming the title Rama IX – Rama, hero of the Hindu epic the *Ramayana*, having been Vishnu's seventh manifestation on earth.

If a Thai wants help in achieving a short-term goal, like passing an exam, becoming pregnant or winning the lottery, then he or she will quite likely turn to the **Hindu pantheon**, visiting an enshrined statue of either Brahma, Vishnu, Shiva, Indra or Ganesh, and making offerings of flowers, incense and maybe food. If the outcome is favourable, devotees will probably come back to show thanks, bringing more offerings and maybe even hiring a dance troupe to perform a celebratory *lakhon chatri* as well. Built in honour of Brahma, Bangkok's Erawan Shrine (see p.139) is the most famous place of Hindu-inspired worship in the country.

Whereas Hindu deities tend to be benevolent, **spirits** (or *phi*) are not nearly as reliable and need to be mollified more frequently. They come in hundreds of varieties, some more malign than others, and inhabit everything from trees, rivers and caves to public buildings and private homes, resulting in the inclusion of a special **spirit house** (*phra phum*) in the vicinity of new buildings as a dwelling for spirits ousted by the construction. Usually raised on a short column to set it at or above eyelevel, the spirit house must occupy an auspicious location – not, for example, in the shadow of the main building – so help from the local temple or village elder is usually required when deciding on the best position. Spirit houses are generally about the size of a doll's house and designed to look like a wat or a traditional Thai house, but their ornamentation is supposed to reflect the status of the humans' building – thus if that building is enlarged or refurbished, the spirit house should be improved accordingly. Little figurines representing the relevant guardian spirit and his aides are sometimes put inside the little house, and daily offerings of incense, lighted candles and garlands of jasmine are placed alongside them to keep the *phi* happy – a disgruntled spirit is a dangerous spirit, liable to cause sickness, accidents and even death. As with any religious building or icon in Thailand, an unwanted or crumbling spirit house should never be dismantled or destroyed, which is why you'll often see damaged spirit houses placed around the base of a sacred banyan tree, where they are able to rest in peace.

# The coastal environment

Spanning some 1650km north to south, Thailand lies in the heart of South-east Asia's tropical zone, its southern border running less than seven degrees north of the Equator. Coastal Thailand's climate is characterized by high temperatures and even higher humidity, a very fertile combination which nourishes a huge diversity of flora and fauna in the tropical rainforests, mangrove swamps and coral reefs that constitute the region's main habitats.

## The habitats

Some of Thailand's most precious coastal habitats are protected as national park, including the steamy jungles of Khao Sok, the coastal mudflats of Khao Sam Roi Yot, the expansive lagoons of Thale Noi and Thale Luang (Khu Khut), all of which are favourite haunts of migrating birds, the turtle-hatching beaches of Ko Surin and Phuket's Hat Mai Khao, and the islands and adjacent coral reefs of Ko Similan, Ko Phi Phi, Ko Tarutao, Ang Thong, Ko Samet and Ko Chang.

### Tropical rainforests

Thailand's **tropical rainforests** occur in areas of high and prolonged rainfall in the southern peninsula, most accessibly in the national parks of Khao Sok, Thale Ban, Tarutao and Khao Luang. Some areas contain as many as two hundred species of tree within a single hectare, along with a host of other flora. Characteristic of a tropical rainforest is the multilayered series of **canopies**. The uppermost storey of emergent trees sometimes reaches 60m, and these towering trees often have enormous buttressed roots for support; beneath this, the dense canopy of 25–35m is often festooned with climbers and epiphytes such as ferns, lianas, mosses and orchids; then comes an uneven layer 5–10m high consisting of palms, rattans, shrubs and small trees. The forest floor in tropical rainforests tends to be relatively open and free of dense undergrowth, owing to the intense filtering of light by the upper three layers.

The family **Dipterocarpaceae** dominate these forests, a group of tropical hardwoods prized for their timber and, in places, their resin. The name comes from the Greek and means "two-winged fruit". Though dipterocarps provide little food for fauna, they play an important role as nesting sites for hornbills, lookout posts for gibbons – and as timber.

Tropical rainforests play host to a plethora of **epiphytes**, of which there are over a thousand species in Thailand. These are plants that usually grow on other plants, though they do not feed from them. Instead they obtain nutrients from the atmosphere, the rain, and decaying plant and animal matter. Some of the commoner epiphytes in Thailand include the golden spiky petalled *Bulbophyllum picturatum*, the bright yellow members of the genus *Dendrobium*, the ivory-coloured *Cymbidium siamensis*, the flame-red *Ascocentrum curvifolium*, and the blue *Vanda coerulea*.

For the early years of its life, the **strangling fig** (*Ficus* sp) is also an epiphyte. The fig's peculiar life starts after the flower has been fertilized by a species-specific wasp host. The ripe fruit must then pass through the gut of a bird or animal and be dropped in a moist spot somewhere near the sunlit canopy of a support tree, often a dipterocarp. After germination, the fig lives a typical epi-phytic lifestyle, but also spreads a lattice of roots down to the ground. Once tethered to the earth, the fig gives up its epiphytic role and feeds normally by extracting nutrients from the soil. After many years, the fig's roots completely enshroud the support tree, and eventually the crown spreads over and above its host, cutting off the support tree's light and thereby hastening its death. The support tree subsequently decomposes, leaving a hollow but structurally sound strangling fig. Strangling figs are excellent places to observe birds and mammals, particularly when in fruit, as they attract hornbills, green pigeons, barbets, gibbons, langurs and macaques.

### Mangrove swamps and coastal forests

**Mangrove swamps** are an important habitat for a wide variety of marine life (including 204 species of bird, 74 species of fish and 54 types of crab) but, like much of Thailand's natural heritage, they have fallen victim to destructive economic policies (see "Environmental issues", p.450). Huge swathes of Thailand's coast used to be fringed with mangrove swamps, but now they are mainly found only along the west peninsular coast, between Ranong and Satun. On Phuket, the Thachatchai Nature Trail leads you on a guided tour through a patch of mangrove swamp, but an even better way of exploring the swamps is to paddle through them in a kayak; several tour operators in Phuket and in the Krabi area can arrange this.

**Nipa palms** share the mangrove's penchant for brackish water, and these stubby-stemmed palm trees grow in abundance in southern **coastal areas**, though commercial plantations are now replacing the natural colonies. Like most other species of palm indigenous to Thailand, the nipa is a versatile plant, its components exploited to the full – alcohol is distilled from its sugary sap, for instance, while roofs, sticky-rice baskets and chair-backs are constructed from its fronds.

Taller and more elegant, **coconut palms** grace some of Thailand's most beautiful beaches. On islands such as Ko Samui, they form the backbone of the local economy, with millions of coconuts harvested every month.

**Casuarinas** also flourish in sandy soils and are common on the beaches of southern Thailand; because they are also fast-growing and attain heights of up to 20m, they are quite often used in afforestation programmes on beaches elsewhere. At first glance, the casuarina's feathery profile makes it look like a pine tree of some kind, but it's actually made up of tiny twigs, not needles.

## The wildlife

In zoogeographical terms, Thailand lies in an exceptionally rich "transition zone" of the Indo-Malayan realm, its forests, mountains and national parks attracting creatures from both Indochina and Indonesia. In all, Thailand is home to 282 species of mammal (over forty of which are considered to be endangered) and 928 species of bird (190 of them endangered). For a guide to Thailand's spectacular array of **marine species**, see the colour section at the beginning of the book.

### Mammals

In the main national parks like Khao Sok, the animals you're most likely to encounter – with your ears if not your eyes – are **primates**, particularly macaques and gibbons.

The latter are responsible for the unmistakable hooting that echoes through the forests of some of the national parks. Chief noise-maker is the **white-handed or lar gibbon**, an appealing beige- or black-bodied, white-faced animal whose appearance, intelligence and dexterity unfortunately make it a popular pet. The poaching and maltreating of lar gibbons has become so severe that a special Gibbon Rehabilitation Project has been set up in Phuket (see p.349).

Similarly chatty, macaques hang out in gangs of twenty or more. The **long-tailed or crab-eating macaque** lives in the lowlands, near the rivers, lakes and coasts of Krabi, Ko Tarutao, Ang Thong and Khao Sam Roi Yot, for example. It eats not only crabs, but mussels, other small animals and fruit, transporting and storing food in its big cheek pouch, when swimming and diving – activities at which it excels. The **pig-tailed macaque**, so called because of its short curly tail, excels at scaling tall trees, a skill which has many of the males captured and trained to pick coconuts – a practice that's very common in Surat Thani (see p.249).

Commonly sighted on night treks in Khao Sam Roi Yot, the **civet** – species of which include the common palm and small Indian – is a small mongoose-type animal which hunts smaller mammals in trees and on the ground; it's known in the West for the powerful smell released from its anal glands, a scent used commercially as a perfume base. More elusive is the **Indochinese tiger**, which lives under constant threat from both poachers and the destruction of its habitat by logging interests, both of which have reduced the current population to somewhere between 150 and 250; for now Khao Sok is the likeliest place for sightings.

The shy, nocturnal **tapir**, an ungulate with three-toed hind legs and four-toed front ones, lives deep in the forest of peninsular Thailand but is occasionally spotted in daylight. A relative of both the horse and the rhino, the tapir is the size of a pony and has a stubby trunk-like snout and distinctive colouring that serves to confuse predators: the front half of its body and all four legs are black, while the rear half is white.

It's thought there are now as few as two thousand wild **elephants** left in Thailand: small-eared Asian elephants found mainly in Khao Sok. The situation is so dire that an organization called the Elephant Help Project Phuket (ⓦ www.elephanthelp.org) has been established with the aim of buying captive elephants from Phuket tourist attractions and releasing them back into the wild via a protected reserve in Northern Thailand.

## Birds

Even if you don't see many mammals on a trek through a national park, you're certain to spot a satisfying range of **birds**. The **hornbill** is the most majestic, easily recognizable from its massive, powerful wings (the flapping of which can be heard for long distances) and huge beak surmounted by a bizarre horny casque. The two most commonly spotted species in Thailand are the plain black-and-white **oriental pied hornbill** and the flashier **great hornbill**, whose monochromic body and head are broken up with jaunty splashes of yellow. Thailand is also home to the extremely rare **Gurney's pitta**, found only in Khlong Thom National Park, inland from Ko Lanta.

**Coastal areas** attract storks, egrets and herons, and the mud flats of Khao Sam Roi Yot are a breeding ground for the large, long-necked **purple heron**. The magnificent **white-bellied sea eagle** haunts the Thai coast, nesting in the forbidding crags around Krabi, Phang Nga and Ko Tarutao, and preying on fish and sea snakes. The tiny **edible nest swiftlet** makes its eponymous nest – the major ingredient of bird's-nest soup and a target for thieves – in the limestone crags, too, though it prefers the caves within these karsts; for more on these swiftlets and their nests see p.379.

## Snakes

Thailand is home to around 175 different species and sub-species of **snake**, 56 of them dangerously venomous. Death by snakebite is not common, however,

## The Gecko

Whether you're staying on a beach or in a town, chances are you'll be sharing your room with a few *geckos*. These pale green tropical lizards, which are completely harmless to humans and usually measure a cute four to ten centimetres in length, mostly appear at night, high up on walls and ceilings, where they feed on insects. Because the undersides of their flat toes are covered with hundreds of microscopic hairs that catch at even the tiniest of irregularities, geckos are able to scale almost any surface, including glass, which is why you usually see them in strange, gravity-defying positions. The largest and most vociferous gecko is known as the *tokay* in Thai, named after the disconcertingly loud sound it makes. Tokays can grow to an alarming 35cm but are welcomed by most householders, as they devour insects and mice; Thais also consider it auspicious if a baby is born within earshot of a crowing tokay.

but all hospitals should keep a stock of serum, produced at the Queen Saovabha Institute in Bangkok.

Found everywhere and highly venomous, the two-metre, nocturnal, yellow-and-black-striped **banded krait** is one to avoid, as is the shorter but equally poisonous **Thai or monocled cobra**, which lurks in low-lying humid areas and close to human habitation. As its name implies, this particular serpent sports a distinctive eye mark on its hood, the only detail on an otherwise plain brown body. The other most widespread poisonous snake is the sixty-centimetre **Malayan pit viper**, whose dangerousness is compounded by its unnerving ability to change the tone of its pinky-brown and black-marked body according to its surroundings.

Non-venomous but considerably mightier, with an average measurement of 7.5m (maximum 10m) and a top weight of 140kg, the **reticulated python** is Thailand's largest snake, and the second largest in the world after the anaconda. Tan-coloured, with "reticulated" black lines it's found especially in the suburbs of Greater Bangkok, and feeds on rats, rabbits, small deer, pigs, cats and dogs, which it kills by constriction; if provoked, it can kill humans in the same way.

## Environmental issues

In 1972 Thailand had just four **national parks**; now there are almost one hundred across the country, plus 37 wildlife sanctuaries, nearly fifty non-hunting grounds and several other protected zones, covering 66,000 square kilometres, or around thirteen percent of the country.

Problems caused by the **touristification of national parks** such as Ko Phi Phi and Ko Samet is a hugely controversial issue, and was highlighted when the Royal Forestry Department allowed a film crew to "relandscape" part of Ko Phi Phi Leh in 1999 for the movie *The Beach*, to vociferous protest from environmental groups. More recently, the RFD began flexing its muscles in the Ko Similan National Marine Park, closing two of the nine islands to all visitors in 2000, imposing tight bureaucratic controls on the boats allowed to bring snorkellers and divers to the other seven and – most controversially – banning local fishermen from the area; the latter injunction caused intense outrage and resulted in two attempts on the life of the national park director involved. While most people understand that the role of the RFD is to conserve vulnerable and precious resources like the Similans, the dramatic hike in entrance fees payable by foreigners to national parks – from B20 up to B200 in 2000 – has been greeted with cynicism and anger, not least because there is little sign of anything tangible being done with the money; see Basics p.69 for more on this.

## Deforestation and infrastructure projects

Undoubtedly the biggest crisis facing Thailand's environment is **deforestation**, the effects of which are felt all over the country. As well as providing shelter and sustenance for birds and animals (a single male tiger, for instance, needs about thirty square kilometres of forest to survive), forests act as an ecological sponge, binding soil and absorbing the impact of monsoon rains. When they are cut down, water and topsoil are rapidly lost, as was demonstrated tragically in 1988, when villages in the south were devastated by mudslides that swept down deforested slopes, killing hundreds of people. A formal **ban** on most **commercial logging** was finally established in the following year, but much illegal activity has continued.

Another major cause of deforestation is development of the country's **infrastructure**. The expanding road network, essential to Thailand's emergence as an industrialized nation, has inevitably damaged the ecology of the country, as have the quarries that supplied the construction boom of the 1980s. But nothing has stirred as much controversy as Thailand's hydro electric schemes, which might be a lot cleaner than the production and burning of lignite – the low-grade coal that's Thailand's major source of energy – but destroys vast areas and, of course, displaces countless people.

The current hot potato is the **Trans-Thai–Malaysia gas pipeline** and gas separation plant project, which the Petroleum Authority of Thailand is planning to construct in Songkhla province, much to the consternation of many local residents.

## Mangroves and coral reefs

In the past, **mangrove swamps** were used by rice farmers to raise **prawns**, using the tides to wash the larvae into prepared pools. Some rice farmers even converted their paddies into prawn farms, but generally the scale of this aquaculture was small and sustainable.

Then, in 1972, the Department of Fisheries began to promote modern technology. Big business swiftly moved in, and today almost all prawn farming in Thailand is in the hands of a few companies. Bad for local farmers, and disastrous for the ecology of the mangroves, large-scale prawn farming uses vast amounts of sea water, which salinates the neighbouring land to the extent that rice farmers who used to produce two crops a year are now reduced to one small harvest. Furthermore, the chemicals used to feed the prawns and ward off disease are allowed to wash back into the swamps, damaging not only the mangroves themselves, but also the water used for irrigation, drinking and washing. Pollution also kills the very industry that produces it, forcing farmers to move their breeding pools along the coast, damaging yet more mangrove. With Thailand now the world's leading producer of tiger prawns, some environmental action groups are calling for an international boycott until there's a proven supply of farmed tropical prawns.

Many of Thailand's **coral reefs** – some of which are thought to be around 450 million years old – are being destroyed by factors attributable to tourism. The main cause of tourism-related destruction is pollution generated by holiday resorts, though the demand for coral souvenirs and irresponsible dive leaders allowing customers to use harpoon guns, both cause terrible damage too. The destruction of coral by tourists is, however, dwarfed by that wreaked by the practice of **dynamite fishing**, which goes on in areas away from the normal tourist haunts.

# Books

The following books should be available in the UK, US or, more likely, Bangkok. Publishers' details for books published in the UK and US are given in the form "UK publisher; US publisher" where they differ; if books are published in one of these countries only, that country's name follows the publisher's name; if books are published in Thailand, the city follows the publisher's name. The designation "o/p" means out of print – consult a library, specialist second-hand bookseller or online out-of-print-books service. Titles marked ⊡ are particularly recommended.

## Culture and society

**Michael Carrithers**, *The Buddha: A Very Short Introduction* (Oxford Paperbacks). Clear, accessible account of the life of the Buddha, and the development and significance of his thought.

**James Eckardt**, *Bangkok People* (Asia Books, Bangkok). The collected articles of a renowned expat journalist, whose interviews and encounters with a gallery of different Bangkokians – from construction-site workers and street vendors to boxers and political candidates – add texture and context to the city.

**Marlane Guelden**, *Thailand: Into the Spirit World* (Times Editions, Bangkok). In richly photographed coffee-table format, a wide-ranging, anecdotal account of the role of magic and spirits in Thai life, from tattoos and amulets to the ghosts of the violently dead.

**Sebastian Hope**, *Outcasts of the Islands: the Sea Gypsies of Southeast Asia* (HarperCollins). Unusual insight into the lives of the chao ley people from a British traveller who spent several months in various sea gypsy communities.

⊡ **William J. Klausner**, *Reflections on Thai Culture* (Siam Society,

Bangkok). Humorous accounts of an anthropologist living in Thailand since 1955; an entertaining mixture of the academic and the anecdotal.

⊡ **Cleo Odzer**, *Patpong Sisters* (Arcade Publishing). An American anthropologist's funny and touching account of her life with the prostitutes and bar girls of Bangkok's notorious red-light district. An enlightening and thought-provoking read, it's a surprisingly enjoyable page-turner too.

⊡ **James O'Reilly and Larry Habegger** (eds), *Travelers' Tales: Thailand* (Travelers' Tales). Perfect background reading for any trip to Thailand: a collection of contemporary writings about the kingdom, some from established Thailand experts, social commentators and travel writers, others culled from enthusiastic visitors with often very funny stories to share.

⊡ **Pasuk Phongpaichit and Sungsidh Piriyarangsan**, Corruption and Democracy in Thailand *(Chulalongkorn University, Bangkok)*. Fascinating study, revealing the nuts and bolts of corruption in Thailand and its links with all levels of political life. Their sequel, a study of Thailand's illegal economy, Guns,

Girls, Gambling, Ganja, co-written with Nualnoi Treerat (Silkworm Books, Chiang Mai), makes equally eye-opening and depressing reading.

**Phya Anuman Rajadhon**, *Some Traditions of the Thai* (DK Books, Bangkok). Meticulously researched essays written by one of Thailand's leading scholars, republished to commemorate the centenary of the author's birth.

**Denis Segaller**, *Thai Ways and More Thai Ways* (Asia Books, Bangkok).

Fascinating collections of short pieces on Thai customs and traditions written for the former Bangkok World newspaper by a long-term English resident of Bangkok.

**William Warren**, *Living in Thailand* (Thames and Hudson). Luscious coffee-table volume of traditional houses and furnishings, with an emphasis on the homes of Thailand's rich and famous; seductively photographed by Luca Invernizzi Tettoni.

# History

**Pasuk Phongpaichit and Chris Baker**, *Thailand's Crisis* (Silkworm Books, Chiang Mai). Illuminating examination, sometimes heavy going, of the 1997 economic crisis.

★ **William Stevenson**, The *Revolutionary King* (Constable, UK). Fascinating biography of the normally secretive King Bhumibol, by a British journalist who was given unprecedented access. The approach is fairly uncritical, but lots of revealing insights emerge along the way.

**William Warren**, *Jim Thompson: the Legendary American of Thailand* (Jim Thompson Thai Silk Co, Bangkok). The engrossing biography of the ex-intelligence agent, art collector and Thai silk magnate whose disappearance in Malaysia in 1967 has never been satisfactorily resolved.

★ **David K. Wyatt**, *Thailand: A Short History* (Yale University Press). An excellent treatment, scholarly but highly readable, with a good eye for witty, telling details.

# Art and architecture

★ **Steve van Beek**, *The Arts of Thailand* (Charles E Tuttle). Lavishly produced and perfectly pitched introduction to the history of Thai architecture, sculpture and painting, with superb photographs by Luca Invernizzi Tettoni.

**Dorothy H. Fickle**, *Images of the Buddha in Thailand* (Oxford University Press, o/p). Clear, concise, though rather arid examination of Thai Buddha images of all periods, and the historical and religious influences which have shaped their development. Well illustrated, with a

short introduction on the life of the Buddha himself.

★ **Sumet Jumsai**, *Naga: Cultural Origins in Siam and the West Pacific* (Oxford University Press, o/p). Wide-ranging discussion of water symbols in Thailand and other parts of Asia, offering a stimulating mix of art, architecture, mythology and cosmology.

★ **Apinan Poshyananda**, *Modern Art In Thailand* (Oxford University Press, Singapore). Excellent introduction – the only one of its kind – which extends up to the early 1990s, with very read-able discussions on dozens of indi-vidual artists, and lots of colour plates.

**William Warren and Luca Invernizzi Tettoni**, *Arts and Crafts of Thailand* (Thames and Hudson). Good-value large-format paperback, setting the wealth of Thai arts and crafts in cultural context, with plen-ty of attractive illustrations and colour photos.

## Natural history and ecology

⭐ **Ashley J. Boyd and Collin Piprell**, *Diving in Thailand* (Times Editions; Hippocrene). A thorough guide to 84 dive sites, detailing access, weather conditions, visibility, scenery and marine life for each, slanted towards the underwater photographer; general introductory sections on Thailand's marine life, conservation and photography tips.

**Margaret S. Gremli and Helen E. Newman**, *Insight Guides Underwater: Marine Life in the South China Sea* (APA). Although not extending to the Andaman coast, Thailand's best snorkelling and div-ing area, this handy, at-a-glance ref-erence guide to reef fish and coral formations covers pretty much everything you'll see there as well as on the Gulf coast. Packed with clear and informative colour photos, yet small enough for a day-pack.

⭐ **Thom Henley**, *Waterfalls and Gibbon Calls* (Limmark, Thailand). Though ostensibly a guide to the flora, fauna and trails of Khao Sok National Park, this book contains so much inter-esting and easily digestible stuff on the plants, animals and birds found all over Thailand that it's worth buying even if you're not going to the park.

⭐ **Eric Valli and Diane Summers**, *The Shadow Hunters* (Suntree, Thailand). Beautifully pho-tographed photo-essay on the bird's-nest collectors of southern Thailand, with whom the authors spent over a year, together scaling the phenome-nal heights of the sheer limestone walls.

## Literature

**Alastair Dingwall** (ed), *Traveller's Literary Companion: Southeast Asia* (Inprint Publishing; Passport, o/p). A useful though rather dry reference book, with a large section on Thailand, with a book list, well-cho-sen extracts, biographical details of authors and other literary notes.

⭐ **Chart Korpjitti**, *The Judgement* (Thai Modern Classics). Sobering modern-day tragedy about a good-hearted Thai villager who is ostracized by his hypocritical neigh-bours. Contains lots of interesting details on village life and traditions and thought-provoking passages on the stifling conservatism of rural communities. Winner of the S.E.A. Write award in 1982.

**Nitaya Masavisut and Matthew Grose**, *The S.E.A. Write Anthology of Thai Short Stories and Poems* (Silkworm Books, Chiang Mai). Interesting medley of short stories and poems by eleven Thai writers who have won Southeast Asian Writers' Awards, providing a good introduction to the contemporary literary scene.

**Rama I**, *Thai Ramayana* (Chalermnit, Bangkok). Slightly stilted abridged prose translation of King Rama I's version of the epic Hindu narrative, full of gleeful descriptions of bizarre mythological characters and supernatural battles. Essential reading if you want anything like a full appreciation of Thai painting, carving and classical dance.

**S.P. Somtow**, *Jasmine Nights* (Hamish Hamilton, o/p). An engaging and humorous rites-of-passage tale of an upper-class boy learning what it is to be Thai.

★ **Khamsing Srinawk**, *The Politician and Other Stories* (Oxford University Press, o/p). A collection of brilliantly satiric short stories, full of pithy moral observation and biting irony, which capture the vulnerability of peasant farmers in the north and northeast.

# Thailand in foreign literature

★ **Dean Barrett**, *Kingdom of Make-Believe* (Village East Books, US). Despite the clichéd ingredients – the Patpong go-go bar scene, opium smuggling in the Golden Triangle, Vietnam veterans – this novel about a return to Thailand following a twenty-year absence turns out to be a rewarding read, with engaging characters and a multidimensional take on the farang experience.

**Botan**, *Letters from Thailand* (DK Books, Bangkok). Probably the best introduction to the Chinese community in Bangkok, presented in the form of letters written over a twenty-year period by a Chinese emigrant to his mother. Branded both as anti-Chinese and anti-Thai, this 1969 prizewinning book is now mandatory reading in school social studies' classes.

★ **Alex Garland**, *The Beach* (Penguin; Riverhead). Gripping and hugely enjoyable cult thriller about a young Brit who gets involved with a group of travellers living a utopian existence on an uninhabited Thai island. Tensions rise as people start to reveal their true personalities, and when the idyll begins to sour the book turns into a mesmerizing page-turner.

**Christopher G. Moore**, *God Of Darkness* (Asia Books, Bangkok). Thailand's best-selling and most prolific expat novelist specializes in intricately woven thrillers packed with incisive detail of contemporary Thai life; this one is set during the economic crisis of 1997, which makes it an especially good read, with plenty of meat on endemic corruption and the desperate struggle for power within family and society.

**Collin Piprell**, *Yawn: a Thriller* (Asia Books, Bangkok). Enjoyable page-turner that spins a good yarn from the apparently disparate worlds of scuba-diving and Buddhist retreats. Set mainly in Pattaya and a thinly disguised Ko Pha Ngan, it stars a Canadian couple and a predictable cast of big-hearted hookers, degenerate expats and an evil godfather figure.

# Food and cookery

**Vatcharin Bhumichitr**, *The Taste of Thailand* (Pavilion; Collier, o/p). Another glossy introduction to this eminently photogenic country, this time through its food. The author runs a Thai restaurant in London and provides background colour as well as about 150 recipes adapted for Western kitchens. **Jacqueline M. Piper**, *Fruits of South-East Asia* (Oxford University Press, o/p). An exploration of the bounteous fruits of the region, tracing their role in cooking, medicine, handicrafts and rituals. Well illustrated with photos, watercolours and early botanical drawings.

# Travel guides

**Naengnoi Suksri**, *The Grand Palace* (Thames & Hudson; River Books). Excellent, authoritative and affordable guide, packed with maps, photos and fascinating background details.

**William Warren**, *Bangkok's Waterways: an Explorer's Handbook* (Asia Books, Bangkok). A cross between a useful guide and an indulgent coffee-table book: attractively produced survey of the capital's riverine sights, spiced with cultural and historical snippets.

# Language

Thai belongs to one of the oldest families of languages in the world, Austro-Thai, and is radically different from most of the other tongues of Southeast Asia. Being tonal, Thai is extremely difficult for Westerners to master, but by building up from a small core of set phrases, you'll soon get the hang of enough to get by. Most Thais who deal with tourists speak some English, but once you stray off the beaten track you'll probably need at least a few words in Thai. Anywhere you go, you'll impress and get better treatment if you at least make an effort to speak a few words.

Distinct dialects are spoken in the north, the northeast and the south, which can increase the difficulty of comprehending what's said to you. **Thai script** is even more of a problem to Westerners, with 44 consonants to represent 21 consonant sounds and 32 vowels to deal with 48 different vowel sounds. However, street signs in touristed areas are nearly always written in Roman script as well as Thai, and in other circumstances you're better off asking than trying to unscramble the swirling mess of symbols, signs and accents. Transliteration into Roman script leads to many problems – see the note in the Introduction.

For the basics, the most useful **language book** on the market is *Thai: a Rough Guide Phrasebook* (Rough Guides), which covers the essential phrases and expressions in both Thai script and phonetic equivalents, as well as dipping into grammar and providing a menu reader and fuller vocabulary in dictionary format.

## Pronunciation

Mastering **tones** is probably the most difficult part of learning Thai. Five different tones are used – low, middle, high, falling, and rising – by which the meaning of a single syllable can be altered in five different ways. Thus, using four of the five tones, you can make a sentence from just one syllable: *mái mài mǎi măi* – "New wood burns, doesn't it?" As well as the natural difficulty in becoming attuned to speaking and listening to these different tones, Western efforts are complicated by our tendency to denote the overall meaning of a sentence by modulating our tones – for example, turning a statement into a question through a shift of stress and tone. Listen to native Thai speakers and you'll soon begin to pick up the different approach to tone.

The pitch of each tone is gauged in relation to your vocal range when speaking, but they should all lie within a narrow band, separated by gaps just big enough to differentiate them. The **low tones** (syllables marked `) , **middle tones** (unmarked syllables), and **high tones** (syllables marked ´) should each be pronounced evenly and with no inflection. The **falling tone** (syllables marked ^) is spoken with an obvious drop in pitch, as if you were sharply emphasizing a word in English. The **rising tone** (marked ~) is pronounced as if you were asking an exaggerated question in English.

As well as the unfamiliar tones, you'll find that, despite the best efforts of the transliterators, there is no precise English equivalent to many **vowel and consonant sounds** in the Thai language. The lists overleaf give a rough idea of pronunciation.

### Greetings and basic phrases

Whenever you speak to a stranger in Thailand, you should end your sentence in *khráp* if you're a man, *khâ* if you're a woman – these untranslatable politening syllables will gain good will, and should always be used after *sawàt dii* (hello/goodbye) and *khàwp khun* (thank you). *Khráp* and *khâ* are also often used to answer "yes" to a question, though the most common way is to repeat the verb of the question (precede it with *mâi* for "no"). *Châi* (yes) and *mâi châi* (no) are less frequently used than their English equivalents.

| | |
|---|---|
| Hello | *sawàt dii* |
| Where are you going? (not always meant literally, but used as a general greeting) | *pai nãi?* |
| I'm out having fun /I'm travelling (answer to pai nãi, almost indefinable pleasantry) | *pai thîaw* |
| Goodbye | *sawàt dii/la kàwn* |
| Good luck/cheers | *chôk dii* |
| Excuse me | *khãw thâwt* |
| Thank you | *khàwp khun* |
| It's nothing/it doesn't matter/no problem | *mâi pen rai* |
| How are you? | *sabai dii reũ?* |
| I'm fine | *sabai dii* |
| What's your name? | *khun chêu arai?* |
| My name is . . . | *phõm (men)/ diichãn (women) chêu . . .* |
| I come from . . . | *phõm/diichãn maa jàak . . .* |
| I don't understand | *mâi khâo jai* |
| Do you speak English? | *khun phûut phasãa angkrìt dâi mãi?* |
| Do you have . . . ? | *mii . . . mãi?* |
| Is there . . . ? | *. . . mii mãi?* |
| Is . . . possible? | *. . . dâi mãi?* |
| Can you help me? | *chûay phõm /diichãn dâi mãi?* |
| (I) want . . . | *ao . . .* |
| (I) would like to . . . | *yàak jà . . .* |
| (I) like . . . | *châwp . . .* |
| What is this called in Thai? | *nîi phasãa thai rîak wâa arai?* |

### Getting around

| | |
|---|---|
| Where is the . . . ? | *. . . yùu thîi nãi?* |
| How far? | *klai thâo rai?* |
| I would like to go to . . . | *yàak jà pai . . .* |
| Where have you been? | *pai nãi maa?* |
| Where is this bus going? | *rót nîi pai nãi?* |
| When will the bus leave? | *rót jà àwk mêua rai?* |
| What time does the bus arrive in . . . ? | *rót theũng . . . kìi mohng?* |
| Stop here | *jàwt thîi nîi* |
| here | *thîi nîi* |
| over there | *thîi nâan/thîi nôhn* |
| right | *khwãa* |
| left | *sái* |
| straight | *trong* |
| north | *neũa* |
| south | *tâi* |
| east | *tawan àwk* |
| west | *tawan tòk* |
| near/far | *klâi/klai* |
| street | *thanõn* |
| train station | *sathàanii rót fai* |
| bus station | *sathàanii rót meh* |
| airport | *sanãam bin* |
| ticket | *tũ˘a* |
| hotel | *rohng raem* |
| post office | *praisanii* |
| restaurant | *raan ahãan* |
| shop | *raan* |
| market | *talàat* |
| hospital | *rohng pha- yaabaan* |
| motorbike | *rót mohtoesai* |
| taxi | *rót táksîi* |
| boat | *reua* |

### Accommodation and shopping

| | |
|---|---|
| How much is . . . ? | *. . . thâo rai /kìi bàat?* |
| How much is a room here per night? | *hâwng thîi nîi kheun lá thâo rai?* |

| | |
|---|---|
| Do you have a cheaper room? | *mii hâwng thùuk kwàa mãi?* |
| Can I/we look at the room? | *duu hâwng dâi mãi?* |
| I/We'll stay two nights | *jà yùu sãwng kheun* |
| Can you reduce the price? | *lót raakhaa dâi mãi?* |
| Can I store my bag here? | *fàak krapão wái thîi nîi dâi mãi?* |
| cheap/expensive | *thùuk/phaeng* |
| air-con room | *hãwng ae* |
| ordinary room | *hãwng thammadaa* |
| telephone | *thohrásàp* |
| laundry | *sák phâa* |
| blanket | *phâa hòm* |
| fan | *phát lom* |

## General adjectives

| | |
|---|---|
| alone | *khon diaw* |
| another | *ìik . . . nèung* |
| bad | *mâi dii* |
| big | *yài* |
| clean | *sa-àat* |
| closed | *pìt* |
| cold (object) | *yen* |
| cold (person or weather) | *não* |
| delicious | *aròi* |
| difficult | *yâak* |
| dirty | *sokaprok* |
| easy | *ngâi* |
| fun | *sanùk* |
| hot (temperature) | *ráwn* |
| hot (spicy) | *pèt* |
| hungry | *hĩu khâo* |
| ill | *mâi sabai* |
| open | *pòet* |
| pretty | *sũay* |
| small | *lek* |
| thirsty | *hĩu nám* |
| tired | *nèu-ai* |
| very | *mâak* |

## General nouns

Nouns have no plurals or genders, and don't require an article.

| | |
|---|---|
| bathroom/toilet | *hãwng nám* |
| boyfriend or girlfriend | *faen* |
| food | *ahãan* |
| foreigner | *fàràng* |
| friend | *phêuan* |
| money | *ngoen* |
| water | *nám* |

## General verbs

Thai verbs do not conjugate at all, and also often double up as nouns and adjectives, which means that foreigners' most unidiomatic attempts to construct sentences are often readily understood.

| | |
|---|---|
| come | *maa* |
| do | *tham* |
| eat | *kin/thaan khâo* |
| give | *hâi* |
| go | *pai* |
| sit | *nâng* |
| sleep | *nawn làp* |
| take | *ao* |
| walk | *doen pai* |

## Numbers

| | |
|---|---|
| zero | *sũun* |
| one | *nèung* |
| two | *sãwng* |
| three | *sãam* |
| four | *sìi* |
| five | *hâa* |
| six | *hòk* |
| seven | *jèt* |
| eight | *pàet* |
| nine | *kâo* |
| ten | *sìp* |
| eleven | *sìp èt* |
| twelve, thirteen, etc | *sìp sãwng, sìp sãam . . .* |
| twenty | *yîi sìp/yiip* |
| twenty-one | *yîi sìp èt* |
| twenty-two, twenty-three, etc | *yîi sìp sãwng, yîi sìp sãam . . ,* |
| thirty, forty, etc | *sãam sìp, sìi sìp . .* |
| one hundred, two hundred, etc | *nèung rói, sãwng rói . . .* |
| one thousand | *nèung phan* |
| ten thousand | *nèung mèun* |

## Time

The commonest system for telling the time, as outlined below, is actually a confusing mix of several different systems. The State Railway and government officials use the 24-hour clock (9am is *kâo naalikaa*, 10am *sìp naalikaa*, and so on), which is always worth trying if you get stuck.

| | |
|---|---|
| 1–5am | *tii nèung–tii hâa* |
| 6–11am | *hòk mohng cháo– sìp èt mohng cháo* |
| noon | *thîang* |
| 1pm | *bài mohng* |

| | | | |
|---|---|---|---|
| 2–4pm | *bài sǎwng mohng–*<br>*bài sìi mohng* | week | *aathít* |
| 5–6pm | *hâa mohng yen–hòk*<br>*mohng yen* | month | *deuan* |
| 7–11pm | *nèung thûm–hâa*<br>*thûm* | year | *pii* |
| | | today | *wan níi* |
| midnight | *thîang kheun* | tomorrow | *phrûng níi* |
| What time is it? | *kìi mohng láew?* | yesterday | *mêua wan* |
| How many hours? | *kìi chûa mohng?* | now | *diǎw níi* |
| How long? | *naan thâo rai?* | next week | *aathít nâa* |
| minute | *naathii* | last week | *aathít kàwn* |
| hour | *chûa mohng* | morning | *cháo* |
| day | *waan* | afternoon | *bài* |
| | | evening | *yen* |
| | | night | *kheun* |

## Vowels

**a** as in dad.

**aa** has no precise equivalent, but is pronounced as it looks, with the vowel elongated.

**ae** as in there.

**ai** as in buy.

**ao** as in now.

**aw** as in awe.

**e** as in pen.

**eu** as in sir, but heavily nasalized.

**i** as in tip.

**ii** as in feet.

**o** as in knock.

**oe** as in hurt, but more closed.

**oh** as in toe.

**u** as in loot.

**uay** "u" plus "ay" as in pay.

**uu** as in pool.

## Consonants

**r** as in rip, but with the tongue flapped quickly against the palate – in everyday speech, it's often pronounced like "l".

**kh** as in keep.

**ph** as in put.

**th** as in time.

**k** is unaspirated and unvoiced, and closer to "g".

**p** is also unaspirated and unvoiced, and closer to "b".

**t** is also unaspirated and unvoiced, and closer to "d".

# Glossary

**Amphoe** District.
**Amphoe muang** Provincial capital.
**Ao** Bay.
**Avatar** Earthly manifestation of a deity.
**Ban** Village or house.
**Bencharong** Polychromatic ceramics made in China for the Thai market.
**Bodhisattva** In Mahayana Buddhism, an enlightened being who postpones his or her entry into Nirvana.
**Bot** Main sanctuary of a Buddhist temple.
**Brahma** One of the Hindu trinity: "the Creator". Usually depicted with four faces and four arms.
**Celadon** Porcelain with distinctive grey-green glaze.
**Changwat** Province.
**Chao ley/Chao nam** "Sea gypsies" – nomadic fisherfolk of southern Thailand.
**Chedi** Reliquary tower in Buddhist temple.
**Dharma** The teachings or doctrine of the Buddha.
**Dharmachakra** Buddhist Wheel of Law (also known as Wheel of Life).
**Erawan** Mythical three-headed elephant; Indra's vehicle.
**Farang** A foreigner; a corruption of the word français.
**Ganesh** Hindu elephant-headed deity, remover of obstacles and god of knowledge.
**Garuda** Mythical Hindu creature – half-man half-bird; Vishnu's vehicle.
**Gopura** Entrance pavilion to temple precinct (especially Khmer).
**Hang yao** Longtail boat.
**Hanuman** Monkey god in the Ramayana; ally of Rama.
**Hat** Beach.
**Hinayana** Pejorative term for Theravada school of Buddhism, literally "Lesser Vehicle".
**Indra** Hindu king of the gods and, in Buddhism, devotee of the Buddha; usually carries a thunderbolt.
**Isaan** Northeast Thailand.

**Jataka** Stories of the five hundred lives of the Buddha.
**Khao** Hill, mountain.
**Khlong** Canal.
**Khon** Classical dance-drama.
**Kinnari** Mythical creature – half-woman, half-bird.
**Ko** Island.
**Laem** Headland or cape.
**Lakhon** Classical dance-drama.
**Lak muang** City pillar; revered home for the city's guardian spirit.
**Lakshaman/Phra Lak** Rama's younger brother.
**Lakshana** Auspicious signs or "marks of greatness" displayed by the Buddha.
**Likay** Popular folk theatre.
**Maenam** River.
**Mahayana** School of Buddhism now practised mainly in China, Japan and Korea; literally "the Great Vehicle".
**Mara** The Evil One; tempter of the Buddha.
**Mawn khwaan** Traditional triangular or "axe-head" pillow.
**Meru/Sineru** Mythical mountain at the centre of Hindu and Buddhist cosmologies.
**Mondop** Small, square temple building to house minor images or religious texts.
**Moo/muu** Neighbourhood within an amphoe.
**Muang** City or town.
**Muay Thai** Thai boxing.
**Mudra** Symbolic gesture of the Buddha.
**Mut mee** Tie-dyed cotton or silk.
**Naga** Mythical dragon-headed serpent in Buddhism and Hinduism.
**Nam** Water.
**Nam tok** Waterfall.
**Nang thalung** Shadow-puppet entertainment, found in southern Thailand.
**Nirvana** Final liberation from the cycle of rebirths; state of non-being to which Buddhists aspire.
**Pak Tai** Southern Thailand.
**Pali** Language of ancient India; the script of the original Buddhist scriptures.

**Pha Sin** Woman's sarong.

**Phi** Animist spirit.

**Phra** Honorific term for a person – literally "excellent".

**Prang** Central tower in a Khmer temple.

**Prasat** Khmer temple complex or central shrine.

**Rama** Human manifestation of Hindu deity Vishnu; hero of the Ramayana.

**Ramakien** Thai version of the Ramayana.

**Ramayana** Hindu epic of good versus evil whose hero is Rama.

**Ravana** Rama's adversary in the Ramayana; represents evil. Also known as Totsagan.

**Reua** Boat.

**Reua hang yao** Longtail boat.

**Rot ae/rot tua** Air-conditioned bus.

**Rot thammadaa** Ordinary bus.

**Sala** Meeting hall or open-sided pavilion.

**Samlor** Passenger tricycle; literally "three-wheeled".

**Sanskrit** Sacred language of Hinduism, also used in Buddhism.

**Sanuk** Fun.

**Sema** Boundary stone to mark consecrated ground within temple complex.

**Shiva** One of the Hindu trinity – "The Destroyer".

**Shiva lingam** Phallic representation of Shiva.

**Soi** Alley or side-road.

**Songkhran** Thai New Year.

**Songthaew** Pick-up used as public transport; literally "two rows", after the vehicle's two facing benches.

**Talat** Market.

**Talat nam** Floating market.

**Talat yen** Night market.

**Tha** Pier.

**Thale** Sea or lake.

**Tham** Cave.

**Thanon** Road.

**Theravada** Main school of Buddhist thought in Thailand; also known as Hinayana.

**Tripitaka** Buddhist scriptures.

**Tuk-tuk** Motorized three-wheeled taxi.

**Uma** Shiva's consort.

**Ushnisha** Cranial protuberance on Buddha images, signifying an enlightened being.

**Viharn** Temple assembly hall for the laity; contains the principal Buddha image.

**Vipassana** Buddhist meditation technique; literally "insight".

**Vishnu** One of the Hindu trinity – "The Preserver". Usually shown with four arms, holding a disc, a conch, a lotus and a club.

**Wai** Thai greeting expressed by a prayer-like gesture with the hands.

**Wat** Temple.

**Yaksha** Mythical giant.

# index

## and small print

# Index

Map entries are in colour

## A

accommodation ......41–43
addresses ...................74
AIDS .................33, 140
airlines
    in Australia and New
        Zealand ..................16
    in Britain & Ireland ...........9
    in North America ...........12
amulets ....................125
Ananda .....................438
Ang Thong National
    Marine Park ...........256
antiques, exporting ......22
Ao Luk .....................361
Ao Nam Mao .............363
**Ao Nang** .........365–369
Ao Nang .....................366
**Ao Phang Nga** ...350–354
Ao Phra Nang ...........362
Ao Thalen ..................361
Aranyaprathet ...........211
ATMs ..........................27
Ayutthaya, history of ..436

## B

baht ..............................26
Ban Chao Mai ...........403
Ban Hat Lek .......209, 210
Ban Pasey Yawo ........431
Ban Phum Riang ........248
Ban Taba ..................429
Bang Niang ........312, 317
Bang Niang ................313
**BANGKOK** ..........79–168
    accommodation ...............96
    airlines ............................161
    airport .............83, 161, 167
    airport accommodation ....86
    amulet market .................125
    Ancient City .....................44
    Ban Kamthieng ...............142
    Bangkok districts .............82
    Bangkok Noi ...........88, 165
    Bangkok Sightseeing Bus
        ...........................................90
    Bangkok Tourist Bureau ...89
    Banglamphu
        ................96, 124, 146, 152

Banglamphu ...............98–99
    bars ................................152
    bicycle tours............ 90, 133
    bookstores ....................160
    Buddhaisawan Chapel ...123
    bus maps ........................90
    bus routes .......................92
    bus terminals ..........88, 165
    canal rides .....................133
    car rental .......................162
central Bangkok .....84–85
    Chatuchak Weekend
        Market ........................143
    Chinatown ......101, 127, 147
    Chinatown ......................128
    city transport ...................90
    clubs ...............................152
    cookery classes .............162
    counterfeit culture ..........157
    culture shows .................155
    cybercafés ......................163
    Democracy Monument ...124
    Don Muang ......83, 161, 167
Downtown: Siam Square &
    Thanon Ploenchit ...103
Downtown: south of
    Rama IV ...................105
    Dusit ..............................135
    elephant museum ...........136
    email services ................163
    embassies ......................162
    Emerald Buddha ............115
    emergencies ...................163
    Erawan Shrine ................139
    express boats .............91, 94
    floating markets .............133
    flower market .................130
    gay bars and clubs ........ 154
    Giant Swing ...................126
    Golden Buddha ..............129
    Golden Mount ................126
    Grand Palace .................111
    highlights ........................80
    hospitals .........................163
    Hualamphong Station
        ...........................87, 165
    immigration office ..........163
    Jim Thompson's House ...137
    Khao Din 136.......................
    Khao San road ........ 96, 124,
        .............................146, 152
    Krung Thep ......................82
    language courses ...........163
    Loh Prasat .....................125
    longtail boats ...................92
    Marble Temple ...............137
    Marsi Gallery .................138
    massage .........................118
    meditation ......................164

    motorbike taxis ................95
    Muang Boran Ancient
        City ...........................144
    National Museum ...........121
    Pahurat ..........................127
    Pak Khlong Talat ............130
    Patpong ..........................140
    post offices .....................163
    Ratanakosin ....................111
    Ratanakosin ....................112
    Reclining Buddha ...........120
    restaurants .....................145
    Royal Barge Museum .....134
    Sampeng Lane ...............129
    Sao Ching Cha ...............126
    shopping .........................156
    Skytrain ............................93
    Soi Issaranuphap ...........129
    Soi Kasemsan 1 .............102
    Soi Ngam Duphli ............104
    Soi Ngam Duphli ...........107
    Suan Pakkad Palace
        Museum ....................138
    Support Museum ...........136
    Taling Chan ...................133
    TAT ..................................89
    taxis .................................95
    telephone offices ............164
    Thai boxing ....................156
    Thai dancing ..................155
    Thanon Sukhumvit
        .......................107, 150, 154
    Thanon Sukhumvit ......... 108
    Thonburi .........................131
    tour operators .................167
    tourist information ...........89
    travel agents ..................164
    travel from Bangkok ......164
    tuk-tuks ...........................95
    vegetarian festival .........148
    Vimanmek Palace ..........135
    Wang Na ........................123
    Wat Arun ........................133
    Wat Benjamabophit .......137
    Wat Ga Buang Kim ........130
    Wat Indraviharn .............124
    Wat Mahathat ................120
    Wat Mangkon
        Kamalawat ...............130
    Wat Phra Kaeo ..............111
    Wat Phra Kaeo & the Grand
        Palace .......................114
    Wat Po ...........................118
    Wat Po ...........................119
    Wat Rajabophit ..............127
    Wat Rajnadda ................125
    Wat Saket .......................126
    Wat Suthat .....................126
    Wat Traimit ....................129

Weekend Market ...........143
zoo .......................................136
Banharn Silpa-archa ...440
banks ................................26
beer ..................................51
Betong ...........................427
Bhumibol Adulyadej ...438
bicycle rental ...............40
bird's-nesting ............. 379
**books** .................452–456
bookshops, travel ........24
boxing, Thai ........ 62, 156
**Buddhism** ..........442–445
budgeting ......................26
bullfighting ..................415
bungalows ....................41
Burma, travel to and
    from ..............................19
buses ............................34

### C

calendar, Thai................58
Cambodia border
    crossings ................210
Cambodia, travel from ...19
camera film ..................75
camping .........................43
car rental ......................39
cashpoints ....................27
Catnet ...........................54
Cha-am ........................233
Chaiya ..........................247
Chak Phra Festival .....251
**Chanthaburi** ......202–205
Chanthaburi ...............203
chao ley .......................308
Chatichai Choonhavan 439
Chavalit Yongchaiyudh 440
children, travel with ......73
Chuan Leekpai ...........440
Chulalongkorn .............437
**Chumphon** .........243–247
Chumphon ......... 244
climate ..........................viii
contact lenses ..............74
contraceptives ..:.........75
cookery classes
    ...75, 162, 264, 328, 357
cookery courses .........328
coral ...............................xvi
costs ..............................26
courier flights .........11, 14
credit cards ..................27
crime ..............................56
currency ........................26
customs regulations .....22

### D

debit cards ....................27
deep south, the ..394–395
dehydration ..................33
dengue fever ...............31
departure taxes ..........164
diapers ..........................73
diarrhoea ......................33
directory enquiries .......53
disabled travel ...............72
dive sites ......................68
diving ..............................67
    Andaman Coast .............323
    Ao Nang .........................365
    Khao Lak ........................315
    Ko Chang .......................213
    Ko Lanta .........................382
    Ko Phi Phi .......................372
    Ko Similan ......................318
    Ko Tao ............................282
    Pattaya ............................183
    Phuket ............................322
Don Muang ..83, 161, 167
doves ............................427
drama .............................61
drinks .............................50
drug smuggling ............56
Dvaravati culture ........435

### E

east coast ....................172
East Railay .................362
Eastern & Oriental Express
    ..........................................20
economic crisis of 1997
    ..........................................440
electricity .......................75
email ..............................54
embassies, Thai ...........22
emergencies .........29, 57
environmental issues .450
etiquette, social ...........65
exchange rates ...........26

### F

faxes ..............................54
ferries ............................37
festivals .........................59
first-aid kit ....................32
flight agents
    in Australia & New Zealand .17
    in Britain & Ireland ...........10

in North America ..............14
flights
    from Australia & New
        Zealand ......................15
    from Britain & Ireland .........9
    from North America ..........12
    in Thailand .........................37
flora and fauna ...447–451
food .........................44–51
food courts ..................45
food etiquette ...............45
fruits ..............................47
fuel .................................39
full-moon parties ........272

### G

gay Thailand .................70
geckoes ......................450
glossary ......................461
guest houses ...............41

### H

Hat Chao Mai National
    Park ...........................402
Hat Kae Kae ...............431
Hat Nopparat Thara... 368
**Hat Rin**.............. 272–276
Hat Rin ........................274
**Hat Yai** ..............415–419
Hat Yai ........................416
health ......................29–34
Hindu deities .............,445
history of Thailand
    ..............................435–441
hitchhiking ...................40
holidays, national .........58
hongs .........................361
hospitals .......................29
hostels ..........................42
hotel booking online ...43
hotels ............................42
**Hua Hin** ..............235–241
Hua Hin .......................236

### I

immigration ..................21
inoculations .................30
insurance ......................28
internet access ...........54
Islamic militancy ........396

# J

Japanese encephalitis ...32
jellyfish bites ................32
Jomtien Beach ...........183
Jomtien Beach ...........184

# K

katoey ...........................70
Kaw Thaung ...............303
kayaking
  v, 6, 9, 257, 361, 366, 373
Khao Kanab Nam ......358
**Khao Lak** ...........312–317
Khao Lak ....................313
Khao Luang National Park
  .................................291
Khao Sam Roi Yot
  National Park ...........241
**Khao Sok National Park**
  .........................309–312
Khlong Yai ..................209
Khmer empire ............435
khon ............................61
Khu Khut Waterbird Park
  .................................425
Khuraburi ...................309
Ko Adang ...................413
Ko Bileh .....................361
Ko Bubu .....................388
Ko Bulon Lae ............414
Ko Chang (Ranong) ...304
**Ko Chang** (Trat) ..211–222
Ko Chang (Trat) ..........212
Ko Chang: Hat Kai Bae
  .................................220
Ko Chang: Hat Sai Khao
  .................................215
Ko Hai .......................403
Ko Hong (Krabi) .........361
Ko Jum ......................389
Ko Kham .....................222
Ko Kham .....................212
Ko Khao Yai ...............414
Ko Kradan ..................405
Ko Kud .......................223
**Ko Lanta** ...........379–388
Ko Lanta .....................380
Ko Lanta: Hat Khlong Dao
  .................................384
Ko Lao Ya ..................223
Ko Libong ..................405
Ko Lidi .......................414
Ko Lipe ......................413
Ko Losin .....................428

Ko Mak .......................222
Ko Mak .......................212
Ko Mook .....................404
Ko Nang Yuan ...........284
Ko Ngai ......................403
Ko Panyi ....................353
**Ko Pha Ngan** .....269–279
Ko Pha Ngan ..............269
Ko Pha Yam ...............306
Ko Phetra National Marine
  Park ..........................414
**Ko Phi Phi** .........369–379
**Ko Phi Phi Don** ...371–378
Ko Phi Phi Don          370
Ko Phi Phi Leh ...........378
Ko Phra Thong ...........309
Ko Pu .........................389
**Ko Samet** ...........191–202
Ko Samet ....................192
**KO SAMUI** .........252–269
  Ang Thong National Marine
    Park .........................256
  Ao Phangka ...............268
  Bangrak ....................260
  Big Buddha ................260
  Bophut .......................259
  Chaweng ...................261
  Chaweng ...................262
  Choeng Mon ..............260
  cookery classes ........264
  Coral Cove ................261
  diving ........................253
  getting there ..............254
  hospital .....................255
  immigration ...............255
  Ko Samui ...................253
  Laem Set ...................268
  Lamai ........................265
  Lamai ........................266
  Maenam .....................257
  Na Muang Falls .........268
  Na Thon ....................255
  tourist office ..............253
  tourist police ......255, 262
  transport ...................254
**Ko Si Chang** ...174–177
Ko Si Chang ...............175
Ko Similan ..................317
Ko Song .....................303
Ko Sukorn ..................406
Ko Surin .....................307
**Ko Tao** ............279–285
Ko Tao ........................280
Ko Tarutao ..................412
**Ko Tarutao National
  Marine Park** ...409–414
Ko Tarutao National Marine
  Park ..........................410
Ko Whai .....................223
Ko Yo .........................424
Koh Kong ...................210

**Krabi** .................354–360
**Krabi beaches** ..360–369
Krabi beaches ............360
Krabi town ..................355
Krung Ching Waterfall 292

# L

Laem Ngop .................209
**Laem Phra Nang** 361–365
lakhon .............................61
language .............457–460
Laos, travel from ..........20
laptops .........................54
left luggage .................75
likay .............................62
longtail boats ...............38
Loy Krathong ...............60

# M

malaria .........................31
Malaysia, travel to and
  from ...20, 408, 417, 429
mangroves .................359
map outlets .................24
maps ...........................23
medications, carrying ..33
meditation centres ......63
menu reader ................48
merit-making ..............445
mobile phones ...........52
monarchy ...................64
Mongkut .....................437
mosquitoes .................31
motorbike rental ..........40
motorbike taxis ...........38
muay thai ............62, 156

# N

**Nakhon Si Thammarat**
  .........................285–291
Nakhon Si Thammarat
  .........................286–287
names, Thai ................66
nang ............................62
nappies .......................73
Narathiwat ..................428
national park
  accommodation ..........2
national parks ......68, 450
newspapers ................55

Ngan Kin Jeh ............327
night markets ..............44
noodles ......................45

# O

online information ........25
opening hours ............58
overland from Southeast
   Asia ..................18–21

# P

Pak Bara ..................411
Pak Meng ..................402
Pattani ......................426
**Pattaya** ............177–190
Pattaya Beach ............178
petrol ..........................39
Phang Nga ................352
pharmacies ................29
Phatthalung ..............396
**Phetchaburi** ......229–233
Phetchaburi ................230
Phibunsongkhram ......438
Phra Ratchaniwet
   Marukhathaiyawan ..235
phrasebooks ..............457
Phraya Taksin ............436
**Phuket** ..............319–350
airlines ....................328
airport ....................321
Ao Bang Tao ............333
Ao Chalong ..............347
Ao Karon ................340
Ao Karon ................341
Ao Kata Noi ............345
Ao Kata Noi ............341
Ao Kata Yai ............345
Ao Kata Yai ............341
Ao Pansea ..............334
Ao Patong ..............336
Ao Patong ..............337
Bang Pae Waterfall ..349
Butterfly Farm ..........326
cookery courses ......328
day-trips ................328
diving ......................322
Gibbon Rehabilitation
   Project ................349
golf ........................328
Hat Kamala ............334
Hat Mai Khao ..........330
Hat Nai Harn ..........346
Hat Nai Thon ..........333
Hat Nai Yang ..........332
Hat Rawai ..............347
Hat Surin ................334

hospitals ..................329
immigration ..............330
Ko Hai ....................347
Ko Maiton ................347
Ko Racha Yai ..........347
Ko Siray ..................348
Laem Panwa ............348
Laem Promthep ........346
Laem Singh ..............335
Ngan Kin Jeh ..........327
Phra Taew National Park 348
Phuket Aquarium ......348
Phuket island ..........320
Phuket town ............324
Phuket town ............325
police ......................30
snorkelling ..............322
Thachatchai Nature Trail 349
Thalang Museum ......348
Ton Sai Waterfall ......349
tourist office ............330
transport ................321
Vegetarian Festival ....327
Wat Phra Tong ........348
police, tourist ............57
post offices ..............52
poste restante ..........52
Prachuap Khiri Khan ..243
Prajadhipok ..............437
Prem Tinsulanonda ....439
Pridi Phanomyong ....437
prostitution ..............140
puddings ....................50

# R

rabies ........................32
radio ..........................55
Railay ......................362
rainfall ......................vii
Rama I ......................436
Rama II ....................436
Rama III ..................437
Rama IV ..................437
Rama V ....................437
Rama VI ..................437
Rama VII ..................437
Rama VIII ................438
Rama IX ..................438
Ramkhamhaeng ........435
Ranong ....................300
Rayong ....................190
rays ..........................xxi
recompression chambers
   ..............................68
reef fish ..................xviii
regional dishes ..........46
rehydration ................33
**religion** ............442–446
restaurants ................44

rice dishes ................46
rock climbing 69, 363, 373
royal family ................64
"royal" Thai cuisine ......45
rubies ......................204

# S

Sa Phra Nang ..........362
Saiburi ....................431
samlors ......................38
*sanuk* ......................66
Saphan Pla ..............303
sapphires ................204
Satun ......................407
scams ........................56
sea gypsies ..............308
sea-canoeing, see kayaking
Seri Thai ..................438
sex industry ..............140
sexual harassment ......57
shadow puppets ........289
share taxis ................36
sharks ......................xxi
Si Racha ..................173
Sichon ....................292
Similan islands ..........317
Singapore, travel to and
   from ......................20
snake bites ................32
snakes ....................449
snorkelling ................67
**Songkhla** ..........419–424
Songkhla ..................420
Songkhla Zoo ..........425
Songkhran ................59
songthaews ..............35
Southern Folklore
   Museum ................425
southern Thai food ......46
Southern Thailand: the
   Andaman Coast 298–299
Southern Thailand: the
   Gulf Coast ............228
spirit houses ............446
Srivijaya empire ........435
Suan Mokkh ............248
Sukhothai, history of ..435
Sungai Kolok ............429
Sunthorn Phu ..........198
**Surat Thani** ......249–252
Surat Thani ..............250
Surin islands ............307
Susaan Hoi ..............360
sweets ......................50

# T

Tak Bai ..........................431
*takraw* ............................63
Taksin Ratchaniwet palace
.....................................432
tampons ..........................75
TAT offices abroad .......23
tax clearance certificates
.....................................22
taxis ...............................38
telephone codes, interna-
tional ...........................53
telephones ....................52
television ...................... 55
Tha Don ........................352
Thai language .....457–460
Thaksin Shinawatra ....441
Thale Ban National Park
.....................................408
Thale Noi Waterbird Park
.....................................398
Tham Lod ......................361
Tham Morakhot ..........404
Than Bokkharani .......361
Thap Lamu .................318
Thong Sala .................271
tipping ...........................75
tour operators
  in Australia and New
    Zealand ......................17
  in Britain & Ireland ............11
  in North America ..............14

in Thailand ...................167
Tourism Authority of
  Thailand ....................23
tourist information ........23
trains .............................36
**Trang town** ........398–401
Trang town ...................399
transliteration ................vii
**transport** .................34–40
transvestites .................70
Trat .............................206
Trat .............................207
travel health centres ....30
travel insurance ............28
travellers' cheques .......27
tuk-tuks ........................38
turtles ..................xxii, 331
TV ..................................55

# U

U-Tapao ......................180

# V

Vajiravudh ..................437
Vegetarian Festival .....327
vegetarian food ............50
Victoria Point ..............303

Vietnam, travel to and
  from ...........................20
Vipassana .....................63
visa extensions ............22
Visakha Puja .................59
visas .............................21

# W

*wai* ...............................65
Wat Chonthara Sing He
.....................................431
Wat Khao Tham .........271
Wat Suan Mokkh ....... 248
Wat Tham Seua (Krabi) 358
water .............................50
weather ..........................vii
websites on Thailand ...25
West Railay ................362
whisky ...........................51
wildlife ...............449–450
wine ..............................51
wiring money ...............27

# Y

Yala .............................427

# Twenty Years of Rough Guides

In the summer of 1981, Mark Ellingham, Rough Guides' founder, knocked out the first guide on a typewriter, with a group of friends. Mark had been travelling in Greece after university, and couldn't find a guidebook that really answered his needs.There were heavyweight cultural guides on the one hand – good on museums and classical sites but not on beaches and tavernas – and on the other hand student manuals that were so caught up with how to save money that they lost sight of the country's significance beyond its role as a place for a cool vacation. None of the guides began to address Greece as a country, with its natural and human environment, its politics and its contemporary life.

Having no urgent reason to return home, Mark decided to write his own guide. It was a guide to Greece that tried to combine some erudition and insight with a thoroughly practical approach to travellers' needs. Scrupulously researched listings of places to stay, eat and drink were matched by careful attention to detail on everything from Homer to Greek music, from classical sites to national parks and from nude beaches to monasteries. Back in London, Mark and his friends got their Rough Guide accepted by a farsighted commissioning editor at the publisher Routledge and it came out in 1982.

The Rough Guide to Greece was a student scheme that became a publishing phenomenon. The immediate success of the book – shortlisted for the Thomas Cook award – spawned a series that rapidly covered dozens of countries. The Rough Guides found a ready market among backpackers and budget travellers, but soon acquired a much broader readership that included older and less impecunious visitors. Readers relished the guides' wit and inquisitiveness as much as the enthusiastic, critical approach that acknowledges everyone wants value for money – but not at any price.

Rough Guides soon began supplementing the "rougher" information – the hostel and low-budget listings – with the kind of detail that independent-minded travellers on any budget might expect. These days, the guides – distributed worldwide by the Penguin group – include recommendations spanning the range from shoestring to luxury, and cover more than 200 destinations around the globe. Our growing team of authors, many of whom come to Rough Guides initially as outstandingly good letter-writers telling us about their travels, are spread all over the world, particularly in Europe, the USA and Australia. As well as the travel guides, Rough Guides publishes a series of dictionary phrasebooks covering two dozen major languages, an acclaimed series of music guides running the gamut from Classical to World Music, a series of music CDs in association with World Music Network, and a range of reference books on topics as diverse as the Internet, Pregnancy and Unexplained Phenomena. Visit www.roughguides.com to see what's cooking.

## Rough Guide Credits

**Text editor** : Clifton Wilkinson
**Series editor** : Mark Ellingham
**Editorial** : Martin Dunford, Jonathan Buckley, Jo Mead, Kate Berens, Ann-Marie Shaw, Helena Smith, Judith Bamber, Orla Duane, Olivia Eccleshall, Ruth Blackmore, Geoff Howard, Claire Saunders, Gavin Thomas, Alexander Mark Rogers, Polly Thomas, Joe Staines, Richard Lim, Duncan Clark, Peter Buckley, Lucy Ratcliffe, Alison Murchie, Matthew Teller (UK); Andrew Rosenberg, Stephen Timblin, Yuki Takagaki, Richard Koss (US)
**Production** : Susanne Hillen, Andy Hilliard, Link Hall, Helen Prior, Julia Bovis, Michelle Draycott, Katie Pringle, Zoë Nobes, Rachel Holmes, Andy Turner

**Cartography** : Melissa Baker, Maxine Repath, Ed Wright, Katie Lloyd-Jones
**Picture research** : Louise Boulton, Sharon Martins, Mark Thomas.
**Online** : Kelly Cross, Anja Mutig-Blessing, Jennifer Gold, Audra Epstein, Suzanne Welles (US)
**Finance** : John Fisher, Gary Singh, Edward Downey, Mark Hall, Tim Bill
**Marketing & Publicity** : Richard Trillo, Niki Smith, David Wearn, Chloë Roberts, Claire Southern, Demelza Dallow, (UK); Simon Carloss, David Wechsler, Kathleen Rushforth (US)
**Administration** : Tania Hummel, Julie Sanderson

## Publishing Information

This first edition published November 2001 by **Rough Guides Ltd** , 62–70 Shorts Gardens, London WC2H 9AH.
Penguin Putnam, Inc. 375 Hudson Street, NY 10014, USA. Reprinted June 2002.
**Distributed by the Penguin Group**
Penguin Books Ltd,
80 Strand, London WC2R ORL
Penguin Putnam, Inc.
375 Hudson Street, NY 10014, USA
Penguin Books Australia Ltd,
487 Maroondah Highway, PO Box 257,
Ringwood, Victoria 3134, Australia
Penguin Books Canada Ltd,
10 Alcorn Avenue, Toronto, Ontario,
Canada M4V 1E4
Penguin Books (NZ) Ltd,
182–190 Wairau Road, Auckland 10,
New Zealand
Typeset in Bembo and Helvetica to an original design by Henry Iles.

Printed in Italy by LegoPrint S.p.A

504pp includes index
A catalogue record for this book is available from the British Library

ISBN 1-85828-829-0

The publishers and authors have done their best to ensure the accuracy and currency of all the information in **The Rough Guide to Thailand's Beaches & Islands** , however, they can accept no responsibility for any loss, injury, or inconvenience sustained by any traveller as a result of information or advice contained in the guide.

## Help us update

We've gone to a lot of effort to ensure that the first edition of **The Rough Guide to Thailand's Beaches & Islands** is accurate and up-to-date. However, things change – places get "discovered", opening hours are notoriously fickle, restaurants and rooms raise prices or lower standards. If you feel we've got it wrong or left something out, we'd like to know, and if you can remember the address, the price, the time, the phone number, so much the better.

We'll credit all contributions, and send a copy of the next edition (or any other Rough Guide if you prefer) for the best letters. Everyone who writes to us and isn't already a subscriber will receive a copy of our full-colour twice-yearly newsletter. Please mark letters: "**Rough Guide Thailand's Beaches & Islands Update** " and send to: Rough Guides, 62–70 Shorts Gardens, London WC2H 9AH, or Rough Guides, 4th Floor, 345 Hudson St, New York, NY 10014. Or send an email to: **mail@roughguides.co.uk** or **mail@roughguides.com**

# Acknowledgements

The authors jointly would like to thank: Ron Emmons and Claire Saunders for their tireless researching and thoughtful updating; Julia Kelly, Nicky Agate and Narrell Leffman for additional Basics research; our editor, Clifton Wilkinson; staff at the Bangkok Tourist Bureau and TAT offices all over the country, especially in Narathiwat and Ko Samui; Tom Vater for the piece on the chao ley; John Clewley for updating the music article; Phil Cornwel-Smith; Randy Campbell; Andrew Spooner; Iain Stewart; Bangkok Airways. Thanks also to Jennifer Speake and Susannah Wight for vigilant proofreading; Mike Hancock, Katie Pringle and Rachel Holmes for typesetting; and Katie Lloyd-Jones and Maxine Repath for maps.

From Lucy, thanks to: Chris Lee and Abi Batalla at London TAT; Mawn in Trat; Tan and Michel in Sukhothai; Mark Read in Khao Yai; Pornprasong and A-No-Thai in Mae Sot; Terry McBroom in Pattaya.

Thanks from Claire to: Navaporn Chuachomket at Narathiwat TAT; Khun Vincent on Ko Libong; Arnat Buathong in Hat Yai; Khun Kannika in Narathiwat; and – especially – to Dick te Brake & Worrawut Wadee in Trang, Khun Natini in Narathiwat, Gareth and Christina in Bangkok, and Ian for selflessly helping research all those beaches. Ron thanks Annette and Pon Kunigagon in Chiang Mai, Shane Beary in Tha Ton, Ung Fhu in Nan and Anirut Ngerncome in Chiang Khong.

Clifton would like to thank Katie, Mike and Rachel for typesetting, Henry for laying out the colour section, Maxine and Katie for the maps, Louise for the cover, Sharon for the lovely photos and Susannah Wight and Jennifer Speake for proofreading.

# Photo Credits

## Cover Credits

front small top picture Grand Palace, Bangkok © Neil Setchfield
front small lower picture Emperor Angelfish © Robert Harding

back top picture Ko Samui © Robert Harding
back lower picture Big Buddah, Ko Samui © Robert Harding

## Interior Picture Credits

Ko Samui sunset © Robert Harding
Long-tailed boats © Y.S. Man
Bar, Railae Beach, Krabi © Ellen Rooney/ Robert Harding
Sea canoe, Krabi © Ellen Rooney/Robert Harding
Tai Chi school, Ko Phangan © Robert Harding
Diver and turtle © Lawson Wood
Sign at Hua Hin train station © B. North/TRIP
Beach scene, southern Thailand © Robert Francis/Robert Harding
Full moon party, Hat Rin, Ko Phangan © Robert Francis/Robert Harding
Seafood curry © Simon Reddy/Travel Ink
Vongduen Beach, Ko Samet © Robert Francis/Robert Harding
Hat Rin, Ko Phangan © Martin Stolworthy/ AXIOM
Songkhla © Paul Gray
Khao Sok National Park © Lucy Ridout
Traditional massage © Robert Harding
Loy Kratong © Robert Harding
Wat Yai Suwannaram, Phetchaburi © Robert Harding

Bay on southwest coast, Ko Tao © Sharon Martins
Diver and coral © Lawson Wood
Street food-stall at night market © Nigel Blythe/Robert Harding
Songkran © Alain Evrard/Robert Harding
Ko Chang, Trat Province © Martyn Evans/ Travel Ink
The Grand Palace, Bangkok © A. Tovy/TRIP
Railae Beach, Aow Pranang © Robert Harding
Krung Ching waterfall © Julia Kelly
Chatuchak Weekend Market © Neil Setchfield
Ko Tarutao © Paul Gray
Phuket © Norma Joseph/Robert Harding
Vegetarian festival, Phuket © Robert Harding
Barracuda © F. Jackson/Robert Harding
Cabbage Patch coral © Robert Harding
Coral polyps, Dead Man's Fingers © Lawson Wood
Sea fan © Lawson Wood
Emperor Angelfish © Robert Harding
Moorish Idol © Robert Harding
Fusiliers © Lawson Wood

SMALL PRINT

The ideas expressed in this code were developed by and for independent travellers.

## Learn About The Country You're Visiting

Start enjoying your travels before you leave by tapping into as many sources of information as you can.

## The Cost Of Your Holiday

Think about where your money goes - be fair and realistic about how cheaply you travel. Try and put money into local peoples' hands; drink local beer or fruit juice rather than imported brands and stay in locally owned accommodation. Haggle with humour and not aggressively. Pay what something is worth to you and remember how wealthy you are compared to local people.

## Embrace The Local Culture

Open your mind to new cultures and traditions - it will transform your experience. Think carefully about what's appropriate in terms of your clothes and the way you behave. You'll earn respect and be more readily welcomed by local people. Respect local laws and attitudes towards drugs and alcohol that vary in different countries and communities. Think about the impact you could have on them.

# Exploring The World – The Travellers' Code

Being sensitive to these ideas means getting more out of your travels - and giving more back to the people you meet and the places you visit.

## Minimise Your Environmental Impact

Think about what happens to your rubbish - take biodegradable products and a water filter bottle. Be sensitive to limited resources like water, fuel and electricity. Help preserve local wildlife and habitats by respecting local rules and regulations, such as sticking to footpaths and not standing on coral.

## Don't Rely On Guidebooks

Use your guidebook as a starting point, not the only source of information. Talk to local people, then discover your own adventure!

## Be Discreet With Photography

Don't treat people as part of the landscape, they may not want their picture taken. Ask first and respect their wishes.

We work with people the world over to promote tourism that benefits their communities, but we can only carry on our work with the support of people like you. For membership details or to find out how to make your travels work for local people and the environment, visit our website.

www.tourismconcern.org.uk

TourismConcern
Campaigning for Ethical and Fairly Traded Tourism

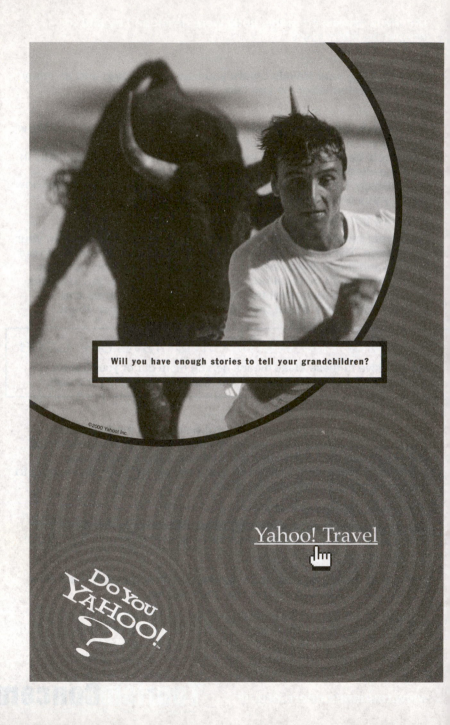

# Don't bury your head in the sand!

# Take cover!

## with Rough Guide Travel Insurance

**Worldwide cover, for Rough Guide readers worldwide**

UK Freefone **0800 015 09 06**
US Freefone **1 866 220 5588**
Worldwide **(+44) 1243 621 046**
Check the web at
**www.roughguides.com/insurance**

ROUGH GUIDES